CW01266821

# THE UNTOLD STORY OF THE PEOPLE OF AZAD KASHMIR

CHRISTOPHER SNEDDEN

# The Untold Story of the People of Azad Kashmir

HURST & COMPANY, LONDON

For the People of Azad Kashmir—Particularly Those Who Lost So Much in the 2005 Earthquake

First published in the United Kingdom in 2012 by
C. Hurst & Co. (Publishers) Ltd.,
41 Great Russell Street, London, WC1B 3PL
© Christopher Snedden, 2012
All rights reserved.
Printed in India

The right of Christopher Snedden to be identified as the
author of this publication is asserted by him in accordance
with the Copyright, Designs and Patents Act, 1988.

A Cataloguing-in-Publication data record for this book
is available from the British Library.

ISBN: 9781849041508 *clothbound*

This book is printed using paper from registered sustainable
and managed sources.

**www.hurstpub.co.uk**

# CONTENTS

| | |
|---|---|
| *Acknowledgements* | xi |
| *Abbreviations* | xv |
| *Glossary* | xvii |
| *List of Tables* | xxi |
| Introduction | 1 |
| *Terminology* | 2 |
| *Documentation* | 3 |

### PART ONE
### JAMMU AND KASHMIR

| | |
|---|---|
| 1. J&K: Disunited People—Undeliverable State | 7 |
| *Introduction* | 7 |
| *The accession issue* | 8 |
| *J&K: diverse and disunited* | 12 |
| *Kashmiris: ambivalent about Pakistan* | 17 |
| *Politicians: differing aspirations* | 22 |
| *Poonch Muslims: martial and disgruntled* | 27 |
| *Jawaharlal Nehru's role* | 32 |
| *Conclusion* | 34 |
| 2. The People: Dividing J&K—Instigating the Kashmir Dispute | 37 |
| *Introduction* | 37 |
| *Events in Jammu: volatile, poorly reported, ignored* | 38 |
| *The evidence: the Poonch uprising* | 41 |
| *The evidence: a 'massacre' of Jammu Muslims* | 47 |
| *The effect: the creation of Azad Kashmir* | 57 |
| *Conclusion* | 63 |
| 3. India and Pakistan: Negating the People's Actions | 65 |
| *Introduction* | 65 |
| *India's negation* | 66 |
| *An examination of India's* White Paper | 70 |
| *A major distraction: Baramulla* | 72 |

## CONTENTS

Pakistan's acquiescence in India's tactic — 74
Conclusion — 77

### PART TWO
### AZAD KASHMIR

4. Pakistan: Integrating the Region — 83
   Introduction — 83
   The post-accession situation in J&K: a brief overview — 85
   Post 1947: Pakistan controls Azad Kashmir — 87
   The Ministry of Kashmir Affairs — 89
   After 1970: legislated dominance — 99
   An examination of the Interim Constitution Act, 1974 — 102
   How the Azad Kashmir Council operates — 108
   Conclusion — 109

5. The Political System: Democratic Shortcomings — 111
   Introduction — 111
   A political overview — 111
   The dominance of the Muslim Conference — 113
   Endemic factionalism, particularly in the 1950s — 117
   Uprisings in Poonch — 121
   The role of biradari — 128
   Seats for refugees and others — 133
   The situation after 1970 — 136
   Conclusion — 138

6. The Administration: Large and Overseen — 141
   Introduction — 141
   Difficult beginnings — 142
   A significant 'loss': the Northern Areas — 146
   From 1949–1971: the reunification dilemma — 148
   After 1971: permanency — 154
   After 1988, and the current administrative situation — 159
   Conclusion — 161

7. The Economy: Poor and Dependent — 163
   Introduction — 163
   The 'loss' of the Jhelum Valley Road — 164
   Dependence on Pakistan — 166
   After 1971: increased support from Pakistan — 171
   Current state of the economy and social wellbeing — 175
   Possible financial independence — 180
   Economic matters related to Indian J&K — 185
   Conclusion — 187

## CONTENTS

8. Elections and Internal Politics since 1970     189
   *Introduction*     189
   *1970 and 1975 elections*     189
   *The military rule period*     191
   *Support for anti-Indian militants*     194
   *The 1990 elections*     199
   *Downfall of a 'shaky coalition' and 1991 elections*     202
   *1996 and 2001 elections*     205
   *2006 elections and Sardar Attique's defeat and return*     210
   *Conclusion*     214

Conclusion     217

### APPENDIXES

| | | |
|---|---|---|
| Appendix I. | The Relationship between the Rajas of Poonch and the Maharajas of Jammu and Kashmir | 229 |
| Appendix II. | Physical, Political and Religious Composition of J&K in 1941 | 239 |
| Appendix III. | Majority Position of Muslims in 1941 | 245 |
| Appendix IV. | Indian Army Soldiers from Poonch, Mirpur | 249 |
| Appendix V. | Physical and Political Composition of J&K after the 1949 Ceasefire | 253 |
| Appendix VI. | Ceasefire Line in J&K | 261 |
| Appendix VII. | Main Office Holders of Azad Kashmir | 265 |
| Appendix VIII. | Azad Kashmir 'Council Legislative List' | 267 |
| Appendix IX. | Composition of the Azad Jammu and Kashmir Council in December 2006 | 271 |
| Appendix X. | Azad Kashmir Administrative Set-up and Functions | 273 |
| Appendix XI. | Azad Kashmir's Actual Administration and Population, 1988–2008 | 289 |
| Appendix XII. | Aspects of the Azad Kashmir Budgets | 291 |
| Appendix XIII. | Crossing Process between Azad Kashmir and Indian J&K | 295 |
| Appendix XIV. | Matters re Azad Kashmir Elections, Particularly in 2006 | 299 |

*Notes*     313
*Bibliography*     405
*Index*     427

# ACKNOWLEDGMENTS

There are two people whose assistance has been invaluable completing this book: my wife, Diane Barbeler, and my former PhD supervisor, Professor Robin Jeffrey. Diane has given me unstinting love and support, particularly as an unpaid editor and an unwavering 'ear' to harangue. I have benefited from Robin's impeccable scholarship, genuine enthusiasm for this book and ongoing friendship. Both have helped me make this a better book.

There are many people in Azad Kashmir and Pakistan to whom I am indebted. I did most of my research in Muzaffarabad, with visits there in 1996, 1998, 1999, 2004 and 2006 (after the terrible 2005 earthquake). Mr Tariq Masud, a former senior Azad Kashmir civil servant who, in his final position, was Azad Kashmir Ombudsman, deserves a special mention. Apart from his ongoing support and generosity, Tariq organised borrowing rights for me at the Khurshid Library (now unfortunately destroyed). Most importantly, he generously gave me a copy of Yusuf Saraf's *Kashmiris Fight—For Freedom*, the two volumes of which are far rarer than 'hen's teeth'. I am unable to thank Tariq sahib enough.

Other helpful people in Muzaffarabad include the staff of the Azad Kashmir Ombudsman's office, particularly Sardar Ashfaq, Mr 'Balti' Hussain and Mr Ayaz Khan. They were always ready with a chat and a *chai* for a lonely scholar away from home. The friendly staff of the Sangum Hotel, particularly the welcoming Mr Shoukat Sheikh and his brother, Tahir, provided an enjoyable place to stay. Helpful staff at Azad Kashmir Tourism gave me useful initial guidance, especially Pirzada Irshad Ahmad. Sardar Sadiq, former Chief Economist and later head of the State Earthquake Reconstruction and Rehabilitation Agency (SERRA), dined me and provided useful economic insights. The staff of the Khurshid Library fulfilled the many requests of this demanding *feringi* (foreigner). In all visits, especially in 2006, senior people in the Azad Kashmir civil service and police were helpful providing me with information, official reports and assistance. While too numerous to name, some include: the former Inspector-General, Azad Kashmir Police, Malik Habib, who organised for me to meet the interesting politician Sardar Qayyum in 1996; Mr Tariq Butt; Dr Syed Asif Hussain; Mr Javaid Ayub; and Mr Muhammad Akram Sohail, who organised for me to meet the Azad Kashmir Prime Minister, Sardar Attique, in 2006. Two people invaluably facilitated the entry of my wife and myself into Azad Kashmir in December 2004: Major General (Retired) Sarfraz Iqbal, Chairman, Azad Kashmir Ehtesab Bureau, and Inspector-General, Azad Kashmir Police, Shahid Hussain Qureshi.

## ACKNOWLEDGMENTS

For help in Pakistan, I thank Professor Samina Yasmeen, her late mother, Mrs Sarfraz *Iqbal*, and her father, Mr Iqbal Malik. Samina is responsible for starting me on my Kashmir 'journey' by inviting me to a conference in Perth in 1990. In 1996, I stayed in Islamabad with her parents when I began my research. While there, Mrs Iqbal 'compelled' me to go to Muzaffarabad when I felt like shirking—she must have sensed that this was my destiny! Mr Khawar Zaman, former High Commissioner for Pakistan in Canberra in the late 1990s, his wife Nighat, and his family, Yusuf (who lived with us in Melbourne for eighteen pleasurable months), Aly, Akbar and Naveed, helped me greatly over the years with friendship, advice and hospitality in Canberra and Lahore, and facilitated my entry to Azad Kashmir at times. In 1999, Khawar arranged for his Muzaffarabad contacts (particularly Asif Hyat, Inspector-General, Azad Kashmir Police) to organise for me to meet Sardar Ibrahim. Spending four hours with this energetic old campaigner at his ancestral home was a highlight of my research. (He died in 2003.) Another highlight was twice meeting the journalist and font of information Mir Abdul Aziz (who died in 2000), in Rawalpindi. Similarly, I am truly grateful to have met the wonderful former senior government official Mr A.M. Salaria, in Lahore. His vivid memories, like those of Sardar Qayyum, Sardar Ibrahim and Mir Abdul Aziz, go back to 1947.

Various other people and organisations have helped greatly. The Institute for Regional Studies at Islamabad has always been welcoming, generous and supportive. In particular, I thank Professor Khalid Mahmud, who invaluably introduced me to his brother, Tariq Masud, in 1998, and Mr Nasir Zaidi, who always willingly helped with historical background and archival material, as did the librarian, Ms Nasreen Naqvi. Thanks also to Colonel (Retired) Aziz, Brigadier (Retired) Bashir Ahmad and Major-General (Retired) Jamshed Ayaz Khan for their support and generosity. The staff at the National Documentation Centre, Islamabad, led by Mr Saleem Ullah Khan, has always been welcoming and responsive. This centre is an excellent—but little known—place to do research in Islamabad.

I cannot thank enough Mr Alexander Evans, Nuffield College, Oxford. Alexander has been exceedingly collegial and generous, giving me invaluable access to contacts and historical information, and very helpful suggestions on my text. Alexander also put me in touch with Mr Ershad Mahmud, now a freelance journalist and formerly of the Institute of Policy Studies, Islamabad, who generously provided contacts, information, collegiality and hospitality. Ershad put me in touch with Justice Manzoor Gilani, who kindly gave me a copy of his book, Administration of Justice in Azad Kashmir. I also thank others who helped with information and formative discussion at times, including John Robinson, Russell Hocking, Colonel (Retired) Brian Cloughley, Tom Weber, Andrew Whitehead, and various officials in Azad Kashmir. I acknowledge a grant in 2004 from The Australian Academy of the Humanities towards my research. Finally, I thank Colonel Darren Kerr, the former Defence Adviser at the Australian High Commission, Islamabad, who generously facilitated my last research trip to Islamabad and Muzaffarabad in 2006.

Last, but not least, I thank all of those unnamed—but very much appreciated—people in Azad Kashmir and Pakistan who have helped me with my research and

# ACKNOWLEDGMENTS

requests and who have facilitated my journeys to, and stays in, their region or country in many significant or small ways. This includes staff in various hotels, drivers who negotiated the rugged Islamabad-Muzaffarabad trip via the sometimes snowbound hill station of Murree, and various friendly doormen who usually stood outside in such snow. I have been fortunate on each of my trips to both locations to enjoy real hospitality, generous help and wonderful conversations—not to mention numerous cups of *chai*! Thank you and God bless you all.

# ABBREVIATIONS

| | |
|---|---|
| AJK | Azad Jammu and Kashmir |
| AK/A.K. | Azad Kashmir |
| APHC | All Parties Hurriyat Conference |
| API | Associated Press of India |
| Ch. | Chaudhri (also Chaudhry) |
| *CMG* | *Civil & Military Gazette*, Lahore |
| GOC | General Officer Commanding, Murree |
| IDPs | Internally Displaced People |
| ISI | Directorate for Inter-Services Intelligence |
| JKLF | Jammu Kashmir Liberation Front |
| J&K | Jammu and Kashmir |
| JUI | Jamiat Ulmah Islam |
| KA&NA | Minister of State (later Minister) for Kashmir Affairs and Northern Affairs |
| kg/s | kilogram/s |
| km/s | kilometre/s |
| kWh | kilowatt hours |
| LOC | Line of Control |
| MAF | million acre feet |
| MKA | Ministry of Kashmir Affairs |
| MMA | Muttahida Majlis-e-Amal (United Council of Action) |
| MQM | Muttahida Qaumi Movement (United National Movement) |
| Muhd | Muhammad |
| MW | megawatts |
| NWFP | North-West Frontier Province (now Khyber Pakhtunkhwa) |
| *NYT* | *The New York Times* |
| p.a. | per annum |
| PML | Peoples [sic] Muslim League-AJK |
| POK | Pakistan-Occupied Kashmir |
| PPP | Pakistan People's Party |
| PPPAK | Pakistan People's Party-Azad Kashmir |
| RIAF | Royal Indian Air Force |
| Rs. | rupees |
| RSS | Rashtriya Swayamsevak Sangh (National Self-Service Society) |
| SCO | Special Communication Organization |
| SERRA | State Earthquake Reconstruction and Rehabilitation Agency |

## ABBREVIATIONS

| | |
|---|---|
| sq. | square |
| *TOI* | *The Times of India*, Bombay |
| UJC | United (or Muttahida) Jihad Council |
| UK/U.K. | United Kingdom |
| UN | United Nations |
| UNCIP | United Nations Commission for India and Pakistan |
| UNSC | United Nations Security Council |
| USD | United States dollar |
| WAPDA | Water and Power Development Authority (Pakistan) |

N.B.: Muslim Conference is an abbreviation for All Jammu and Kashmir Muslim Conference.

# GLOSSARY

| | |
|---|---|
| Azad | 'Free' or 'liberated'; initially from Maharaja Sir Hari Singh's rule, then from Indian rule. |
| *Azadi* | Freedom or independence (from India and Pakistan). |
| Azad Jammu and Kashmir | Full title for Azad Kashmir; one of the two regions of J&K administered by Pakistan. |
| Azad Kashmir | Commonly used popular term for Azad Jammu and Kashmir. |
| Azad Kashmiri | Resident of Azad Kashmir. |
| Baltistan | Geographic area in the former Frontier Districts Province. |
| *biradari* | Brotherhood or tribe, as in Azad Kashmir's tribal-based politics. |
| Ceasefire Line | Heavily-militarised line that divided J&K from 1949 until 1972; now known as the Line of Control (LOC). |
| Dogra | Ethnic group in Jammu from which J&K's ruling family came. |
| Gilgit | Geographical area in the former Frontier Districts Province. |
| Gilgit-Baltistan | Name for the Northern Areas since 2009. |
| Gilgiti | Individual from the Gilgit area. |
| hydel | Hydro-electricity. |
| Indian J&K | Those areas of J&K under direct Indian control: Jammu, the Kashmir Valley, Ladakh. |
| *jagir* | Autonomous area not under the direct control of the Maharaja of J&K. |
| Jagirdar | Head of a *jagir*. |
| Jammu | Home province of Maharaja Hari Singh in 1947; since 1947, one of the three regions of Indian J&K; also sometimes shorthand for Jammu City (also called Jammu Tawi), the capital of Jammu. |
| Jammuite | Individual from the Jammu Province area of J&K; since 1947, an individual from the Jammu region of Indian J&K. |

# GLOSSARY

| | |
|---|---|
| Jammu and Kashmir | The territory that comprised the (former) princely state of Jammu and Kashmir; popularly called 'Kashmir'; claimed in its entirety by India because Maharaja Hari Singh acceded to India on 26 October 1947; this accession is disputed by Pakistan. |
| Kashir | Term that Kashmiris use for their homeland, the Kashmir Valley. |
| Kashmir | The region that comprises the Kashmir Valley and its immediate surrounds; often also used to describe the former princely state of J&K or all of what currently comprises J&K, e.g. the 'Kashmir' dispute. |
| Kashmir Valley | Most important and most populous of the three regions controlled by India in Indian J&K. |
| Kashmiri | A person who is ethnically a Kashmiri or who is a resident of the Kashmir Valley region; often also used to describe a subject of the princely state of J&K or a resident of J&K. |
| Kashmiriness | Practice prevalent in the Kashmir Valley of acceptance and tolerance of people from all religions; see also 'Kashmiriyat'. |
| Kashmiriyat | A name derived from Arabic and Persian that more recently is being used instead of the older term 'Kashmiriness'. |
| Ladakh | One of the three regions of Indian J&K. |
| Ladakhi | Individual from the Ladakh area of Indian J&K. |
| Line of Control (LOC) | Heavily-militarised dividing line in J&K that separates Pakistan-Administered J&K from Indian J&K; prior to 1972, the LOC was known as the Ceasefire Line; LOC ends at map point NJ 980420 in north-eastern J&K, beyond which is the disputed Siachen Glacier, on which India and Pakistan have stationed forces. |
| Maulia | follower of the Agha Khan; also known as an 'Ismaili'. |
| Mirpuri | Individual from the Mirpur area. |
| Mohammaden/Muhammaden | Another name for a Muslim. |
| Mujahid | Freedom fighter in 1947; holy warrior on *'jihad'* (holy war). |
| *naibat* | Sub-*tehsil*. |
| *naib tehsildar* | Head of a sub-*tehsil* or *naibat*. |
| Nawab | Muslim ruler of a princely state. |
| Northern Areas | One of the two regions of J&K administered by Pakistan. |

# GLOSSARY

| | |
|---|---|
| Pakistan-Administered J&K | Those regions of J&K administered by Pakistan: Azad Kashmir and the Northern Areas. The term 'Pakistani J&K' is inappropriate as Pakistan is supposed only to be administering these two regions until a UN-supervised plebiscite determines whether J&K, in its entirety, will join India or Pakistan. |
| Pakistan-Occupied Kashmir (POK) | India's term for Pakistan-Administered J&K; Sometimes (confusingly) used to refer only to Azad Kashmir or to the Northern Areas. |
| Pandit | Most commonly, a Hindu Kashmiri living in the Kashmir Valley; also a Hindu whose descendants were originally from the Kashmir Valley, e.g. 'Pandit' Jawaharlal Nehru. |
| Pathan | British name for a Pukhtoon (see 'Pukhtoons' below). |
| Praja Sabha | Limited legislative assembly in J&K that Maharaja Hari Singh established after, and as a result of, the 1931 uprising in Kashmir. |
| Pukhtoons | Tribesmen from NWFP; many invaded J&K in October 1947; also called Pakhtoons, Pashtuns, Pushtoons, Pathans, etc. |
| Rajput | Hindu caste in Jammu, to which many Dogras belong/ed. |
| Sardar | Tribal chieftain. |
| Sudhan/Sudhozai | One of the main tribes of (southern) Poonch, allegedly originating from Pashtun areas. |
| Sufi | Practitioner of a mystical strand of Islam. |
| *tehsil* | Sub-district. |
| *Tehsildar* | Head of a sub-district. |
| Vale of Kashmir | Another name for the Kashmir Valley region. |

# LIST OF TABLES

1.1 The Princely State of Jammu and Kashmir in 1941.
1.2 Numbers of Muslims and Hindus in each province of Princely J&K, and as percentages of each province, as percentages of J&K, and as percentages of each respective religious group.
1.3 Muslims and Hindus in Jammu Province as percentages of their Respective Districts.
2.1 Population of Muslims and Hindus in certain Muslim-majority and non-Muslim-majority District Groups, and as percentages of Jammu Province, their District Group and their religious group.
2.2 Some incidents of violence against Muslims in Jammu Province as reported by some 'Englishmen' in *CMG*, 18 December 1947.
5.1 Differences in Voter Numbers for Constituencies in Azad Kashmir in 1996, 2001, 2006.
6.1 Districts of Azad Kashmir, 1988: their area, populations (1972 and 1981), population density, urban percentage of population, average population growth and percentage change in populations (1972–81).
6.2 Administrative makeup of Azad Kashmir in 1951 and 2008.
7.1 Crops in Azad Kashmir from 1982 to 1987 and in 1997–98, including average area cropped per annum and average yield per annum, compared with average yield per annum in Pakistan and for the world leader during the 1982–87 period.
7.2 Amounts allocated by Pakistan from 1955 to 2006 to Azad Kashmir for Development Programs.
7.3 Allocations to the Azad Kashmir Budget of Amounts Controlled by Islamabad (in Rs. millions).

# INTRODUCTION

This book offers a new perspective about who started the dispute over the international status of Jammu and Kashmir (J&K). Most accounts claim that Pukhtoon tribesmen from Pakistan instigated this dispute. This book documents how people from the Jammu Province of J&K—Jammuites—actually started it. After Partition in 1947, Jammuites engaged in three significant actions. The first was a Muslim uprising in the Poonch area of western Jammu Province against the unpopular Hindu ruler, Maharaja Sir Hari Singh. The second was serious inter-religious violence throughout the province that killed or displaced large numbers of people from all religious communities. The third was the creation of Azad (Free) Jammu and Kashmir in the area of western Jammu Province that the 'rebels' had 'freed' or liberated. These significant actions all took place before the Maharaja acceded to India on 26 October 1947. They divided 'his' Muslim-majority state and confirmed that it was undeliverable in its entirety to either India or Pakistan. They instigated the ongoing dispute between India and Pakistan over which state should possess J&K—the so-called 'Kashmir dispute'.

This book also provides new information and analysis about the least known area of disputed J&K: Azad Kashmir, a narrow strip of territory in south-western J&K populated by Muslims and administered by Pakistan. Few books have ever been written about this region. None are contemporary.[1] This is despite the role that people who later came to be called Azad Kashmiris played in instigating the Kashmir dispute, despite ongoing Indian claims to ownership of this region, and despite Pakistani oversight of it until J&K's international status is finally resolved. We know little about this region and how its people have fared since 1947 politically, economically, administratively, and in their relationship with Pakistan. This book (partially) remedies this deficiency. It shows that Azad Kashmir is heavily involved with, and dependent on, Pakistan and suggests that Azad Kashmir's *de facto* status as being part of Pakistan should be made *de jure*.

The Kashmir dispute has bedevilled India-Pakistan relations since 1947. The book's Conclusion suggests a possible framework to resolve this seemingly intractable issue. Following Maharaja Hari Singh's accession to India in 1947, the Indian and Pakistan governments, and then the United Nations, resolved to consult the people of J&K about their state's international status. This would be done via a United Nations-supervised plebiscite. This poll has never been held—nor is it likely to be held. Despite being marginalised since about mid-1948, the people of J&K are still legitimate stakeholders in the Kashmir dispute. Indeed, given India's and Pakistan's inability to resolve this bitter dispute, only the people of J&K appear to have the will and sufficient interest to do so. This reaffirms the lapsed proposition to resolve the Kashmir dispute: 'Let the People Decide'.

There are two parts to this book. Part I has three chapters. Using primary source material wherever possible, it discusses the instigation of the Kashmir dispute and the creation of Azad Kashmir. Chapter 1 analyses the disparate religious and political situation in J&K in 1947. Chapter 2 provides evidence that substantiates the claim that Jammuites engaged in three significant actions in 1947. Chapter 3 shows how India has denied these peoples' actions and how Pakistan has acquiesced in India's tactic.

Part II has five chapters. These provide new information about how Azad Kashmir and Azad Kashmiris have fared since 1947. Chapter 4 discusses how Pakistan has controlled and integrated this disputed region. Chapter 5 analyses Azad Kashmir's political system, and associated phenomena. Chapter 6 discusses Azad Kashmir's structure and administration. Chapter 7 looks at Azad Kashmir's economy and some social aspects. Chapter 8 examines elections and internal politics in Azad Kashmir since 1970.

A Conclusion ends the narrative, after which fourteen appendixes provide information not appropriate for the text. A bibliography and index follow.

*Terminology*

The terms 'Kashmir' and 'Kashmiri' mean different things to different people, particularly in the subcontinent. Except when used in the term 'the Kashmir dispute', I use 'Kashmir' to refer to the Kashmir Valley. I use the term 'Kashmiri' to refer to the people who populate this region and people with ancestors from it (for example, Jawaharlal Nehru's forebears were ethnic Kashmiri (Hindu) Pandits). To avoid confusion, I use the term 'J&K' to refer to the territory that comprised the former princely state of Jammu and Kashmir, the popular shorthand for which was 'Kashmir'.

In terms of J&K's five regions, I refer to the actual area of J&K under India's control (Jammu; Ladakh; the Kashmir Valley) as 'Indian J&K'. I refer to the area of J&K that Pakistan is administering (Azad Kashmir; the Northern Areas) as 'Pakistan-Administered J&K'. I generally use the popular term 'Azad Kashmir' throughout this book, even though the region's full title is 'Azad Jammu and Kashmir'. Likewise, I use the term 'Azad Kashmir Government'. In August 2009, Pakistan renamed the Northern Areas 'Gilgit-Baltistan'.[2] Nevertheless, I use the older term 'Northern Areas' throughout, except in the Conclusion, as this was the region's name for most of the period covered by this book. Similarly, I use 'North-West Frontier Province' (NWFP) instead of Khyber Pakhtunkhwa.[3]

It is also important to know what India and Pakistan call the territory of J&K under the other nation's control. Indians call the area that Pakistan is administering 'Pakistan-Occupied Kashmir' ('POK'). Confusingly, Indians use this term regardless of whether they are referring to all of Pakistan-Administered J&K, or to Azad Kashmir, or to the Northern Areas. In return, Pakistanis call Indian J&K either 'Indian-Occupied Kashmir' ('IOK') or 'Indian-Held Kashmir' ('IHK'). Confusingly, when Pakistanis are talking about 'Held Kashmir', they often mean the Kashmir Valley, as they have almost no interest in Jammu and Ladakh. I use none of these loaded terms in this book, except when quoting.

INTRODUCTION

*Documentation*

Because there is a dearth of good quality documents discussing Azad Kashmir, I have had to access a wide range of sources. One source has been interviews. I have enjoyed meeting and interviewing senior and interesting people with long involvement with Azad Kashmir. Chiefly, but not exclusively, these have been politicians, journalists and bureaucrats. I have accessed newspapers that have reported about Azad Kashmir, such as the (defunct) *Civil & Military Gazette (CMG)* and *Dawn*. I have also used some official documents. While somewhat dry, these have veracity as they form a legal basis for operations in Azad Kashmir. Similarly, some rare primary and secondary sources may lack balance. Nevertheless, they offer a useful perspective about Azad Kashmir, Azad Kashmiris, and their issues. I have also accessed Internet sites, although some websites may no longer exist, particularly for two former prime ministers involved in the four extraordinary prime ministerial changes that occurred in Azad Kashmir in 2009–10.

Wherever possible, I have based my narrative on primary source documents. Two stand out: the comprehensive 'restricted' *Report of the Sub-committee on Western Kashmir*, 1949, of the United Nations Commission for India and Pakistan (UNCIP),[4] and the 'secret' *Census of Azad Kashmir, 1951*.[5] Information from these 'warts and all' documents has rarely been published before. Another important document is the 'restricted' 'Rules of Business 1985',[6] without which it would have been difficult to discuss Azad Kashmir's post-1979 administration.[7] These Rules appear to be current.

# PART ONE

# JAMMU AND KASHMIR

# 1

# J&K

## DISUNITED PEOPLE—UNDELIVERABLE STATE

*Introduction*

In 1947, a strong perception existed that the princely state of Jammu and Kashmir was a unified and indivisible entity capable of being delivered, in its entirety, to either India or Pakistan. This led to an expectation that, with the British departure from the Indian subcontinent, J&K would unite with one of the new dominions. Events soon after Partition showed that J&K was not a unified entity. Even so, the perception that J&K was an indivisible entity persisted, and this was a major impediment for many years in attempts to resolve the dispute over J&K's international status. As the discussion in this chapter shows, the perception was false.

There are a number of reasons why the perception arose that J&K was a unified, indivisible entity capable of delivery to India or Pakistan. Autocratic Dogra maharajas, strongly supported by the British acting as paramount power, had ensured that this entity cohered with few major political problems. People expected that this entity would continue to cohere. Powerbrokers in 1947 also were influenced by the method used to decolonise Princely India (as against British-controlled India), whereby each ruler was deemed to have the power—and, indeed, was expected—to accede to either India or Pakistan. Princely states therefore were considered to be indivisible and without any independent future. Neither the departing British nor the future leaders of India and Pakistan sought partition of any princely state along religious lines, nor would they countenance independence for any of them. Instead, the British encouraged each princely ruler to consider geographical factors and the will of his subjects in deciding his accession. Even though the accession would clearly impact on all of the prince's subjects, nevertheless there were no legal requirements or popular pressures for the ruler to consider either factor. He alone would decide the accession. Once it was decided, the expectation was that all of his princely state would, along with the ruler, join the new dominion of his choice.

This chapter discusses J&K's indivisibility and shows that this concept was flawed. For a start, J&K was an artificial entity constructed by the British and the first Dogra ruler, and supported thereafter by British paramountcy. Only the unpopular autocratic rule of the ruler of J&K, Maharaja Sir Hari Singh, and his regressive regime compelled the disparate people of J&K to cohere. These 'peoples' had major geographical, ethnic, religious, historic, cultural and political differences, divisions, and desires—especially for J&K's future international status, on which significant issue some had little inclination to compromise. The present discussion especially focuses on people who lived in the Kashmir Valley and in western parts of Jammu Province, particularly in the Jagir of Poonch, where large Muslim majorities were located. It does so because the Maharaja's regime and practices impacted negatively on these people most of all. Individuals in both places also played the most significant roles as politicians, leaders and activists in the period leading up to the Maharaja's accession to India on 26 October 1947, and thereafter in divided J&K.

*The accession issue*

With the departure of the British from the Indian subcontinent in August 1947, all Indian princes were faced with a momentous decision: to join their domains with either India or Pakistan. The Indian Independence Act, 1947, provided the legal basis for the British departure. In essence, it allowed for the partition of British India into India and Pakistan, with the Islamic dominion comprising eastern and western wings, and for the lapse of British paramountcy over princely states. This latter provision appeared to suggest that the multitude of these states, including J&K, essentially became independent after 15 August 1947.[1] However, the departing British and the leadership of both new dominions made it clear that they expected each ruler to make an accession. The British also made it clear that their government would not recognise as a dominion any princely state that declared independence.[2] When the British finally departed the subcontinent on 15 August 1947, most princes had acceded to India, with a few opting to join Pakistan. (It was impossible to accede to Pakistan before the new dominion actually came into existence on 15 August 1947.) The Maharaja of J&K was one of only a few princes who had not made an accession. Others of significance included the Nizam of Hyderabad in southern India and the Nawab of Junagadh in the Kathiawar peninsula.[3] Nevertheless, the expectation was still that Hari Singh would make an accession.

For Maharaja Hari Singh, accession to Pakistan was, in terms of J&K's geography, feasible, even desirable. This was because almost all of J&K's major geographical, communication and economic links were with areas of western Punjab and the North-West Frontier Province that were to become part of the new Muslim-majority state of Pakistan. Geographically speaking, the only railway line that entered J&K was a branch of the North Western Railway from Sialkot, some twenty-five miles away in Pakistan, to J&K's winter capital, Jammu City. As for motorable roads, J&K had few. Like the railway line, the main road to Jammu City was from Sialkot. Of the three roads to Srinagar, J&K's summer capital, two entered J&K from areas that were to become part of Pakistan.[4] The first was the all-weather Jhelum Valley Road, which ran alongside the Jhelum River for 132 of its 196 miles.

## J&K: DISUNITED PEOPLE—UNDELIVERABLE STATE

This road began in Rawalpindi, where there was a railhead, and then went via Murree and Domel, near Muzaffarabad, to Srinagar. A second road went from the NWFP rail terminus of Havelian, seventy-one miles further north of Rawalpindi, via Abbottabad, to Muzaffarabad, and then to Srinagar. A third, 'more picturesque' road was an extension of the Sialkot-Jammu road. This route went for 203 miles from Jammu City to Srinagar via the Banihal Pass, which was often snowbound during winter from December to April[5] and was 'notoriously liable to gullying and landslips'.[6] In terms of communications, J&K's post and telegraphic links invariably followed the major road or rail links that entered the princely state. These also originated in, or traversed through, areas that were to become part of Pakistan.

Economically speaking, accession to Pakistan was feasible as J&K's links with areas that were to become part of this new dominion were highly important. Indeed, the J&K economy was heavily integrated with, and dependent on, these areas. Up to 98 per cent of the non-timber exports from the Kashmir Valley went via the Jhelum Valley Road to Rawalpindi,[7] the city considered the 'warehouse' for goods transiting to and from the Kashmir Valley.[8] J&K timber exports were floated down the Jhelum and Chenab rivers to points downstream in (Pakistani) Punjab. (Equally, these rivers' headwaters controlled vitally important water flows from J&K into the downstream (Pakistani) Punjab canal system.) Goods from J&K freighted by rail from Jammu City or Rawalpindi were carried on the western rail network to Karachi, the traditional port for the princely state. Owing to its proximity, Karachi enjoyed a 65 per cent freight advantage over goods sent to Bombay or Calcutta.[9] Finally, even in the 1940s, Kashmir Province was a popular tourist destination, with tourism 'of vast economic importance'. In 1940, almost all of the province's 29,292 visitors, who comprised 8,367 Europeans and 20,925 Indians,[10] would have entered J&K by roads coming from areas that were to become part of Pakistan, chiefly the Jhelum Valley Road.

For geographical and economic reasons, accession to Pakistan may therefore have been desirable. It even looked likely when the J&K Government sought and agreed a 'Standstill Agreement' with the Pakistan Government just before partition.[11] J&K's dependency on Pakistani Punjab was highlighted after the delivery of essential goods and services from this region, including petrol, wheat and salt, to J&K was severely curtailed in September 1947.[12] The Standstill Agreement made this curtailment unfortunate. As J&K and India saw it, the Pakistan Government was seeking to pressure the J&K Government on the accession issue.[13] Conversely, the Pakistan Government claimed to be unable to compel reluctant, unprotected lorry drivers to drive through turbulent areas where they would possibly confront personal danger and severe looting.[14] Under the Indian Independence Act, a Standstill Agreement was supposed to enable various existing agreements and arrangements relating to economic activities and the provision of services between a princely state and British India to continue with the new dominion until new ones were put in place. This gave a princely state's ruler more time to determine to which dominion he ultimately would accede. With most of J&K's services and economic activities occurring with Pakistan, and given that the J&K Government had sought and obtained the Standstill Agreement just before the British departed, many Pakistanis apparently believed that J&K would, at some time in the future, accede to it.[15] This hope was false. The J&K Government had openly offered the same agreement to India, but New Delhi had been non-committal.[16] India's stance was not a pressing issue for J&K as almost all of its significant geographical and economic links were with Pakistan.

For Maharaja Hari Singh personally, the accession issue posed a major dilemma: he was the Hindu ruler of a Muslim-majority state. In 1947, J&K had a population of just over four million (see Table 1.1), 77 per cent of whom were Muslims. Muslims also constituted a clear majority in all three of J&K's provinces: Jammu, Kashmir, and the Frontier Districts. If the partition method used by the British in British India, whereby Muslim-majority areas became part of Pakistan, was any guide, Hari Singh should have chosen to unite his princely state with Pakistan. Nevertheless, despite the fact that J&K had a Muslim-majority population, the political inclinations of the people of J&K were far more complex and uncertain. As we shall see, some significant Hindus believed that J&K should join Pakistan. Even more important, some, perhaps many, Muslims—nobody knows for certain how many—did not favour J&K joining Pakistan. This uncertainty about the political wishes of the people of J&K arises because neither the Maharaja nor the governments of India and Pakistan have ever asked Muslims, or any other people in J&K, in any meaningful or inclusive way, what status they wanted for J&K. Also, no opinions polls or other attempts to gauge public opinion were conducted at the time.

Table 1.1: The Princely State of Jammu and Kashmir in 1941.[17]

| Province | Area (sq. miles) | Population | Religious Composition | Number |
|---|---|---|---|---|
| Jammu | 12,378 | 1,981,433 | 61.19 per cent Muslims | 1,212,405 |
| | | | 37.19 per cent Hindus | 736,862 |
| | | | 1.41 per cent Sikhs | 27,896 |
| | | | 0.21 per cent Others (Jains, Christians, Buddhists etc.)★ | 4,270 |
| Kashmir | 8,539 | 1,728,705 | 93.48 per cent Muslims | 1,615,928 |
| | | | 4.95 per cent Hindus | 85,531 |
| | | | 1.56 per cent Sikhs | 27,001 |
| | | | 0.01 per cent Others★ | 245 |
| Frontier Districts | 63,554 | 311,478 | 86.86 per cent Muslims | 270,539 |
| | | | 12.89 per cent Buddhists | 40,164 |
| | | | 0.25 per cent Hindus, Unspecified Others and Sikhs★★ | 775 |
| State total | 84,471 | 4,021,616 | 77.06 per cent Muslims | 3,098,872 |
| | | | 20.46 per cent Hindus | 822,955 |
| | | | 1.37 per cent Sikhs | 54,975 |
| | | | 1.01 per cent Buddhists | 40,684 |
| | | | 0.10 per cent Unspecified Others | 4,130 |

Source: *Census of India 1941*, Volume XXII, Jammu & Kashmir State, Part III, Village Tables, Srinagar, R.G. Wreford, Editor, Jammu and Kashmir Government, 1942.

Key: ★ Breakdown of figures not provided.
★★ Only the Ladakh District had Hindus, Sikhs or Unspecified Others.[18]

## J&K: DISUNITED PEOPLE—UNDELIVERABLE STATE

Instead of making a bold accession that would have resolved the issue of his state's international status, Maharaja Hari Singh vacillated. This was partially understandable: rather than it being a simple 'either/or' choice, the background to, and the ramifications of, this decision were complex. Furthermore, joining either dominion was a stark proposition given the awful upheavals and brutal killings that each was experiencing in adjacent Punjab. Hari Singh's situation in J&K was relatively more peaceful—but personally more difficult. The fact that the majority of his subjects were Muslims was offset by the fact that he was a Hindu from Jammu whose position, power and influence would likely be curtailed if he joined Pakistan. He and many of his Hindu and Sikh subjects, especially those located in Jammu Province, felt not only that a union with Muslim Pakistan was 'repugnant' on religious grounds, but also that they faced being politically, and physically, overwhelmed in any such union. These non-Muslims would have resisted this union strongly and with force.[19]

The Maharaja also confronted other factors that added complexity to the accession issue. Some Kashmiri Muslims apparently were ambivalent about joining Pakistan, although whatever political possibility they offered Hari Singh was lessened because their leader, Sheikh Mohammad Abdullah, was a politician whom he disliked. A popular, secular and influential Kashmiri, Abdullah had played a significant part in Kashmiri politics since he became known as the 'Lion of Kashmir' during the 1931 anti-Maharaja uprising in Kashmir. Abdullah, in turn, was strongly supported by another man whom Hari Singh disliked intensely: the Prime Minister of India, Jawaharlal Nehru. With Kashmiri (Hindu) Pandit forebears, Nehru was a great lover of Kashmir. He also wanted the princely state to join India. Conversely, a few influential Kashmiri Pandits wanted J&K to join Pakistan. They possibly included Ramchandra Kak, the Maharaja's Prime Minister until Hari Singh sacked him just before Partition, possibly because of Kak's alleged pro-Pakistan leanings. Similarly, Muslims in western Jammu Province, particularly in Poonch, many of whom had martial capabilities, and Muslims in the Frontier Districts Province strongly wanted J&K to join Pakistan. Finally, some individuals, including the ruler himself and, at times, Sheikh Abdullah, wanted independence for J&K.[20] This was not an impossible proposition given J&K's size and its unique strategic setting of sharing international borders with China and Afghanistan. Conversely, J&K lacked the military capability, economic independence and support from the new dominions to make independence practicable.

The India-Pakistan border announced on 17 August 1947 further complicated the Maharaja's accession, chiefly because it made the option of joining India realistic. Surprisingly, India obtained three of the four *tehsils* in the Muslim-majority Gurdaspur District of Punjab.[21] This gave India a narrow land corridor across its part of Punjab to J&K's Kathua District, in the eastern corner of Jammu Province. Within this corridor, a poor road already connected the rest of India with J&K, while a railway line from Pathankot town was extendable to Kathua, and beyond.[22] This fortuitous strategic land bridge meant that the Hindu-led princely state could directly access the Hindu-majority dominion. Without this strategic link, J&K and/or India would have had to construct a new road from Kangra, in the hilly part of Indian Punjab, via difficult terrain, to eastern Jammu. J&K's access to India became much easier after the existing road was upgraded and the railway line was extended. This reduced J&K's almost total reliance on its existing road and rail links from Pakistan.

The Maharaja's vacillation did nothing to reduce the complexity—and anxiety—surrounding the accession question. Hari Singh's son has explained his father's ability to vacillate. For Karan Singh,[23] the Maharaja faced a 'once-in-a-millennium historical phenomenon' where four major forces or their leaders opposed him: the hurriedly departing and therefore impetuous British; Nehru's Indian National Congress; Muhammad Ali Jinnah's Muslim League (and its local 'affiliate', the All J&K Muslim Conference); and Abdullah's All J&K National Conference. Some or all of them were applying pressure to Hari Singh, either directly through consultations and visits (India, particularly, and the British) or subtly through activities such as economic blockades (Pakistan), cross-border military activity (Pakistan), and internal politicking (Muslim Conference and National Conference). The Maharaja's decision on the future international status of J&K, whatever it was, would not satisfy all of these groups and people. Karan Singh also considered that his father suffered from the 'feudal virus' of indecisiveness. This 'disinclination to take a firm decision one way or the other' only increased people's suspicions and encouraged some of them, particularly Muslims and Hindus in Jammu Province, to take actions after 15 August 1947 to ensure that J&K joined the dominion of their choice. This involved an uprising in Poonch and serious internal inter-religious violence in Jammu Province.

On 26 October 1947, Maharaja Hari Singh finally made an accession—to India. Ostensibly, he was compelled to accede to India in order to receive Indian military assistance to defend J&K from an invasion by Muslim Pukhtoon tribesmen from Pakistan that began on 22 October 1947. However, by then J&K was already physically divided by internal fighting, chiefly in Jammu Province, to such an extent that it was actually undeliverable in its entirety to India (or, indeed, to Pakistan, had Hari Singh acceded to it). Hence, India and Pakistan's perceptions of J&K's indivisibility and deliverability were flawed. They underestimated the disunited J&K people's deep religious differences and strongly held, but differing, political desires, as a result of which neither India nor Pakistan was guaranteed majority popular support. Their stance also ignored J&K's unique social diversity and complexity and its divisive political situation in which the Maharaja's forces had been the only unifying factor. The next section explores these points.

*J&K: diverse and disunited*

The princely state of Jammu and Kashmir was an artificial political entity created by the British in 1846. Throughout its 101-year existence, little held this diverse and disunited state together, except autocratic rule by Dogra maharajas. The British constructed J&K in conjunction with Maharaja Gulab Singh, a Rajput Dogra from Jammu. Gulab Singh was an opportunist, intriguer and ambivalent participant with his supposed allies, the Sikhs, in their (losing) war against the East India Company forces in 1845–46. The British established their paramountcy over Gulab Singh via the 1846 Treaty of Amritsar in which he unequivocally acknowledged the 'supremacy of the British Government'.[24] In return, the British sold him indefeasible title to hereditary and other land that comprised Gulab Singh's existing domain as Raja of Jammu,[25] to land he held in Ladakh, and to the Kashmir Valley and land located in what was later called J&K's Frontier Districts Province. In consideration for his 'territorial windfall',[26] Gulab Singh paid the British Rs. 7.5 million. Following some territorial adjustments soon after, the second maharaja, Ranbir Singh, finally and fully incorporated the rebellious northern Gilgit area of the Frontier Districts into J&K in the late 1870s.[27] The modern entity known as Jammu and Kashmir had fully emerged.

The areas that the Dogra maharajas acquired had never been effectively united under a single local ruler before, nor did their state naturally cohere as an entity. The princely state needed a strong ruler to hold it together. With the exception of the Kashmir Valley, the areas acquired by the Dogras had never had settled government. Given the diversity of the population, J&K's difficult geography and its lack of a shared history, it was 'by no means an easy task' to consolidate this construction.[28] To ease this burden, and their own fears about possible Russian (later Soviet) incursions into India via J&K, the British strongly supported all four Dogra rulers who ruled J&K from 1846 to 1947 under the supervision, and protection, of British paramountcy. Overall, the convenient British-Dogra relationship maximised the maharaja's rule over J&K and minimised internal forces that might have challenged it. This ensured that the colonial entity cohered, thus enhancing J&K's defensibility. Equally important, this prevented problems on Britain's strategically important northern frontier.

When J&K did cause the British problems, they intervened. In 1889, after accusing Maharaja Pratap Singh of maladministration, the British essentially ruled J&K directly until 1905 through a Council of State and a British resident.[29] While the resident acted as the 'final arbiter' in J&K's affairs,[30] he only interceded on behalf of the British 'when events were so obvious that they could not escape publicity'.[31] In 1931 the British helpfully intervened in J&K to support Dogra rule. The (British) Indian Army helped Hari Singh quell a major uprising in Srinagar which, in terms of casualties and property damage, 'was possibly the most serious communal outbreak in India between the Moplah rebellion of 1921 and the Calcutta riots of 1946'.[32] Hari Singh was displeased when British meddling thereafter compelled him to make some administrative changes and give his subjects some political representation.[33] Nevertheless, these changes did little to reduce Hari Singh's overall power and internal control. Indeed, the British allowed Hari Singh to engage in practices that kept the majority of his subjects politically unempowered and with no effective role in determining the fate of their lives or the lands on which they lived. To obtain responsible government, 'nothing less than a political and social revolution' would have been required for the people of J&K.[34]

Following his Dogra forebears' traditions, the fourth Maharaja, Maharaja Sir Hari Singh, dominated J&K. While the British were satisfied with this arrangement, it also meant that Hari Singh did not develop a popular constituency to fall back on when times became tough—as they did when the British left the subcontinent in 1947, after which he was on his own. Until then, Hari Singh's rule was difficult to challenge. It is therefore necessary to examine the nature of Hari Singh's regime in 1947 and the extent of his power and influence.

# THE UNTOLD STORY OF THE PEOPLE OF AZAD KASHMIR

In 1947, Maharaja Hari Singh controlled all of his regime's organs of violence, power or influence, either directly or by making senior appointments to them, or by passing laws that ensured the superior position of him and his religious community. He usually appointed Hindus to his administration, police and army, certainly at the senior levels. Frequently, these Hindus were from the same geographical area of eastern Jammu as the ruling Dogra clan,[35] or they regarded themselves as part of the ruler's 'royal clan', or they were indebted to the ruler for their wealth and wellbeing.[36] Muslims were under-represented in these bodies, particularly at senior levels. By April 1945, they comprised 40 per cent of J&K's civil service.[37] In 1932, they comprised 45 per cent of the 1,500-strong Department of Police, only outnumbering non-Muslims at the constable level (460 to 430). Of the other 600 men with any rank, only 200 were Muslims (35 per cent); of the thirty-seven men holding the rank of inspector and above, only two were Muslims.[38] The 'Jammu army',[39] which comprised 9,100 men in 1939,[40] was even more heavily dominated by non-Muslims: a maximum of 25 per cent of its soldiers were Muslims; much of the remainder (63 per cent) were Hindus from the maharaja's Dogra community.[41] Kashmiris, almost all of whom were Muslims, were debarred from military service as they were 'considered a non-martial race'.[42] Equally discriminatory, the J&K Arms Act 1940 allowed only (Jammu-based) Rajput Dogras to own and use firearms.[43] To discourage further conversions to Islam, particularly among Kashmiris, Hari Singh passed laws that compelled converts to forfeit all ancestral property.[44] This was a further sign of the Hindu Maharaja's overwhelming power.

Maharaja Hari Singh also dominated J&K's media and the princely state's limited consultative political body, the Praja Sabha (People's House). J&K's media comprised newspapers only. The Maharaja had only allowed their publication in J&K since 1934.[45] Prior to that, any newspapers in J&K came from Punjab, particularly Lahore. J&K's Praja Sabha was only established in 1934 after Hari Singh, following British 'encouragement', deigned to grant J&K a constitution. This followed his agreement in 1932 to allow overt political activity and public protest. However, the Maharaja tightly controlled the seventy-five-seat Praja Sabha via forty-two official or nominated seats and by allowing certain qualified subjects from selected sectors to elect the other thirty-three seats.[46] By 1939, this representation had changed (slightly) to forty members being directly elected.[47] Of these, twenty-one came from Muslim constituencies, ten from Hindu constituencies, two from Sikh constituencies, six from 'special constituencies' for landed interests, and one from a pensioner constituency. Given that all non-Muslim seats were usually pro-Maharaja, Hari Singh had effective control of this body. Furthermore, the limited debate that the ruler allowed on certain issues did not lessen his authority, power or control: it was unlawful for the Praja Sabha to consider ten major reserved matters that dealt with the regime and its practices.[48] The Praja Sabha's sitting time also was brief—thirty days in 1938.[49] The ruler could prorogue the body at any time. Overall, the Maharaja's rule was rarely scrutinised, or challenged.

At the beginning of 1947 therefore, Maharaja Hari Singh dominated J&K—and his subjects could do little about it. His position rapidly changed in August after the guarantors of his rule, the British, had left the subcontinent. Hari Singh then confronted two major challenges: continued Dogra rule and the accession issue.

## J&K: DISUNITED PEOPLE—UNDELIVERABLE STATE

The only constituency that strongly supported the continuance of his rule was that of his Hindu co-religionists, particularly in eastern Jammu Province. The leaders of India and Pakistan—Jawaharlal Nehru, whom Singh disliked, and the autocratic Muhammad Ali Jinnah—probably did not want Dogra rule to continue. Additionally, Hari Singh had never sought, nor obtained, support from his predominantly Muslim subjects that may have helped the continuance of his rule. Some of these subjects had local and regional influence. They could lobby leaders such as Nehru and Jinnah for support. They also could create significant political and physical obstacles to Dogra rule in J&K. Hari Singh and his regime now had to counter these forces on their own.

Regarding the second challenge, under the J&K Constitution, the accession decision was the Maharaja's alone.[50] However, before Partition, two of the most influential men in India had encouraged Hari Singh to take the desire of his subjects into account. After meeting Maharaja Hari Singh in early August 1947, Mahatma Gandhi publicly stated that 'the will of the Kashmiris was the supreme law' in J&K and the Maharaja had 'readily acknowledged the fact'.[51] In July 1947, the Viceroy of India, Lord Mountbatten, had privately suggested to the Maharaja that he 'should consult the will of the people and do what the majority thought best for the State'.[52] Hari Singh ignored these exhortations. He also had no mechanisms in place to consult the people of J&K, or their representatives, in any inclusive or meaningful way on the accession—even if the autocrat had wanted to. The Praja Sabha was largely useless: it was unrepresentative and pro-Maharaja. No electoral roll existed that listed all adults in J&K eligible to vote in any universal adult suffrage poll or referendum on the accession. Finally, all of the leading, popular J&K politicians were in jail. The decision on J&K's future status remained the Maharaja's alone.

Because the people of J&K were not asked about the future status of their state, it is impossible to state definitively what their aspirations were on this matter. Clearly however, this issue was divisive throughout 1947. Despite a lack of any polling, we have some contemporary indications of the perceived desires of the people of J&K—although the veracity of these is impossible to determine. On 13 August 1947, the presumably apolitical British Resident in Srinagar believed that the 'bulk' of J&K's population 'if consulted would probably favour Pakistan especially [those in the] Mirpur, Poonch and Muzaffarabad area'.[53] An assessment of newspapers that actively reported on J&K in 1947 also suggests that many people wanted J&K to join Pakistan.[54] In a *CMG* report on 28 October 1947, the former editor of the Srinagar-based *Kashmir Times*, G.K. Reddy, a South Indian, who had recently been expelled for advocating J&K's accession to Pakistan, believed that 'the vast majority of the State people want that Kashmir State should accede to Pakistan'.[55] On 20 November 1947, almost a month after the unpopular invasion by Muslim Pukhtoon tribesmen from Pakistan, *The Times* stated that there was 'little doubt that the bulk of the Muslim population' desired to join Pakistan.[56] This may have been so, although, equally, some Kashmiris under National Conference influence had different desires for J&K's international status (see below).

The question of whether J&K should join Pakistan or India was not simple. Although J&K had a Muslim majority, the state was a polyglot entity whose people enjoyed little religious homogeneity, interaction or unity, and had differing

15

desires for the future status of J&K. While the vast majority of J&K's residents were Muslims, they did not comprise a unified, monolithic community. Most Muslims were Sunnis, but Shias and 'Maulias', followers of the Agha Khan (also called 'Ismailis'), were strong in the large and lightly populated Frontier Districts Province. In the Kashmir Valley, liberal, tolerant, Sufi-inspired Sunni Islam was practised. It allowed the veneration of saints, individuals, and even objects considered holy, including a relic in Srinagar's Hazratbal shrine said to be a hair of the Prophet Muhammad; about this, a Kashmiri verse states with much seeming unorthodoxy, 'Whosoever has seen the sacred hair of Muhammad, [h]as had in reality the vision of the Prophet'.[57] Other religious groups represented in J&K included Hindus, who comprised a diverse collection of various castes and Untouchables, Buddhists, Sikhs, Jains and Christians. The 1941 Census provides evidence of J&K's diversity. In it, people either classified themselves, or were classified, as Dogras, Rajputs, Brahmins, Thakkars, Jats, Untouchables, Gujjars, Bakarwals, Poonchis, Syeds, Afghans, Punjabis, Maliks, Mians, Sikhs, Kashmiris, Pandits, Bodhs, Baltis, Shins and Yashkins.[58] While some of these categories represented ethnic groups, a number also had clear religious affiliations, including Brahmins, Untouchables and Pandits (Hinduism), Syeds (Islam), Sikhs (Sikhism) and Bodhs (Buddhism).

In a straight choice between India and Pakistan, most non-Muslims probably favoured joining India. Non-Muslims comprised 23 per cent of J&K's population. The largest of these pro-Indian elements was Jammu Hindus, who were 18 per cent of J&K's population. The most important among this group was the Maharaja, a Hindu Dogra from eastern Jammu Province, the only area of J&K which had a large Hindu population (see Table 1.2) and where the ruler enjoyed genuine popularity. For religious reasons, Hindus in this area favoured joining India. Other probably pro-Indian, non-Muslim elements in J&K included Hindu Pandits in the Kashmir Valley (2.1 per cent of J&K's population), Sikhs in Jammu or Kashmir provinces (1.4 per cent), and Buddhists (1 per cent) who, despite being numerically few, comprised a large majority in the Ladakh *tehsil* and a small minority in the Kargil *tehsil* of Ladakh District. The most important of this agglomeration of pro-Indian, non-Muslims was the Hindus who lived in eastern Jammu. They engaged in some significant actions after Partition that were clearly pro-Indian and anti-Muslim. These are discussed in Chapter 2.

A significant factor in 1947 for the Maharaja to ponder was that Muslims had differing aspirations for J&K. Had Muslims been united in wanting J&K to join Pakistan in 1947, it would have been exceedingly difficult for Hari Singh to oppose their wishes. The fact that J&K Muslims were not united allowed him to consider accession to India. We can determine the predilections of some J&K Muslims by their actions before and after Hari Singh's accession to India on 26 October 1947. Many Muslims in the *jagir* of Poonch and Mirpur District, both of which were located in western Jammu Province, were clearly anti-Maharaja and pro-Pakistan. These Muslims shared close geographical, historical, economic and cultural links with areas of western (Pakistani) Punjab and NWFP. Led by some pro-Pakistan Muslim Conference politicians, they engaged in some significant actions in September-October 1947 to ensure that J&K joined Pakistan. These actions included instigating an anti-Maharaja uprising in Poonch and starting the Azad (Free) Kashmir movement. Similarly, early in November 1947,

## J&K: DISUNITED PEOPLE—UNDELIVERABLE STATE

Gilgit Muslims in J&K's Frontier Districts Province revolted, imprisoned the Maharaja's governor who had recently arrived, and opted to join Pakistan.[59] Soon after this, Karachi sent an administrator to govern this area. These actions are discussed below.

Conversely some, perhaps many, Kashmiri Muslims were ambivalent about joining Pakistan—an important fact. Indeed, some were actively pro-Indian. Led by Sheikh Abdullah and his secular National Conference, these Muslims' distaste for Pakistan was heightened by the Pukhtoon invasion of Kashmir Province in October 1947. Kashmiris opposed this invasion. Consequently many also supported Hari Singh's accession to India, an act in which Abdullah played a major part. Because of its prestige, importance and attractiveness to both India and Pakistan, an examination of the most prized part of J&K—the physically isolated and culturally insulated Kashmir Valley—is important. So also is an examination of the leading role that Kashmiri politicians played in 1947, as not all of them were in favour of J&K joining Pakistan. These examinations confirm that J&K was a disunited and essentially undeliverable entity in 1947.

### Kashmiris: ambivalent about Pakistan

The Kashmir Valley region—or Kashmir, as it has been popularly called—was the most famous and important region of J&K. It was acclaimed because of its physical beauty and its popularity with outsiders. The most famous of these was the Mughal Emperor Jehangir, a devotee who exuberantly called 'paradise' the Kashmir kingdom captured by his father, Akbar, in 1586.[60] Kashmir also was famous because of well-known 'old' Kashmiris such as Jawaharlal Nehru and the famous subcontinental poet Muhammad Iqbal, whose ancestors were Kashmiris. The Kashmir Valley was important because Srinagar, the political centre and summer capital of J&K, was located there. With a 1941 population of 208,000, Srinagar was J&K's largest city (Jammu City had a population of 50,000). It was also the largest city north of Lahore and the twentieth largest city in India.[61] In addition, Srinagar was Sheikh Abdullah's stronghold and the centre of activities of the party that he led, the National Conference. In mid-1947, political attention was focused on Srinagar as the Maharaja was in residence; because of his involvement with Srinagar-based politicians, particularly Sheikh Abdullah, Nehru appeared to assume that circumstances in Srinagar reflected the overall state of affairs in J&K. This practice caused him to misread the political situation that existed throughout the diverse princely state.

A further reason why the Kashmir Valley was important was the numerical strength of the Muslims living in this geographically small, but ethnically homogeneous, region of Kashmir Province. In 1947, Kashmir Province had three districts: Anantnag, Baramulla and Muzaffarabad.[62] The Kashmir Valley, which was some eighty-four miles long by twenty to twenty-five miles wide,[63] straddled the Anantnag and Baramulla districts. Most Muslims residing in these two districts were ethnic Kashmiris; they comprised about 1.4 million of the 1.6 million Muslims living in Kashmir Province. A 'considerable number' of Kashmiri Muslims also lived in the more rugged, mountainous, western Muzaffarabad District, but

17

they were dispersed and outnumbered by Muslim shepherds, chiefly ethnic Gujjars and Bakarwals who, conversely, comprised small minorities in more mountainous areas surrounding the Kashmir Valley.[64] Very small numbers of Kashmiri Muslims also lived elsewhere in J&K, most notably in the Frontier Districts Province. Kashmiri Muslims living in the Kashmir Valley were politically significant as they enjoyed a substantial degree of ethnic homogeneity and cultural unity. In the event of a poll ever being held to ascertain the people of J&K's wishes on J&K's international status, anyone able to successfully woo the majority of Kashmir Valley Muslims was potentially in a powerful political position. Indeed, in any such poll, the votes of these Muslims could have been decisive.[65]

An important trait evident among Kashmiris partially explains why Kashmiri Muslims were ambivalent about Pakistan in 1947. Called 'Kashmiriness' or 'Kashmiriyat', a newer term with Perso-Arabic roots, this trait was a fundamental and apparently long-held part of Kashmiri identity and culture.[66] Kashmiriness emphasises 'the acceptance and tolerance of all religions among Kashmiris'.[67] It is 'manifested in the solidarity of different faiths and ethnic groups in the state'.[68] The concept was apparently epitomised by the patron saint of Kashmir, Sheikh Noor-ud-Din, a Muslim born in 1375 of a Hindu convert to Islam.[69] Popularly known as Nund Rishi, he repeatedly poses a question in a poem: 'How can members of the same family jeer at one another?'[70] The answer is the essence of Kashmiriness: Kashmiris, whoever they are and whatever their religious backgrounds and practices, are all members of one indivisible Kashmir Valley 'family'. It is a recipe—or even a requirement—for tolerance.

One significant consequence of Kashmiriness was that, compared with Hindus and Muslims in Jammu or northern India, Kashmiri Muslims and Kashmiri Hindus (Pandits) had relatively few social divisions or antagonisms. While they nevertheless had disputes and rivalries, the two groups generally were more liberal and more tolerant and, in many cases, had amicable, even close relations. This harmony arose because both shared the same ethnicity, language and geographical region and the same recent history under repressive rulers comprising Muslim Afghans (Durranis), Punjabi Sikhs (Ranjit Singh's empire) and Jammu Hindus (Dogras), although the latter was less repressive for Pandits. It was important that Kashmiri Muslims and Kashmiri Pandits also enjoyed a similar culture, including revering each other's religious figures and festivals, eating *halal* mutton instead of beef or pork (even though Pandits were of the Brahmin or priestly caste that elsewhere usually practised vegetarianism), and not being particular about 'defilement or pollution by touch'.[71] As a leading Pandit put it, 'Racially, culturally and linguistically the Hindus and Muslims living in Kashmir [were] practically one'.[72] That said, Kashmiri Pandits also enjoyed greater influence and economic wellbeing than Kashmiri Muslims. This was due to the Pandits' position as Hindu subjects of a Hindu ruler, from which flowed benefits such as being landowners and their numerically large involvement as state employees. Nevertheless, relations between Kashmiri Muslims and Kashmiri Pandits were generally far more amicable than relations between Hindus and Muslims in Jammu Province.

One significant result of the concept of Kashmiriness was that Kashmiris may have been naturally attracted to secular thinking. This was partly because they were apparently not afflicted by 'the majority-minority complex' that was evident

Table 1.2: Numbers of Muslims and Hindus in each province of Princely J&K, and as percentages of J&K, and as percentages of each respective religious group.

| Province | Muslims | %P | %JK | %M | Hindus | %P | %JK | %H | Total |
|---|---|---|---|---|---|---|---|---|---|
| Jammu | 1,212,405 | 61.19 | 30.15 | 39.12 | 736,862 | 37.19 | 18.32 | 89.54 | 1,981,433 |
| Kashmir | 1,615,928 | 93.48 | 40.18 | 52.15 | 85,531 | 4.95 | 2.13 | 10.39 | 1,728,705 |
| Frontier | 270,539 | 86.86 | 6.73 | 8.73 | 562 | 0.18 | 0.01 | 0.07 | 311,478 |
| Total J&K | 3,098,872 | | 77.06 | — | 822,955 | — | 20.46 | — | 4,021,616 |

Source: *Census of India 1941*, Volume XXII, Jammu & Kashmir State, Part III, Village Tables, Srinagar, R. G. Wreford, Editor, Jammu and Kashmir Government, 1942.

Key: H  Percentage of Hindu population.
 JK  Percentage of J&K population.
 M  Percentage of Muslim population.
 P  Percentage of population in province.

among Muslims in other parts of the subcontinent, and partly because they were 'a deeply religious people who abhor[red] political exploitation of their faith'.[73] Hence, the stance of the major pro-Pakistan party in J&K, the Muslim Conference, and its Pakistan ally the Muslim League was not automatically popular with Kashmiri Muslims. To join Pakistan simply because it would be a Muslim homeland was an insufficient reason. Furthermore, as the secular Sheikh Abdullah noted, more Muslims would remain in India (40 million) than would join (neighbouring) West Pakistan (25 million). If 'one Muslim is as good as another, the Kashmiri Muslims ... should choose the forty million living in India'.[74] Using the same logic, they could have joined Pakistan.

Equally, another result of the concept of Kashmiriness was that one or two important or influential Hindu Pandits believed that, because of the demographic and geographical compulsions discussed above, J&K should join Pakistan. One was Prem Nath Bazaz, leader of the Kashmir Kisan Mazdoor Conference (Peasants and Workers Conference). A smaller 'non-communal party', it supported J&K's accession to Pakistan, 'a State run on Islamic principles'.[75] While Bazaz had stood unsuccessfully for election to the Praja Sabha in early 1947,[76] his defeat probably reflected the situation whereby few peasants and workers were entitled to vote in such selections. On 9 October 1947, his party called upon the Maharaja to accede to Pakistan.[77] In 1951, Bazaz still supported this stance: 'Kashmir is preponderantly Muslim. It is therefore just and rational as well as democratic that it should be allowed to accede to Pakistan'.[78]

Another possibly pro-Pakistan Pandit—according to his political opponents—was the Prime Minister of J&K, Ramchandra Kak.[79] (Other Muslim opponents considered him pro-independence.)[80] The first state subject to hold this position,[81] as well as 'the one man who had the intellectual capacity to make some coherent effort towards an acceptable settlement' of the accession issue,[82] Kak was dismissed by Hari Singh on 11 August, possibly because he may have impeded J&K's accession to India.[83] Equally, there was much intrigue surrounding the Maharaja's relationship with the supposedly mystical and highly influential religious figure Swami Santdev, who both disliked Kak and heavily influenced Hari Singh.[84] Kak's replacement, General Janak Singh, was related to the Maharaja. In mid-October, he was replaced by the strongly pro-Indian Justice Mehr Chand Mahajan. As Kak himself (somewhat immodestly) noted, 'Loyalty is a great virtue, but as the Maharaja soon found, it [did] not compensate for lack of ability'.[85] Had Kak remained in office, 'events might have followed a different course' and J&K may well have joined Pakistan.[86] Equally, the state may have survived as a single, undivided political entity.

Certainly, Kashmiriness and the 'secular thinking' of Kashmiris were significant reasons why the Kashmir Valley experienced almost no communal violence during 1947. Kashmiris were more tolerant, their practice of Islam and Hinduism more liberal, and their inter-communal relationships more involved and harmonious than those in other parts of the princely state. The lack of disruption in the Kashmir Valley in 1947 was assisted by Muslims being an overwhelming majority that did not feel threatened by the small Hindu Pandit minority. Equally, the Pandits could not threaten the majority Muslim community. Consequently, Kashmiris living in the Kashmir Valley were less susceptible to, and involved in, divisive communal politics and activities than Muslims and Hindus elsewhere, particularly in Jammu Province, where there was substantial communal violence during 1947 (discussed below).

A further factor that caused Kashmiris to be ambivalent about Pakistan was the significant role played in 1947 by Sheikh Abdullah and the political party that he dominated, the National Conference. For over fifty years (1931–82), he was Muslim Kashmiris' most popular politician, whether in power or denied it. (Abdullah was jailed for long periods by the Maharaja, by Bakshi Ghulam Mohammed, his successor as Prime Minister in J&K, and by the Indian Government.) According to his autobiography, Abdullah's political career began as early as 1926, when he joined the 'relentless struggle between the oppressor and the oppressed', desiring to become the people's saviour, began to oppose the Maharaja's regime and its practices on an individual basis.[87] He disliked a number of the Maharaja's practices, including discrimination on religious grounds, exploitation of the people through taxation, corruption, the inequitable land system, and the people's lack of political freedom.[88] Abdullah sprang to prominence in 1931 during the major anti-Maharaja agitation in Srinagar, an event of seminal importance that temporarily—but severely—challenged Hari Singh's rule.[89] Indeed, it was due to Abdullah's bold part in this uprising that he became known as the Lion of Kashmir. A further consequence of this major uprising was that, as a result of the Glancy Commission formed in order to investigate the uprising's causes, the Maharaja allowed the formation of the first political party in J&K. In October 1932, the All J&K Muslim Conference was formed in order to safeguard Muslim interests in J&K.[90] Abdullah, a Muslim, later renamed this party the All J&K National Conference. Espousing secularism, it would later play a significant role in delivering a large part of J&K to India and in ending the Maharaja's rule.

Because Sheikh Abdullah had a strong aversion to autocracy, he regarded the concept of Pakistan negatively. Abdullah disliked the Maharaja's absolutism. The United States' Consul in Lahore agreed: 'according to all disinterested informants [the maharaja] has never displayed the slightest interest in the welfare of the people over whom he has maintained an autocratic rule.'[91] For Sheikh Abdullah, both Jinnah and the Islamic Pakistan that the autocratic Muslim League leader envisaged establishing therefore were also unappealing.[92] The influential Kashmiri leader considered that Pakistan was the result of an emotional Muslim reaction to Hindu communalism and 'an escapist device'. Abdullah and his colleagues, many of whom were Muslims, also perceived (correctly) that Pakistan would be dominated by feudal elements, as well as being a society in which Kashmiris and their reform agenda would have little power: 'Chains of slavery will keep us in their continuous stranglehold.'[93] Conversely, Abdullah considered that secular India would be different. It would have people and parties, including India's major party, the Indian National Congress, whose views largely coincided with Abdullah's and his party's. India also represented an option that would accept the National Conference's 'enlightened and progressive ideas'. It embraced more democracy than either Pakistan or the Jinnah-dominated Muslim League, whose leader had 'a very high opinion of himself'.[94] Abdullah was not ambivalent about Pakistan—for him, it was totally unappealing. To this end, he both opposed the rival pro-Pakistan

Muslim Conference and worked against its desire to have the princely state join Pakistan. Abdullah's opposition to both factors increased political divisions in J&K, as well as its undeliverability.

*Politicians: differing aspirations*

Political divisions within J&K are a further factor that suggested that J&K was a disunited and essentially undeliverable entity in 1947. From as early as 1941, rivalry between Muslim politicians from J&K's diverse Muslim 'community' reflected the struggle in British India between Muslims and secularists that eventually resulted in the creation of India and Pakistan. In 1947, J&K's political scene was dominated by two parties: the All J&K National Conference (commonly called the National Conference) and the All J&K Muslim Conference (commonly called the Muslim Conference). Each conference had a different aspiration for J&K's status: the National Conference opposed J&K joining Pakistan; the Muslim Conference favoured this option. While it is impossible to quantify the exact support that either party enjoyed, between them they had over 20,000 paid-up members.[95] The National Conference was strongest in the Kashmir Valley, where perhaps as many as 50 per cent of all Muslims and many Hindus supported this party; conversely, outside the Kashmir Valley its support was much less, with perhaps five to 15 per cent of the population supporting it.[96] The Muslim Conference had a lot of support in Jammu Province and much less in the Kashmir Valley. Even though their leaders were not responsible for the actual accession, these two parties and their leaders played important roles in 1947 influencing the people of J&K on whom the Maharaja's decision would have a direct and major impact.

In 1939, the All J&K Muslim Conference was renamed the All J&K National Conference. This was seven years after the Muslim Conference had been formed. It was supposed to have been made in order to reflect a secular leaning among some of the Muslim Conference's leadership and to encourage non-Muslims to join the party. Chiefly, it occurred because of Sheikh Abdullah's secularism. Abdullah had been influenced by a burgeoning friendship with the strongly secular Jawaharlal Nehru, whom he first met in 1938 and who thereafter would play a significant, and partisan, role in J&K. Abdullah believed that if Kashmiri leaders wanted the support of the Indian National Congress in their anti-Maharaja struggle, the Muslim Conference would have to change its name and constitution.[97] He also believed that the Maharaja was oppressing people of all religions, not just Muslims. Abdullah was able to convince his colleagues to secularise the party, thus making it accessible to, and representative of, all religions present in J&K; hence the name change. Thereafter, in terms of political ideology and leanings, Abdullah, Nehru and their respective secular parties, the National Conference and the Indian National Congress, would have strong, if informal, links.

In a move that anticipated the division of J&K into pro-Pakistan and pro-Indian areas, some disgruntled Muslims revived the Muslim Conference in 1941 as a political vehicle for Muslims. Hence, by 1941, two conferences existed in J&K: the All J&K National Conference and the All J&K Muslim Conference. The old Muslim Conference was revived because some Muslim members of the National

Conference were disenchanted with the party's secularism, which they believed diluted Muslims' power in that party. (Even so, Abdullah and most of the National Conference's top leadership were Muslims.) They also disliked Abdullah's close friendship with Nehru and the National Conference's support for the Indian National Congress and its ideals. Equally, there were aspects of regional and personal rivalry behind the revival of the Muslim Conference: Chaudhry Ghulam Abbas, a Jammuite, who became president of the Muslim Conference, and Mirwaiz Yusuf Shah, a religious preacher and senior party figure from Srinagar, had been Abdullah's intermittent political rivals since 1931 (both later became leading politicians in Azad Kashmir). Abbas and 'his group from Jammu' had resigned from the National Conference 'as a protest against toeing the Congress line' after Nehru visited Srinagar in May 1940 as a guest of the National Conference.[98] More likely, Abbas's stance related to the Muslim League's Lahore Resolution of March 1940 that called for separate states where Muslims were in the majority in the subcontinent, that is, for Pakistan. Although the secular National Conference was dominated by Muslims, it did not favour this concept. The Muslims who revived the Muslim Conference did.

Another reason why the Muslim Conference was revived was that some Muslims considered Hindus 'were not liberal enough to see the liquidation of the autocratic rule of a Hindu Maharaja'.[99] They believed that self-interested Hindu clients of the Maharaja, particularly in Jammu Province, wanted the regime of their co-religionist Maharaja to continue, as he would look after their interests better than non-Hindu politicians.[100] Given J&K's strong Muslim majority, the Hindus' concern may have been reasonable. Equally, Muslims felt that the Muslim Conference needed to be revived not only to oppose the secular, pro-Indian National Conference, but also as a political vehicle for Muslims to pursue their wellbeing. Because Muslim interests needed to be advanced in J&K, 'The old Muslim Conference, with its ideal of working for the amelioration and betterment of the Muslims of the State, was revived ... This body then identified itself, in ideology, with the Muslim League programme in the Indo-Pakistan [sic] Sub-Continent.'[101] Thereafter, although the Muslim Conference would claim otherwise, it was a communal organisation, if only because it was unattractive to non-Muslims.

In many ways, the avowedly anti-Maharaja National Conference was all that the Muslim Conference was not: secular, well organised, disciplined, bravely led, certain, anti-Pakistan, friendly with India, and populist (although not necessarily more popular). In 1947 Sheikh Abdullah, the National Conference's undisputed leader, was almost certainly the most popular and influential politician in the Kashmir Valley, and possibly in all of J&K. This is impossible to verify as both Abdullah, who was then in jail, and the National Conference boycotted the 1947 Praja Sabha elections, thereby missing an opportunity to confirm their popularity among the limited and selective electorate that voted.[102] (Conversely, the Muslim Conference won sixteen of the twenty-one J&K Muslims seats, including some in the Kashmir Valley, although voter turnout was low.)[103] Equally, Abdullah's 1946 'Quit Kashmir' campaign (discussed below) had made him popular. Furthermore, Kashmiris, in particular, related to Abdullah because of his unprivileged upbringing and his inspiring oration and recitations of the Koran in Kashmiri. They admired him because of the sacrifices he had made since 1931 in the struggle against the despotic Dogras. They liked him because he advocated land reform to the detriment of absentee Dogra landlords and debt alleviation to the detriment of Hindu moneylenders. Abdullah's secularism also resonated with the ideals of Kashmiriness, while his opposition to J&K joining Pakistan appealed to some Kashmiris, particularly Hindu Pandits, although this support is impossible to quantify. Abdullah's influence and pro-India leanings were a major reason why Kashmiri Muslims were ambivalent about joining Muslim Pakistan.

Conversely, the Muslim Conference appeared to have a narrow agenda: to advance Muslim welfare and join Pakistan, although not necessarily in that order. Its agenda appeared to be popular with many Muslims in Jammu Province and with some, perhaps many, Muslims in the Kashmir Valley. (Neither party appeared to attract much interest or support in the distant and lightly populated Frontier Districts Province.) Abdullah, who was released from jail on 29 September 1947,[104] had, according to *The Times* of 10 October, possibly lost popular support to the Muslim Conference, the 'only other effective political organization' in J&K. During Abdullah's detention, the Muslim Conference's rallying cry of 'Islamic India' (as recorded in the report in *The Times*, which surely meant 'Islamic Pakistan') had become so popular that it 'may defeat him' if a plebiscite were held. This was because 'the simple Muslim hillmen [of J&K] might well forget newly found political theories and allow the dictates of religious and communal prejudice to influence his vote'.[105] Even so, the Muslim Conference faced a major challenge in the numerically and politically important Kashmir Valley: it lacked a charismatic Kashmiri-speaking politician who could rival Sheikh Abdullah and his coterie of Kashmiri colleagues. The Muslim Conference's stance also was unpopular elsewhere, especially among the non-Muslim majority in eastern Jammu, as its killings of Muslims (discussed in Chapter 2) were clearly showing.

While the National Conference appeared to enjoy much popularity in the Kashmir Valley, and while the Muslim Conference had problems in garnering support there, the National Conference was not necessarily the most popular party there. The two parties in favour of J&K joining Pakistan, the Muslim Conference and Prem Nath Bazaz's Kisan Mazdoor Conference, also had (unquantifiable) support. According to *The Times*' Special Correspondent in late October 1947, it was 'a moot point how far Abdullah's influence extends among the Kashmiri Muslims ... but in Srinagar his influence is paramount'.[106] The *CMG*, the best-informed English-language newspaper on J&K affairs, on 21 October 1947 reported that the southern Kashmir Valley, which apparently was the 'stronghold' of the Kisan Mazdoor Conference, 'last week witnessed a massive upsurge in favour of Pakistan'.[107] However, the *CMG*'s report predated the tribal invasion of Kashmir Province by one day, after which support for pro-Pakistan parties may have lessened, at least in the short term, even though southern Kashmir was not directly affected by this invasion.

The different approaches of the National Conference and the Muslim Conference on the issue of resolving J&K's international status portended future problems in J&K, particularly in relation to the option of independence. The National Conference had agonised over whether J&K should join Pakistan or India or pursue independence.[108] Not prepared to 'brook dictation from Pakistan or coercion from India', it first wanted to attain 'freedom from autocracy' by ending the

## J&K: DISUNITED PEOPLE—UNDELIVERABLE STATE

Maharaja's rule,[109] then to replace this with self-government, presumably under National Conference leadership. This stance essentially meant *de facto* independence for J&K. On 9 October 1947, Sheikh Abdullah, stated: 'Our prime concern at this stage is the emancipation of the four million people living in this State. We can consider the question of joining one or the other Dominion only when we have achieved our objective. We cannot decide it as long as we are slaves.'[110] Although this statement was made seventeen days before the Maharaja acceded to India, Abdullah's independent attitude and his attitude towards independence would later pose serious problems for India, especially after Abdullah was removed from office in 1953.

The issue of independence in 1947 also showed that some in J&K favoured the princely state not being delivered to either dominion. On this, Sheikh Abdullah and Maharaja Hari Singh were seemingly in agreement; in reality, both were seeking options other than joining Pakistan where their positions would be weaker. Both before and after his accession, Hari Singh seriously considered independence. His stance was initially supported by both the Muslim Conference (see below) and by the Jammu-based, and locally strong,[111] Jammu and Kashmir Rajya Hindu Sabha which did not want the 'Hindu State' to 'merge its identity in a secular India'.[112] In July, the *CMG* reported that 'The Kashmir State has finally decided to declare independence after the lapse of paramountcy next month. It is learned from official quarters that an announcement to this affect is expected in a fortnight'.[113] In late 1947, Hari Singh 'nodded [his] assent' when Abdullah told the J&K Prime Minister, Mahajan, that it would be a good thing 'if India and Pakistan were made to recognise the State as an independent unit like Switzerland'.[114] This unity was misleading. As *The Times* noted on 10 October, Abdullah and Hari Singh had 'basically dissimilar [aims], but both are anti-Pakistan'.[115] The reality of their dislike for joining Pakistan was shown when the Pukhtoon tribesmen invaded J&K. Faced with physical and political annihilation, the Maharaja quickly acceded to India. Similarly confronted, Abdullah just as quickly concurred with his decision.

The Muslim Conference's approach to the issue of J&K's international status was eventually to favour J&K joining Pakistan, although a temporary ruse for independence in 1947 obfuscated its stance. On 11 May 1947, the acting Muslim Conference President, Chaudhry Hamidullah (Ghulam Abbas was in jail), believed that Muslims would 'readily acclaim [the Maharaja] as the first constitutional king of a democratic and independent Kashmir'.[116] He again spoke of independence for J&K in Srinagar on 21 May.[117] On both occasions, Hamidullah may have been acting on written directions received from Ghulam Abbas in jail.[118] By 22 June, a somewhat prescient Hamidullah cautioned Hari Singh from acceding to India, on the grounds that Muslims would revolt (as they later did) and declare independence. He claimed that the Muslim Conference still wanted Pakistan but had 'sacrificed' joining it 'to allay the fears and suspicions of the minorities'.[119] The most important of these minorities were J&K Hindus, who were the Maharaja's strongest supporters—and major opponents of the Muslim Conference. The Muslim Conference quickly dropped what one correspondent called its 'ruse to trap the Maharaja' and 'absorb' J&K into Pakistan.[120] On, and consistently from, 22 July 1947, Hamidullah called on the Maharaja to accede to Pakistan.[121] On 29 July, the

Muslim Conference's Muslim League ally also suggested that: 'The only sensible course for Kashmir is ... to join the Pakistan Dominion ... We trust that Sir Harri [sic] Singh will soon make his choice and come down on the right side of the fence on which he has so long been occupying an uncertain and precarious perch.'[122] This reflected an unequivocal return of the pro-Pakistan forces to the position that J&K should join Pakistan. Meanwhile, Hari Singh continued to sit on his precarious perch.

The Muslim Conference's advocacy of independence for J&K reflected the control that the charismatic—for Muslims, at least—Jinnah and his colleagues already had over a party that was really their surrogate. Equally, it revealed the Muslim Conference's desire to follow the Muslim League's line and do whatever was needed to ensure that J&K joined Pakistan. Both parties would continue this unequal relationship after Azad Kashmir was created. Although Jinnah (falsely) believed that J&K would fall into Pakistan's 'lap like a ripe fruit' once the Maharaja realised his and the people's interests and acceded to Pakistan,[123] and although he was prepared to allow the Maharaja's 'autocratic government' to continue,[124] support for independence enabled pro-Pakistan forces to woo the decision maker rather than the people. This approach was pragmatic. However, it also made the Muslim Conference appear keen to gain the Maharaja's support at any cost. Although this tactic adhered to Jinnah's statement in July 1947 that princely rulers were free to join Pakistan, India or remain independent,[125] many Muslim Conference members wanted their party's support for independence reversed.[126] Also, by allowing the ruler to decide the issue, the Muslim Conference enabled its National Conference rival to advance the populist—and eminently more 'sellable'—view that the people should be given self-government so that, 'armed with authority and responsibility, [they] could decide for themselves where their interests lay'.[127] Apart from advancing its own popularity, the National Conference's stance also served to reveal the Muslim Conference as simply an appendage or surrogate of the Muslim League—as it was.

The Muslim Conference's pragmatic approach towards the Maharaja built on a previous stance Jinnah instigated during the National Conference's 'Quit Kashmir' campaign that started on 20 May 1946 with the aim of ridding J&K of Dogra rule. This campaign was significant as, apart from directly challenging the Maharaja, it highlighted a difference between the positions of Jinnah and Nehru on J&K. Jinnah opposed Quit Kashmir as a movement 'engineered by some malcontents'.[128] This stance, coupled with his lack of criticism of J&K's unpopular ruler, particularly when compared with criticisms made by Nehru and the Indian National Congress, made Jinnah appear pro-Maharaja. This lost the Muslim League leader support among Kashmiri Muslims,[129] especially among the 'malcontents', most of whom were National Conference members. Indeed, one such National Conference member, Mir Qasim (who later became a Chief Minister of Indian J&K), believed that Jinnah's unpopular and insensitive attitude 'killed the chances of Kashmir going to Pakistan'.[130] It also affected the Muslim League's surrogate, the Muslim Conference. The Muslim Conference lost credibility because it did not initially oppose the Maharaja when Quit Kashmir commenced in May 1946—a policy Jinnah ordered because he believed that the party would do better working through constitutional channels. After July 1946, the Muslim Conference began a more aggressive anti-Maharaja stance by calling for a constitutional assembly to frame a democratic constitution for J&K. The Maharaja responded by banning the Muslim Conference's annual conference scheduled for October and arresting its leader, Ghulam Abbas, on 23 October 1946. Thereafter, the Muslim Conference appeared to steadily lose support, certainly in the Kashmir Valley, owing to poor leadership and increased factionalism; conversely, support for the National Conference increased because it was united and had strong leadership.

One of the most significant aspects of the Quit Kashmir movement was the seminal impact it had on the future Prime Minister of independent India, Jawaharlal Nehru, and, as a consequence, on his party. To counter Quit Kashmir, the Maharaja declared martial law, arrested 900 political leaders during and after May 1946, including Sheikh Abdullah, and forced other political activists to flee the princely state.[131] The Maharaja and his Prime Minister, Ramchandra Kak, who hated Nehru 'with a bitter hatred' for supporting the anti-Maharaja forces in J&K,[132] arrested him in June 1946 while he was travelling to Srinagar in his capacity as a lawyer to defend Abdullah. According to Karan Singh, there was 'no doubt that [Nehru's] arrest was the turning point in the history of the State'.[133] An indignant Nehru, who only reached Srinagar in July and was thus unable to secure the release of his client, Sheikh Abdullah, apparently never forgave Hari Singh for Abdullah's sentence of three years' rigorous imprisonment for sedition. Perhaps even more significantly, Nehru's visit to J&K put the issue of the state's post-British status firmly on the Indian National Congress's agenda. On 15 August 1946, Sardar Patel informed Kak that the Working Committee of the Indian National Congress had considered 'Nehru's report about his visit to Kashmir' for a 'long time'.[134] Importantly, exactly one year before the British departure from the subcontinent, members of the future Indian dominion already were focused on J&K's future. Only much later would Muslims favouring the creation of a Muslim-majority state or J&K's accession to Pakistan realise this situation and react to it

Hence, from mid-1946, by which time it was clear that British paramountcy was soon going to end in India, J&K was politically disunited by forces that had strong—and differing—post-British desires for the princely state's status. In an attempt to limit political activities and the influence of outside parties in J&K, the Maharaja's administration jailed local politicians, stifled debate and dissent, and censored news about the increasingly topical issue of J&K's future status. The British, who mostly condoned the ruler's activities, sought to fulfil their obligations to the Maharaja by keeping certain Indian politicians away from J&K. While Hari Singh's actions shored up his position in the short term, they neither endeared him to his people nor helped him build a consensus with them on the important, and divisive, issue of J&K's post-British status. As a result, after mid-1946, the Dogra regime increasingly needed to rely on the use of force to hold its domain together and to keep its subjects in line. Little else unified them.

## Poonch Muslims: martial and disgruntled

Another factor affecting J&K's divisibility and deliverability was the role that aggrieved Muslims in western Jammu, especially in the *jagir* of Poonch, could and did play in 1947. While Muslims comprised an overall majority of Jammu Province's population, they were numerically strongest in the province's three western districts of Mirpur, Reasi and Poonch. (Muslims were a minority in Jammu Province's eastern districts of Jammu, Udhampur, Kathua and the Chenani *jagir*; see Table 1.3.) Poonch *jagir* was an important district in J&K. Comprising 1,627 sq. miles, it was by far the larger of J&K's two jurisdictional *jagir*s. (The other was the tiny Chenani *jagir*.) Indeed, it was larger than many of India's princely states, including high profile ones such as Cochin (1,418 sq. miles) and Cooch Behar (1,318 sq. miles).[135] Even so, landholdings in the *jagir* were usually small, with poor soil. With little work available locally, many Poonchis sought employment outside the *jagir* working in Punjab, working on the railways, joining the (British) Indian Army, which they did in large numbers, or joining the British merchant navy in Bombay.[136] Ramifications of working in the latter two areas would later prove to be of significance in the creation and sustenance of Azad Kashmir.

One reason why Muslims in western Jammu Province were pro-Pakistan was their geographical, historical, ethnic, cultural and economic connections with, and reliance on, Punjab and NWFP. With homelands located in the foothills and highlands that abutted the end of the Punjab plains, people in western Jammu spoke dialects of Punjabi, such as Hindko and Pahari (as against Dogri in eastern Jammu). For them, western Punjab and NWFP's Hazara region located on the western side of the Jhelum River that divided the constructed entity of J&K from British India (later Pakistan) were geographically closer and more accessible than the remainder of Jammu Province located east of the Chenab River. To travel to the Kashmir Valley involved crossing the difficult Pir Panjal mountain range via longer and more difficult routes that were often snowbound in winter. For Poonchis, Rawalpindi, which was connected by road and rail to Lahore, was closer and

Table 1.3: Muslims and Hindus in Jammu Province as percentages of their Respective Districts.

| District | Muslims | %D | Hindus | %D | District Pop* |
|---|---|---|---|---|---|
| Chenani Jagir | 2,205 | 18.70 | 9,581 | 81.22 | 11,796 |
| Jammu | 170,789 | 39.60 | 248,173 | 57.53 | 431,362 |
| Kathua | 45,000 | 25.33 | 132,022 | 74.31 | 177,672 |
| Mirpur | 310,900 | 80.41 | 63,576 | 16.44 | 386,655 |
| Poonch | 379,645 | 90.00 | 37,965 | 9.00 | 421,828 |
| Reasi | 175,539 | ±68.06 | 80,725 | 31.30 | 257,903 |
| Udhampur | 128,327 | 43.62 | 164,820 | 56.02 | 294,217 |
| Total JP | 1,212,405 | | 736,862 | | 1,981,433 |

Source: *Census of India 1941*, Volume XXII, Jammu & Kashmir State, Part III, Village Tables, Srinagar, R.G. Wreford, Editor, Jammu and Kashmir Government, 1942.

Key: JP   Jammu Province.
 Pop Population.
 ±   The census gives this figure as 'over 67 per cent' (p. 151).
 *   Includes 27,896 Sikhs and 4,270 Others: Indian Christians, Jains, Buddhists and unspecified others.

considerably easier to reach than Jammu City. For Mirpuris, Jhelum town, which was on the same railway line, was closer and easier to get to than Jammu City. In 1947, therefore, the closest historical, cultural and fraternal links for western Jammuites were with Punjab and NWFP, with Lahore being the principal city to which they looked for work, trade and culture.

Another reason why Muslims in western Jammu Province were pro-Pakistan was that Poonch Muslims, and to a lesser extent Mirpur Muslims, disliked Dogra rule.[137] In the case of the Poonchis, their dislike apparently began in the 1830s-40s when Gulab Singh militarily imposed Dogra rule on their forebears with much brutality. In doing so, he engaged in unsavoury acts such as killing the previous ruler (a Muslim), his son and his nephew and displaying their bodies in 'an iron cage'[138] and 'flay[ing] alive' some local rebel leaders whose rebellion against Dogra rule Gulab Singh suppressed with 'extreme cruelty'.[139] Possibly 5,000 Sudhans, members of one of the main tribes of Poonch, were slaughtered; a similar number of captured women and children died from starvation, exposure, or were enslaved.[140] Poonchis apparently never forgot this Dogra barbarity.[141]

A further reason for Poonchis' dislike of Dogra rule was that they were subjected to a dual system of autocracy, or 'dual control'.[142] This comprised the Maharaja's overlordship or suzerainty,[143] plus local rule by the subordinate Raja of Poonch. For Poonchis, this dual arrangement was relatively new, and somewhat unpopular. It resulted from a long history of dislike and disputation between the rajas of Poonch and the maharajas of J&K going back to the late 1830s-early 1840s. In 1925, it intensified when Hari Singh became Maharaja of J&K, after which he sought to bring the Raja of Poonch, a distant cousin and spiritual heir to the late Maharaja Pratap Singh, under his direct control. This demotion involved an agreement in 1928 between Maharaja Hari Singh and Raja Jagatdev Singh when the former installed the latter as ruler of Poonch.[144] This arrangement was 'enhanced' (to Hari Singh's advantage) in 1936–37 after the British not only dismissed a protest by Raja Jagatdev Singh but also confirmed his subordinate position. It was completed in 1940 when Jagatdev Singh died. Hari Singh then fully asserted himself over Jagatdev's heir, Shiv Ratandev Singh, who was still then a minor.[145]

With British acquiescence, Maharaja Hari Singh, via his officials, was now fully in control of Poonch, although this absolute dominance of Poonch disgruntled Poonchis.[146] Although the Raja of Poonch remained an 'Illaqadar or an independent Jagirdar' (or head)[147] of an autonomous district ('*illaqas*'), his autonomy was curtailed by an administrator appointed by, and responsible to, the (superior) Maharaja.[148] Although the Poonch administration had its own officials, including a bureaucracy, police and a standing army of one company[149] that had once comprised 'about 1,200 men' equipped with a battery of guns,[150] the Maharaja further exercised his control and influence through officers of his administration that he 'lent' to Poonch (a system Pakistan would adopt with Azad Kashmir).[151] While the Raja's courts had jurisdiction in all petty cases, all serious crimes were referred to Srinagar. The Raja of Poonch lost the prestige and power he had enjoyed before Hari Singh imposed himself. He became a (junior) feudatory under the control of his distant cousin, the (senior) Maharaja. On 30 July 1940, a 'huge gathering' of the 'Poonch Public' expressed 'profound sorrow and deep indignation and resentment' that Hari Singh had described Poonch as a *jagir* and their 'beloved' Raja as a Jagirdar. The gathering passed a resolution that called on the people of Poonch 'to unite and continue the struggle in a constitutional and peaceful manner, until Poonch State is free from the bondage and absolutely unwarranted yoke and interference of the Kashmir durbar'.[152]

Dual autocratic rule in Poonch imposed heavy taxation on Poonchis. Indeed, they were 'burdened with still heavier taxes' in order to support both the rule of the Maharaja and the Raja.[153] Certainly, the Maharaja was the major beneficiary of the Raja's demotion, chiefly because Hari Singh acquired direct control over 420,000 taxable subjects,[154] particularly after 1941 when a number of new taxes were imposed, some of which only applied to Muslims.[155] The Raja also apparently levied his own taxes, out of which he paid a yearly tribute of Rs. 231 to the Maharaja on whom he attended on state occasions.[156] According to Richard Symonds,[157] resentful Muslim Poonchis, particularly soldiers returning from fighting fought in World War II—but not Hindus or Sikhs—were forced to pay a number of (imaginative) taxes:

- The Tirni Tax, on Muslims only, of rupees 1.4 on every cow and rupees 1 on every buffalo;
- The Bakri Tax of 10 annas per sheep and 4 annas per goat;
- The Chula Tax, introduced in 1947, of 8 annas on every hearth;
- A Wife Tax of 8 annas on every wife over and above the first;
- The Zaildari Tax, introduced in 1947, of one and a half paisa per rupee of Revenue Tax to support the Zaildar, a minor tax collector;
- A Widow Tax of 4 annas per widow;
- A Forest Tax;
- Import and export taxes, e.g. 75 per cent on toilet soap, and silk.[158]

Poonchis also paid other 'strange' taxes, such as a horse tax on 50 per cent of the purchase price.[159] In addition, 'Dogra troops were billeted on the Poonchis to enforce collections',[160] while also they requisitioned supplies locally from the Poonchis who were paid with 'worthless chits'.[161] If that was not enough, Poonchis also had to endure the Raja appropriating up to 40 per cent of the *jagir*'s average annual income of Rs. 1 million a year,[162] almost all of which appeared to have been raised by taxes.[163]

Two factors added to the taxation issue in Poonch: disgruntled local officials and an increasing cost of living.[164] Local officials in the Poonch administration, the bulk of whom were Hindus, were discontented with receiving lower pay than their counterparts in either the J&K state or Indian administrations and abnormally slow rates of promotion. As a result, they were inefficient and corrupt. Poonchis also suffered from an increasing cost of living, a situation made worse by the unproductive nature of their lands and the heavy taxes levied on them. Many Poonchi men worked outside the *jagir* to alleviate this situation. While this practice brought considerable economic benefits to their families, particularly during World War II when many men served in the Indian Army, it also informed Poonchis of how relatively backward their area was when compared with the 'far higher standards of living prevailing outside the State'. For this reason, some Poonchis had sought the integration of Poonch into British India long before Partition was proposed, a major uprising in 1938 among Sudhans being the most pronounced example of this desire. The uprising ended after two battalions of J&K State Forces were sent into the *jagir* and the leader of the unrest was politically placated. Significantly, the J&K State Forces stayed in the area thereafter.

A further negative factor for Poonchis was that Dogra rule denied them important land reforms granted to other state subjects after the 1931 uprising in the Kashmir Valley. When proprietary rights were granted to landholders in J&K in 1933 as a result of the Glancy Commission, Poonchis were excluded.[165] This probably occurred because the Raja of Poonch then still enjoyed considerable autonomy; also, the 1931 uprising occurred in 'the Maharaja's domain, not in Poonch. Nevertheless, the Raja was able to retain his position as the holder of proprietary rights to all land in Poonch *jagir*. The actual 'holders of land' neither could be, nor were, recognised as the owners of the land—they were considered '*assamis*' (agents) of the Raja.[166] Poonchi peasants, particularly in Bagh and Sudhnoti *tehsil*s, had been dissatisfied about this situation from as early as 1905 when they had begun an agitation to obtain ownership rights.[167] Their dissatisfaction also may have arisen because, for 'unknown causes', some cultivators in Poonch's Mendhar *tehsil* had apparently been granted ownership rights in 1906.[168] Bagh and Sudhnoti peasants were further aggrieved when they were not granted proprietary rights in 1933, a situation that caused them to harbour 'widespread and deep-rooted grievances' with Dogra rule.[169]

Importantly, many Poonchi men possessed significant military capabilities that could challenge Dogra rule. Most had obtained this as soldiers in the Indian Army in World War I and World War II, not as members of the Maharaja's Hindu/Dogra-dominated military. Many Poonchis, along with neighbouring Mirpuris, had volunteered for the Indian Army, although not for patriotic reasons alone. Small farms, limited local economic opportunities and heavy taxes encouraged men in Mirpur and Poonch, particularly, to go elsewhere to obtain work. Apart from working at various occupations in Punjab, Muslims in these districts had a reputation for enlisting in the Indian Army: 'It was particularly said about Punch [Poonch] that every male Muslim in the Jagir was, had been, or when old enough would be a soldier in the Indian Army … the Mirpur-Punch area [was] the great recruiting area of the Indian Army'.[170] The location of Poonch and Mirpur close to major military recruiting regions in Punjab, such as Sialkot, on which the Indian Army consistently drew, assisted this process. Indeed, many Poonchis enlisted as 'Punjabi Musalmans' (Muslims) mainly in the Punjab Regiment.[171] While not ethnically Punjabis, Poonchis and Mirpuris focused on Punjab and felt more of an affinity with it than with other areas of J&K.

While it is difficult to quantify, both in terms of absolute numbers and service occupations, large numbers of Poonchis served as soldiers in the Indian Army. The 1941 Census gives no figures, but a close analysis of this document reveals that six of Jammu Province's seven districts provided men to either the Indian Army or to the J&K Army.[172] During World War I, of the 31,000 men from J&K who served in the Indian Army, Poonch was 'particularly prominent' in supplying recruits.[173] For World War II, a reasonable figure for Poonchi and Mirpuri servicemen would seem to be at least 50,000.[174] These figures meant that, in 1947, Muslim men in Poonch and Mirpur with military experience and training outnumbered the strength of the Maharaja's armed forces. Significantly, they were concentrated in one area. By comparison, in 1939 the J&K State Army had 9,100 men,[175] although by 1947 this had probably increased slightly owing to World War II. Eight battalions of infantry were dispersed throughout J&K via four commands: Kashmir (for Kashmir Province, Leh, Skardu), Jammu (Bhimbar to Kathua), Poonch (Poonch, Rawalakot) and Mirpur.[176] Immediately after World War II, the Maharaja was recruiting 'Gurkas, Sikhs and even untouchables'—but, it was alleged, not Muslims—for an extra four battalions.[177] Fighting in World War II had given Poonch and Mirpur Muslims useful skills, broad experiences, new ideas and additional reasons to be disgruntled when they returned to their backward districts: the soldier who came back 'was no longer so docile as to submit easily to "begaar". He was defiant and almost in a mood to revolt'.[178] (*Begaar* was a device used by the regime whereby men were press-ganged into unpaid service for the Maharaja, usually to carry loads up the notoriously bad Gilgit road.) As a result of both world wars, particularly World War II, the Maharaja had individuals in his domain who had developed the ability—and desire—to oppose him.

As a military officer, Lieutenant-General Hari Singh was well aware of the Poonchis' martial capabilities, if not of their grievances over taxes and land.[179] From 21 to 25 April 1947,[180] he made a 'whirlwind tour' of western Jammu and Poonch where many ex-servicemen lived.[181] He met retired officers and saw large groups of pensioners from the Indian Army who had been summoned for the occasion. The military potential of these Muslim ex-servicemen and their location in south-western J&K just across the border from the future Pakistan meant that these Muslims potentially posed a difficult problem for the Maharaja's small, predominantly Hindu, armed forces to control—and to disarm and subdue, if need be. His army's task would be harder if the Muslims gained succour from, or took refuge in, Pakistan. Additionally, those who needed arms could purchase these from arms bazaars in NWFP. The only way the Maharaja could possibly appease Poonch Muslims would be to accede to Pakistan; they would not have settled for anything less.

In summary, not only did Poonch Muslims want to join Muslim Pakistan for religious, fraternal and geographical reasons, they also saw it as an opportunity to divest themselves of oppressive Hindu Dogra rule. Of all of the people in 1947 wanting to end Dogra rule in J&K, Poonchis were the most important. Their grievances against, and dislike of, the Dogras, coupled with their martial experiences, meant that only they had the intent and the capability to oppose Maharaja Hari Singh's rule: 'it was only from Poonch that a serious and effective challenge to the Dogra Government could originate and flourish'.[182] This came after 15 August 1947 when Poonchis empowered themselves during a brief 'window of opportunity' while the ruler was vacillating on his accession. The Poonchis' important actions, which physically and militarily divided J&K, are discussed in Chapter 2.

*Jawaharlal Nehru's role*

A final factor that must be discussed in relation to J&K's divisibility and deliverability is the significant role that Jawaharlal Nehru played in J&K before and after

# J&K: DISUNITED PEOPLE—UNDELIVERABLE STATE

Maharaja Hari Singh's accession to India. J&K's future had been on Nehru's mind since the Maharaja arrested him in J&K in June 1946. However, in seeking to obtain J&K for India, Nehru ignored realities such as J&K's Muslim-majority population, its physical links with Pakistan and the strong pro-Pakistan feelings of some, perhaps many, of its people. Instead, he was blinded by his emotional attachment to the Kashmir Valley, heavily influenced by his friendship with Sheikh Abdullah, and poorly informed about affairs outside Srinagar—to the detriment of other places and events in J&K. Nehru's involvement in J&K heightened the state's political divisions and increased volatility around the accession issue.

Nehru had two major failings in relation to J&K. First, his Kashmiri blood created an emotional attachment to the Kashmir Valley that clouded his ability to examine the issue of J&K's status dispassionately.[183] Indeed, Nehru's genealogical link with Kashmir overrode 'considerations of policy and ideology' in relation to J&K.[184] Nehru was proud of his Kashmiri heritage: 'I told my audience with becoming modesty, that during the fifty-five years of the life of the Indian Congress, for seven years Kashmiri Pandits had been president—a remarkable feat for a handful of people who had migrated from Kashmir to the plains below'.[185] These Kashmiri Pandits were Nehru's father, Motilal, and himself. Nehru also felt a strong link with Kashmir and Kashmiris. As he indicated to Sheikh Abdullah's wife, Begum Abdullah, in June 1947: 'Nothing that can happen can break these strong bonds that tie me to Kashmir and its people, and their welfare will ever remain a first priority with me'.[186] This made Nehru keen about J&K's inclusion in the Indian Union.

Nehru's second failing was that, owing to his strong friendship with Sheikh Abdullah, he was overly influenced by this Kashmiri Muslim and excessively focused on events in Srinagar. This led Nehru to make incomplete, or incorrect, conclusions. Nehru saw a pro-Indian bent among Kashmiris that was based on his own experiences in Srinagar, his friend's activities there, or on communications that Nehru received from there. Some evidence of his excessive focus on the Kashmir Valley comes from a lopsided report discussing J&K that Nehru gave to the Viceroy, Lord Mountbatten, on 17 June 1947.[187] Nehru reported almost exclusively about Kashmir Province and the National Conference. He dismissed Jammu as 'largely a continuation of the Punjab' and negated Abdullah's rivals as 'reactionary Hindu and Muslim groups', with the Muslims allied to the Muslim League and with 'little influence in the State'. While Nehru's geographical assessment of Jammu was correct, other aspects of his report were false, incomplete or misleading. Jammu was a significant part of J&K: it was the princely state's most populous province. The Hindu ruler came from, and had significant support, there. Muslims may have been allied to the Muslim League, but they also had their own party in J&K, the Muslim Conference. This party had significant levels of support both in Jammu (as pro-Pakistan Muslim elements allied with the Muslim Conference would later show) and, although this is difficult to quantify, in the Kashmir Valley.

Nehru's report to the Viceroy also either misread or ignored the overall political situation in J&K. The report's final paragraph shows this: 'The normal and obvious course appears to be for Kashmir to join the Constituent Assembly of India. This will satisfy both the popular demand and the Maharaja's wishes. It is absurd to think that Pakistan will create trouble if this happens'.[188]

The first sentence reflects Nehru's desires rather than a realistic analysis. Given J&K's Muslim-majority population and its significant geographical and economic links with the future Pakistan, the 'normal and obvious course' was for the princely state to join that dominion. The second sentence may have been correct in relation to the Maharaja, although, unless the Indians knew otherwise, he had not yet decided his accession in June. As for 'the popular demand', this was—and has always been—difficult to ascertain. Nehru's claim most likely reflected the National Conference's desire and its significant local popularity in Srinagar. This ignored the Muslim Conference's popularity and the aspirations of Muslims outside, and possibly also inside, the Kashmir Valley. The final sentence was wishful thinking. With intrigue increasing around J&K's future, Nehru hoped that Pakistan, whose name was an acronym in which the 'k' stood for 'Kashmir', would not create trouble if Muslim-majority J&K joined India. This contradicted Nehru's advice to the viceroy in April: 'the future of Kashmir might produce a difficult problem'.[189]

As well as his pre-Partition involvement with the Viceroy, Nehru's role in J&K itself was important. After Partition, he pressured Maharaja Hari Singh to give Sheikh Abdullah a position of power in J&K. Abdullah's release from jail in late September 1947—long before that of any of his political rivals—and his concurrent induction into the Maharaja's administration are largely attributable to Nehru's influence and actions. In elevating Abdullah, Nehru ignored the wishes of many Muslims and weakened the position of Muslim Conference politicians, many of whom were still in jail. Equally, he ignored the desires of Jammu Hindus and Ladakhis not to be dominated by Kashmiris. Nevertheless, from 31 October 1947, the Nehru-Abdullah duumvirate effectively ended Hari Singh's autocratic rule of his domain. Power was split between the Maharaja and the Abdullah-led Emergency Administration, with the latter directly in charge of Nehru's beloved Kashmir Valley.[190] This came after India received the Maharaja's accession on 26 October 1947, although by this time, as we shall later see, J&K was already politically, militarily and physically divided. Thereafter, the Indians quickly found that they could not and would not obtain J&K in its entirety.

*Conclusion*

In 1947, the British withdrawal from the subcontinent unleashed a difficult situation in which the indecisive ruler of Jammu and Kashmir had to determine the future status of his princely state. In this volatile and unstable environment, many Indians, Pakistanis and people in J&K were expectantly waiting with some sense of optimism for Maharaja Hari Singh to make an accession. His choice was made more difficult because 'his' people had different accessional desires and aspirations. Furthermore, after Partition, his regime and power were the only unity that J&K possessed.[191] Formerly, the people of J&K had cohered in this constructed princely state because Hari Singh and his administration, with British support, compelled them to do so. Now, when the aloof, unpopular autocrat needed his people's support most, this was not forthcoming. Only non-Muslims—Hindus, Sikhs and Buddhists, chiefly—desired Dogra rule to continue. Owing to the lack of any genuine and inclusive democracy in J&K, others had little sense of being a citizen of J&K, or of wanting to be such a citizen. Even though Hari Singh only, and clearly, had the power to accede, his lack of popularity meant that there was little guarantee that 'his' people would accept his choice. This was compounded by Hari Singh's total failure to consult the people of J&K in any way on the future of what was also their state. With the ruler's power seriously waning in the post-British political environment, and given that many of the people of J&K were strongly desirous of becoming Pakistanis or Indians, his accession inevitably would, and did, inspire division.

Despite J&K's inherent disunity, Hari Singh's accession would have been much simpler had Muslims in J&K been united in their desire for the state's future status. Indeed, Muslim disunity is one of the most significant explanations of why the so-called Kashmir dispute began—and continues. The political division among Muslims, and especially among their leaders, made it possible for the Maharaja to avoid acceding to Pakistan. According to *The Times*, the Maharaja had originally been resigned 'to Kashmir's accession to Pakistan because of geographical contiguity, economic dependence, and ties of religion'.[192] Hari Singh's resigned attitude changed when he realised that some J&K Muslims supported accession to India. It also changed after the Gurdaspur land corridor was awarded to India. Nevertheless, had J&K Muslims, who comprised 77 per cent of J&K's population, been united and unequivocal in their desire for the princely state to become part of Pakistan, Hari Singh would have had little choice but to accede to the new Islamic dominion.[193] This is because, with the exception of the eastern part of Jammu Province, Muslims physically dominated all areas of J&K. Serious Muslim opposition, political or physical, therefore would have been very difficult for the Maharaja's army and police to contain, let alone subdue. Muslim unity for J&K's accession to Pakistan also would have made it hard for outsiders to meddle or peddle influence in the princely state via associates or surrogates. Similarly, India's desire to obtain J&K, and to act there after accession, would have been made very difficult.

However, even if Muslim unity had compelled the Maharaja to accede to Pakistan, this decision would not have satisfied the 23 per cent of residents of J&K who were non-Muslims. Nor would such a decision have guaranteed the delivery of J&K in its entirety to Pakistan (just as Hari Singh's actual accession did not deliver the entire state to India). Those Hindus and Sikhs who comprised a majority in the eastern parts of Jammu Province were strongly pro-Indian. Their dislike of Pakistan and of pro-Pakistani J&K Muslims was further heightened by the arrival of angry and agitated Hindu and Sikh refugees from western (Pakistani) Punjab after 15 August 1947. Accession to Pakistan therefore, would almost certainly have seen these people either fight to retain their land or take flight to India. In the event of accession to Pakistan, Hindu Pandits and Sikhs in the Kashmir Valley, most of whom probably favoured J&K joining India, might also have fled to pro-Indian parts of J&K, or to India. Although their position is less clear, Ladakhi Buddhists probably favoured India also. However, Ladakh's physical remoteness meant that it was politically remote in 1947, although not undesired, given its strategic location close to China.

Thus, disregarding the Maharaja's autocracy, unpopularity and vacillation on the accession question in 1947, the core of the problem in J&K was its people. They were ethnically, religiously and culturally diverse, diffuse and different; they lacked religious and political unity; they were divided in their aspirations for J&K's future international status. All of these factors, including the division of the people of J&K along pro-Pakistan and pro-Indian lines, were in place before the British left the subcontinent on 15 August 1947. Inherently, the state was undeliverable to either India or Pakistan. This was confirmed when it quickly fragmented after Partition (as detailed in the next chapter). The state then became what it still is today—a divided and disputed entity.

2

# THE PEOPLE

DIVIDING J&K—INSTIGATING THE KASHMIR DISPUTE

*Introduction*

In 1947, people in Jammu Province engaged in three major actions that divided Jammu and Kashmir and confirmed that the princely state was not deliverable in its entirety to India or Pakistan. The first was a pro-Pakistan, anti-Maharaja uprising by Muslim Poonchis in western Jammu that 'liberated' large parts of this area from the Maharaja's control. The second was major inter-religious violence in the province that caused upheaval and death, including a possible massacre of Muslims. The third was the creation of the Provisional Azad (Free) Government in areas liberated or 'freed' by the Poonch uprising. This region soon popularly became known as 'Azad Kashmir'.[1] These three actions all occurred during the ten-week interregnum between the creation of India and Pakistan on 15 August 1947 and Maharaja Hari Singh's accession to India on 26 October 1947. Each was initiated, and then largely undertaken, by J&K state subjects—local people of J&K who had a legitimate right to be in the princely state. The only exception was the inter-religious violence which, while initiated by state subjects, was also fuelled by the arrival of refugees, external and internal, moving into or through Jammu Province, especially via the Sialkot-Jammu-Pathankot corridor.

The Jammuites' three actions in 1947 were highly significant. They caused a large number of deaths, many casualties and much dislocation. They divided Jammu Province politically, physically and militarily into pro-Pakistan and pro-Indian areas. They instigated the ongoing dispute over J&K's international status—the so-called Kashmir dispute—before Maharaja Hari Singh's accession to India. Indeed, as the evidence below shows, the dispute over whether J&K should join India or Pakistan began almost immediately after 15 August 1947 and was well under way in September 1947. During the short post-Partition, British-free, pre-accession period, Hari Singh struggled to prevent the princely state's physical and political disintegration. He failed. When the Maharaja acceded to India on 26 October 1947, his armed forces had lost control of large parts of 'his' princely domain. By then, J&K was a divided state.[2]

# THE UNTOLD STORY OF THE PEOPLE OF AZAD KASHMIR

While the Jammuites' post-Partition actions in 1947 were significant, we know little about them. This is partly because India, especially, and Pakistan have generally ignored them (as discussed in Chapter 3). Since 1947, India has consistently claimed that all of the violence that occurred in J&K only began after, and as a result of, the invasion of Kashmir Province on 22 October 1947 by 'outsiders': Muslim Pukhtoon tribesmen from Pakistan.[3] Unable to deflect India's accusations of being involved in the Pukhtoons' invasion, Pakistan acquiesced in India's tactic. Pakistan could have countered India's accusations by publicising the actions taken in J&K by 'insiders': state subjects in Poonch or violence against Muslims, but it chose not to. This is why it is important to discuss the Jammuites' actions in 1947.

There are serious information gaps concerning these events. Few scholars have discussed the Poonch uprising or the creation of Azad Kashmir in any depth. People have been reluctant to delve into the embarrassing inter-religious violence in Jammu in 1947. Consequently, we know little about the violence committed against Muslims in eastern Jammu—not to mention significant violence committed against Hindus and Sikhs in western Jammu. While I have sought to use primary sources where possible, some of the information presented below may be *post factum* justifications for actions and atrocities committed against, or by, 'the other community'. Equally, some suggests official involvement in violence. Overall, the evidence below confirms the Jammuites' three actions: the Poonch uprising, inter-religious violence and the creation of Azad Kashmir. It shows that these actions were under way before the Pukhtoons' invasion of J&K. Indeed, the Jammuites' actions may have partially inspired that invasion.[4] Most important, the evidence confirms that the people of J&K—and not outsiders—instigated the Kashmir dispute.

*Events in Jammu: volatile, poorly reported, ignored*

The British departure from the subcontinent in August 1947 caused two significant changes in J&K. The ramifications of these changes impacted on Jammu Province most of all. First, Maharaja Hari Singh lost his guarantor, the British. No longer could he impose his will, almost with impunity, on the people of J&K, knowing that the British would support him or, at worst, ignore his actions. Nor could he rely on the (British) Indian Government to control subcontinental politicians, particularly in the Indian National Congress, and neighbouring populations, particularly Punjabi Muslims wanting to politically or physically assist J&K Muslims. He could not call on the support of (British) India's military to quell internal uprisings, as he had done in 1931,[5] or to police J&K's porous borders and keep out intruders. Instead, Hari Singh came under increasing pressure from the new leaders of India and Pakistan over the accession issue, over the welfare of the people of J&K, and over the release of each dominion's respective political surrogates then languishing in J&K jails.

A further result of the British departure was that the Maharaja was placed in a position where, in a volatile and increasingly insecure environment, he was charged with determining J&K's future status. This decision took on added signifi-

## THE PEOPLE

cance after Muslim-majority Pakistan and secular (but Hindu-dominated) India were created. Partition confirmed that Hari Singh was now British-free—and on his own. Equally, it created expectations among the people of J&K that soon they also would be joining one of these new dominions. Their expectations were heightened when, by 15 August 1947, almost all of the rulers of Princely India had made accessions to India or Pakistan. This, in turn, put further pressure on Hari Singh to make an accession.

In J&K, the partition process and its impacts affected Jammu Province most of all. This province was contiguous to Punjab, where violent and brutal inter-religious activity was occurring. Millions of Hindus and Sikhs were moving eastwards from the new dominion of Pakistan to India while conversely, Muslims from India went westwards to Pakistan. Some of these dislocated souls travelled via a major land route that ran from Sialkot, through Jammu City, to Pathankot, thus connecting the two new dominions. The presence of these refugees and their harrowing stories further agitated Jammuites who, like their Punjabi neighbours, were highly volatile throughout 1947. However, unlike the Kashmir and Frontier Districts provinces where Muslims comprised an overwhelming majority, Jammu Province had a Muslim majority in the west and a Hindu majority in the east (see tables 1.3, 2.1). The majorities—and minorities—in each area were very restive in 1947; if their post-Partition activities are any indication, Jammu Province was the province whose residents had the most divisive political inclinations in J&K. Muslims acutely wanted J&K to join Pakistan; non-Muslims, comprising Hindus and Sikhs, strongly favoured union with India.

After 15 August 1947, pro-Pakistan and pro-Indian elements in Jammu Province engaged in considerable violence. Much of this was not widely reported, even though the violence in Jammu may have been worse than in Punjab, where perhaps up to one million people were killed.[6] Comparatively speaking, as a percentage of the relative populations involved, deaths in Jammu Province may have been greater.[7] Despite this, many subcontinental newspapers, even if they were aware of events in Jammu Province, chose not to publish stories about violence there. There were two reasons for this lack of reporting. First, communications to and from J&K were disrupted by events in newly-divided Punjab.[8] Second, subcontinental attention was focused on the well-reported communal events occurring in Punjab, or Bengal. In Calcutta, for example, stories about the 'large-scale insurrection by the tough Muslim peasants ... around Poonch' were rarely published in newspapers because there was a lot happening there and this insurrection was 'important but remote'. Furthermore, to have published stories about a possible Muslim massacre in Jammu might have incited further bloodshed and started individuals 'once more slaughtering one another'.[9] This is plausible, given the widespread religious volatility throughout northern parts of the subcontinent in 1947.

In relation to J&K, attention was focused on Kashmir Province, particularly Srinagar, and not Jammu Province. Maharaja Hari Singh was residing in J&K's summer capital pondering his accession; many political leaders were in jail there. Traditionally, most political activity took place in J&K's largest city, Srinagar, where the warm summer weather was more conducive to action than winter months when Jammu City was J&K's capital. Reporting was easier from Kashmir

Province also because of its compactness, better roads, and communications with metropolitan India, particularly via the all-weather Jhelum Valley Road. Owing to Srinagar's size and Kashmir's prestige, which the presence of many foreign, heat-averse holidaymakers enhanced, Kashmir Province invariably received better press coverage. Conversely, Jammu Province drew few tourists and few journalists, particularly to areas outside Jammu City. The southern province was even less attractive when the Maharaja was not in residence in Jammu City. Poor roads and communications also made it difficult for journalists to travel in, and report from, Jammu Province.

Another reason why the Jammu events were poorly reported in 1947 was that the Maharaja's government suppressed, adulterated or hindered news collection and reporting activities. Hari Singh's administration was waging a 'ceaseless war against newspapers and Journalists [sic] that [we]re in favour of Kashmir's accession to Pakistan'. By 7 October, it had imposed 'rigorous pre-censorship on all news and views' published in at least four 'leading' local newspapers; it had banned the entry of four daily newspapers from West Punjab, and forced the 'Muslim "Kashmir Times" to cease publication'[10] after instructing its editor 'not to publish matter advocating Kashmir's accession to Pakistan'.[11] The newspaper suspended publication in protest. In early October, the Maharaja's government interned the correspondent for Associated Press of India (API), a major source of news about J&K.[12] On 21 October, Lahore's *Civil & Military Gazette*, which often took API reports, pointedly rebuked the J&K Government for its 'censorship of news in Kashmir when reports were in circulation of severe repressive measures adopted by the military forces of the State in Poonch'.[13] In a crude form of censorship, J&K's former Prime Minister, Ramchandra Kak, a possible advocate of accession to Pakistan, was prevented officially from leaving Srinagar as his departure was 'likely to prove prejudicial to the interests of the State'.[14] With such influential and well-informed individuals constrained, significant events in J&K concerning lesser-known people received scant, or no, coverage.

Another reason why little has been written about the major events in Jammu Province in 1947 is Indian and Pakistani neglect. Both goverments have been engrossed in their war of words over J&K rather than factually determining what—or who—instigated the Kashmir dispute. Indian analysis of J&K invariably begins with, or conveniently focuses on, Pakistan's 'aggression by force' in J&K that started when Pakistan 'attacked' J&K on 22 October 1947 using Pukhtoon tribesmen.[15] It then deals with the international aspects of the Kashmir dispute or discusses the Kashmir Valley and its important coterie of pro-Indian Muslims, where India, initially at least, appeared in a better light than Pakistan. Jammu Province is rarely discussed. Generally speaking, Pakistanis are uninterested in what happened in Jammu Province in 1947. Rather, they focus on the pro-Pakistan action in Gilgit in November.[16] The India and Pakistan governments also have political reasons for ignoring, negating or even denying the events that occurred in Jammu Province in 1947. These are discussed in Chapter 3. Nevertheless, the evidence below confirms that the Poonch uprising, the inter-religious violence in Jammu Province and the formation of Azad Kashmir all occurred.

# THE PEOPLE

*The evidence: the Poonch uprising*

The Poonch uprising has been 'glossed over in virtually all accounts of the origins of the Kashmir dispute'.[17] This serious and significant anti-Maharaja uprising by Muslims living in the *jagir* of Poonch was a response to a number of factors. These included their dislike of the Hindu Maharaja and his repressive regime, their need to obtain protection from some anti-Muslim activities that the Maharaja's army engaged in soon after Partition, and their desire for J&K to join Pakistan. Additional factors included the provocative stationing of Dogra forces in Poonch in 1947, the 'invasion of Jammu by Sikhs' and other militant non-Muslims after Partition,[18] and disenchantment with corruption surrounding an unpaid per capita grant for personnel who had served in the Indian Army or the labour corps during World War II.[19] Poonchis, the vast majority of whom were Muslims, were also disenchanted with the dual system of autocracy and heavy taxation inflicted on them by the Maharaja and their local Raja. Similarly, disgruntled unemployed Poonchi men developed 'hatred for the person and the rule of the Maharaja' because Muslims were unable to enlist in the J&K army, despite its recruiting of an additional four battalions.[20]

A further factor concerned the Poonchis' weakening ability to defend themselves. Hari Singh was aware that many more Poonchis and Mirpuris had military capabilities and experience than the numbers serving in his army. He also had been 'specially impressed and alarmed' by a gathering of some 40,000 men, 'almost all ex-Servicemen of the British Army from Sudhnutti and Bagh Tehsils of Poonch, assembled to greet him on 21 April 1947 at Rawalakot' during his tour of the 'frontier areas' of J&K.[21] In July, the 'spooked' Maharaja's government 'encouraged' military-capable Poonchis and Mirpuris to disarm,[22] including those 'on leave with arms and ammunition' from the Pakistan Army.[23] These Muslims then became alarmed when the J&K Police, with whom they had deposited their arms, redistributed these to Sikhs and Hindus for self-defence.[24] Their alarm was understandable, given the inter-religious violence then occurring in Punjab.

A further factor motivating Poonchis was the creation of Pakistan and the Maharaja's reaction to their support for it. The transfer of British power to the new dominions of India and Pakistan, coupled with Hari Singh's vacillation on the accession, inspired much interest, even fervour, among the people of J&K. In Poonch, many people were already identifying themselves with Pakistan. From 14 August, the day before Pakistan became a legal entity and a physical reality, pro-Pakistan, anti-Maharaja meetings took place in Poonch, even though public meetings were banned. Many Poonchis declared their desire for J&K to join Pakistan, particularly on 'Pakistan Day' (14 August 1947) when they raised Pakistan flags and supported the Muslim Conference's (by now unequivocal) pro-Pakistan stance.[25] Poonchis were pro-Pakistan partly for reasons of religious solidarity. Additionally, some repressive measures undertaken against them by the Maharaja's army and anti-Muslim elements, particularly Sikhs,[26] convinced them that 'if they did not rise in revolt, they would be massacred or pushed into Pakistan'.[27] This was plausible, given the concurrent large-scale inter-religious bloodletting in Punjab and religious tensions in Jammu.

Motivated by these various factors, disgruntled Poonchis engaged in actions against the Maharaja to protect themselves. Anti-Maharaja activity possibly commenced as early as February,[28] and almost certainly was occurring by June 1947,[29] when Poonchis mounted a 'no tax' campaign.[30] A press note issued on 12 September by the J&K Government confirms this campaign: 'Early in August in ... Poonch Jagir, evilly disposed persons launched a violent agitation against the administration of the jagir in favour of civil disobedience and No Tax Campaign'.[31] The Muslim unrest may also have included a 'no rent' element, a distinct possibility, given the Poonchis' grievances over land.[32] The Maharaja and his armed forces moved to suppress this campaign. Around 15 August, they may also have begun to repress Muslims, by killing them or by forcefully disarming them. A 1948 publication stated that 'hundreds' of people in Bagh, a district in Poonch, were killed at a hoisting of the Pakistan flag to celebrate Independence Day.[33] Two short telegrams to Jinnah on 29 August from the 'Muslims of Poonch' and the 'Muslims of Bagh' also spoke of anti-Muslim brutality by the Maharaja's forces around the same time.[34] The Muslim Conference politician who became the foundation President of Azad Kashmir, Sardar Muhammad Ibrahim Khan from Rawalakot in Poonch, was quoted by a 1949 publication as stating that the Maharaja had unleashed a 'reign of terror' on 24 August 1947 that killed 500 people.[35] While the number of casualties cannot be confirmed, 'shoot-on-sight' orders were apparently issued to army officers on 2 September 1947.[36]

The reaction of the ruler's predominantly Hindu army to Poonch Muslims' pro-Pakistan activities boosted the anti-Maharaja 'cause' in Poonch and incited Poonchis to take further action. In response to incidents around Poonch that invariably involved Muslims, the Maharaja's army fired on crowds, burned houses and villages indiscriminately, plundered, arrested people and imposed local martial law.[37] Indeed, because 'trouble continued ... the State forces were compelled to deal with it with a heavy hand'.[38] Until such oppressive actions, the anti-Maharaja cause probably had little backing.[39] 'Substantial men' told Symonds that 'they would never have joined such a rash enterprise' opposing the Maharaja 'but for the folly of the Dogras who burnt whole villages where only a single family was involved in the revolt'.[40] Such folly motivated some Poonch Muslims to organise a people's resistance movement. Towards the end of August, it became an armed revolt.[41] Sardar Abdul Qayyum Khan, twenty-four years old and with Indian Army military experience,[42] apparently 'set the [military] ball rolling in Kashmir'.[43] 'In six weeks the whole district except Poonch city itself was in rebel hands'.[44] (While these pro-Pakistan forces continued to retain this area after the accession to India, they were never able to capture Poonch City.) In response, the Maharaja's army mounted an offensive in September and October 1947 against Poonchis 'who had shown some rebellious activities', and against Muslims in the predominantly Dogra areas of Jammu Province.[45]

Hari Singh, in a move that portended or inspired a similar stance by India, blamed Pakistan for his problems in Jammu Province. He accused the new dominion on 4 September of infiltrating fully armed men into J&K, and in early October of mounting an economic blockade that deprived J&K of vital supplies. Pakistan denied both charges.[46] While the J&K armed forces realised that local men were doing the fighting, they believed that the 'trouble was being fomented by infiltration of armed gangs from Pakistan'.[47] Nevertheless, the J&K Government could provide little solid supporting evidence, nor could the Indian Government do so retrospectively. Its 1948 *White Paper on Jammu & Kashmir* provided only one piece of hard evidence of cross-border activity (although an official 1949 Indian publication found 25 instances between 3 September and 20 October 1947).[48] The author of the report in the *White Paper* was significant: Major-General Scott, the long-term Chief of Staff of the J&K State Forces.[49] On 4 September 1947, he reported to J&K's Deputy Prime Minister that 'Reliable reports' from unnamed informants stated that 'a band of up to 400 Sattis—Muslim residents mainly in Kahuta Tehsil of Rawalpindi District' were infiltrating into J&K 'in the area of Owen, eleven miles east of Kahuta', with the purpose of 'looting and attacking minority communities'.

Scott's report of cross-border activity may have been accurate—there almost certainly was some support from Pakistanis for J&K Muslims. Equally, borders were porous in 1947, with many cross-border connections between people and little military patrolling. While 'Sattis' were Pakistani tribesmen, they could have been mistaken for Poonchis or Mirpuris, who were of similar Punjabi ethnicity,[50] perhaps returning home from visits or stays in Pakistan or fighting with guerrilla bands using Pakistan for sanctuary. Many Poonchis and Mirpuris worked in nearby cities such as Lahore and Rawalpindi. In addition the J&K-Pakistan border was very porous southwards from around Mirpur. It no longer enjoyed the natural divide of the Jhelum River; instead, it was an artificial line that superficially separated the northern end of the Punjab plains into Pakistani and J&K territory. A number of large Pakistani towns located near this border, including Jhelum, Gujrat and Sialkot, were closer to Mirpur than Jammu City. Similarly, Poonch was closer to Murree and Rawalpindi, than to Jammu City or Srinagar. Furthermore, strong cross-border links enabled J&K locals to strategically 'retire' to Pakistani territory when needing to avoid the Maharaja's forces or to obtain succour and support.[51] Equally, the porous border allowed 'raids into Pakistani territory by armed Dogra gangs and non-Muslim refugees', as Pakistan claimed was happening in October 1947.[52]

It is unlikely that Pakistanis were creating all of the Maharaja's troubles in western Jammu. Indeed, a number of factors suggest that the Poonch uprising was an indigenous affair. Pakistan was fully occupied dealing with the almost overwhelming physical, administrative and emotional ramifications of Partition. Any Pakistani support or leadership for Jammuites was probably not officially sanctioned. Rather, Punjabi or NWFP Muslims, with whom Jammu Muslims had close ethnic, familial, cultural, geographical and economic links, would have provided support on that basis. For example, some '*sudhans*' from Poonch considered themselves to be '*sudho zai* Pathans' (Pukhtoons), which for them, explained why 'the Pathans lost no time' coming to help J&K Muslims.[53] Furthermore—and importantly—Poonch Muslims had the capability, given their military abilities and experiences, and the intent, given their anti-Maharaja grievances, to foment and sustain anti-Maharaja actions themselves. They did not need any Pakistani encouragement or assistance.

Geography also suggests that the Poonch uprising was an indigenous affair. The region that Poonchis inhabited was a remote, highland area difficult to access. The *jagir* was east of the border created by the Jhelum River, which, flowing southwards from a point west of Muzaffarabad to near Mirpur town, physically separated Pakistan and J&K. Poonch was much higher and more difficult to enter than the undulating Mirpur lowlands at the end of the Punjab plains. After crossing of the Jhelum at Kohala, 'the mountains of Poonch rise very steeply'.[54] Furthermore, a person seeking to enter Poonch surreptitiously needed to secure transport to cross the swift-flowing Jhelum and avoid Kohala bridge, which the Maharaja's armed forces guarded. These forces made the task even more difficult when they 'cut off Poonch from direct communication with Pakistan' by destroying the six ferries that facilitated Jhelum crossings.[55] Outsiders wanting to enter Poonch and create 'mischief' therefore needed to engage in a degree of planning and logistics, and to have some local knowledge and support—factors unnecessary for crossing the porous southern part of the Pakistan-J&K border.

After Muslims in western Jammu rearmed in August, they initially fought the Maharaja's forces locally until some leading Poonchis organised them into an 'army'. Poonchis had begun preparing to retaliate after the ruler's brutal suppression of their 'no tax' campaign.[56] They started to rearm themselves in August, chiefly by purchasing weapons from NWFP arms bazaars.[57] Thereafter, 'some sectors were organised for fighting the Dogras', but mostly the anti-Maharaja struggle 'consisted of the uncoordinated efforts of each village, with its own band of guerrillas, taking care of the immediate military requirements'.[58]

These small, distant and often disparate 'village bands'[59] were frequently commanded by all-powerful, self-promoting local leaders who, in some cases, promoted themselves up to the rank of field marshal.[60] In early September, Sardar Ibrahim and others began to form a unified command post in Murree to direct these various irregular people's forces. This nearby hill station was strategically, and safely, located in Pakistani Punjab on the main Rawalpindi-Srinagar road, part of which bordered Poonch. Ibrahim and his organisers received help from a number of sources including sympathetic Muslim soldiers in the J&K Army; ex-Indian National Army officers; ex-Indian Army officers; and, as the Maharaja had long suspected, members of Pakistan's army and its bureaucracy as well as other Pakistani volunteers. It is uncertain if the Pakistanis' assistance was sanctioned at senior levels. Once fully organised, this motivated military force would pose the Maharaja, then India, significant problems.

According to Sardar Ibrahim, during September 1947, some 50,000 men were organised into a people's militia variously known as the 'Azad Army',[61] 'Azad Forces' or 'Azad Kashmir Regular Forces'. This locally-officered volunteer 'army' comprised 90 per cent ex-servicemen, except in Bagh, where the percentage was lower.[62] A 'very small percentage of Pakistani volunteers' fought with them,[63] as may have twelve women.[64] According to the Azad Kashmir Defence Minister, Colonel Ali Ahmad Shah (a former captain in the J&K State Force), the 'Azad Forces had been recruited locally or had risen spontaneously'.[65] They comprised 'seasoned troops' with experience fighting in both world wars and the serious 'Waziristan Operations' (1920–21).[66] After Azad Kashmir came into being, its 'Defence Council' assumed administrative control of 'Azad Jammu and Kashmir Forces'. This council comprised seven members: two ministers (Defence, Finance); one bureaucrat (Defence secretary); two soldiers (commander-in-chief, chief of staff), and two 'public representatives' (members of the Muslim Conference).[67] 'Soldiers' were paid Rs. 10 per month from accumulated donations, although many men apparently refused wages.[68] Clothing came from donations from local supporters and Pakistanis. The 'main problem' was a lack of arms, with some soldiers fighting with 'axes, spears and swords'.[69] Most used arms and ammunition 'captured from the enemy in major and minor engagements' or obtained from Muslim deserters from the Maharaja's army.[70] Communications were an issue, with men fighting 'in separate groups on many fronts … [with] no links with each other'.[71] Couriers carried messages between Muzaffarabad and Bagh; elsewhere, post and telegraphic exchanges went via locations in Pakistan.[72]

Initially confined to Jammu Province, the Azad Army's area of operation expanded into Kashmir Province. The Frontier Districts Province was omitted because 'the Gilgit organization was separate',[73] with the Gilgit Scouts already including pro-Pakistan dissidents. Following their uprising, Pakistan sent a 'Political Agent' to the Gilgit area on 16 November 1947.[74] The Azad Kashmir region was thus confined to the 'liberated' areas of Jammu and Kashmir provinces. This comprised two sectors: Jammu to Bhimber; Bhimber to Muzaffarabad. After about three months, the Azad Army was united under the leadership of 'General Tarik', by which time its enemy was Indian forces.[75] Tarik subsequently was identified as Colonel Akbar Khan, a Pakistan Army regular determined to deliver J&K to Pakistan. In 1951 Khan, now a major-general, and some co-conspirators attempted to overthrow the Pakistan Army high command which they considered complacent in pursuing J&K's liberation. They were court-martialled in the 'Rawalpindi Conspiracy' case.[76]

Benefiting from shorter supply lines, rugged terrain and local knowledge, support and high morale, the Azad Army built on the Poonch uprising to further oppose the Maharaja.[77] By 22 September 1947, the Azad Army's military structure was functioning so well that Major-General Scott reported that the Maharaja's armed forces were losing control over large parts of J&K.[78] The Maharaja's opponents were doing well, despite 'miserably lack[ing] a regular line of communication, and a regular supply of arms and ammunition'.[79] By mid-to-late October, they controlled large parts of Poonch and Mirpur, while much of Muzaffarabad *tehsil* was being cleared of non-Muslims elements, including 'Sikhs, Dogras and R.S.S [Rashtriya Swayamsevak Sangh] cut-throats'.[80] This latter activity mirrored anti-Muslim religious violence occurring in Jammu.

The Azad Army's success was significant: when Pukhtoon tribesmen entered Kashmir Province on 22 October 1947, most of western Jammu Province had already been liberated from the Maharaja's forces.[81] Two days after the Pukhtoons' invasion—as India correctly called it—and possibly prompted by it, some anti-Maharaja elements in Poonch and Mirpur managed to form a government in the area outside the Maharaja's dwindling control. On 24 October, they formed the Provisional Azad Government. This followed an unsuccessful attempt to form a similar body earlier that month (discussed below). This 'government' came into being two days before Maharaja Hari Singh's accession to India on 26 October 1947.

From 4 September 1947, newspapers started reporting an uprising in Poonch. These included *CMG* (4 September and 2, 5, 19, 21 October 1947); *The Times* (8 September and 25, 30 October 1947); and *TOI* (15, 17, 19, 20, 26 October 1947). On 8 September, *The Times* stated that, according to 'unconfirmed reports',

## THE UNTOLD STORY OF THE PEOPLE OF AZAD KASHMIR

Muslim demonstrators in Poonch had 'been involved in clashes with Hindu troops of the State forces, large numbers being killed'.[82] On 2 October, *CMG* carried a copy of a telegram from the Kashmir Association, in Lahore, to Muhammad Ali Jinnah asking him to intervene because Muslims in Poonch were being 'butchered' and because Muslims elsewhere were 'greatly harassed by Dogra atrocities'.[83] *CMG* carried a statement on 19 October by 'the Government of Kashmir' that confirmed trouble in Poonch allegedly assisted, but not instigated, by Pakistan: 'Disturbances aided by armed people from the Pakistan Dominion in the Poonch and Mirpur areas have been reported for some days'. These had been 'causing hardships to law-abiding people', but the 'situation is now fully under control'.[84]

Two days later—and with the situation not under control—*CMG* reported details of a telegram from the J&K Government to Pakistan. The telegram complained about atrocities committed against 'Kashmiris' by Pakistanis and 'difficulties created for the Kashmir Government by the Pakistan Government'.[85] This ignored the antagonistic role played by the Maharaja, and the role played by local, disenchanted anti-Maharaja Muslim elements in Jammu. By 28 October, *CMG* editorialised that:

> With regard to Kashmir, it is an established fact that killings and burnings in Poonch started long before the 'invasion' of Kashmir along the Jhelum road by tribesmen from the northwest. The presumption may be that neither India nor Pakistan had any standing 'vis-a-vis' the happenings in Poonch, these being an 'internal affair' in the hands of the Kashmir Government.[86]

*CMG* was in no doubt as to the sequence of events in relation to this 'internal affair'.

Other press reports confirmed the role of Muslims in Poonch and Mirpur. On 25 October, *The Times* reported that 'in recent weeks' friction in J&K 'had taken the form of armed rebellion against the Maharaja by the Muslim peasantry of the western districts of Poonch Province [sic; it was a district of Jammu]'.[87] The report continued that 'rebellious Muslims of the Bagh district [sic; it was a *tehsil*] ... have succeeded in forcing the Kashmir State troops (mainly Hindu Dogras) to withdraw to the town of Poonch'. An editorial in *The Times* on 30 October reiterated this report: an 'insurrection broke out among the Muslim tribesmen of the western province [sic] of Poonch, the rebels protesting against the [Maharaja's] presumed intention to adhere to India'.[88] Sheikh Abdullah, whose party many Poonchi Muslims strongly opposed, confirmed in New Delhi on 22 October the 'present troubles' in Poonch: 'The people of Poonch ... had started a people's movement for the redress of their grievances. It was not communal. The Kashmir State sent their [sic] troops and there was panic in Poonch ... The present position was that the Kashmir State forces were forced to withdraw in certain areas'.[89] This important statement by J&K's leading politician was made on the day that Pukhtoon tribesmen entered J&K. This news would reach New Delhi a few days later.

By 28 October 1947, the Pukhtoons' invasion was being widely reported. In a portent of ongoing attempts to ignore or deny the Poonch uprising, all anti-Indian forces fighting in J&K thereafter were usually described as 'raiders'. The (incorrect) connotation was that all of them were from outside J&K. Nevertheless, on 28 October *The Times*, while referring to the anti-Indian 'raiding forces', was still able to identify four elements among the 3,000 or so 'Muslim rebels and tribesmen' in J&K: 1) 'Muslim League agents and agitators from Pakistan'; 2) 'villagers who have raised the Pakistan flag and attacked Kashmir officials'; 3) 'Pathan [Pukhtoon] tribesmen'; 4) 'Muslim deserters from Kashmir State forces who have taken their arms with them'.[90] Given that the Muslim League had no branch in J&K, the first element may have been local pro-Pakistan Muslim Conference politicians and members. The second element certainly comprised people who were J&K state subjects, as almost certainly were members of the fourth element. These residents of J&K had every right to be in the (disintegrating) princely state, unlike the first and third elements. These state subjects also had commenced their anti-ruler activities well before the Pukhtoons invaded Kashmir Province on 22 October 1947.

Given the increasing use of the term raiders to connote all anti-Maharaja, anti-Indian elements fighting in J&K after the Pukhtoons' invasion, it is important to deal with the issue of 'state subjects'. State subjects, such as Poonchis, Mirpuris, Kashmiris, Gilgitis and Ladakhis, were the only people who had any right to live and own immovable property in the princely state of Jammu and Kashmir. Their unique status arose as a result of some local unease with 'outsiders'—educated and trained Punjabi Hindus—whom Maharaja Hari Singh and his uncle, Pratap, had employed in their administrations, including at higher levels. Maharaja Pratap Singh 'imported' the Punjabis to fill a void in trained personnel when he reorganised his bureaucracy along 'modern lines'.[91] The Punjabis' presence in J&K was unpopular: it hindered local peoples' ability to obtain civil service positions, particularly those in the small, well-educated Hindu Pandit community. In 1889 Pratap changed the official court language from Persian to Urdu, thus (temporarily) disadvantaging Pandits trained in Persian.[92] After an anti-Punjabi agitation that began as early as 1910 under Pratap, Hari Singh passed a law in 1927 that specifically defined a state subject[93] and four classifications within this.[94] This satisfied local residents by limiting the ability of outsiders to live and work in J&K. It also meant that anyone who was a state subject had a legitimate right to be in J&K. (Equally, Hari Singh used this law as a device to assert his control over land: after 1928, only state subjects could purchase non-movable property in J&K.)[95] Therefore, Poonchis and Mirpuris who opposed the Maharaja were not raiders or outsiders, as this term connotes. They were local J&K citizens with every right to be in the princely state.

The evidence above shows that there was significant Muslim unrest and anti-Maharaja activity in the Poonch area after 15 August 1947. While these J&K Muslims may have received some help from people and relations in Pakistan, they had sufficient local grievances and adequate indigenous capabilities to mount, and then sustain, their significant anti-Maharaja activity. The actions of these state subjects certainly predated the intervention of outsiders (Pukhtoons) into Kashmir Province on 22 October 1947.

*The evidence: a 'massacre' of Jammu Muslims*

Significant inter-religious violence took place in Jammu Province in 1947. Pro-Indian Hindus and Sikhs murdered and harmed Muslims; pro-Pakistan Muslims harmed and murdered Hindus and Sikhs. Although Indians and Pakistanis have largely ignored this violence, the evidence below suggests that non-Muslims killed large numbers of Muslims in Jammu around October 1947. Equally, many Jammu Muslims fled to safer areas nearby in Pakistan or to western areas of Jammu Province controlled by pro-Pakistan Poonchis and Mirpuris. There were about half a million such Muslim refugees. Conversely, Muslims killed many Hindus and Sikhs in other parts of Jammu Province and in the Muzaffarabad District of Kashmir Province. Many non-Muslims also fled to safe areas in J&K where their community was in the majority, or to India.[96] The inter-religious violence discussed below received little attention in 1947, although it was a significant precursor to the Pukhtoon invasion.

While inter-religious violence in Jammu Province affected all communities, this section largely, but not totally, focuses on a possible 'massacre' of Muslims in Jammu's four eastern, Hindu-majority districts. This event was important: it inspired Jammu Muslims to defend themselves and to form the Azad Kashmir movement in the 'liberated' Muslim-majority areas of western Jammu Province. It also caused a substantial decrease in the number of Muslims in eastern Jammu. The loss of these Muslims through death or flight to Pakistan and Azad Kashmir, plus the arrival of Hindus and Sikhs internally displaced within J&K or to a lesser extent as refugees from Pakistan, resulted in Hindus becoming a strong majority in eastern (now Indian) Jammu. Significantly, after fighting ended in J&K in 1949, Jammu Province's reduced size, due to the loss of western areas to Azad Kashmir and its net loss of population, saw the Muslim-majority Kashmir Valley become the most populous region of Indian J&K. Thereafter, Jammu played second fiddle to Kashmir.

Anti-Pakistani and pro-Indian elements in J&K were responsible for the killing of Muslims in J&K. These included: Maharaja Hari Singh and some members of his predominantly non-Muslim armed forces; local Hindus, including right-wing RSS members and Hindus and Sikhs displaced from other parts of J&K. These non-Muslims strongly disliked the creation of Pakistan and, by implication, Muslims in favour of this Islamic dominion, including Jammu Muslims, whom they perceived (correctly) to be pro-Pakistan. Others involved in anti-Muslim activities in Jammu Province may have been emulating events in adjacent East Punjab where large numbers of Muslims had been encouraged to leave, or they were seeking revenge for Hindus and Sikhs cleared from Muslim-majority areas in West Punjab. 'Thousands' of Hindu and Sikh 'refugees were pouring over the State borders from India and Pakistan daily',[97] with at least 70,000 Hindu and Sikh refugees in Jammu in early September.[98] Indeed, nearly 60,000 Hindu 'Dogras and Sikhs from Gujrat district', which was close to Jammu Province, may have arrived in one week near the end of September.[99] Many of these would have been in transit from West Punjab, via Jammu and Kathua districts, to north-west India. Some of these non-Muslim refugee arrivals were 'victims of frenzied savagery'.[100] Equally frenzied, they took revenge, or inspired others to take revenge on Jammu Muslims, particularly those more vulnerable because they lived in Hindu-majority areas in eastern Jammu Province. A further motive to attack people in these turbulent and lawless times was the opportunity to loot, pillage and accrue booty. The creation of India and Pakistan offered a once-in-a-lifetime opportunity to exploit members of the other community or to settle old scores.

Writing in 1948, some Muslims believed there had been a plot in 1947 to eliminate them from Jammu Province and—a somewhat unrealistic idea—from all of J&K. While it is impossible to confirm this plot, these writings offer important perceptions about how Muslims felt. According to an Azad Kashmir Government publication, Hari Singh intended to seal J&K's borders and then 'massacre the Moslems [sic] of Kashmir', as per the master plan of his 'fellow tyrants' in East Punjab where '[m]illions' of Muslims 'had been massacred'.[101] Apart from their pro-Pakistan leanings, another reason for the extermination of J&K Muslims was to make room for Sikhs displaced from western Punjab and, apparently invited by the Maharaja, to make J&K their new home.[102] Any attempt to clear Jammu Province—let alone all of J&K—of its Muslims was highly ambitious. Borders were impossible to seal, while Muslims comprised 61 per cent of Jammu Province's population. Muslims were even larger majorities in the other two provinces. The only area where such an action might have succeeded was in Jammu Province's four eastern districts where Muslims comprised a 38 per cent minority and were physically vulnerable. (Equally vulnerable were Hindu and Sikh minorities in Jammu's three western districts.) Much of the territory that comprised the districts of Jammu, Kathua, Udhampur and Chenani Jagir was located east of the Chenab River, a significant natural division within Jammu Province. Jammu Hindus and Sikhs may have been looking to a future partition of their province along this line, or as far west as it could be pushed. Violence against Muslims in Jammu may have been an attempt to alter the religious balance to this effect.

Muslims perceived that large numbers of them were killed in Jammu Province in 1947. There is some evidence for these claims, although the bias of each document's author or organisation must be considered. This paragraph discusses pro-Pakistan sources. A 1948 Azad Kashmir Government publication stated that:

Killing, looting, arson and rape by the Hindu Dogra troops, R.S.S. Storm Troopers, Hindu and Sikh civilians, went on unabated in [Jammu and] Kashmir during August, September and October 1947 ... No less than 200,000 Moslem men, women and children were killed. At least, twenty-seven thousand women were abducted ... About 200,000 Moslem refugees from Kashmir are now in Pakistan territory.[103]

Another 1948 publication discussing 'massacres' in Jammu Province has an appendix detailing ninety anti-Muslim incidents in J&K between 8 August 1947 and 12 December 1947.[104] A tally of the death and abduction figures for the seventy-three incidents for which the publication provides figures shows that 118,459 Muslims were killed and another 13,360 were abducted in J&K during this period. At least 80,000 of these alleged Muslim deaths occurred before the Pukhtoons' invasion on 22 October 1947, with all incidents related to these deaths involving 'state' or 'Dogra' troops, often assisted by 'non-Muslim civilians', that is Hindus and Sikhs.[105] Other contemporary publications discussed or provided accounts of anti-Muslim violence in Jammu, although none provided any figures for the number of Muslims killed or abducted.[106]

A more objective source is UNCIP's 1949 *Report of the Sub-committee on Western Kashmir*. It stated that 'Many of the Muslim refugees have lively recollections of the Jammu massacres of November 1947'.[107] Buried deep in the report was mention of a *zaildar* (revenue collector) who informed UNCIP that 'on 20th of October 1947, he heard the Maharajah, while visiting [Bhimber] tehsil, give orders that

Table 2.1: Population of Muslims and Hindus in certain Muslim-majority and non-Muslim-majority District Groups, and as percentages of Jammu Province, their District Group and their religious group.

| District Group | Pop. | %JP | Muslims | %DG | %JP | %M | Hindus | %DG | %JP | %H |
|---|---|---|---|---|---|---|---|---|---|---|
| Muslim-majority Mirpur and Poonch* | 808,483 | 40.80 | 690,545 | 85.41 | 34.85 | 56.97 | 101,541 | 12.56 | 5.12 | 13.83 |
| Muslim-majority districts: Mirpur, Poonch, Reasi | 1,066,386 | 53.82 | 865,904 | 81.20 | 43.70 | 71.43 | 182,266 | 17.09 | 9.20 | 24.82 |
| Hindu-majority districts: Jammu, Kathua, Udhampur, Chenani | 915,047 | 46.18 | 346,321 | 37.85 | 17.48 | 28.57 | 552,126 | 60.34 | 27.87 | 75.18 |
| Total JP | 1,981,433 | | 1,212,225 | – | 61.18 | – | 734,392 | – | 37.06 | – |

Source: *Census of India 1941*, Volume XXII, *Jammu & Kashmir State*, Part III, *Village Tables*, Srinagar, R.G. Wreford, Editor, Jammu and Kashmir Government, 1942.

Key: DG  District Group: Muslims or Hindus as a percentage of the population for the specific District Group.
 H   Hindus as a percentage of the total population of Hindus in Jammu Province.
 JP  Jammu Province.
 M   Muslims as a percentage of the total population of Muslims in Jammu Province.
 Pop. Population.
 *   Significant parts of these areas became Azad (Free) Jammu and Kashmir.

the Muslims were to be exterminated and had seen His Highness shooting two or three'.[108] While these two occurrences in the UNCIP report were significant, the report was after the event and not for public consumption.

Newspaper coverage of anti-Muslim activity in Jammu Province began as early as 26 September 1947. On this day, *CMG* carried an isolated, but startling, API report headlined 'Exodus of Muslims from Jammu'. It stated that 'Jammu will almost be free of Muslims if the present speed of evacuation continues unchecked. It is estimated that 50,000 Muslims have migrated to the West Punjab, while nearly 50,000 [sic] Muslims start towards Pakistan every day.[109]

Although the report did not explain why Muslims were leaving, one reason almost certainly was the unsettled conditions prevailing. Another was a possible 'impending' famine (which also would have affected non-Muslims),[110] although in early October *CMG* reported there was 'No Imminent Danger of Famine' in J&K.[111] A further reason may have been that displaced Muslims from outside J&K were traversing the state going from India to Pakistan.

From 19 October 1947, *CMG* began regularly reporting incidents of violence against Jammu Muslims, particularly in Poonch.[112] Initially, these were based on press releases or communiqués from pro-Pakistan sources such as the Muslim Conference or the Pakistan Government. (Concurrently, the J&K Government was accusing Pakistan of sponsoring unrest in J&K, an allegation Pakistan 'emphatically and categorically' denied.)[113] On 26 October 1947, the first report from a source not obviously pro-Pakistan appeared on *CMG's* front page.[114] Quoting 'latest messages', it stated that 'The exodus of Muslims from Kashmir State [sic] as a result of recurring attacks by Dogra troops continues apace', with some 5,000 Muslims entering Pakistan on 23 and 24 October. The report appeared under a headline querying whether there was a 'Pogrom Against Kashmir Muslims?'. However, it also appeared with a report from the (pro-Pakistan) West Punjab Director of Public Relations who claimed that 'Muslim villages in Jammu State [sic] territory are being subjected to a furious campaign of arson and killing by Sikh and Dogra mobs and the State troops'. In addition, the Director accused the J&K Government of crossing the border and burning houses and killing people in West Punjab.[115]

On 28 October 1947, *CMG* carried two API reports about anti-Muslim violence in Jammu. One stated that Jammu Muslims were pouring into Sialkot bringing 'harrowing' stories of 'wholesale looting, killing and kidnapping of men and women by State troops and [RSS] members'.[116] The second report confirmed this situation. It detailed an interview given by the former editor of the *Kashmir Times*, G.K. Reddy, who had left Srinagar in mid-October after being exiled from J&K for advocating its accession to Pakistan. (While disenchanted with the Maharaja and his regime, he was not necessarily disenchanted with Pakistan or India.) After leaving Srinagar, Reddy was detained for ten days at Domel, the customs point on the Jhelum Valley Road located near Muzaffarabad town. After that, he was 'secretly removed under military escort' to Kathua and expelled. Reddy arrived in Lahore on Sunday 26 October. When interviewed about his experiences in 'the disturbed areas of Jammu', he related that he had seen a 'mad orgy of Dogra violence against unarmed Muslims [that] should put any self-respecting human being to shame'. This included seeing 'armed bands of ruffians and soldiers shooting down and hacking to pieces helpless Muslims refugees heading towards Pakistan'; watching officials and military officers 'directing a huge armed mob against a Muslim refugee convoy [that it] hacked to pieces'; and, in Jammu City, counting 'as many as twenty-four villages burning one night [while] all through the night rattling fire of automatic weapons could be heard from the surrounding refugee camps'. Reddy concluded by warning the J&K Government that 'by such methods of mass murder they [sic] cannot alter the population scales of the State'.

From around the beginning of November, press reports of violence against Muslims in Jammu largely, but not totally, disappeared. The reason for this was simple: most news was about the high profile tribal invasion of J&K. Reporting then increasingly dealt with the political, diplomatic and military battle between pro-Pakistan and Indian forces in, and for, J&K. It particularly focused on the Kashmir Valley, including reports on some diabolical Pukhtoon actions there, especially in Baramulla (discussed in the next chapter). Newspapers did report anti-Muslim violence in Jammu, but invariably this was retrospective.[117] For example, on 21 November, *CMG* reported that a party of (unnamed) Englishmen, after interviewing 200 wounded refugees in Sialkot, was 'convinced that there has been a disgraceful massacre of Muslims in Jammu'.[118] On 26 November, *The New York Times* stated that Jammu had been 'the scene of massacres against Mohammedans' in retaliation for Hindu and Sikh deaths in West Punjab.[119]

On 18 December 1947, *CMG* published a detailed account, possibly officially sanctioned, by the above-mentioned Englishmen about anti-Muslim activity in Jammu Province in previous months, including attacks against police and women.[120] This provided the most credible, useful and significant account to date. The Englishmen, possibly pacifist Quakers and seemingly not ideologically driven,[121] had visited Jammu Province recently and interrogated Muslim refugees and officials. Their subsequent report was considered a 'factual report jointly submitted by two foreigners who ... were commissioned for this purpose by the Governments of India and Pakistan'.[122] It provided comprehensive information about anti-Muslim violence in Jammu Province in 1947.

The Englishmen detailed ten separate violent incidents that had occurred between the beginning of October and 9 November. Some suggested official complicity. Six of the incidents took place before Maharaja Hari Singh acceded to India, meaning that his government was solely responsible—and largely culpable. The other four incidents took place after the accession, but before the Maharaja began to share power in Jammu Province with Sheikh Abdullah's Emergency Administration instigated in late October 1947 and initially restricted to the Kashmir Valley. When Abdullah visited Jammu on 16 November, the ongoing violence there inspired him to take five 'emergency advisers' to 'create confidence among Muslims'.[123] Before Abdullah's visit, the Maharaja's forces were still the pre-eminent—if disorganised and antagonistic—force in Jammu Province.

Three incidents described by the Englishmen involved the J&K Police, a force traditionally dominated by Hindus, particularly at the senior level.[124] These incidents, while not specifically describing anti-Muslim violence, nevertheless were disturbing. The first occurred early in October when police operating around the Kathua area seized some arms and ammunition from Hindu and Sikh 'smugglers' entering J&K from nearby Gurdaspur. Hindu state officials then took the arms from the police and returned these to the smugglers. The second incident occurred on 22 October when all Muslim members of the J&K Police in Jammu City were disarmed and ordered to go to Pakistan. The third reported incident took place on the same day, when some policemen went to help Muslims being attacked in Daghiana, near Jammu City. The 'State troops aimed their rifles at the police, and ordered them to turn back'. These incidents suggested a pro-Hindu, anti-Muslim bias among senior J&K officials.

Table 2.2: Some incidents of violence against Muslims in Jammu Province as reported by some 'Englishmen' in *CMG*, 18 December 1947.

| Inct | Date (1947) | Location | Total Muslims killed | Women separated? | PE Taken? | Survived |
|---|---|---|---|---|---|---|
| 1 | 20 October | Near Kathua | 8,000 | No | No | 40 |
| 2 | 20 October | Akhnur Bridge | 15,000 | No | No | 100 |
| 3 | 22 October | Sambha | 14,000 | All women | No | 15 |
| 4 | 23 October | Maogoan | 25,000 | All women | Yes | 200 |
| 5 | 5 November | Jammu City | 4,000 | Young women | Yes | 900 |
| 6 | 6 November | Jammu City | *2,800 | No | No | 3 |
| 7 | 9 November | To Suchetgarh | *1,200 | Seven | Yes | 1,193 |
| Total | | | 70,000 | | | 2,448 |

Source: Based on 'Englishmen's Account of Kashmir Muslims' Plight', *Civil & Military Gazette*, 18 December 1947.
Key: Inct Incident number.
    PE Personal effects and/or luggage taken from Muslims.
    * Estimated (convoy numbers; respectively seventy and thirty trucks at forty person per truck).

Of the seven specific incidents of anti-Muslim violence that the Englishmen alleged, all but two involved a massive loss of Muslim lives.[125] Incidents One and Two (Table 2.2) occurred before the tribal invasion; Incidents One to Four took place before the Maharaja acceded to India (and before details of the tribal invasion were well known in Jammu). The killers supposedly included 'state' or 'Dogra' troops in all instances. In Incident Three, the Maharaja was also implicated directly. In two reported incidents involving 8,000 Muslims near Kathua (Incident One) and 15,000 Muslims at Akhnur Bridge (Incident Two), only forty and 100 Muslims respectively survived. 'Dogra troops and armed Sikh civilians ... slaughtered' the first group; 'Rajput and Dogra soldiers' the second. In Incident Three involving a siege of 14,000 Muslims at Sambha village near Jammu City, 'all the Muslim women in the village were apparently taken away by the State troops, and the men were slaughtered with the exception of fifteen survivors, who escaped to Sialkot'. This action was supposed to have occurred almost immediately after a visit to Sambha by the Maharaja himself. In Incident Four, the 'State Government' allegedly ordered 25,000 Muslims gathered at Maogoan awaiting evacuation to Pakistan to walk to the new dominion: 'But as they were doing so, their women and all their personal belongings were taken away from them by the Dogra troops, and the rest made to stand in a line, whereupon they were riddled with machine-gun bullets.' Only about 200 men apparently made it to Pakistan.

# THE UNTOLD STORY OF THE PEOPLE OF AZAD KASHMIR

The alleged Incidents Five, Six and Seven in the Englishmen's account occurred after the Maharaja's accession to India. While the number of deaths in these incidents was relatively fewer than in the first four events, J&K State troops were involved in Incidents Five and Six. On 21 November, in a telegram to Liaquat Ali Khan, Nehru acknowledged that these post-accession attacks, all of which involved convoys taking Muslims to Pakistan, had occurred. Nehru believed each attack was undertaken 'chiefly by non-Muslims refugees'. The third convoy mentioned in Incident Seven had been guarded by Indian troops who repelled and killed 150 of the attackers.[126] The Englishmen, who stated that this convoy was 'escorted by Dogra and Madrasi troops' (south Indians), confirmed Nehru's position.

Of the seven incidents, Incidents Three, Four, Five and Seven included operations where some or all of the women, particularly young women, were separated from the group. (Muslim groups presumably included children, but the Englishmen do not mention minors.) The kidnapping, rape and killing of females in 1947 has largely been forgotten or overlooked. Nevertheless, it was a significant problem, in J&K among other places. On 2 December 1947 the J&K Muslim Conference, applauding a reported initiative of the National Conference's Controller of Jammu to 'recover' abducted women, believed that 'about 5,000' was 'a rough estimate' of the number of Muslim 'girls' abducted in Jammu Province.[127] Pukhtoons abducted an unknown number of Kashmiri women. India and Pakistan were keen to find and repatriate abducted women. On 2 December, Nehru asked Liaquat to take all possible steps to rescue 2,000 'unfortunate' Hindu women abducted from the Bhimber area 'being sold like cattle at about Rs. 150 each' in nearby Gujrat.[128] The J&K Maharaja and Maharani made a similar plea in Jammu on 16 December,[129] although Hari Singh may have been complicit in such abductions. According to Sheikh Abdullah, while he and his cohorts were trying to defuse tension in Kashmir Province from the tribal invasion, Hari Singh and his wife were 'fanning communalism' in Jammu.[130] A later commentator also blamed the ruler for 'prosecuting so disgraceful a campaign of persecution ... [that was a] systematic modification of the population in favour of the non-Moslem [sic] elements'.[131]

The incidents discussed above suggest a large loss of Muslim life in Jammu in 1947.[132] They are also a disturbing indictment of autocratic power and may partially explain why the J&K regime prevented information about state happenings being freely collected and published. Concerning the abovementioned pre-accession incidents (Incidents One to Four), some tentative but unverifiable, calculations can be made about the number of deaths. In Incidents One and Two, in which women were not separated from either group, only 140 Muslims were supposed to have survived. In Incidents Three and Four, for which exact figures are lacking for the number of women separated, assuming that 50 per cent of the total of 39,000 for the two groups comprised females and that all were separated from the group, then some 19,500 females 'disappeared'; that is, they fled or were abducted, with many later possibly raped and/or killed. Some women probably survived, but we do not know how many or in what state—physical, psychological, religious or political. (Abductees often ended up in their captors' dominion and religion.) Of the 19,500 Muslim males in Incidents Three and Four, only 215 were supposed to have survived. Similarly, before accession, of some 62,000 Muslims congregated in Jammu Province for evacuation to Pakistan, perhaps as few as 345 made it to the new Muslim dominion.

## THE PEOPLE

Some Muslims believe that 200,000 Muslims were affected by anti-Muslim activities in Jammu. In January 1948, Horace Alexander was one of the first to quote this figure. In late November 1947, when 'disquieting stories were current of massacres of civilians on both sides', the governments of India and J&K asked him 'to investigate the condition of Muslims in Jammu'.[133] Alexander's report appeared a couple of months after the alleged 'massacres'.[134] Comparing the Jammu events with the horror of the tribal intervention in Kashmir Province, Alexander noted that: 'Hindus and Sikhs of Jammu area, led largely by refugees, but once again, apparently with at least the tacit consent of State authority, had driven many thousands of their Muslim neighbours from their homes, and some two hundred thousand are, as Mr Gandhi with his usual courageous candour has admitted, not accounted for'.[135] Despite Alexander's exhortations not to forget the anti-Muslim actions in Jammu, this soon happened.

Mahatma Gandhi, in his 'usual courageous candour', confirmed that atrocities had been committed against Jammu Muslims. Speaking on 27 November 1947, Gandhi noted the 'considerable' and 'unreported' Hindu 'excesses' in Jammu.[136] The next day, he spoke of Hindus and Sikhs killing Muslims in Jammu.[137] Gandhi did so in the presence of Sheikh Abdullah, who had recently been to Jammu. When Abdullah confirmed the Jammu atrocities, Gandhi reproached the Kashmiri for 'betraying' his people's trust by not having the Maharaja's powers curtailed.[138] On 25 December, Gandhi stated that he held the Maharaja 'responsible for the happenings in his state',[139] including the 'murders of numberless Muslims and abduction of Muslim girls in Jammu'.[140] After meeting Gandhi in December 1947, Ian Stephens believed that the Mahatma's 'despairing mood' before his assassination on 30 January 1948 could be explained more by his knowledge of Hindu 'excesses' in Jammu than by carnage in Delhi.[141] Abdullah concurred: the Maharaja's 'fanning of communal hatred [in Jammu] slashed the Mahatma's soul'.[142]

On 10 August 1948, an informed Special Correspondent of *The Times* provided an exact figure of 237,000 for the number of Muslims who disappeared from Jammu.[143] Under the subtitle 'Elimination of Muslims from Jammu', he provided detailed information about the Muslim population of eastern Jammu, which for him comprised the districts of Jammu, Udhampur and Kathua and the eastern part of Reasi district. Out of a total population of 411,000 Muslims, the Special Correspondent believed that '237,000 Muslims were systematically exterminated—unless they escaped to Pakistan along the border—by all the forces of the Dogra State, headed by the Maharaja in person and aided by Hindus and Sikhs. This happened in October 1947, five days before the first Pathan invasion and nine days before the Maharaja's accession to India'.

Although no calculations for this exact figure were given and it was not broken down into deaths and escapes, the writer concluded that this 'elimination of two-thirds of the Muslims last autumn has entirely changed the present composition of eastern Jammu Province'. This report had some veracity given the writer's background knowledge of J&K.[144] Since the figure of '237,000' Muslims being 'exterminated' first appeared in *The Times*, numerous official Pakistan documents and pro-Pakistan writers have cited this report as evidence of a Muslim 'massacre'. Their citations usually include an incorrect report date of 10 October 1948; this was a Sunday, and the only day of the week on which *The Times* was not published.

# THE UNTOLD STORY OF THE PEOPLE OF AZAD KASHMIR

While an unknown number of Muslims were certainly killed in Jammu Province in 1947, thousands also fled to Pakistan to escape the violence. Although many refugees hoped to go home once normalcy returned to J&K or after it had eventually joined Pakistan as they believed it would, most did not return.[145] Documents by pro-Pakistan sources indicate the numbers involved. In 1948, the Muslim Conference claimed that nearly 200,000 Jammu Muslims had migrated to Pakistan.[146] In 1952, the Pakistan Government believed it was caring for over 600,000 Muslim refugees from J&K.[147] Their arrival began as early as September 1947 when 'more well-informed' J&K Muslims 'apprehending trouble' began to arrive at Sialkot 'in small unnoticeable batches every day'.[148] In January 1951, a comprehensive report in *Dawn* noted that 'During October-November, 1947, the genocide of the Muslims of [J&K] and their expulsion began according to plan, and as a result about 200,000 Muslims were forced to take refuge in Pakistan.'

This was the first of two waves that saw some 400,000 refugees move from J&K to Pakistan. The second wave occurred in April-July 1948 as Indian forces mounted a successful offensive in J&K. About half of the arrivals sought asylum in nearby Sialkot District, a logical place from which to quickly return to Jammu Province when normalcy returned. Equally, refugees expected to be able to return home after the plebiscite (promised by India when receiving Hari Singh's accession) was held, as a result of which, they believed, J&K would unite with Pakistan. *Dawn* also reported that a 'sensus' (census) taken from May to July 1949 registered 355,000 J&K refugees in West Pakistan. Of these, 334,000 came from the Indian-controlled portion of J&K and 21,000 were from Azad Kashmir. Azad Kashmir itself had 'about 150,000 refugees and displaced persons'. Such large numbers of Muslims would not have left Jammu Province had conditions been stable.

It is important to remember that, although much evidence exists of anti-Muslim activity in Jammu Province in 1947, indisputably Muslims also committed acts of violence against Hindus and Sikhs in J&K in 1947. They were also poorly reported, even less is known about them and their perpetrators, than about anti-Muslim violence. According to one pro-Indian writer (and given that there is little evidence to support or counter this claim), 'If the ruthless killings in [the] Jammu area could be called genocide, it was a genocide of the Hindus and not of the Muslims'.[149] The Indian *White Paper* discusses one incident of violence and kidnapping in and around Mirpur on 25 November 1947, with 'Pathans' the perpetrators.[150] A further alleged—and if true, abysmal—incident of anti-Hindu violence took place in Mirpur. This was the 'liquidation of over twenty thousand non-Muslims on and after 25 November 1947 out of a total of twenty-five thousand' gathered in Mirpur for shelter and protection.[151] A 'greatly shocked' Sardar Ibrahim painfully confirmed that some Hindus were 'disposed of' in Mirpur in November 1947, although he does not mention any figures.[152] Certainly, by March 1949, the number of non-Muslims in Azad Kashmir had greatly decreased. Out of a population of 700,000 people (plus an estimated 200,000 refugees) there, non-Muslims numbered 'less than 2 per cent as contrasted with approximately 12.5 per cent prior to 1947'.[153] This decrease presumably was due to migration, flight, kidnapping of women, natural causes—and deliberate murder.

By 1951, there were even fewer non-Muslims living in Azad Kashmir than in 1949. In the 1941 Census, 10 per cent of the population of Poonch *jagir*, about 60 per cent of which later became part of Azad Kashmir, consisted of non-Muslims.[154] In Mirpur District, about 90 per cent of which became Azad Kashmir, some 20 per cent of the 1941 population comprised non-Muslims. Collectively, non-Muslims in both districts amounted to almost 102,000 people. Muzaffarabad *tehsil*, all of which became Azad Kashmir, had about 12,000 Hindus and Sikhs in 1941, with many Sikhs living in Muzaffarabad town. By 1951, the Azad Kashmir Census stated that, out of Azad Kashmir's total population of 886,153, only 790 people or less than 0.09 per cent, were non-Muslims.[155] This appallingly low figure was presumably one reason why the 1951 Azad Kashmir Census, which was 'done under the aegis of Pakistani authorities', was classified 'Secret' and for 'limited distribution'.[156] Thousands of Hindus and Sikhs had been killed, abducted or had fled.[157] Some ended up in Poonch city, or in the eastern Hindu-majority parts of Jammu Province, or in Kashmir Province. The 1961 Census of India—there was no 1951 census of J&K owing to its disrupted conditions—does not specify figures for non-Muslims displaced in 1947 living in Indian J&K. It does mention 'large scale migration and immigration from and into [Poonch] town' and Sikhs in Srinagar, some of whom 'hail[ed] from Muzaffarabad and other areas now on the other side of the Cease-fire Line'.[158] Certainly, J&K Hindus and Sikhs also suffered from inter-religious violence.

The deaths, two-way emigration and internal movement of Jammu Muslims, Hindus and Sikhs changed the religious composition of Jammu Province in and after 1947. Muslims fleeing eastern areas of Jammu Province were replaced by Hindu and Sikh refugees fleeing Pakistan and other areas of J&K, particularly from Poonch, Mirpur and Muzaffarabad districts. Areas west of the Chenab River were virtually free from non-Muslims; in areas east of this river, Hindus had become a large majority.[159] While the 1961 Census of India did not mention how many Muslims left or were killed in this area, it noted that Muslim populations had decreased in Udhampur and Kathua districts. There also had been 'a phenomenal fall in the rural population of [the] Muslim community in Jammu district during the last two decades as a result of the mass migration to Pakistan of most of the Muslims ... The total population of this community in the district as a whole ... is about one-third of what it was in 1941'.[160]

Despite general ignorance about the serious inter-religious violence that occurred in Jammu Province in 1947 and regardless of the actual number of deaths that occurred, much of the Jammuites' violence predated the tribal invasion of J&K. One result of the specific violence against Muslims in Jammu was the largely forgotten, or overlooked, formation of the Azad Kashmir movement in areas liberated by Poonchis and Mirpuris. We now discuss this movement.

*The effect: the creation of Azad Kashmir*

A third significant, but neglected, event involving the people of Jammu Province in 1947 was the creation of the anti-Maharaja Azad (Free) Kashmir movement. Arising from actions that occurred in Jammu after 15 August, an increasingly organised people's militia, the Azad Army, opposed the Maharaja's autocratic rule. Political forces opposed to the Maharaja, chiefly pro-Pakistan Muslim Conference politicians, supported and organised it. Initially, the Azad Kashmir movement did not seek full political autonomy or independence for J&K. Rather, it wanted J&K to be *azad*, or free, from the Maharaja's control. On 4 October 1947, an unsuccessful attempt was made to create an alternative government for J&K. On 24 October, at the second attempt, senior Muslim Conference politicians successfully formed a Provisional Azad Government. (Although this was unstated, it was to be provisional until J&K's international status was determined.) While this government was created two days after, and possibly because of the Pukhtoons' invasion of Kashmir Province on 22 October, the activities that encouraged its formation came before this invasion and were possibly a catalyst for it. The politicians who successfully formed the Provisional Azad Government had been opposing the Maharaja long before the Pukhtoons entered J&K. Nevertheless, the Pukhtoons' arrival certainly boosted their physical and military—but not their political—causes.

One major reason for the formation of the Azad Kashmir movement was fear. As noted, from the start of anti-Muslim violence in Jammu Province, some Muslims believed that Maharaja Hari Singh had a plan to 'take quick and strong action, [and] liquidate the whole Moslem population by massacring large numbers and pushing out the rest into Pakistan'. Hari Singh first planned to deal with the '100,000 ex-servicemen' living in areas close to Pakistan, then he would 'turn [his attention] to the rest of the Moslem population' whom, Muslims believed, he intended to massacre.[161] The ruler would then allow the 'surplus Sikh' population from West Punjab to replace the Muslims.[162] If true, Hari Singh's plan was ambitious: he would have to kill or expel over three million J&K Muslims. Nevertheless, the Muslims' fear had some basis: Hindus and Sikhs, sometimes acting with official sanction, were ridding eastern Punjab of much of its Muslim population. This involved attacking, looting, arson, and raping and killing Muslims.

Muslims' perception of a possible massacre increased following the Maharaja's apparent declaration of martial law around August—which concurred with anti-Muslim atrocities in Punjab. This made Jammu Muslims 'mentally prepared for the worst'.[163] Sensing danger, some decided to organise. Many Poonchi Muslims were clear that 'only by force of arms could they remove the Maharaja's oppressive army occupation, and save their own lives'.[164] Soon after violence against Muslims started in Jammu Province and conditions had become 'intolerable', some Muslims organised a people's resistance movement by 'mobiliz[ing] all of our able-bodied population'. This movement was the Azad Army. Members of the Muslim Conference led by Sardar Ibrahim, were the political force behind this body. By late September, this Azad Army controlled much of Poonch and Mirpur districts in Jammu Province. 'By the middle of October the military initiative passed into [Azad Army] hands'.[165] As a result of its military successes, the political organisation known as the Azad Kashmir movement developed.

Politically, a major impetus for pro-Pakistan elements in J&K was the establishment of a provisional government in the princely state of Junagadh on 1 October 1947. Junagadh's religious and political situation was the reverse of J&K's: a Muslim Nawab ruled an 80 per cent Hindu population. Unlike J&K, Junagadh's scattered territory was close to, but not contiguous with, Pakistan, although direct sea communication was possible from coastal areas. The Nawab had acceded to Pakistan on 15 August 1947. Indian National Congress members of the local assembly, supported by India, repudiated this accession on 1 October, after which they sought to govern Junagadh via a provisional government. This action inspired some patriotic but timid Muslim Conference workers in J&K. On 4 October, they announced the formation of a 'provisional revolutionary government on the Junagadh model'.[166] From supposed headquarters at Muzaffarabad, the proclamation signed by the president 'Mr. Anwar' stated that 'all laws, orders and instructions promulgated or issued by the Provisional Republican Government of Kashmir State shall be respected and obeyed'.[167] Anyone disobeying this 'duly constituted Government of the people of Kashmir' or aiding and abetting the 'ex-Maharaja' would be guilty of 'high treason' and 'dealt with accordingly'.[168]

Even though the people of J&K apparently received this new government enthusiastically, it failed. One reason was that the President, after making his proclamation, apparently went to Srinagar to arrest the Maharaja but instead was arrested himself and imprisoned for thirteen months.[169] Equally, the provisional government failed because it was formed at 'a municipal and limited level' without the knowledge of the Muslim Conference's 'top brass'. They were not prepared to support this action by impetuous lower-level members: the circumstances were not right and they were not ready.[170] The provisional government therefore never saw 'the light of day'. Its formation also may have been a feint by inexperienced political forces designed to inspire or cajole other pro-Pakistan forces into further action to ensure that J&K joined Pakistan.

Despite failing, the first 'Provisional Republican Government of Kashmir State' energised more senior Muslim Conference elements. Soon afterwards, they established another provisional government, possibly with Pakistan's support. Towards the end of October, it was 'more propitious' to engage in decisive political action. Relations between Pakistan and the J&K Government had deteriorated, with Srinagar accusing Karachi of withholding vital supplies, which the J&K Government stated it might seek to obtain elsewhere. This could only mean from India, a proposition that made both Pakistan and pro-Pakistanis in J&K wary lest India try to take the princely state by stealth. A further propitious factor was the Maharaja's 'wholesale arrests of patriots in the [Kashmir] Valley [that caused] a high wave of resentment'.[171] Pro-Pakistan politicians felt that they could capitalise on this resentment.

Another important factor was that, on 21–22 October 1947, pro-Pakistan 'traitors' in the Maharaja's army,[172] probably inspired by Azad Army elements, rebelled at Domel and took control of the strategic bridge over the Jhelum River that controlled entry to the Kashmir Valley beyond.[173] This facilitated the invading Pukhtoons' move down the Jhelum Valley Road towards J&K's summer capital.[174] Many in the fledgling Azad Kashmir movement believed probably naively, that these poorly trained, undisciplined, irregular, booty-hungry tribesmen would quickly capture Srinagar and Maharaja Hari Singh and entice him to accede to Pakistan.[175] Had the Pukhtoons succeeded, pro-Pakistan elements would have gained control of the prized Kashmir Valley, including Srinagar and its airport (whose strategic significance Pakistan would later understand). This would have allowed this region—and all of J&K had they obtained Hari Singh's accession—to join, or be joined, with Pakistan. Also, given that bitter winter snows were expected soon to envelop Kashmir Province, the weather would have prevented any serious Indian military response. A new government for J&K would have been needed; the provisional government would have been this body.

The final propitious factor that enabled a provisional government to be established, and sustained, was the emergence of some Muslim Conference members full of 'daring and infused with a spirit of revolutionary adventure'.[176] They were led by Sardar Ibrahim, a little known thirty-two-year-old barrister from Rawalakot, Poonch (who would go on to play a role in Azad Kashmir politics for over fifty years).[177] One of the few Muslim barristers in J&K in 1947, Ibrahim had worked as 'an unknown assistant District Advocate in the Maharaja's Government'.[178] In January 1947, he had been elected unopposed from the 'Bagh Sadnooti [sic; Sudhnuti] Muslim' constituency to the Praja Sabha,[179] where he served as Chief Whip of the Muslim Conference.[180] On 22 July 1947, he gained prestige after 200 Muslim Conference leaders 'passed unanimously' a resolution in his Srinagar home,[181] a dangerous act of hospitality given the volatile times and Srinagar being a National Conference stronghold. This resolution urged Hari Singh to join Pakistan. It warned him that, if he acceded to India, 'the people of Kashmir will stand as one man against such a decision and launch a struggle with all the power at their command'.[182] This resolution ended the Muslim Conference's temporary stance of independence and anticipated the formation of the Azad Kashmir movement. It was designed to deter the Maharaja who, according to a rumour related in *CMG* on 3 July, had a 'deep-seated desire' to join India.[183] While *CMG* noted that the rumour had little veracity, it was sufficient to engage pro-Pakistan Muslim minds.

Sardar Ibrahim had three advantages. First, he was available for a leadership role simply because he was not in jail. Police crackdowns throughout 1946 and 1947 had jailed many senior Muslim Conference members, forced them to flee J&K, or deterred them from leadership roles. Second, his 'single minded fanaticism and fiery eloquence quickly gave him the lead' among his peers.[184] He appeared to be passionate, with a clearer vision and less fear about advancing the pro-Pakistan cause than some of his colleagues, such as Chaudhry Hamidullah (see below). Third, he was a leading figure of the Sudhan tribe, a main and martial tribe of dissident Poonch. In this and other areas that came to comprise Azad Kashmir, people's tribal affiliations were important. After July 1947, when the establishment of Pakistan was a certainty, Poonchis' 'intense tribalism' meant that 'only one of them could have commanded their complete loyalty and Sardar Ibrahim was doubtlessly the only choice'. Along with Muslims from neighbouring Bagh, Sudhans formed the backbone of the anti-Maharaja, pro-Pakistan forces in western Jammu. When the Pukhtoons invaded on 22 October 1947, they already were 'fighting actively' and rather successfully 'on [sic] various sectors except Muzaffarabad'.[185]

In a portent of Azad Kashmir's factionalised politics, Ibrahim mistakenly believed he had authority to act as Muslim Conference leader and head of any provisional government. Chaudhry Hamidullah, Muslim Conference leader in the Praja Sabha,[186] had been acting President since Ghulam Abbas, the actual Muslim Conference President, was jailed in September 1946 (Abbas was released on 28 February 1948).[187] Because Hamidullah feared imminent arrest as a result of the j&k government serving him with expulsion orders,[188] he consulted his available Muslim Conference colleagues, and then apparently sent Ibrahim a letter of authority dated 17 September 1947 appointing the barrister as his successor. According to Ibrahim, this letter gave him (Ibrahim) great power: 'you will be perfectly competent to receive and deliver goods on behalf of the Muslim Conference. You can negotiate with any party or organization, and arrive at any understanding you deem fit and proper. The Muslim Conference will be bound by your acts and words'.

A postscript boosted Ibrahim's power: 'as long as I am not arrested, you are even now, quite competent to act on my behalf outside the State'.[189] However, a month later, when Ibrahim announced the formation of the Provisional Azad Government, Hamidullah questioned his authority. Although Hamidullah wished to avoid being 'Chief Rebel', he told Saraf that Ibrahim's 'announcement was unauthorised' and should have been ignored. Nevertheless, on 4 November 1947, Hamidullah met Ibrahim and offered to support him.[190]

Ibrahim says little about the formation of what was a 'parallel independent government' in J&K, except that it was 'declared to have been established' on 24 October.[191] This was two days after the Pukhtoons first invaded Kashmir Province—and two days before Maharaja Hari Singh's accession to India on 26 October 1947. Nevertheless, the build-up to the Provisional Azad Government's creation predated the Pukhtoons' invasion. On 24 October Ibrahim's group, acting as the reconstituted 'Provisional Azad Government which the people of Jammu and Kashmir had set up a few weeks ago', announced that it was 'assuming the administration of the state'.[192] On 28 October 1947, *TOI* published a report dated 27 October about the new government's existence: 'About ten days ago ... [Poonch] insurgents succeeded in overwhelming the Government forces and thereafter the rebels established a "Provisional Azad Kashmir Government", with its seat in Poonch'.[193] *TOI*'s 'authentic version' of events meant that the Azad Kashmir Government was actually established on 17 October 1947, five days before the tribal invasion of J&K. More likely, its establishment was a rushed response to the Pukhtoons' entry into the already physically and politically divided princely state.[194] Feeling euphoric, anti-Maharaja forces wanted a government in place before—as they anticipated—the Pukhtoons took Srinagar, captured Maharaja Hari Singh and obtained his accession. After that, the Provisional Azad Government would administer J&K.

This second, or reconstituted, Provisional Azad Government released an uncertain communiqué on 24 October 1947.[195] Instead of naming the Muslim Conference as the body behind the government, it deferentially mentioned both Nehru and the National Conference's 1946 'Quit Kashmir' campaign, and made some negative statements about the people's common enemy, the Maharaja. This was an attempt at either inclusiveness or obfuscation, to lessen the impact of the then little known Pukhtoons' intervention about which the Muslim Conference certainly knew—and from which it had benefited (initially, at least). In either case, those familiar with local politics would have known that 'Mr. Ibrahim, Barrister-at-Law, of Poonch', who was mentioned in the communiqué's first paragraph as the government's 'provisional head', was a Muslim Conference member. Additionally, for a movement both pro-Pakistan and anti-Indian, the communiqué displayed remarkable equanimity towards both dominions. Its authors may have wanted to leave the decision on J&K's future status to the people of J&K, or else wanted independence for J&K (which the communiqué inferred). Another reason may have been temporary ambivalence towards Pakistan, which was not providing the help that Azad Kashmiris believed they were entitled to receive in order to wage their anti-Maharaja struggle. Most probably, the communiqué was a quickly constructed document that reflected the provisional government's insecurity and political inexperience during a turbulent, fast-changing situation.

While the second Provisional Azad Government sought to establish itself in the liberated area that now comprised Azad Kashmir, it soon had another, non-aristocratic, rival in J&K. As early as 1 November 1947, the 'Azad Kashmir Government', feeling more confident, dropped the word 'provisional' from its title.[196] Its physical survival was helped by the Azad Army's control of large parts of western Jammu Province and by the Pukhtoons' presence in western areas of Kashmir Province. Equally, India and its Kashmiri surrogates benefited from the Pukhtoons' invasion. On 26 October, New Delhi won the Maharaja's accession when he was compelled to accede to India to obtain its defensive help against the Pukhtoons. For Karachi, the accession was 'based on fraud and violence'.[197] However, Hari Singh's accession gave India—unlike Pakistan—the legal right and moral justification to despatch forces to J&K on 27 October. They flew into the (uncaptured) Srinagar airfield and began to repulse the pro-Pakistan Pukhtoons who, distracted by looting, were only then reaching Srinagar's outskirts. On 31 October, the Indian Government hobbled the Maharaja's regime by creating an Emergency Administration that empowered Sheikh Abdullah and some National Conference members.[198] This placed these pro-Indian Kashmiris directly in charge of the prized, but threatened, Kashmir Valley. Thereafter, the Azad Kashmir Government had a rival body seeking to administer J&K.

Statements issued by the Azad Kashmir Government reflected its change of fortune. For two days—24 and 25 October 1947—it 'ruled' unchallenged, except for the Maharaja's weak regime. Hari Singh's accession to India on 26 October changed this situation. The Azad Kashmir Government. seemingly unaware in its remote capital of the accession, on 27 October inclusively extended its 'fullest co-operation to all classes' and 'especially' to Sheikh Abdullah, whom it requested to return to J&K and 'play his rightful role in the battle of liberty'.[199] (He was in New Delhi having discussions with senior Indian leaders.) Two days later, after Abdullah sided with India and Hari Singh, the 'despot' against whom he had raised the Quit Kashmir slogan,[200] the 'Provisional Government of Azad Kashmir' issued a strong statement aimed clearly at its opponents: 'may he be a raja or any of his henchmen, our Government does not recognise the authority of any oppressor or traitor. We have launched a fight to overthrow an alien ruler and we are determined to fight it to the finish.'[201]

The battle lines were drawn. Thereafter, pro-Pakistan Azad Kashmiris engaged pro-Indian forces supporting the National Conference in a fight that proved to be inconclusive.

When Azad Kashmir was created on 24 October 1947, its founders were probably looking only to the immediate or short-term future. They expected J&K's international status to be resolved by the Maharaja acceding to Pakistan or by the Pukhtoons capturing the Kashmir Valley for Pakistan. Azad Kashmiris would then provide the political and administrative elite to govern J&K—or at least the Mus-

THE PEOPLE

lim areas under their control. Two days after Azad Kashmir's creation, their outlook changed following the Maharaja's accession to India. It changed again on 27 October 1947 when Indian military forces started arriving in J&K. They gradually threatened the physical survival of Azad Kashmir, and as a consequence the Pakistan Army officially entered J&K in May 1948.[202] The provisional government united all pro-Pakistan forces in J&K, including the Pukhtoons, under its leadership and control and ensured that Azad Kashmir survived until the United Nations ceasefire on 1 January 1949 ended the fighting in J&K. Thereafter, the dispute over possession of J&K increasingly became a contest between India and Pakistan, with the Azad Kashmir Government still in existence, but on the periphery.

*Conclusion*

The evidence above confirms that the people of J&K commenced, and sustained, the violent activities that occurred in J&K between Partition on 15 August and Maharaja Hari Singh's accession to India on 26 October 1947. During this significant ten-week period, the Maharaja confronted two major law and order crises involving Jammuites: first, the Poonch uprising, which his forces could not control; second, inter-religious violence in Jammu Province, including a possible massacre of Muslims, which the ruler and his forces could not control—and may have been involved in. The Poonch uprising, the Muslim 'massacre' and the resultant formation of the Azad Kashmir movement were attempts by some Jammuites either to free themselves from autocracy, to impose their collective will locally, or to join J&K with Pakistan or India. Regardless of the specific motivation for each event, the evidence above confirms that these were local events undertaken and led by state subjects with every right to be in J&K. Similarly, this evidence shows that the Poonch uprising and the violence against Muslims in Jammu Province commenced, and were well under way, before Pakistani Pukhtoons invaded J&K on 22 October 1947. Indeed, these actions may have inspired the Pukhtoons' invasion.

These actions by the people of J&K are significant for two reasons. First, they directly led to the physical and political division of J&K before the Maharaja acceded to India. Second, and most important, they instigated the ongoing dispute over whether J&K should join India or Pakistan—the so-called Kashmir dispute. The evidence shows that the people of Jammu and Kashmir themselves began the Kashmir dispute. Pukhtoon raiders or outsiders did not start it, as India has repeatedly stated since 1947. India used this argument to strengthen its position in the Kashmir dispute, but Pakistan's acquiescence in it is surprising. These matters are discussed in the next chapter.

3

# INDIA AND PAKISTAN

## NEGATING THE PEOPLE'S ACTIONS

*Introduction*

Since 1947, India has deliberately denied or ignored the significant pre-accession actions by the people of Jammu and Kashmir that divided the princely state and instigated the dispute over it. Instead, to enhance its own position and to weaken Pakistan's, India has mounted an argument that Pakistan started the Kashmir dispute. The Indian argument, which is now the accepted—but incorrect—view, goes like this: on 22 October 1947, Karachi deliberately sent Muslim Pukhtoon tribesmen into Muslim-majority J&K to physically seize the princely state for Pakistan. New Delhi, after obtaining Maharaja Hari Singh's accession on 26 October and with the support of secular Kashmiri Muslims, magnanimously deployed Indian military forces to J&K on, and after 27 October 1947, to defend and free J&K from these 'raiders'. The Pakistani action of sending the Pukhtoons initiated all of the troubles in J&K and instigated the dispute between India and Pakistan over which should possess this state.

While it is indisputable that Pukhtoons invaded J&K in 1947, there is contention about whether the Pakistan Government was responsible for despatching these Pukhtoons or not. It is outside the scope of this book to determine this issue.[1] What can be said is that, by focusing on the raiders—as India called those Pukhtoons—and their often deplorable actions in J&K against people of all religions, India was able to seriously embarrass Pakistan. Additionally, New Delhi negated the independent actions of pro-Pakistan J&K Muslims by including them with those despicable Pukhtoons. Karachi could not fend off India's pointed accusations that Pakistan had sent the raiders. Curiously, it also was unwilling to strengthen its case by highlighting the pre-accession actions by the people of J&K. Instead, Pakistan sought—unsuccessfully—to broaden the argument by questioning the legitimacy of Hari Singh's accession and by raising associated issues, such as the status of the (also disputed) princely states of Junagadh and Hyderabad and India's role in these. Pakistan's ploys failed. Instead the Indian view of history prevailed, and Pakistani Pukhtoons (incorrectly) came to be seen as instigators of the Kashmir dispute, not the people of J&K. Equally, the people's significant post-Partition, pre-accession actions discussed previously were forgotten or deliberately ignored.

This chapter examines why, and how, India and Pakistan overlooked or negated the three significant actions taken by the people of J&K in 1947. It provides evidence to confirm that India's political leaders knew that the Jammuites' actions predated the Pukhtoons' invasion of J&K, and instigated the dispute over whether J&K should join India or Pakistan. It shows how Pakistan was unable to prevent itself from acquiescing in India's tactic of propagating the view that Pakistanis instigated the Kashmir dispute.

*India's negation*

Since 1947, India has consistently claimed that all violence in J&K started when Pukhtoon raiders sent by Pakistan entered Kashmir Province on 22 October. As Bazaz noted, for 'Nehru and his supporters aggression [in J&K] begins from the moment tribesmen entered Kashmir'.[2] However, the evidence confirms that India's leaders were aware of J&K's internal situation well before the Pukhtoons invaded Kashmir Province. Sheikh Abdullah, who knew about the Jammu violence provided information to the Indians, particularly to Jawaharlal Nehru.[3] Details for members of the Indian Government were, as Nehru informed his Pakistani prime ministerial counterpart, Liaquat Ali Khan, 'derived largely from statements appearing in the press'.[4] By 22 October 1947, there had been a number of press reports published about events in Jammu Province. Some appeared in early September; more appeared in October. Specifically, reports published about events in Poonch before the Pukhtoons' invasion included *CMG* (4 September and 2, 5, 19 and 21 October 1947); *The Times* (8 September); and *TOI* (15, 17, 19 and 20 October 1947). Reports published about Jammu's inter-religious violence before the Pukhtoons' invasion included *CMG* (26 September and 19 and 21 October). *CMG* was one of the best sources for news about J&K—and a newspaper that Nehru, given his interest in J&K, certainly read on occasions. On 30 December, Nehru informed Patel that this Lahore-based paper had the 'latest evidence' on a 'conflict' between the Muslim Conference and the Azad Kashmir movement.[5]

Nehru and Patel also knew through other sources what had been happening in J&K before the Pukhtoon invasion. On 2 October 1947, Patel wrote to Maharaja Hari Singh stating that he (Patel) was 'expediting' telegraph, telephone, wireless and roads links between J&K and India as 'we fully realize the need for despatch and urgency and ... we shall do our best' to fulfil these.[6] Patel wrote this letter twenty days before the Pukhtoons' invasion and twenty-six days before the Maharaja's accession. He may have been trying to help J&K with its difficulties obtaining supplies, including petrol, from Pakistan, although Patel does not mention this.[7] Rather, it appears he was preparing for Hari Singh's alignment with, or even his accession to, India—something Nehru had five days earlier (on 27 September) suggested to Patel should be achieved 'as rapidly as possible'.[8] Patel also mentions in his letter to Hari Singh that he (Patel) had personally delivered the ruler's letters to 'justice

## INDIA AND PAKISTAN: NEGATING THE PEOPLE'S ACTIONS

Mahajan' in Amritsar, and that Patel understood the (pro-Indian) Mahajan would 'very shortly' join the ruler's staff (as Prime Minister). Patel made his extraordinary personal efforts because he had been in search of a 'proper person' to be 'a good man in Kashmir' for India since late August 1947.[9] Patel also was 'pleased' that the Maharaja had proclaimed a general political amnesty—which actually applied only to National Conference members. Hari Singh had released his old adversary Sheikh Abdullah, something Patel had been seeking since April 1947.[10]

Nehru, for whom J&K's future was 'both a personal and public' matter, knew what was actually happening in J&K, as a letter to Sardar Patel on 5 October 1947 shows.[11] Nehru enclosed a report about J&K from Dwarkanath Kachru, Secretary of the All-India States Peoples' Conference, who had been in Srinagar for four days.[12] Kachru made nineteen points. His first and second were that: the National Conference had 'decided for the Indian Union'; this decision had not been announced. Kachru's fifth point was that the recently released Abdullah was delivering speeches saying that the 'killings of Hindus and Muslims [we]re un-Hindu and un-Islamic'. As there was almost no communal violence in the Kashmir Valley, Abdullah was clearly referring to other areas, chiefly Jammu, where inter-religious violence was then worsening. Kachru's eighth point discussed 'the utter collapse of [J&K's] administrative and government machinery'. Three weeks before the Pukhtoons' invasion, India was reliably informed that Hari Singh had lost control of his princely domain.

There also is evidence that India and its Prime Minister, Jawaharlal Nehru, knew that many so-called raiders active in J&K were not from outside J&K—as the term raiders infers. India knew that the Maharaja's opponents comprised of local men from J&K who were state subjects entitled to be there. As noted previously, Abdullah stated in New Delhi on 22 October—before news of the Pukhtoons' invasion had broken outside western J&K—that the 'present troubles in Poonch' were because of 'a people's movement for the redress of their grievances'.[13] Abdullah did not mention raiders or outsiders. Indeed, his explanation of events in Poonch suggested where possible Indian confusion about raiders arose:

most of the adult population of Poonch ... had close connections with the people in Jhelum and Rawalpindi. They evacuated their women and children, crossed the frontier and returned with arms supplied to them by willing people. The present position was that the Kashmir State forces were forced to withdraw in certain areas.[14]

Abdullah confirmed the close links between Poonchis and their neighbours. When re-entering the princely state, Poonch men may have appeared—to the uninformed or prejudiced eye—to be from outside J&K. But, as Abdullah knew and stated publicly, many were J&K citizens returning to defend their homes and land from the unpopular Maharaja's actions.

The most important point about Sheikh Abdullah's statement is that, if he knew what the people of Poonch were doing when he spoke in New Delhi on 22 October 1947, almost certainly he would have informed his secular colleagues. In particular, Abdullah probably would have discussed this issue with his close, pro-Kashmir friend, Jawaharlal Nehru, whose interest in Kashmir and its future was, as he had informed Abdullah, 'of the most intimate personal significance'.[15] Hence, if Abdullah knew, so too did Nehru. On 2 November 1947, soon after the Pukhtoon invasion, Nehru sent a letter to his 'prime ministers' showing he had listened to Abdullah. Reflecting Abdullah's statement, Nehru informed them that 'the actual tribesmen among the raiders are probably limited in numbers, the rest are ex-servicemen.[16] Part of the Muslim element in the Kashmir [armed] forces has also gone over [to the pro-Pakistan forces]'.[17] By 'tribesmen' Nehru meant Pukhtoons; by ex-servicemen, he meant Poonchis, some 60,000 of whom had served in the (British) Indian Army.[18] Nehru also knew that the 'Muslim element in the Kashmir [armed] forces' were state subjects, usually Muslim Rajputs from Jammu.

In statements made later in 1947, Nehru clearly understood that (outside) raiders were not responsible for all violent incidents in J&K in 1947. Speaking in the Indian Constituent Assembly on 25 November, he noted that some Jammuites, chiefly Hindus and Rajputs who lived near the J&K-Pakistan border, were responsible for taking 'retaliatory measures' against Muslims and driving them out of villages in various 'border conflicts'.[19] In a letter to Maharaja Hari Singh on 1 December, Nehru spoke of 'the raiders and the Poonchi rebels' and said that, in the event of a plebiscite, there was 'little doubt' that the mass of Poonch's population would 'likely be against the Indian Union'.[20] On 30 December, the Prime Minister also pointedly told Hari Singh that the anti-Muslim policy 'recently pursued' in Jammu Province had 'alienated' Muslims 'very greatly': 'a large part of our difficulties [in J&K] is due to previous wrongs policies and mistakes ... The occurrences in Jammu and roundabout [sic] towards the end of October and early in November are associated ... with Mr. Mahajan's administration and they have had a disastrous result'.[21]

In Mountbatten's record of a conversation on 8 December involving Nehru, Liaquat and others, Mountbatten stated that Nehru had said that, if India withdrew its troops, J&K would be 'at the mercy of the armed men of Poonch'.[22] Writing to Mountbatten on 26 December, Nehru acknowledged that the 'inhabitants of Poonch' were a different element from the outside raiders.[23] Thus, while Nehru usually spoke publicly about raiders, he knew that a significant proportion of men engaging in anti-Maharaja, then anti-Indian, activities in J&K comprised a large local J&K element.

India's leaders were also aware of a possible Pukhtoon invasion of J&K beforehand. As early as 27 September 1947, Nehru wrote to Patel 'about Kashmir' telling Patel that he (Nehru) was aware of what was going on from the many reports he received.[24] This included information that the Muslim League in Punjab and NWFP—the Pakistan Government was not mentioned—were 'making preparations to enter Kashmir in considerable numbers'. (Nehru's speech in the Indian Constituent Assembly on 25 November confirmed India's awareness in September of these preparations.)[25] Nehru told Patel that, owing to the forthcoming onset of winter, the intruders would enter Kashmir Province via the Jhelum Valley Road 'by the end of October or, at the latest, the beginning of November'. The 'Pakistan strategy [wa]s to infiltrate into Kashmir now and to take some big action as soon as Kashmir is more or less isolated because of the coming winter'. Nehru concluded that 'time [wa]s of the essence' and that the accession of J&K to India should be brought about 'as rapidly as possible with the cooperation of Sheikh Abdullah'. Patel obviously believed Nehru for he (Patel) in turn, wrote to India's Defence Minister, Sardar Baldev Singh, asking him to immediately send arms and ammunition to J&K, by air if necessary. 'There [wa]s no time to lose', because it appeared that the Pakistani intervention was 'going to be true to [the] Nazi pattern'.²⁶ Presumably this meant swift, overwhelming and brutal. Patel wrote to Singh on 7 October 1947, a fortnight before the Pukhtoons entered J&K.

Despite India's foreknowledge of events in, and related to, J&K, Indian statements after the Maharaja's accession on 26 October almost always only talked of raiders—and not Poonchis, Mirpuris, or men from J&K. India's intention was twofold: first, to infer that these raiders were outsiders from J&K who had every intention of doing harm; second, to show that the raiders had mounted all anti-Maharaja operations in J&K, and not any locally disgruntled J&K state subjects. On 3 November 1947, Prime Minister Nehru set the tone in a broadcast about 'events in Kashmir'. His foreign policy statement entitled 'Invasion of Kashmir' in the Constituent Assembly followed on 25 November.²⁷ In his radio address, Nehru stated that 'considerable parts' of J&K had been 'overrun by raiders from outside'.²⁸ Referring to Jammu's problems before the Pukhtoons' invasion, he stated that India did not 'interfere' in Jammu 'even though a part of Jammu Province was overrun by these raiders'. He also claimed that ninety-five villages were destroyed by 'the raiders from Pakistan' and that 'a considerable part of Poonch and Mirpur areas [wa]s in possession of the raiders'. Nehru deduced that 'the struggle in Kashmir [wa]s a struggle of the people of Kashmir against the invader ... We talk about the invaders and raiders in Kashmir ... All of these have come across and from Pakistan territory'. For Nehru, it was emphatically clear: the people causing problems in J&K were raiders supported by Pakistan.

Nehru was obfuscating. He knew that people in J&K themselves had opposed the Maharaja, by military means among others. Nehru had been aware of the actual situation in J&K before the Pukhtoons' invasion. The main physical struggle there had been a fight by people in Jammu Province against the Maharaja and his armed forces. Their struggle had begun well before the Pukhtoons' invasion. A further action was the serious inter-religious violence that began in Jammu in September 1947, possibly with the ruler's connivance (as discussed previously), and which may have inspired the Pukhtoons' invasion. The 'rebels' involved with the Poonch uprising almost certainly received some support from their Pakistani brethren across the porous border, some of whom were related by blood or marriage, particularly in the Hazara region of NWFP. Nevertheless, very few of these rebels were raiders who had come 'across or from' Pakistan territory. Most were men from Jammu Province entitled to be in J&K.

From late October 1947 onwards, official Indian publications usually spoke only of raiders when referring to anti-Maharaja, then anti-Indian, activities in J&K after 15 August 1947. Indeed, by mid-1948, use of this terminology appeared to be official government policy, with the Government of India's 1948 *White Paper on Jammu & Kashmir* setting the standard. Its summary of 'Events Leading up to the Accession of Jammu and Kashmir to India' did not mention the violence in Jammu and the formation of the Azad Kashmir movement; even though, in a report from New Delhi dated 27 October 1947, *TOI* reported that 'About ten days ago ... [Poonch] insurgents ... established a "Provisional Azad Kashmir Government", with its seat in Poonch'.²⁹ As it was a Bombay-based newspaper and as the story emanated from New Delhi, the *TOI's* report was available to Indian

Government officials. The *White Paper* also dismissed the Poonchis' anti-Maharaja activities as being instigated and led by 'armed gangs from Pakistan'.[30] A New Delhi communiqué of 1 November 1947 went further: these activities were 'feints in the Poonch area to disguise the line of the main [Pakistani] attack'.[31] The *White Paper* did (inadvertently?) include one press report from Palandari, the headquarters of the 'organised Muslim military and political rebellion aimed at driving Kashmir to Pakistan'—that is, the Azad Kashmir movement. Dated 11 November 1947, the report significantly suggested that the 6,000 rebels comprised local state subjects, including 'a few Pakistan Army Officers who have taken leave to fight with their [Azad Kashmiri] people'.[32] This was highly likely given how many Poonchis had martial experience and given that Poonchis serving in the Pakistan Army probably had a strong desire to defend their homelands in 1947.[33]

Similarly, an official Indian Government publication of 1949 entitled *Defending Kashmir* claimed that cross-border harassment by 'raiders from Pakistan' provided the prelude to the Pukhtoons' entry.[34] According to it, from 3 September until the full-scale invasion began on 20 October 1947 (Pukhtoons actually entered Kashmir Province on 22 October), these raiders pierced the border 'at several points almost every day'. The only mention of Poonch in *Defending Kashmir* was in the chronology of 'Border Incidents before 27 October 1947'. This noted, almost certainly correctly, that on 4 October '[Sardar] Ibrahim Khan of Punch [Poonch] ... was trying to send arms and ammunition to Punch' from Murree.[35] Equally, there was probably other cross-border support from Pakistanis for Poonchi and Mirpuri rebels. Nevertheless, local J&K Muslim men almost certainly undertook the bulk of the anti-Maharaja actions. Apart from the significant instability in Punjab itself, Pakistan and Pakistanis had few resources to spare in 1947. Conversely, Pakistan may also have confronted serious cross-border activity across the Sialkot-Jammu border in 1947. This involved killings of Muslims mainly, but also of some Dogras and Sikhs, destruction of property and crops, and loss of property. 'Kashmir State Forces' allegedly committed some of this violence.[36]

Indian writers soon began emulating 'official' Indian terminology of raiders. In 1950, D.F. Karaka claimed that 'After partition, when the British had quit, His Highness [Maharaja Hari Singh] found himself confronted with a new situation ... a savage tribe of raiders which had appeared on the borders of his state were soon pressing inwards towards Srinagar.'[37]

Following the Indian tactic, Karaka made no mention of any anti-Maharaja or inter-religious activity anywhere in Jammu Province prior to the Pukhtoons' arrival. For 'astonished' Indians like Karaka the situation was that, first, Pukhtoon raiders suddenly arrived in J&K unannounced; second, Pakistan had inspired and induced and/or ordered them to seize peaceful J&K from the pacific Maharaja for Pakistan, and third, the Pukhtoons' invasion of J&K marked the beginning of all anti-Maharaja, then anti-Indian, violence in J&K. It was a simplistic and inaccurate portrayal of events that Pakistan would find impossible to counter.

*An examination of India's* White Paper

India's use of the term raiders to describe the Maharaja's opponents in J&K before the Pukhtoons' invasion was incorrect and unsubstantiated, as an examination of

## INDIA AND PAKISTAN: NEGATING THE PEOPLE'S ACTIONS

India's *White Paper on Jammu & Kashmir* shows.[38] Tabled in March 1948, the *White Paper* was the Government of India's first detailed and official document about the Kashmir dispute. It sought, in four parts, to provide 'factual information, backed by the relevant documents' about events leading up to: Part I) the accession; Part II) 'the invasion … by raiders from Pakistan'; Part III) Pakistan's 'complicity' in this, and Part IV) India's objectives in J&K.[39] In relation to Part I, the *White Paper* presented thirty-one documents. Of these, only one provided any evidence of people from outside J&K entering the state before 22 October 1947 (after which date outsiders indisputably did enter J&K in large numbers). This document was a copy of Major-General Scott's report on 4 September about '400 Sattis' entering J&K from Kahuta.[40] As discussed previously, this could have been correct or it could have been a case of 'mistaken identity'.

The *White Paper's* introduction to Part One also provided some startling information. It spoke of some 'four to five thousand raiders in green uniforms' in the Mirpur area on 15 October and 'heavy fighting' taking place 'along the Kotli-Poonch road' on 18 October.[41] If true, this described an extraordinary situation that predated the Pukhtoons' invasion of J&K and which was of an equal magnitude to it, perhaps even greater. Somewhat surprisingly, the Maharaja did not seek defensive help from India, nor did India publicise this important intrusion by alleged foreigners. There is a simple explanation for this: the 'raiders in green uniforms' were not outsiders. Almost certainly they were local Muslims wearing their old Indian Army uniforms who had gathered to oppose the—by then highly unpopular—Maharaja. Furthermore, for such a large force from Pakistan to reach, then breach, the Kotli-Poonch road and thereafter maintain this position would have been very difficult, given J&K's poor infrastructure and the relatively isolated and sometimes difficult terrain through which this road traversed.[42] Local knowledge and local connections would have been needed.

An analysis of the *White Paper* further shows that its introduction to Part II belies India's inference that all of the so-called raiders fighting in J&K were from outside the state.[43] Simply entitled 'The Invasion', Part II provided eleven documents. All dealt retrospectively with the events. According to the introduction to Part II, the composition of the 'attacking force' had been determined on the basis of operations around 'Nowshera' (Naushera), north-east of Mirpur, in December 1947 and a subsequent body count. It comprised 70 per cent 'Pathans and Muslims from Dir and Swat States' in NWFP, 20 per cent 'deserters from State Forces', 5 per cent 'from Poonch' and 5 per cent 'Sundas', which may possibly have meant Sudans/Sudhans from Poonch. The percentage of Pukhtoons seemed excessively high, given how far 'Nowshera' was from NWFP. As for the remaining 30 per cent of the attacking force, these men were almost certainly not external raiders at all. Poonchis were state subjects, as were 'Sundas' (Sudhans), from Sudhnoti *tehsil* in south-eastern Poonch Jagir. Most 'deserters' were probably J&K Muslims given that, apart from 1,000 Gurkhas, the Maharaja's military force comprised Hindus (predominantly) and Muslims from Jammu.[44]

Similarly, parts III and IV of the *White Paper* provided no hard evidence that advanced India's case, or implicated Pakistan. The introduction to Part IV blandly stated that there was 'abundant circumstantial evidence to show that Pakistan has aided and abetted the "Tribal" invasion' of J&K.[45] The evidence was just that—

circumstantial. Part III, entitled 'Complicity of Pakistan in the Invasion of Kashmir', provided twenty-one documents. All were dated after 22 October 1947, except for one press item dated 16 September, reporting that an NWFP Muslim group would engage in a '*Jehad*' if the Maharaja acceded to India. Part IV, entitled 'India's Objectives', which comprised forty-five of the *White Paper's* eighty-nine pages, provided thirty-eight documents. All dealt with India's and Pakistan's activities in, or stances on J&K. This was possibly the *White Paper's* best feature: it provided an excellent and comprehensive account of both dominions' early official exchanges—and vastly differing stances—on what by now had become known as 'the Kashmir dispute'.

*A major distraction: Baramulla*

One factor enabled India to successfully overlook the role that the people of J&K had played fomenting unrest in J&K before, and after, the Maharaja's accession. This was the inexcusable excesses committed by Pukhtoon invaders in Kashmir Province, including in Muzaffarabad, Uri and particularly, Baramulla.[46] Pukhtoons attacked, looted and killed not only Hindus and Sikhs, but also fellow Muslims and foreigners. The press later reported this violence widely—and sometimes wildly. It was easy for India to berate Pakistan for sending these despicable raiders to Kashmir. This reporting of Pukhtoon atrocities irretrievably tipped the publicity scales in the Kashmir dispute in India's favour.

Immediately after the Pukhtoons entered Kashmir Province on 22 October 1947, they committed brutal acts which, unlike the Poonch uprising, the press began reporting soon after they occurred. These acts justified the Pukhtoons being called raiders, for raiding is what they mostly did: looted, pillaged and took their booty to their tribal homes. The tribesmen committed many excesses against non-Muslims as they headed towards Srinagar. One (probably Muslim) *lambardar* (headman of a village, probably Kashmiri) detailed some of these incidents and claimed that 'nearly 22,000 Hindus and Sikhs were killed in villages *en route* from Kohala to Uri'.[47] Sardar Ibrahim, who was in Muzaffarabad at the time (probably facilitating the Pukhtoons advance to Srinagar), 'ha[d] no hesitation' in bemoaning some unjustified 'killing' by 'our tribal brethren' that he witnessed 'on or about the 22nd, 23rd and 24th of October'.[48]

The most widely reported of the Pukhtoons' excesses occurred in Baramulla where they pillaged heavily and murdered a number of local people. 'Surviving residents' told Robert Trumbull, the correspondent for *The New York Times*, that they estimated that 3,000 people had been 'slain' (an unverifiable figure).[49] On 4 November 1947, *The Times* contained an early and brief report of atrocities. It had particular shock value as it discussed the killing of Europeans: two British subjects, a retired colonel from the Indian Army and an assistant mother superior from the Roman Catholic convent.[50] After Indian forces recaptured Baramulla on 9 November, Trumbull reported more fully, and sensationally, that:

This quiet city ... was left smoking, desolate and full of horrible memories by invading frontier tribesmen who held a thirteen-day saturnalia of looting, raping and killing here. The city had been stripped of its wealth and young women before the tribesmen fled ... Hardly a single article of value or usefulness was left in Baramula [sic].[51]

Trumbull also stated that 'only 1,000 were left of a normal population of about 14,000'. This did not mean that 13,000 people had been killed: many would have fled to try to save themselves.[52] Six days later, the *NYT* published two photos of the Baramulla area. One was of captured 'Pathans' (Pukhtoons); the other was of Sikh soldiers digging in before (unseen) 'marauding Pathan tribesmen'.[53] These reflected India's argument that Pukhtoons had been, and still were, the major problem in J&K.

While Pukhtoons had been indisputably, and unacceptably, 'forthright and ruthless' in Baramulla, it is impossible to verify the number of people they killed, nor have any official documents attempted to do so.[54] Apart from the above-mentioned figure of 3,000 deaths in Baramulla, the Indian *White Paper* does not provide any other figures for deaths or injuries. Instead, it concentrates on reports detailing the Pukhtoons' activities that justified them being labelled raiders. Lamb calculates that about '400 people [were] killed', a 'not unreasonable figure'.[55] Furthermore— though this does not excuse the Pukhtoons' actions—their 'dramatic but overnotorious happenings' in Kashmir were on a much lesser scale than the poorly reported anti-Muslim violence in Jammu Province.[56] By cleverly using the foreign and domestic press, India successfully focused local and international attention on its Pukhtoon opponents' brutal activities in Kashmir Province and away from ongoing violence in Jammu Province, particularly that committed (somewhat embarrassingly) by Hindus and Sikhs against Muslims. India did so even though the number of deaths in Kashmir had neither been established nor verified.

Put simply, India successfully demonised its pro-Pakistan opponents in Kashmir. It did so despite fresh violence that took place in Jammu Province after the Pukhtoons actually committed their atrocities in Baramulla, and which India chose not to publicise. Privately, Nehru informed his chief ministers on 15 November 1947 about the 'fierce communal passion' going on in Jammu Province that involved RSS, Akali Dal and Muslim League elements and was full of 'explosive possibilities'. On 16 November, Sheikh Abdullah and five advisers flew to Jammu as communal feelings were (still) 'running high … and clashes [were] occurring between Muslim villagers and Hindu and Sikh refugees'.[57] On 21 November, India's Prime Minister expressed deep regret to his Pakistani counterpart, Liaquat Ali Khan, for the 'heavy casualties' suffered by Muslims early in November when two convoys of them were 'brutally attacked' in Jammu.[58] Nehru confirmed his statement in the Indian Constituent Assembly on 25 November.[59] But for him, the Jammu violence compared (unfavourably) with the concurrent 'remarkable communal unity' in the Kashmir Valley, where Muslims, Hindus and Sikhs had 'demonstrated cohesion of purpose and effort in the face of a common danger'—the Pukhtoon raiders sent by Pakistan.[60]

Reporters such as Robert Trumbull assisted India to demonise its opponents and to overlook local involvement in events in J&K. Journalists enjoyed greater access to the Kashmir Valley than to Jammu because of the former's compactness, better main roads and relatively better communications. They were aided when, after accession, Sheikh Abdullah and his National Conference, with strong support from Nehru, gained control of J&K's media. It was advantageous for these pro-Indian/anti-Pakistani elements to have visiting journalists report on Pukhtoon brutality in Kashmir Province. However, most journalists could not distinguish between the various elements that comprised the anti-Indian forces in J&K. Invariably, they merged rebel Poonchis with Pukhtoon raiders.[61] Until early 1948 *The Times*, on occasions, could still discriminate between rebels and raiders, but these moments became increasingly rare. In early January 1948, despite talking about the raiders previously, its 'Delhi Correspondent' stated that 'According to a reliable estimate the Azad forces consist of about 60 per cent Poonchies [sic] and other Kashmiri Muslims, 35 per cent Pathan tribesmen, and 5 per cent Punjabi Muslims.'[62] That is, 60 per cent of these forces comprised men from J&K.

Apart from the Baramulla brutalities, there is little record of any other atrocities being committed by Pukhtoons. Indeed, after they 'became more disciplined, and when the[ir] outrages ceased the Muslim population increasingly rallied to their support', India's military forces were then 'fighting in hostile country, and much outnumbered'.[63] This altered situation may have reflected the strong desire that many J&K Muslims, including those in the Kashmir Valley, had to join Pakistan.

In India's defence, one reason why it may have focused on the Pukhtoons was that it and Pakistan had different perceptions and experiences of what happened in J&K in 1947. While Pakistanis were enraged by what happened to Muslims in Jammu, Indians had 'largely and undeservedly forgotten' the 'Poonch rebellion':

Indian minds are not haunted by recollections of burning and killing by the Maharajah's Dogras [in Jammu]. They see the situation as saving the lovely Vale of Kashmir ... from the fate of Baramula [sic], which was sacked by tribesmen. Thus no real argument takes place between the two Dominions, because they are talking about different situations.[64]

That said, Indians also told only selective truths about what had happened in J&K. These assisted their nation's cause significantly. Indeed, India's tactic of making the Pukhtoon raiders the object of aversion in J&K successfully made the National Conference appear to be the most popular, and decent, political party in J&K. As one pro-Pakistan writer writing in 1948 bemoaned, it was 'the greatest travesty of facts when India put up the hoax of [the] "raiders" to come to the help of the Maharaja against his people'.[65]

*Pakistan's acquiescence in India's tactic*

After, and as a result of, the negativity associated with the Pukhtoons' invasion of Kashmir Province in October 1947, Pakistan soon found itself under pressure from India to deny having sent these raiders. Unable to fend off India's accusations, Pakistan acquiesced in India's tactic of defining all troublemakers in J&K as raiders and blaming all of J&K's internal problems on them. Pakistan did so by failing to do three things. First, it failed to successfully publicise the vital role that Muslims in Poonch, particularly, and Mirpur played instigating the anti-Maharaja violence in J&K before the ruler's accession to India on 26 October 1947. This would have highlighted these state subjects' primary role in opposing a harsh autocrat, and it might have overshadowed, or at least put into perspective, the much briefer role that non-state subjects (Pukhtoon Muslims) played. Second, Pakistan failed to highlight the large number of Muslims killed or made homeless by significant anti-Muslim violence in Jammu Province in 1947, particularly the violence committed before Hari Singh's accession, some of which the ruler may have sanctioned, knew about or been involved with. This could have counterbalanced the negative effects of the Pukhtoons' opportunistic—in terms of looting and pillaging—actions in Kashmir. Third, Pakistan failed to grant *de jure* recognition to the Azad Kashmir Government. As it lacked legitimacy in Pakistani eyes, the new government's ability to promote itself as the only true representative of the people of J&K was severely hindered. It was also unable to rival the Indian-sponsored Abdullah government that New Delhi successfully promoted as the true J&K government after, and as a result of, the Pukhtoons' brutality.

Despite their inept performance, Pakistan's leaders certainly knew about what had been happening in Jammu Province after Partition, particularly in Poonch. Like the Indians, they had access to press reports. Another source of information was reports about local events received from Muslim Conference members and other pro-Pakistan elements in J&K.[66] These included a report by 'G. Mohamed' as early as 25 August 1947 about the tense inter-religious situation in J&K.[67] He specifically mentioned the situation in Poonch where 'there is already trouble where some arrests have been made and civil disobedience has been started by the Muslim Conference'. (Presciently, Mohamed deplored the Pakistan Government's 'most appeasing and conciliatory' attitude and the Muslim League's disinterest and silence on J&K's future which could cause J&K 'to be lost' by Pakistan.) On 29 August, Pakistan's Governor-General, Muhammad Ali Jinnah, received two brief telegrams from 'Muslims of Poonch' and 'Muslims of Bagh'. The former spoke of being 'ruthlessly slaughtered by [the J&K] State military'; the latter stated that an estimated 'five hundred lives' were lost when the J&K Government opened fire on the 'Muslim public'.[68] On 13 September, the Muslim Conference informed Jinnah by telegram of the '[a]trocious military oppression in Poonch' in which the public was 'being looted and shooted [sic] at random'.[69] On 30 September, the 'Kashmir Muslims Association' sent Liaquat a similar telegram stating that Muslims were being 'ruthlessly butchered in Poonch'.[70] These various communications informed Pakistani officials about what was happening in Jammu Province. The language used should have alarmed them.

Public utterances and diplomatic exchanges also confirm that senior Pakistanis knew about anti-Muslim violence in Jammu Province in 1947. On 26 October, Jinnah wrote to the Maharaja about the J&K Government's policy of 'suppressing the Mussalmans in every way' and of 'atrocities ... being committed by [J&K] troops' that were driving Muslims out of J&K.[71] Liaquat, based in Lahore, appeared to be even better informed. On 18 October, he complained to J&K's Prime Minister about the 'mounting exigence [sic] of ruthless oppression of Muslims'.[72] On 1 November Liaquat complained to India's Governor-General, Lord Mountbatten, about the Maharaja allowing his troops to 'massacre Muslims in the Poonch and Mirpur' areas.[73] On 4 November, in a broadcast about J&K, Liaquat informed the Pakistan public of 'bestial deeds perpetrated on the people of Kashmir', especially the Poonch uprising.[74] By early December, after receiving 'first-hand evidence' from refugees he had recently met in Sialkot and Rawalpindi, Liaquat believed that the loss of life among Jammu Muslims ran into 'six figures'.[75] Pakistan knew that considerable anti-Muslim violence had occurred in Jammu.

Pakistan's leaders also knew about the formation of the Azad Kashmir Government, although they did not wish to recognise it. The Pakistan Prime Minister's

# THE UNTOLD STORY OF THE PEOPLE OF AZAD KASHMIR

'Statement' of 16 November 1947 confirmed his knowledge of Azad Kashmir's existence.[76] According to Liaquat, Pakistan had no control over the forces of the 'Provisional Government of Kashmir', although Pakistan was prepared, in conjunction with India, to 'make war' on the Azad Kashmiris if they did not obey a ceasefire that Liaquat was proposing. This position was important. J&K was part of the strategic 'game' Pakistan was playing with India in 1947–48 to obtain the three contested princely states of J&K, Junagadh and Hyderabad. Karachi did not want to jeopardise its position on J&K by supporting an unelected government in a part, while conversely, seeking a plebiscite for all of J&K. Recognising the Azad Kashmir Government also would have contradicted Pakistan's position in Junagadh where Karachi already had rejected the unelected pro-Indian Provisional Government. (Chapter 4 discusses the issue of Azad Kashmir's recognition.) Similarly, such recognition would have contradicted Pakistan's position on Junagadh and Hyderabad—and its original stance on J&K—whereby only the ruler decided the accession issue. Pakistan had to deal with some major double standards and incompatible inconsistencies.

Guilt or embarrassment is the main reason why Pakistan was unable to prevent itself from acquiescing in India's tactic of blaming all of J&K's internal problems on raiders. The Pukhtoons invaded J&K after coming from and through Pakistan. Thereafter, Karachi had to defend itself from New Delhi's allegations—which had credence—that Pakistan had organised, or at least allowed, the undisciplined Pukhtoons to cross its territory and illegally invade J&K.[77] As New Delhi saw it, generous India and its armed forces, with much courage, were repelling and protecting the poor people of Kashmir from the Pakistan-inspired raiders. Confronting such Indian virtue and such Pakistani guilt, Karachi sought to obfuscate the role that Pakistan had played in supporting any Muslim activities in J&K, regardless of whether these activities were by local people or by outsiders. Pakistan broadened its agenda with India to include matters such as the legality of the Maharaja's accession to India, India's role in this (which Karachi saw as devious), and the Junagadh issue.[78] This stance began as early as 16 November 1947 when Liaquat, in his 'Statement', spoke about Junagadh in detail before discussing J&K.[79] This marked a change from his long radio address on 4 November when Liaquat kept fairly strictly to J&K matters.[80] By broadening the range of India-Pakistan issues, Pakistan deflected some attention from its role assisting raiders in J&K.

In broadening the range of India-Pakistan issues, Pakistan could not avoid acquiescing in India's tactic of blaming all of J&K's internal problems on raiders. After New Delhi involved the United Nations in the Kashmir dispute in late December 1947, India and Pakistan engaged in a bitter diplomatic, legal and propaganda battle. This was fought over issues such as the proposed plebiscite and how to implement the various United Nations resolutions, and associated issues such as India's unilateral integration of Junagadh and Hyderabad. By 1950, for Pakistan, its dispute with India was about their mutual peace and prosperity and maintaining international peace; the people of J&K had become peripheral.[81] Pakistanis were pursuing an international role, not promoting the J&K people's anti-Maharaja actions in 1947. Not only did Karachi therefore effectively acquiesce in New Delhi's tactic: the legitimate role played by the people of J&K, particularly Muslims, in dividing J&K and instigating the dispute over J&K's

## INDIA AND PAKISTAN: NEGATING THE PEOPLE'S ACTIONS

international status was also obliterated. This marginalised the people of J&K. Thereafter, they had little involvement in attempts to resolve the dispute over what was, after all, their homeland.

Further evidence of Pakistan's inability to successfully highlight Muslim activities in J&K in 1947 comes from public utterances by major Pakistan spokesmen from about 1950. Very little was said before then. Zafrullah Khan, Pakistan's Foreign Minister, and Mushtaq Ahmad Gurmani, Minister for Kashmir Affairs, failed to publicise the 1947 activities by, and against Muslims in J&K. Both also overlooked the anti-Maharaja, pro-Pakistan uprising by J&K Muslims in Gilgit in early November 1947. Only in 1950 did Zafrullah mention that 'a vigorous freedom movement had already started within the State and had made considerable progress before the tribal incursion took place'.[82] Talking of the 'massacre' of J&K Muslims, Zafrullah used *The Times'* report that quoted the 'extermination' of 237,000 Muslims in Jammu. Not only did he give the incorrect publication date, but in addition this was only a secondary source. Zafrullah also failed to mention the Azad Kashmir movement, although he did mention the 'Azad Kashmir Forces'. Given that Zafrullah was Pakistan's spokesman at the United Nations, this incompleteness was telling. In 1952, Gurmani spoke briefly of the Poonch uprising and the 'massacre' of Jammu Muslims, although he also quoted secondary sources: the estranged Kashmiri, Prem Nath Bazaz, and *The Times'* report (mentioned above).[83] Tellingly, Gurmani spoke neither of the formation of Azad Kashmir nor of the Pukhtoons' intervention. Both men's statements were in keeping with Pakistan's desire to broaden its dispute with India and to divert attention from Pakistan's negative actions in J&K.

A further issue that India was able to take advantage of was the clandestine entry of Pakistan's army into J&K in May 1948. Although India claimed that Pakistani soldiers were fighting in J&K long before that, Pakistan initially refuted this allegation by stating, probably correctly, that such soldiers were J&K locals, chiefly Poonchis, on leave from the Pakistan Army.[84] This stance became ineffectual when 'hostile elements' (Pakistani Pukhtoons) breached international law by invading J&K in October 1947. To prevent India's increasingly successful military from overrunning local pro-Pakistan elements during its spring offensive, the Pakistan Army entered J&K 'during the first half of May [1948]'.[85] To its discredit, Karachi only informed the United Nations Commission for India and Pakistan, the body formed in April 1948 to investigate India and Pakistan's dispute over J&K, between 7 and 9 July 1948.[86] This was three weeks after this 'material change in the situation' in J&K.[87] Pakistan's deceitful lack of disclosure further discredited it—and boosted India's credibility.

*Conclusion*

By focusing on the Pukhtoons' invasion, India deliberately neglected the highly significant roles that the people of J&K played in Jammu Province in 1947. Instead, India successfully claimed that Pukhtoon tribesmen—or raiders—instigated the anti-Maharaja violence in J&K. By cleverly using this tactic, India obtained a number of benefits. First, India successfully accused Pakistan of breaking international law by unilaterally sending Pukhtoons across an international border. It then blamed Pakistan for causing the troubles in J&K that encouraged Maharaja Hari Singh to accede to India in order to obtain Indian assistance to defend J&K. This, secondly, shifted attention from any underhand role that New Delhi played obtaining the Maharaja's accession to India and instead, enabled India to sanctify its involvement in J&K as the protector of the invaded people. Third, India was able to focus attention on the endangered Kashmir Valley where India was (temporarily) popular in 1947 and whose residents New Delhi could clearly show had (briefly) been brutalised by Pukhtoons, thus making Pakistan unpopular. Fourth, it enhanced the position of pro-Indian forces in J&K to the detriment of pro-Pakistan rebels and highlighted the National Conference's position as, according to Indian officials, the 'largest and most influential political party' in J&K.[88] Fifth, it enabled India (and Pakistan) to internationalise the issue, marginalising the people of J&K from any active involvement in resolving the dispute over their homelands.

India's consistent—and disingenuous—reference to the various anti-Indian forces in J&K as raiders, raiders from Pakistan or invaders incorrectly grouped all internal anti-Maharaja, then anti-Indian, elements in J&K with people from outside J&K who, indeed, were raiders: Pukhtoon tribesmen. The term 'raider' suggested that the Maharaja's and India's opponents were not legitimate state subjects with a genuine and legal right either to be in J&K or to agitate for J&K to join Pakistan. Rather, they were anti-social outsiders making trouble at Pakistan's behest. This overlooked the genuine disgruntlement that many people of J&K had felt with the Maharaja and his administration and then, after accession, with India's involvement in J&K. Large numbers of these disgruntled people were certainly pro-Pakistan. Some almost certainly received help from neighbouring Pakistan and Pakistanis before and after, the Pukhtoons' invasion. Many could legitimately be called rebels. But, few, if any, actually were Pakistanis. This explains why India was unable to defeat opponents that New Delhi considered external raiders: India's armed forces were actually fighting internal 'patriotic forces' with local support, local knowledge and a strong will to win, or at least to protect their homes, lands and families.[89] India's position in J&K would have been much easier if its opponents had been outsiders devoid of local concerns, commitments, connections—and a strong will to oppose.

In addition, the use of the term raider deliberately neglected the role that the Azad Kashmir movement had played—and could have continued to play—representing those in J&K opposed to the Maharaja and to successor regimes. Pakistan's inability to grant *de jure* recognition to Azad Kashmir also hampered its cause. This lack of recognition, coupled with a lack of physical support from the Pakistan Government, impaired the Azad Kashmir Government's ability to strengthen and publicise its position as the true representative body for the people of J&K. Similarly, India considered the Azad Kashmir Government an illegal, irrelevant body, and ignored it.[90] Following the two dominions' stances, the United Nations recognised the Azad Kashmir Government only as a 'local authority': one with limited power, control and influence.[91] This belittled the Azad Kashmir movement and totally overlooked the role that it, and people under its influence or leadership, had played in instigating and then sustaining, the Kashmir dispute.

# INDIA AND PAKISTAN: NEGATING THE PEOPLE'S ACTIONS

In 1947–48, there were (at least) two struggles in J&K: a physical fight between the pro- and anti-Pakistan forces, and a concomitant publicity struggle. The first was indecisive, whilst pro-Pakistan forces clearly lost the second. The people of J&K were casualties of India's consistent use of the term raiders. India's tactic, and Pakistan's acquiescence in it, advanced the perception that these people had been politically inactive prior to the Pukhtoons' arrival. Their role as instigators of the Kashmir dispute was forgotten. Their status as legitimate stakeholders in this dispute was ignored. They were effectively marginalised. Fairly quickly, the Kashmir dispute became a bitter military, diplomatic and propaganda struggle solely between India and Pakistan. Indeed, by mid-1948, India and Pakistan's feud over which should possess J&K had come to dominate everything to do with the former princely state. Nevertheless, there was one indisputable fact concerning J&K: Azad (Free) Jammu and Kashmir had come into existence. The rest of this book focuses on this overlooked region.

# PART TWO

# AZAD KASHMIR

4

# PAKISTAN

## INTEGRATING THE REGION

*Introduction*

This chapter discusses the relationship between Azad Kashmir (the region) and Pakistan (the nation). The title 'Azad Kashmir' is a misnomer. 'Azad' means 'free'. However, Azad Kashmir is 'free' only in the sense that people freed themselves from Maharaja Hari Singh's control in 1947, and then, after his accession to India on 26 October, they remained free from India's control. Azad Kashmir was never free in the sense that people enjoyed, or wanted to enjoy, the political freedom to fully and freely determine their own destiny and international status. Instead, Azad Kashmiris strongly wanted J&K to become part of Pakistan, subjecting to all of the rights and responsibilities that a relationship with, and incorporation into, this new dominion would demand. Perhaps not surprisingly, therefore, Pakistan and Pakistanis have essentially dominated Azad Kashmir and Azad Kashmiris virtually since the region came into existence in 1947.

The political entity of Pakistan became involved with J&K when Maharaja Hari Singh's government agreed a Standstill Agreement with the Pakistan Government on the day that it came into existence: 15 August 1947.[1] This allowed various existing agreements and arrangements, regarding economic activities and the provision of services between J&K and newly-created Pakistan, to continue until new ones superseded them. The Standstill Agreement also gave Hari Singh more time to decide his accession. Further, Pakistan became involved with J&K when Jammuites fought to ensure that the princely state joined Pakistan, and when large numbers of Muslims fled Jammu Province for Pakistan. In October 1947, Pakistanis became physically involved in J&K when Pakistani Pukhtoons invaded Kashmir Province. Similarly, in November 1947, Muslims in Gilgit removed the Maharaja's governor, asked to join Pakistan, and soon afterwards welcomed a Pakistani administrator. In May 1948, the Pakistan Army officially entered J&K, chiefly to support pro-Pakistan forces.[2] Its presence in Azad Kashmir and the Northern Areas meant that Pakistan quickly became the predominant power in the areas of J&K not under Indian control.[3]

## THE UNTOLD STORY OF THE PEOPLE OF AZAD KASHMIR

Finally, Pakistan became involved with J&K via the United Nations after India involved the UN Security Council on 1 January 1948, hoping to have Pakistani aggression in J&K condemned.[4] This did not happen. Instead, the UN sought to conduct 'a free and impartial plebiscite' so that the people of J&K could determine whether to unite J&K, in its entirety, with India or Pakistan. No other options were offered. A 1949 UNCIP resolution on the plebiscite, which India and Pakistan accepted, required three things to happen before it could be held: 1) Pakistan was 'to use its best endeavour [sic] to secure the withdrawal ... of tribesmen and Pakistani nationals ... who have entered the [J&K] State for the purpose of fighting'; 2) Pakistan was 'to withdraw its troops' from J&K; 3) UNCIP was to notify India that the Pukhtoons had withdrawn and that the Pakistan forces were being withdrawn, after which India was to 'withdraw the bulk of its forces' from J&K in stages to be agreed with UNCIP.[5] Much argument and many fruitless negotiations followed the UNCIP resolution. While the Pukhtoons did withdraw from J&K, largely of their own accord, the other actions did not happen. Consequently, the plebiscite has never been held. Nevertheless, Pakistan is still involved in J&K because of these, and other, UN Security Council resolutions, although its involvement is based on more than just UN resolutions.[6]

Despite Pakistan being involved with Azad Kashmir since 1947, the region has never officially or legally joined this nation. Indeed, Azad Kashmir's international legal status is still unresolved because the region is part of the disputed state of Jammu and Kashmir. Pakistan's position has been that it is administering Azad Kashmir, along with the Northern Areas, until the plebiscite, initially promised by India in October 1947 and reiterated by the United Nations, gives 'the people of Jammu and Kashmir ... the right of self-determination'.[7] Theoretically therefore, Azad Kashmir is legally free and autonomous from Pakistan. Practically, as we shall see, Azad Kashmiris need, and want, Pakistan. Since April 1949, various formal and legal arrangements have prescribed the Azad Kashmir-Pakistan relationship. Generally, these have tied Azad Kashmir to Pakistan, ensured the nation's superior position, and decreased Azad Kashmir's autonomy. Pakistan has also been able to assert itself using local surrogates and via its powerful Ministry of Kashmir Affairs (MKA).

Azad Kashmiris have acquiesced in their relationship with Pakistan, chiefly because they have wanted strongly to join this nation. Pakistan's control however, has significantly reduced Azad Kashmiris' ability to determine their own destiny, although Pakistan has acted no differently with Azad Kashmir than with its own princely states and provinces. Indeed, it may have been harder in these latter: consider the brutal integration of princely Kalat into Baluchistan in 1948.[8] Equally, the role of Pakistani governments based in Karachi, then Rawalpindi, then finally Islamabad, in relation to Azad Kashmir has been contradictory. While Pakistan has aspired since 1947 to become a rational-legal, democratic nation-state, it has also used practices to control and incorporate Azad Kashmir that typify some of Hari Singh's autocratic methods. Indeed, Pakistan has totally manipulated a pliant Azad Kashmir population and denied them meaningful power. Given Azad Kashmiris' noted martial capabilities, their total acquiescence in this process is surprising. Pakistan's superior position has had two important consequences: it has diluted the issue of Azad Kashmir's undecided international status—the region is, to all intents and purposes, part of Pakistan—and it has negated Azad Kashmir's

# PAKISTAN: INTEGRATING THE REGION

standing as a genuine rival government to that in place in Indian J&K. This also is surprising, given that the Azad Kashmir Government established itself—and still theoretically sees itself—as an alternative government for all of J&K.

*The post-accession situation in J&K: a brief overview*

After Maharaja Hari Singh's accession to India, Azad Kashmir is virulently opposed India—whose military forces entered J&K on 27 October 1947—and have remained there ever since. Pakistan supported the Azad Kashmiris, especially after the Pakistan Army officially entered J&K in May 1948. Pro-Pakistan forces then fought India's armed forces until a United Nations-negotiated ceasefire came into effect on 1 January 1949. Thereafter, as discussed below, Azad Kashmir became more closely involved with, and dependent upon, Pakistan.

Before dealing with the Azad Kashmir-Pakistan relationship, it is worth discussing post-accession activities in other parts of J&K. On 1 November 1947, 3,000 Muslims in Gilgit with 'Islamic spirit in their heart'[9] and armed with various weapons[10] 'revolted against the Maharaja's government'.[11] The 'quiet transfer' by the British of their area back to Hari Singh's regime on 1 August 1947, without being asked, displeased them.[12] Equally, they disliked the Maharaja's accession to India 'without [him] having consulted them'.[13] The Pukhtoons' invasion of neighbouring, but distant, Kashmir Province may also have inspired Gilgitis (who would have heard about this via Gilgit's telegraph or telephone links with Peshawar).[14] Anti-Maharaja elements in Gilgit formed a 'provisional government' under the presidency of an 'influential local personality', the former soldier, Shah Rais Khan.[15] They may also have declared a republic.[16] Concurrently, the local Gilgit Scouts, under the command of a British officer, Major Brown,[17] took the Maharaja's governor, Gansara Singh, and some other non-Muslims into 'protective custody'. This action apparently saved their lives.[18] On 16 November 1947, Karachi sent an administrator to govern the area.[19] Thereafter, Gilgitis, along with neighbouring Baltis from the Frontier Districts Province, resisted Indian military forces physically trying to capture these recalcitrant areas.[20] The Gilgitis' 'operations' in northern J&K were separate from the Azad Army's in south-western J&K,[21] and remained so.[22]

Concurrently with the Gilgit uprising, Maharaja Hari Singh started to lose power to the Indian Army and to Sheikh Abdullah. One immediate and significant consequence of Hari Singh's accession was that New Delhi was able 'legally and constitutionally to send military assistance to halt the wanton invasion', allegedly 'by Pakistan', of J&K.[23] By 31 October 1947, these invaders were believed to be sixteen miles from Srinagar.[24] However, the day after Singh's accession, India had begun deploying military forces to its newly-acquired territory. The Indian Army, confronting possibly '10,000 persons spear-headed by a well-armed and organized striking force' supposed to be armed with guns and mortars,[25] moved quickly to protect Kashmiris from the advancing Pukhtoons.[26] Thereafter, it did most of the fighting against the Pukhtoons, although Abdullah claimed that his government's newly-established People's Militia 'when called to the front ... proved unassailable'.[27] By 2 November, the Indian Army was 'strong enough to hold the central Vale of Kashmir and the capital city against any threat by the invaders'.[28]

## THE UNTOLD STORY OF THE PEOPLE OF AZAD KASHMIR

To succeed in the Kashmir Valley, India needed 'the cooperation of [Indian] troops with the civil population'.[29] This situation empowered Sheikh Abdullah. He could 'enlist the support of the masses ... to present a united front to the threat of deposition and the declaration of a "free Kashmir Government" by the raiders'. Pragmatically, the J&K Chief Justice hastily swore in Abdullah as 'head' of the National Conference-dominated administration on 31 October.[30] This came after India's Prime Minister, Jawaharlal Nehru, on 27 October, gave the Maharaja's Prime Minister, Mehr Chand Mahajan, three conditions on which India would advance military help 'at such a critical juncture'. The third of these was that Abdullah 'should be taken in[to] the administration and made responsible for it along with the Prime Minister'.[31] The pressured Maharaja had little option but to agree. After 31 October, Indian J&K was administered by Abdullah in Srinagar and, in a 'face-saving gesture' to Hari Singh,[32] by Mahajan in Jammu City.[33] As Chief Emergency Administrator, Abdullah headed an unrepresentative, but pro-Indian, Emergency Administration comprising seven cabinet members and sixteen emergency officers. Only five were the Maharaja's appointees.[34] This administration controlled the political situation in its stronghold, the Kashmir Valley, to which area it was largely restricted because of the onset of winter and road closures, and because the Indian Army was still securing territory. Its position was boosted by the Pukhtoons' despicable actions in Baramulla, which made pro-Pakistan elements temporarily unpopular in the Kashmir Valley.[35]

Hari Singh's appointment of his bitter foe, Sheikh Abdullah, as Chief Emergency Administrator advanced the end of Dogra rule in J&K. On 5 March 1948, Indian J&K's 'experiment with dyarchy' ended.[36] Hari Singh, after interference by Nehru[37] who feared 'reactionary elements' would become popular should Abdullah be disempowered,[38] proclaimed the formation of a 'National Interim Government' to administer Indian J&K.[39] Sworn in on 18 March 1948, this new government basically comprised the old Emergency Administration, but with only one representative of the Maharaja. The ruler became a constitutional head; Abdullah became Prime Minister.[40] By 1 January 1949, this new body was administering those areas of J&K under Indian military control: eastern Jammu Province; most of Kashmir Province, minus Muzaffarabad District; the Ladakh area of the Frontier Districts Province.[41] On 20 June 1949, Hari Singh left J&K and, simultaneously, devolved his (dwindling) powers to his son, Karan Singh, at Nehru's 'intervention'.[42] By pressuring him to leave, Nehru, Sardar Patel and Abdullah had essentially 'deposed' the ruler.[43] Hari Singh's departure effectively ended 103 years of Dogra rule in J&K. Thereafter, until his removal in 1953, Abdullah was all-powerful within Indian J&K.

The 1949 ceasefire changed the nature of the J&K entity and the dispute over it. The ceasefire confirmed J&K's division into the pro-Indian area under India's control and the pro-Pakistan area comprising Azad Kashmir and the Northern Areas.[44] On 27 July 1949, Indian and Pakistani military officials formalised this division in Karachi by defining the actual ceasefire line 'to mark the effective limit of the sovereignties of the two States'.[45] Despite this militarily-enforced division, India continued to claim all of J&K because of Hari Singh's accession. Pakistan, which rejected the accession as fraudulent, did not seek legally to integrate 'its' area of J&K into Pakistan. Rather, Karachi would administer this area until the

United Nations-supervised plebiscite was held. Hence Pakistan was only in temporary possession of a part of J&K which, theoretically, it could lose in the plebiscite. This potential loss of territory equally applied to India. With much at stake and with the use of force unacceptable, the struggle to obtain J&K moved to an ongoing political and diplomatic one. India and Pakistan took total control of this struggle; they effectively marginalised the people of J&K and seemingly became the only parties to this dispute. Divided by the ceasefire line, J&K increasingly existed only on paper.

After the 1949 ceasefire, the only 'outsiders' to whom landlocked Azad Kashmiris could turn were Pakistanis. Mountainous terrain separated Azad Kashmir from the Northern Areas; severed road links and the heavily-militarised 1949 ceasefire line effectively ended contacts with Indian J&K; the quickest way to travel between major Azad Kashmir centres was (and is) via Pakistan. Because Azad Kashmiris have invariably wanted to be with Pakistan, they have accepted Pakistan's increasing control over them and their region. Pakistan's greater financial, administrative and military support has also helped Azad Kashmir to survive Indian aggression. After the ceasefire, Azad Kashmiris' desire to unite with Pakistan was satisfied practically—although not legally—when the region was, to all intents and purposes, quickly integrated into Pakistan. Since then, most Azad Kashmiris have never seriously challenged their region's international status in the way militant anti-Indian Kashmiris have been doing since 1988. Indeed, from the moment the British talked seriously of creating a subcontinental Muslim dominion, most Muslims in what now comprises Azad Kashmir have predominantly wanted to become Pakistanis.

*Post-1947: Pakistan controls Azad Kashmir*

Azad Kashmir's relationship with Pakistan since 1947 has largely been one in which the nation has progressively subsumed the region. This process commenced with the Pakistan Army's entry into J&K. Initially, Karachi had involved Azad Kashmiris in its dispute with India over possession of J&K, but from mid-1948 Pakistan increasingly took sole responsibility for this issue, with little direct Azad Kashmiri involvement after late 1949.[46] In 'the last quarter of 1948', the 'Azad Army' militia opposing Indian forces officially became part of the Pakistan Army.[47] In 1949, this army comprised 35,000 men.[48] After the ceasefire, and with the UN plebiscite seemingly imminent, large parts of the Azad Army were disbanded or amalgamated into the Pakistan Army. (In 1951, the Pakistan Army Act was applied to all Azad Army remnants as they 'needed to be put on a regular footing and brought under some military code of discipline'.)[49] With few economic opportunities at home, the disposition of Azad soldiers posed the Azad Kashmir Government serious problems,[50] although the Azad Kashmir Defence Minister believed (correctly) that demobilised soldiers would happily return to their farms.[51] The loss of the motivated Azad Army was significant. It stifled the Azad Kashmir movement's physical ability to liberate all of J&K from Indian control. It also made it easier for Pakistan to control Azad Kashmir.

While Pakistan began manifesting its control over Azad Kashmir from about mid-1948, Azad Kashmiris acted assertively in their early relationship with Pakistan. In early November 1947 the initial Azad Kashmir President, Sardar Ibrahim, bemoaned Pakistan's lack of support: it should 'now recognise our Government and cease supporting the alien Government of Hari Singh'.[52] In May 1949, Ibrahim repeated his call for *de facto* recognition for Azad Kashmir.[53] Around July 1948, a statement by Ibrahim showed that Azad Kashmir still had foreign policy aspirations. Ibrahim told UNCIP that, as the Azad Kashmir Government controlled over half of J&K, the Security Council's 'failure' to hear an Azad Kashmir representative 'was a serious injustice' to the people of J&K. He continued assertively:

> I must emphasize that the Azad Kashmir Government will not accept any settlement to which they are not a party, and that Pakistan, though keenly interested in the future of Jammu and Kashmir, cannot bind the Azad Kashmir Government or commit them to a course of action without their previous approval.[54]

At that time, Pakistan agreed with Ibrahim. In September 1948, it informed UNCIP that Pakistan 'cannot make commitments on behalf of the Azad organization'.[55] While differences over foreign policy matters would be sorted out after the 1949 ceasefire, Azad Kashmiris enjoyed local political and administrative autonomy until about 1950. Thereafter Pakistan, acting through its Ministry of Kashmir Affairs, or derivatives thereof, and its military, increasingly asserted itself.

Although the Azad Kashmir Government wanted to legally join Pakistan, Pakistan has been unable to confirm Azad Kashmir's position *de jure* in this way,[56] although the Azad Kashmir Government's *de facto* position was 'recognized'.[57] Pakistan's inability relates to the wider issue of obtaining all of J&K. A unilateral *de jure* absorption of Azad Kashmir would have meant that Pakistan obtained a sector of J&K without consulting, via a plebiscite, this sector's people about what international status they wanted.[58] This precedent could have negated Pakistan's demand for a plebiscite for all J&K citizens to determine whether J&K, in its entirety, would join India or Pakistan. To resolve its quandary, Pakistan is 'administering' those areas of J&K under its control until the plebiscite decides their fate, and the fate of all of J&K. Pakistan appears confident that, ultimately, J&K will join it. The 1962 Pakistan Constitution was unequivocal: 'a person deriving his nationality [sic] from the state of Jammu and Kashmir shall be deemed to be a citizen of Pakistan' (Article 241).[59] The current Pakistan Constitution states that: 'When the people of the State of Jammu and Kashmir decide to accede to Pakistan, the relationship between Pakistan and the State shall be determined in accordance with the wishes of the people of that State.[60] Despite such expectations, the status of Azad Kashmir and the Northern Areas remains unresolved.

Azad Kashmir's lack of recognition enabled its status to be reduced internationally, regionally, and with Pakistan. UNCIP, whose primary relationships were with the Indian and Pakistan governments, refused to recognise the Azad Kashmir Government as the ruling and independent entity, free from Pakistani control, in Azad Kashmir. In 1948, it downgraded Azad Kashmir's status to a 'local authority'. (The Northern Areas that Pakistan directly administered did not pose this problem.) Until August 1948, Pakistan had always referred to the 'Azad Kashmir Government' in dealings with the UN.[61] India objected. In March 1948, New Delhi claimed (falsely) that the Azad Kashmir Government existed 'largely on paper' and was 'from eye-witness accounts ... a facade put up for external consumption'.[62] India wanted the National Conference-led government in Indian J&K to be recognised as the only legitimate administration in J&K. Despite Pakistan's insistence that *de facto* recognition be given to Azad Kashmir, UNCIP 'wriggled out of this problem'[63] by stating on 13 August 1948 that the Azad Kashmir Government was (only) a 'local authority'.[64] Ten months after its creation, the Azad Kashmir Government no longer had any international, or subcontinental, status and legitimacy as an alternative government for, and in, J&K. Thereafter, it was considered internationally as a type of municipal or district body controlling limited functions in its area of supervision.

Indian pressure aside, UNCIP 'demoted' Azad Kashmir because no nation, not even Pakistan, had formally recognised this entity. UNCIP concluded that, 'having no international standing, the [Azad Kashmir Government] can have no international responsibility'.[65] One reason why Pakistanis agreed to this 'demotion' was that they believed, as did Azad Kashmiris, that the promised plebiscite would soon resolve J&K's status.[66] Equally, Pakistan had assumed responsibility for all Pakistani aspects of the Kashmir dispute and wanted no local rival. The UN thereafter dealt only with the Pakistan Government on all J&K matters. This empowered Karachi to take binding decisions on Azad Kashmir without having to consult the Azad Kashmir Government. Azad Kashmiris could do little about their reduced status and legitimacy and their marginalisation.[67]

*The Ministry of Kashmir Affairs*

With the relationship changed in Pakistan's favour following UNCIP's 'demotion' of Azad Kashmir, Pakistan began to totally control Azad Kashmir (and the Northern Areas). Pakistan's greatest instrument in this process was its Ministry of Kashmir Affairs. In late 1947, Pakistan realised there was 'the problem of relations with the recently formed Azad Kashmir' and that it needed 'a trusted agent of the Pakistan government in Rawalpindi to handle these problems on the spot'.[68] In January 1949 the Ministry of Kashmir Affairs was created to fill this need,[69] although its creation may not have been announced then.[70] The MKA was also created to help Pakistan deal with the UN's increasing involvement in the Kashmir dispute,[71] including conducting the plebiscite.[72] The MKA had a 300-man Secretariat in Rawalpindi and Directorates of Public Relations, Refugee Rehabilitation, Movements and Quartering, Civil Supplies, and Coordination at Murree. It would help Pakistan communicate with and administer those areas and people of J&K not under Indian control.[73] Rawalpindi was chosen for the MKA's Secretariat because it was the closest and best-connected urban centre to Azad Kashmir and 'the centre of the [pro-Pakistan, anti-Indian] Kashmir freedom movement'.[74] Murree was midway between Rawalpindi and Muzaffarabad.

The first head of the Ministry of Kashmir Affairs was the 'Minister of State without portfolio [sic]', Mushtaq Ahmad Gurmani.[75] He was important for Pakistan. Previously, Gurmani had been involved with Azad Kashmiris and J&K refugees.[76] One of Gurmani's first official duties was to meet UNCIP officials on 13 March 1949.[77] During his tenure as MKA head,[78] Gurmani established the ministry's culture and typified its attitude and style. A man 'trained in the pre-partition feudal school of politics' while serving as Prime Minister of Bahawalpur,[79] the 'ubiquitous' civil servant, 'ardent Muslim Leaguer'[80] and 'redoubtable Punjabi'[81] was the major reason why Pakistan, acting through the MKA, effectively asserted its authority over Azad Kashmir.[82] From the outset, Gurmani divided and ruled Azad Kashmir's disunited politicians, particularly those in leading positions: Chaudhry Ghulam Abbas and Sardar Ibrahim.[83] This tactic ensured his, the MKA's, and Pakistan's supremacy. Conversely, for Azad Kashmiris, Gurmani and his ilk had an 'extremely poor image'.[84] Apart from their overbearing demeanours, MKA machinations resulted in Azad Kashmir having seven presidents from May 1950 until K.H. Khurshid's presidency in May 1959.[85] This rapid turnover involved five men, with two 'recycled' by the MKA for second terms. By comparison, after General Ayub Khan's military takeover in Pakistan in October 1958, Azad Kashmir had two presidents in the next ten years. This reflected the overall political stability that the Ayub regime was able to impose on the nation and the region.

Pakistanis involved with Azad Kashmir, seemingly informed by former British bureaucrats, engaged in autocratic practices. MKA manipulation meant that it went 'without saying' that no Azad Kashmir president could 'sanely, think of keeping himself in [the] saddle if and when the Government of Pakistan wants him to quit'.[86] They stayed in office, or left, on MKA orders. The Supreme Head of the Azad Kashmir Movement, Ghulam Abbas, complained to Liaquat Ali Khan in late 1950 that the MKA gave 'scant regard' to the region's government: 'very often' the MKA issued orders 'regarding day-to-day administrative matters without any reference to, or consultation with, the Azad Kashmir Government'.[87] Azad Kashmiris considered that 'Pindi' (Rawalpindi) bureaucrats saw Azad Kashmir as a 'fiefdom'.[88] The joint secretary heading the MKA 'had the best claim to being the real head of the Azad Kashmir government'.[89] This Pakistani bureaucrat and his colleagues ensured that Pakistan's writ applied throughout Azad Kashmir. They also treated the Azad Kashmir president and senior Azad Kashmir Government officials as second-class citizens. It was 'quite normal' that Azad Kashmir 'chief executives' should wait outside the office of the joint secretary, who theoretically was subordinate to the Azad Kashmiris, before they were 'called in' at his pleasure.[90] Azad Kashmiris had to accept such belittling treatment. Their region lacked international recognition and it was dependent on Pakistan for many things, including financial, military and physical support, such as food grains and basic staples.

One of the MKA's first—and most significant—acts was to conclude an agreement that formalised Pakistan's relationship with Azad Kashmir. Very much in Pakistan's favour, this deprived Azad Kashmiris of significant powers and responsibilities. The 'Heads of Agreement' document was signed around April 1949.[91] Its signatories were: M.A. Gurmani, then Pakistan's Minister without portfolio; Ghulam Abbas, President of the All Jammu and Kashmir Muslim Conference; and Sardar Ibrahim, President of the Azad Jammu and Kashmir Government. The agreement, which comprised three parts, delineated the respective jurisdictions and functions for the three organisations these men headed. Part I covered the actual structure and operation of the 'Civil Administration of [the] Azad Kashmir Area', which related to how Azad Kashmir should govern itself. Part II dealt with 'Financial Arrangements' by which Pakistan would advance money to the Azad

Kashmir Government. Part III was entitled 'Division of functions between the Governments of Pakistan, the Azad Kashmir Government and the Muslim Conference'.

Part III was the most important part of the agreement as it clearly delineated each of the three organisations' responsibilities. It contained three sections: A, B and C. Section A listed those 'Matters within the Purview of [the] Pakistan Government'. Pakistan was allocated eight important matters:

i) Defence, including complete control over Azad Kashmir Forces;
ii) Negotiations with UNCIP;
iii) Foreign policy of the Azad Kashmir Government;
iv) Publicity in Pakistan and foreign countries;
v) Coordination of arrangements for relief and rehabilitation of refugees;
vi) Coordination of publicity and all arrangements in connection with the plebiscite;
vii) All activities within Pakistan itself with regard to Kashmir such as the procurement of food and civil supplies transport, running of refugee camps, medical arrangements etc.;
viii) All affairs of the Gilgit and Ladakh areas under the control of the political agent at Gilgit.[92]

Sections B and C of the agreement clearly listed 'Matters within the Purview' of the Azad Kashmir Government and the Muslim Conference respectively. The former was allocated (only) four functions, three of which primarily gave it responsibility for policy, and to administer and develop economic resources within Azad Kashmir. The last function was to give 'advice' to the Minister without portfolio 'with regard to negotiations' with UNCIP. The Muslim Conference was assigned eight functions, six of which gave it responsibility to organise and publicise political activities, including the plebiscite, within Azad Kashmir, 'the Indian occupied areas of the State' and 'among Kashmir refugees in Pakistan'. The seventh function was to give 'general guidance' to the Azad Kashmir Government. The last function was identical to the Azad Kashmir Government's last function: to give 'advice' to the Minister without portfolio 'with regard to negotiations' with UNCIP.[93]

The Heads of Agreement ensured Pakistan's dominance over Azad Kashmir. It confirmed the Azad Kashmir Government's role as being a local authority and limited this role to the rump territory of Azad Kashmir. The Azad Kashmir Government 'lost' the Gilgit and 'Ladakh' areas, which also were free (*azad*) from Indian control and which Azad Kashmir had previously sought to govern theoretically, but not practically, on account of its self-perceived status as the alternative government for J&K. Pakistan secured total control over foreign affairs, including all United Nations matters and all aspects to do with J&K. Pakistan obtained total control of the defence of Pakistan-Administered J&K, including control over the Azad Army. Pakistan was in charge of all major matters to do with non-Indian J&K. The Azad Kashmir Government no longer had any international role resolving the Kashmir dispute, nor any military capability, and had little to do outside the small territory of Azad Kashmir. The clear delineation of powers meant that Azad Kashmir was subordinate to Pakistan. Karachi had attained this ascendancy through Gurmani and 'his' Ministry of Kashmir Affairs.

## THE UNTOLD STORY OF THE PEOPLE OF AZAD KASHMIR

The Azad Kashmir Government and the Muslim Conference accepted the Heads of Agreement for a number of reasons. Being pro-Pakistan, both bodies wanted Azad Kashmir to join Pakistan, something they expected to happen soon via the promised plebiscite (although Sardar Ibrahim believed the agreement was only temporary until the plebiscite was held).[94] Both were prepared to accept Pakistan's political, economic and military leadership. Azad Kashmir's treatment was similar to Pakistan's relationship with its provinces, with Karachi in the superior position. The region had a fledgling administration attempting to grapple with a poor, rural environment and without the resources, personnel and skills to engage in international affairs and diplomacy. Logically, Pakistan should control these matters. Azad Kashmir's links with the liberated areas in the Frontier Districts Province were weak, while the difficult terrain dividing the two regions made it easier for Pakistan to administer the Northern Areas, from Peshawar or Rawalpindi, than for Azad Kashmir to do so. Additionally, in September 1947, Azad Kashmiris had accepted that these areas were outside their control.[95] In terms of liberating J&K, Azad Kashmir had many willing and able personnel, but it lacked resources to mount and sustain a war against India. Only Pakistan, with its greater manpower, resources and strategic depth, might do so. Finally, leaders of the Muslim Conference and Azad Kashmir Government were rivals trying to limit each other's power. Gurmani took advantage of this dynamic—and both groups lost equally.[96]

As well as controlling financial and other resources that Pakistan advanced to Azad Kashmir, the Ministry of Kashmir Affairs gained ascendancy over the region by changes made to a document called 'The Rules of Business of Azad Kashmir 1950'.[97] Because Azad Kashmir rejected the J&K constitution, because it was not legally part of Pakistan and because it lacked international standing, the region had no constitution or formal set of rules to regulate its activities. In late 1950, with Azad Kashmir having moved from a 'War Council' to a fully-fledged administration,[98] Azad Kashmiris belatedly framed some Rules of Business to guide the running of their 'State' and government. The Supreme Head of the Azad Kashmir Movement, Ghulam Abbas, issued these Rules on 28 December 1950.[99] In them, power flowed from the Supreme Head of the Azad Kashmir Movement downwards. Indeed, the Supreme Head sanctioned the rules, with some protesting that this gave Abbas more power than Hari Singh had ever had.[100] Abbas appointed the Azad Kashmir president and other subordinate government members who held office 'during his pleasure' and were responsible to him.[101] The 1950 Rules of Business also gave Azad Kashmir a Pakistan-free status. They made no mention of this nation, or of the MKA. Seemingly, 'the Government of Azad Kashmir was a powerful Government unrestricted of any limitation'.[102] It was supposed to be in charge of its own destiny—or at least Abbas was.

In October 1952, Azad Kashmir's Rules of Business were revised.[103] The revisions dramatically changed the region's situation, and made it abundantly clear that Pakistan was in charge of, and in, Azad Kashmir. The 1952 Rules of Business were issued under the signature of the President of Azad Kashmir, Colonel Sher Ahmad Khan, a politically inexperienced Sudhan with little support among his powerful tribe or in Azad Kashmir. Indeed, he was 'totally dependent' on the Ministry of Kashmir Affairs[104] and may have 'bartered away' Azad Kashmir's Pakistan-free status

## PAKISTAN: INTEGRATING THE REGION

'in return for offices and honours'.[105] The 1952 Rules established a system in which Pakistan's control of Azad Kashmir via the MKA was total. The MKA was mentioned fifteen times in the Rules. It controlled everything. This started with the body that appointed the president: the 'general council of the All Jammu & Kashmir Muslim Conference duly recognised as such by the Government of Pakistan in the Ministry of Kashmir Affairs'.[106] To semi-empower this body, the MKA 'abolished' the office of the 'Supreme Head of the Azad Kashmir Movement', a position not mentioned in the 1952 Rules.[107] The MKA was to be consulted on almost all matters by the Azad Kashmir Government; it was to supervise the region's Executive; the MKA's Joint Secretary was the final arbiter on all appeals. The Azad Kashmir Government was to act through a body called the Azad Kashmir Council, comprising the president and other ministers. Any legislation the Council passed only had the 'force of law' after it received the MKA's concurrence. It was crystal clear: the MKA was now legally and practically all-powerful in its relationship with Azad Kashmir. Conversely, four years after being a belligerent anti-Indian fighting force, the Azad Kashmir movement was emasculated. It now was a supplicant, not a surrogate.

Another way that Pakistan asserted itself in Azad Kashmir was by providing 'lent officers' from its administrative staff to the Azad Kashmir administration. This arrangement was not specifically mentioned in the Rules of Business, nor did it have any legal basis. Rather, it was based on 'mutually accepted traditions and trust'.[108] This arrangement helped Azad Kashmir overcome a serious lack of experienced administrative personnel due to the 'disappearance' of Hindus, who had dominated the J&K and Poonch administrations, soon after Partition. The practice also replicated a local tradition whereby the Raja of Poonch 'borrowed' officers from the Maharaja's administration.[109] Officers on loan from Pakistan filled most senior positions in the Azad Kashmir administration; their loyalties, however, ultimately lay with Pakistan. With the benefit of such officers and the Rules of Business 1952, the MKA and successor organisations were able to maintain their pre-eminent position in Azad Kashmir until about 1970.

Apart from the efforts of the 'feudal' Gurmani and the MKA,[110] Pakistan's change of attitude towards Azad Kashmir between 1950 and 1952, may partially be explained by Liaquat Ali Khan's tragic assassination in October 1951. Thereafter, Pakistan experienced difficult times as less 'towering' men ruled. A pliant Azad Kashmir was therefore best. During the 1950s, Pakistani politics was riven by rivalry between ambitious men such as Khwaja Nazimuddin, Ghulam Muhammad, Iskander Mirza, Muhammad Ali Bogra, Chaudhry Muhammad Ali, H.S. Suhrawardy, Ibrahim Ismail Chundrigar, Firoz Khan Noon and General Muhammad Ayub Khan.[111] Their struggles abated only after Ayub finally 'won' power in 1958.[112] After Liaquat, Pakistani politicians wrestled with major issues: Pakistan's constitution, which was finally approved on 23 March 1956;[113] religious problems, including Ahmadiyya 'apostasy', which put pressure on Pakistan's (Ahmadi) foreign minister, Zafrullah Khan;[114] transforming Pakistan in 1955 into East and West Pakistan from a polyglot provincial structure comprising Bahawalpur, Baluchistan, East Bengal (Pakistan's most populous province), Khairpur, NWFP, Sind and West Punjab, plus Karachi and the Tribal Areas of NWFP, which, with Baluchistan, were under central jurisdiction;[115] placating unruly provinces, particularly Baluchistan, with Baluchis fighting the Pakistan Army in 1948 and 1958;[116] land reform; physically and politically accommodating Pakistan's refugees, who comprised ten per cent of the population;[117] and major foreign policy decisions, including joining some United States-led military alliances in the early 1950s, which made India fear that Pakistan might seek a 'military solution' to the Kashmir dispute.[118] Confronting such an array of issues, Pakistan needed a pliant Azad Kashmir.

A number of events on 'the other side' also encouraged Pakistan to assert itself in Azad Kashmir. The 1951 election in Indian J&K of a Constituent Assembly to frame a constitution made the promised plebiscite appear less likely. Such suspicions were confirmed when, on 6 February 1954, the Indian J&K Constituent Assembly unanimously reaffirmed Hari Singh's accession to India and requested closer formal links with J&K.[119] Pakistan was also concerned that, with Indian J&K's new constitution reserving twenty-five seats for 'PoK' residents,[120] Azad Kashmiris might develop insatiable desires for democracy. In July 1952, the 'Delhi Agreement' between Abdullah and Nehru changed the status quo in J&K. It confirmed that Indian J&K was part of the Indian Union, but with certain unique privileges, particularly Article 370 of the Indian Constitution that (supposedly) guaranteed its autonomy.[121] Nevertheless, after Abdullah was sacked on 8 August 1953 for advocating independence for J&K and 'gravely jeopardiz[ing]' Indian J&K,[122] India steadily, and relentlessly, eroded the state's 'unique privileges' and integrated it into the Union. Given such developments, Pakistan needed to shore up its position in Azad Kashmir.

Events around 1951 provided the most important reason for Pakistan to assert itself in Azad Kashmir. Rumours arose that J&K's two senior political leaders, Sheikh Abdullah in Indian J&K and Ghulam Abbas in Azad Kashmir, were trying to conclude an internal settlement to the Kashmir question.[123] As early as April 1950, with the demilitarisation issue stalling the plebiscite, Abbas made a 'sporting offer' to Abdullah saying that he (Abbas) was prepared to have both Azad Kashmir and 'Abdullah Kashmir' completely demilitarised, after which J&K, for the 'duration of the plebiscite', would be under the control of a 'militia of the Muslims from [Indian]-occupied Kashmir'.[124] The two leaders may also have been in contact from mid-1952 to mid-1953.[125] Sheikh Abdullah, disenchanted with India, was advocating independence for J&K: 'Kashmir belongs to neither India nor Pakistan but to Kashmiris who reside in Kashmir'.[126] In Azad Kashmir, disenchantment also had been increasing. The United Nations had been unable to conduct the plebiscite, despite the attempts of two UN Representatives for India and Pakistan, Sir Owen Dixon (May-September 1950) and Frank P. Graham (September 1951-February 1953). There was also disenchantment with Pakistan's lack of action on the Kashmir issue. Finally, owing to Sardar Ibrahim's removal as Azad Kashmir President in May 1950, there was considerable unrest within the Muslim Conference.[127]

While Abbas and Abdullah may have been communicating, they did not meet until 1964. The ceasefire line (later the Line of Control, LOC) that physically, militarily and psychologically divided J&K after 1949 discouraged contacts between almost all J&K residents on different sides of the line.[128] Some lower-level contacts across the long, rugged, often remote ceasefire line did occur, but these were unknown or were ignored by sympathetic authorities.[129] Official contacts between J&K leaders only occurred outside the subcontinent at the United Nations during early attempts to resolve the Kashmir dispute,[130] among the broader 'Kashmiri' diaspora in the United Kingdom and elsewhere,[131] or at the Haj in Saudi Arabia.[132] In May 1964, Hajj Sheikh Abdullah did make an extremely rare visit to the 'other side' of J&K (and to Pakistan)—perhaps the only such official visit since 1949.[133] Nehru encouraged his 'sensitive' visit, partially to encourage Pakistan to enter negotiations with India over J&K's status. Abdullah met Ayub Khan, Ghulam Abbas, Mirwaiz Yusuf Shah, and a 'young' Zulfikar Ali Bhutto. In Muzaffarabad, a fellow Kashmiri, K.H. Khurshid, and a 'sea of humanity' greeted him.[134] Nehru's death on 27 May 1964 cut short Abdullah's visit. The 1965 India-Pakistan war soon followed, with no J&K leaders 'taken into confidence' beforehand about General Ayub's (flawed) plans to infiltrate men into Indian J&K to foment a popular uprising,[135] even though most '*jihadis*' were from Azad Kashmir and the Northern Areas.[136] After this war, direct contacts between people in J&K became almost non-existent.

Concurrently with the Abbas-Abdullah rumours of the early 1950s, Azad Kashmiris displayed discontent with Pakistan's stance on the Kashmir dispute. The so-called 'first freedom fighter', the pro-Pakistan Sardar Abdul Qayyum Khan, formed an 'Independent Party' in early 1951 while 'again preparing to cross the ceasefire line, and resume our war of liberation' for J&K.[137] His move was associated with the 'Rawalpindi Conspiracy'.[138] In April 1952, a Muslim Conference convention urged the 'Reorientation of Pakistan's Kashmir policy', since otherwise the party 'would be forced to declare itself shorn of all of its international obligations pertaining to the ceasefire and take the initiative … once again'.[139] In May 1952, Sardar Ibrahim, on being elected Muslim Conference president, stated that the post-ceasefire 'stalemate' on the Kashmir issue was 'becoming nauseating [sic]' and that Azad Kashmiris were 'simply fed up with it'. At the same meeting, Colonel Sher Khan, who would become Azad Kashmir President in June, urged Pakistan 'to pursue [its] Kashmir policy more vigorously'.[140] In July 1952, Ibrahim and other Muslim Conference members sought to create a broad-based 'All-Pakistan Kashmir Liberation Union' to represent people 'impatient over the problem of [the] accession of J&K and her freedom'.[141]

Meanwhile, for Pakistan, Azad Kashmir's status was far from settled and there appeared to be uncertainty about what to do. By the time Dixon arrived in Pakistan in June 1950, the Prime Minister of Pakistan usually took the lead on the international aspects of the Kashmir dispute (as did his counterpart in India). Following Liaquat's assassination in October 1951, Pakistan's new Prime Minister, Khwaja Nazimuddin, did defer to Pakistan's capable Foreign Minister, Zafrullah Khan. However, from April 1953, Nazimuddin's prime ministerial successor, the 'confirmed political non-entity' Muhammad Ali Bogra, reverted to leading on J&K and had discussions during his term with Nehru that 'aroused great expectations; but achieved little'.[142] In November 1955 Bogra's successor, Chaudhry Muhammad Ali, held a major 'All Parties Conference on Kashmir' in Karachi.[143] This 'great step' may have been the largest conference ever called on Kashmir matters by the Pakistan Government.[144]

Chaudhry Muhammad Ali held his 1955 'Conference on Kashmir' to discover 'the views of the Pakistanis and the [Azad] Kashmiris on the Kashmir issue and the existing situation of Azad Kashmir' and 'to achieve a national consensus on Kashmir'.[145] He may also have been trying to placate Azad Kashmiris. There had been significant disagreements in the Muslim Conference, while Sudhans had staged a major uprising shortly before Ali's conference (as discussed in the next chapter).[146] Equally, the troublesome events in Indian J&K may have inspired Chaudhry Muhammad Ali, or he may have wanted to weaken Ghulam Abbas's long-held opposition to Azad Kashmir being given popular forms of political participation. Some delegates, such as Sardar Qayyum, supported Abbas in the ongoing 'democracy versus freedom movement' debate. They were against diverting and 'damag[ing] the liberation movement by indulging in electoral strife'.[147] Nevertheless, after deliberating, the conference determined that Azad Kashmir would have a legislative assembly and elections, both of which Sardar Ibrahim had 'vigorously campaigned for'. Ibrahim had also wanted the unpopular Ministry of Kashmir Affairs dissolved, but he failed to achieve this, despite promises at the conference that this would happen.[148] Such Azad Kashmiris pursuing democracy, while possibly genuine democrats, also may have been using it as a device to weaken their opponents or to obtain political power. Nevertheless, the Awami League did establish a branch in Azad Kashmir in 1956–57, possibly because its leader, Suhrawardy, was then Pakistan's Prime Minister.[149] In any case, Ayub Khan's military coup in 1958 abruptly finished the idea of conducting popular, universal franchise elections in Azad Kashmir (and in Pakistan).

Pakistan's need for a pliant Azad Kashmir was helped because, for about ten years, it only confronted a single organisation, the manipulable Muslim Conference, which had a fractious leadership. In the 'disturbed conditions' following accession,[150] this party focused on liberating J&K, among other activities by supervising the Azad Kashmir movement. The Muslim Conference was the supreme body to which the subordinate Azad Kashmir Government reported, although both bodies were really aspects of the same organisation. Immediately after the ceasefire, the Muslim Conference maintained its monopoly control of the Azad Kashmir Government; it also secured exclusivity in Azad Kashmir as the only political organisation that Pakistan recognised.[151] While this ensured the party's longevity, it also meant that, once Karachi achieved control of the Muslim Conference, it achieved control of the Azad Kashmir Government. The Muslim Conference's fractious leadership unwittingly assisted Pakistan. While leaders were supposed to answer to the party's Working Committee, the 'supreme leader', Ghulam Abbas, had unpopular autocratic aspirations. He was reluctant to share power, or to institute a multi-party democracy in Azad Kashmir. This situation made the MKA's job easier: it took advantage of the divisions and disgruntlement within the Muslim Conference to take charge of Azad Kashmir.

The Muslim Conference had a number of factions after the 1949 ceasefire. The two main factions centred on Abbas, whose political career gave him power and prestige, and on Ibrahim, whose position arose from the liberation movement and his powerful Sudhan tribe in southern Poonch.[152] Abbas's supporters were chiefly refugees from eastern areas of Jammu; Ibrahim's supporters were chiefly Poonchis and Mirpuris. Some Poonchis also liked the youthful freedom fighter Sardar Qayyum, from the Bagh area of northern Poonch; Qayyum was a strong Abbas supporter.[153] A smaller, third faction comprised ethnic Kashmiris including the prominent Mirwaiz Yusuf Shah and, later, K.H. Khurshid. The Azad Kashmir Government needed to include token members from all J&K groups to show that it was a truly representative, and genuine alternative, government for J&K. Because of this need for inclusiveness—and MKA manipulation—five men served as the seven presidents of Azad Kashmir between 1950 and 1959. Two were Sudhan Poonchis (Ibrahim, twice; Sher Ahmad Khan); one was from Bagh (Qayyum); one was a Mirpuri (Ali Ahmad Shah); one was a Kashmiri (Yusuf Shah, twice). The length of each one's term invariably depended on their ability to satisfy the MKA.

Significantly for the MKA, Azad Kashmir's two major leaders, Ghulam Abbas and Sardar Ibrahim, could be played off against one another, while a lesser figure, such as Yusuf Shah, could be made president when necessary. For Gurmani, the Abbas-Ibrahim situation was a boon: the minister played the factions off and 'wittingly or unwittingly' divided the entire liberation movement.[154] Indeed, Gurmani's ministry 'played havoc' with the Azad Kashmir movement and had it 'liquidated to the satisfaction of all bureaucrats in Pakistan' by late 1951 when Mirwaiz was appointed President of Azad Kashmir.[155] Azad Kashmiris' fractiousness was not about the accession issue: all three factions wanted J&K to join Pakistan. Nor was it ideological: no faction 'had any positive programme either for the liberation of occupied Kashmir or for the betterment of the lot of Azad Kashmir inhabitants'. It was to do with obtaining power and influence:

> It is true that the MKA, especially after Mr. Gurmani graced it with his feudal presence ... must share a part of the blame for the division in our ranks but it is also true that a larger part of the blame squarely rests on the shoulders of our leaders—one and all ... each faction tried to enlist the support of the MKA against the other faction, with the result that all got destroyed.[156]

Fractiousness became an ongoing problem in Azad Kashmir politics (as discussed later). To Pakistan's discredit, it did not seek to discourage this by enabling a multi-party democracy in Azad Kashmir. This disinclination reflected Pakistani politics. Following the untimely deaths of Jinnah and Liaquat, Pakistani politicians were also fractious. Between 1950 and 1958, Pakistan had seven prime ministers.[157] The difference from Azad Kashmir, however, was that no outside body had imposed these changes on Pakistan.

The MKA's poor treatment of Azad Kashmir's leaders changed only after the reasonably influential K.H. Khurshid accepted General Ayub Khan's request to become Azad Kashmir's President. Khurshid was President from 1 May 1959 until 5 August 1964. He had status: he had been Jinnah's private secretary from 1944 to 1947; he was arrested twice in 1947 by Sheikh Abdullah's Emergency Administration for 'activities prejudicial to the welfare of the State';[158] his contacts included General Ayub, a powerful patron while ruling Pakistan (1958–69), and Jinnah's sister, Fatima, the 'First Lady of Pakistan' and 'Mother of the Nation'.[159] Khurshid's standing and connections meant that he was not prepared to be treated as a supplicant. Equally, he benefited by being Azad Kashmir's President while Pakistan endured political impotency under military rule; that situation curtailed even the MKA's activities.

Nevertheless, Khurshid fell out with the Ministry of Kashmir Affairs after being branded as 'difficult and uncooperative'.[160] He was not helped by an 'extremely strained' relationship with Azad Kashmir's Chief Secretary, a senior officer on loan from the Pakistan Civil Service.[161] Despite General Ayub's controlled 1961 Basic Democracy elections confirming his presidency, Khurshid was replaced in 1964 before the end of his term. (In the Basic Democracy system, people elected (supposedly) apolitical 'Basic Democrats'; (supposedly) more politically astute, they then elected other representatives as president and members of the Azad Kashmir Council.) Khurshid's removal followed MKA intrigue. The MKA was displeased with the Kashmiri's direct contact with General Ayub and its inability to dominate him. While in Rawalpindi ostensibly to attend a Development Board meeting, the 'furious but helpless' Khurshid was sacked.[162] He was then temporarily incarcerated in a Rawalpindi jail.[163]

Hence, by about 1965, the Ministry of Kashmir Affairs had successfully subordinated Azad Kashmir. This included ensuring that Azad Kashmir's 1958 Rules of Business confirmed Pakistan's domination.[164] Unable or unwilling to resist, Azad Kashmiris also allowed the Azad Jammu and Kashmir Government Acts of 1964 and 1968 to further Pakistan's position.[165] These 'humiliating' acts downgraded Azad Kashmir's administration to 'municipal committee status',[166] with members unable to pass laws or spend money without the approval of a Pakistani joint secretary and an all-powerful, Pakistan-appointed Chief Advisor.[167] The acts allowed the election of an eight member 'State Council', although after it was elected, the Chief Advisor selected the Azad Kashmir president from among those elected—and then controlled him.[168] The only benefit for Azad Kashmiris was that, unlike previous Pakistani ministers, the military was less inclined to engage in manipulative politics. Under Ayub, the Pakistan Army did not need to; it was all-powerful, had a clear chain of command, and had no polls to fear.

In the late 1960s, General Ayub's power waned. Pakistan's concurrent struggle towards democracy had positive effects for Azad Kashmiris, including the lessening of the MKA's impact. Ayub's popularity started to decline after the inconclusive 1965 India-Pakistan war; duped Pakistanis disliked their 'diet of victory reports'.[169] Thereafter, politicians dragged Pakistan towards a democracy. In 1967, the rising but manipulative Zulfikar Ali Bhutto, who had urged Ayub to fight India,[170] formed the Pakistan People's Party (PPP). The same year, Sheikh Mujibur Rahman's Awami League sought more autonomy and power for East Pakistanis. In 1969, even a disgruntled former Pakistan Air Force chief (and Kashmiri refugee),[171] Air Marshal Muhammad Asghar Khan, formed a political party: Tehrik-i-Istiqlal (Solidarity Movement).[172] Finally, 'popular disturbances' in Pakistan in late 1968 and early 1969, and pressure from bodies such as the Democratic Action Committee, which sought to replace Ayub's centrist system with a devolved federal system, led to Ayub's resignation in March 1969. Undemocratically and without 'any legal foundation', he devolved power to General Yahya Khan, his successor as Chief of the Pakistan Army. Under the 1962 Constitution, the Speaker of the National Assembly should have taken over.

General Yahya Khan was a 'sincere but politically inept general'.[173] Under him, Azad Kashmiris and Pakistanis experienced democracy, followed by turmoil. By mid-1968, during the increasingly turbulent political situation confronting Pakistan, three major political parties existed in Azad Kashmir: the All J&K Muslim Conference; the J&K Liberation League; and the Azad J&K Muslim Conference. Emboldened by increasing efforts to make Pakistan a democracy, 'all [sic] factions of political and civil society' in and outside Azad Kashmir (unusually) came together to demonstrate against the disliked 'Azad Jammu and Kashmir Government Act' of 1968.[174] On 5 August 1968, Sardar Qayyum, K.H. Khurshid and Sardar Ibrahim signed a joint declaration calling for the 're-constituted Azad Kashmir Government [to] be treated as [the] full sovereign, [and] successor to the Government of Maharaja Hari Singh for the whole state'.[175] Their efforts succeeded when, under pressure, Yahya became tired of his army having to deal with agitated Pakistanis and Azad Kashmiris.[176] On 7 October 1969 the Azad Kashmir President, Khan Abdul Hamid Khan, resigned to enable the 'framing of a constitution for ... the people of Kashmir'.[177] A man with important military connections, Abdul Rehman Khan, a retired brigadier from Bhimber, replaced him.[178] Rehman took over as interim Azad Kashmir President promising efficiency, a neutral government, the framing of a new constitution, and elections.[179] In October 1970, Azad Kashmiris voted in presidential and general elections (discussed below).

In December 1970, Pakistan held its first universal suffrage elections for national and provincial assemblies.[180] J&K refugees living in Pakistan were entitled to vote in these.[181] These elections were significant. They delivered a divisive result that 'laid bare' the 'long-established political cleavages between East and West Pakistan'. Serious trouble followed. Of the 300 seats contested, Bhutto's PPP won 81 of the 138 seats in West Pakistan, which gave it a majority in the west, while Mujibur Rahman's Awami League won 160 of the 162 seats in East Pakistan, which gave it an overwhelming majority in the east, plus an overall majority nationally. Thereafter, the inability of West Pakistanis, particularly Bhutto, to allow the Awami League to govern Pakistan led to seriously disenchanted Bengalis, including the Indian-supported Mukhti Bahini guerrilla group, staging a rebellion. The Pakistan Army brutally tried to suppress this uprising, killing many Bengalis in the process. After India officially became involved in November 1971, its military forces defeated Pakistan's in a two-week war. The Indian Army captured 93,000 Pakistani soldiers; Pakistan lost 'half of its navy, a third of its army and a quarter of its air forces'—plus 'its' eastern wing.[182] East Pakistan became the nation of Bangladesh. As discussed below, this war also changed the way that Azad Kashmiris and Pakistanis related to each other.

*After 1970: legislated dominance*

In the 1970s, Azad Kashmir was better treated by Pakistan. This was chiefly because Islamabad's (tight) control of the region was generally enforced using established legal processes. These replaced Ministry of Kashmir Affairs bureaucrats imposing their will or military personnel asserting themselves during martial law. Such legal instruments and matters are discussed below. They are important as many are still in place in the Azad Kashmir-Pakistan relationship.

In 1970, a major change in Azad Kashmir occurred when General Yahya Khan granted Azad Kashmir a rudimentary constitution: 'The Azad Jammu and Kashmir Government Act, 1970' (hereafter called the '1970 Act').[183] It generously—or naively—gave the region a presidential system of government, a legislative assembly, and considerable autonomy: the Azad Kashmir Government controlled everything except foreign affairs, defence and currency. In June 1970, the Pakistan Cabinet also issued an instruction 'for observance by all Ministries and Departments of the Central Governments [sic]'.[184] It instructed that, despite Azad Kashmir not being a part of Pakistan according to the Pakistan Constitution, 'it should for all practical [reasons] be treated like any other province ... Azad Kashmir should be brought into the main stream of the general administration'. The exclusive oversight of Azad Kashmir by the 'Kashmir Affairs Division' was to be replaced by 'Central Ministries' dealing with the region 'as if it were another administrative unit of the country'. In May 1971, the Pakistani Cabinet Secretary, Ghulam Ishaq Khan, finally informed the Azad Kashmir 'Secretary' of this decision. He gave no reason for the 11-month delay.

The Azad Kashmir-Pakistan relationship enacted by the 1970 Act gave Azad Kashmir the greatest autonomy the region ever experienced. On 5 September 1970, a 'Government Order' promulgated this act as 'Act I of 1970'.[185] It established a presidential system of government in Azad Kashmir that gave the region 'absolute internal autonomy'.[186] J&K state subjects living in Azad Kashmir and Pakistan directly elected, on the basis of adult suffrage, a legislative assembly and the president. The authority of the president, who had to be a Muslim male at least 35 years old, was broad. His only restrictions were that he must exercise power without 'imped[ing] or prejudic[ing]' Pakistan's responsibilities under UNCIP resolutions or for the defence and security of Azad Kashmir; on these matters, the president was to liaise with a Pakistan Government adviser. This, seemingly, was his only contact with Pakistan. The president was also in a powerful political position: the only way to remove him from office was by a no-confidence motion supported by two-thirds of the Legislative Assembly (which later became an issue, as discussed in Chapter 5). The Legislative Assembly could make laws on all matters related to Azad Kashmir and for all state subjects, wherever they were domiciled. It had the same restrictions as the president, and in addition was not able to legislate on currency-related matters.[187]

The 1970 Act obtained credence because Azad Kashmiris had been involved in formulating it—Pakistan did not simply impose it.[188] While this act gave Azad Kashmir considerable freedom and autonomy, the region additionally operated under Rules of Business (discussed in Chapter 6). The 1970 Act also prohibited Azad Kashmiri leaders from doing anything but supporting Azad Kashmir's accession to Pakistan. This was despite its preamble (contradictorily) talking of the people deciding the issue of J&K's accession. Instead, the act required senior Azad Kashmiri office bearers to swear they would 'remain loyal to the country and the cause of accession of the State of Jammu and Kashmir to Pakistan'.[189] (It was unclear what was meant by 'the 'country'.) While this legal requirement reflected many of Azad Kashmiris' aspirations, it was undemocratic and contrary to the either/or choice the UN plebiscite would offer to all J&K people. This requirement sought to stymie people such as K.H. Khurshid, who possibly favoured an 'independent Kashmir'.[190] For Sardar Qayyum, this 'deception of independence' negated people's sacrifices to unite Azad Kashmir with Pakistan and diminished the concept of a united Muslim community joining Pakistan, a nation created for Muslims.[191]

Azad Kashmir's relatively liberal and essentially Pakistan-free presidential system came into being before Pakistan's devastating loss in its 1971 war with India. This war, most of which was fought outside J&K,[192] had four important consequences for Azad Kashmir. First, in December 1971, following Yahya Khan's 30 months in power, the politically capable Zulfikar Ali Bhutto assumed office in Pakistan. This (temporarily) restored the supremacy of civilian politicians over (defeated and subdued) soldiers. On 14 August 1973, after much politicking, consultation and agreement, Bhutto introduced a new constitution that gave Pakistan a parliamentary system of government in which the prime minister was supreme, not the president.[193] This influenced Azad Kashmiris' desires for a similar system,[194] with a local PPP faction lobbying Bhutto for this change.[195] Second, Bhutto was thought to have India's approval to provincialise Azad Kashmir. He obtained this via an oral—but secret and unwritten—agreement made with India's Prime Minister, Indira Gandhi, as part of their post-war Simla Agreement of 1972. Without consulting the people of J&K, New Delhi and Islamabad would settle the Kashmir dispute by dividing J&K along the renamed 'line of control', after which India and Pakistan would fully incorporate their respective parts of J&K.[196] Azad Kashmir would then become a fully-fledged province of Pakistan,[197] something Bhutto possibly initiated when he came to power. Third, the Simla Agreement stated that all 'differences' between India and Pakistan, including the Kashmir dispute, were bilateral issues.[198] This seemingly negated the promised plebiscite. Fourth, Pakistanis and Azad Kashmiris perceived (realistically) that, owing to India's size, population and military strength, Pakistan's military could not liberate J&K.[199] These third and fourth factors made Azad Kashmiris consider their situation and matters such as democracy, their own development and their inevitable relationship with Pakistan—rather than just agreeing to be the 'base camp' to liberate Indian-J&K.[200]

While there is little direct evidence that Pakistan was going to provincialise Azad Kashmir, Pakistan gave itself the legal scope to do so. After the 'loss' of East Pakistan in 1971 and the promulgation of its 1973 constitution, Pakistan's national structure comprised the provinces of Baluchistan, NWFP, Punjab and Sind, plus the Federally Administered Tribal Areas and the Islamabad Capital Territory, plus 'such States and territories as are or may be included in Pakistan, whether by accession or otherwise'.[201] This latter category included Azad Kashmir. Nevertheless, Bhutto's messages on this issue were mixed. On 27 September 1974, he stated that the Northern Areas 'could not be made a province of Pakistan, for the time being, because of the Kashmir dispute with India'.[202] The same applied to Azad Kashmir. Furthermore, to become a province of Pakistan may have been unappealing for Azad Kashmiris. The Pakistan Army had brutally repressed East Pakistan and was suppressing Baluchistan, with Baluchis possibly inspired by the Bengalis'/Bangladeshis' victory.[203] Similarly, the Punjabi-dominated Pakistan Army was leading the 'Punjabisation' of Pakistan.[204] However, had Azad Kashmir become a province of Pakistan, this might have resolved the issue of the region's status—provided that this was part of an overall resolution of the Kashmir dispute.

Talk of making Azad Kashmir a province of Pakistan also offered Bhutto advantages. He was able to assert Pakistan's ongoing control by ensuring that Azad Kashmir had a subordinate constitution that ensured Pakistan's primacy and a 'matching' prime ministerial system. Bhutto also allowed, even encouraged, external political parties, particularly the Pakistan People's Party, to operate in Azad Kashmir. Previously, only locally based parties had existed, the rationale being to keep Azad Kashmiris focused on the freedom struggle—a stance that the locally popular Muslim Conference supported. If Bhutto did, indeed, want to provincialise Azad Kashmir, he may have needed a strong PPP presence in Azad Kashmir to weaken the Muslim Conference's position.[205] Equally, a local PPP presence provided reasons, and allies, for Bhutto to intervene in Azad Kashmir—something non-PPP politicians such as Sardar Qayyum did not want.

In 1974, Azad Kashmir repealed the 1970 Act and enacted a constitution 'framed' by Pakistan with a prime ministerial system that could have enabled Pakistan to easily provincialise the region.[206] This was 'The Azad Jammu and Kashmir Interim Constitution Act, 1974' (hereafter called the 'Interim Constitution'), which the Pakistan Government 'authorised' the Azad Kashmir President to introduce in the Azad Kashmir Legislative Assembly 'for consideration and passage'.[207] The Legislative Assembly passed this act on 24 August 1974.[208] This constitutional change was agreed after 'prolonged parlays' between Bhutto and leading Azad Kashmiri politicians, including President Sardar Qayyum,[209] who was politically distant from Bhutto.[210] Apart from effects of the 1971 India-Pakistan war—particularly Bhutto's pre-eminence—the constitutional difficulty involved in removing the Azad Kashmir president also encouraged constitutional change. The new Interim Constitution granted Azad Kashmir a lower house, the Legislative Assembly, based in Muzaffarabad, similar to lower houses existing in Pakistan. Uniquely, Azad Kashmir received another house, the Azad Kashmir Council, based in Islamabad. This superior body, which comprised Pakistani and Azad Kashmiri members, effectively tied the region to Pakistan and regulated contact between senior Pakistanis and Azad Kashmiris. Importantly, the Pakistan prime minister was Council chairman. In 1974, this was the 'charismatic and demagogic' Bhutto, a man at the height of his power and popularity.[211]

The Interim Constitution also formalised how Azad Kashmir and Pakistan would relate. Indeed, it provided certainty—disregarding military coups—about this relationship, with Pakistan again in charge and with constitutional clauses (discussed below) to ensure that this situation continued. The Interim Constitution was 'interim' until Azad Kashmir's status was resolved by the promised plebiscite or by other means, like the supposed secret Bhutto-Gandhi agreement; then, it would be replaced by a permanent constitution. More pointedly than its 1970 predecessor, the Interim Constitution insisted that all Azad Kashmiris seeking office should support and swear to J&K's accession to Pakistan.[212] Individuals and/or political parties in Azad Kashmir, in addition, were prohibited from 'propagat[ing] against, or tak[ing] part in activities prejudicial or detrimental to, the ideology of the State's accession to Pakistan'.[213] This made it clear: it was illegal for Azad Kashmiris to favour Azad Kashmir becoming anything but part of Pakistan. This stronger stance was to diminish support for groups like the Kashmir National Liberation Front which, in the name of freeing J&K, successfully hijacked an Indian Airlines aircraft in January 1971. As noted in Chapter 8, this group was 'no subservient tool' of Pakistan or Azad Kashmir.[214]

*An examination of the Interim Constitution Act, 1974*

Since 1974, the Interim Constitution has ordered the Azad Kashmir-Pakistan relationship and tied the region to the nation 'in form as well as fact'.[215] While the

Interim Constitution mostly determines how 'to provide for the better Government and administration' of Azad Kashmir,[216] significant sections detail the Azad Kashmir-Pakistan relationship, in which Pakistan is in the superior position. Indeed, an examination of the Interim Constitution shows that Pakistan, particularly when under military leadership, has used sections within it to impose its will in Azad Kashmir—or to justify this imposition. Azad Kashmiri politicians have had little option but to comply.

The Interim Constitution established an unusual bicameral situation for Azad Kashmir, comprising the Azad Kashmir Legislative Assembly and the Azad Kashmir Council. This was supposed to give Azad Kashmir 'parity' with Pakistan's provinces as per Pakistan's 1973 Constitution. However, the reconstituted Azad Kashmir Council was a collective body unique in the subcontinent and not 'akin or equal to an upper House or the [Pakistan] Senate'.[217] It regulated relations between Azad Kashmir and Pakistan and defined Islamabad's power 'so as to avoid day-to-day friction that had existed since 1948'.[218] The Council also gave Azad Kashmiris more higher-level representation at the federal executive level than any province, and it ensured that senior Azad Kashmiri politicians, unlike provincial chief ministers, had regular access to Pakistan's prime minister. Conversely, the Interim Constitution significantly reduced Azad Kashmir's autonomy. Pakistani leaders who followed Bhutto, particularly General Zia-ul-Haq but also Nawaz Sharif,[219] used the constitution to make, or justify, changes to Azad Kashmir's leadership. Sometimes Azad Kashmiri politicians, often under duress, aided the Pakistanis.

Section 21 of the Interim Constitution deemed that: 'There shall be an Azad Jammu and Kashmir Council'.[220] It would comprise 14 voting members: six Pakistanis and eight Azad Kashmiris. Four members were *ex-officio*: the prime minister of Pakistan, chairman; the Azad Kashmir president, vice-chairman; the Azad Kashmir prime minister, member; and, Pakistan's 'Minister of the [sic] State for Kashmir Affairs and Northern Affairs' (KA&NA), adviser.[221] Pakistan's prime minister appointed four other members; the Azad Kashmir Legislative Assembly elected six members for five-year terms, or until their successors took office. The chairman could appoint three other advisers. All advisers could take part in proceedings, but were not entitled to vote—although voting on issues may have been a formality, or simply ignored, with Pakistan, in the minority position, imposing decisions. The six 'elected' Azad Kashmir members and the 'Federal Minister in-charge of the Council Secretariat' (usually KA&NA), would elect the Azad Kashmir president via a 'joint session' with the Legislative Assembly.[222] This was the only time KA&NA voted. KA&NA's inclusion as an *ex-officio* member assisted Pakistan: he brought specific portfolio expertise; he led the Council when Pakistan's prime minister was absent;[223] he was 'in-charge' of the Council Secretariat, its staff and affairs; and he delegated tasks and duties to three subordinate advisers.[224] This reflected how the Council operated: it decided and legislated; KA&NA's Secretariat provided support and administered.[225]

While Azad Kashmiris comprised the majority of the Azad Kashmir Council's 14 members, this was their sole advantage. The Pakistan prime minister was chairman. The Interim Constitution gave him/her the power to 'regulate' the Council's business 'for the convenient transaction of that business'.[226] Islamabad therefore determined what would be on the agenda and when it would be discussed. The Pakistan prime minister's nominees also comprised ministers with influential ministries: Interior; Foreign Affairs; Media and Information Development; Education; KA&NA.[227] Conversely, the Azad Kashmir president or prime minister did not nominate any members. Additionally, they and the six elected Azad Kashmir members may have been from different political parties with varying political loyalties and aspirations in relation to Islamabad powerbrokers. These differences worked to Pakistan's advantage. Similarly, the Council always sat in Islamabad, which enabled Pakistani politicians to put pressure on Council members, distribute largesse to them via the 'Development Programme', or coerce them. Pakistan also had significant control over Azad Kashmir's revenue, one of the Council Secretariat's main functions being the 'collection of income tax from the territory of Azad Kashmir' (as discussed below).[228]

The Interim Constitution itself enhanced Pakistan's legal ability to control Azad Kashmir. The Azad Kashmir Council's areas of responsibility were clearly shown in the Interim Constitution's 'Third Schedule … Council Legislative List', which contained 'virtually everything of any importance'.[229] It exhaustively listed 52 matters for which only the Azad Kashmir Council could legislate.[230] While similar to the Pakistan Constitution's 'Fourth Schedule' that provides the 'Federal Legislative List' and the 'Concurrent Legislative List', the Third Schedule was more restrictive as no item was concurrent.[231] It included all aspects of foreign affairs, transport, communications, financial and economic matters, nuclear energy, planning, police, electricity (one of Azad Kashmir's few economic assets), and 'Election to the [Azad Kashmir] Council'.[232] The Azad Kashmir Legislative Assembly could legislate on everything 'not enumerated' in the Third Schedule.[233] This was little—and local. Pakistan effectively had control of Azad Kashmir's affairs, plus a veto power on important issues, including foreign affairs, nuclear matters and law and order. This ensured that, as per the 1948 UNCIP resolution, the Azad Kashmir Government comprised a local authority with limited functions. The Azad Kashmir 'Rules of Business 1985', Schedule II, 'Distribution of business among Departments', confirms this situation.[234] It details the Azad Kashmir Government's various municipal-type functions.

Three sections of the Interim Constitution that related to Pakistan also ensured its superior position: sections 31, 53 and 56. Section 31 discussed 'Legislative Powers'. Its Sub-section 3 stated that neither the Azad Kashmir Legislative Assembly nor the Azad Kashmir Council could make laws concerning:

a) the responsibilities of the Government of Pakistan under the UNCIP Resolutions;
b) the defence and security of Azad Jammu and Kashmir;
c) the current coin or the issue of any bills, notes or other paper currency; or,
d) the external affairs of Azad Jammu and Kashmir including foreign trade and foreign aid.[235]

The Interim Constitution did not state which body should make laws in relation to these matters, but it inferred that this body should be Pakistan. Section 56 stated that nothing in the Interim Constitution 'shall derogate' from Pakistan's responsibilities specified in Section 31, or prevent it 'from taking such action as it may consider necessary or expedient for the effective discharge of those responsibilities'.[236] Section 56 effectively gave Pakistan the power to do whatever it wanted in Azad Kashmir. Two Pakistanis, General Zia-ul-Haq and Nawaz Sharif, would later invoke it (see below).

Section 53, 'Power to issue proclamation', dealt with 'grave' emergency situations where Azad Kashmir's security was 'threatened by war or external aggression or by internal disturbances'. In such situations, the president of Azad Kashmir, 'if so advised' by the chairman of the Azad Kashmir Council, should issue a 'proclamation of emergency'. While a joint sitting of the Azad Kashmir Legislative Assembly and the Azad Kashmir Council had to confirm any proclamation within thirty days, if the former was dissolved, the proclamation could remain in force for four months. Otherwise, it remained in force until a joint sitting negated the proclamation. Section 53 is still current.[237]

A temporary but related—and draconian—Section 53-A, 'Proclamation to provide for Interim Government', was inserted into the Interim Constitution in 1977.[238] This occurred soon after Pakistan's Chief of Army Staff, General Zia, and the Pakistan Army staged a coup in Pakistan on 5 July because Pakistan was in 'danger of a full-scale civil war'[239] after rigged elections in March 1977.[240] To control Azad Kashmir, the all-powerful Zia had six amendments made to the Interim Constitution.[241] These were instituted following an important 'Heads of Agreement' on 27 July 1977 between Zia, as Chief of Army Staff and Chief Martial Law Administrator, and the heads of the Pakistan People's Party-Azad Kashmir (PPPAK)[242] (Pir Ali Jan Shah), the Muslim Conference (Sardar Qayyum) and the Azad Muslim Conference (Chaudhry Noor Hussain). Zia ensured that these intimidated politicians had the Interim Constitution 'and other relevant laws amended ... by 6th August 1977'.[243] The two most important changes were an amendment to Section 21 and the insertion of Section 53-A. An addition to Section 21 enabled Zia to become Chairman of the Azad Kashmir Council:

> The words 'The Prime Minister of Pakistan' wherever occurring ... shall be deemed to include the person for the time being exercising the powers and performing the functions of the Chief Executive of Pakistan.[244]

Section 53-A determined that the Azad Kashmir president:

> shall, if so advised by the Chairman of the [Azad Kashmir] Council [i.e. General Zia], issue a Proclamation to make such provisions as may be necessary for dissolving the Assembly before [the] expiry of its term, cessation of elected members of the Council, holding of elections thereof, appointment of a person as Chief Executive of Azad Jammu and Kashmir to perform the functions of and exercise the powers vested in the Government under this Act, ... [until a new] Prime Minister enters upon his office, and for matters incidental or connected herewith.

This essentially imposed martial law on Azad Kashmir in 1977, a situation that Zia and the military that he commanded, which had a large presence in Azad Kashmir, could enforce.

On 11 August 1977, President Sardar Ibrahim duly issued his Proclamation. In accordance with the Heads of Agreement that enabled Ibrahim to continue as 'interim President provided he does not seek election for any office', he dismissed the various elected Azad Kashmir office holders and their advisers, including the

Azad Kashmir Prime Minister. Except for Ibrahim, every elected official in the Azad Kashmir Council or the Azad Kashmir Legislative Assembly, and their assistants, ceased to hold office. Ibrahim then appointed Major-General (Retired) Abdul Rehman Khan as the 'Chief Executive' of Azad Kashmir, with all of the prime minister's and Legislative Assembly speaker's powers.[245] Rehman, who had occupied this position during General Yahya's martial law regime, served until 30 October 1978.

On 31 October 1978, Zia invoked Section 56 of the Interim Constitution to dismiss Sardar Ibrahim. Zia issued a proclamation which stated that, 'for the better government and administration' of Azad Kashmir, he was 'pleased to relieve' Ibrahim of his office and to appoint Brigadier (later Major-General) Muhammad Hayat Khan as President of Azad Kashmir 'in addition to his duties as Chief Executive of Azad Jammu and Kashmir'.[246] Ibrahim's dismissal was unpopular with Sudhans who (again) created 'disturbances',[247] although it was surprising that Zia had allowed this pro-Bhutto politician to remain President of Azad Kashmir for a further 15 months. Hayat served until February 1983, when Rehman returned as Azad Kashmir President following some rare local dissent: 'a great movement and agitation against Mr. [sic] Hayat' occurred because people were disenchanted with him and Pakistan.[248] Rehman served until 1985 when Sardar Qayyum took over as President. Meanwhile, Ibrahim had challenged his dismissal. On appeal from the Azad Kashmir High Court,[249] he won a case in the Azad Kashmir Supreme Court.[250] However, Ibrahim's victory came in 1990, two years after Zia's death and the end of martial law.

Section 53-A was supposedly temporary until elections were held for the Azad Kashmir Legislative Assembly. According to Ibrahim's Proclamation, these were due in October 1977.[251] The powers vested in Section 53-A would then automatically end when a new prime minister was inducted into office.[252] In relation to elections Zia promised much, but delivered little. After his coup in July 1977, he assured Pakistanis that free and fair elections would be held in October 1977; they were held in February 1985.[253] Similarly, on 3 October 1977, the Azad Kashmir Government postponed Legislative Assembly elections because all political activity was banned in Pakistan, which made it impossible for J&K refugees living there to participate in electing their 12 Legislative Assembly representatives.[254] Section 53-A was finally deleted from the Interim Constitution following military-supervised elections in June 1985 in Azad Kashmir, as a result of which two Zia sympathisers, Sardar Sikandar Hayat Khan and Sardar Qayyum, became Prime Minister and President respectively.[255] While Section 53-A enabled the continuation of Zia's military rule, Section 56-A cleverly accounted for the eight-year delay in elections being held. Inserted into the Interim Constitution in 1975, it stated that the 'Failure to comply with requirement as to time does not render an act invalid'.[256] Section 53-A no longer applies; Section 56-A remains current.[257]

Possibly inspired by General Zia, a second Pakistani also used Section 56 to dismiss a senior Azad Kashmiri. In 1991, Pakistan's Prime Minister, Nawaz Sharif, dismissed Azad Kashmir's Prime Minister, Mumtaz Hussain Rathore.[258] Following elections in May 1990, Rathore, the leader of the Pakistan People's Party-Azad Kashmir, formed a large and shaky coalition. In August 1990 his ally, Pakistan's Prime Minister Benazir Bhutto, was sacked, which put Rathore under further pressure. To consolidate his position, he called elections in June 1991. To Rathore's surprise, the Muslim Conference, which was aligned with Sharif's Muslim League, resoundingly won. Believing rigging had occurred, Rathore declared the 1991 elections null and void, after which Sharif dismissed him in July 1991 and the Muslim Conference formed a government.[259] Rathore had little option but to accept his sacking. Section 56 is still in the Interim Constitution.[260] Interestingly, no corresponding provision exists in the constitutions of Pakistan, India or Indian J&K.[261]

Pakistan's reversion to democracy in 1988 changed the way Pakistan related to Azad Kashmir. The Interim Constitution still regulated relations and the Azad Kashmir Council's operations, but otherwise it was rarely invoked. Unpopular martial law ended in August 1988, following General Zia's fatal air crash, after which the Chairman of the Pakistan Senate, Ghulam Ishaq Khan, duly took over as President. Following elections, Benazir Bhutto and her Pakistan People's Party came to power in December 1988. Then followed 11 years of civilians 'experiment[ing] with democracy'.[262] Bhutto was Prime Minister twice (December 1988-August 1990; October 1993-November 1996), as was Nawaz Sharif, leader of the Pakistan Muslim League (November 1990-July 1993; February 1997-October 1999). This 'merry-go-round' occurred because civilian presidents invoked the Pakistan Constitution's Eighth Amendment to dismiss 'unsavoury' prime ministers: Ishaq Khan dismissed Bhutto in 1990 and Sharif in 1993 (although a Supreme Court verdict later reinstated him); Farooq Leghari dismissed Bhutto in 1996.[263] As discussed in Chapter 8, Pakistan's elected leaders influenced Azad Kashmir's politics through their membership of the Azad Kashmir Council, by manipulating Azad Kashmir Legislative Assembly elections via constituencies for J&K refugees located in Pakistan, and by supporting local surrogates. Consequently, their dismissals invariably put pressure on Azad Kashmir politicians of a different political persuasion to Islamabad's replacement prime minister.

On 12 October 1999, General Pervez Musharraf came to power in Pakistan via a military 'counter-coup'.[264] He strengthened Pakistan's position over Azad Kashmir, albeit without referring to the Interim Constitution. Despite imposing military rule and then a 'command democracy' (military-dominated rule) throughout Pakistan from 1999 to 2007, Musharraf allowed elected civilians to govern Azad Kashmir, under military supervision. He also allowed the first major elections during his tenure to be held in Azad Kashmir on 5 July 2001, after which Sardar Sikandar returned as Prime Minister. To ensure Sikandar's compliance, Musharraf had Major-General (Retired) Sardar Mohammed Anwar Khan elected as Azad Kashmir President on 1 August 2001. This was Islamabad imposing its will in a blatant way. Three days beforehand, Anwar was still Vice Chief of the General Staff of the Pakistan Army;[265] two years should have elapsed from the end of his military service before he could stand for such a position.[266] Musharraf imposed Islamabad's 'man' in Azad Kashmir to stem corruption, to maximise its control of the region, and because of Anwar's 'dedication to the liberation of Kashmir'.[267] Finally, in the 2006 Azad Kashmir elections, in an important step Musharraf granted his imprimatur for Sardar Qayyum's son, Sardar Attique, to become Azad Kashmir's Prime Minister. This confirmed Pakistanis' superiority and the tradition whereby Azad Kashmiri politicians seek and/or need Islamabad's approval to be in power (see Chapter 8).

## How the Azad Kashmir Council operates

Despite the Azad Kashmir Council existing since 1974, little pertinent information exists about how this important body has functioned. The Council has a (scant) website,[268] but other material is scarce or available only to 'insiders'. In 2006, the Azad Kashmir Council appeared to be functioning adequately, despite its members not meeting often.[269] The Council apparently meets two to three times a year, with each meeting lasting between 1.5 and two hours. In 2005, it met three times. This suggests that Council members are very efficient or have little business, possibly because of the Council Secretariat's role and efficiency. The Secretariat is based in Islamabad. In 2005, its staff comprised 542 officers, including one secretary, one joint secretary and four deputy secretaries.[270] Pakistanis heavily dominated this body: all officers had been seconded from the Pakistan civil service for five-year terms. All were under the control of the Minister for Kashmir Affairs and Northern Affairs, who is the main Pakistani dealing with Azad Kashmiris and their region.

Importantly, the Azad Kashmir Council undertakes all income tax, excise and sales tax collection for Azad Kashmir, and collects all Pakistani taxes and duties imposed by the Azad Kashmir Government.[271] The Council does so via its Board of Revenue and the Commissionerate of Income Tax. The Commissionerate has offices in Azad Kashmir's seven districts; its officers collect revenue.[272] It also collects 'central excise duty, education cess [tax], sales tax and other provincial taxes/duties' for the Azad Kashmir Government. In 2000–01, the 'relentless and dedicated efforts' of the Commissionerate's officers were so successful that they collected Rs. 61 million over the Azad Kashmir Government's revenue target.[273] The Azad Kashmir Council releases 80 per cent of the revenue collected to the Azad Kashmir Government 'straight-away',[274] as per 'the distribution of revenue and grant-in-order, 1975' formula, which the Pakistan Government approved.[275] It does not deduct any service charges. The remaining 20 per cent goes to the Council's 'consolidated [sic] Funds'[276] to meet the Secretariat's operating expenses and for a 'Development Programme'.[277] Development projects are proposed by the Council's vice-chairman, elected members, the relevant minister, and the Secretariat.[278] While the Council's tax collection provides a useful service for the Azad Kashmir Government, local officers could collect taxes. This process gives Islamabad significant control over Azad Kashmir's finances.

The Azad Kashmir Council's Development Programme is interesting.[279] In 2006–07, allocations to Council members from Azad Kashmir, except the prime minister, provided them with considerable financial largesse 'to spend locally'.[280] In 2006–07, the Programme's budget was Rs. 900 million.[281] This comprised Rs. 360 million for 'ongoing projects' and Rs. 540 million for 'new projects'. One new project was the 'Members Development Programme', for which Rs. 90 million was allocated. This was divided into Rs. 20 million for the vice-chairman, Rs. 10 million for the 'Minister Incharge' (KA&NA), and Rs. 60 million for the six Azad Kashmir members. No details were provided about how they would spend 'their' money. Each would receive a further Rs. 5–10 million in the 2007–08 budget. This money offered these Azad Kashmiris the opportunity to garner support locally by devolving 'favours'. Equally, they were beholden to Islamabad for providing this money.

The Development Programme also allocated money to be spent outside Azad Kashmir. A 'Package to Kashmiri refugees' of Rs. 38.7 million was for projects in Jhang District, Punjab, to be undertaken by the Pakistan Works Department. There were also some funds in the 'Office Buildings' and 'Community Uplift Schemes' categories, with the latter category having the Development Programme's most expensive project: construction of the 'Ch. Ghulam Abbas Kashmir Housing Colony Purab, Distt Sheikhupura', Punjab, costing Rs. 209.5 million.[282] The Azad Kashmir Government may have 'inherited' this land from Maharaja Hari Singh,[283] and/or received it from the Punjab Government.[284] Money being spent outside Azad Kashmir reflects the fact that refugees from the former Jammu and Kashmir provinces of princely J&K living in Pakistan also elect members of the Azad Kashmir Legislative Assembly. This political situation is discussed in later chapters.

*Conclusion*

Since about 1949, Pakistanis have tightly controlled the people of Azad Kashmir. Azad Kashmiris have generally accepted what Pakistan and Pakistanis have done to them and their region. Given Azad Kashmiris' martial capabilities, they might have opposed some of the negative actions inflicted on them, particularly those by overbearing bureaucrats in the Ministry of Kashmir Affairs. However, the Azad Army's disappearance after the 1949 ceasefire limited their physical ability to do so. Equally, Karachi may have wanted to disband this potent anti-Indian force because it could have opposed Pakistan. Two further factors limited Azad Kashmiris' ability to oppose Pakistan. First, with no other nation to turn to, Azad Kashmiris were almost totally dependent on Pakistan for their survival and well-being. Second, Azad Kashmiris had always wanted to be part of this nation. They therefore accepted what Pakistan did to them, which, in any case, varied little from how most Pakistanis were treated. More positively, Azad Kashmiris were participating in the nation-building exercise of establishing and sustaining the Islamic Republic of Pakistan. They may not have been part of this nation legally, but they were with it, and for it, in all other ways. In a choice between India and Pakistan, Azad Kashmiris' choice was clear: be with Pakistan.

For its part, Pakistan had little to fear from a pro-Pakistan Azad Kashmir population devoid of options. Consequently, and often thoughtlessly, Pakistan imposed its will through the MKA, through its military or, after 1970, through its politicians, the Interim Constitution and associated measures. In doing so, Pakistan failed to empower 'its' people in Azad Kashmir, only allowing genuine self-government for a short period in the early 1970s via Azad Kashmir's presidential system. In the context of the Kashmir dispute, Pakistan's autocratic treatment of Azad Kashmiris is surprising. Pakistan claims to be administering 'its' part of J&K until the UN-supervised plebiscite resolves the Kashmir dispute. This means that the people of J&K, including Azad Kashmiris, could reject Pakistan in this poll, and that Pakistan's administration of Azad Kashmir (and the Northern Areas) is possibly temporary. But in fact, Pakistan's actions in Azad Kashmir, and the legal instruments that Pakistan has imposed to order the relationship with Azad Kashmir, suggest that Pakistan is integrating this region. As the Interim Constitution shows, all Azad Kashmiris and all of their political parties have no choice but to be pro-Pakistan: 'No person or political party in Azad Jammu and Kashmir shall be permitted to propagate against, or take part in activities prejudicial or detrimental to, the State's accession to Pakistan'.[285]

Although most Azad Kashmiris have not considered any option other than joining Azad Kashmir with Pakistan, the Interim Constitution gives them no choice. Hence, while Azad (Free) Kashmiris certainly are free from Indian control, they are, conversely, heavily dominated and almost totally controlled by Pakistan. Indeed, in all senses except legally, Azad Kashmir is fully integrated into Pakistan.

5

# THE POLITICAL SYSTEM

## DEMOCRATIC SHORTCOMINGS

*Introduction*

This chapter examines Azad Kashmir's political system and why it has major shortcomings. After Azad Kashmir's creation on 24 October 1947, Azad Kashmiris had to establish, then sustain, a political system. This has involved three phases. The first was the period immediately after the establishment of Azad Kashmir when the Muslim Conference dominated. The second was from about 1950 until 1970, when a heavily constrained, largely non-participatory and Pakistan-controlled system existed. The third was after 1970, when Azad Kashmiris received some say in their political affairs via a multi-party system and adult suffrage elections. Following the 1970 elections, polls were held in 1975, 1985, 1990, 1991, 1996, 2001 and 2006. All were 'influenced' by Islamabad. Chapter 8 discusses these elections.

For much of its existence, Pakistan's politicians and soldiers have directly ruled or indirectly influenced Azad Kashmir. Nevertheless, Azad Kashmiris have aspired for democracy, if only because people in Indian J&K have a form of this system, Pakistanis seemingly want it, and Indians enjoy it. While Pakistan is chiefly responsible for ensuring that Azad Kashmiris have not received a fully participatory, autonomous democracy, local politicians are also partly responsible. They have been disunited, engaging in rivalry to do with political leanings, age, status, geographical background and *biradari* or tribal connections (*biradari* is a Persian word meaning brotherhood, clan, tribe or fraternity;[1] it is explained below). They have succumbed to Pakistani manipulation or pressure. Furthermore, until India decisively defeated Pakistan in 1971, they could not decide whether to focus on liberating J&K or on making Azad Kashmir democratic and strong. Since then, while Azad Kashmiris have voted many times, Pakistani oversight still heavily influences their political system.

*A political overview*

J&K's division by fighting in the 'disturbed conditions' after Partition, meant that separate political systems were needed on both 'sides' of J&K.[2] This was easier to develop in Indian J&K: its international legal status as part of India was settled, while its leadership was unified and better focused. From late October 1947, Sheikh Abdullah's National Conference, backed by Jawaharlal Nehru and the Indian military, usurped Maharaja Hari Singh's regime, including the Praja Sabha which, while highly flawed, was a somewhat pluralistic body. Thereafter the National Conference, or derivatives of it, dominated Indian J&K's political system, by means including manipulation of elections, until the anti-Indian uprising began around 1988. The 100-seat Constituent Assembly established after elections in August 1951 reserved twenty-five seats for potential members in constituencies located in 'Pakistan-Occupied Kashmir': Azad Kashmir and the Northern Areas. This was because Kashmiri leaders also expected that the plebiscite would soon reunify J&K and that these people would need representation. With polls only held in areas under Indian control, these seats were never filled. It was therefore a sham in 1954 when the Constituent Assembly unanimously reaffirmed the legality of the Maharaja's accession to India.[3] It was not a fully representative body: people in Pakistan-Administered J&K had neither voted for or sent members to this body, nor had they been consulted on this specific issue.

In Pakistan-Administered J&K, there was no political system in which people could readily participate. No remnants of the Praja Sabha existed. After the Gilgit uprising in November 1947, Pakistan sent an administrator. He directly ruled this region, with no thought of popular participation for Gilgitis and Baltis previously ruled by local monarchs. In Azad Kashmir, the Muslim Conference dominated. After fighting divided J&K in 1947, the plurality of political parties in J&K diminished. The Muslim Conference became concentrated in Azad Kashmir; its main rival, the National Conference, dominated in Indian J&K. By April 1950, some 300,000 (about 25 per cent) of all J&K state subjects living either in Azad Kashmir or Pakistan had joined the Muslim Conference.[4] But it disappeared—or was forced to disappear because of its intolerable pro-Pakistan stance—from Indian J&K,[5] which benefited the National Conference. Equally, the National Conference's absence in Azad Kashmir, even though it had enjoyed little popularity in this area, deprived Azad Kashmiris of any effective political opposition. Consequently, each party was able to dominate its own area of J&K for a long period of time.

A further difficulty for participatory politics in J&K was the lack of a strong democratic tradition. This made it difficult—on both sides of J&K—to develop robust, inclusive democracies that allowed freedom of speech and regular free and fair elections. Political leaders of both conferences were less than democratic, with Muslim Conference leaders arguably worse due to the influence of Jinnah's aloof, dictatorial style as Muslim League leader compared with Nehru's more inclusive style. Hari Singh's autocratic rule also informed both conferences' leaders. Those who had been 'selected' to sit in the Praja Sabha had been powerless and never consulted; many former activists had been denied free speech and jailed for unacceptable views; all were without experience of a fully participatory democracy. Equally, few people in J&K pined for a 'democratic' system about which most, knew very little. Equally, few could recognise that many of their leaders' actions and practices were undemocratic. In Azad Kashmir, leaders and freedom fighters intent on liberating J&K also saw no virtue in installing a democracy that would distract people's attention from the freedom struggle. Nevertheless, apart from

## THE POLITICAL SYSTEM: DEMOCRATIC SHORTCOMINGS

providing a 'safety valve' for dissent, a robust democracy could have made Azad Kashmir attractive to people on the other 'side' of J&K allegedly suffering from Indian subjugation.

Other reasons exist for Azad Kashmir's lack of participatory democracy. The region was frequently led by a small coterie of male rivals—Azad Kashmir's leaders have always been men—whose priority was to obtain power, not develop a democracy. From October 1947 until about 1950, Azad Kashmir was essentially self-governing. Thereafter Pakistan came to the fore, imposing various systems on Azad Kashmir, including[6] one-party domination by the Muslim Conference, with intrusive oversight by the Ministry of Kashmir Affairs (1950–58); General Ayub Khan's martial law and (supposedly) partyless Basic Democracy elections in 1961 (1958–69); General Yahya Khan's brief martial law period which delivered a multi-party presidential system following Azad Kashmir's first genuine universal suffrage elections in 1970 (1970–74); a multi-party prime ministerial system that Zulfikar Ali Bhutto imposed in 1974, with elections in 1975 (1974–77); General Zia-ul-Haq's martial law, with (supposedly) multi-party elections in 1985 to a military-supervised 'legislature' (1977–88); a return to the multi-party prime ministerial system, with elections in 1990, 1991 and 1996; and a continuation of this system, with elections in 2001 and 2006, but with General Musharraf and the Pakistan military heavily overseeing it after October 1999. Leadership in these situations invariably reflected an unwritten 'law': Azad Kashmir's prime minister should be in favour with Pakistan's leader and reflect his/her political persuasion.

Overall, politics in Azad Kashmir has largely involved determining which pliable or acceptable Azad Kashmiri politician would be in power. Equally, Pakistan's often democratically unstable or military-dominated situation has not helped Azad Kashmir to develop a truly democratic system. Ironically however, it was a Pakistani military dictator, General Yahya Khan, who gave Azad Kashmir its first participatory political system in 1970, albeit after significant popular pressure near the end of a long period of unpopular military rule. In 1974, this presidential political system was changed to a prime ministerial system. This regularised Pakistan's relationship with Azad Kashmir and furthered Islamabad's control. Since then, Azad Kashmiri political leaders have been spending increasing amounts of time in Islamabad seeking Pakistani leaders' political 'blessings' to obtain or retain power. This was still happening in the 2006 election, the last election this book discusses.

### The dominance of the Muslim Conference

Azad Kashmiris' inability to develop a genuine participatory democracy stems from the way that the Azad Kashmir movement was founded in 1947, and run thereafter. From the outset, Muslim Conference members always led the anti-Maharaja, then anti-Indian, Azad Kashmir movement. This party was popular in Azad Kashmir; it had no local rival and there were no divergent views. In January 1949, pro-Pakistan J&K Muslims considered it their 'sole representative' and the only body with 'the authority to act on their behalf'.[7] While this exclusive situation was acceptable during the difficult period fighting against India, after the 1949 ceasefire Azad Kashmir's leaders had to engage in peacetime political and administrative activities until the promised plebiscite supposedly re-unified J&K and delivered it to Pakistan. Nevertheless party leaders, used to the Muslim Conference's dictatorial monopoly rule and expecting the plebiscite to be held soon, felt no need to establish a participatory political system. Thereafter, the major political issue locally was which individual would control the party, and subsequently control Azad Kashmir. This ongoing rivalry developed into divisive factionalism, a situation worsened because this 'government in exile', which comprised a single political party, had 'too much time for intrigue and backbiting'.[8] Factionalism would become a major and ongoing feature of Azad Kashmir politics.

The most obvious sign of the Muslim Conference's dominance was that, from 1947 to 1960, it appointed the Azad Kashmir president. He was always a party member 'holding the confidence' of the party's senior Working Committee.[9] Until 1952, he definitely ruled Azad Kashmir; thereafter, the Ministry of Kashmir Affairs was in effective control. The Muslim Conference's dominance arose from its prestige as the only political party in J&K willing to fight to join this state with Pakistan. Karachi also recognised the Muslim Conference-backed Azad Kashmir Government as the easiest option for Pakistan. Until the early 1950s, the Muslim Conference was unchallenged in Azad Kashmir. Indeed, its only rival was the MKA, whose desire to hobble it was simplified by the Muslim Conference's hierarchical structure and the party's increasingly divided leadership. However, the rudiments of a democratic system were absent—and unwanted. The only place where differences of opinion could be aired, shared or opposed was in the fledgling, but controlled, Azad Kashmir press (see below).[10] This stifled any Azad Kashmiris with differing views. It became an issue as the promised plebiscite receded and as Azad Kashmiris faced more pressing issues—about which various opinions and ideas existed. In the late 1950s, some Azad Kashmiris began to challenge the Muslim Conference's pre-eminent position in Azad Kashmir by forming other political parties. Martial law in 1958 ended these parties' existence—and the Muslim Conference's superior political position. Conversely, military rule enabled Azad Kashmiris to participate in a limited political process via the (supposedly) partyless Basic Democracies method (discussed below).

The Muslim Conference's dominance instituted and sustained an undemocratic tradition in Azad Kashmir politics. Procrastination about the plebiscite also discouraged the establishment of permanent political institutions. But perhaps the most significant anti-democratic force in Azad Kashmir was the spoiling role played by the Muslim Conference leader, Chaudhry Ghulam Abbas. As he was the Supreme Head of the Azad Kashmir Movement, a position higher than the Azad Kashmir president, power flowed downwards from the dictatorial Abbas. Until the MKA became all-powerful, he was able to control major appointments made in the region. These included nominating the Azad Kashmir president and attendees at the important All-Parties Kashmir Conference in Karachi in November 1955. From this conference, Azad Kashmir was supposed to get an elected legislature—a 'radical demand' that Abbas's major rival, Sardar Ibrahim, whose name Abbas had not approved to attend, 'vigorously' supported, partly to weaken Abbas.[11] Ibrahim opposed Abbas because Abbas would not share power, and perhaps had never contemplated this possibility. Equally, Abbas may have declined to head the Azad Kashmir administration and chose to live at Murree, midway between Rawalpindi

# THE POLITICAL SYSTEM: DEMOCRATIC SHORTCOMINGS

and Muzaffarabad, because he wanted to concentrate on leading the 'freedom movement'.[12] He therefore strongly opposed an elected legislature as, without such a body, Abbas's rivals would remain politically unempowered.[13] Equally, Abbas and his ally, Sardar Qayyum, considered that a multi-party system would distract Azad Kashmiris and weaken the Azad Kashmir movement's drive to unify J&K with Pakistan.[14] While seemingly pragmatic, this stance was undemocratic—but not surprising, as Abbas had been heavily influenced by Hari Singh's autocratic and undemocratic practices since at least 1931.

Ghulam Abbas's dictatorial tradition was later emulated by at least three Azad Kashmir presidents. Sardar Ibrahim governed without a Council of Ministers (or cabinet) for the first sixteen months of his second presidency (April 1957-April 1959). Ibrahim was in a strong position after being put 'on the throne' by direct order of Pakistan's Prime Minister H.S. Suhrawardy, from whom Ghulam Abbas was estranged.[15] Two other presidents, K.H. Khurshid (May 1959-August 1964) and Khan Abdul Hamid Khan (August 1964-October 1969), also governed without a cabinet. Khurshid adopted this system 'absolutely on his own', a 'bad precedent' that 'violated democratic norms practised the world over'.[16] However, having been installed by soldiers who disliked politicians and political parties, Khurshid may have chosen to emulate the military's effective, but undemocratic, command practices. He may also have been seeking to consolidate his position, as Abbas had supported Khurshid to prevent Ibrahim from retaining the presidency.[17] By ruling alone, Khurshid had no pro-Abbas or pro-Ibrahim cabinet colleagues to contend with. For Hamid Khan, the Kashmiri former Chief Justice of the Azad Kashmir High Court, there was no obligation to form a Council of Ministers.[18] The martial law regime had made him Azad Kashmir's president—not any political process. He also followed the precedent of his presidential predecessor, Khurshid.

While Khurshid did not advance participatory democracy, his sole rule of Azad Kashmir showed that Muslim Conference predominance had weakened and that military backing provided stability. Before martial law, Azad Kashmir had seven presidents in less than twelve years.[19] Conversely, Khurshid was in power for five years and three months, the longest period ever served by an Azad Kashmir president. Khurshid also was respected, even revered, by Azad Kashmiris, chiefly as he was strongly pro-Azad Kashmir,[20] although, in later years, he may have favoured independence for J&K.[21] Khurshid also defied the Muslim Conference and Abbas, with whom he fell out around 1960. Having endured the charade of being nominated president by the Muslim Conference[22]—a party which believed it had an almost divine right to provide Azad Kashmir's political leadership—after assuming office, Khurshid did not 'abide by [the party's] directives', despite an understanding that he would.[23] Khurshid could resist the Muslim Conference as he had his own contacts, particularly the all-powerful General Ayub. Equally, Abbas ignored the reality that Pakistani leaders would always support their surrogate in Azad Kashmir before deferring to the Muslim Conference.

Another issue for participatory democracy was Pakistan's ability to 'buy off' Azad Kashmiris. Muslim Conference leaders, particularly Ghulam Abbas, wanted to 'usurp political power' in Azad Kashmir 'without any elections'. This practice 'always succeeded, thanks to the various short-sighted governments of Pakistan' and Azad Kashmiris' desire to remain unified on the issue of J&K's international status.[24] But in addition, Pakistan basically bought off Muslim Conference politicians by offering them senior positions, or by getting the MKA to pay allowances that made them dependent on Pakistan. The MKA paid Ghulam Abbas an 'annual honorarium of Rs 25,000', and Mirwaiz Yusuf Shah Rs. 1,000 a month, and there were allowances ranging from Rs. 300 to 500 per month for more senior political workers, and Rs. 30 per month for the lowest category political workers. This largesse, along with the 'issuing of free rations', continued until the late 1950s,[25] but not without some leaders allegedly acquiring 'illegotten [sic] wealth and properties'.[26] Azad Kashmiri politicians appeared to put obtaining power and privilege via this 'institutionalised patronage' before other principles,[27] or before any desire to obtain a legislative assembly: 'as soon as [these politicians] were offered [the] loaves and fishes of power by others through undemocratic channels, even they forsook all their slogans and ate the booty'.[28] This partially explains why Azad Kashmir had so many presidents before the martial law period. It also explains why K.H. Khurshid, who apparently did not succumb to such temptations, was popular with Azad Kashmiris.

Azad Kashmir's lack of democracy caused disgruntlement but there was no outlet for this.[29] Throughout the 1950s, discontent was increasing. The plebiscite looked unlikely because of the United Nations' inability to get India-Pakistan agreement on demilitarising J&K. Dislike of Pakistan's stance on J&K was increasing. Events in Indian J&K, such as Abdullah's sacking and the reaffirmation of the Maharaja's accession to India, caused unease. There were few effective ways to accommodate, or diminish, dissident views. The press was weak and located outside Azad Kashmir. Some political parties had been operating, such as the Kisan Mazdoor Conference, but their existence was brief or they 'lacked teeth'.[30] Around 1951 Sardar Qayyum, disenchanted with Ghulam Abbas's conservative leadership of the Muslim Conference, formed the 'Independent Party' because Abbas 'was not prepared to take any risk' to liberate J&K.[31] Eventually a major political party, the Awami League (People's League), started a branch in Azad Kashmir in 1956.[32] Chaudhry Noor Hussain, a wealthy, politically astute Jat from Mirpur, convened it.[33] Members included Mirwaiz Yusuf Shah, a later president, and Chaudhry Hamidullah, a later general secretary; an important ally was Suhrawardy, Pakistan's Prime Minister from September 1956, who led the Awami League.[34] However, all overt political activity ended in 1958 when General Ayub imposed martial law on Pakistan and Azad Kashmir.

The Muslim Conference's fixation on J&K joining Pakistan also hindered the establishment of a democratic Azad Kashmir political system. This stance conveniently shifted attention from the region's deficiencies, with Azad Kashmiris' democratic rights getting 'lost into the jumble of the jargon of the accession issue'.[35] Many Azad Kashmiris, especially their leaders, were obsessed—to the detriment of almost everything else, including their own internal political freedom—with reuniting J&K and delivering it to Pakistan.[36] Their rallying cry was '*Kashmir Bane ga Pakistan*': 'Kashmir has to become Pakistan'.[37] Reflecting this obsession and believing they had a right to meet their 'brethren' living in Indian J&K, Azad Kashmiris attempted, on occasions, to cross the ceasefire line. This political gesture was a convenient way to distract attention from Azad Kashmir's deficiencies, including its lack of democracy. Azad Kashmiris knew that the Pakistan Army

## THE POLITICAL SYSTEM: DEMOCRATIC SHORTCOMINGS

would not allow anyone to breach the heavily-fortified ceasefire line, as this could lead to unforeseen consequences and the possible killing of protesters by Indian Army mines or gunfire.[38]

The 1958 Kashmir Liberation Movement made the most significant attempt to cross the ceasefire line. Initiated by Ghulam Abbas, its rallying cry was '*Kashmir Chalo*': 'Let's go to Kashmir'.[39] This slogan was surprising. For Azad Kashmiri participants such as Colonel Sher Ahmad Khan, Sardar Qayyum and K.H. Khurshid, they already were in 'Kashmir', with the Azad Kashmir Government the true administration for this state. Presumably they meant 'Let's go to the Kashmir Valley'. Such politicians seemingly wanted to protest because they were displeased with Sheikh Abdullah's rearrest in Indian J&K soon after release from five years' detention without trial.[40] Possibly they were dissatisfied with Pakistan's inability to liberate J&K and its inertia over resolving the Kashmir dispute. Most probably this was an attempt by Abbas and Qayyum to undermine their rival, Sardar Ibrahim, then Azad Kashmir President.[41] The imposition of martial law in 1958 emasculated this movement.[42]

Azad Kashmiris' obsession with the single issue of uniting J&K with Pakistan was short-sighted. It stifled the development of indigenous institutions as Azad Kashmiris waited for the promised plebiscite to resolve things. It discouraged Azad Kashmiris' political involvement, with dissent or opposition, including opposition through constructive political parties, hardly arising or needing to be accommodated. It meant that Azad Kashmir did not develop any positive political alternatives, democratic or otherwise, to those on offer in Indian J&K. Equally, Azad Kashmiris did not develop abilities or traditions of political argument, policy analysis and constructive criticism. This lack of political maturity was unhealthy for a region with leaders informed by the Maharaja's autocracy and already having a dictatorial political structure. Finally, it allowed Pakistan, which had its own major democratic shortcomings, to dictate the political system—democratic, martial or otherwise—that Azad Kashmir should have. Azad Kashmiris willingly accepted this because they were keenly pro-Pakistan: 'For us Pakistan is a model, positive or negative. We follow her blindly'.[43]

*Endemic factionalism, particularly in the 1950s*

A major consequence of the Muslim Conference's domination of Azad Kashmir was factionalised politics. This prevented the development of a stable democratic system. Factionalism began as early as 24 October 1947 when Sardar Ibrahim became Azad Kashmir President, an appointment some senior Muslim Conference leaders rejected. Once Ghulam Abbas arrived in Pakistan in March 1948 after his release from jail in Indian J&K,[44] he immediately became involved in Muslim Conference politics. Thereafter, a political struggle with Sardar Ibrahim continued for many years. Following Abbas's death from cancer on 18 December 1968,[45] his political ally Sardar Qayyum, became the unequivocal leader of the anti-Ibrahim faction. Reputed to be the 'man who set the [military] ball rolling in Kashmir',[46] Qayyum, who had been leader of the Muslim Conference for some time,[47] proved to be a capable grassroots politician. He rejuvenated this party, continued his faction's rivalry with Ibrahim, and won the 1970 Azad Kashmir presidential election.[48] Because of the longevity of these factions and their leaders—Ibrahim and Qayyum were still politically active into the 2000s—it is important to examine the issue of factionalism, particularly in the 1950s, when it was endemic.[49]

Factionalism began when Sardar Ibrahim became leader of the Azad Kashmir movement in 1947. With the Muslim Conference President, Ghulam Abbas, in jail, few party members wanted this role because the movement might fail or because Hari Singh would punish them for being 'Chief Rebel'.[50] These included Chaudhry Hamidullah and Mirwaiz Yusuf Shah, who both claimed divisively to be acting party president after Abbas was jailed in September 1946.[51] After Ibrahim became Azad Kashmir President and then succeeded in sustaining the fledgling anti-Maharaja movement, some Muslim Conference members became envious of the younger man's success. Age and status are important factors in Azad Kashmir's tribal- or *biradari*-based politics.[52] Within a few months, the sardar (tribal leader) was so successful he became the hero of the Azad Kashmir movement. This was 'a meteoric rise' comparable with Abdullah's 'emergence' as the Lion of Kashmir during the 1931 anti-Maharaja uprising.[53] Ibrahim's popularity and prestige were enhanced by his inclusion in the first Pakistan delegation to the UN in early 1948. He became so popular that even Liaquat Ali Khan was 'getting uneasy' and 'wanted to eliminate or at least disgrace him'.[54] Apart from such senior Pakistanis, Ibrahim's only other real rival was Ghulam Abbas. An older man with a much longer political career, Abbas was still in jail.

Competition between the Muslim Conference and its governmental arm, the Azad Kashmir Government, quickly formed a basis for factionalism. As early as December 1947, *CMG* reported a 'sensational political upheaval' in Azad Kashmir with rivalry between the supposedly superior Muslim Conference and the supposedly subordinate Azad Kashmir Government.[55] Pro-Abbas elements, mainly from eastern Jammu Province and jealous of Ibrahim (as may have been Abbas), controlled the party.[56] The 'junior man' from Poonch, Sardar Ibrahim, led the government.[57] The Muslim Conference had

> snarled its protest against what it considers to be the 'dictatorial' attitude of the [Ibrahim-led] Azad Cabinet. The latter, it is learned, has not seen eye to eye with the Muslim Conference on certain matters of policy and their reported defiance of the Muslim Conference nominees in no way helps to make a brighter picture.[58]

Prophetically confirming Azad Kashmir's future factionalism, *CMG* reported that 'Chaudhry Hamidullah, the Muslim Conference Acting President, nominated by the President, Chaudhry Ghulam Abbas ... was given a grim reception at the last meeting at Azad Kashmir headquarters, which was supposed to act as a taste of things to come'.[59] The Azad Kashmir President, Sardar Ibrahim, controlled these 'headquarters'; his government's relationship with the Muslim Conference would cause further problems.

In March 1948 factionalism became entrenched when the actual Muslim Conference President, Ghulam Abbas, arrived in Pakistan, reclaimed his position and quickly sought to assert himself—especially over Sardar Ibrahim. For a few weeks, Azad Kashmir had two leaders: Abbas as Muslim Conference President, and Ibrahim as Azad Kashmir President. On 9 April 1948 the older, more prestigious

## THE POLITICAL SYSTEM: DEMOCRATIC SHORTCOMINGS

Quaid-i-Millat (leader of the community)[60] imposed himself—supposedly 'at the request of the Azad Kashmir Cabinet'—as 'Supreme Head of the Azad Kashmir Movement', after which Abbas allowed Ibrahim to retain his (thereafter inferior) position as 'President of the Azad Kashmir Government'.[61] Yielding to pressure from Abbas, his colleagues and Pakistan, Ibrahim capitulated.[62] With due supplication, he stated that Chaudhry Ghulam Abbas

> undoubtedly, is the supreme head of the whole organisation of the Muslim Conference and also the Azad Government, which is directly under the Muslim Conference. I, as the President of the Azad Kashmir Government have placed myself and the Government at the complete disposal and direction of Chaudhry Ghulam Abbas Khan and I have also placed all matters at his disposal including reshuffling and reconstruction of the Government in any matter Chaudhury Saheb [sic] likes. There [sic] has been complete unanimity on all points that have been discussed and on all decisions that have been agreed upon.[63]

While still Azad Kashmir President, Ibrahim was under Abbas in his newly-created position of 'supreme head [of] the whole organisation of the Muslim Conference and also the Azad Kashmir Government' with 'full powers to reconstitute the Azad Kashmir Cabinet if necessary'.[64] This arrangement established a hierarchy within the Azad Kashmir movement whereby all power actually (until 1952) or theoretically (until martial law in 1958) resided with the head of the Muslim Conference. Initially, this empowered Abbas.

The Abbas-Ibrahim arrangement did not end this matter. Indeed, Abbas's assertiveness, Ibrahim's subjugation and the separation of powers created further rivalry. Portending future disenchantment Sardar Ibrahim, when returning to Trarkhel, then Azad Kashmir's capital, was greeted in Muzaffarabad by some 10,000 people.[65] Disingenuously, he told bureaucrats there 'to regard themselves as servants of the people not as agents of an imperialistic regime', by which he possibly meant Abbas's regime.[66] The Abbas-Ibrahim arrangement also displeased people in J&K. For Prem Nath Bazaz, the Kashmiri politician jailed by Abdullah for favouring J&K's accession to Pakistan, Ibrahim's capitulation was

> resented by all progressive and secular minded Kashmiris ... It was evident to the revolutionists that [the] Azad Kashmir movement had ceased to be what it professed to be and was now only a tussle between two designing politicians for capture of power ... Azad Kashmir ... was no more a democratic Government of the areas liberated from the Dogra rule, but a piece of land where power hungry political workers were fighting against each other to become rulers more despotic than the hated Dogras.[67]

For Bazaz, this was factionalism.

The Abbas-Ibrahim arrangement divided the Azad Kashmir movement. Within the bureaucracy, government employees 'immediately divided into pro-Ibrahim and pro-Abbas factions with the result that Azad Kashmir had two parallel administrations'. This became 'an almost permanent feature of the [Azad Kashmir] administration'.[68] On the basis of geography, factions grouped around either leader. Jammuites, many of whom were refugees, crowded around Abbas, who as chairman of the powerful 'Kashmir Refugees Committee', helped find and resettle displaced people.[69] Poonchis involved in the Azad Kashmir movement and its early activities rallied around Ibrahim. A smaller third group comprised ethnic Kashmiris, most of whom had left or been forced out of the Kashmir Valley for political reasons. Some hovered around the religious figure Mirwaiz Yusuf Shah, and the 'Kashmir Muslim Conference' formed around September 1949.[70] Other people outside these groups, such as Baltis from the Northern Areas dislocated by fighting in 1947–49, had no obvious leader.

While Ghulam Abbas had major advantages over Sardar Ibrahim, the junior man also had strengths. The older Abbas had more prestige, having been a 'towering personality in J&K Muslim politics since 1931' who was jailed a number of times for political activities.[71] In 1941 Abbas, with his colleague and rival Mirwaiz Yusuf Shah, revived the Muslim Conference. In a precursor to Azad Kashmir's later factionalism, both were disenchanted with Sheikh Abdullah and his National Conference's secularism. From 1941, Abbas was the Muslim Conference's President, the senior party position. He lost this position only when Hari Singh jailed him (again) in 1946. The understanding then was that, when he was freed, both the presidency and undisputed party leadership would revert to Abbas. When this happened in 1948, many senior Muslim Conference members were conveniently still in Indian J&K, which meant that Abbas, as President, could wield his power 'unquestioned'.[72] Finally, Abbas knew the major political figures in J&K, Pakistan and India, and they knew him, if only by reputation. They included Liaquat Ali Khan, which was important. Indeed, Abbas was so highly thought of that he may have been one of Jinnah's two nominated political successors.[73] Overall, Abbas was more important, more experienced and better connected than the relative newcomer, Ibrahim. He was the only serious rival in J&K to the high profile, popular Abdullah. Furthermore, being in jail during a period of significant change in the subcontinent had whetted his appetite for power.

Conversely, Ibrahim's inexperience and the method of his appointment denied him the political authority to immediately challenge Abbas as undisputed leader of the Azad Kashmir movement. Nevertheless, his prestige and 'recent fame' as leader of this movement and as Azad Kashmir's initial President, plus his own important support base among Poonch's powerful, military-capable Sudhan tribe where he was the 'uncrowned king', made him a serious rival.[74] Another factor that increased Ibrahim's position over time was the autocratic Abbas's declining popularity.[75] While Ibrahim's yielding to Abbas resolved their relationship initially, it ultimately led to further political difficulties and 'polemics'.[76] By January 1949, rumours appeared about 'differences' between them.[77] These rumours, involving 'obstruction, intrigue and false propaganda',[78] proved correct. M.A. Gurmani tried to salve the Abbas-Ibrahim relationship in late 1949 but failed, which probably suited Gurmani's divisive agenda.[79] The politicians' rivalry continued, with varying support from Pakistani leaders, depending on who was in power in Karachi. Ultimately, the only thing the two men had in common was that they were lawyers. This was a recipe for an argument, not an alliance.

The Abbas-Ibrahim rift was complete by 30 May 1950 when Abbas announced a reconstituted Azad Kashmir Government that did not include Ibrahim.[80] According to Ibrahim, Abbas had not consulted him about this new government,[81] although Gurmani discussed it with Ibrahim and advised him to resign.[82] Ibrahim was replaced as President by the former Defence Minister, Colonel Ali Ahmed Shah, a Mirpuri with pretensions given his self-promotion to 'Captain General'.[83] Ibrahim's removal occurred shortly after, and perhaps because of, Gurmani's pro-

## THE POLITICAL SYSTEM: DEMOCRATIC SHORTCOMINGS

motion to Minister for Kashmir Affairs in April 1950.[84] Equally, pro-Pakistan forces wanted to present a unified front before the United Nations' Special Representative, Sir Owen Dixon, arrived in Karachi on 1 June 1950.[85] Conveniently, Dixon's visit diverted attention from Ibrahim's diminution by the 'Supreme Head', who was seen by some as 'unconstitutional, unwanted and Franco-minded'.[86] Equally, Abbas was seeking to resolve 'diametrically opposite views' on the future of the Muslim Conference and Azad Kashmir.[87] Abbas wanted the region to be politically unified to maintain the party's stance on J&K and to prosecute the 'freedom movement'; Ibrahim wanted it to be more democratic.[88] Ibrahim's sacking set the factional tone for the decade.

*Uprisings in Poonch*

Abbas's sacking of Ibrahim in May 1950 provoked an uprising in the Poonch area where Sardar Ibrahim, many ex-servicemen and many demobilised Azad Army soldiers lived. This was possibly the most serious anti-government episode in Azad Kashmir's history. I say 'possibly' as few primary or secondary source documents exist about violent events in Poonch in the 1950s. Only a few Azad Kashmiris, including brave journalists such as Mir Abdul Aziz, wrote about these events. Yusuf Saraf's book discusses them, but it was published twenty years after they took place. There are many reasons for this lack of information. The parts of Poonch where troubles occurred were remote and difficult to access, for journalists among others. Pakistan and Azad Kashmir authorities 'discouraged' reporting,[89] while they 'understandably withheld' details of any uprising to avoid appearing to be suppressing pro-Pakistan people.[90] Indeed, Pakistan displayed 'extreme reticence' to report a 'problem' in Azad Kashmir 'causing concern to the authorities', while at the same time it provided 'extensive publicity' about negative events in Indian J&K.[91] Given India's actions against Kashmiris, Pakistan did not want to embarrass pro-Pakistan forces in J&K and negate their morally superior position. If the 1955 Poonch uprising is any guide, according to H.S. Suhrawardy, Pakistan's Minister of Law, 'a dozen or more restrictive laws', including the 'Official Secrets Act' and the 'Safety Act against the Press', prevented Pakistani journalists from reporting certain such sensitive matters.[92]

A final reason why news about events in Poonch was scarce is that no printing presses existed in Azad Kashmir to publish newspapers. The 'dozen newspapers' run by Azad Kashmiris or J&K refugees had offices located in 'border districts of the Punjab'—that is, within Pakistan.[93] This made timely news collection in Azad Kashmir difficult. The Ministry of Kashmir Affairs also prevented '[Azad] Kashmiri journalists' from 'enjoying more freedom and facilities'. It subjected newspapers to intrusive censorship; its selective advertising revenue had 'political strings' attached that threatened the viability of non-conformist newspapers; it controlled the release of newsprint. The vagaries of Pakistan's postal system also made getting newspapers and periodicals to Azad Kashmiris a slow, difficult, uncertain process.[94] Hence, authorities did not need to hide news about Poonch; it was unobtainable or newspapers chose not to report it.

The following provides a limited understanding of events in Poonch in 1950–51. From around the end of 1949, divisions and disenchantment increased among

Azad Kashmiris. Some were frustrated that the plebiscite was not happening; some believed Pakistan could do more to resolve the Kashmir dispute. Politically, Ghulam Abbas's installation of 'The Rules of Business of Azad Kashmir 1950' gave him enormous power,[95] as power flowed downwards from the dictatorial Supreme Head of the Azad Kashmir Movement.[96] Sardar Ibrahim, in addition, did not take his 1950 sacking gracefully. After learning of his dismissal when it was announced on the radio,[97] he 'reacted forcefully',[98] 'stirring up an agitation ... throughout Azad Kashmir. Its major effect was in Poonch, and people there were poised for rebellion'.[99] A major uprising occurred around the Rawalakot area of Poonch amongst displeased Sudhans, which Ibrahim claimed lasted for seventeen months. The Pakistan Army's 12th Division fought in this area and apparently had 500 soldiers taken prisoner.[100]

After the 'bomb-shell' of Ibrahim's dismissal,[101] Colonel (Retired) Sher Ahmad Khan, a *sardar* and 'scion of the Sudhan tribe [and] the senior most military officer from Poonch', was made a cabinet minister with responsibility for defence, education and health.[102] This was done to placate Sudhans and weaken Ibrahim's leadership.[103] In a speech on 4 June 1950, the new minister, seeking to stem divisions growing around Abbas or Ibrahim, 'appealed to Kashmir Muslims to stand united under the banner of their sole representative body—the All-Jammu and Kashmir Muslim Conference'. Similarly, the new Finance Minister, 'Syed Nazir Hussain Shah, ... appeal[ed] for one leader, one organisation and one ideal'—all of which were unspecified—as 'the only guarantee of success'.[104] On 2 June,[105] Colonel Sher Ahmad tellingly resigned because 'his community, the Sudhans, were strongly opposed to his appointment in view of the practical dismissal of their Chief, Sardar Ibrahim'.[106]

Concurrently, 'defiance of Authority [sic] ... began to grow in strength' in Poonch.[107] In September 1950, *The Times* reported that 'for some weeks past, there have been sporadic disturbances in Poonch ... and shooting and fighting between the factions'. The 'problem has proved sufficiently unyielding and of sufficient significance' that Liaquat Ali Khan was to visit Rawalpindi 'with the settling of the trouble [in Poonch] as one of the main objects of his visit'.[108] By the beginning of 1951, violent demonstrations had occurred,[109] particularly in the Rawalakot and Palandri areas of Poonch,[110] where Sudhans displeased with the sacking of their 'man', Ibrahim, opposed the replacement government.[111] There also had been a 'show-down between the Sudhans and the [Pakistan] Army contingents posted in the area', which 'caused great concern to the Central Government'.[112]

By the beginning of 1951, there was 'practically no Government in large areas of Poonch, particularly in the tehsils of Pallandri and Rawalakot'.[113] In June 1951 Sardar Ibrahim, Colonel Sher Ahmad, Mir Abdul Aziz and others, formed a parallel government in Poonch.[114] It tried to democratise Azad Kashmir politics,[115] something Ibrahim and Aziz had sought since the late 1940s. At the same time, some opponents of Abbas raised the slogan of 'democracy or death', called for the Muslim Conference's 'reorganisation', for 'constitutional and democratic methods' to elect Azad Kashmir governments, and engaged in civil disobedience in which 'nearly 500 persons were arrested'.[116] This possibly included the 'large scale arrests' of followers of Sardar Ibrahim, who had been interned at his residence in September 1950, but had later escaped.[117]

## THE POLITICAL SYSTEM: DEMOCRATIC SHORTCOMINGS

The Poonch situation became so bad that the Azad Kashmir Police could not control it. Members of the Punjab Constabulary were brought in. The Pakistan Army's 12th Division, with headquarters in Murree and with forces already deployed in Azad Kashmir,[118] joined in the suppression, declaring martial law in September.[119] The fighting was not one-sided. Some Sudhans captured 120 soldiers from Mianwali, in Punjab, and their arms.[120] This improved Sardar Ibrahim's position when he later negotiated with Gurmani, whom Liaquat had ordered to 'work out a peaceful agreement providing for the return of the confiscated arms in return for the dismissal of the Muslim Conference Government in Muzaffarabad'. Indeed, Liaquat was about to dismiss this government in Rawalpindi on 16 October 1951 but was shot first. By then, events in Poonch appeared to have calmed down, although Sudhans were not fully placated, nor had factionalism ended.

Liaquat's assassination meant that Karachi did not immediately resolve Azad Kashmir's factional problems. Three of the four prime ministers who followed Liaquat were Bengalis: Nazimuddin, Bogra and Suhrawardy. Ghulam Abbas lost an ally in Liaquat, while his replacements were less interested in the Kashmir dispute and in local leadership struggles. Furthermore, they were possibly more inclined towards democracy, a factor that further challenged Abbas. In the post-Liaquat era, Abbas's position appeared to weaken. Dixon's mission had failed; Graham's mission was failing; Ibrahim, as former Azad Kashmir President, had been actively making statements, sometimes provocative;[121] Gurmani had become Minister for Interior; and elections in Indian J&K had elected its Constituent Assembly. Likewise, in Azad Kashmir, pressure was increasing for some internal democracy. Such demands were not new. When Abbas had first arrived in Pakistan, he received a memorandum signed by 200 Muslim Conference workers 'expressing the need for a provisional legislative assembly for Azad Kashmir'.[122]

Towards the end of 1951, Pakistan's Prime Minister, Khwaja Nazimuddin, had 'longs talks with [the] Azad Supremo', Abbas, and other Azad Kashmir leaders[123] about creating an all-party government.[124] In early December 1951, the Azad Kashmir Government resigned and was replaced by a transitional government led by Mirwaiz Yusuf Shah.[125] Noting that the 'absence of a full representative government [wa]s a very painful situation', Mirwaiz intended to resolve the 'existing discords' by 'cleansing and clarifying the internal politics of Azad Kashmir' and 'taking them out of the context of personal rivalries'.[126] At the same time, Abbas decided with a 'heavy heart' to withdraw from politics, providing no reasons why.[127] In April 1952, he clarified his position: he had withdrawn from 'Kashmir politics' not 'Kashmir policies'.[128] This presumably meant he would continue to try to influence Karachi on J&K matters and look after issues such as refugee welfare. Similarly, as part of Nazimuddin's talks, Ibrahim may have agreed to renounce immediate attempts to become Azad Kashmir president.

On 5 December 1951, the Muslim Conference announced elections to its general council.[129] These were finally held on 18 May 1952 in Muzaffarabad, with Sardar Ibrahim elected Muslim Conference president for 1952–53. A tearful Ibrahim told 200 delegates that he 'would serve [the] Kashmir cause most selflessly and most faithfully'.[130] He called on Mirwaiz's caretaker government to resign to give way to 'a popular, duly-elected Government', which it did on 19 June 1952.[131] Despite Ibrahim's statement, Karachi had imposed this new government on Azad Kashmir. The new cabinet acknowledged as much on 22 June: 'look[ing] to the people, from whom [it] derived strength', it thanked 'Khwaja Nazimuddin, Prime Minister of Pakistan and Dr Mahmud Hussain, Minister for Kashmir Affairs, for the great encouragement received from them on the eve of the new Cabinet assuming control of the administration'.[132] Karachi was back in control in Azad Kashmir.

In a pragmatic conciliatory gesture to appease the factions, the new government sworn in on 21 June 1952 had 'representatives of various interests and sections of Azad Kashmir and Jammu and Kashmir'.[133] The President was the Sudhan Poonchi, Colonel Sher Ahmad, who was possibly a compromise candidate because Ibrahim was unacceptable.[134] Ministers included the Mirpuri Jat, Noor Hussain and the rising Sardar Qayyum, an Abbasi (or Dhond/Dhund) from Bagh.[135] (The term 'Abbasi' does not refer to Qayyum's political links with Ghulam Abbas.) Others were the Jammuite Chaudhry Hamidullah, and a Kashmiri, Pir Zia-ud-Din, from the 'Abbas group'.[136] With tension still present amongst Azad Kashmir politicians, Sher Ahmad's sole focus was to 'intensify the struggle for the freedom of occupied Kashmir and for the betterment of my brethren already liberated, particularly refugees, by bringing together representatives from various sections in Azad Kashmir and Jammu and Kashmir'.[137]

Sher Ahmad was well placed to do this: he claimed to have no affiliations with any group, including the Muslim Conference's Working Committee.[138] His Sudhan ethnicity helped as it was 'considered essential to have a Sudhan as Head of the government' to appease Poonchis still displeased with Ibrahim's earlier sacking and given the 'uncertain and unhappy' law and order situation in Poonch.[139] Poonchis appear to have accepted Sher Ahmad: 'several thousand' World War I and World War II veterans gave him a rousing reception in Palandri in early July.[140]

Sher Ahmad quickly became a captive of his main supporter, the Ministry of Kashmir Affairs, which had initially placed him in power. During Ahmad's tenure, the MKA secured its position as the most powerful and best organised 'faction' in Azad Kashmir. This included getting Ahmed to revise Azad Kashmir's Rules of Business in October 1952 in favour of Pakistan and the MKA. Thereafter all officials, including the president, served in Azad Kashmir at the MKA's pleasure.[141] Mirwaiz Yusuf Shah, who had become an 'Honorary Adviser to the Minister for Kashmir Affairs in regard to the matters pertaining to the Kashmir Valley', may have helped this revision.[142] This reflected an aspect of Azad Kashmir's factionalism. The Muslim Conference, despite the mild-mannered Sher Ahmad being in power, was still divided into the Abbas, Ibrahim and Mirwaiz factions. The last-named was the weakest; it was prepared to offer the MKA assistance in return for support and to weaken its opponents. Ahmad's supplicant relationship with the MKA partly explains his longevity at the top: he lasted from June 1952 to May 1956, then an unprecedented term as Azad Kashmir president.

However, Sudhans again displayed displeasure in 1955 when they 'rose up against the [Sher Ahmad] regime set up by the MKA'.[143] As with the 1950–51 Poonch uprising, we know little about this 1955 uprising. One source of Sudhan displeasure was the Azad Kashmir Government, which Gurmani and the MKA reconstituted in 1954; it was possibly engaging in corruption, bribery and embezzlement.[144] Another source was the lack of a plebiscite, with some senior Azad

# THE POLITICAL SYSTEM: DEMOCRATIC SHORTCOMINGS

Kashmiris calling for 'direct action' in September 1953 'to wrest control of Kashmir from India's hands'.[145] A third was Sudhans' continuing displeasure with Ibrahim's 1951 sacking. A fourth was the lack of an 'elected legislature' for Azad Kashmir,[146] as the Sudhans' 'uncrowned king', Ibrahim, and others had campaigned for since mid-1954.[147] Their actions seemed vindicated when the All-Parties Kashmir Conference in Karachi in November 1955 seemingly concurred with their desire. Even though for Ibrahim the second Poonch uprising was more of an agitation, with big meetings, many protests, taxes not being paid and few casualties,[148] conversely, the disturbing events in Poonch actually may have inspired the holding of the All-Parties Kashmir Conference. Even so, Azad Kashmir was denied a legislature. Apart from MKA obstructionism, Ghulam Abbas and Sardar Qayyum also opposed an elected body as it might weaken the liberation movement's efforts.[149]

On balance, it seems that the 1955 Poonch uprising involved an 'armed rebellion' to support Ibrahim's strong demand to have the Azad Kashmir president directly elected.[150] Sudhans' anti-government actions started in February 1955 with an assassination attempt in Poonch on the Azad Kashmir President, Sher Ahmad, from which he had a 'miraculous escape'. Matters escalated when police sought to arrest an 'absconding accused' by entering a mosque at Palandri. Thereafter, Sudhans clashed with the Pakistan Army, possibly soldiers from XV Corps, and the Punjab Constabulary, which dealt with the insurrection brutally.[151] Similarly, the Punjab Prosecuting Agency was 'a terror' to Azad Kashmiris, particularly those incarcerated.[152] On 3 July 1955, *CMG* reported that the situation in Poonch was 'very grave indeed'.[153] According to Saraf, the troubles in Poonch lasted 'several months', during which time the Sudhans again set up a 'parallel' government. Some Sudhan fighters were former soldiers. As punishment for their rebellious actions, General Ayub Khan had 'the pensions of ex-servicemen [living] in the tehsils of Pallandri and Rawalakot' withheld until 1960.[154]

The Pakistan Army, Punjab Constabulary and Punjab Prosecuting Agency were alleged to have committed atrocities in 1955 in Poonch. Some were detailed in 1956 in two documents: a *Memorandum to Members of the Pakistan Constituent Assembly* by the 'All-Jammu and Kashmir Muslim Conference', and a 'Humble Appeal' to the Members of the Constituent Assembly of Pakistan.[155] Published by the Indian Information Service, the two documents could have been clever Indian forgeries—although India submitted them to the United Nations in 1957, which suggests otherwise.[156] The first document's author was Ghulam Mohammad, 'Publicity Secretary', a Kashmiri with seven years of involvement in the Muslim Conference, who was exiled from Srinagar in 1949 and became Azad Kashmir's Revenue Minister on 13 June 1950.[157] Three of the four people who signed the 'Humble Appeal' appear in Saraf's and Aziz's books: (Khwajah) Abdus Salam Yatu, (Khwajah) Ghulam Nabi Gilkar Anwar and Mir Abdul Aziz, who surprisingly, did not write elsewhere about this major event. The signatories were Kashmiris, not Sudhans. On balance, these documents have some veracity.

The two documents detailed some events in Poonch in 1955, probably from stories heard, people met, or secondary sources. Sardar Qayyum's observations below about events in 1955 corroborate the documents' claims. Ghulam Mohammad spoke of: 'great terror and terrorisation' in Poonch—the Azad Kashmir Government, under MKA instructions, 'deliberately and malafide subjected the people of Poonch during the last few months to ruthless suppression'—and of 'disturbances' and 'tragic happenings' in Poonch. He claimed that: 'a dozen houses were blasted with dynamite'; and there had been 'Ruthless shelling and random firing by mortar guns ... resulting in many deaths'. Other events detailed: the 'imposition of martial law'; police raids on villages; plundering; arrests of 400 people who were under detention in 'the concentration camp at Pullandri'; arrests without warrants; additional 'concentration camps' at Bagh, Bari and Sarsawah; women being 'arrested and subjected to unbecoming and insulting treatment'; 'teen-aged boys having been subjected to unnatural vices by men of Platoon 14 of the P[unjab] C[onstabulary] in Soon village'; looting and robbery; confessions being extracted under torture; and lawyers being 'overawed' and threatened by the police. Perhaps worst of all—from the (embarrassed) point of view of Azad Kashmir freedom fighters—was the document's statement that 'terrorised by the situation [in Azad Kashmir] 3000 people have gone over to the Indian side of the cease-fire line'. The 'Humble Appeal' document was shorter and more general, but it also mentioned a 'prison at Pullandri' that housed 340 men when its capacity was thirty-six prisoners. Both documents called for a commission of inquiry and for Azad Kashmir to receive a legislative assembly. It was not surprising that the Indian Information Service published such embarrassing documents.

Sardar Qayyum also provides details about the 1955 Poonch uprising.[158] Ibrahim was part of the problem: he had been 'busy stirring up agitation ... throughout Azad Kashmir' (although Ibrahim does not discuss either of the Poonch incidents in his book).[159] Qayyum also states that a parallel government was 'crushed by military action', with the 'whole area [of Poonch] given over to the control of the [Pakistan] Army'. This saw 'an exchange of firing between the army and the people' at 'Rawalakot, Palandri and Baral', after which the 'Punjab Constabulary was also summoned'. It 'indulged in excesses in order to crush the armed revolt'. These included dragging dignitaries through bazaars; making some people 'bark like dogs' or 'mew like cats'; floggings; cramming small jails with excessive numbers of people; and, tormenting and humiliating people in various others ways, including all day detention and pulling of ears. Qayyum believed that some actions may have been justified to restore law and order as Poonch also had lawlessness—people refusing to pay taxes or openly carrying arms, detention of government officials, unauthorised cutting of forest trees, and damage to property. Had India attacked then, Qayyum believed Azad Kashmiris 'would have been unable to repel [it]'.[160] Overall for Qayyum, the 1955 Poonch uprising was 'a bad spot in our history', while the way in which the Punjab Constabulary 'dealt with the insurrection [wa]s a matter of great shock and sorrow'.[161]

Troubles in Poonch appear to have subsided when the important 'All Parties Conference on Kashmir' took place in Karachi in November 1955. Equally, this inclusive conference may have helped placate disgruntled Azad Kashmiris. Certainly, by mid-1956, Azad Kashmir officials had 'given instructions to their own people and sympathisers across the cease-fire line not to resort to violence'. In Azad Kashmir, these were 'strictly enforced; the former guerrillas ha[d] been disarmed (by show of force where necessary), [and] agitation for the renewal of hostilities severely curbed'.[162] In 1957, Poonch returned to normalcy when Ibrahim regained power.

# THE POLITICAL SYSTEM: DEMOCRATIC SHORTCOMINGS

Despite events in Poonch, Sher Ahmad continued his long presidency. His cabinet was reconstituted 'a number of times' between 1952 and 1956, with Sardar Qayyum leaving in 1952, Chaudhry Hamidullah in 1953 and Noor Hussain in 1954.[163] They were replaced by Chaudhry Abdul Karim, a Mirpuri, Mohammed Abdul Hamid, from Muzaffarabad, and Khwaja Ghulam Mohammad, a Kashmiri.[164] After a self-enforced break, Ghulam Abbas returned to political activities around March 1953. The reason for his political reinvigoration was unknown. It was possibly that the Pakistan Government had not recognised the 1952 election of Muslim Conference officials as the 'sole representative body' for Azad Kashmiris; or he may have been a simple lust for power.[165] Ghulam Abbas may have been inspired by events in Indian J&K where Sheikh Abdullah started to challenge Indian rule.[166] By 1956, three factions still existed in the Muslim Conference: Abbas's, Ibrahim's, and the smaller Mirwaiz faction.[167]

In May 1956, the Azad Kashmir presidential merry-go-round recommenced. Mirwaiz Yusuf Shah, with the MKA's approval, served again for a short period as caretaker President, during which the MKA 'pushed through' its 'Political Parties Settlement scheme'[168] to 'merge' and reunify the Muslim Conference's three factions. At a conference in Muzaffarabad in September 1956 attended by a 'jointly-agreed list of 150 political workers, mostly of [the] pre-1947 period', Sardar Ibrahim was 'elected' President of the 'united Muslim Conference', with Sardar Qayyum, from Abbas's faction, elected Azad Kashmir President.[169] On Qayyum's agenda was a more 'active' policy to try to reunify J&K.[170] The MKA, with the consent of Pakistan's Prime Minister, Chaudhry Muhammad Ali, had predetermined this 'election'.[171] In April 1957, Qayyum resigned as President, possibly because Pakistan's latest Prime Minister, Suhrawardy, disliked him;[172] equally, the MKA abhorred his disobedience to instructions,[173] while some 'colleagues' in the supposedly reunified Muslim Conference opposed him having power, including Ghulam Abbas, Qayyum's supposed ally.[174]

With some reluctance[175] but on the insistence of Suhrawardy,[176] Sardar Ibrahim replaced Sardar Qayyum after the Muslim Conference Working Group 'elected' him President on 12 April 1957.[177] This did not end factionalism in Azad Kashmir. Indeed 'inter-group strife again became vocal', possibly because Ibrahim ruled without a cabinet for sixteen months.[178] Ghulam Abbas soon complained to Suhrawardy in Rawalpindi;[179] in 1958 he organised the Kashmir Liberation Movement's attempt to cross the ceasefire line, to undermine Ibrahim.[180] Conversely, Abbas was unpopular with Azad Kashmiris wanting democracy: the slogan 'Obstruction Thy Name is Abbas suggested their disdain.[181] Despite Azad Kashmir's factionalism, Ibrahim served for two years until K.H. Khurshid, with Ayub Khan's approval, became president in May 1959.

Azad Kashmir politics received an indirect 'boost' from the Muslim Conference's contrived 1956 reunification and Ibrahim's autocracy.[182] Some non-Muslim Conference politicians were empowered to form a 'Jammu and Kashmir United Front'. It comprised five groups: the J&K Kisan Mazdoor Conference, under Abdus Salam Yatu's leadership; the Azad Kashmir Awami Conference, led by Abdul Khaliq Ansari from Mirpur; the J&K People's Conference, led by Abdul Majeed Malik, from Mirpur; the Kashmir Republican Party, led by Khwaja Ghulam Nabi Gilkar, the alleged founder of the first Azad Kashmir Government on 4 October

# THE UNTOLD STORY OF THE PEOPLE OF AZAD KASHMIR

1947;[183] and Anjuman-i-Naujvanan-i-Kashmir, led by Sheikh Muhammad Iqbal Jafari, a Jammuite from Sialkot. 'Captain General' Ali Ahmad Shah, Azad Kashmir's President in 1950–51, advised the United Front. It demanded a 'democratic legislature' for Azad Kashmir, which was 'the need of the hour'. The United Front fought for this until martial law came into place in 1958, after which the partyless Basic Democracy system was imposed on the region.

## The role of biradari

People's support in Azad Kashmir politics for Ghulam Abbas, Sardar Ibrahim or Mirwaiz Yusuf Shah was roughly along geographical lines: Jammuites supported Abbas; Poonchis supported Ibrahim; Kashmiris supported Mirwaiz. This focus on leaders reflected and entrenched, an important, ongoing factor in Azad Kashmir politics: the role of the tribe or *biradari*. *Biradari* means brotherhood, clan, tribe, fraternity or kinship network. This inherent social organisation has impacted on all political systems that Azad Kashmir has had. Indeed, 'politics in Azad Kashmir is largely tribal',[184] with *biradari* playing an important role determining election outcomes. People of a *biradari* vote for 'one of their own'—not always, but noticeably. Other factors can come into play: a candidate's reputation and influence; what he can offer a tribe or region (in Azad Kashmir, most elected representatives are men); current issues; factionalism, rivalry or unresolved issues within a *biradari* that may dilute a 'vote bank'; the role of outsiders, either to 'influence' a voter, usually by endorsing a candidate or possibly by offering largesse, or to 'manipulate' or rig an election. Such matters are discussed in Chapter 8.

With little in common among Azad Kashmiris apart from shared geography, religion and their desire for Pakistan, the tribe or *biradari* has acted as another faction in Azad Kashmir, albeit usually a local or loose one. Azad Kashmiris are disparate: '[a] person living in the extreme South [of Azad Kashmir] has as much in common with a person living in the extreme North as a Negro with an Eskimo'.[185] Southern Azad Kashmiris are heavily influenced by Punjab; in northern Azad Kashmir, people use 'half a dozen different languages', with Urdu used for inter-group communications.[186] One consequence of this diversity is that Azad Kashmiri politics has tended to devolve to the lowest common denominator of the tribe or brotherhood—to the *biradari*. Very little has been written specifically about *biradari* in Azad Kashmir. For Saraf, 'tribalism plays an important role in the affairs of the community' of the people both of Azad Kashmir and of Jammu—unlike the Kashmir Valley which is fairly homogeneous ethnically.[187] The 1951 Azad Kashmir Census confirms this understanding: Azad Kashmiris who found employment outside the region 'migrated only temporarily and remained rooted to their homelands for various reasons, chief among them being the one of the tribe or the clan'.[188]

The British scholar Alexander Evans, and organization Human Rights Watch, consider *biradari* very important in Azad Kashmir. In 'Kashmiri Exceptionalism',[189] Evans states that many Azad Kashmiris 'feel most keenly tied to clan/*biraderi* identities (e.g. being Sudhan, Rajput, or a Sayyid)'. He then argues that *biraderis* 'continue to play the leading role in social organization in Pakistani-administered

## THE POLITICAL SYSTEM: DEMOCRATIC SHORTCOMINGS

Kashmir' and many senior politicians accept that they continue to exercise greater influence on electoral politics there than political parties—'though some, particularly the more progressive PPP, argue this is changing rapidly'.[190] For Human Rights Watch, 'The biradari is the overriding determinant of identity and power relationships within the Azad Kashmiri sociopolitical landscape'. This 'Cultural practice in Azad Kashmir has more in common with the Punjab than with the Kashmir valley',[191] a factor reinforced since 1947 because J&K's division ended Azad Kashmiris' official connections with the Kashmir Valley and focused them on Pakistan, particularly Punjab. This probably strengthened *biradari*. With specific data lacking for Azad Kashmir *biradari*s, I extrapolate based on data for Pakistan.

In its narrowest sense, *biradari* 'denote[s] notions of common ancestry or a social network of related tribes'.[192] This ancestry is patrilineal, with members often located in, or coming from, a specific geographical area.[193] This is an important, perhaps inherent, factor for Muslims, particularly when arranging marriages.[194] These require a prospective couple to have complementary religious, ethnic and tribal affiliations (and, increasingly in urban areas, economic factors like occupation). Overall Pakistanis, and probably most Azad Kashmiris, still prefer endogamous unions (marriage within a given tribe or social group) and consanguineous unions (marriage to someone with the same descent: to a second cousin or closer). In a representative study made in the 1990s, 62 per cent of Pakistani marriages were consanguineous. In another study, 47 per cent were consanguineous, while 38 per cent occurred within a specific *biradari*.[195] Such marriages were important, partly because of 'the pride associated with staying within the bounds of biraderi or social group identity as well as economic factors and the ease of arranging marriages within the family'.[196] Consanguineous unions were even better, as the 'property exchanged at marriage then stays within the patrilineage'.[197]

In political terms, *biradari* is significant. General Zia's 1985 elections in Pakistan provide an example. Despite the 'partyless nature of [the] elections and the ban on traditional means of electioneering (through public rallies and speeches)', the 'personal influence of the candidates, the ties to clan, tribe, or biradari and feudal social bases, in particular, largely determined the outcome'.[198] There was a clear link between voters, *biradari* and votes. Nevertheless, *biradari*s are not social, or voting, monoliths, and other factors influence election outcomes. People from the same *biradari* may compete against each other in elections. Nevertheless, a Pakistani political party must understand the composition of local *biradari*s and select appropriate candidates, as *biradari*s can be 'motivated' to vote for, or against, a certain person.[199] There is a strong kinship-voting link in Pakistan: 'people cast votes on the basis of Biradari. The ratio of casting vote[s according] to Biradari in the elections of local government [in the 1990s] was 50 per cent'; similarly, the 'percentage of vote casting to the candidates of Biradari was 23 per cent in the elections of national and provincial assemblies'.[200] Similar links between voters, *biradari* and votes would apply to Azad Kashmir: between a quarter to a half of Azad Kashmiris in a constituency would vote for a candidate from their *biradari*, if only because he is a tribal representative.

Specifically, *biradari* appears to have three levels in Azad Kashmir. In the strictest endogamous or consanguineous sense (the first level), one such *biradari* would consist of members of Sardar Ibrahim's Sudhan (or Sudhozai) tribe based around the former Sudhnoti Tehsil of the Poonch *jagir*.[201] Another would comprise Sardar Qayyum's Abbasi tribe located in the *jagir*'s former Bagh *tehsil*, north of Sudhnoti. People in these areas would vote for a political figure from their tribe, regardless of 'his' political party. A broader, second level *biradari* could include individuals united by perceived membership of some type of historical, cultural or former Hindu caste group, such as Rajputs from the Kshatriya (warrior) caste. Some second-level *biradari*s include Jats, Rajputs and Gujjars for Jammuites and Mirpuris; Maldail, Gujjar, Tezial and Awans for Poonchis;[202] Gujjars, Khakas, Bambas, Kashmiris, Mughals and Ghakars in Muzaffarabad District;[203] or Saeeds (Sayyeds; Syeds) in the Chilian and Tehwal areas of the Neelum Valley, divided by the LOC from brethren in Indian J&K.[204]

At a third level, *biradari* could comprise loose or broader 'tribes' that unify around some sense of shared belonging: for example, Jammuites, Poonchis, Baghis, Muzaffarabadis, Mirpuris, etc. Given their relative homogeneity, ethnic Kashmiris resident in Azad Kashmir and Pakistan comprise a loose *biradari*.[205] However, the term 'Kashmiri' is problematic—and increasingly self-defined, with non-ethnic 'Kashmiris' using this term to describe themselves. Mirpuris in Azad Kashmir and, more particularly, the 450,000 Mirpuri Jats living in the United Kingdom called 'Pakistanis', increasingly are calling themselves 'Kashmiris' or 'Pakistani Kashmiris'. This self-identification does not relate to their ethnicity or *biradari*. Rather these 'new Kashmiris' are referring to their status as citizens of the former princely state of J&K popularly called 'Kashmir'. They are seeking to obviate 'perceived condescension from Punjabis' and create 'a rhetorical basis for a stronger sense of self-respect'.[206] Equally, they may suffer from a 'strong sense of disillusionment about the way in which Pakistan has treated them'. Conversely, some Sudhans are 'enthusiastic about identifying themselves as Kashmiris' because of pride in instigating the anti-Maharaja rebellion in 1947 and their desire 'to bring the whole of Kashmir into a wider Pakistan'.[207]

*Biradari* is not to be confused with the Hindu concept of caste (*varna*). Islam, which is the 'State religion' of Azad Kashmir,[208] does not sanction *biradari* in the Koran as some Hindu scriptures, such as the Vedas and the Laws of Manu, sanction caste. Nor is there supposed to be any hierarchy of *biradari*; that would be un-Islamic. Unlike members of a caste or sub-caste who are expected to perform a certain function, no specific occupations are associated with, or sanctioned for, a *biradari*. Individuals may, and do, carry on a range of occupations, although 'many high-strung clans of Azad Kashmir will not take to certain professions which they regard as below their dignity'.[209] Equally, Gujjars 'as a rule are pastoral people' with 'an atavistic flair for cattle-breeding', while Bakarwals 'breed goats only and are a nomadic people who are regarded as the arch-enemies of the forests'.[210] If anything, *biradari* is similar to the concept of *jati*, or a group united by kin and/or shared blood.

The 1998 Azad Kashmir Census provides the most recent information—albeit surprisingly brief—about 'Ethnicity and Tribes' in Azad Kashmir.[211] It states that 'the majority' of Azad Kashmir residents 'judging by the castes they retain, are descended from ancient Hindus, most commonly Brahmins, but Mughals, Afghans and Sayyeds are quite common[,] as are also convert[s] to Islam from Kshatriya Hindus'. Seemingly, there were no Muslim converts from low castes, even though

## THE POLITICAL SYSTEM: DEMOCRATIC SHORTCOMINGS

the Interim Constitution felt the need to abolish 'Untouchability'.[212] The Census briefly discusses Kashmiris, Gujjars and Bakarwals, and mentions that, besides these 'tribes', there are Bamba/Khakka and Mughal in Muzaffarabad District, Sudhans in Sudhnoti and Poonch districts, Maldail, Dhond (Abbasi), Rathore and Narma Rajas in Bagh District, and Rajput, Jat and Sayyed in Mirpur District. The Census also provides brief information about languages spoken in Azad Kashmir.[213] The official language is Urdu, as in Pakistan. Other than Urdu, 'regional languages viz Kashmiri, Pahari, Gojri, Punjabi, Kohistani, Pushto and Sheena are frequently spoken in Azad Kashmir'. These suggest larger cross-border or cross-LOC *biradari* groupings.

The overall significance of *biradari* in Azad Kashmir politics is that it is an inherent social construction which, used politically, has empowered Azad Kashmir politicians. Azad Kashmiris appear inherently able to identify the specific or local *biradari* of their member or preferred electoral candidate. In a fifteen-minute conversation in December 2006, an electoral official in Muzaffarabad quickly identified the *biradari* of forty of the forty-one directly-elected members of the Azad Kashmir Legislative Assembly. These comprised fourteen *biradari*s: Abbasi (one member); Awan (one member); Gillani (one); Gujjar (six); Jarral/Mirza (one); Jat (six); Kashmiri (three); Khokhar (one); Malik (one); Mughal (two); Pathan (one); Rajput (eight); Sudhan (six); Syed (two); and one unknown (possibly Jat or Gujjar).[214] While this appears clinical, *biradari* members compete: for example, Sardar Ibrahim and Sardar Qayyum, both Poonchis (but respectively from Rawalakot and Bagh); two Kashmiris, K.H. Khurshid and Mirwaiz Yusuf Shah; and, election candidates since 1974, when constituencies have been localised. *Biradari* members seek to ensure that 'their' politicians and people obtain sufficient cabinet and bureaucratic appointments.[215] Azad Kashmir politics also seeks to avoid *biradari* angst, such as that which provoked the Sudhan uprising in 1950–51. Finally, politicians have benefited because Azad Kashmiris, aware of *biradari* they have chosen, or felt compelled, to often vote for affiliates with whom they identify, even in supposedly partyless elections.

The 1961 Basic Democracy elections provide an excellent example of how *biradari* has operated in Azad Kashmir. With the military less inclined to 'pander' to *biradari*s, factions and political parties, General Ayub sought to conduct partyless elections. People's awareness of *biradari*s and *biradari* leaders negated his efforts. In the partyless, but 'vigorous', elections for the Azad Kashmir president,[216] voting apparently was on tribal, or *biradari*, lines. Apart from knowing candidates' *biradari*s, 'Sudhans, Muslim Rajputs[,] Khakhas, Jats, Muslims and Gujjars vot[ed] … at the bidding of the tribal sardars': others voted for an 'outsider' *biradari* comprising refugees from Indian J&K.[217] Khurshid, Azad Kashmir President and a Kashmiri with strong links with ethnic Kashmiris, expected to win 'an overwhelming majority of Kashmiri-speaking votes'.[218] With some politicians, including Ghulam Abbas, disqualified, others, such as Mirwaiz Yusuf Shah and Sardar Qayyum, were allowed to participate.[219] Owing to their high profiles, both were able to translate their reputations and *biradari* support into votes (although Mirwaiz, with the advantage or disadvantage of being a religious figure, competed with another ethnic Kashmiri, Khurshid). On the basis of the numerical strengths of Azad Kashmir's various *biradari*, Qayyum should have got, and possibly did get, the most number of votes in 1961. But, in another factor that became entrenched in Azad Kashmir politics, votes of J&K refugees settled in Pakistan were possibly manipulated so Khurshid 'won' this party-free—but almost certainly not military-free—poll.[220]

After martial law, *biradari* continued to be an important factor in Azad Kashmir elections. Indeed, from 1970 onwards, geographically-based constituencies enabled a voter to easily elect a member from his or her own *biradari*. Similarly, politicians with a strong local *biradari* in Azad Kashmir, such as Sardar Qayyum, Sardar Sikandar and Barrister Sultan Mahmood Chaudhry, generally became more important than refugee politicians. Azad Kashmiri *biradari*s were tighter, geographically and socially, than broad refugee *biradari*s of Jammu and Kashmir refugees dispersed throughout Pakistan. Also, refugees lacked leaders of the stature of Ghulam Abbas (died 1968), Yusuf Shah (died 1968) and K.H. Khurshid (died 1988). With the plebiscite a non-event and refugees not going 'home' soon, they inevitably became entrenched in Pakistan geographically, administratively, politically, economically and emotionally. Because of this, local Azad Kashmir *biradari*s have supplied all elected Azad Kashmir presidents and prime ministers after 1977.

Since 1970, Azad Kashmir political parties have often been affiliated with Pakistani political parties. While heavily influenced by Islamabad, Azad Kashmir's political system did not simply reflect Pakistan's. Rather, it was still 'closely related' to Azad Kashmir's traditional *biradari* system.[221] Hence, individuals who chose to vote for Sardar Qayyum of the Muslim Conference most likely did so because he was an Abbasi or a Baghi, not necessarily because of his political affiliations with Nawaz Sharif or the Muslim League, with which the Muslim Conference was affiliated. That said, such an affiliation also could garner support within Azad Kashmir and, importantly, within Pakistan, as it gave Qayyum status and influence, particularly when Sharif was in power and able to dispense largesse to his Azad Kashmiri affiliates or *biradari*. Similarly, Azad Kashmiris associated with the Pakistan People's Party, such as Sardar Ibrahim, benefited when one of the Bhuttos, Zulfikar or Benazir, held power. This system changed after the Pakistan military instituted its 'command democracy' from October 1999. Azad Kashmir politicians then had to align themselves with the greater 'military' *biradari*. Of all the 'tribes' involved in Pakistan and Azad Kashmir, it is the most unified, potent and wilful.

The nature of *biradari* can even point to manipulated Azad Kashmir elections. Politicians can woo broad *biradari*s, such as refugees, or narrow *biradari*s, such as a specific tribe like the Sudhans, whose members are united by blood, marriage and location. In seats where members of one *biradari* comprise a clear majority of electors, their candidate, if solidly endorsed by tribal leaders, would be expected to win. In the 1990 elections, a journalist identified various *biradari*s and suggested 'a split mandate' and how many seats each party would win.[222] His results were confirmed when candidates from the local, numerically-dominant *biradari* usually won, as was expected,[223] but with neither the Muslim Conference nor the Pakistan People's Party-Azad Kashmir gaining a majority.[224] Mumtaz Rathore's PPPAK and various political partners then formed a cabinet of seventeen ministers, the largest ever in Azad Kashmir politics—and essentially its own *biradari*.[225] This replaced the previous Raja *biradari*-dominated cabinet for which Azad Kashmir was nicknamed 'Rajastan'.[226] The PPPAK was allied with the Pakistan People's Party, from which it received help to govern. In August 1990 Benazir Bhutto was sacked, after which Nawaz Sharif's Muslim League government, with which the

## THE POLITICAL SYSTEM: DEMOCRATIC SHORTCOMINGS

Muslim Conference was aligned, took over. Under increasing pressure, Rathore held elections in June 1991. To his 'dismay', the PPPAK lost to the Muslim Conference, which won a staggering 80 per cent of directly-elected seats: thirty-two of forty seats.[227] With many voters liking Rathore because he was opposing Islamabad's dominance and manipulation, his loss appeared to result from 'massive intervention by Pakistan'. There was proof for this claim: candidates who were not from the numerically-dominant *biradari* won in almost half of the seats, which suggested significant electoral manipulation.

*Seats for refugees and others*

Another issue related to *biradari*, in its broad sense, is the discriminatory advantage that refugee *biradari*s have in Azad Kashmir elections. There is no official definition of a refugee but by inference, he/she is a state subject who has moved, or fled, from J&K to Pakistan since 1947.[228] A State Subject is 'as defined in the late Government of the State of Jammu and Kashmir Notification No. 1-L/84, dated the 20th April, 1927'.[229] There are two refugee classifications: Kashmiris from the 'occupied areas' of the former Kashmir Province as it existed on 14 August 1947 who reside in Pakistan's four provinces; 'Jammu & Others' from areas of J&K apart from Kashmir Province (mainly from Jammu Province) and from Azad Kashmir who reside in Pakistan's four provinces. Curiously, Islamabad is not mentioned as a location where state subjects may reside and then vote in Azad Kashmir elections. Refugees from J&K living in Azad Kashmir itself vote in constituencies within Azad Kashmir. Refugees living in Pakistan elect twelve representatives to the Azad Kashmir Legislative Assembly: six for Kashmiris; six for 'Jammu & Others'. These are generally known as 'refugee seats'. This arrangement exists because the Azad Kashmir Government considers itself the successor to Hari Singh's regime, which means that it must provide representation for all people in J&K. Allowing refugees to elect members to the Legislative Assembly also keeps alive their 'attachment' to 'Kashmir and [the] Kashmir issue'.[230] It reminds refugees that their ancestral homelands in Indian J&K are 'occupied'.[231]

Refugee seats offer opportunistic Azad Kashmiri politicians possibilities. While Abbas, Mirwaiz and Khurshid were clearly refugees, some candidates who have contested refugee seats appeared to be temporary residents from Azad Kashmir. In 1990, Sardar Sikandar Hayat Khan, Azad Kashmir's Prime Minister and a proud resident of Kotli, from where he contested an Azad Kashmir constituency, also contested a refugee seat in Rawalpindi (probably Jammu & Others VI). This offended some people.[232] Sikandar possibly did so because, like many wealthy Azad Kashmiris, he had a residence in the Rawalpindi-Islamabad area. This entitled him to stand in this constituency because the Jammu & Others category includes state subjects from Azad Kashmir 'now residing' in any province of Pakistan.[233] Azad Kashmir's Supreme Court later found Sikandar's nomination illegal,[234] possibly because an elector can only be enrolled in one electorate.[235] Sikandar was elected from Kotli anyway.[236] In 2001 Sardar Attique Ahmad Khan, whose ancestral home is in Bagh, contested and won the Jammu & Others I seat.[237] This seat was reserved for state subjects living in Baluchistan, Sind and Punjab Province's divisions of

## THE UNTOLD STORY OF THE PEOPLE OF AZAD KASHMIR

Bahawalpur, Multan, Dera Ghazi Khan, Faisalabad, Sargodha and Lahore.[238] Attique possibly contested this seat because his father, Sardar Qayyum, was entrenched in their 'home' seat, Bagh I (which Attique won in 2006).[239] Like Sikandar, Attique was legally entitled to stand in this constituency; the doubt in 2001 was about where Attique was 'now residing'.[240] His win appeared to go uncontested.

The inclusion of Pakistani-based refugees in Azad Kashmir elections has disproportionally favoured them over Azad Kashmir residents. In the partyless 1961 election conducted under the Azad Kashmir Basic Democracies Act, 1960,[241] voters from Azad Kashmir's population of 1,065,000 people[242] elected 1,200 Basic Democrats, while 109,000 Jammu refugees elected 600, as did 10,000 Kashmir Valley refugees.[243] These 2,400 Basic Democrats then elected twelve members to the Azad Kashmir Council on the same 2:1:1 formula.[244] In 1968, Azad Kashmiri representation on the Council rose to eight, with refugees' representation dropping to four.[245] Elected members of 'Union Councils, Union committees and Town committees' elected the eight Azad Kashmiri representatives under the Basic Democracies regime; the (Pakistani) Chief Adviser appointed the four refugees.[246] The imbalance on a per capita basis was still obvious. In the 1970 elections, the same formula was followed: Azad Kashmir voters elected sixteen of twenty-five members; Jammu & Others elected four members; Kashmir refugees elected four. These members then elected the twenty-fifth member, a woman, to a reserved seat.[247] Since 1974, Azad Kashmir has a larger Legislative Assembly. From 1975 to 2005, there were forty directly-elected members. In 2006, this became forty-one.[248] Directly-elected members later elect a further eight members (discussed below), bringing the total number of members to forty-nine. Of the forty-one directly-elected seats, six are for Jammu & Others, six are for Kashmir refugees, twenty-nine are for Azad Kashmiris. As explained below, refugee seats are easier to win; and the more refugee seats that a party wins, the fewer Azad Kashmir seats it needs to secure government.

Azad Kashmir Legislative Assembly elections have anomalies that favour refugees, particularly Kashmiris. In the 1990 elections, 1.2 million Azad Kashmiris and 400,000 refugees voted.[249] Each Azad Kashmir constituency averaged 43,000 electors; refugee constituencies averaged 33,000 electors. This was an improvement from the 1961 situation, although it still discriminated in favour of refugee voters living in Pakistan (who were also entitled to vote in national and provincial elections).[250] In the 1996, 2001 and 2006 elections (see Table 5.1), Kashmiris were greatly favoured, with Jammu & Others voters worse off. Indeed, relatively speaking, Jammu & Others refugees were under-represented in the Legislative Assembly while Kashmiri refugees were over-represented, a continuing phenomenon supposed to be aimed at showing solidarity with Kashmiris in Indian J&K. A further electorate bias indirectly relates to refugees, with average Mirpuri electorates having fewer electors than other Azad Kashmir electorates. This is supposed to provide a 'cushion' for the 800,000 Mirpuris living abroad, mainly in the United Kingdom.[251]

Another factor that skews results in favour of refugees is lower voter turnouts. It takes far fewer voters to secure a refugee seat than an Azad Kashmir seat.[252] In the 1996 elections, the average voter turnout was 69 per cent for all constituencies, comprising 74 per cent for Azad Kashmir constituencies and 57 per cent for

# THE POLITICAL SYSTEM: DEMOCRATIC SHORTCOMINGS

Table 5.1: Differences in Voter Numbers for Constituencies in Azad Kashmir in 1996, 2001, 2006.

| EY | Total: AK | Total: Ref | AK Cons | Ref Cons | J&O Cons | K Cons |
|---|---|---|---|---|---|---|
| 1996 | 1.2 million | 408,000 | 43,000 | 34,000 | 62,400 | 5,500 |
| 2001 | 1.6 million | 499,000 | 56,700 | 41,600 | 77,800 | 5,300 |
| 2006 | 1.8 million | 581,000 | 62,900 | 48,400 | 91,000 | 5,900 |

Source: Table XIV 6: Differences in Electorate Sizes in Azad Kashmir in 1996, 2001, 2006, in Appendix XIV: Matters re Azad Kashmir elections, particularly in 2006.

Key: AK   Azad Kashmir.
     Cons   Constituencies (averaged).
     EY   Election year.
     J&O   Jammu & Others.
     K   Kashmir refugees.
     Ref   All refugees (comprising Jammu & Others and Kashmir) living in Pakistan.
     Total: AK   Total number of registered Azad Kashmir voters.
     Total: Ref   Total number of registered refugee voters.

refugee constituencies. On average, a victor had to win more overall votes to secure an Azad Kashmir seat than a refugee seat. In the 2001 elections voter turnouts slumped, possibly because of disenchantment with military rule and the military-run elections. The average voter turnout was 49 per cent for all constituencies, comprising 54 per cent for Azad Kashmir constituencies and 41 per cent for refugee constituencies. On average, a victor had to win more overall votes in an Azad Kashmir seat than in a refugee seat. Best off were Kashmir refugee constituencies, where candidates had small electorates and low voter turnouts.

An important consideration is that refugee seats offer Pakistanis opportunities to manipulate Azad Kashmir elections, because Islamabad can 'influence' voting conducted in Pakistan by refugees. Refugees live in disparate constituencies 'spread all over Pakistan'.[253] Their remoteness tends to favour the party or military body in power in Islamabad and its Azad Kashmiri surrogate, which is not necessarily the party in power in Muzaffarabad. The Pakistan Election Commission is responsible for compiling electoral rolls and for conducting elections in refugee seats, not the Azad Kashmir Election Commission.[254] This means that Pakistani politicians, soldiers and bureaucrats can influence results. This can be done through rigging and other methods: intimidating and disenfranchising candidates before nominating or during campaigning; intimidating or enticing voters not to vote, or to vote a certain way; capturing polling stations to prevent or influence voting; stuffing completed voting slips in ballot boxes; manipulating counting and falsifying results. Chapter 8 discusses instances where Pakistani interference in voting for refugee seats has influenced outcomes.

Since 1986, directly-elected members have elected a further eight members to the Azad Kashmir Legislative Assembly.[255] This system reflects the former Maharaja's controlled franchise. Five reserved seats are for women, which does not preclude them from seeking direct election to the Legislative Assembly, although this is rare in Azad Kashmir's male-dominated political environment: two women were directly elected in 2001, one in 2006.[256] One reserved seat is for a 'technocrat and professional': 'any person having special education in any branch of knowledge' (agriculturists, economists, educationists, lawyers, doctors, engineers, scientists), with at least ten years of experience. One reserved seat is for a religious scholar or Muslim cleric (Ulema-e-Din or Mushaikh) 'Well-versed with the teachings of Islam'. One seat is for 'Jammu and Kashmir State Subjects residing abroad', although the current incumbent's address is given as 'Kotli'.[257]

'Reserved seats' usually strengthen the ruling party's position in the Legislative Assembly. In 2006, the Muslim Conference won six of the eight reserved seats. This boosted its position from twenty-two of forty-one directly-elected seats to twenty-eight of forty-nine total seats, thus improving its slender majority. Reserved seats can also be used to insert special people into the Legislative Assembly. In 1991, the Muslim Conference blatantly used its overwhelming majority to ensure that Sardar Qayyum was elected to the reserved seat for a religious scholar or Muslim cleric. While Qayyum was a devout Muslim keen to Islamise Azad Kashmir,[258] he was neither a religious scholar nor a Muslim cleric. He 'could not have had the time for any formal training or education as a religious scholar' because, since serving as a 'havaldar clerk' in the Maharaja's forces (from which he deserted),[259] he had been heavily involved in Azad Kashmir politics. On 30 July 1991, the Legislative Assembly elected Qayyum Prime Minister, which was the ultimate aim of the strategy.[260]

Overall, the system of disproportional representation in the Azad Kashmir Legislative Assembly involving refugees has been unfair. The large disparity in constituencies for Azad Kashmiris, Jammu & Others and Kashmiri refugees has not altered greatly since 1949. This is despite additional refugees coming to Azad Kashmir or Pakistan after India-Pakistan wars in 1965 and 1971 and since the anti-Indian uprising began in the Kashmir Valley in 1988.[261] Jammu & Others electorates on average remain larger, while Kashmir refugee votes remain the most 'valuable'. Refugee seats also remain a valuable device for Islamabad to use to ensure its preferred candidate or party does well in Azad Kashmir elections.

*The situation after 1970*

In 1970, Azad Kashmir obtained a presidential system of government. This was a watershed. It resulted from the dispirited Pakistan military's keenness to remove itself from political processes. It followed some rare agreement between three of Azad Kashmir's highest profile, most ambitious leaders. It delivered maximum autonomy to the region and its people. The initial, and only, election held under this system using universal adult suffrage was considered free and fair. But the presidential system only lasted briefly; in 1974 Pakistan's Prime Minister, Zulfikar Ali Bhutto, replaced it with a prime ministerial system. This re-established close Pakistani supervision of Azad Kashmir and provided more predictable election outcomes for Islamabad. This prime ministerial system continued thereafter, except during General Zia's martial law.

In 1968, the military was under increasing pressure in Pakistan. In August Sardar Ibrahim (Azad Muslim Conference), Sardar Qayyum (Muslim Conference) and K.H. Khurshid (J&K Liberation League),[262] made a joint declaration calling for a

## THE POLITICAL SYSTEM: DEMOCRATIC SHORTCOMINGS

constitution and representative government for Azad Kashmir. Their unanimity concurred with a 'wave of indignation' among Azad Kashmiris after General Ayub's Government Act of 1968 made Azad Kashmir a municipality, rather then promoting it to provincial level, as many Azad Kashmiris wanted.[263] After General Yahya Khan's martial law regime replaced Ayub's discredited government in March 1969, Yahya appointed Abdul Rehman Khan, an apolitical retired army brigadier, Azad Kashmir president in October 1969.[264] Under pressure, Yahya instructed Rehman to 'give them [politically] what they want'.[265] Rehman's 'foremost task' was to frame a new constitution and hold adult suffrage elections. To help him with his 'onerous responsibilities', Ibrahim, Qayyum and Khurshid each nominated a representative who, in turn, was made a minister.[266] This gave Rehman room to move, and it allowed leaders to have input into the region's political future. The result was the 1970 Government Act. This delivered a presidential system of government to Azad Kashmir with 'absolute internal autonomy to the Azad State' and limited Pakistani control.[267] The future Azad Kashmir President would liaise with a Pakistan Government adviser. This was seemingly his only contact with Pakistan.

Despite its achievements obtaining genuine autonomy, Azad Kashmir's presidential system had one significant problem: constitutionally, the only way to remove the president was by a no-confidence motion supported by two-thirds of the Legislative Assembly's twenty-five members, that is, by seventeen members. For the fractious rivals of Sardar Qayyum, who was then President, this was a major impediment. The Muslim Conference had fifteen seats in the Legislative Assembly; Khurshid's Liberation League had five; Ibrahim's Azad Muslim Conference had one; there were three independents; and an indirectly-elected female representative whose political affiliations were unclear.[268] Until Qayyum's opponents could unify, they could never oust him. This situation enabled Qayyum to rule with 'absolute power' and 'relish' for over four years.[269] Imitating some of his autocratic predecessors, he ruled without a cabinet for the first three months in office.[270] This situation was one reason why the presidential system was changed to a prime ministerial system. Qayyum's ascendant position meant that Pakistan had no provisions to remove an unacceptable Azad Kashmir president. This became an issue after Bhutto turned his attention to Azad Kashmir after finalising the Simla Agreement in June 1972. Bhutto, who had been Minister for Kashmir Affairs in the early 1960s,[271] disliked Qayyum and his alignment with Pakistan's Jamiat-i-Islami and Pakistani generals. To ensure Pakistan's control over Azad Kashmir, Bhutto imposed a prime ministerial system of government via the 1974 Interim Constitution.

The Azad Jammu and Kashmir Interim Constitution Act, 1974, was presented to, and passed by, the Azad Kashmir Legislative Assembly on 24 August 1974.[272] President Qayyum ratified it on the same day. The prime ministerial system had two benefits for Pakistan; first, only a simple majority was required to oust the prime minister;[273] second, a number of constitutional provisions ensured Pakistan's superior position, particularly the Azad Kashmir Council. Qayyum's term as President, which was due to finish in November 1974, continued until 16 April 1975, when fresh elections were called and the Legislative Assembly passed a previously-agreed no-confidence motion against Qayyum. The assembly's four-year term had been due to expire in November 1974. Qayyum's extension resulted from an all-party agreement that added a special provision to the Interim Constitution on 24 August 1974 to enable a smooth transition from the presidential to the prime ministerial system. After Qayyum left office, the Speaker of the Legislative Assembly, Manzar Masood, constitutionally acted as president until 29 May 1975 when Sardar Ibrahim was elected to this more titular position.

Azad Kashmir's prime ministerial system only began to operate after the assembly and presidential elections in May 1975.[274] A senior Pakistani official, Hayat Muhammad Khan Tamman, who was Bhutto's Political Adviser, 'managed' the results.[275] A displaced Sardar Qayyum and the Muslim Conference boycotted both polls. Unsurprisingly the Pakistan People's Party's local affiliate, the Pakistan People's Party-Azad Kashmir, easily won the elections, after which its leader, Khan Abdul Hamid Khan, became Prime Minister. A few days before, as the Interim Constitution required, a joint sitting of the Azad Kashmir Legislative Assembly and the Azad Kashmir Council elected Sardar Ibrahim unopposed as President. Following an invitation from Bhutto, Ibrahim joined the PPPAK.[276] Azad Kashmir's new political system created two executive positions for politicians to covet: the presidency and the prime ministership, which was beneficial. The president's position was largely titular, although he also was vice-chairman of the powerful Azad Kashmir Council; the prime minister held the superior political and administrative position. Hence, even though Ibrahim may have been better known because of his reputation and connections, Hamid Khan had more power.

So began Azad Kashmir's modern prime ministerial political system. Apart from General Zia's martial law intervention (1977–88), this has been the region's political system since mid-1975. Chapter 8 discusses events and elections in Azad Kashmir since 1970, including the period of Zia's rule.

*Conclusion*

Frequently the political systems established in Azad Kashmir have not fully empowered Azad Kashmiris. Despite establishing their own provisional government in October 1947 in the 'liberated' areas of south-western J&K, Azad Kashmiris soon came under Pakistan's control. Until 1970, local leaders supervised by Pakistan's intrusive Ministry of Kashmir Affairs or its military, or under the sway of prestige and Pakistan's largesse, led Azad Kashmir. The people had little say in their own affairs. Briefly after 1970, Azad Kashmiris experienced genuine autonomy via a presidential system devolved by General Yahya's military regime. In 1974, Pakistan under Bhutto reasserted itself. Once again, Azad Kashmiris were tied closely to Pakistan, this time via the Interim Constitution and its various pro-Pakistan provisions, including the important Azad Kashmir Council. While Bhutto imposed a prime ministerial system of government on Azad Kashmir, General Zia's military rule interrupted this system by ruling Azad Kashmir directly through military appointments. The 1990 elections fully restored Azad Kashmir's prime ministerial system, which Azad Kashmiris have since enjoyed, even during General Musharraf's control of Pakistan.

# THE POLITICAL SYSTEM: DEMOCRATIC SHORTCOMINGS

There are many reasons why it took so long for Azad Kashmir to obtain a participatory political system. These include Azad Kashmiris' own actions: their excessive focus on liberating J&K, initially via the promised plebiscite, which meant that development of an inclusive political system was stifled in order to achieve this aim; ongoing factionalism and rivalry among leaders, which enabled intrusive Ministry of Kashmir Affairs domination; and, entrenched and sometimes reactionary *biradari* politics, as displayed by Sudhans in the 1950s. Pakistanis also are to blame: they 'demoted' Azad Kashmir to 'local authority' level, rather than empowering it as a genuine and dynamic alternative government for all of J&K; MKA actions were autocratic; and military rule, apart from devolving the 1970 presidential system to Azad Kashmir, has generally disempowered Azad Kashmiris. A further issue has been the perceived need to include refugees in any political system, which causes discrepancies in election results, some due to Pakistani meddling. However, Azad Kashmiris' stance of representing all of the people of J&K is spurious, if only because Azad Kashmir and the Northern Areas have been kept separate since at least 1949. Additionally, most 'refugees' are now heavily entrenched in Pakistani society. Should the Kashmir dispute ever be resolved, few would return to Indian J&K, where evacuee properties were long ago distributed among the local population. These *de facto* Pakistanis should now be made *de jure* Pakistanis.

The 1971 India-Pakistan war marked a turning point in Azad Kashmir politics: thereafter Azad Kashmiris realised that the Pakistan military could not liberate J&K from Indian control. Equally, because of the Simla Agreement, the plebiscite was no longer an option. This meant that Azad Kashmiris had little choice but to be with Pakistan—and to accept what it wanted. The 1971 war also empowered Bhutto, who had the political capital and dynamism to impose a new, but restrictive, constitution on Azad Kashmir that enhanced Pakistan's position. However, as Bhutto's overthrow and execution by Zia's military regime show, when it comes to democracy, Azad Kashmiris should not look to Pakistan for inspiration. For more than half of its existence, Pakistan has endured martial law or military-dominated 'command' political systems. This has not stopped Pakistanis with poor or non-existent democratic records, supported by Azad Kashmiris often being denied democracy, calling for the UN plebiscite to be held so that the people of J&K could democratically decide the issue of 'their' state's international status.[277] Such calls have been hypocritical.

6

# THE ADMINISTRATION

## LARGE AND OVERSEEN

*Introduction*

This chapter discusses the formation, consolidation and continuation of Azad Kashmir's administration. The Provisional Azad Kashmir Government was created on 24 October 1947. It had two purposes. First, it saw itself as a rival to Maharaja Hari Singh's rule and administration and then, after the accession to India, to the National Conference administration in Indian J&K. Second, it needed to administer the 'liberated' areas of western Jammu Province and those areas of Muzaffarabad District in western Kashmir Province captured by the invading Pukhtoons. It did not administer any 'liberated' areas in the Frontier Districts Province under Pakistan's control.

From its inception, the Azad Kashmir Government confronted major problems in developing an administration. Three days after coming into existence, Azad Kashmir had to fight against, and protect itself from, a new enemy: India's military forces. They constituted a far more potent and resilient adversary than the Maharaja's over-stretched army. The new government, which had few trained and experienced personnel except policemen, also had to create an administration essentially from nothing, during a period of war. It had to locate this within Azad Kashmir, and not Pakistan, in order to show that the Azad Kashmir movement was truly indigenous and not a figment of the Pakistan press. This fledgling, inexperienced administration confronted some immediate and important tasks. These included organising and supplying the Azad Army, tending to the local population's needs, and protecting the numerous refugees under its control. Because these tasks posed major challenges, Azad Kashmiris were compelled to look to Pakistan, to which they were politically and emotionally inclined, for assistance. Seeking Pakistan's help also reflected Azad Kashmir's geo-strategic circumstances: hostile Indian forces to the east and a mountain barrier to the north compelled Azad Kashmiris to go to west to Pakistan.

With an acute lack of administrative personnel and a severe shortage of resources, building the Azad Kashmir administration was an *ad hoc* process. After the 1949 ceasefire ended the fighting in J&K, the Azad Kashmir Government faced a further—and major—dilemma. Would it put down solid administrative roots, by establishing an alternative capital for J&K among other steps, or maintain a temporary administration until the promised plebiscite determined J&K's status and allowed its people to be physically and administratively reunified? By the mid-1950s, the plebiscite seemed unlikely to be held. Nevertheless, Azad Kashmiris continued to maintain an administration with sufficient capacity to run all of J&K when it was reunified and united with Pakistan—as they still believed would happen. Meanwhile, the Azad Kashmir Government would administer those areas of J&K under its control. In 1949 it created three districts: Mirpur, Muzaffarabad and Poonch. These reflected the Maharaja's administrative arrangements. By 2008 Mirpur, Muzaffarabad and Poonch had become divisions, under which there were eight districts. Inexplicably, Azad Kashmir had also increased in area.

*Difficult beginnings*

The Azad Kashmir administration has had three distinct periods: from its inception in 1947 until the ceasefire in 1949; from then until the 1971 India-Pakistan war; and the period after 1971. During the first period, the main task of influential local officials, who comprised senior members of the Muslim Conference or local military commanders, was to prosecute war. This was against the Maharaja's army, then against India following Hari Singh's accession on 26 October, two days after Azad Kashmir's creation. In the second period, the administration's main focus was to act as an alternative government for J&K, including maintaining a capacity to administer J&K after the promised plebiscite reunited the state and delivered it to Pakistan. Muslim Conference members largely staffed this administration; Pakistan increasingly controlled it through its Ministry of Kashmir Affairs and its military. The third period commenced as a result of the India-Pakistan war in 1971. Pakistan's defeat made Azad Kashmiris realise that Pakistan's armed forces could not obtain Indian J&K through military conquest. Since then, Azad Kashmir has been treated more like a province of Pakistan and Azad Kashmiris have sought to develop their region administratively and economically. (Chapter 7 discusses Azad Kashmir's economy.)

On 24 October 1947, the 'Provisional Azad Government' came into being. It faced significant difficulties. Initially, it sought to show that it was a rival government to the Maharaja's, especially after Hari Singh's accession to India compelled him to combine with his former—and the Muslim Conference's ongoing—political rivals, the National Conference. However, the Azad Kashmir Government's capabilities, particularly non-military, were limited. Effective control rested with local commanders rather than with a government whose administration functioned throughout all of the liberated area. Indeed, the Azad Kashmir Government essentially operated as an *ad hoc* War Council whose chief objective was to rid J&K of Dogra, then Indian, rule.[1] To achieve this objective, it faced major obstacles. For a start, it 'did not inherit any civil service. [Azad Kashmiris] had no offices, no records and not even a type writer [sic] to carry on the work of the Government'.[2] It had to develop an organisation 'almost from scratch under the greatest handicaps' to replace the severely depleted local administration thrown 'completely out of gear' by the activities of the Maharaja and his forces in Jammu Province.[3] This new organisation needed to administer those areas of Poonch and Mirpur already under its control, plus the area of Kashmir Province captured—and devastated—by marauding Pukhtoons. Muslim Conference personnel monopolised this new organisation, a situation that would continue until the late 1960s. While the party aspired to 'work for the peoples [sic] benefits and ... be responsible to the people',[4] in reality it had little inclination to be accountable.

The execution of the Azad Kashmir Government's primary objective of waging war revealed three significant drawbacks from which Azad Kashmir still suffers. First, it has never been able to secure international recognition and has been treated as a 'local authority', by Pakistan among others. Chapter 4 discussed this issue. Second, apart from the limited resources that it could muster internally, Azad Kashmir was dependent on Pakistan. Prior to August 1947, the region's traditional and most important links—but not its only links—were with areas in western Punjab and NWFP that became part of Pakistan after Partition. Fighting in 1947 divided J&K and severed Azad Kashmir's links with other areas of the state, after which the region's only outside links were with Pakistan. Indeed, Azad Kashmir thereafter had no other options but to be involved only with Pakistan. The Pakistan Government 'readily' provided assistance to this clearly pro-Pakistan area deficient in resources.[5] This assistance began the process whereby Azad Kashmir would become dependent on Pakistan for physical, administrative and military support. It also enabled Pakistanis to control Azad Kashmiris. This control was enhanced after the Pakistan Army officially entered J&K in May 1948; it then took command of all anti-Indian forces and their activities.

The third significant drawback for Azad Kashmir was a severe lack of strategic depth. This hampered the region's ability to prosecute war and increased its dependence on Pakistan. From 27 October 1947 when Indian military forces entered J&K, the Azad Kashmir Government had to deal with this new enemy. The Azad Army, utilising local knowledge and support, with the advantage of shorter supply lines and being acclimatised to J&K's difficult terrain and harsh climate, initially contained its ground-based opponent. It struggled to cope when the Royal Indian Air Force (RIAF) joined the fray in November.[6] As Azad Kashmiris lacked strategic depth, RIAF bombing and strafing caused damage and made it difficult to establish a capital from which Azad Kashmiris could safely administer their region. Because Azad Kashmir lacked a suitable or safe urban area, Azad Kashmiris had initially established operations in thick forests around Palandri, the first place 'surrendered by the Dogras', in remote southern Poonch.[7] After 'heavy and indiscriminate' RIAF bombing,[8] they moved the capital to thicker forests at Trarkhel, further east in Poonch.[9] Large-scale government and administrative operations probably started in these areas in mid-November. Before that, the Azad Kashmir Provisional Government mainly operated from a building in Rawalpindi until early November 1947.[10]

The Azad Kashmir Government selected Palandri/Trarkhel for strategic and tactical reasons, although not all organisations associated with the Azad Kashmir movement and its administration were located there. Strategically, being located in Poonch provided credibility, something that had been a problem for Azad

Kashmiris. Although the second, or reconstituted, Provisional Azad Government released its communiqué on 24 October 1947 from 'Pulandari' in Poonch,[11] elements of this government, particularly its unified command, were located in places in Pakistan, such as Murree or Rawalpindi. Equally, the Pakistan Government and its army, which neutral British officers still led, were reluctant to be seen to be providing support in Pakistan for the Azad Kashmir movement. Once Azad Kashmir's capital and many elements of government were located inside the region, the Azad Kashmir movement's credibility as an indigenous movement improved, thus partly countering India's tactic of blaming Pakistan for all of the violence occurring in J&K.

Tactically, the Palandri/Trarkhel area was ideal. It was located in the heart of the former Poonch *jagir*, which provided the bulk of the Azad Army's soldiers. It was close to the front line, where this 'army' was fighting. It was less vulnerable to land attack, as the few roads servicing this area were poor, the easiest land access being from Hazara (NWFP) or western (Pakistani) Punjab—not from Indian J&K. Nevertheless, some government bodies were located away from Palandri/Trarkhel for safety reasons and because of a lack of facilities. For example, the Muslim Conference's headquarters were in Sialkot until February 1949.[12] The office of the Supreme Head of the Azad Kashmir Movement was still in Murree in late 1950, as evidenced by the issuing of Azad Kashmir's first 'Rules of Business' from there.[13]

Many tasks confronted the new Azad Kashmir administration. These included building a civil organisation, supporting the Azad Army, restoring 'completely disrupted' communications, procuring and distributing civil and military supplies, and reviving trade.[14] The Azad Kashmir Government needed:

> porters, labourers, volunteers, recruits, as also material aid in the shape of arms, ammunition, clothes, food etc. for the fighters on the front. Taxes had to be collected; land revenue recovered; forest royalties realised; custom [sic] dues levied ... a civilian authority having political roots, was essential for settling disputes, maintaining law and order and dispensing justice ... hospitals and dispensaries had to be set up to look after the health problems of the local population, whether staying back at home or fighting on the front ... School [sic] and colleges had also to be reopened to enable students to continue their studies so far as possible.[15]

So Azad Kashmir confronted many issues.

Azad Kashmir also had a refugee problem. In 1949, about 200,000 Muslim refugees had been internally displaced from, or had chosen to leave, areas of J&K. They were scattered all over Azad Kashmir, with the main concentrations in Kotli, Hajira, Bagh and Muzaffarabad.[16] There also were smaller concentrations of Hindu and Sikh refugees, totalling some 10,000 people, waiting to leave the region.[17] A further 600,000 J&K refugees were in Pakistan. The Azad Kashmir Government had to accommodate, feed and protect all of its refugees. It had to distribute departing refugees' immovable property to arriving refugees. Authorities were also trying to locate missing relatives, particularly young females, a large number of whom were victims of rape, abduction and murder by members of other religious communities in 1947. In 1949–50, the Azad Kashmir Government allocated Rs. 8 million 'for refugee purposes'—more than half of its Rs. 13.7 million budget.[18] In 1951, Azad Kashmir still had 150,000 Muslim refugees.[19]

## THE ADMINISTRATION: LARGE AND OVERSEEN

For the new Azad Kashmir Government, finding and enlisting qualified personnel was a major problem; the usual remedy—asking Pakistan for help—established the ongoing tradition of Pakistanis' administrative involvement in Azad Kashmir. Muslim Conference forces in control of Azad Kashmir's administration did not inherit very much, if any, of the previous regime's bureaucracy. The Maharaja's administration was largely based in Srinagar in summer and Jammu City in winter; the local Raja of Poonch's administration, which was 'inferior to the [J&K] State Service',[20] was headquartered in Poonch City. All three locations were outside Azad Kashmir's physical control. Furthermore, senior officers and many ordinary officers in these administrations were pro-Maharaja Hindus. Many Hindus located in areas that became Azad Kashmir had fled or been killed. So, even if Azad Kashmiris had been able to induce Hindus to join the fledgling administration, few were physically available to serve. The Muslim Conference, the Azad Army and Muslims in the former Poonch administration did provide some experienced personnel; otherwise, few individuals in Azad Kashmir 'had any experience of administration'.[21] This shortage of experienced officers was partially remedied after the Azad Kashmir Government made a request to Pakistan's Deputy Commissioner at Sialkot. He is supposed to have sent 'lorry-loads' of refugee administrators originally from Jammu; they were 'immediately recruited' to Azad Kashmiri versions of their 'previous departments'.[22]

Despite these difficulties, the new Azad Kashmir administration began to function, establishing different departments 'in the crudest of forms' during November-December 1947.[23] Conditions were primitive,[24] with office accommodation so basic that 'ministers were living in tents or [rough] huts ... disposing [of] files while sitting on charpaies [beds]'. Cabinet staff worked in 'rickety huts ... having poor ventilation ... infested with bugs and crammed with specially obnoxious insect[s]'. Apart from Trarkhel's extreme cold, living conditions were poor, with bathing difficult and food supplies spartan. Initially, all staff comprised volunteers who received rations as pay. Later, salaries were paid, although these were subjected to a 'heavy deduction', sometimes up to 50 per cent, as subscriptions to 'the Liberation Fund'. This was acceptable as most personnel 'worked in a spirit of patriotism and self-denial'. Senior office holders fared better: 'Each Minister was paid a monthly salary of Rs. 300 which was raised to Rs. 500 in March, 1948'. Those who received such pay included Chaudhry Hamidullah and dependents of the jailed Chaudhry Ghulam Abbas.[25]

While the Azad Kashmir President, Sardar Ibrahim, believed his government had become 'a well run administration' within its first six months,[26] it had already developed some poor practices. In May 1948, a meeting of departmental secretaries in Trarkhel discussed a long list of diverse issues that needed addressing. These included:

civil supplies, procurement drive, extension of medical aid, postal and transport facilities to civil areas, vigorous policing, encouragement of import and export trade, collection of customs, land revenues, advance of 'takkavi' loans to poor peasants, rehabilitation of refugees from Rajauri, civil administration of [the] liberated area, country-wide round up of fifth column agents, and intesification [sic] of propaganda and publicity.[27]

A general directive was issued to all department secretaries to place 'special emphasis on co-operation, speed and courtesy to members of the public'.[28] Addi-

# THE UNTOLD STORY OF THE PEOPLE OF AZAD KASHMIR

tionally, the Azad Kashmir Government had started a 'drive against corruption and mal-administration' and was making efforts 'to introduce reforms in the territory'.[29] The Azad Kashmir administration had surmounted many obstacles, but it needed to improve its performance.

## A significant 'loss': the Northern Areas

Apart from Azad Kashmir, the other area where anti-regime activity took place in 1947 was in the Frontier Districts Province. The 'liberated' area came to be known as the Northern Areas, although not necessarily by that title initially.[30] This region comprised of the Astore District; a small area of Baramulla District; Gilgit (Leased Area); the Gilgit Agency, consisting of the *illaqa*s (districts) of Hunza, Nagar, Punial, Yasin, Kuh Ghizar, Ishkuman and Chilas; and 'Baltistan', a previously undefined region comprising Skardu *tehsil* and part of the Kargil Tehsil from Ladakh District.[31] Except for Baramulla, which was in Kashmir Province, these areas had been under Maharaja Hari Singh's direct, albeit tenuous, control on 15 August 1947 as his Frontier Districts Province. This included both Gilgit (Leased Area) and the Gilgit Agency, which the British had administered on behalf of the J&K Government until 31 July 1947.[32] On 1 August 1947, the departing paramount power retroceded both areas to Hari Singh.[33]

In November 1947 pro-Pakistan Muslim Gilgitis staged an uprising and 'of their own accord' joined with Pakistan.[34] They may have mounted their own indigenous, usually uncoordinated, struggles against the Maharaja from as early as October 1947 but, owing to poor communications, these were not reported until January 1948. Nevertheless, on 1 November 1947, Gilgit Muslims disenchanted with Hari Singh's accession to India formed a provisional government. Concurrently, the local Gilgit Scouts placed the Maharaja's governor under protective custody and took control.[35] On 16 November 1947, Karachi sent a political agent in response to the provisional government's invitation;[36] thereafter, he had 'exclusive authority' to administer these areas.[37] By 1 January 1949, his domain had extended to all the non-Indian areas of the Frontier Districts Province.[38] From then on, Pakistan directly administered this region as the Northern Areas.

Theoretically, the Northern Areas, which also were 'free' from India, could have become part of Azad (Free) Kashmir—particularly given that the Azad Kashmir Government claimed to be the legitimate government for all of J&K. Had Azad Kashmir included the Northern Areas, this would have added substance to the Azad Kashmiris' claim, and it would have made Azad Kashmir a more credible territorial rival to the Indian J&K regime: Azad Kashmir comprised only 4,500 sq. miles, the Northern Areas comprised 25,000 sq. miles,[39] and Indian J&K 54,000 sq. miles.[40] Furthermore, given its borders with China and Afghanistan, the Northern Areas' strategic importance would have enhanced Azad Kashmir's status—although this was one reason why Pakistan wanted to separate the two regions. The 'loss' of the Northern Areas restricted Azad Kashmiris to governing the 'rump' area of Jammu and Kashmir provinces under their actual control. As a result, Azad Kashmir never comprised—nor did it appear to comprise—a realistic alternative government for all of J&K.

## THE ADMINISTRATION: LARGE AND OVERSEEN

However, the 'freed' areas of the Frontier Districts Province were, from the outset separate—and separated—from Azad Kashmir, as Azad Kashmiris themselves recognised in 1947. The Northern Areas' 'peculiar geographical position' meant that its people had few, if any, links with Azad Kashmir and Azad Kashmiris.[41] There was no direct land route between the two regions and the easiest place for people from both regions to meet was in third locations, usually Rawalpindi, Lahore or in Pakistan's (then) capital, Karachi.[42] The two regions also had few religious or cultural connections: in the Northern Areas, people were predominantly Shia Muslims or followers of the Agha Khan (Ismailis/Maulias); most Azad Kashmiris were Sunni Muslims with links with Punjab. When establishing the Azad Army, Sardar Ibrahim and his anti-Maharaja colleagues accepted that the Frontier Districts Province was outside their domain.[43] In addition, the Azad Kashmir Government never had any 'political control over the Gilgit Agency and Baltistan'.[44] Indeed, it would have been extremely difficult for Azad Kashmiris based in Poonch to administer the vast, isolated and lightly populated Northern Areas, especially as they lacked resources and spare personnel. Gilgit and Baltistan were simply beyond the Azad Kashmiris' reach—physically, militarily, administratively and politically.

Apart from being relatively better resourced, Pakistan was able to establish its control in the Northern Areas because it enjoyed popular support there—unlike Azad Kashmir and India. The anti-Maharaja Gilgit uprising showed that people in this area wanted to become part of Pakistan, not part of Azad Kashmir. So too did their local rulers and leaders. Early in November the Mir of Hunza, the Mir of Nagar, the Raja of Punial and the governors of Kuh Ghizar and Yasin, whose populations comprised the bulk of the Gilgit Agency, announced their intentions or desires, in the governors' cases, to accede to Pakistan.[45] While these were admirable gestures, these rulers were legally unable to accede as they were under Maharaja Hari Singh's suzerainty and only he could accede.[46] Karachi was not prepared to formally accept any such 'accessions' as this would have complicated and weakened Pakistan's ability to obtain the entire state of J&K via the promised plebiscite. In the interim, Pakistan administered the Northern Areas as a territory under the jurisdiction of a central government ministry, usually the Ministry of Kashmir Affairs.

Generally, the Azad Kashmir Government accepted that the Northern Areas were outside its jurisdiction. Privately, as early as 1950, Ghulam Abbas wrote to Liaquat Ali Khan telling him that the Working Committee of the Muslim Conference had passed a resolution about the 'unsatisfactory state of affairs prevailing at present in Gilgit and Baltistan'. It 'demand[ed] that the control over these areas be immediately transferred to the Ministry of Kashmir Affairs and the Azad Kashmir Government',[47] a surprising prospective arrangement explicable at this stage because Azad Kashmiris were not yet subservient to the MKA. However, this resolution had been withheld from 'both the press and the public' and from Liaquat: a tentative Abbas only informed him about the resolution two months after it was passed.[48] Liaquat's response is not known, although nothing changed because Pakistan continued to administer the Northern Areas directly through a bureaucrat sent by Karachi/Rawalpindi/Islamabad. Azad Kashmir accepted this ongoing situation.

## THE UNTOLD STORY OF THE PEOPLE OF AZAD KASHMIR

In 1993, Azad Kashmir's lack of control over the Northern Areas was challenged. The Azad Kashmir High Court upheld a petition that the Northern Areas should be annexed to, and administered by, the Azad Kashmir Government.[49] On 8 March 1993, the High Court directed the Azad Kashmir Government to 'immediately assume the administrative control' of the Northern Areas and to annex it to the Azad Kashmir administration.[50] The Pakistan Government, through its Ministry of Kashmir Affairs and Northern Affairs, appealed against the High Court's (totally unenforceable) decision. In 1994, the Azad Kashmir Supreme Court overturned the High Court's decision and dismissed its directive.[51] The Supreme Court's judgment stated that the Northern Areas were 'not a part of Azad Jammu and Kashmir as defined in the Interim Constitution Act, 1974'. It also deemed that the Azad Kashmir High Court did not have the 'necessary jurisdiction' to order Pakistan to give control of the Northern Areas to the Azad Kashmir Government.[52] Pakistan therefore retained its control of this region, as it still does.[53]

*From 1949–1971: the reunification dilemma*

Immediately after the 1949 ceasefire, Azad Kashmiris (and Pakistanis) faced a dilemma: should Azad Kashmir put down permanent administrative roots or wait until the UN plebiscite was held, after which J&K would be reunited and centrally governed again?[54] In the interim, Azad Kashmiris focused on meeting the 'political and ideological aspirations of the ... artificially divided' people of J&K.[55] This included developing an administration—at least for Azad Kashmir. They also contemplated how, after a plebiscite, their administration would subsume Indian J&K and its National Conference-led administration, an ongoing desire that was not really extinguished until Pakistan's defeat in the 1971 India-Pakistan war. By the mid-1950s, with the plebiscite looking unlikely to be held, some Azad Kashmiris still believed that the Azad Kashmir Government needed to maintain 'machinery' that could 'at a moment's notice' take over all of J&K 'in the event of a decision whenever it comes'.[56] Even after the Simla Agreement, when the plebiscite was removed from the India-Pakistan agenda, the first point in the preamble to Azad Kashmir's 1974 Interim Constitution stated that the UN-supervised poll should be conducted.[57] After General Zia seized power in 1977, he reinstated the plebiscite as Pakistan's preferred way to resolve the Kashmir dispute. This rekindled some Azad Kashmiris' aspirations to maintain an adequate administration in case J&K was ever reunified. By then, most Azad Kashmiris recognised that reunification would not happen quickly, if at all.

Disregarding the plebiscite issue, after the 1949 ceasefire the Azad Kashmir Government was compelled to change from a war council opposing Indian forces to a peacetime administration governing Azad Kashmir. By March 1949, UNCIP noted that, according to the Azad Kashmiris, there was a 'functioning "government" throughout the entire area of Western Kashmir'. It sought to perform all administrative functions, except the provision of post and telegraph services and controlling the Azad Army, both of which were under the respective control of the Pakistan Government and the Pakistan Army.[58] This 'government' comprised

## THE ADMINISTRATION: LARGE AND OVERSEEN

a five-man cabinet and a civil secretariat. Cabinet members were Sardar Ibrahim, President; Colonel Ali Ahmad Shah, Defence Minister; Nazir Hussain Shah, Finance; Mirwaiz Yusuf Shah, Health and Education; and, Ghulam-ud-Din Wani, Revenue.[59] The civil secretariat had eight departments: General Secretariat; Law and Order; Finance; Revenue and Public Works; Development; Health and Education; Defence; and Foreign Affairs, to liaise with the 'outside world'. There also was a fairly autonomous district-based administration that had 'withstood the impact of the fighting and disturbances reasonably well'.[60] A District Magistrate and subordinates administered each of Azad Kashmir's three districts of Muzaffarabad, Mirpur and Poonch, and associated *tehsils*.[61] Within Azad Kashmir, 200 elected Panchayat councils covered some 500 villages, and Muzaffarabad had a Town Area Committee.[62]

While there was, overall, generally a 'shortage of trained personnel' in Azad Kashmir,[63] this did not apply to the police force. Of the region's seventy to eighty administrative personnel, about three-quarters had previously been in government service, principally in the Maharaja's bureaucracy. The new regime upgraded their ranks and responsibilities.[64] The Azad Kashmir Police comprised eighty-eight officers and 1,013 men. Relative to its 1947 strength, its presence had increased in this area. Of these policemen, 95 per cent had served in the J&K Police Force; many were promoted from their previous ranks.[65] UNCIP considered the Azad Kashmir Police 'well disciplined and armed, and [it] appeared capable of maintaining law and order in the area under present conditions'. Azad Kashmir also had a forest patrol, a customs patrol and a 'Home Guard' of about 500 personnel. The Home Guard was 'organized and directed by the Muslim Conference', although not very well.

One of the Azad Kashmir administration's first peacetime requirements was to create a new capital away from the former front line. Following a 'frantic search',[66] administrators chose 'war battered' Muzaffarabad as the new capital on 8 February 1949.[67] Although this district headquarters had been considered the unattractive 'Siberia' or 'Coventry' of the Maharaja's regime,[68] its strategic location made it the 'obvious choice'.[69] Muzaffarabad was near Poonch, where many of Azad Kashmir's leaders and defenders lived. It had good road connections with Rawalpindi, Murree and Abbottabad in Pakistan. Its selection 'by implication' served as 'a constant reminder' of the Azad Kashmir movement's real objective, Srinagar,[70] only 111 miles down the motorable Jhelum Valley Road—had it been open.[71] Muzaffarabad was also the only place in Azad Kashmir that resembled an urban area or 'continuous habitation' with a population of 5,000 or more.[72] The only other district headquarters in Azad Kashmiri hands was Mirpur, which had been Jammu Province's second biggest town and the town with the easiest access to Pakistan. But Mirpur was 'a city of the dead'. Before Azad Kashmiris captured it on 25 November 1947, fleeing Dogras, departing Hindu and Sikh residents and heavy RIAF bombardment had 'devastated' Mirpur.[73] UNCIP, whose members visited Mirpur on 19 March 1949, confirmed that the town was 'very severely damaged both in fighting and the subsequent bombing'.[74] In Muzaffarabad, however, some brick buildings, including the district court and lock-up, had survived the RIAF's attacks.[75]

As part of becoming a peacetime administration, on 28 December 1950, the Azad Kashmir Government framed some Rules of Business with which to guide and govern Azad Kashmir.[76] These were replaced by new rules in 1952, then 1958, after which came a series of legislative acts. The Supreme Head of the Azad Kashmir Movement, Ghulam Abbas, who was then based in Murree, issued the 1950 Rules of Business. While confirming that power flowed downwards from him, they also provided, 'broad principles and regulations for the functioning of the [Azad Kashmir] Administration' and regulated 'the classification and distribution of the business of the Government among the officers of the Government'.[77] This enabled Azad Kashmiris to operate their own administration largely unhindered. In October 1952, the Rules of Business were heavily revised.[78] This revision established an ongoing system in which ultimate political and administrative power rested with Pakistan's Ministry of Kashmir Affairs. The Azad Kashmir Government was to consult it on almost all matters and the Joint Secretary of the MKA was the final arbiter on all appeals. While this put Pakistan in a powerful position, it also regularised Azad Kashmir's relationship with its metropolitan power.

In 29 November 1958 Sardar Ibrahim, as Azad Kashmir President, enacted a revised set of Rules of Business to 'regulate the Constitution of the Azad Kashmir Government' and for the 'distribution of the Business of the Government'.[79] These Rules maintained the MKA's superior position, with the Muslim Conference having some say, subject to MKA approval, in who should be Azad Kashmir's president. He would 'hold office during the pleasure' of the Muslim Conference 'duly recognised as such by the Government of Pakistan in the Ministry of Kashmir Affairs'.[80] While the MKA was effectively in charge of Azad Kashmir, in the final paragraph Ibrahim seemingly had the final word: 'Notwithstanding anything contained in the foregoing sections, the President' alone could constitute 'the Government without any other members ... [and] will exercise all the powers of Council of Ministers'.[81] Given the MKA's dominance, this would only have occurred in a dire emergency, such as a full-scale attack on Azad Kashmir by India. Equally, given that these rules were formulated soon after General Ayub Khan's martial law regime took power in Pakistan, the MKA could have appointed a new president of its choosing to rule Azad Kashmir autocratically, if necessary.

The 1958 Rules made one major change: a 'Council' was formed that comprised the 'President and other Ministers of the Azad Kashmir Government'.[82] The Azad Kashmir president was president of this Council and of the government. However, a Pakistani 'lent officer' (see below) acting as Secretary-General effectively ran the Council. He controlled the Council's deliberations; all orders were issued over his signature.[83] He also dealt with the MKA, from which he specifically had to seek advice in relation to: 'i) State [sic] Budget; ii) Public debts and loans; iii) Foreign Relations; iv) Town Improvements and Development Schemes; and, v) Levy of new taxes and abolishing of existing ones'. An MKA 'Chief Adviser' could attend all Council meetings and 'tender advice on any matter under discussion'. The Secretary-General also had to seek the Chief Adviser's advice before submitting any matter to the Council, and on a range of other matters. These included legislation and laws, state property, internal security, civil supplies and rehabilitation, forests, public works over Rs. 100,000, and evacuees and their property.

From 1960, the situation changed as Azad Kashmir moved slowly towards a more participatory form of government. In 1961, Azad Kashmiris indirectly

## THE ADMINISTRATION: LARGE AND OVERSEEN

elected 'their' president and an Azad Kashmir Council under Ayub Khan's Basic Democracies system. The Presidential Election Act, 1960, superseded the Rules of Business and functioned in lieu of an Azad Kashmir constitution.[84] The subsequent Azad Jammu and Kashmir Government Act of 1964[85] and the Azad Jammu and Kashmir Government Act of 1968[86] determined Azad Kashmir's system of government. Local power was essentially invested in the Azad Kashmir president. The Azad Jammu and Kashmir Government Act, 1970, instituted a legislative assembly for Azad Kashmir for the first time. This was replaced by the current act, the Azad Jammu and Kashmir Interim Constitution Act, 1974, which provided a parliamentary system of government in Azad Kashmir 'on the pattern evolved in Pakistan'.[87] This was important as it seemingly diminished the MKA's direct control.

While the Rules of Business and their various replacements were supposed to allow Azad Kashmiris to govern themselves, in reality Pakistan heavily supervised, if not controlled, this process from 1952. Pakistan used two mechanisms: its Ministry of Kashmir Affairs and lent civil service officers. The intrusive MKA's joint secretary exercised 'general supervision' of all departments of the Azad Kashmir administration to ensure that employees discharged their duties 'properly'.[88] The MKA's 'advice' had to be obtained on a broad list of fifteen items before a matter could be submitted to the Azad Kashmir Council.[89] This list had six items that included the word 'all'. The first three items on the list were broad and extensive: 'All questions of general policy'; 'All important matters involving heavy financial commitments'; 'All matters relating to legislation, statutory rules, regulations and by laws'. The other twelve items ranged from foreign affairs, through budgetary, taxation and expenditure matters, to internal security. Finally, legislation or rules passed by the Azad Kashmir Council only had the 'force of law' after they had received the MKA's 'concurrence'.[90]

The second mechanism that ensured Pakistan's control was 'lending' of officers from its administration to the Azad Kashmir administration. These 'lent officers' followed a tradition whereby the Raja of Poonch 'borrowed' officers from the Maharaja's service for his own administration.[91] In 1949, there were 'only thirteen Pakistani nationals … serving as executive officials in the Azad administration', although they may have been employees, not lent officers.[92] They helped Azad Kashmir meet its serious lack of able, experienced or qualified personnel. Being outsiders, the Pakistanis also helped to overcome some tribal or *biradari* issues in the Azad Kashmir bureaucracy that arose on account of the region's diverse social structure and the early Abbas-Ibrahim political split in which the bureaucracy took sides and 'parallel administrations' emerged.[93] Invariably however, lent officers' loyalties lay with Pakistan. Such senior Pakistanis were not always popular with Azad Kashmiris who perceived that many lent officers, particularly in the 1950s, 'lived as High-caste Brahmins in what they considered a society of untouchables'.[94] The Pakistanis felt superior; Azad Kashmiris were inferior.

As Azad Kashmiris' skills advanced, the number of Pakistani lent officers reduced. Nevertheless, they heavily 'influenced' Azad Kashmir's administration by serving in five very senior administrative positions (a situation that continues, not necessarily with popular local approval). Of the eleven most senior 'Category 1' positions in the Azad Kashmir administration,[95] Pakistanis served in the important and influential positions of: Secretary General/Chief Secretary; Finance Secretary;

Accountant-General; Inspector-General of Police; and Chief Engineer/Development Commissioner.[96] The Secretary General was very powerful as he was in charge of the overall administration and its personnel, including all Category 1 officers.[97] He determined what matters were presented to the Azad Kashmir Council, and after 1955 could, 'at his discretion', call for any file or case and issue orders or take actions in relation to it as he considered 'necessary or appropriate', while obtaining the Council's approval only 'where necessary'.[98] The term 'where necessary' was not qualified. Overall, Pakistani lent officers had control of the Azad Kashmir Council, the Azad Kashmir administration and its associated financial arrangements, as well as law and order.

While the arrangement of lent officers in Azad Kashmir was based on 'mutually accepted traditions and trust',[99] their actual legal position is unclear as none of the various 'Rules of Business' specifically mention such roles. Lent officers appear to have been under the Ministry of Kashmir Affairs' control in its role 'exercis[ing] general supervision' over Azad Kashmir's administration to ensure that 'Government employees discharge their duties properly'.[100] Certainly in 1981, the MKA was involved with lent officers, with performance evaluation reports for 'Federal Government Officers in Azad Kashmir' to be 'countersigned' by the Minister for Kashmir Affairs.[101] Similarly, a Section Officer (Kashmir) in the (Pakistan) Kashmir Affairs Division was responsible for 'All matter [sic] relating to the Lent Officers posted in Azad Kashmir'.[102] As 'members of the Central Superior Services', lent officers were probably paid by the Pakistan Government, although I cannot confirm this.[103]

In a sign of the integrated nature of Pakistan-Azad Kashmir relations, Azad Kashmiris have been able to join the Pakistan Central Superior Service for some time.[104] As early as 1949, the Pakistani body applied a federal quota system to recruit 80 per cent of its staff, with the other 20 per cent recruited on merit. From all positions, 15 per cent were allocated to individuals from Sind, Khairpur, NWFP, the Frontier States and Tribal Areas, Baluchistan, Azad Kashmir and Kashmir refugees. After August 1973, Azad Kashmir was allocated two per cent of all Federal Public Service Commission positions. Azad Kashmir was unable to fill its quota because not enough Azad Kashmiris with suitable qualifications were applying. It was therefore under-represented numerically and in the number of higher positions held. Nevertheless, the two-way flow of people between the bureaucracies of Pakistan and Azad Kashmir suggested that Azad Kashmir's status was not as unresolved as Pakistanis and Azad Kashmiris suggest.

Until 1970, Azad Kashmir's executive and legislative functions were exercised by the Azad Kashmir 'President with his Council of Ministers' and later by the 'President's Council' under a Supreme Head. These bodies overcame Azad Kashmir's initial lack of laws by taking them from elsewhere, including from Dogra and Pakistani laws.[105] The latter included some laws in force in (Pakistani) Punjab to do with land[106] and criminality,[107] which Azad Kashmir adopted by its 'Adaptation of Laws Act, 1948'.[108] In 1959, the Azad Kashmir Government enacted the 'very important piece of legislation' known as 'the Azad Kashmir Adaption [sic] of Laws Act, 1959'.[109] This brought the region into line with laws in force in West Pakistan and effectively bound it to Pakistan's legal system. Nevertheless, by 1965 the Azad Kashmir legal system still comprised 'laws of the old [Dogra] regime', laws of

## THE ADMINISTRATION: LARGE AND OVERSEEN

Pakistan or of the 'former Punjab specifically adapted', and laws enacted by the Azad Kashmir Government.[110] This composite legal system was workable, although outside laws sometimes caused problems; for example, the J&K Land Revenue Act, which was based on the Punjab Land Revenue Act, had to be amended to protect the mulberry tree, a valued item in J&K but not in Punjab. Otherwise, Azad Kashmiris' reliance on others' law reflected the uncertain state of affairs caused by their wait for the promised plebiscite. Alternatively, Azad Kashmiris knew that, when J&K did eventually join Pakistan, the application of Pakistan's laws would be easier as they were already using some of them.

Revenue collection was a major issue in Azad Kashmir chiefly because, from the outset, finances were scarce.[111] In 1949–50, the administration's estimated revenue was Rs. 3.825 million, comprising sales of forest products from the state-owned forest monopoly, 60 per cent; customs duties, 20 per cent; land revenue, 13 per cent; 'State property outside the State' (revenue earned from the Maharaja's confiscated property in Pakistan), 3 per cent; and various smaller revenue sources, such as stamps and income tax (levied on government servants whose remuneration exceeded Rs. 2000 per month). An 'indeterminable' amount was received from donations. UNCIP was informed that, in the six months to March 1949, a deficit of nearly Rs. 10 million was 'almost equalled by voluntary private donations'. In 1949–50, expenditure would be Rs. 13.7 million, of which Rs. 8 million was 'earmarked for refugee purposes'. Again, a Rs. 10 million deficit would be met by private donations and by asking the Pakistan Government for assistance.

While Azad Kashmir's Revenue Department occupied a 'vital position' in Azad Kashmir's administration, it faced three initial problems. First, before August 1947, most J&K revenue officers were Hindus; their subsequent disappearance from areas that became Azad Kashmir created a 'vacuum' in the Revenue Department, which started functioning with the few Muslim officers remaining.[112] Second, during the fighting in J&K between October 1947 and January 1949, some revenue records were destroyed, while others were unobtainable because they were in Indian J&K.[113] (Conversely, seeking to impress, Azad Kashmir told UNCIP that 'pre-existing land records ha[d] been preserved and kept up to date for revenue purposes', a factor that 'should prove helpful' in identifying 'bona fide' residents, i.e. state subjects.)[114] Third, it was 'extremely difficult' for the Azad Kashmir administration 'to float a loan' to pay for its financial requirements, particularly to care for and rehabilitate refugees. This was because 'the "Government [of Azad Kashmir]" was not recognized'. Over time, this issue would diminish as Pakistan provided donations or loans to the deficit financial area of Azad Kashmir, a policy that meshed with the use of Pakistani currency in Azad Kashmir.[115] In 1949, the Revenue Department was reorganised under a commissioner (Financial Commissioner in 1965) and three deputies.[116] The commissioner was a Category 1 officer.[117] His three deputies administered Azad Kashmir's three districts of Mirpur, Muzaffarabad and Poonch. Each district was divided into *tehsils* headed by a *tehsildar* and further sub-divisions controlled by *naib* (assistant) *tehsildars*.[118] In 1965, Mirpur District had three *tehsils* and one separate *naibat*, Muzaffarabad District had two *tehsils* and one separate *naibat*, and Poonch District had three *tehsils*.[119] Acting as revenue collectors and local magistrates, officials controlling these areas were locally powerful.[120]

# THE UNTOLD STORY OF THE PEOPLE OF AZAD KASHMIR

By 1965, President Hamid Khan believed that the Azad Kashmir Government's achievements 'may not be spectacular' but they were 'by no means small either', given its limited resources and its primary objective of freeing the remainder of J&K 'from the unscrupulous aggressor'.[121] His government's 'ultimate goal' was (still) to 'liberate the Indian Occupied area' of J&K, with the reconstruction work 'done or being done' in Azad Kashmir as 'a step forward towards that goal'.[122] Reflecting this goal, Azad Kashmir had an 'effective' but 'elaborate' and 'top heavy' administrative machinery'.[123] In 1958, this comprised seventeen departments and numerous gazetted officers.[124] There was a court system, with a High Court that acted as a court of appeal, with 'three High Court Judges to hear the appeals of two Sessions Judges, and seven Secretaries to the Government'.[125] Hamid Khan gave no figures for the number of government employees. However, Azad Kashmir's administration had three deputy commissioners and their staffs of assistant commissioners, *tehsildars* and revenue assistants. All were gazetted officers. Some Azad Kashmiris 'stoutly' defended this 'top heavy' structure. Like the President, they believed that, after a plebiscite, their 'ideological state' would need to expand to assume the administration for all of J&K.[126] Conversely, this focus on its 'primary objective' of liberating the rest of J&K enabled Azad Kashmiri leaders to conveniently shift their citizens' attention away from their own region's shortcomings.

## After 1971: permanency

The aftermath of the 1971 India–Pakistan war changed Azad Kashmir's administration. With Pakistan's military forces unable to 'liberate' J&K and the plebiscite unlikely, permanent administrative arrangements were needed. At the same time, Pakistan paid greater attention to developing Azad Kashmir politically and economically. Until the late 1980s, information was scarce about administrative developments in Azad Kashmir, although little appears to have happened between Azad Kashmir's 1972 Census and 1981 Census.[127] In the late 1980s, Azad Kashmir authorities became more forthcoming. This may have reflected the region's better democratic practices, better organisation, or more openness. From the late 1980s, the Azad Kashmir Government regularly produced pamphlets such as *Azad Kashmir at a Glance*, which provided general information about the region's economy and administration.[128] Documents such as censuses and Azad Kashmir Planning and Development Department publications also contain much information, although their restricted classification and limited distribution make them hard to procure. More recently, official Internet sites provide much information about Azad Kashmir,[129] although they do not discuss the politics behind administrative decisions. The 2000s are not covered in detail below: information about this period is now available on official websites (although these often 'recycle' sometimes inaccurate information from older official paper publications).

Some time after 1972, two new districts were created in Azad Kashmir: Bagh and Kotli.[130] Along with Mirpur, Muzaffarabad and Poonch districts, this brought the total to five. The Azad Kashmir Government was unsure exactly when these new districts were created: 'Between 1972 and 1981'—between census times— Kotli was 'carved out' of Mirpur District,[131] while Bagh was 'carved out' of

## THE ADMINISTRATION: LARGE AND OVERSEEN

Poonch District 'a number of years after the [1981] Census took place'.[132] No reason for creating these new districts was given, although it may have been to appease important local politicians: Sardar Qayyum was from Bagh, Sardar Sikandar was from Kotli. More likely, it was to deal with population increases. By 1981, Azad Kashmir's population was 1.98 million. This was a 26 per cent increase over the 1972 figure of 1.6 million. The population was projected to continue to grow at a rate of 2.7 per cent per annum and reach 2.6 million in 1991.[133] In 1981, Muzaffarabad District remained Azad Kashmir's largest district. It also had become the most populous district, although Poonch District's population growth, which was both higher and for a much smaller area, overshadowed Muzaffarabad's. By comparison, Mirpur District had a low population growth rate, which probably reflected its greater overall affluence and possible emigration (see next chapter). Almost 92 per cent of Azad Kashmir's 1.98 million people lived in rural areas.[134]

From 1958 to 1975, it is unclear under which exact legal instrument Azad Kashmir's public sector operated. The Azad Kashmir Council was involved in administering the region, but to what extent and how this actually happened is not known. After 1975, Azad Kashmir operated under the 'Rules of Business, 1975'.[135] These would have been created under Section 58 of the Interim Constitution, which states that the 'President may make rules for carrying out the purposes of this Act'.[136] From 1 June 1985, the major document that guided the Azad Kashmir administration in its functions and operations was the 'Rules of Business 1985'. This was a restricted document 'in supersession' of the 'Rules of Business, 1975'.[137] It was also one of the last acts passed under Azad Kashmir's Chief Executive/President, Major-General (Retired) Rehman Khan, before his military-backed regime handed power to Sardar Sikandar's 'elected' government. Indeed, the Rules were instituted in the period between election day (15 May 1985) and when the Legislative Assembly elected Sardar Sikandar Prime Minister (16 June 1985). While the President was 'Pleased to make the following rules for transaction of the business of government', Rehman did not sign the document. A middling Category II bureaucrat, 'Chaundry Mohammad Latif, Joint Secretary, Services & General Administration Department', signed it.[138] The Rules appear to have been updated in 2002,[139] but not superseded.[140] Given this, we may assume that Azad Kashmir's Rules of Business 1985, despite being imposed by a military president, have operated reasonably effectively.[141]

The Rules of Business 1985 were far more comprehensive than previous Rules. They distributed 'business' ranging from the 'Eradication of Social Evils' (to the Local Government, Rural Development and Social Welfare Department), through 'Public order and internal security' (to the Home Department), to the actual 'Framing and alteration of Rules of Business for Azad Kashmir Government and allocation of business among Ministers' (to the all-powerful Services and General Administration Department). They detailed various political and administrative functions, departmental procedures and services, cabinet procedures, legislative procedures, the administration's relations with the Legislative Assembly, and miscellaneous provisions, and had nine detailed schedules listing administrative matters.[142] Unlike previous Rules, the 1985 Rules did not mention the Ministry of Kashmir Affairs. After the establishment of the Azad Kashmir Council in 1984, the MKA dealt with Azad Kashmir via this higher body.

155

# THE UNTOLD STORY OF THE PEOPLE OF AZAD KASHMIR

According to the Rules, the Azad Kashmir prime minister was the major political figure in the Azad Kashmir administration. He was head of the cabinet, co-ordinated all policy matters, allocated all business, determined departments and assigned them to ministers, and could seek any case or information from any office or department.[143] Ministers ran their departments, submitted cases to the prime minister when required, and kept him informed of important issues. There was also a chief secretary, who invariably was a Pakistani lent officer—although the Rules did not mention this aspect.[144] He was secretary to the cabinet, coordinated all departmental activities and cases from or submitted to the prime minister, was 'generally responsible for all matters affecting public tranquillity', and like the prime minister, could seek any case or information from any office or department. Under him came various secretaries who assisted the minister to formulate and execute policy, ran their departments and allocated tasks, and kept the minister and chief secretary informed of important cases. All business was disposed of by the Services and General Administration Department, of which the chief secretary was head, via 'Secretariat Instructions'. These orders were made in writing.

The Rules of Business also detailed the administrative structure and ranks of Azad Kashmir administrative officers. Schedules I and II respectively listed twenty-three departments and their subsidiary bodies, and the distribution of business among them.[145] Schedule IX provided a list of 'Administrative Authorities' that had five categories: the twelve 'Heads of Administrative Department', then categories I-IV, with administrative responsibility decreasing from I to III.[146] Category IV, 'All other Gazetted Officers', was the lowest category. Surprisingly, given his status as a lent officer, the chief secretary was ranked sixth in the 'Head of Administrative Department' category, coming after the chief justices of Azad Kashmir's major courts (Supreme, High, Shariat), the chairman of the Council of Islamic Ideology and the chief election commissioner. Also surprisingly, the chairman of the powerful 'Prime Minister's Inspection Team' was ranked last. This was despite—or perhaps because of—two of the Inspection Team's seven tasks being to inspect all government departments and bodies and to undertake 'Special assignments under the orders of the Prime Minister' to which 'Any requisition made or assistance sought ... shall be complied with promptly by all concerned'.[147] This may have been difficult to achieve, given that the chief secretary outranked the chairman of the Inspection Team.

The Rules of Business also detailed the specific roles and relationship of the president and prime minister. 'All executive actions of Government' were taken in the name of the president.[148] He did not attend cabinet, although Schedule V listed seventeen 'Cases to be submitted to the President for his Approval before issue of Orders'.[149] These cases related to Legislative Assembly matters (summoning, proroguing, dissolving), changing the Rules of Business, promulgating ordinances, the Advocate General, high-level financial matters, courts (Supreme, High, Shariat), Islamic ideology, the public service commission, petitions, staff, mercy petitions, and high-level university matters. Another schedule, Schedule VI, ensured that the president received all periodical reports of a political nature or relating to law and order or by department heads, special reports by officers about matters that 'seriously affect the peace and tranquillity of the territory', official press notes, and intelligence reports.

## THE ADMINISTRATION: LARGE AND OVERSEEN

The Rules of Business provided the prime minister with similar schedules that detailed his role. Schedule III listed twenty-two 'Cases to be submitted to the Prime Minister for Approval before issue of [O]rders'.[150] These cases related to day-to-day ministerial, business, budget, and expenditure and staffing matters that the prime minister had to address, including changing the Rules of Business and granting honours and awards. Interestingly, Schedule III had five items about matters that may involve the 'Federal Government' (of Pakistan), including any 'officer on deputation from the Government of Pakistan' (a lent officer) or 'members of all Pakistan Services' (possibly members of the Pakistan military). A further interesting item was 'All cases which may have a bearing on relations with a Foreign Government' which, given Azad Kashmir's geo-strategic situation, probably meant India. Rather surprisingly however, while the prime minister dealt with Pakistan, the Azad Kashmir president who was also vice-chairman of the Azad Kashmir Council under Pakistan's prime minister as chairman, did not deal with, or need to be informed about, any matters to do with the 'Federal Government' or a 'Foreign Government'. A further schedule, Schedule IV, ensured that the prime minister was provided with the same information as the president, but with the addition of access to reports of government-appointed committees.

In terms of administrative matters and information flows—or lack thereof—the Rules of Business 1985 made it appear that the prime minister was administratively superior to the president, as it should be in a prime ministerial system. The prime minister could control the president's access to many business matters and to information. Conversely, the president dealt with higher-level matters. He was in the superior titular and ceremonial position, with access to, and control over, high-level appointments and significant Legislative Assembly matters—but not during a state of emergency, when control appeared to lie with the prime minister.[151] The president was also in the superior position in the Azad Kashmir Council, of which the prime minister was an *ex-officio* member.

Arguably, the chief secretary was more administratively powerful than both the president and prime minister. Indeed, as the senior bureaucrat, he appeared to be the most powerful individual in the Azad Kashmir administration. He controlled the administration, what business and cases it undertook, which sections specifically did these, ensured that they reported back to him, and chose officers to run administrative branches and sections (via transfers, promotions). He was the funnel through which all decisions and cases descended from the prime minister or cabinet and through which all information, cases and reports ascended to them.[152] Through 'his' all-powerful Services and General Administration Department, to which all departments deferred, the chief secretary had his 'finger on the pulse' and in all administrative 'pies'. Given that this person was invariably a Pakistani lent officer, this put Pakistan in a powerful position. Equally, it reflected the situation whereby Azad Kashmir 'should for all practical [purposes] be treated like any other province'.[153]

By 1988, when General Zia's overbearing military oversight of Azad Kashmir finally ended, the region's administration had grown substantially from its impoverished beginnings. It had twenty-three departments[154] and an administrative set-up that comprised five districts, thirteen *tehsils*, twenty-nine police stations, thirty *markaz* councils (a *markaz* is a central body for a cluster of union councils, the area of which often mirrors a police district), seven municipal committees, ten town committees, 180 union councils, and 1,644 villages.[155] The urban areas that acted as district headquarters and their respective populations were: Muzaffarabad (Muzaffarabad District), 37,400; Bagh township (Bagh District), 3,600; Rawalakot (Poonch District), 15,800; Kotli (Kotli District), 15,800; and, Mirpur City (Mirpur District), 57,300.[156] Muzaffarabad was still Azad Kashmir's capital. Mirpur City's size reflected its district's greater affluence.

Table 6.1: Districts of Azad Kashmir, 1988: their area, populations (1972 and 1981), population density, urban percentage of population, average population growth and percentage change in populations (1972–81).

| District* | Area** | Pop. (1972) | Pop. (1981) | PD | %U | AGR | %Chge |
|---|---|---|---|---|---|---|---|
| Muzaffarabad | 6,117 | 349,216 | 466,297 | 76 | 10.0 | 3.42 | 33.53 |
| Bagh (E) | 1,368 | 243,667 | 314,834 | 342 | 2.0 | 2.40 | 29.21 |
| Poonch (E) | 1,424 | 300,068 | 407,180 | 218 | 6.0 | 3.40 | 35.70 |
| Kotli | 1,862 | 293,890 | 364,558 | 196 | 4.3 | 2.55 | 24.05 |
| Mirpur | 2,526 | 406,945 | 427,197 | 169 | 18.1 | 1.25 | 4.98 |
| Total AK | 13,297 | 1,593,786 | 1,980,066 | 149 | 8.1 | 2.74 | 25.90 |

Source: *Azad Kashmir Statistical Year Book 1990*, Muzaffarabad?, Statistics Section, Planning & Development Department, Azad Government of the State of Jammu & Kashmir [1992].

Key: AGR   Annual growth rate of population, 1972–1981.
     AK    Azad Kashmir.
     Chge  Change; percentage change in population, 1972–1981.
     E     Estimated population figures.
     Pop.   Population.
     PD    Population density per square kilometre.
     U     Urban; percentage of population that lived in urban areas.
     *     Districts listed from north to south.
     **    Area in square kilometres.

The Azad Kashmir administration had been busy since its inception. Within its five districts were 3,210 primary schools (educating 220,000 students), 792 middle schools (126,000 students), 425 high schools (135,000 students), 35 intermediate colleges (6,900 students) and 13 degree colleges (7,000 students).[157] Even so, only 28 per cent of Azad Kashmiris were literate: 43 per cent of males; 12.5 per cent of females.[158] While this was an increase on the 1951 figures of 11.6 per cent literacy (20 per cent of males; 2.6 per cent of females), female illiteracy was an ongoing issue owing to the need to provide separate schools for girls.[159] Azad Kashmir also had 11 hospitals (1,000 beds), 327 dispensaries (226 beds), 18 rural health centres (188 beds), 26 TB clinics and one TB hospital (50 beds), and 366 doctors.[160] This health system treated 745,000 patients, and dealt with 235 people injured and 84 people killed in 97 road accidents.[161] These resulted from 16,000 motor vehicles using 2,600 kms of high-type (1,400 kms) and low-type (1,200 kms) roads.[162]

## THE ADMINISTRATION: LARGE AND OVERSEEN

*After 1988, and the current administrative situation*

Surprisingly, given its role to deliver meaningful statistics and information, the 1998 Azad Kashmir Census only devotes three pages to Azad Kashmir's 'Administrative Set Up'. A major, but unexplained, administrative change occurred some time before this census: Azad Kashmir was demarcated into the divisions of Mirpur and Muzaffarabad.[163] This was done possibly to obtain greater efficiency, because of population increases, or as a response to political pressure. In 1995, Mirpur Division comprised Mirpur and Kotli districts; Muzaffarabad Division comprised Muzaffarabad, Poonch and Bagh districts.[164] Azad Kashmir's administrative set-up included seventeen *tehsils*, thirty police stations, thirty *markaz* councils, two municipal corporations, five municipal committees, twelve town committees, 202 union councils, and 1,646 villages. In 1996, two new districts were created: Bhimber District in Mirpur Division and Pallandri District in Muzaffarabad District. This led to the creation of two new *tehsils*, one within each newly created district.[165]

By 2008, Azad Kashmir's administrative structure had increased to three divisions and eight administrative districts.[166] Ironically, this administrative set-up superficially reflected the region's composition of three districts in 1947 (see Table 6.2), albeit with a third level of bureaucracy. The new division was Poonch, comprising Poonch, Bagh and Sudhnuti districts. Mirpur Division now had Mirpur, Bhimber and Kotli districts; Muzaffarabad Division comprised Muzaffarabad and Neelum districts. Neelum was a new district established in 2004 in the remoter northern parts of the previous large Muzaffarabad District. Azad Kashmir had twenty-seven subdivisions (or *tehsils*), forty-three police stations, thirty-one *markaz* councils, two municipal corporations, eleven municipal committees, five development authorities, 189 union councils (202 in 1998), and 1,654 villages (1,653 in 1998), each with elected local councils. No explanation was given for the decrease in union councils.

Although the various figures provided above for the administration were relatively impressive given the low base from which the region started in 1947, Azad Kashmir still had some major issues. The average annual population growth rate was 2.41 per cent, with the region's population increasing from 886,000 in 1951 to an estimated 3.77 million in 2008. As officially noted in 2007,[167] 'indicators of social sector improvement, particularly health and population welfare have not shown much proficiency'. Despite wanting to 'bring the fruits of development to the common man', the same official document showed that Azad Kashmiris experienced a population density of 277 persons per sq. kilometre, an infant mortality rate of fifty-six per 1,000 live births, an average per capita income of USD 908, 'inadequate' health care, and high unemployment. This latter is a major issue, particularly in relation to generating meaningful employment outside the government sector. Basically, Azad Kashmir had a large, and increasing, population that it was struggling to fully care for. The one bright spot was a credible, and improving, literacy rate of 64 per cent.

One result of Azad Kashmir's burgeoning administrative structure is that the government is the major employer in the region, with many Azad Kashmiris dependent on it for work. In 1988, 48,000 Azad Kashmiris worked directly in the Azad Kashmir bureaucracy's forty-one divisions.[168] By 1998, Azad Kashmir had 98,000 government employees, comprising 90,000 males and 8,000 females. A further 7,000 people worked in autonomous bodies.[169] The ten-year growth in the number of government employees is inexplicable. There was an increase in police strength from 4,500 (which figure included Home Department, jail and civil defence staff) in 1988 to 6,300 (police only) in 1998.[170] The 1988 figure is also only for 'sanctioned positions'—that is, permanent government positions—while the 1998 figure was for 'a person who works in any Government/Semi-Government Organization for pay'.[171] Nevertheless, in 1998, out of Azad Kashmir's total of 377,000 people in employment in 'all occupation groups', one in four employed Azad Kashmiris (28 per cent) worked directly or indirectly in government service. This preponderance was more pronounced in urban areas, where 43 per cent of employed people (26,000) worked for the government or autonomous bodies, compared with 25 per cent (79,000) in rural areas. This preponderance did not reflect Azad Kashmir's urban: rural population ratio of 12:88.[172] The region's latest administrative reorganisation into three divisions and various additional districts and sub-districts will likely generate further government jobs.

While Azad Kashmiris are dependent on government employment, many government activities and functions appear to be worthwhile. The 1998 Census does not provide sufficient detail to determine what does what among government employees. However, the *Statistical Year Book 1988* provides specific information about the Azad Kashmir Government's 48,000 employees in sanctioned posts.[173] The majority of these appear to be in productive or useful areas. In 1988, 52 per cent worked in the education sector, either for the Education Department (24,000) or for the University of Azad Jammu and Kashmir (850). The next largest departments were Home (4,500), which included police and jail staff responsible for dealing with 3,300 reported crimes,[174] Health (4,300), Electricity (2,000), Public Works (2,000) and Forestry (1,900). Work to do with religion and Islamic practices employed 525 people.[175] The smallest departments were the Election Commissioner (35), Provincial [sic] Transport Association (21), Public Service Commission (21), Sports (18), and the Election Commissioner for Local Bodies (eight staff). In 1985, Category 1 positions had increased markedly to 28 (11 in 1952), while there were 19 Category 2 officers (14 in 1952) and 49 Category 3 officers (who comprised all other officers in 1952).[176]

Apart from population growth, the major change in Azad Kashmir since 1947 is an increase in area (Table 6.2). In 1951, the Azad Kashmir Census officially stated that Azad Kashmir's area was 4,494 sq. miles.[177] Official publications now give its area as 13,297 sq. kilometres, or 5,134 sq. miles.[178] This additional 640 sq. miles represents a 14 per cent increase in Azad Kashmir's since 1947. It does not relate to a specific division or district. This upward revision possibly involved Azad Kashmir's Revenue Department, given its role of 'Territorial adjustments and changes'.[179] It could be due to unpublicised changes in boundaries, presumably with Pakistan, or to more accurate measurements being made. The revision appears to have been made between the 1972 and 1981 censuses. The official figure of 4,494 sq. miles was used in 1979.[180] The *Statistical Year Book 1988* confusingly provided an area of 11,642 sq. kilometres for Azad Kashmir in 1972 and an area of 13,297 sq. kilometres for 1981—on opposite pages.[181] By 1988, the revised figures of 13,297 sq. kilometres, or 5,134 sq. miles, were being used.[182] Thereafter, only these two figures appear in official publications. Somewhat suspiciously, the 1998 Census does not mention anywhere Azad Kashmir's actual area.

## THE ADMINISTRATION: LARGE AND OVERSEEN

Table 6.2: Administrative makeup of Azad Kashmir in 1951 and 2008.

| District | 1951 area sq. miles [sq. kms] | 1951 Pop. | Division | 2008 area [sq. miles] sq. kms | | 2008 Pop.* |
|---|---|---|---|---|---|---|
| Muzaffarabad | 2,082 [5,392] | 220,971 | Muzaffarabad | [2,362] | 6,117 | 983,000 |
| Poonch | 969 [2,510] | 293,723 | Poonch | [1,078] | 2,792 | 1,263,000 |
| Mirpur | 1,443 [3,737] | 371,459 | Mirpur | [1,694] | 4,388 | 1,528,000 |
| Total | 4,494 [11,639] | 886,153★ | Total | [5,134] | 13,297 | 3,774,000 |

Sources: 1) *Census of Azad Kashmir, 1951*, Murree?, Iftikhar Ahmad, Chief Enumeration Officer, Government of Azad Kashmir [1952].
2) *Azad Kashmir at a Glance*, 2008, Muzaffarabad, Planning & Development Department, Azad Govt. of the State of Jammu & Kashmir, 2008, www.pndajk.gov.pk/glance.asp [accessed 15 September 2010].
Key: Pop. Population.
     kms kilometres.
     sq. square (miles or kilometres).
     ★ Projected, 2008.
All figures in square brackets are conversions from the original measurement.

*Conclusion*

Azad Kashmiris have had little option but to be administratively dependent on Pakistan. Apart from the new Azad Kashmir administration's severe lack of trained and experienced personnel when it came into existence in 1947, Azad Kashmiris had no other choice but to turn to Pakistan for military and administrative support and assistance. They needed such help to ensure their region's survival and to continue their struggle to liberate J&K from Indian control. This fight was far more important than the need to develop a fully-fledged administration. After the 1949 ceasefire, Azad Kashmiris still retained their desire to liberate all of J&K. The major difference was that the UN-supervised plebiscite would now be the liberation vehicle. Because Azad Kashmiris saw their administration as an alternative government for J&K, they needed to develop an organisation that could successfully administer J&K when, as they believed, it was inevitably reunified after the plebiscite. This administration would need to be able to replace and liquidate the National Conference-dominated administration in Indian J&K. In 1952, Azad Kashmir's administrative situation changed greatly. With the plebiscite increasingly unlikely and with Pakistan having consolidated after the trauma and disruptions of Partition, Pakistan fully asserted itself in, and over, Azad Kashmir. It did so via its Ministry of Kashmir Affairs and the Business Rules that Karachi imposed on Azad Kashmir. As a result of both measures, the MKA became the driver and arbiter of Azad Kashmir's administrative agenda. This did not hinder the development of Azad Kashmir's administration, although increasingly, it became a moot point whether it was capable of administering all of J&K. Should the plebiscite ever be held, a relevant question would be, is it possible to actually amalgamate or disband this large and inveterate body?

# THE UNTOLD STORY OF THE PEOPLE OF AZAD KASHMIR

In 2010, with the plebiscite an issue only for senior Pakistani and Azad Kashmiri politicians, the Azad Kashmir administration is irretrievably entrenched as a necessary, permanent and ongoing entity in its own right. It now knows far more about itself and Azad Kashmiris than it did when the region started 'almost from scratch' in 1947.[183] Much of this information is publicly available through open Internet sources. Administratively, Pakistan still controls Azad Kashmir through two devices: the Azad Kashmir Council and, importantly, through the five lent officers that Islamabad continues to embed in the Azad Kashmir administration. These Pakistanis still fill the most senior positions in the Azad Kashmir administration—even though there are sufficiently skilled Azad Kashmiri officers now able to administer this region. Pakistani lent officers in Azad Kashmir act as Secretary General/Chief Secretary, Finance Secretary, Accountant-General, Inspector-General of Police, and Chief Engineer/Development Commissioner.[184] Between them, they control the most important aspects of Azad Kashmir's financial, bureaucratic and law and order agendas. From personal experience, Azad Kashmiris dislike this situation, partly because it prevents them from obtaining the most senior position in their particular service. The lent officers institution is evidence of the actual power that Pakistan continues to exercise in Azad Kashmir and over Azad Kashmiris.

7

# THE ECONOMY

## POOR AND DEPENDENT

*Introduction*

From the outset, Azad Kashmir's economy has been backward. Apart from forests and water, the region lacks physical assets and resources that could fuel significant economic growth. It also suffers from poor agricultural land, a lack of industry and related unemployment. In 1947 geographical, historical and familial links meant that a lot of economic activity was already heavily involved with areas in Pakistani Punjab and NWFP. People were reliant on these areas for physical support, including the provision of transport, communications and food, and for permanent and temporary employment. Even so, the loss by fighting of connections with Indian J&K from 1947, particularly the Jhelum Valley Road that carried tourists and trade between Rawalpindi and the Kashmir Valley, reduced Azad Kashmir's economic options. Azad Kashmir was also an unattractive investment destination because of its location immediately east of the heavily-militarised ceasefire line/LOC across which the Indian and Pakistan armies have had numerous and serious exchanges of fire since 1949. Consequently, Azad Kashmir has been totally dependent on Pakistan for defence, employment, goods and markets, food, and financial support. This has been an acceptable situation for Azad Kashmiris, given their preference to join Pakistan. That said, Pakistan has controlled the two factors that they could have exploited to reduce their region's dependency: hydroelectricity ('hydel') and foreign remittances. This chapter discusses these economic matters and some associated social aspects.

It is difficult to assess the depth and breadth of Azad Kashmir's economic and financial dependency on Pakistan and whether Pakistan has exacerbated this situation. Pakistani scholars and authors have written little about Azad Kashmir's economic situation, possibly because of a lack of information. Similarly, official Pakistan publications rarely publish data in national accounts about amounts of aid or assistance allocated to Azad Kashmir and their disbursement. This dearth of information is possibly because Pakistan does not regard Azad Kashmir as being legally part of Pakistan—even though, practically, this region is well integrated into the nation. This chapter's examination of Azad Kashmir's economy shows that, while the region is dependent on Pakistan, this is not necessarily a bad thing—Azad Kashmir needs all the help that it can get. Pakistan receives a return on its 'investment' from the significant amounts of water and hydro-electricity that it obtains from areas upstream in Azad Kashmir. Equally, given Pakistan's numerous political, economic and social challenges, a dependent, and therefore pliant, Azad Kashmir, may be to Islamabad's liking.

*The 'loss' of the Jhelum Valley Road*

In 1947, the Azad Kashmir economy—while not then a distinct or integrated entity—was considered to be on a 'subsistence level'.[1] The fight against India further damaged this situation, particularly in relation to food production, with military operations and RIAF activity making farming difficult and forcing peasants to leave large tracts of land fallow.[2] Nevertheless, in the early years, some Azad Kashmiris were highly optimistic about their economic prospects. In 1948, Hafizullah visualised: 'Kashmir flowing with milk and honey ... ribboned with thousands of miles of metalled roads and covered with brisk rail and road communications ... her cities bustling with trade and commerce and her skies streaked with the wandering smoke of her mills'.[3]

This dream would be financed by savings made from no longer having to support the Maharaja and his family, his army, and the 'fat salaries' paid to his officials. These consumed an 'unnecessary' Rs. 20.2 million of J&K's budget of Rs. 27.7 million.[4] New revenue sources, such as water and minerals, could also supplement the state's income. Consequently, J&K would soon 'radiate with knowledge, bliss and prosperity and become a veritable Queen of Asia'.[5] However, Hafizullah's dream was unrealistic. J&K has never reunified; Azad Kashmir remains underdeveloped and dependent on Pakistan.

The closure by fighting of the important and popular Jhelum Valley Road in October 1947 was a major loss, in economic terms, to northern Azad Kashmir. This 'windpipe' through which the Kashmir Valley 'breathed' went from Srinagar to Rawalpindi, via Domel and Murree.[6] Domel was situated at the confluence of the Jhelum and Kishenganga (now Neelum) rivers, near Muzaffarabad, which then had a large Sikh population and acted as the transport, urban and administration centre for Muzaffarabad District.[7] Postal and telegram services used the Jhelum Valley Road which was the 'most convenient route' into Kashmir Province.[8] Up to 98 per cent of the Kashmir Valley's non-forest exports, such as woollens, silks, curios, fruits and wood products,[9] went via this route to Rawalpindi,[10] which was the nearest railhead and an important storage centre for goods from Kashmir. Equally, locally-refined kerosene and petrol,[11] salt (for domestic and industrial purposes),[12] cooking oils and fats, sugar and manufactured goods,[13] were transported from Rawalpindi to Kashmir. The Jhelum Valley Road acquired even greater significance, and traffic, when the difficult road from Jammu City to Srinagar via Banihal Pass was blocked in winter because of rain and associated landslides or inundations of snow, as often happened.[14] Then, the all-weather Jhelum Valley Road via Domel was the only way out of, or into, the Kashmir Valley.[15]

## THE ECONOMY: POOR AND DEPENDENT

Considerable numbers of people also moved along the Jhelum Valley Road. Kashmiris seeking work in places such as Murree, Rawalpindi or Lahore, invariably left the Kashmir Valley via this road, as did men in northern Poonch seeking work outside J&K, taking up, or returning to, positions in the Indian Army. So too did people entering Kashmir Province for rest or recreation in the scenic Kashmir Valley. In 1947, Kashmir Province was a popular tourist destination, with 40,000 tourists and an industry worth Rs. 1.5 million.[16] Many holidaymakers came from West Punjab, where the only major summer health resort or hill station was the 'comparatively small' Murree.[17] To control the movement of people visiting J&K via Kashmir Province, J&K Customs Service had posts at Kohala, on the Jhelum River border with NWFP and at Domel, at which custom tolls were paid. Domel had a dispensary, hospital, petrol pump and 'Hindu kitchen'. Both locations had post and telegraph facilities and 'dak bungalow' accommodation.[18] With Rawalpindi being the closest railway station to Kashmir Province and with plane travel to Srinagar generally not an option, the Jhelum Valley Road via Domel was the easiest and quickest way to get to Srinagar.

From late October 1947, fighting closed the Jhelum Valley Road. This fighting was between the various pro-Pakistan forces, including Pukhtoon tribesmen who entered Kashmir Province along this road, and India's armed forces. The 1949 ceasefire line formalised this closure and J&K's division, with 'the economic disruption caused by the *de facto* partition [of J&K] along the Cease Fire line [being] deplorable'.[19] Apart from the Jhelum Valley Road, other major roads, such as between Rawalakot and Poonch City, Kotli and Poonch City, and Bhimber and Rajouri, were no longer accessible. These closures ended any trade—and most formal and informal links—between people in these areas. J&K's division also ended the traditional floating of large quantities of timber from the Kashmir Valley along the Jhelum River, via Domel and Kohala, to Punjab; this was collected at, and distributed from, Jhelum town.[20] Given that the main markets for J&K timber were also in areas that became part of India in 1947,[21] the ending of this timber trade represented an economic loss for Azad Kashmir. Similarly, the closure of the Jhelum Valley Road deprived the Azad Kashmir Government of transit and other revenues that it could have obtained from travellers and traders using this route.

Following J&K's division by fighting, then by the formal ceasefire line, Azad Kashmiris' only choice thereafter was to be involved physically and economically with Pakistan. As it was sandwiched between the ceasefire line and Pakistan, previous locations that had been venues for undertakings by Azad Kashmiris, such as Srinagar, Jammu City or Poonch City, were no longer accessible; nor was India. Pakistan was the only outside place to which Azad Kashmiris could travel and with which they could trade. After the actual ceasefire line was demarcated in July 1949, a Pakistani 'timber curtain', not unlike the 'iron curtain', descended around Azad Kashmir and the Northern Areas, while an Indian 'timber curtain' descended around Indian J&K.[22] These effectively ensured that Pakistan-Administered J&K and Indian J&K thereafter had no formal, and little informal, contact. The Pakistani 'curtain' also cocooned Azad Kashmir and prevented it from having any outside economic relations with any place but Pakistan.

# THE UNTOLD STORY OF THE PEOPLE OF AZAD KASHMIR

*Dependence on Pakistan*

From its inception, the region that came to comprise Azad Kashmir suffered from physical and economic disadvantages. Azad Kashmir had poor transport and communication networks. Its hilly-to-mountainous terrain intersected by powerful rivers and waterways made development difficult. Its agricultural land was not highly productive, because of poor soil and small landholdings. It lacked exploitable raw materials. It had little industry. These factors, coupled with a lack of urban centres, meant that Azad Kashmiris lacked internal employment opportunities. Furthermore, Azad Kashmir had few comparative advantages that made it an attractive destination for investment and industry. Its only abundant assets were water, human beings and forest products. However, Azad Kashmiris were often unskilled and inexperienced in business, they suffered from a lack of business planning on their behalf.[23] The Azad Kashmir Government was otherwise 'saddled with twin tasks': 'rehabilitating' its war-ravaged economy and 'initiating schemes of development to raise the standard of living of the people'.[24]

Azad Kashmir's physical location was also a disincentive to economic investment, development, and even the provision of aid. Because Azad Kashmir was only 200 miles long and forty-five miles wide at its widest,[25] the entire region was located in the general proximity of the heavily-armed and highly volatile military zone that straddled the ceasefire line. The western border of Poonch District was furthest from the ceasefire line, but the furthest parts of Muzaffarabad District were only fourteen miles away from it. Proximity to the ceasefire line was rarely discussed as an impediment to development, although a 1965 Azad Kashmir Government publication did state that the biggest handicap facing the region was 'the presence of an armed enemy along the ceasefire line and its ever-increasing aggressive activities disrupting the smooth functioning of life in the liberated areas'. Consequently, an 'all embracing' economic programme was not conceivable 'unless the entire State is cleared of the enemy'.[26] Vulnerability to Indian military activity, including small arms and artillery fire, discouraged aid agencies from accessing Azad Kashmir because it was a 'sensitive area'.[27] This vulnerability was also a strong disincentive to the establishment of major industrial undertakings in the region.

In the early years and despite its dependency on Pakistan, Azad Kashmir maintained financial separation. In 1949, Azad Kashmir-Pakistan trade was worth Rs. 10 million, with Azad Kashmir's exports including timber (the largest export earner), forest products, fruit (fresh and dry), herbs and chillies, forest grass, sheep and goats, and hides and skins.[28] Imports from Pakistan included consumer goods and cloth.[29] Until April 1951, the Azad Kashmir Government levied customs duties on all goods entering Azad Kashmir, and on some goods leaving. Although this provided an annual income of Rs. 1.2 million, these customs duties were abolished as they opposed 'the spirit of the freedom movement which aimed at [the] accession of the entire state to Pakistan'.[30] By 1960–61, Azad Kashmir's new Taxation and Excise Department that replaced the Customs and Excise Department was collecting eight taxes, of which four delivered most of the region's Rs. 846,000 revenue: income tax; road toll; registration fees, licence fees and motor tax; and excise duty on tobacco. Other taxes comprised duties on entertainments and opium, radio licence fees, and miscellaneous taxes. Grants from Pakistan prob-

## THE ECONOMY: POOR AND DEPENDENT

ably made up the Azad Kashmir Government's revenue shortfall arising from its loss of customs duties. By 1963–64, the region's tax revenues of Rs. 1,468,000 exceeded customs duties collected in 1951.[31]

Primarily, Azad Kashmir's status as a dependent economic region arose from its inability to produce sufficient food. Azad Kashmir had a 'huge deficit in food grains' that only Pakistan could supply. It was thus 'unavoidable' for Azad Kashmir to import 'enormous quantities of food grains every year' from Pakistan.[32] This dependency was recognised early. In 1949, UNCIP reported that Azad Kashmir had 'never been more than approximately 50 per cent self sufficient in food grains, [with] the present figure given as 40 per cent'.[33] According to the Azad Kashmir Government, this deficiency was due to the 'loss' of Rajouri and Mendhar, 'the grannaries [sic] of Azad Kashmir'. Consequently, Azad Kashmir was importing 5,000–10,000 tons of grain per month, with Mirpur importing about half of its total grain requirements, and Poonch and Muzaffarabad importing more than three-quarters.[34] In 1951, the census queried whether Azad Kashmir had 'the means' to support the number of people inhabiting the region, or 'even for a lesser number' minus refugees: 'Unfortunately, the answer … is in the negative and that too of an emphatic nature'.[35] While agriculture, which included forestry, was the 'mainstay' of Azad Kashmir,[36] in terms of producing edible foodstuffs, the region could not support its population.

One significant, and ongoing, reason for Azad Kashmir's food deficiency and consequent dependency on Pakistan, was a lack of cultivable land in this hilly-to-mountainous region, with landholdings small, uneconomic and 'mainly dependent on rainfall'.[37] Cultivable land was defined as land 'assessed to land revenue, which includes fallows and lands on which no crops can be raised but are held by individual farmers for grass for their livestock'.[38] In 1951, out of Azad Kashmir's total area of 2.9 million acres, only 527,000 acres (18 per cent) was land assessed for land revenue. Mirpur District had the most cultivable land, with 269,000 acres (30 per cent of the district); Poonch District had 151,000 acres (24 per cent), whilst Muzaffarabad District had 107,000 acres (8 per cent).[39] By 1990, cultivable land had decreased to 14.6 per cent of Azad Kashmir's total area, probably because of increased urbanisation. By 2005–06,[40] this figure was 13 per cent, or 410,000 acres (166,000 hectares), with 92 per cent of cultivable land dependent on rainfall. About 84 per cent of all households had land-holdings, but these were small: the average farm area was 2.7 acres (1.1 hectare) per family, or per capita 0.37 acres (0.15 hectares); the average cultivated area was 1.43 acres (0.58 hectares) per family, and per capita 0.2 acres (0.08 hectares). Only two per cent of Azad Kashmiris did not own land, which meant that, unlike Pakistan, Azad Kashmir did not suffer from oppressive feudalism. Conversely, the 'unyielding conservativeness of a considerable section of the agricultural classes' meant that small landholdings continued to be subdivided among (mainly male) heirs, causing further inefficiencies and houses being built on scarce land.[41]

A further reason for Azad Kashmir's food deficiency and dependency on Pakistan was Azad Kashmir's poor soil and low productivity. This latter was due partly to Azad Kashmir's cold climate that mostly allowed only a single crop each year, and partly to a general lack of irrigation, despite the presence of some significant rivers in the region: the Jhelum, Neelum and Poonch. Between 1982 and 1987,[42] based on average hectares cropped per annum,[43] Azad Kashmir's most important crops were maize and wheat, with rice grown also. As Table 7.1 shows, per annum yields were low between 1982 and 1987, and again in 1997–98, although rice yields for this one-off year had reduced markedly.[44] These low yields were despite Azad Kashmir's farmers possibly having benefited by then from advances in agriculture, such as better seed varieties, fertilisers and mechanisation. Additionally, by 1997–98, only 8,800 hectares in Azad Kashmir were irrigated, chiefly in the cooler Muzaffarabad District (6,200 hectares), then in the temperate Mirpur/Bhimber areas (1,400).[45] Some farmers, probably in the irrigated areas, produced two crops each year: *rabi* (harvested in spring) and *kharif* (harvested in autumn). By 2005–06,[46] the total cropped area was 240,000 hectares, with the irrigated area having increased to 15,500 hectares.[47]

Table 7.1: Crops in Azad Kashmir from 1982 to 1987 and in 1997–98, including average area cropped per annum and average yield per annum, compared with average yield per annum in Pakistan and for the world leader during the 1982–87 period.

| Crop | Av. Area* '82–87 | AY AK '82–87 | AY Pak '82–87 | AY WL '82–87 | Area* '97–98 | AY AK '97–98 |
|---|---|---|---|---|---|---|
| Maize | 123,000 | 1,100 | 1,300 | 7,400: US | 121,500 | 1,000 |
| Wheat | 82,000 | 1,000 | 1,650 | 5,600: France | 86,000** | 1,000 |
| Rice | 6,800 | 1,500 | 2,800 | 6,200: Japan | 4,500 | 670 |
| Total | 211,800 | – | – | – | 212,000 | – |

Sources: 1) *Statistical Year Book 1988*, Muzaffarabad?, Planning & Development Department, Azad Government of the State of Jammu and Kashmir, [1989].

2) *1998 Census Report of Azad Kashmir*, Islamabad, Population Census Organization, Statistics Division, Government of Pakistan, July 2001.

Key: Av. Average.
AK Azad Kashmir.
AY Average yield per annum in kgs. per hectare during the period.
Pak Pakistan.
WL World leader for the specified crop during the period 1982–1987.
\* Hectares per annum.
\*\* Figure (incorrectly) stated in census as '851,566' hectares.

Despite Azad Kashmir having low productivity and little land under irrigation, the 1951 Azad Kashmir Census report had expressed the belief that theoretically, the region could become self-sufficient in food production, although internal distribution would be a problem.[48] It believed that a large-scale irrigation scheme was needed in the more temperate, and therefore more productive, agricultural areas of Mirpur and Bhimber *tehsils* of Mirpur District abutting the productive Punjab plains. Given that the Jhelum and Poonch rivers were nearby, water availability was not an issue, although physically accessing it was. Nevertheless, even if this irrigation scheme was developed and food produced, a major problem was the ability to distribute this using Azad Kashmir's '150 miles of tortuous fair-weather roads'. The report considered it 'extremely doubtful' that grain transported internally from Mirpur to northern Azad Kashmir could compete in price with grain

## THE ECONOMY: POOR AND DEPENDENT

imported from Punjab, particularly given that the easiest route from Mirpur to Muzaffarabad was via Rawalpindi.[49] The only solution to the region's food problem was to instigate 'small-scale schemes to develop each locality on its own lines'.

Despite these intentions, Azad Kashmir was significantly dependent on Pakistan for its additional needs for food, especially grains, a situation that Azad Kashmir's population growth would exacerbate. During the period 1983–88, Azad Kashmir produced an annual average of 76,400 tonnes of wheat per year. However, it imported almost double this amount: an annual average of 142,500 tonnes. This amounted to an average increase of 6.5 per cent per year during this period.[50] Clearly, Azad Kashmir was significantly dependent on grain imports from Pakistan, the only place from which such imports could be made. The region's inability to feed itself also would have continued if and when J&K reunified and joined Pakistan, given that Indian J&K had imported 56,000 tons of cereal grains from India in 1949 and 26,000 tons in 1950—and no doubt thereafter.[51]

The 'realistic' view of the 1951 Azad Kashmir Census report was that, in order to stem Azad Kashmir's need to produce more food, widespread contraception, about which 'no forbidding religious injunction is known to exist', was badly needed to curb Azad Kashmir's population growth.[52] In 1951, Azad Kashmir's population was 887,000 people, comprising 461,000 males and 426,000 females.[53] Although the census did not explain this gender imbalance—which was probably worse, given that many men worked outside Azad Kashmir—it provided a hint: 'Sometimes methods that have always been regarded as vice are practised in desperation to do away with the expected child'.[54] These 'methods' were abortion or infanticide, particularly of females. As the 1998 Azad Kashmir Census report officially notes, families show 'no signs of rejoicing' when a girl is born, but there is 'great rejoicing' when a boy is born, with his birth 'celebrated with distribution of sweets etc. among relatives'.[55] Later population figures confirmed Azad Kashmir's gender imbalance. By 1981, the region's population had more than doubled to 1,980,000, comprising 1,022,000 males and 958,000 females.[56] Average annual growth rates were 1.9 per cent for the period 1951–61 (compared with 2.4 per cent in Pakistan), 3.4 per cent for 1961–72 (3.7 per cent in Pakistan), and 2.7 per cent for 1972–81 (3 per cent).[57] There are no details about whether Azad Kashmir's lower growth rates were due to a successful contraception campaign or to other reasons, legitimate or nefarious.

In terms of Azad Kashmir's few physical assets, forests were important. As one of the former princely state's greatest economic assets, forests were one of two items that Maharaja Hari Singh protected. (The other was cattle, with cows sacred to his Hindu religion.)[58] In 1965, of J&K's 10,700 sq. miles of forests, 'about' 2,800 sq. miles (1,800,000 acres) 'fell on the Azad Kashmir side'.[59] This gave Azad Kashmir a 26 per cent share of J&K's total forests. More specifically,[60] demarcated forests comprised 62 per cent of Azad Kashmir, or 1,569,000 acres. The area of undemarcated forests was not stated. The Azad Kashmir Forest Department controlled these forests, which comprised 643,000 acres of commercial forests (41 per cent) and 926,000 acres of non-commercial forests (59 per cent). With 929,000 acres, Muzaffarabad District had 59 per cent of Azad Kashmir's demarcated forests, which comprised 70 per cent of the district's area. Next was Poonch District with 29 per cent of Azad Kashmir's demarcated forests (459,000 acres; 74 per cent of its area), followed by Mirpur District with 12 per cent (181,000 acres; 20 per cent). Mirpur lacked forests because it had the largest amount of Azad Kashmir's arable land. Conversely, Muzaffarabad District was less arable, with less conducive weather for cropping. By 1990,[61] Azad Kashmir's total area of forests had decreased to 1,367,000 acres, or 42 per cent of its area. (By comparison, 3 per cent of Pakistan was under forests.) In 2000,[62] the Azad Kashmir Forest Department controlled an (unexplained) increased area of 567,000 hectares of forest (1,401,000 acres; 48 per cent of Azad Kashmir). This area comprised 154,000 hectares of 'wild forests' (27 per cent), 225,000 hectares of 'other trees or rangelands' (40 per cent) and 188,000 hectares of 'non-productive forest' (33 per cent). Some of the forest areas were 'still virgin'.

While 'forest-working' was very important in 1951, there was virtually no other industry in Azad Kashmir 'worth the name'.[63] This made Azad Kashmir dependent on Pakistan for many manufactured goods and employment opportunities. In 1949, UNCIP noted that there were 'no factory industries and few cottage industries' in Azad Kashmir, with 'the area being predominantly agricultural'.[64] In 1951, the forest industry provided 90 per cent of Azad Kashmir's revenue.[65] By 1961, this figure was 'about' 80 per cent, with an annual income 'fluctuating' between Rs. 8–9 million.[66] However, the forestry industry could not provide jobs for the many small landowners and refugees seeking employment. With few other options, Azad Kashmiri men invariably 'yielded to the urge' to seek employment outside Azad Kashmir.[67] Mirpuris and Poonchis located close to Punjab did so in large numbers. They were employed in Pakistan's defence forces, with 'some 15,000 Poonchis' already serving in the Pakistan Army in 1949.[68] They also were employed in the Pakistan police, in the merchant navy, on the railways, and as domestic servants and labourers. There are no details about any Muzaffarabadis' outside employment. Azad Kashmiris' employment in Pakistan meant that money was remitted to the region, some of it via the National Bank of Pakistan after it opened its first branch in Azad Kashmir at Muzaffarabad in 1953–54; at the same time it 'propose[d] to set up another Branch at Mirpur'.[69] Equally, Azad Kashmir's revenue base was reduced because no taxes were collected from people working outside its territory.

Azad Kashmir's lack of industry is a problem that the Azad Kashmir Government has unsuccessfully sought to address. Between 1951 and 1961, steps were taken 'to improve the economic condition of the population' via industrial development.[70] By 1963, any development was still 'pitifully small' and there was 'an atmosphere of deepening poverty, neglect and stagnation'.[71] While Azad Kashmir was an 'agricultural country [sic]',[72] its low productivity meant the region had no surpluses to sell or trade to obtain capital or equipment for development. Also, 'almost the entire area is mountainous and access to markets is not so easy'. This made it unsuitable for heavy industry. Given this situation, the Azad Kashmir Government considered it 'advisable' to focus on 'small and cottage industries', particularly ones for which 'skilled labour and raw material [sic] are wholly or partially available' locally.[73] It therefore sought to develop cottage, sericulture, fruit and other small-scale industries. It tried to promote tourism, although Azad Kashmir's inaccessibility and 'the presence of an armed enemy' nearby were strong disincentives.[74] It began considering the possibility of developing irrigation, min-

## THE ECONOMY: POOR AND DEPENDENT

ing and hydel.[75] Nevertheless, before 1970, most Azad Kashmiris were employed outside the region in Pakistan, or worked in agriculture, largely on a semi-subsistence basis, or were employed in the (burgeoning) Azad Kashmir administration.

By 1970, the Pakistan Planning Commission assessed that Azad Kashmir's economy had 'stagnated over the past twenty years'. This was partly because, between 1947 and 1968, only Rs. 92.6 million—or Rs. 4.00 per capita, p.a.—had been invested in the region.[76] Azad Kashmir's natural resources had not been fully explored, although some coal, mica, limonite and fireclay were being produced. Industrial development had been patchy, with Mirpur District being the main beneficiary. It had textile, ghee and light engineering industries.[77] Otherwise, Azad Kashmir's industrial production was limited, with the main industrial enterprises being cotton-based products (yarn, cloth, cotton seed oil), woollen blankets or yarn, ice, light engineering products, and vegetable ghee.[78] The region was still backward and dependent on Pakistan.

*After 1971: increased support from Pakistan*

Economic development in Azad Kashmir increased after, and because of, the 1971 India-Pakistan war.[79] Indeed, it was only in the early 1970s that Azad Kashmir's 'economic development ... started in earnest'.[80] (This date was later revised (incorrectly) to suggest that economic development began in the 'early 60's [sic]'.)[81] One attempt to decrease Azad Kashmir's economic backwardness was an instruction by the Pakistan Cabinet in June 1970 that the region 'should for all practical [reasons] be treated like any other province' of Pakistan. It was to be brought into the 'main stream of the general administration (of the country)' with 'a view to mounting ... a concerned attack on its development problems and to being [sic] about a speedy improvement in the economic conditions of its people'.[82] Beforehand, Azad Kashmir (and Pakistani) leaders' priority—and obsession—was to reunite J&K and deliver it to Pakistan. They were 'not interested in tackling the economic problems of their part of the state'.[83] Azad Kashmir's poor industrial development confirms this, as does the fact that the Azad Kashmir Government established a planning and development department only in 1970.[84] Since then, Azad Kashmir has experienced some economic development, although the region is still dependent on Pakistan. Azad Kashmiris believe they could have lessened this dependency in two ways: first, if Pakistan had paid more for electricity generated in Azad Kashmir and enabled Azad Kashmir to generate its own hydel; second, if Azad Kashmir had been allowed access to remittances in Pakistani banks from so-called 'Pakistanis', and their descendants living overseas, many of whom are people originally from Mirpur District.

After losing the 1971 India-Pakistan war, Pakistan seriously began to integrate Azad Kashmir economically. The 1972 Simla Agreement possibly gave Pakistan some sense of security that it could now invest in Pakistan-Administered Kashmir without fear of losing Azad Kashmir or the Northern Areas—and any Pakistani investment—to India. After Simla, the plebiscite was off the India-Pakistan agenda, while any Indian attempt to capture Pakistan-Administered Kashmir was unlikely to occur, or succeed. Equally, Azad Kashmiri leaders, realising that Pakistan was unable and unwilling to fulfil their obsession to reunify J&K and deliver it to Pakistan, encouraged their region's (further) economic integration into Pakistan.[85] Subsequently, Azad Kashmir received substantial financial assistance from Pakistan. Its generosity began after Prime Minister Bhutto's 'extensive tour of Azad Kashmir in 1973', during which he 'met people in remote areas to create an awakening and consciousness for active participation in fashioning their destiny'. Bhutto was concerned to uplift Azad Kashmiris socially and economically and 'bring them at par with their brethren in Pakistan'. This reflected his 'firm belief that social and economic development of a people provide [a] firm foundation for assertion of its political rights'.[86] Given Azad Kashmir's sheer lack of economic assets and resources, this development would be difficult to achieve.

While Bhutto appeared to instigate Pakistan's generosity, later official publications showed that Pakistan had allocated money to Azad Kashmir from Pakistan's first five-year plan in 1955–60.[87] In 1976, the Pakistan Government claimed to have allocated Azad Kashmir Rs. 327 million since Bhutto assumed office in 1971.[88] This compared favourably with the figure of Rs. 137 million allocated to Azad Kashmir under Pakistan's (military-dominated) first, second and third five-year plans,[89] although an earlier source claimed Azad Kashmir received 'about Rs. 40 million' under the second five-year plan and would receive a 'huge allocation of Rs. 150 million' under the third five-year plan from July 1965.[90] Nevertheless, the Bhutto government's allocation to Azad Kashmir increased from a low base of Rs. 16 million in 1971–72 to Rs. 120 million in 1975–76. This trend of increasing financial allocations to Azad Kashmir continued. It suggested that Pakistan, indeed, had financially neglected Azad Kashmir, and that Islamabad was fully integrating the region into the nation. A report to the Pakistan Planning Commission stated as much: 'allocation in A.K. through-out has been extremely insufficient and as such no substantial gains were made in any sector of the economy'. It called for a (staggering) per annum allocation to Azad Kashmir of Rs. 720 million.[91]

Hence, Pakistan became a generous benefactor to Azad Kashmir after 1971 by providing large amounts of funding to supplement the region's deficit budget. Indeed, over a fifty-year period (1955 to 2006), Pakistan made Rs. 44 billion available to Azad Kashmir as development aid, with amounts increasingly substantially after 1970 (Table 7.2). Azad Kashmir utilised over Rs. 40 billion of this money. The Azad Kashmir Government's 'utter dependence' on Islamabad 'for financial support' has increased. In 1987–88, under the 'very accommodating' Zia regime, Pakistan provided 'grants' (not loans) that covered nearly Rs. 2.1 billion of Azad Kashmir's Rs. 2.5 billion budget. Under the subsequent, more austere Benazir Bhutto government, Pakistan still granted Azad Kashmir Rs. 1.94 billion of its Rs. 2.76 billion budget in 1989–90, but the remainder was loans.[92] Equally, Azad Kashmir thereafter became 'entirely dependent upon [the] Government of Pakistan for the financing of its development outlays'.[93]

Apart from development outlays, Table 7.3 shows that, from the early 1990s, Azad Kashmir relied on Islamabad to allocate up to 69 per cent of its spending on non-development matters.[94] This money was used to meet various 'Department' spending requirements (as, for example, Table 2 of Appendix XII details for 2005–06).[95] Azad Kashmir's financial dependence on Pakistan is confirmed by figures contained in recent government documents. From the early 2000s, *Azad Kashmir*

## THE ECONOMY: POOR AND DEPENDENT

Table 7.2: Amounts allocated by Pakistan from 1955 to 2006 to Azad Kashmir for Development Programmes.

| Period | Total Allocation | Utilisation | Percentage Utilisation |
|---|---|---|---|
| 1st Five Year Plan (1955–1960) | 10.00 M | 10.00 M | 100% |
| 2nd Five Year Plan (1960–1965) | 39.42 M | 39.40 M | 100% |
| 3rd Five Year Plan (1965–1970) | 88.10 M | 88.00 M | 99% |
| Non Plan Period (1970–1978) | 604.10 M | 576.00 M | 95% |
| 5th Five Year Plan (1978–1983) | 1,216.80 M | 1,215.50 M | 99% |
| 6th Five Year Plan (1983–1988) | 3,174.00 M | 3,102.30 M | 98% |
| 7th Five Year Plan (1988–1993) | 4,916.00 M | 4,709.90 M | 96% |
| 8th Five Year Plan (1993–1998) | 8,277.30 M | 7,768.90 M | 94% |
| Non Plan Period (1998–2001)* | 6,368.77 M | 6,102.85 M | 97% |
| 2001–2002 to 2004–2005** | 14,199.64 M | 13,136.59 M | 93% |
| 2005–2006 | 5,214.34 M | 3,994.69 M | 77% |
| Total | 44,108.47 M | 40,774.12 M | 92% |
| MTDF (2005–2010) | 39,700.00 M | – | – |

Sources: 1) *Azad Kashmir at a Glance*, undated, Muzaffarabad, Planning & Development Department, Azad Govt. of the State of Jammu & Kashmir, 2007?, www.pndajk.gov.pk/glance.asp [accessed 25 February 2009], p. 1.
2) *Public Sector Development Programme 2006–2007*, Planning & Development Department, Azad Government of the State of Jammu and Kashmir, Muzaffarabad, 2007?, p. v.

Key: M Millions (figures rounded).
  MTDF Medium Term Development Framework, 2005–2010. Started after the Pakistan Government abandoned the Ten Year Perspective Plan and approved MTDF.
  * The 9th Five Year Plan could not be approved by the Pakistan Government and funds were allocated on a year-to-year basis.
  ** Allocated under the Ten Year Perspective Plan.

*at a Glance* publications provide sub-totals for revenue that appears to be raised locally and for revenue determined or dispensed by Islamabad. The three largest estimated revenue receipts in any Azad Kashmir budget are all issued or controlled by Islamabad. These are 'Federal Aid for Deficit Budget', 'Share of Federal Taxes' and 'Income from AJK Council' ('AK Council' in later years). Two newer budgetary amounts issued and controlled by Islamabad are 'Net Capital Receipts' and 'Mangla Dam Royalty'. The former appeared for the first time, and without explanation, in the Revised Estimates of 2002–03.[96] Islamabad appears to allocate these 'receipts' to supplement Azad Kashmir revenues when needed—with the use of

Table 7.3: Allocations to the Azad Kashmir Budget of Amounts Controlled by Islamabad (in Rs. millions).

| FY | Budgeted Revenue for Azad Kashmir | 1. Mangla Dam Royalty | 2. Income from AJK Council# | 3. Share of Federal Taxes | 4. Federal Aid for Deficit Budget | 5. Net Capital Receipts | Total Amount & % from Pakistan |
|---|---|---|---|---|---|---|---|
| 1994–1995 | 4,055 M | Nil | 726 M 17.9% | 830 M 20.5% | 1,194 M 29.4% | 8 M 0.2% | 2,758 M 68.0% |
| 1995–1996 | 4,246 M | Nil | 726 M 17.1% | 993 M 23.4% | 1,191 M 28.0% | 8 M 0.19% | 2,918 M 68.7% |
| 2002–2003** | 9,215 M | Nil | 1,769 M 19.2% | 1,983 M 21.5% | 2,317 M 25.1% | 60 M 0.65% | 6,129 M 66.5% |
| 2003–2004 | 9,372 M | 900 M | 1,725 M 18.4% | 2,303 M 24.6% | 2,287 M 24.4% | Nil | 7,215 M 77.0% |
| 2004–2005 | 11,183 M | 938 M 8.4% | 1,880 M 16.8% | 2,534 M 22.7% | 1,926 M 17.2% | 620 M 5.5% | 7,898 M 70.6% |
| 2005–2006 | 12,748 M | 900 M* 7.0% | 2,065 M 16.2% | 2,888 M 22.7% | 2,766 M 21.7% | [915 M]* [6.8%]* | 8,619 M 67.6% |
| 2006–2007** | 13,931 M | 663 M 4.8% | 2,272 M 16.3% | 3,317 M 23.8% | 3,158 M 22.7% | Nil*** | 9,410 M 67.6% |

Sources: 1) *Azad Kashmir at a Glance* 1995, Muzaffarabad, Planning & Dev [sic] Department, Azad Govt. [sic] of the State of Jammu & Kashmir, 1996?, p. 28;
2) *Azad Kashmir at a Glance* 1996, Muzaffarabad, Planning & Developmnet [sic] Department, Azad Govt. [sic] of the State of Jammu & Kashmir, 1997?, p. 28;
3) *Azad Kashmir at a Glance* 2003, Muzaffarabad, Planning & Dev. [sic] Department, Azad Govt. [sic] of the State of Jammu & Kashmir, 2004?, p. 27;
4) *Azad Kashmir at a Glance* 2004, Muzaffarabad, Planning & Development Department, Azad Government of the State of Jammu & Kashmir, 2005?, p. 29;
5) *Azad Kashmir at a Glance* 2005, Muzaffarabad, Planning & Development Department, Azad Government of the State of Jammu & Kashmir, 2006?, p. 29.
6) *Azad Kashmir at a Glance*, undated, Muzaffarabad, Planning & Development Department, Azad Govt. of the State of Jammu & Kashmir, 2007?, www.pndajk.gov.pk/glance.asp [accessed 25 February 2009], p. 1.

Key: FY Financial year.
M Million.
\# In 2002–2003, and thereafter, this was shown as '80 per cent Share From AK Council'.
% Percentage of overall Budgeted Revenue for Azad Kashmir.
* Figures from Revised Estimates (2005–2006); actual Mangla Dam Royalty was Rs. 696.6 M; actual total revenue was Rs. 13,305 M; Rs. 915 M was 6.8 per cent of this figure.
** Figures from the (later) Revised Estimates (not the (earlier) Budget Estimates): 2002–2003; 2006–2007.
*** No Revised Estimate available for this figure.

the word 'capital' providing a nice *double entendre*. Mangla Dam royalties have been paid since 2004. This may have been the result of lobbying by Azad Kashmiris. It also may have been Islamabad appeasing them because of raising the height of the wall of the contentious Mangla Dam (see below).

There are two interesting aspects to the Azad Kashmir budgetary figures given—or not given—in Table 7.3. The first is the doubling in actual revenue receipts between 1995–96 and 2002–03. The reasons for this revenue increase are not clear. While some of it comes from natural economic growth and inflation, in both Azad Kashmir and Pakistan, the Azad Kashmir Government also significantly increased its local revenue collection. That said, the Pakistan Government's contributions also rose accordingly. The second interesting aspect is that the Azad Kashmir Council's Development Programme (discussed in Chapter 4) is not mentioned anywhere. Presumably, this is because these funds do not directly come to Azad Kashmir or because they are not always spent in this region. Additionally, the Azad Kashmir Government and the Azad Kashmir Council, while linked via the participation of Azad Kashmiris on the Council, are separate bodies.[97]

*Current state of the economy and social wellbeing*

Azad Kashmir's economy is neither self-sufficient nor vibrant. A 2006 official brief revealed an economy confronting some serious, and longstanding issues.[98] The Azad Kashmir Government's established 'development strategy' seeks to address or provide better roads; hydel and rural electrification; tourism; access to, and improvement in the quality of, education; health services; piped water and sanitation facilities; and information technology, including computer literacy programmes. It also seeks to maintain assets already created. Looking positively, the Azad Kashmir Government saw the region's 'Potential and Resources' as hydel power; forests; tourism; mineral resources; foreign remittances by expatriates; fisheries; and, cottage/small scale industry. Looking negatively, it saw the region's 'Constraints' as inadequate physical infrastructure; overpopulation; small landholdings; lack of private sector employment opportunities; fast depletion of forest resources; land erosion by fast water run off and human encroachment; location and geographical disadvantages; proximity to the LOC; and shortages of skilled manpower. The region's 'Issues' are uncertainty along the LOC due to firing by Indian forces;[99] unemployment of educated youth; inadequate infrastructure; a short working season; the 'indecisiveness of implementing agencies due to fear of accountability'; and non-professional contractors. The latter two points may be euphemisms for corruption, which has been an 'endemic' problem for some time,[100] with some contractors earning 'a bad professional reputation'.[101]

In 2006, the Azad Kashmir Government noted some achievements since 1947.[102] Educational facilities at all levels had significantly increased: primary schools, from 254 in 1947 to 4,265 in 2004; middle schools, thirty to 1,029; high schools, six to 596; and there were 168 new institutions, ranging from forty-two higher secondary schools to three new universities, with two in the private sector. Student enrolments in the five to nine years age bracket were 95 per cent for boys (90 per cent in Pakistan) and 87 per cent for girls (61 per cent in Pakistan). Literacy was 64 per cent

(54 per cent in Pakistan). Health improvements included: an increase in hospital beds from thirty in 1947 to 1,781 in 2004; fifteen civil hospitals and thirty-three rural health centres; a further 530 basic health units (eleven in 1947); an increase in medical personnel from twenty in 1947 to 4,129 in 2004. The infant mortality rate was fifty-six deaths per thousand (eighty-two in Pakistan). Water supply coverage had increased, with 62 per cent of rural areas and 88 per cent of urban areas now covered. In transport and communications, metalled roads had increased from 100 kms in 1947 to 3,642 kms in 2004, 'fair weather roads' had increased from 165 kms to 3,896 kms, two airports now existed, and there were 38,000 telephone connections and 2,100 mobile connections (none in 1947). From having no power anywhere in 1947, Azad Kashmir had six hydel stations in 2004, and a grid capacity of 283 megavolt amperes (MVA) that electrified 1,620 villages (97 per cent coverage) and provided 315 kilowatt hours (kWh) of electricity per capita per year (247 kWh in Pakistan) to 2.3 million people. Negatively, the population per hospital bed was 1,940 for Azad Kashmir (1,540 in Pakistan), the population per doctor was 5,750 for Azad Kashmir (1,400 in Pakistan) and the immunisation coverage was 86 per cent for Azad Kashmir (93 per cent in Pakistan).

Azad Kashmir's most recent census (1998) provides further information about the region's economy and society, although it also suffers from four defects. First, this scanty document includes much irrelevant information, such as seven pages about 'Important/Historical Places' in Azad Kashmir and thirteen (unnumbered) pages of associated photographs.[103] Furthermore, its brief historical coverage of events in 1947 is incomplete. Surprisingly, the census report does not mention the Poonch uprising. Rather, it states that it was the Maharaja's accession to India that 'sparked the liberation movement of the Muslim population of the state against Dogra and India forces in Kashmir';[104] the accession occurred two days after the official creation of Azad Kashmir. Second, the census' statistics are generally for Azad Kashmir as a whole, with very few tables providing divisional, district or *tehsil*-level statistics; this gives an incomplete picture of the region.

A third defect of the census is that it appears to have been hastily produced. Supposedly an 'important national activity', the census was delayed from March 1991 until March 1998 owing to a 'lack of consensus among the provinces on the dates, procedures etc.'. With the previous census having been in 1982 and another one (long) overdue, this document with information for 1998 was finally published in July 2001.[105] A fourth defect is that it displays some Pakistani bias, possibly because the Population Census Organization within Pakistan's Statistics Division conducted it.[106] On p. 29, the census report states that Urdu is the official language of the Government of Azad Kashmir, with Kashmiri, Pahari, Gojri, Punjabi, Kohistani, Pushto and Sheena 'frequently spoken in Azad Kashmir'.[107] Yet, when surveyed about their 'Mother Tongue', Azad Kashmiris' choices were limited to selecting from Pakistan's major languages: Urdu, Punjabi, Sindhi, Pushto, Balochi, Saraiki and 'Others'; not surprisingly, 2.18 million of Azad Kashmir's 2.97 million people chose 'Others'.[108] When dealing with migration, the census returns provide much detail as to where migrants have come from in Pakistan and elsewhere, but none about their destinations in Azad Kashmir.[109] Despite these limitations, the 1998 Census was restricted 'For Official Use Only'.[110] The information contained within may therefore be considered reasonably accurate.

## THE ECONOMY: POOR AND DEPENDENT

The 1998 Census had some useful statistics about aspects of Azad Kashmir society, particularly Azad Kashmiris' religious persuasions and migration. Muslims comprised 99.48 per cent (2.96 million) of Azad Kashmir's population of 1.49 million men and 1.47 million women[111] (99.91 per cent in 1951).[112] (While it is not mentioned in the census, most Muslims are Sunnis.) The small non-Muslim 'community', whose members are not obvious in Azad Kashmir, comprised 5,700 unspecified 'Others' (2,800 men; 2,900 women); 5,200 'Qadiani (Ahmadi)' (2,800 men; 2,400 women); 3,700 Christians (2,100 men; 1,600 women); 600 'Hindu (Jati)' (240 men; 360 women); and 310 Scheduled Castes (140 men; 170 women).[113] Azad Kashmir had 103,000 migrants (59,000 men; 44,000 women), or 3.5 per cent of the population, over half of whom (55,000) had been in their place of 'continuous residence' longer than ten years.[114] Most were from Punjab (39,000), followed by internal migrants from Azad Kashmir (24,000) and 'Other countries' (22,000). Most migrants came with their family (32,000), for other (unspecified) reasons (22,000), for/with employment (21,000), for marriage (15,700, of whom 15,300 were females), or for business (7,000, of whom 6,200 were men). Other reasons were study (3,000), returning home (2,000, which possibly included some Mirpuris from the United Kingdom) or health (200). Surprisingly, the census had no figures for Azad Kashmiris estimated to be temporarily living and working outside the region. The closest it got was to note that 'Many people have gone abroad and contribute to the development of the country [sic]'.[115]

The 1998 Census had three sections that discussed Azad Kashmir's economy. 'Industry and Trade' provided information from government departments mostly from 2000—although the census was supposed to be for 1998. This confirmed an 'emphasis on handicrafts and small scale industry' due to Azad Kashmir being 'mostly hilly' and not producing raw materials for major industry.[116] Mirpur was best developed and best served because of its proximity to Punjab. Indeed, of Azad Kashmir's 915 industrial units (911 private; four public),[117] 313 units were in Mirpur District, which also had two of the region's four public industries. Otherwise, Muzaffarabad District had 206 private industries (and one public), Bhimber 128, Kotli 126 (one public), Poonch fifty-nine, Bagh fifty-three, and Sudhnoti thirty. In terms of industrial activity, the census had twenty-three categories. Apart from 426 'miscellaneous' units, there were 100 wood works and furniture houses, ninety poultry farms, seventy steel and welding works, fifty-two food industries and bakeries, thirty-two crushing machines, seventeen printing presses, and fifteen main hotels. There was also one 'vespa factory' and six 'arms factories' which, given the anti-Indian uprising in the Kashmir Valley since 1988, might be cause for Indian angst.

A second section of the 1998 Census that dealt with Azad Kashmir's economy, 'Economic Characteristics', showed low participation and high unemployment.[118] The economically active population, or labour force, comprised 'persons aged 10 years and above ... engaged in some work for pay or profit including un-paid family helpers and ... those not working but looking for work' during the census period.[119] In 1998, 19 per cent (559,000 people) of Azad Kashmir's 2.97 million population were in the labour force: 96.7 per cent males; 3.3 per cent females. The other 81 per cent were economically inactive, comprising domestic workers (35 per cent, of whom two thirds were women), children (30 per cent), students

(11 per cent), and 'other categories' (five per cent). The labour force participation rate was 27 per cent: 52 per cent for males; 2 per cent for females. This gave Azad Kashmir a 'very low overall participation rate compared to other countries'. This possibly reflects a cultural or male aversion to females working in paid employment outside the house; equally, females may choose to stay at home. Of the employed Azad Kashmiris, 52 per cent were self-employed, 26 per cent were in government service, and 16 per cent were in private sector employment. Azad Kashmir's unemployment rate was 32.6 per cent: 33.4 per cent for males; 8.7 per cent for females. An official publication confirmed this high figure, stating that unemployment ranged from '35 to 50' per cent.[120] There were no figures for under-employment or for the 'huge migratory workforce' that leaves Azad Kashmir, permanently or for work reasons, on account of high unemployment.[121]

A third section, 'Agriculture and Related Sectors', provided government information about land use and livestock. This confirmed that Azad Kashmir had 'an agricultural economy [that] mainly depends upon rainfall' but with 'tremendous [unenunciated] possibilities of fruit and vegetable cultivation'.[122] Nevertheless, despite 'planners' having 'made good efforts in laying down a proper path for the rapid development of the area',[123] Azad Kashmir's economic activity was rudimentary.

One factor the 1998 Census did not discuss was destructive natural calamities. Apart from the loss of human and animal life, torrential rain and floods, avalanches and earthquakes have an economic impact on Azad Kashmir. The region experienced bad floods in 1929, 1959 and 1992, with the latter causing 260 deaths, significant losses of property, livestock and saleable timber, and Rs. 580 million damage to bridges and infrastructure.[124] Avalanches after heavy snowfalls cause problems, with thirty-two people killed in the Neelum Valley in 1996.[125] Azad Kashmir's most devastating natural calamity was the earthquake measuring 7.6 on the Richter scale that struck the region (and parts of Indian J&K and northern Pakistan) on 8 October 2005.[126] There were over 500 aftershocks in the following week, including one measuring 5.0 on the Richter scale.[127] With the onset of winter, heavy rains and snows also began to fall. The figures are staggering. The earthquake affected 7,000 sq. kms of Azad Kashmir and 1,050 of its 1,313 villages.[128] It impacted on 1.8 million Azad Kashmiris, killed 47,000 of them, injured 33,000, and damaged 330,000 houses.[129] Muzaffarabad District was worst affected, with 36,000 deaths, 23,000 injuries and 169,000 damaged or uninhabitable houses. Bagh District had 9,000 deaths and 91,000 damaged houses, while Poonch District had 1,000 deaths and 56,000 damaged houses. The least affected districts were those remotest from the earthquake: Sudhnuti (four 4 deaths; 2,500 houses damaged) and Mirpur (six deaths; no damage). There was significant public sector damage: 2,700 educational and 176 health institutions needed reconstructing; 2,600 kms of roads and numerous bridges needed rebuilding or repairing; 800 official residences needed repairing or rebuilding; 1,600 rural water supply and waste management systems were damaged.

To deal with the 2005 calamity, the Azad Kashmir Government established the State Earthquake Reconstruction & Rehabilitation Agency (SERRA), while Pakistan established the Earthquake Reconstruction & Rehabilitation Agency (ERRA).[130] Apart from efforts drawing on Azad Kashmir's own resources and Paki-

## THE ECONOMY: POOR AND DEPENDENT

stan's civil and military resources, assistance came from other nations, large organisations (such as the World Bank), fifty-two NGOs and, controversially, 'militant *jihadi* groups' who, 'in many cases [were] the first to arrive on the scene to assist in rescue and relief efforts following the earthquake'.[131] On the other hand, the earthquake may have killed 500–2,000 militants—not to mention 1,000 Pakistani soldiers—and destroyed fifteen of the fifty-five militant camps that 'Indian security sources' claimed existed around Muzaffarabad.[132] Rescue efforts involved fifty helicopters flying 19,000 sorties until April 2006, the establishment of 220 camps for 117,000 displaced people (94,000 of whom were repatriated to their original locations around March 2006), 855 tons of medicines, 76,000 tons of rations, 400,000 tents, and 6 million sheets of galvanised iron. People received free transport facilities to return to their original locations, while 9,200 people were shifted to camps because their areas were 'high hazardous zones' possibly subjected to landslides, etc.

After the earthquake, there were numerous issues and constraints. These included town planning deficiencies; shortages of land, finance and affordable construction materials; lack of managers, engineers, consultants and labour, skilled and unskilled; and poor logistics, including the inadequate state of Muzaffarabad Airport and the Muzaffarabad-Kohala-Islamabad Road.[133] This road, which is also called the 'Islamabad-Muzaffarabad Expressway (N-75)' project,[134] was 'still incomplete after ten years and eating up more than Rs. 14 billion'.[135] Nevertheless, by April 2006, all other primary and secondary roads had been reopened and communications restored, and no reports had been received of any epidemic or infectious diseases. By mid-2006, 30,000 people were living in forty-four camps; 90 per cent of people affected were in semi-permanent or permanent shelters; 55 per cent had started reconstructing permanent houses.[136]

The economic cost of the 2005 earthquake was enormous, although SERRA believed that this calamity also created opportunities.[137] Estimated total losses were Rs. 125 billion: Rs. 64 billion for the public sector, and Rs. 61 billion for the private sector. Rs. 34 billion was paid in compensation: Rs. 1.7 billion in cash grants of Rs. 3,000 per month for six months to 112,000 people; Rs. 4.5 billion to survivors for injury and family death/s; Rs. 27.7 billion as a first housing instalment of Rs. 25,000 to 299,000 people, and as a second instalment of Rs. 50,000–100,000 to 277,000 people. (While helpful, a two-room, earthquake-resistant house was estimated to cost Rs. 442,300 in 2006.)[138] Rs. 25 billion was allocated to reconstruct Muzaffarabad, with suggestions made to relocate it or build accommodation elsewhere.[139] SERRA talked of 'Converting [the] Earthquake into Opportunity'. It perceived increased economic activity; construction of better houses, schools, health facilities and urban settlements; involvement of, and interaction with, the international community; and the improvement of Azad Kashmir's disaster management capacity. Significantly, 70,000 people had received skills training, one million new jobs had been created and the unemployment rate was supposed to have dropped below 6.5 per cent.[140]

One positive result of the 2005 earthquake was the deregulation of Azad Kashmir's telecommunications sector.[141] Mobile telephones were finally permitted in Azad Kashmir in 2003—long after Pakistan. The region's delay was because of its difficult terrain and because the conservative Special Communication Organization (SCO), 'an organ of the Pakistan Armed Forces since 1976', was reluctant to allow this technology in a strategically vulnerable area close to the LOC. The earthquake badly damaged SCO's infrastructure; to satisfy Azad Kashmir's 'urgent communications needs', the Pakistan Telecommunication Authority allowed the widespread, and temporarily unregulated, release of mobile telephone technology. User numbers grew exponentially: 3,000 (2003–04); 5,000 (2004–05); 53,000 (2005–06); 912,000 (2006–07); 1,600,000 (2007–08). By 2008, over one third of Azad Kashmiris had mobile phones, with coverage available in 80 per cent of the region. Five companies, plus SCO, provided services via 514 'cell sites', with 'huge proceeds'—Rs. 1.2 billion by 2008—available to the Azad Kashmir Council from licensing the commercial providers. Azad Kashmir had entered a 'new era of better connectivity and economic growth'.[142] The former appeared to be true; the latter remained to be seen.

*Possible financial independence*

Azad Kashmir has been 'conspicuously unsuccessful in stimulating its own finances'.[143] The region is dependent on Pakistan for most funding, although not all Azad Kashmiris are happy with this situation. Some claim that had Azad Kashmir received all revenues from sales of hydro-electricity generated by the Mangla Dam, the region would have been more economically viable and possibly not financially dependent on Pakistan at all. The Mangla Dam stores and controls the waters of the Jhelum and Poonch rivers, just before they unite and exit Azad Kashmir for the (Pakistani) Punjab plains below. In upgrading from a barrage structure, the overall construction of the dam, powerhouse and associated facilities was a joint venture between the governments of Pakistan and Azad Kashmir, which would 'offer great scope for employment' and as a result of which Azad Kashmiris would 'get their share of hydel energy and water'.[144] A new town was built to replace old Mirpur town, which the 100 sq. mile waters of the new dam flooded. Pakistan and the World Bank provided most of the finance for the project,[145] which in 1957 was expected to cost Rs. 1 billion.[146] Although India protested to the UN Security Council in 1957 against Pakistan's involvement building this dam in 'Indian territory',[147] construction went ahead. Completed in 1967, the dam had a gross storage capacity of 5.9 million acre feet (MAF).[148]

Pakistan and Pakistanis were the main beneficiaries of the Mangla Dam—not Azad Kashmir and Azad Kashmiris. Although the project's aim was 'to provide and enlarge irrigation and hydel facilities for a considerable area and vastly to improve the economic condition of the people living there',[149] much of this area and most people were in Pakistan. Pakistanis downstream benefited from flood mitigation and better-regulated irrigation water, with Mangla water expected to irrigate three million acres of (Pakistani) land.[150] Another benefit was cheaper electricity, with the dam's power station having a capacity of 300 megawatts (MW). Indeed, as Pakistan's second largest source of hydel after the Tarbela Dam (on the Indus River near Abbottabad) and the major water storage facility for Punjab's irrigation system, the Mangla Dam was 'critical to the success of the Pakistani economy as a whole'.[151]

Conversely, Azad Kashmiris upstream gained little and lost a lot. One of their (few) gains was cheap electricity, which Pakistan's powerful Water and Power

## THE ECONOMY: POOR AND DEPENDENT

Development Authority (WAPDA) spent Rs. 20 billion subsidising until January 1998,[152] but for which the Azad Kashmir Government paid Rs. 4.9 billion in 1999.[153] In 2000, agitated Azad Kashmir Council members also lodged a 'strong protest' because Rs. 1.4 billion of the Council's funds were unilaterally paid by the 'Minister Incharge of Azad Jammu and Kashmir Secretariat', Abbas Sarfaraz Khan, to WAPDA to clear the Azad Kashmir Government's outstanding bill.[154] Otherwise, of 42,000 acres affected by the dam's rising waters, Mirpuris lost 22,000 acres (8 per cent of cultivable land in their district), they suffered physical and emotional upheaval as rising water levels affected 122 villages, and they had major infrastructural disruptions, including poor road access to nearby Punjab for some years.[155] Most Mirpuris tolerated such difficulties for patriotic reasons: 'How can those who have given their blood for Pakistan, grudge water to their brethren?' Similarly, Azad Kashmiris believed the Mangla Dam project would lead to local economic, agricultural and industrial progress, new employment opportunities and to a higher standard of living.[156]

Some Azad Kashmiris believed their region would have been better off had it obtained total control of all hydel and associated royalties generated by the Mangla Dam.[157] This would have enabled the Azad Kashmir Government to develop further projects within the region. Azad Kashmiris believed their region was entitled to receive all hydel royalties as the Mangla Dam and its power station are located wholly within Azad Kashmir. (However, in that case, Pakistan would be entitled to seek compensation for costs incurred constructing and running this project.) In 1998, Mangla generated 1,000 MW electricity at a production cost of Rs. 1.50 per MW. Azad Kashmiris believed total royalties from selling such electricity were worth about Rs. 1 billion p.a.[158] Traditionally, Pakistan has taken 70 per cent of royalties; Azad Kashmir has received the rest (although these amounts did not appear in budgetary documents until recently). Even if Azad Kashmir had received all royalties, these would not have made the region financially self-sufficient, although they would have reduced its dependency on Pakistan. Equally, Mirpuris could have sought a greater share of any extra funds received, given that the Mangla Dam is wholly located within Mirpur District.

Azad Kashmiris have partly been appeased. Since 2003, Azad Kashmir has inexplicably received an annual 'Mangla Dam Royalty' payment (Table 7.3), possibly because Azad Kashmiris had been agitating for such royalties since at least 1998.[159] Such payments may also serve to satisfy Azad Kashmiris disenchanted because Pakistan decided in 2004 to spend Rs. 64 billion on raising the height of the Mangla Dam by 30 feet (to 1,240 feet).[160] (This decision may have been made as early as September 2002.)[161] The dam's capacity had dropped to 4.7 MAF (from 5.9 MAF) owing to sedimentation; further silting would reduce this to 4.5 MAF by the project's envisaged completion date of June 2007.[162] Silting has been a major problem for Mangla, made worse by deforestation, post-earthquake landslides, and increased urbanisation reducing catchment areas. Annually, 42,000 acre feet of sediment enter the Mangla Dam, meaning that it could be completely silted in 100–110 years.[163] Raising the dam wall would mean more areas of Mirpur District being flooded, with 40,000 'affectees' to be resettled in a WAPDA-built 'city near Mirpur and four towns as close as possible to the affected area'.[164] Some Mangla Dam royalties would be used to rehabilitate 'affectees', while Azad

Kashmir would benefit from parts of Mirpur and Bhimber districts being brought under irrigation.[165] No funds had been allocated to address the ongoing issue of sedimentation.

A further way for Azad Kashmir to become more financially independent would be to generate its own (non-Mangla Dam) hydel and sell this to Pakistan. The Azad Kashmir Government is aware of this potential,[166] having established a Hydro Electric Board headed by a former WAPDA official in 2004.[167] Azad Kashmir has three rivers with hydel potential: the Jhelum, which flows north-westerly through northern Azad Kashmir and then, deviating southwards, provides the border with NWFP, then with Punjab; the Neelum, its longest river, which flows roughly adjacent to the LOC through Neelum and Muzaffarabad districts, joining the Jhelum at Muzaffarabad; and the Poonch, which rises in the Pir Panjal mountains and flows southwards into Mangla Dam. Given that Azad Kashmir's annual rainfall averages fifty-six to eighty inches (1,400–2,000 millimetres),[168] these fast-flowing rivers carry large volumes of water. Utilising them and their tributaries, the region could generate 5,000–7,170 MW of hydel; Azad Kashmir consumers' requirements are only 250 MW.[169] Of Azad Kashmir's 'identified potential', only thirty-six MW had been developed by December 2006, with the Hydro Electric Board considering 2,220 MW of proposals: 980 MW in the public sector; 1,240 in the private sector.[170] The major scheme developed was the thrity-one MW Jagran Hydel Power project in Neelum District.[171] By August 2010, Azad Kashmir had seven 'small and mini hydropower stations' operating, including Jagran, with 'cumulative installed capacity of 37.6 MW'.[172] These stations are dwarfed by WAPDA's proposed Neelum-Jhelum scheme to divert water from the Neelum to the Jhelum via a thirty-two-km tunnel, generating 960 MW of hydel via this diversion. Contentiously, this project is threatened by a similar Indian project upstream to divert water from the Kishenganga (Neelum in Azad Kashmir) to the Jhelum.[173] India and Pakistan are now in dispute about which nation is entitled to this river's water under the 1960 Indus Waters Treaty.[174]

To their displeasure, Azad Kashmiris have faced problems generating hydel in Azad Kashmir since at least the 1980s. Islamabad allocates development finance to Azad Kashmir and controls the Azad Kashmir Council, which legislates with respect to electricity.[175] Until the abovementioned Neelum-Jhelum project, Islamabad displayed a cautious, even negative, attitude towards the development of public or private sector hydel projects in Azad Kashmir. This could be because water is a sensitive issue with India, especially for downstream Pakistan, or because of Azad Kashmir's unresolved international status and the possibility that any investment would be lost if Azad Kashmir ended up in India, or because Pakistan has invested heavily in building existing dams, such as Mangla and Tarbela, that provide power. Pakistan's attitude has displeased Azad Kashmiris. In 1989 Prime Minister Sardar Sikandar, who claimed to have initiated the development of hydel schemes in Azad Kashmir, deplored 'red-tapism' surrounding WAPDA's Kohala Dam project on the Jhelum River because the river acts as the Azad Kashmir-Pakistan border.[176] Sikandar was further concerned that Azad Kashmir was buying expensive Pakistani electricity when local schemes could have supplied cheap, clean electricity. Surplus power could have been sold to Pakistan's expanding market and reduced Azad Kashmir's financial dependence on Pakistan. Azad Kash-

## THE ECONOMY: POOR AND DEPENDENT

miris were being prevented from making use of one of their few cheap, clean, environmentally safe and abundant natural resources—water.[177]

A second way for Azad Kashmir to become more financially independent of Pakistan would be to gain access to funds remitted to Pakistani banks by Azad Kashmiris, particularly those from the (former) Mirpur District.[178] (In 1949, most of Mirpur District was in Azad Kashmir; it now comprises three districts: (northern) Kotli; (central) Mirpur; (south-eastern) Bhimber.)[179] Long before Pakistan existed, Mirpuris looked outside their area for work. The 1941 Census report mentions that large numbers of men from Mirpur, particularly, and Kotli *tehsils*, regularly left Mirpur District for employment: 'They join the army in large numbers as well as the mercantile marine operating from Indian ports'.[180] By the end of the nineteenth century, Mirpuris provided a high proportion of workers in engine rooms and stokeholds on merchant ships. Since 1947, many unskilled Azad Kashmiris have emigrated from 'less agriculturally prosperous' areas, some going to the United Kingdom. They joined Mirpuri seamen who gained jobs ashore during UK's labour shortage in World War II. Britain's post-war boom boosted Mirpuri numbers, as did the construction of the Mangla Dam, after which more Mirpuris joined brethren in the UK. Consequently, most UK immigrants from 'Pakistan' are actually people from the former Mirpur District. Indeed, about 'two-thirds of all British Pakistanis are in fact of Azad Kashmiri origin' with 'the overwhelming majority ... [from] Mirpur district, or from the southern part of Kotli district'. The level of emigration from these areas has been 'truly massive', with well over half of the population in many villages in Mirpur District now living overseas—and often remitting money home.

Since 1947, 'Pakistanis' in the United Kingdom—many of whom could be considered Azad Kashmiris—have contributed significantly to Azad Kashmir and Pakistan, particularly via remittances. In the 1970s, spending by the 'overseas Mirpuri diaspora' in Mirpur caused a 'spectacular, if highly localised and very temporary economic boom'.[181] Population figures partly confirm this: urban Mirpur's population grew from 8,500 (1961) to 43,500 (1972) to 57,000 (1981), and it displaced Muzaffarabad (37,500 in 1981) as Azad Kashmir's largest city.[182] Azad Kashmiris' remittances reached their peak in 'the early 1980s', when 'they provided well over 50 per cent of [Pakistan's] foreign exchange earnings'.[183] In 1988, according to Pakistan's Finance Minister, Azad Kashmiris' deposits in Pakistani banks amounted to Rs. 2.4 trillion.[184] This was 960 times the size of Azad Kashmir's 1987–88 budget of Rs. 2.5 billion. In 2007–08, UK remittances of US$459 million were 7 per cent of Pakistan's total US$6.5 billion foreign remittances.[185] This official figure did not include unknown, but significant, amounts hand-carried or sent via the unofficial and cheaper *hundi* or *hawala* systems.[186] Assuming that 'two-thirds of all British Pakistanis are ... of Azad Kashmiri origin' and that they remit to Pakistan according to this proportion,[187] Azad Kashmiris sent US$306 million in 2007–08. Given Azad Kashmir's estimated 2006 population of 3.5 million, this amounts to $87 per capita, or 10 per cent of the average $847 per capita income.[188]

Nevertheless, the Azad Kashmir Government has not been able to access the trillions of Azad Kashmiris' remittances, either to borrow them or to invest them to obtain income. Pakistan, which oversees Azad Kashmir's fiscal policy and monetary situation, including banking, has not allowed this.[189] Equally, until 2006, no Azad Kashmir owned or operated bank existed that could accept international remittances—only Pakistani banks could do so. In November 2006, the Azad Kashmir Government instigated the commercial Bank of Azad Jammu & Kashmir, in which it has 51 per cent ownership, with Rs 2 billion capital. Set up to advance savings and development, it now has thirty-eight branches in Azad Kashmir and an arrangement with a Pakistan bank 'to facilitate distribution of home remittances'.[190] Before 2006, an Azad Jammu & Kashmir Cooperative Bank Ltd also existed, but it only operated for cooperative societies.[191] Such societies have existed since 1947, with 'more than 600' in 1965,[192] but (inexplicably) only 400 in 1985–86: 325 agricultural, seventy-five non-agricultural.[193] Had the Azad Kashmir Government been allowed direct access to foreign remittances from Azad Kashmiris, if only through borrowings, the prudent use and investment of them could have eased Azad Kashmir's financial dependency on Pakistan. However, turning such borrowings into proper, productive and profit-generating assets would have been difficult, given Azad Kashmir's drawbacks as a destination for investment and industry.

Some Azad Kashmiris, particularly Mirpuris, have been disgruntled with Pakistan's treatment of them and Azad Kashmir. Mirpuris 'control one-third of total liquid assets estimated at $60 billion held by Pakistanis abroad'. Some live in the 'superior' city of Mirpur, which is 'primarily based on savings made by Mirpuri earners overseas'.[194] While wealthy, Mirpuris lack influence. Despite personal dislocation to make way for the Mangla Dam and their contribution to the Pakistan economy through remittances, 'no serious effort had been made to stimulate economic and infrastructural development in … Mirpur district, or indeed in Azad Kashmir as a whole'. The benefits of Mangla Dam electricity had been felt in Lahore and Karachi 'long before powerlines began to be installed in rural Mirpur' to power Mirpuris' expensive overseas equipment.[195] While Mirpuris were Azad Kashmir's largest consumers of electricity in 1987–8, both in numbers (56,000) and amount consumed (46 million kWh), Mirpur District only had 2,600 telephone connections for its population of 466,000. (Muzaffarabad District was next: 34,000 electricity consumers; 27 million kWh consumed; 2,000 telephone connections, but more were automatic.)[196] Abutting the Punjab plains, Mirpur could have easily been integrated into northern Pakistan's economic zone.

By 2003, the Azad Kashmir Government had (finally) developed a 'comprehensive strategy' to encourage foreign investment by 'overseas Pakistanis and especially the Kashmiri [sic] expatriates based in the United Kingdom'.[197] In 1970, a report to the Pakistan Planning Commission had suggested that 'Azad Kashmir nationals living in U.K. [be] permitted to export machinery etc., … [to] set up small industries in A.K.'.[198] In 2003, the government's intention was 'to bring about [an] industrial revolution in Azad Kashmir',[199] including ventures in Mirpur Dry Port and the Software Development Centre at Mirpur.[200] This had some limited success. By 2009, Mirpur had 'an industrial area with textile, ghee, garments, engineering, cosmetic and other units'. But Mirpur appeared to be an atypical subcontinental city in appearance, affluence and its population's exposure to international experiences and connections.[201]

To assuage their disenchantment, some Mirpuris, particularly in the overseas diaspora, started supporting political movements such as the Jammu Kashmir Liberation Front. Seeking independence for all of J&K (see the next chapter),[202] JKLF may have 20,000–30,000 members and 'hundreds of thousands of supporters', with support strongest in Mirpur, Bagh and Poonch.[203] However, its economic agenda is rudimentary and Kashmir Valley-centric. 'Kashmir' can become 'the most prosperous country of the region' by 'invit[ing] millions of tourists every year' to the 'Switzerland of Asia' and 'Nature's Show-Window'; generating electricity on a large scale and selling this to 'neighbouring countries'; exploiting fruit, timber, minerals and herbs; developing Srinagar's 'small scale' watch-making industry; and utilising the 'valuable asset' of Kashmiri handcrafts.[204] This thinking is reminiscent of Hafizullah and various Azad Kashmir governments. Furthermore, supporting the JKLF may not be in Mirpuris' interests. Mirpuris have more in common with Punjabis than with Kashmiris, whose population, through sheer weight of numbers, and leaders would dominate if ever 'Kashmir' won independence. Furthermore, Srinagar would become the capital, which might not appeal to distant Mirpuris for whom Islamabad and Rawalpindi would continue to be significantly easier to access than Srinagar, Muzaffarabad or Jammu City; Islamabad also has a fully functioning international airport.[205] Mirpuris' support for the JKLF may have been a (largely unsuccessful) ploy to extract resources from Islamabad and Muzaffarabad to satisfy their desire for more local economic development.

*Economic matters related to Indian J&K*

Under the 1974 Interim Constitution, Pakistan controls all matters to do with 'the external affairs of Azad Jammu and Kashmir including foreign trade and foreign aid'.[206] From 1949, the Azad Kashmir Government has only been able to offer advice to Pakistan on such matters. Since late 1947, Azad Kashmir has remained cut off from Indian J&K. This isolation has been enforced by the Line of Control dividing J&K and by the Pakistani (and Indian) military forces that patrol the LOC. In recent years, two events have established closer contacts between Azad Kashmir and Indian J&K. First, because of the anti-Indian uprising in the Kashmir Valley since 1988, Azad Kashmir now houses more people from Indian J&K. Second, improved India-Pakistan relations resulting from the Composite Dialogue that began in 2004 established some significant cross-LOC links. This section discusses these two issues, both of which have economic ramifications for Azad Kashmir.

The number of 'Internally Displaced People' (IDPs) from Indian J&K living in Azad Kashmir has steadily risen since 1989.[207] (These people are IDPs as they 'have not crossed an international border'; this term also distinguishes them from Kashmiris who arrived in Azad Kashmir and Pakistan in 1947, or soon thereafter.)[208] Soon after Kashmiris began their anti-Indian uprising in 1988, IDPs started arriving in Azad Kashmir. They did so in a steady stream.[209] In 1997, Azad Kashmir housed 2,500 families, or 12,440 people from Indian J&K.[210] In 2006 there were 5,860 families, or 27,000 people.[211] Of these IDPs, 90 per cent were ethnic Kashmiris from the Kashmir Valley; the others were from the Poonch area of Indian J&K. IDPs were housed in fifteen camps: nine in Muzaffarabad District (2,000 families), four in Bagh District (980 families), two in Kotli District (1,140 families). Some families lived in rented properties: 1,630 in Muzaffarabad; ninety in

Mirpur; twenty in Rawalakot. IDPs' conditions were often rudimentary, with many 'living in extremely grim situations with no access to safe drinking water, regular food supplies, schooling for their children or adequate shelter'.[212] Many were engaged in 'small time jobs, selling fruit and readymade garments on the roadside to support themselves'.[213]

By 2008, IDPs from Indian J&K had increased to 7,000 families, comprising 31,000 people, housed in thirty-four camps or locations.[214] They were dispersed as follows: 4,800 families (19,000 people) in Muzaffarabad District; 1,100 families (6,300 people) in Kotli District; 1,000 families (5,200 people) in Bagh District; eighty families (400 people) in Mirpur; and twenty families (100 people) in Rawalakot. In 2002, every person was being paid Rs. 1,500 per month as a 'subsistence allowance'.[215] The Azad Kashmir Government gave each family a one-off grant of Rs. 1,000–2,000 on arrival in Azad Kashmir; each person received a 'Subsistence Allowance' of Rs. 1,000 per month; Rs. 1,090 per month was paid to the 'Head of the Family'.[216] (Another source states that IDPs were only paid Rs. 750 per month.)[217] It provided medical facilities, the installation of electricity, drinking water, education and books, free of charge. Students attending sixth to tenth class received an allowance of Rs. 150 per month; those undertaking higher education received Rs. 300 per month; those 'Memorising the Holy Quran' received Rs. 100 per month. The Azad Kashmir Government also apparently provided mosques, schools and industrial centres in each camp.

It is unclear how costs for IDPs have been met. Pakistan may have paid, or the Azad Kashmir Government could have provided for IDPs in the 'General Admin', 'Miscellaneous' or 'Rehabilitation' sections of its budget.[218] In its 'Development Programme 2006–2007', the Azad Kashmir Council listed an amount of Rs. 38.7 million as a 'Package for Kashmiri Refugees'. This was almost certainly for who people who arrived in Azad Kashmir and Pakistan in 1947, or soon thereafter— not the new IDPs.[219] Surprisingly, the 1998 Census does not mention IDPs, even though there were 12,440 people from Indian J&K living in Azad Kashmir in 1997.[220] This reflects the Azad Kashmir Government's dilemma: it has an obligation to look after people from 'Occupied' J&K, but it does not want too many of them. IDPs also confront a difficult situation: many want to return to their homes and families across the LOC, but, being unable currently to do so, are becoming more entrenched in Azad Kashmir's society and economy.

More recent cross-LOC contacts have established closer contacts between Azad Kashmir and Indian J&K. In 2004, the India-Pakistan Composite Dialogue began, with positive benefits for both nations and 'their' respective parts of J&K. This included agreeing some 'Kashmir-related Confidence Building Measures', among them: cross-LOC bus and truck services; the opening of LOC crossing points; providing LOC meeting points for divided families; and 'greater interaction among Kashmiri leadership on both sides of the LOC'.[221] On 5 April 2005, a ground-breaking—literally and figuratively—monthly bus service began operating between Muzaffarabad and Srinagar.[222] Since then, a Rawalakot-Poonch bus service has commenced,[223] with the Indian and Pakistani foreign ministers talking in May 2008 of increasing the frequency of both bus services to weekly.[224] A number of LOC crossing points were opened after the 2005 earthquake to enable J&K relatives to visit one another more easily—provided they could obtain the necessary permissions from both authorities and wait for the assigned crossing day. The five LOC crossings are (north to south, with the Azad Kashmir side listed first): Nauseri-Tithwal; Chakoti-Uri; Hajipur-Uri; Rawalakot-Poonch; Tattapani-Poonch. Only three crossings were operational in 2008.[225] Appendix XIII provides information for crossings in 2005–06 and about the processes involved.[226]

Despite a downturn in relations after General Musharraf's resignation, India and Pakistan agreed in May 2008 'to finalise modalities for intra-Kashmir trade and truck service'.[227] This cross-LOC trade and associated truck services began in October 2008 for a narrow range of twenty-one predetermined items on a twice-weekly basis via the Muzaffarabad-Srinagar and Rawalakot-Poonch routes.[228] Customs duties would not be levied, trade being conducted on a barter basis. While this was a positive move, traders were concerned about excessive bureaucratic procedures,[229] poor cross-LOC communications and inadequate infrastructure, and the lack of any bank with branches on both sides of the LOC to remove the need for barter. This trade is unlikely to boost Azad Kashmir's economic situation greatly. Nevertheless, it does offer some economic opportunities: Azad Kashmiris have access to another market, although two-way trade will probably favour Indian J&K; their region could become a trade corridor, although this will be limited because of the narrow range of tradeable items; both situations could create employment.[230] Such developments also rely on India-Pakistan relations remaining good and on a concomitant lack of military exchanges over the heavily-militarised LOC.

*Conclusion*

Since 1947, the resource-poor Azad Kashmir economy has been dependent on Pakistan for defence, food and other imports, employment, transport links, and financial assistance. While Pakistan overlooked Azad Kashmir's financial needs from 1947 until 1971, this was largely because Azad Kashmiris and Pakistanis were focused on reuniting J&K and delivering it to Pakistan. From the early 1970s, Azad Kashmir's economic situation began to improve, chiefly because Pakistan allocated large amounts of financial assistance to this deficit region. This did not lead to the region's industrialisation, something (still) needed to create jobs for unemployed or underemployed Azad Kashmiris living on small landholdings and/or generally needing to work in Pakistan or overseas. Instead, Azad Kashmir remained a deficit and backward region. Azad Kashmir's industrialisation will always pose problems. The region is an unattractive investment destination because of its location along the heavily-militarised LOC. Cross-LOC trade since late 2008 offers Azad Kashmiris some new, but limited, opportunities—and hope. But this situation is captive to India-Pakistan relations remaining stable. Similarly, significant industrialisation in Azad Kashmir is unlikely to occur until the Kashmir dispute is resolved.

Of all the economic issues confronting Azad Kashmir, financial dependence on Pakistan was, and is, the most difficult. Pakistan has provided large amounts of assistance to help Azad Kashmiris to survive. Nevertheless, some Azad Kashmiris believe—probably falsely—that had Azad Kashmir received more money from hydel sales from the Mangla Dam, had it been able to generate its own hydel and sell it to Pakistan, and had it been able access to Azad Kashmiris' investible overseas remittances, these could have been used to make Azad Kashmir economically self-sufficient. This, it is believed, would have led to greater prosperity—perhaps most importantly, it might have made Azad Kashmir the most prosperous of J&K's five regions. This would have advanced Azad Kashmir's ability to provide, and independently fund, a genuine alternative government for all of J&K. However, as things stand, Azad Kashmir remains economically backward, with high unemployment or under-employment, and with few prospects of developing into the advanced region of which some Azad Kashmiris have dreamed. Landlocked, devoid of any major resources and deficient in food and finances, it is, and will remain, heavily dependent on Pakistan.

8

# ELECTIONS AND INTERNAL POLITICS SINCE 1970

*Introduction*

In 1970, Azad Kashmir's constitution fully enfranchised the people of Azad Kashmir and enabled them to vote in multi-party elections. Genuinely free and fair presidential and general elections were held in October. There were further elections in Azad Kashmir in 1975, 1985, 1990, 1991, 1996, 2001 and 2006. Martial law from 1977 to 1988 interrupted Azad Kashmir's democracy, although the military did hold the heavily-controlled 1985 elections. The anti-Indian uprising in the Kashmir Valley after 1988 impacted on elections in 1990, but not thereafter. Despite General Musharraf's military rule, elections were held in 2001. This chapter discusses the various elections held in Azad Kashmir in and after 1970, and some of the politics surrounding these.

*1970 and 1975 elections*

On 30 October 1970, voters in Azad Kashmir participated in the presidential election, which, possibly, was the only genuinely free and fair election ever held in Azad Kashmir—and possibly in J&K. (By 1970, of Indian J&K's four elections, none was as free and fair as the 1970 Azad Kashmir presidential election.) For the only time, Azad Kashmiris directly elected the Azad Kashmir president. Universal suffrage was used for the first time.[1] The candidates were the respective party presidents: Sardar Ibrahim (Azad Muslim Conference); K.H. Khurshid (Liberation League); Sardar Qayyum (Muslim Conference); and Muhammad Sharif Tariq (J&K Plebiscite Front).[2] The result was: Qayyum, 229,512 votes; Khurshid, 163,865 votes; Ibrahim, 114,894 votes; and the less well known Tariq, 12,906 votes, with his votes coming mainly from his Gujjar *biradari*.[3] While the politically-weary Pakistan military, distracted by worsening events in East Pakistan and keen to devolve civilian rule to Azad Kashmir, felt disinclined to manipulate the election, they did prefer Sardar Qayyum as only he and his party were 'irrevocably committed' to J&K's accession to Pakistan.[4] Sardar Ibrahim believed General Yahya's regime helped Qayyum;[5] another observer, Yusuf Saraf, considered that Qayyum had campaigned hard and won the presidential election 'on merit'.[6]

189

## THE UNTOLD STORY OF THE PEOPLE OF AZAD KASHMIR

Little other information is available about the 1970 elections, presidential or general (discussed below). Apparently 'arson caused by rioters during 1977 in the Election Commission's Office at Rawalpindi' destroyed many records.[7]

The next day, on 31 October 1970, Azad Kashmiri voters participated in general elections to elect twenty-four members to the Azad Kashmir Legislative Assembly: seven from Mirpur; five from Poonch; four from Muzaffarabad; four Jammu & Others; and four Kashmir refugees. Qayyum's Muslim Conference won fifteen seats: twelve in Azad Kashmir and three refugee seats. Khurshid's Liberation League won five seats: one in Azad Kashmir, four refugee seats. Three independents were elected: two in Azad Kashmir, one refugee. Ibrahim's Azad Muslim Conference won the final seat, in Azad Kashmir. Thereafter, the indirectly-elected 'Reserved Lady Seat' went to Saeeda Khanam;[8] there is no indication of her location and party affiliation. The Muslim Conference had done well, both in Azad Kashmir through its extensive rural connections and in securing refugee seats. The Liberation League, whose leader was a Kashmiri refugee, was strong in refugee areas, where it won four of its five seats; otherwise, it failed to capitalise on Khurshid's charisma. The Azad Muslim Conference did poorly, possibly because Ibrahim was out of favour in Islamabad—a factor that has influenced all Azad Kashmir elections.[9]

Following the enactment of the Interim Constitution in 1974, elections were held on 18 May 1975 for the Azad Kashmir Legislative Assembly.[10] (Voters no longer elected the Azad Kashmir president.) There were forty directly-elected constituencies: twenty-eight in Azad Kashmir, twelve for refugees.[11] A 'United Front' alliance comprising the Pakistan People's Party-Azad Kashmir (PPPAK), the Liberation League and the Azad Muslim Conference contested the elections. The Front's major rival—Sardar Qayyum's powerful and well-organised Muslim Conference—boycotted the elections because of intimidation by the Pakistan Army and the police, and because of restrictions placed on their political activities and movements.[12] There were 1,407 polling stations: 961 in Azad Kashmir; 446 in Pakistan.[13] In a change of fortune, the PPPAK won twenty-six seats, and a majority, in the forty-two-seat Legislative Assembly. The Liberation League won five seats; Chaudhry Noor Hussain's Azad Muslim Conference won three seats; three rebellious Muslim Conference members won seats; and three independents were elected. Thereafter, Begum Zamurd Sharif and Farhat Shaheen were indirectly elected to the assembly in the Special Seats for Women.[14] There is no indication of these women's location and party affiliation.

The Pakistan People's Party-Azad Kashmir, which was the local affiliate of Zulfiqar Ali Bhutto's Pakistan People's Party, was the major beneficiary of the 1975 elections. While the PPPAK may have won many of its seventeen seats in Azad Kashmir on merit, its winning of nine (of twelve) refugee seats appeared dubious. Indeed, its overall victory possibly resulted from Bhutto's Political Adviser, Hayat Muhammad Khan Tamman, closely 'supervising' and 'managing' the actual results to ensure the 'correct' people were 'elected'. Basically, the elections were rigged. The PPPAK's victory reflected the dominance that its political patron, Bhutto, enjoyed in Pakistan and, vicariously, Qayyum's isolation from Bhutto. Later, Bhutto acknowledged his adviser's excessive zeal when he told a restricted gathering that Pakistan's 1977 general elections would not be like Azad Kashmir's 'Tammani elections'.[15] Unsurprisingly, Qayyum believed that the 1975 elections were a fraud and that 90 per cent of electors had not voted.[16] However, other factors were responsible for Qayyum's 'loss', including a desire for change, given that the Muslim Conference had been involved in running Azad Kashmir since 1947.

Using its majority in the Legislative Assembly, and ignoring the other United Front members, the PPPAK formed a government on its own. Khan Abdul Hamid Khan, elected from a Kashmir refugee seat, became Prime Minister. A joint sitting of the Azad Kashmir Legislative Assembly and the newly-constituted Azad Kashmir Council then elected Sardar Ibrahim Azad Kashmir President.[17] A five-member cabinet was formed comprising Hamid Khan, Mumtaz Rathore (elected from a Poonch seat) as Senior Minister, Chaudhry Sohbat Ali (Mirpur), Mian Ghulam Rasool (Muzaffarabad) and Sardar Khan Bahadur (Poonch). Bhutto had wanted Khurshid to become prime minister. Apart from his displeasure with the rigged elections,[18] Khurshid could not overcome opposition from the majority PPPAK and the significant support given to Hamid Khan by his brother, a former Chief Minister of NWFP.[19]

*The military rule period*

Azad Kashmir's next elections were due in mid-1980, after the government completed its five-year term. However, on 5 July 1977, General Zia's martial law administration brought Azad Kashmir under its compelling control. Zia became Chairman of the Azad Kashmir Council, while Major-General (Retired) Rehman was appointed Chief Executive of Azad Kashmir. Sardar Ibrahim remained President until 31 October 1978 when Zia made Brigadier Hayat Khan President and Chief Executive of Azad Kashmir. Rehman and Hayat essentially usurped Azad Kashmir's legislature and executive, and ruled by military-initiated ordinances.[20] This caused 'a long pause in the political process' in Azad Kashmir 'during which all representative institutions remained petrified' and elections were 'thwarted'.[21] 'Elections' were finally held in 1985.

Early in its rule, the military considered holding elections for Azad Kashmir. On 11 August 1977, in accordance with 53-A of the Interim Constitution, Sardar Ibrahim issued a presidential proclamation dissolving the Legislative Assembly and ordering elections for October 1977.[22] In a second proclamation on 8 October 1977, he instructed that Azad Kashmir elections should be held 'within ten days' of the proposed 1977 general elections in Pakistan. Preparations were made, including acceptance of 260 nominations. However, the 1977 elections, and a further attempt in November 1979, were postponed, chiefly because a distrustful Zia wanted politicians made more accountable before allowing elections in Pakistan,[23] after which elections could be held in Azad Kashmir. The 1977 postponement was acceptable. There was uncertainty about dated electoral rolls, particularly for refugee seats: 'enlightened public opinion was sceptical about their accuracy' owing to some old and obsolete—and some bogus new—entries.[24] The second postponement caused 'dismay'. Azad Kashmir elections had become 'subservient' to the 'ten day rule' to conduct elections soon after Pakistan's general elections; no elections in Pakistan meant no Azad Kashmir elections. But all was not wasted: electoral rolls updated in 1978 were used that year to conduct elections to 'various tiers of local bodies … after a lapse of about fifteen years'.[25]

## THE UNTOLD STORY OF THE PEOPLE OF AZAD KASHMIR

In September 1979, the 'Political Parties Ordinance' was promulgated 'to regulate ... [all] political parties' in Azad Kashmir. While not as draconian as Pakistan's Martial Law Regulation 48 by which all political parties in Pakistan simply 'ceased to exist',[26] it possibly inspired President Hayat Khan's announcement on 31 October 1980 that a Council of Ministers and an Advisory Council (Majlis-e-Shoora) would be elected on a non-party basis.[27] This did not occur and political parties were permitted, but regulated. To register under the Ordinance, a party had to have published its foundation document or constitution, have periodic elections of principal officers, subscribe to the ideology of Pakistan and J&K's accession to it, submit accounts for audit, and not be aided by, or associated with, a foreign country or foreign political party.[28] The PPPAK refused to register and challenged the Ordinance's constitutionality, a challenge that the Election Commissioner rejected. The party then neither formally registered nor was allocated an electoral symbol with which to contest elections.[29] By 1985, when elections finally appeared imminent, eleven political parties had qualified to participate.[30] These included the Muslim Conference, the Azad Muslim Conference, the Plebiscite Front and the J&K Tehrik-i-Amal Party.[31] The PPPAK and five minor parties had not registered.[32] Interestingly, Hayat Khan, the former military-appointed Azad Kashmir President (1978–83), led Tehrik-i-Amal. Despite an overbearing disposition towards politicians and political parties, he had reversed his unpopular 1980 stance against non-party elections. Equally, he had recovered from agitation in 1983 that resulted in his resignation and replacement by Major-General Rehman.[33]

The 1985 Azad Kashmir elections took place on 15 May—more than ten days after Pakistan's February non-party elections, because Azad Kashmir was only free from snow by then.[34] The elections generated 'unusual enthusiasm'—and security. Officials deployed police, reserve police, Pakistan Rangers, Janbaz militia, Razakars (militia), Forest Guards, twenty platoons of Punjab Police, five platoons of Frontier Police and, as a 'precautionary measure', 'units' of Army personnel near potential places of trouble.[35] There were 201 candidates for forty seats: 122 candidates contested twenty-eight seats in Azad Kashmir; forty-nine contested six Jammu & Others seats; thirty contested six Kashmir Valley seats.[36] Partywise, there were eighty-one independents, forty Muslim Conference, twenty-nine Azad Muslim Conference, twenty-five Tehrik-i-Amal Party, twenty-three Liberation League and three Muslim Conference (Ghazi Group). First-past-the-post voting took place in 1,780 polling stations (1,357 in Azad Kashmir; 423 in Pakistan) for 1,310,000 voters (1,007,000 in Azad Kashmir; 284,000 Jammu & Others; 19,000 'Kashmir Valley' refugees),[37] with a 59 per cent voter turnout.[38]

Officially, despite 'foreboding' by 'some prophets of doom', the 1985 elections were free, fair, competitive and peaceful—and 'an ample testimony of the political sagacity of the common man'.[39] The Muslim Conference won nineteen seats (40 per cent of the vote), Tehrik-i-Amal won eight seats (19 per cent), independents seven seats (17 per cent), the Liberation League four (14 per cent), the Azad Muslim Conference two (10 per cent), and the Muslim Conference (Ghazi Group) no seats (0.13 per cent).[40] Four Kashmir Valley candidates won seats by 'securing between 435 and 700 odd votes'.[41] Some independents were possibly PPPAK members who stood in this category because the unregistered PPPAK was distant from the military and had boycotted the elections, as did Jamiat-i-

# ELECTIONS AND INTERNAL POLITICS SINCE 1970

Islami, because it perceived (probably correctly) official favouritism for the Muslim Conference.[42] The military-dominated Azad Kashmir Election Commission created an oppressive pre-poll disincentive by obliging parties taking part in the elections to 'secure' 12.5 per cent of total votes polled and five per cent of votes polled in each district, or be de-registered.[43] This deterred six registered parties from contesting while, after the elections, three parties had to 'show cause' why they should not be de-registered: Azad Muslim Conference, Muslim Conference (Ghazi Group) and Tehrik-i-Amal Party. The latter had done well in the overall vote, but poorly in Mirpur District only. After some bitter public agitation and a successful petition to the Azad Kashmir High Court, the Election Commission backed down, thus preventing an 'unsavoury aftermath ... after a long eclipse of [the] democratic process'.[44]

After the elections, the Muslim Conference's position improved. On 1 June 1985, members of the Legislative Assembly elected two women members (from five candidates) in reserved seats.[45] On 16 June, members elected Sardar Sikandar Prime Minister by twenty-four votes to seventeen, over an independent.[46] On 25 July, six members (from nine candidates) were elected to the Azad Kashmir Council.[47] On 30 September, a joint Council-Legislative Assembly sitting elected Sardar Qayyum president over Mian Ghulam Rias.[48] Qayyum's election was contentious: only twenty-nine of forty-nine eligible members voted at the joint sitting, one absentee being the 'Federal Minister incharge [sic] of the Council Secretariat'. Nevertheless, Qayyum secured all votes and the requisite majority. The presidential election was also late: it should have been held thirty days after the Legislative Assembly results were published on 2 June 1985, but the Pakistan President was unavailable beforehand to witness members being sworn in (and thereby made eligible to vote in the presidential election) as Council Chairman, as the Interim Constitution required. This delay was acceptable under the constitution's 'catch all' clause of 56-A (see Chapter 4).[49]

The Muslim Conference government had few problems until 1988. Qayyum enjoyed 'a total understanding with the Centre'[50] and 'unusual proximity' to Zia.[51] Qayyum liked the military, partly because he considered his government a quasi-military 'movement whose main aim was to liberate [Indian] Kashmir'.[52] He hoped India would attack Azad Kashmir, because then 'nine million [sic] Kashmiris will rebel' and the resultant war 'would seal and decide matters for ever' in the Kashmiris' favour, after which they would accede to Pakistan.[53] This was rhetoric. Qayyum had no forces, nor would Pakistan—and its military—have allowed any such rival organisation in Azad Kashmir. Qayyum's cosy political situation changed after some unexpected events in 1988: Zia's death in August; severe unrest in Indian J&K; and Benazir Bhutto's election victory. Qayyum was critical of the popular Bhutto and her Pakistan People's Party, and she and Qayyum had a difficult relationship,[54] although Bhutto did not sack the Azad Kashmir Government after securing power.[55] Instead, she used her superior position as Azad Kashmir Council 'Chairman' to impose strict conditions on Pakistan's financial assistance to Azad Kashmir and the Ministry of Kashmir Affairs to rebuild the PPPAK and enhance its *biradari* links.[56] These positioned 'her' party well for the 1990 Azad Kashmir elections in which voters had 'great dissatisfaction' with Muslim Conference corruption.[57]

# THE UNTOLD STORY OF THE PEOPLE OF AZAD KASHMIR

*Support for anti-Indian militants*

By 1990, the political situation had changed dramatically in Azad Kashmir, and in Indian J&K also. From 31 July 1988, the Kashmir Valley experienced a 'sudden eruption of violence' as motivated Kashmiris wanting *azadi* (independence from India and Pakistan) unexpectedly instigated an anti-Indian uprising.[58] With a serious downturn in India-Pakistan relations, the Pakistan and Azad Kashmir governments were trying to comprehend the militancy and decide what to do. In Azad Kashmir, demonstrations of popular support occurred, with Azad Kashmiris hopeful that India would be forced to leave the Kashmir Valley. Most Azad Kashmiris wanted this region to join Pakistan; some also wanted independence for J&K.

Before discussing Azad Kashmir and Pakistan's support for anti-Indian militants, some important antecedents are worth noting. These relate to the Jammu Kashmir Liberation Front. Its ideology is 're-unification and complete independence of Kashmir'—by which it presumably means J&K. Militarily, the JKLF claims, with some justification, to have started the anti-Indian uprising in the Kashmir Valley in 1988 'to attract world attention to its cause'.[59] Politically, the JKLF claims to be 'functioning in Indian held Kashmir, Azad Kashmir, Gilgit Baltistan, Middle East, Europe and USA'. In Azad Kashmir, it enjoys some popularity, mainly around Mirpur, Poonch and Bagh,[60] although its actual popularity is impossible to confirm as the party is electorally untested. As discussed below, the JKLF's pro-independence stance prevents its candidates from contesting Azad Kashmir elections.

Anti-Indian activities by people associated with JKLF began as early as 1965. That year, 'fragments' from Pakistan's failed 'Operation Gibraltar' (which provoked the 1965 India-Pakistan war) formed the Plebiscite Front.[61] These included the politically-active Mirpuri, Abdul Khaliq Ansari, and two Kashmiris, Maqbool Butt, 'a charismatic but mysterious figure',[62] and Amanullah Khan,[63] a former major in the 'Azad Kashmir Armed Forces'.[64] (The Azad Kashmir Plebiscite Front had no connections with the Indian J&K Plebiscite Front formed in 1953.)[65] In 1966, Butt organised 'secret cells and train[ed] locally-enlisted workers' in the Kashmir Valley for anti-Indian 'sabotage'.[66] In 1971, he was involved in hijacking an Indian Airlines aircraft from Srinagar to Lahore.[67] On 29 May 1977, Butt and Amanullah formed the JKLF in England,[68] with one objective being armed struggle. It evolved from the Kashmir National Liberation Front, which arose from the Plebiscite Front.[69] In 1986, JKLF personnel 'received [covert] armed training' in Pakistan, after which they 'returned to Kashmir to declare war on the Indian forces, thus launching the armed struggle'.[70] They were partially 'galvanized' by India's hanging in 1984 of Maqbool Butt, whose 'only crime' was 'his exemplary Kashmiri patriotism'.[71] India's 'ferocious' suppression of subsequent Kashmiri protests helped their cause.[72]

While the JKLF may have instigated the anti-Indian uprising in the Kashmir Valley, it was soon sidelined. The JKLF, possibly through its armed wing, the Kashmir Liberation Army which predated the formation of other anti-Indian armed militant groups,[73] was active militarily early in the anti-Indian uprising. However, by December 1991, after the Front had been supposed to be 'the only organization in the field of armed struggle for over eighteen months', and because it favoured 'complete independence of Kashmir',[74] Pakistan's insidious Directorate for Inter-

Services Intelligence (ISI) began 'directing assassinations and attacks ... to remove [JKLF] as a military force'.[75] Amanullah complained that 'the pro-Pakistan Hizb[ul Mujahidin] was killing JKLF workers'[76] and that JKLF had taken a 'secondary position' to 'religious militant organizations'. He (optimistically) saw this as 'a temporary phase' until India, Pakistan and the international community saw 'reason and realize[d] their responsibilities', in relation to J&K and JKLF's 'way to ensure permanent peace, prosperity and tranquillity for [the] entire South Asia'.[77]

A more controversial matter is support from Azad Kashmir and Pakistan for anti-Indian militants. This includes arming and enabling militant organisations to train and operate in Azad Kashmir, and assisting their operatives to transit through the region into Indian J&K. For Pakistan, India's 'baseless' claims are 'an attempt to malign Pakistan and the Kashmiri freedom movement' and shift attention away from (unacceptable) human rights violations in the Kashmir Valley.[78] Despite a lack of reliable information, India's claims have much basis in fact, as the evidence below shows, discussing two aspects: covert support to anti-Indian militants and overt support to their political organisations and the anti-Indian cause.

The Azad Kashmir Government appears to have had little involvement in supporting anti-Indian militants since 1988, despite President Qayyum's claim to have a 'strategy' to 'organize resistance on both sides' of the LOC.[79] Expressing a contrasting view, Qayyum considered that it would be 'better and safer if, instead of an active liberation effort, Muslims ... [in Indian J&K] tr[ied] to protect and maintain their Islamic culture and their separate identity'. Realistically, Azad Kashmiris were 'not in a position' to offer Kashmiris the 'required assistance', although they would give them 'full moral support'.[80] Equally, Azad Kashmiris knew that assisting militants was Pakistan's responsibility.

Pakistan's covert support for anti-Indian militants has taken various forms, including providing training to militants at camps in Azad Kashmir (at which only 15 per cent of trainees have been Azad Kashmiris).[81] Brian Cloughley, an expert on the Pakistan Army, is unequivocal: 'Pakistan, never loath to capitalise on India's discomfort or difficulties, took the opportunity, through the army, to foster various groupings that were intent on creating mayhem on the Indian side of the Line of Control. Their efforts grew, year by year, and there was no doubt they had official backing from within Pakistan'.[82]

The Pakistan Army's assistance to anti-Indian militants included: treating militants in army hospitals in Azad Kashmir; providing them with 'abundant military assistance, much of it funded through ISI'; supplying them with arms; delivering training programmes; turning 'a blind eye to armed line-crossers'; and giving them 'covering fire by use of small arms and even artillery'.[83] A former Pakistan government official states that Lashkar-i-Taiba, the 'militant wing' of 'Markaz Dawat-ul-Irshad (MDI—Center for Religious Learning and Propagation)', provides 'guerrilla warfare training in military camps, located mostly in Pakistani-controlled Kashmir'.[84] Lashkar's 'successful sabotage operations against Indian forces in Kashmir' have ensured it immunity from Pakistan's intelligence and law enforcement agencies, without which 'running military training camps inside Pakistan would not be possible'. Lashkar-i-Taiba has won 'the goodwill of the army leadership for achieving what they could not' in Indian J&K, plus its help in operational matters, with ISI providing 'sensitive maps and access to arms and ammunition'.

## THE UNTOLD STORY OF THE PEOPLE OF AZAD KASHMIR

A moot point is not whether there are training camps Pakistan in Azad Kashmir for anti-Indian militants, but how many there are. Figures vary. In 2001, *Strategic Comments* claimed that Pakistan had 'failed to eliminate the 180 training camps and supply bases in its Azad (Free) Kashmir province used by insurgents'.[85] This number was almost certainly reduced after 9/11 when a pressured Pakistan reacted to world disgust against nations supporting terrorism—of which it was considered to be one. More particularly, Islamabad responded to an alleged US threat to bomb Pakistan 'back to the Stone Age' if it continued to support terrorists, particularly, but not exclusively, the Taliban.[86] A chastened Pakistan joined the US-led 'Global War on Terror' and reduced its involvement in 'terror' operations, including those against India. The US also wanted better India-Pakistan relations to ensure Pakistan would focus on its Taliban-infested western border area, not on India. Concurrently, improved India-Pakistan relations saw their eight-topic 'Composite Dialogue' begin, which included discussions on 'terrorism and drug trafficking' and J&K. Four rounds of discussions took place from February 2004 until India suspended the dialogue after the Mumbai terrorist attacks on 27 November 2008.[87] India blamed Pakistanis, particularly 'fundamentalist' Lashkar-e-Taiba operatives, for these attacks. Later, Pakistan's Interior Minister, Rehman Malik, publicly admitted that they were partly planned in Pakistan and that 'suspects from the banned Lashkar-e-Taiba militant group had been held and may be prosecuted'.[88]

In 2009, India identified 'forty-two terror-training camps directed against India … in Pakistan and PoK'. Using data from Indian intelligence agencies, India's Multi-Agency Centre assessed there were thirty-four 'active' and eight 'holding' camps located evenly between Azad Kashmir and Pakistan/the Northern Areas.[89] Active camps in Azad Kashmir were at: 'Kotli, Garhi Dupatta, Nikial, Sensa, Gulpur, Forward Kahutta, Peer Chinasi, Jhandi Chauntra, Bhimbher, Barnala, Skardu [sic; in the Northern Areas], Abdullah Bin Masud, Tattapani, Samani and Shavai Nallah'. Other camps were located in NWFP, 'with the densely-forested hilly Manshera [Mansehra] region, in particular, housing several madrasas, which also double up as training camps',[90] and in 'Pakistan and [the] Northern Areas' at 'Muridke, Sialkot, Beesian, Garhi Habibullah [in Mansehra District, NWFP] and Jalogali'. Some of these camps outside Azad Kashmir were located close to this region, particularly those in Mansehra District, which borders Muzaffarabad and Neelum districts, and Sialkot, which is close to Mirpur. According to the Indian assessment, militant camps housed 'round 2,200 militants', with 'around 300 belong[ing] to Lashkar-e-Taiba, 240 to Jaish-e-Mohammed and 130 to Huji [*Harkat-ul-Jihad-al-Islami*], with the rest 'of "mixed" origins'. Many camps were 'makeshift' and could be 'translocated very quickly to evade scrutiny … [with] the real leaders of the various tanzims [militant organisations]' based in Islamabad and Lahore. Such mobility is likely as each camp, on average, accommodated fifty to fifty-five men.

Three non-Indian sources confirm that Azad Kashmir housed camps for anti-Indian militants. First, in May 2007, Sardar Qayyum stated that 'the Mujahideen's training camps not only existed in Azad Kashmir but were also operational in Pakistan'; indeed, 'it would be a lie' to say otherwise.[91] This countered his earlier braggadocio that 'Those who are prepared to die for a cause need no training'.[92] Second, General Musharraf stated that a suicide bomber who attacked him in

2003 was 'Mohammad Jamil ... from a village in Rawalakot in Azad (Independent [sic]) Kashmir'. According to Jamil's relatives, as Musharraf quoted them, Jamil 'received training from a terrorist organization in the Kotli area of Independent [sic]) Kashmir'.[93] That Azad Kashmir was 'independent' would have been news to Azad Kashmiris. In October 2010, Musharraf publicly confirmed that Pakistan had formed 'militant underground groups to fight India in Kashmir' and that it was 'the Pakistani security forces that trained them'.[94]

The third source confirming that Azad Kashmir housed camps for anti-Indian militants is reports after the 2005 earthquake detailing how militant groups engaged in rescue and relief very soon after the earthquake struck. Given their presence in Azad Kashmir, it was 'no accident that militant groups were the first on the scene dispensing relief goods and other aid after the earthquake'.[95] Groups immediately able to help were 'reportedly the Islamic militant or "*jihadi*" groups already based in the [Azad Kashmir] area at camps used to train anti-Indian Kashmiri militant groups'. These included Hizbul Mujahidin, Jamiat-al-Ansar (formerly Harkatul Mujahidin), Jamaat ud-Dawa (formerly Lashkar-i-Taiba) and Al-Rashid Trust. Indeed, 'as many as seventeen groups ... banned by the Musharraf government or placed on its terrorism watch-list ... [were] involved in relief activities'. With people turning a 'blind eye' to their presence, militant groups did good work in the difficult post-earthquake period. Apart from the immediacy of their help, 'members of *jihadi* groups, many of whom had been trained at camps for Kashmiri militant groups in the earthquake-affected areas of NWFP and PaK [Pakistan-Administered J&K], had the tremendous advantage of knowing the terrain and the people, and having close ties with and support from the Pakistan Army'.[96] Indeed, the Pakistan military was keen to enlist militants' support, including to help its own personnel. It also 'saw the earthquake as an opportunity to craft a new image for the militant groups rather than ... to disband them'.[97]

The second aspect to discuss is Azad Kashmir and Pakistan's overt support for militants' political organisations and their anti-Indian cause. Apart from unofficial people's rallies, protests and general strikes showing solidarity with the Kashmiris' cause,[98] overt support has taken two forms. The first is anti-Indian propaganda efforts. In early 1990, the Azad Kashmir Government established the Kashmir Liberation Cell in Muzaffarabad. Its responsibilities included printing anti-Indian literature, distributing this in Azad Kashmir and Pakistan, and smuggling it into Indian J&K.[99] The Cell has been ineffective. It has lacked direction, drive and skilled personnel, partly because Azad Kashmiri leaders appointed unqualified party workers to positions.[100] Its unsophisticated publications lack appeal, except for biased anti-Indian readers.[101] It may even have closed for some time.[102] In 2010, the Cell was still sluggish, its main effort being an Internet forum for 'users' to discuss the Kashmir dispute and associated issues. As Farooq Haider, Azad Kashmir's then Prime Minister, noted: the Cell needed 'services rules ... to make [it] more active and dynamic'.[103] A model might be the propagandist radio station operating in Azad Kashmir since 1960; in 1994, apparently it was so successful publicising the 'freedom movement' that the Indians banned listening to it and sought to jam its signal.[104]

Another way in which Azad Kashmir has overtly supported anti-Indian militants is to allow the United Jihad Council (UJC) to operate in Muzaffarabad.[105]

# THE UNTOLD STORY OF THE PEOPLE OF AZAD KASHMIR

There is little information available about this body, a situation that reflects ISI's ability to dominate militants and control information about their activities, by means including intimidation of Azad Kashmiri journalists:[106] 'We are ... at the mercy of Pakistani jihadis and the dreaded ISI here. But the problem is, we are all compromised. If the ISI call me and ask me whether I spoke to you, I will probably tell them everything', said a journalist who spoke on 'condition of anonymity' astride the noisy Neelum River in Muzaffarabad 'to ensure he was not overheard'. Similarly: 'Virtually all independent commentators, journalists, as well as former and serving militants, Pakistani military officers and Pakistan-backed Azad Kashmir politicians speaking off-the-record told Human Rights Watch that there was continuing militant infiltration from Azad Kashmir into Jammu and Kashmir state, but were not willing to be quoted for fear of reprisal from the ISI'. ISI is all-powerful in Azad Kashmir.

The United Jihad Council was created in 1994[107] by the Pakistan military 'to ensure unity of command and control' over anti-Indian militants.[108] 'Syed Salahuddin', a Kashmiri from the Kashmiri-dominated Hizbul Mujahideen, led it.[109] Hizbul is the largest militant group in the 'umbrella' organisation, whose members 'follow their own strategies and fight ... for resources and the patronage of the Pakistani government', chiefly ISI, which employs a 'divide-and-manage' control strategy.[110] When it started, the UJC had fourteen members: Hizbul Mujahideen, Harkatul Mujahideen (previously Harakat al-Ansar), and twelve minor groups of the hardline 'Deobandi persuasion'.[111] Two large militant groups operating in Azad Kashmir, Lashkar-i-Taiba and Jaish-i-Mohammed, joined later, possibly after Pakistan reorganised the UJC.[112] By 1999, only four groups were considered effective: Lashkar-i-Taiba, Hizbul Mujahideen, Al Badr Mujahideen and Harkatul Mujahideen.[113] Both the UJC and Hizbul Mujahideen may be affiliated with the activist Islamic religious organisation, the Jamaat-i-Islami,[114] which has made 'deep inroads into Kashmiri Muslim society'.[115] The UJC was in contact with the Kashmir-based All Parties Hurriyat Conference (APHC),[116] although not always amicably. Apart from differing agendas, the APHC had difficulties with Salahuddin's idiosyncratic Hizbul Mujahideen,[117] which in 2000 declared a unilateral ceasefire then rescinded it when India refused its demands.[118] An APHC chapter comprising 'about thirty-four freedom fighting groups' was also located in Azad Kashmir.[119] Its links with the Kashmir APHC were unknown.

After 9/11, the UJC 'ceased to operate publicly' and some militant groups changed their names.[120] Thereafter, it appears to have been fairly low key. However, in 2010 the UJC was obviously active. Militant activity was increasing in Indian J&K owing to the downturn in India-Pakistan relations, with Pakistan supporting militants to pressure India and insecure militant groups (such as Lashkar-i-Taiba) seeking to show they could not be easily suppressed. In January 2010, emboldened militants met in Muzaffarabad at a meeting co-chaired by the noted anti-Indian 'hawk' and former ISI chief, Hamid Gul.[121] In March 2010, the UJC Chairman, Syed Salahuddin, stated that the 'unsuccessful' resumption of India-Pakistan talks at the secretary level was an Indian 'ploy',[122] after which he and 5,000 'hardline' militants met in Kotli and 'vowed to wage a holy war to liberate ... Kashmir from Indian control'. Those attending included Hizbul Mujahidin and Jamaat-ud-Dawa, 'a charity widely viewed as a front for banned Islamist group

Lashkar-e-Taiba'.[123] The UJC now comprises a 'loose alliance of thirteen guerrilla groups',[124] although an Indian organisation identified sixteen members: Hizb-ul-Mujahideen; JKLF; Harkat-ul-Ansar; Tehrik-e-Jehad; Tehreek-ul-Mujahideen; Jamiat-ul-Mujahideen; Al Jehad; Al Umar Mujahideen; Jammu Kashmir Islamic Front; Muslim Janbaz Force; Hizbullah; Al Fatah; Hizb-ul-Momineen; Lashkar-e-Toiba; Jaish-e-Mohammed; Al-Badr Mujahideen.[125]

It is difficult to determine what presence the UJC actually has in Azad Kashmir. While it has issued statements from Muzaffarabad, many militant leaders probably live elsewhere and only visit provincial Muzaffarabad for meetings or protests. Hizbul Mujahideen's office is 'in a middle-class neighbourhood in Rawalpindi';[126] other groups, like Lashkar-i-Taiba and Jaish-e-Muhammad, are based in Punjab.[127] For Pakistan, it is helpful having militants located where it can 'keep an eye on them'. Equally, Islamabad takes all decisions on anti-Indian activities, not Muzaffarabad. Finally, for Azad Kashmir, bodies like the UJC are Pakistan's responsibility.[128] Nevertheless in 2003, to ensure 'public order', the Azad Kashmir Government 'prohibited' the leader of the banned and 'defunct Jaish-i-Mohammad group from entering [its] territory'. In reality, it was the Pakistan Government's responsibility to deal with this group.[129]

An abysmal aspect of militant activity involves suicide attacks in Azad Kashmir. From June 2009 to February 2010, five suicide attacks made against the military,[130] against Shias during Muharram,[131] and against the general public killed eighteen people, including ten army or police personnel,[132] and injured 101 people.[133] Groups involved were the banned Tehrik-i-Taliban Pakistan (Student Movement of Pakistan)[134] and Lashkar-e-Zil (Shadow Army), a 'loose alliance' of anti-US al-Qaeda and Taliban groups of which 'the Azad Kashmir chapter of the Harkat-ul-Jihad al-Islami (Huji) led by Commander Ilyas Kashmiri' is a member.[135] Kashmiri is an ex-Pakistan Army commando from Kotli, where his organisation once had a training camp.[136] On 6 January 2010, a Huji operative undertook the suicide attack near a military installation at Trarkhel that killed four soldiers. The military was possibly targeted because of the Azad Kashmir Regiment's involvement in anti-Taliban operations in Pakistan. Equally, the attacks suggested Taliban frustration, or opportunism, by striking at (possibly softer) targets in Azad Kashmir. The attacks do not appear to directly involve UJC members, most of whom are anti-Indian, not anti-Pakistani.

*The 1990 elections*

The unexpected anti-Indian insurgency by Kashmiris after July 1988 influenced the 1990 Azad Kashmir elections (but few elections thereafter). Many Azad Kashmiris supported the Kashmiris, with the Jammu Kashmir Liberation Front and the Pakistan People's Party-Azad Kashmir leading this support. Conversely, the Muslim Conference was bewildered. Being in government (Sardar Qayyum was President, Sardar Sikandar was Prime Minister), it needed to act cautiously and responsibly, unlike its increasingly popular political rivals. In mid-1989, with support for Kashmiris almost euphoric, 'eleven political and religious parties' formed the Kashmir Liberation Alliance to show solidarity with Kashmiris.[137] These included the Muslim Conference and the JKLF, but not the PPPAK. Tehrik-I-Amal's President, Hayat Khan, was convenor. One surprising item on the Alliance's six-point agenda was that all people in J&K should be allowed to choose whether J&K should join India, join Pakistan or be independent.[138] While the panicky Muslim Conference's decision to join the Alliance displayed its pro-Kashmiri credentials and enabled it to monitor its rivals, the decision was ill-considered. Membership contradicted the Interim Constitution's requirement that all Azad Kashmir politicians must favour J&K's accession to Pakistan. This may explain why the Alliance soon became inactive.

With the PPP in power in Pakistan, Sardar Ibrahim's PPPAK played an interesting role in Azad Kashmir. To support the Kashmiris' nascent uprising, 'big public rallies' were held in Muzaffarabad, Mirpur, Kotli and Bagh. The PPPAK organised these 'show[s] of strength that could not be matched by other political parties'.[139] Equally, the JKLF was receiving popular support, chiefly because its fighters were at the forefront of the anti-Indian uprising.[140] It had links with Yasin Malik's Kashmir Valley JKLF, but these ended in 1995 when Amanullah sacked Malik as JKLF president for unilaterally offering a ceasefire. Malik, in turn, removed Amanullah as JKLF chairman.[141] While Ibrahim and the PPPAK had no constraining responsibilities of office, its partner in Islamabad, Benazir Bhutto's PPP Government, confronted three significant challenges: to placate a restive population strongly supportive of the Kashmiris' struggle; to pacify an angry India accusing Pakistan of sending and supporting anti-Indian militants; and to control military elements keen to use the uprising to avenge Pakistan's humiliating defeat in the 1971 India-Pakistan war.[142] These issues also affected Azad Kashmir.

With an election imminent in May 1990, the uncertain Muslim Conference government had issues. Its rivals' popularity was ballooning. There was 'controversy' over independent Kashmir that the JKLF, the 'dominant force in the present campaign', was pushing. And while Qayyum was supposed to want to 'get the occupied valley liberated from India' first,[143] Ibrahim trumped him by proposing to raise 100,000 'commandos' to do this.[144] (Pakistan opposed this 'lashkar to liberate Kashmir', to prevent giving agitated India any excuse to start new 'hostilities culminating in war'.) On 26 January 1990, India's Republic Day, '2,000 enraged Azad Kashmiri youth' attempted to cross the LOC but were stopped when the Pakistan Army fired on them.[145] (A later report claimed Indian forces killed two youths.)[146] The Muslim Conference was unsure about how to negate such popular support for the anti-Indian cause. Indeed, some politicians were reluctant to support Kashmiris because, if J&K were reunited, the centre of politics would shift to Srinagar and ethnic Kashmiris would regain their dominance.[147] Another issue was that distraught Kashmiris increasingly started to cross the LOC in 1990.[148] 'All [sic] of them' had a 'strong desire' to obtain arms and return to the Kashmir Valley to 'wage a *jihad*'.[149] In February, 'some twenty to twenty-five' IDP families[150] were housed 'in a madrasah [sic]' in Bagh district;[151] by April, a 'sizeable influx' of IDPs had occurred;[152] by May, there were 'more than 10,000 people', mostly young men. Many considered Azad Kashmir to be the 'base camp for the liberation struggle',[153] a reasonable expectation given that it 'was increasingly dotted with militant camps' in the 1990s.[154] Three weeks before polling day, there was little political activity in Azad Kashmir.[155] Apart from the Ramadan fasting period, the presence of 'thousands of young [Kashmiri] boys' seeking support subdued high-spirited electioneering at this 'crucial juncture in [J&K's] history'. Some politicians wanted the election postponed, which was possible for up to twelve months under the so-called 'law of necessity'.[156] For the JKLF, the elections would only divide Azad Kashmiris into small ethnic groups and *biradari*s when unity was needed to continue the anti-Indian 'struggle'. While an elected government in Azad Kashmir would compare favourably with Indian J&K's lack of democracy, some Kashmiri IDPs were 'not fighting for democracy, but independence'. After five years in power, the Muslim Conference Government had 'lost its credibility' because of nepotism and corruption, particularly among the 'raja' *biradari* who dominated cabinet. Many Azad Kashmiris also perceived that their region might obtain extra development funds if governments of similar persuasions were in power in Islamabad and Muzaffarabad. The 'general impression' was that the PPPAK would 'most probably outmanoeuvre its rivals' and secure government.

While the main struggle was between the Muslim Conference and the PPPAK, six other parties participated in the 1990 elections: Tehrik-i-Amal; the J&K Liberation League; the Azad J&K Muslim Conference of a future Prime Minister, Barrister Sultan Mahmood Chaudhry;[157] the All J&K Jamiat-e-Ulema-e-Islam; the J&K People's National Party; and Jamiat-e-Ulema J&K.[158] A large number of independents also stood. Pragmatically, the JKLF boycotted the elections. Apart from its focus on the Kashmiris' liberation struggle, its candidates would have been disqualified by the electoral requirement for all candidates to confirm J&K's 'accession to Pakistan'.[159] The requirement has regularly prevented pro-independence candidates from groups such as JKLF and J&K People's National Party from contesting Azad Kashmir elections.[160]

Elections to the fourth Azad Kashmir Legislative Assembly occurred on 21 May 1990. They were considered to be reasonably fair, at least in Azad Kashmir constituencies.[161] There were forty directly-elected seats: twenty-eight in Azad Kashmir, twelve for refugees. Of the 244 candidates, 125 were from the eight contesting parties; 119 were independents.[162] Voter turnout was 63 per cent, up slightly from 1985.[163] The Muslim Conference and the PPPAK each won sixteen seats; the Azad J&K Muslim Conference won three seats; two independents won seats; Tehrik-e-Amal secured one. Two refugee seats were decided after polling day; the winners' party affiliations were unknown, although they may have been Muslim Conference and PPPAK.[164] Significantly, the Muslim Conference did poorly in Azad Kashmir electorates, winning only eight seats; it was 'saved' by winning eight refugee seats, although Punjab's Chief Minister had 'publicly "assured"' the ruling party' he would deliver it all ten refugee seats.[165] On 29 June the PPPAK's Mumtaz Rathore defeated the Muslim Conference's Sardar Sikander twenty-nine votes to fifteen to become Prime Minister.[166] President Qayyum, from the rival Muslim Conference, initially refused to swear in Rathore and his seventeen-member cabinet,[167] possibly because of the 'horse-trading' involved in creating this body. The issue was resolved after the PPP government in Islamabad applied pressure. However, Qayyum's action presaged future difficulties for Rathore, with tension between the two major parties continuing throughout 1990.

In a surprising post-election move, Amanullah Khan, the leader of the seemingly popular JKLF, unilaterally declared that a provisional government for J&K

had been formed, complete with a twenty-four-member cabinet. The JKLF's (previously uninformed) 'Working Committee' was to meet on 30 June to approve or reject their leader's announcement.[168] Amanullah's act 'disturbed' people, especially in Pakistan, which was about to have talks with India 'to defuse tensions'. Azad Kashmir leaders questioned the 'need' for a provisional government 'in the presence of a working administration in Azad Kashmir'. Bhutto talked with Qayyum about forming a Muslim Conference-PPPAK coalition government to deal with this 'very serious issue'. While Qayyum was possibly willing, his ally and Bhutto's opponent, Nawaz Sharif, was opposed and nothing came of it.[169]

*Downfall of a 'shaky coalition' and 1991 elections*

During the next nine months, Mumtaz Rathore led a 'shaky coalition'.[170] Its major problem was its unwieldy seventeen-member cabinet. Other problems included the sacking of Benazir Bhutto's PPP government on 6 August 1990 and its replacement by Nawaz Sharif's unfriendly Muslim League; Sardar Qayyum's re-election on 26 August 1990 as Azad Kashmir President by a joint sitting of the Azad Kashmir Legislative Assembly and the Azad Kashmir Council, now chaired by Sharif, with Qayyum defeating the PPPAK's nominee, Sultan Mahmood, by 32 votes to twenty-three.[171] A constitutional dispute in January 1991 between the heads of state (Qayyum) and government (Rathore) over the appointment of three additional judges to the Azad Kashmir High Court, and an increasingly divided bureaucracy acting in true *biradari* style to implement or resist orders from Rathore or Qayyum also caused issues.[172] Conversely, Rathore wooed the Pakistan Army. It preferred his government to the corrupt and nepotistic pre-1990 Muslim Conference government, particularly while waging a proxy war with India.

Rathore's position was shaky. His government survived three no-confidence motions by exploiting Muslim Conference disunity over fear of defeat in the consequent elections and rivalry about its prime ministerial candidate: Qayyum or Sikandar.[173] However, a new challenge emerged in the form of a Jat *biradari* based around Sultan Mahmood and the Liberation League, a party formed from the post-election merger of the J&K Liberation League and Azad J&K Muslim Conference. Its proposed no-confidence motion looked likely to succeed—with Muslim Conference support. Qayyum's son, Sardar Attique, may have convinced his friend Rathore of a secret Mahmood-Qayyum 'deal' concerning this motion, and of Rathore's decreasing popularity and political isolation.[174] Under pressure, Rathore decided to dissolve the Legislative Assembly, which he did on 31 March 1991. While this surprised some, he wanted to ease the temptations, especially financial ones, 'encouraging' his allies to defect.[175] There was also talk of the elections being postponed or a coalition government being formed to show solidarity with Kashmiris,[176] whose anti-Indian militancy was still raging. Nevertheless, elections were called for 29 June 1991.

The electoral period saw significant political manoeuvring in Muzaffarabad and Islamabad between self-interested politicians seeking to maximise their positions.[177] The charismatic Rathore sought to exploit his relationship with the Pakistan Army; Qayyum garnered support from Sharif and his government.[178]

These manoeuvrings occurred when India-Pakistan relations were severely strained by the anti-Indian uprising in Indian J&K. One result of this tension was major exchanges of fire between Indian and Pakistani forces across the LOC in May 1991.[179] Another was the need to conduct the Azad Kashmir elections on schedule to score 'a vital point' against India, given that the unpopular Indian J&K governor, Jagmohan Malhotra, had imposed direct rule.[180] Islamabad was an important 'player' in these elections—although out of self interest, not to ensure democracy—with one Pakistani paper editorialising that, in Azad Kashmir, power flowed 'from without rather than from within'.[181] Other papers were now comparing Islamabad's interference in the 'labyrinthine nature of Azad Kashmir politics' with Kashmiris struggling against Indian domination and interference.[182] Islamabad's 'cavalier approach' towards Azad Kashmir was weakening Pakistan's moral and legal superiority over India because of its actions in Kashmir.[183] *The News* suggested that, in the national interest, the Azad Kashmir 'house should be quickly put in order to pursue with complete single-mindedness the cause of Kashmiri self-determination'.[184] Azad Kashmir needed a government with a strong majority.

Elections on 29 June 1991 did put Azad Kashmir's political 'house ... in order', although not in a way Rathore envisaged or would initially accept.[185] Reflecting the political heat following the Legislative Assembly's dissolution, the election was the 'bloodiest' ever held in Azad Kashmir, with twenty people killed at polling booth 'shoot-outs'.[186] Voter turnout was 63 per cent, as in 1990.[187] But surprisingly—especially for Rathore—the PPPAK was routed. Overall, the Muslim Conference won thirty-one of forty seats, including eleven of twelve refugee seats.[188] The PPPAK won three seats, two of which Rathore contested;[189] the anti-PPP, Jamhoori Ittehad, won four seats; there were two independents.[190] The PPPAK's defeat was compounded when the Muslim Conference won all eight reserved seats, giving it a massive thirty-nine seats in the forty-eight-seat assembly.[191] Upset about Azad Kashmir being treated like a 'colony', Rathore denied the result.[192] In his capacity as caretaker Prime Minister, he declared the elections a 'massive fraud' and 'null and void', ordered an inquiry into the 'massive rigging' (as discussed in previous chapters), and called 'fresh elections' for 27 September 1991. He expelled two Pakistani lent officers whom he considered responsible for the rigging, the Chief Secretary and the Inspector-general of Police. He disbanded the Election Commission and established a high-level judicial commission to probe the 'massive rigging'.[193] But Rathore failed to note one important factor: the Pakistan Army was no longer supporting him. Confronting angry Indian forces across the LOC, it needed stability in Azad Kashmir. Furthermore, if free and fair elections had actually been held, the Muslim Conference probably would still have won.[194]

Rathore's defiance embarrassed Islamabad.[195] His stridency and unilateral actions surprised many, including Pakistan's Prime Minister, Nawaz Sharif, the Minister for Kashmir Affairs, Mehtab Abbasi, and some senior PPP leaders with whom Rathore had not consulted. A 'defiant' Azad Kashmir bureaucracy under the influence of Islamabad and Sardar Qayyum refused to implement Rathore's orders. On 4 July 1991 in Muzaffarabad, a defiant Rathore talked alarmingly—and in terms reflecting events in Kashmir—of using 'the bullet to restore the sanctity of the ballot'. The situation in Azad Kashmir had become intolerable and untenable. Similarly, Rathore's response to the elections had given India a propaganda opportunity. The next day, after some hesitation—because of sensitivities about how Azad Kashmiri events would look in Indian J&K—the Pakistan military seized Rathore and removed him to Islamabad. The Election Commissioner (and acting Chief Justice) was appointed caretaker Prime Minister. Section 56 of the Interim Constitution, which essentially enables Pakistan to do whatever it wants in Azad Kashmir, was used to justify deposing Rathore.

With the silencing of the 'mercurial' Rathore, Azad Kashmir quickly returned to normalcy.[196] Rathore was detained for some time 'outside the boundaries of the state'. After his release, he sought to challenge Pakistan's actions in the Azad Kashmir High Court, but soon withdrew his action because the process would take too long and could put the judges on trial.[197] Given Sardar Ibrahim's experience with the Azad Kashmir courts in a similar case, Rathore's reasons for his self-instigated withdrawal were plausible,[198] although other (unnamed) forces or 'incentives' from Islamabad also probably come into play. Surprisingly, he seemed to be the only person experiencing real angst about his sacking; equally, few wanted to give India any more propaganda opportunities. In any case, the 1991 election results stood, and Rathore faded. His party's miniscule presence in the Legislative Assembly and his lack of support from the Pakistan military gave him no platform from which to launch political action. Furthermore, by the time of the 1996 election, the younger, ambitious, up-and-coming politician Sultan Mahmood had joined the PPPAK and become its leader.[199]

With Azad Kashmir politics becoming less volatile, the Legislative Assembly conducted its first session on 30 July 1991. One of Azad Kashmir's wiliest politicians, Sardar Qayyum, was elected Prime Minister. Shortly before, he had resigned from the presidency, and then had been elected in a reserved seat as a religious scholar, despite apparently lacking formal religious qualifications. The Sharif Government may have encouraged Qayyum's manoeuvre because the experienced politician could ensure stability after Rathore's volatile demise. In August, Sardar Sikandar was elected Azad Kashmir President. By reversing their roles of 1985–90, this seemingly resolved some rivalry between the two *sardar*s, although Sikandar was now under Qayyum's nominal control, having to act in 'accordance with the advice of the Prime Minister and such advice shall be binding'.[200] Consequently, Sikandar became a 'signing machine' to complete legislative processes.[201]

After the presidential elections, Azad Kashmir was politically quiet. One exception was Amanullah Khan's commemoration of Maqbool Butt's 1984 execution by an attempt to cross the LOC in 1992, which gained him some popularity and attention.[202] Otherwise, the Muslim Conference's strong position in the Legislative Assembly, plus the presence of its ally, Nawaz Sharif, in power in Pakistan, ensured calm until Benazir Bhutto's re-election in mid-October 1993. Azad Kashmir also needed to display stability and democracy to highlight Indian J&K's lack of these.[203] This benefited Sardar Qayyum, particularly after Bhutto's re-election, after which moves were made to oust him and the Muslim Conference Government. Qayyum survived by playing the 'magic card': don't destabilise Azad Kashmir because it will look bad in Indian J&K.[204] Islamabad desisted from meddling in Azad Kashmir. Instead, it caused the region financial difficulties, with the Azad Kashmir Government having to 'borrow heavily' to pay its employees because of the 'erratic flow of funds' from Pakistan.[205]

# ELECTIONS AND INTERNAL POLITICS SINCE 1970

*1996 and 2001 elections*

In 1996, for the first time, a democratically elected Azad Kashmir government completed five years in office. On 30 June, elections were held. These occurred soon after the otherwise estranged Azad Kashmir President (Sardar Qayyum) and Prime Minister (Sardar Sikandar) did some clever politicking. Sikandar resigned as President because of 'mental pressure' before the elections; then, suddenly feeling better, he was re-elected President by the outgoing electoral college for another five-year term.[206] The Muslim Conference engaged in this ploy because the forthcoming elections would be close and it needed its 'man' as president, and vice-chairman of the Azad Kashmir Council, during this period. Equally, the party realised that it had become discredited and unpopular. This was due to a number of factors:[207] the supposed extravagance and misuse of public funds, including spending on overseas travel; an 'unwieldy cabinet of over two dozen ministers' that governed more from Islamabad than Muzaffarabad; alleged rampant corruption, including purchasing so many vehicles that Azad Kashmir was nicknamed 'Pajero-land'; alleged 'large-scale corruption';[208] employment of 486 Gazetted Officers without 'due process'; and party dissensions, especially between Qayyum and Sikandar. Finally, a monetary shortfall in 1991 of Rs 1.2 million had grown to Rs 1 billion in 1996. For the government's critics, these factors supposedly typified the 'incredibly lavish and reckless manner in which resources were squandered'.[209]

The 1996 elections were a triumph for the Pakistan People's Party-Azad Kashmir. The results were a reversal from 1991: the PPPAK won thirty-seven seats, the Muslim Conference nine seats, the Pakistan Muslim League (Junejo) one, and Jamaat-e-Islami one.[210] Voter turnout was 69 per cent. Both parties obtained a similar percentage of votes: 28 per cent for the PPPAK, 25 per cent for the Muslim Conference. (No other party, and no independent, got into double figures.)[211] The surprise was how these percentages translated into a two-thirds majority for the PPPAK in the Legislative Assembly. The vagaries of first-past-the-post voting helped, but rigging was also an issue, particularly in the twelve refugee seats in Pakistan, of which the PPPAK won eleven. In Azad Kashmir, Pakistani lent officers had given 'top-priority' to implementing the electoral policies of 'their parent government',[212] although the Muslim Conference-dominated administration hindered their efforts. But in refugee seats, Muslim Conference candidates boycotted the polls 'as it was clear' that Pakistan 'had decided which way the results should go'.[213] The Muslim Conference's election debacle was largely due to its unsavoury record. However, with the Pakistan People's Party in power in Pakistan, many Azad Kashmiris followed 'their best interests' and elected a party with Islamabad's backing—and 'financial support'.[214] On 12 August 1996, the PPPAK used its (convenient) two-thirds majority to fulfil the constitutional requirement and ousted Sardar Sikandar as Azad Kashmir President.[215] In his place the old campaigner Sardar Ibrahim was elected to his final public office as President, even though he belonged to a breakaway PPPAK faction led by his son, Khalid Ibrahim.[216]

Prime Minister Sultan Mahmood's government functioned reasonably well until 2001, although it did confront some political challenges. In late 1997, Mumtaz Rathore, then Speaker of the Legislative Assembly but wanting to replace Mahmood as prime minister,[217] re-emerged as the leader of some PPPAK dissidents. With Islamabad's support, Mahmood successfully offered 'incentives', including ministries, to the (supposed) twenty-six pro-Rathore dissidents in order to defeat Rathore's no-confidence motion.[218] Mahmood's ministry had expanded from nine members (August 1996) to seventeen (August 1996) to nineteen (December 1997).[219] After Rathore's party membership was cancelled,[220] the Legislative Assembly conclusively passed a no-confidence motion against him as Speaker in June 1998.[221] The factionalised Muslim Conference 'opposition', with five members led by Qayyum and four by Sikandar, supported this motion.[222] It did so because Rathore, now reconciled with his 1991 nemesis, Nawaz Sharif, had tried to encroach on the Muslim Conference's political territory by establishing a branch of Sharif's Pakistan Muslim League (Nawaz) in Azad Kashmir.[223] Rathore then became a leading figure in the 'tamed' opposition.[224]

Another issue for Sultan Mahmood was his relationship with Islamabad. This was fine while Bhutto, who was of the same political persuasion, was in power. However in February 1997, Nawaz Sharif's party won its large majority—although Mahmood's ongoing 'obedience' encouraged Sharif not to destabilise him.[225] Adroitly, Mahmood did not raise 'even a cautious objection' to any of Islamabad's stances on the Kashmir issue, including its stances during the controversial Kargil 'war' in mid-1999 between Pakistani 'militants' and Indian forces.[226] He cleverly used the 'magic card': 'Don't destabilise Azad Kashmir because it will look bad in Indian J&K'.[227] To enhance his position, he spent lots of time in Islamabad, although Azad Kashmiris disliked this practice,[228] especially departmental secretaries who needed Mahmood's permission to leave Azad Kashmir.[229] Locally, he sought to garner support by obtaining more funds for Azad Kashmir, among other means by seeking all water and electricity royalties from the Mangla Dam, which was located near his Mirpur electorate.[230]

For Mahmood, General Musharraf's military takeover of Pakistan on 12 October 1999 might have posed a big challenge. But, surprisingly, military rule was not extended to Azad Kashmir, possibly because Mahmood was not of the same political persuasion as the objectionable Sharif. Equally, despite military rule in Pakistan, Islamabad may have wanted to keep Azad Kashmir under democratic rule to highlight the poor state of this commodity in Indian J&K, thereby best serving the 'freedom struggle'.[231] Nevertheless, Mahmood's government was basically 'a lame duck ... with no powers'.[232] Islamabad already had significant control through Musharraf's chairmanship of the Azad Kashmir Council, through the funds it disbursed to the deficit region, and through Pakistan's palpable military presence. While Mahmood was 'mentally relaxed' about Pakistan's military rulers, they wanted him to provide 'good governance'. Musharraf twice directed Mahmood to reduce the size of his large cabinet.[233] Mahmood was also encouraged to curb spending, check corruption and the misuse of government vehicles, reduce the number of advisers and enforce merit in administrative appointments, and to govern from Azad Kashmir.[234] Mahmood's ministers and senior officials were spending too much time in new office accommodation (Kashmir House) in comfortable Islamabad, rather than 'killing flies in Muzaffarabad'.[235]

Most important, the military scrutinised Azad Kashmir's expenditure far more closely than civilian regimes. By March 2001, a new Ehtesab (Accountability) Bureau was planning 'to nab at least twenty legislators ... for their alleged involvement in corruption'. The Chief Secretary had instructed senior staff to fully cooperate and send 'references against those officials who committed irregularities'.[236] Nevertheless, the Ehtesab Bureau faced many challenges, especially collusion between 'present and past corrupt rulers and politicians'.[237] Keen to keep corrupt politicians from power, the Ehtesab Bureau asked the Pakistan Government to delay the 2001 Azad Kashmir elections by twelve months so it could continue its work unhindered.[238] Its request was rejected.[239]

Preceding the 2001 elections, four important issues were finalised. First, after consideration of abolishing one of Azad Kashmir's two executive positions (president or prime minister) to ensure more efficient, less expensive government, no change was made, although the Pakistan military flagged its involvement in future appointments.[240] Second, an amendment was made to the Legislative Assembly (Elections) Ordinance, 1970, to ensure that all candidates had matriculation as a minimal education qualification;[241] this seemingly weakened Sardar Qayyum as fire had destroyed his matriculation certificate 'a long time ago'.[242] (He later stood for, and won, the seat of Bagh I.)[243] Third, to deter corrupt candidates, the same amendment made all election candidates submit a list of their property and assets, moveable and immoveable.[244] The Ehtesab Bureau examined the probity of these, then made their declarations public.[245] These revealed some wealthy candidates, but many (possibly corrupt) 'old hands' were still able to stand for election. Fourth, the Election Commission rejected 40 JKLF candidates' nominations because they refused to affirm their support for J&K's accession to Pakistan, as the Interim Constitution required. This was significant as, arguably, the party's popularity had been increasing, particularly among Mirpuris and younger voters.[246] This increase was due partly to the JKLF's support for the Kashmiris' popular anti-Indian uprising, to some disenchantment with Pakistan's inability to solve the Kashmir dispute and reunite J&K, and to Azad Kashmir's economic backwardness.

There was thought to be 'genuine enthusiasm' for elections held on 5 July 2001—although voter turnout was only 49 per cent, the lowest since 1985. The Election Commission believed that 'the most transparent, peaceful and fair ... elections' in Azad Kashmir's history were due to the lack of 'adulteration of any bogus voting' in the count—that is, the absence of rigging.[247] (It later found irregularities: 33,000 bogus votes in one Kotli and three Mirpur constituencies; voting lists, particularly for refugee seats, needed heavy revision.)[248] With Qayyum and Sikandar reuniting their factions, the Muslim Conference won 21 seats (five from refugee seats), the PPPAK won 15 (four refugee seats), there were three independents (two refugee seats), and a Pakistan Muslim League member (from a refugee seat).[249] This result reflected 'the fairness of the polls'.[250] In the elections for reserved seats, the Muslim Conference, supported by the four non-PPPAK members,[251] collected six seats, the PPPAK two.[252] This gave the Muslim Conference and its allies 31 seats in the Legislative Assembly; the PPPAK had 17. After 'guidance' from General Officer Commanding (GOC) Murree, Major-General Shahid Aziz, the Pakistan general in charge of Azad Kashmir affairs,[253] the more acceptable Sardar Sikandar was elected Prime Minister, defeating Sultan Mahmood by 13 votes. Inspired by his victory—and GOC Murree—Sikandar resolved to deliver good governance and to work for the success of the Kashmiris' freedom struggle.[254]

The widely-accepted 2001 elections were significant for three reasons. First, they were the first elections that Musharraf conducted anywhere since his 1999 coup, although they did coincide with local government elections in Pakistan; as such, the Azad Kashmir elections comprised an 'experiment in holding parliamentary elections' for the military.²⁵⁵ Second, the results suggested that Azad Kashmir was establishing a genuine two-party political system. This was due to factors such as the entrenchment of the Muslim Conference and the PPPAK as Azad Kashmir's two dominant parties, coupled with many smaller parties being soundly defeated; the 'generally religious and conservative' Azad Kashmiris not voting for, or empowering, religious parties; and the *biradari* factor being less important.²⁵⁶ Third, the lack of rigging was possibly 'a prelude for the establishment of a vibrant, democratic ... society' in Azad Kashmir.²⁵⁷ The region's political system was reaching 'political maturity', with the 'smooth transitions of power since 1985' in 'sharp contrast' to military-dominated Pakistan²⁵⁸ and turbulent Indian J&K.

Conversely, a negative event quickly followed the 2001 elections: the Pakistan military imposed one of its own as Azad Kashmir President, Major-General (recently Retired) Sardar Mohammad Anwar Khan. The Muslim Conference concurred, with Anwar its representative in the presidential election on 1 August 2001, even though Sardar Qayyum still looked the likely candidate on 27 July.²⁵⁹ A 'scion of [a] proud Sudhan clan of Poonch',²⁶⁰ the 56-year-old general had a major—and controversial—problem: three days before becoming President, he was still Vice Chief of the Pakistan Army.²⁶¹ According to Section 5 (2) (ix) of the Azad Kashmir Legislative Assembly (Elections) Ordinance, 1970, he should have been retired from military service for two years before standing for election; but this section was rapidly amended on 28 July 2001 to 'unless he retires from service' before standing for election.²⁶² In the presidential election, Anwar received 36 (of 54) votes to defeat PPPAK's Chaudhry Latif Akbar.²⁶³ His appointment was a 'surprising development'—except in Islamabad. Anwar had powerful and influential military allies there acquired over 35 years of service, including service in the 'famous Azad Kashmir Regiment',²⁶⁴ and most recently as Musharraf's deputy. His appointment satisfied the Pakistan military's 'tendency' to seek 'jobs for the boys' on whom it could rely, and its desire to stem corruption.²⁶⁵ Anwar could improve the poor performance of Azad Kashmir's administrators on whose salaries and 'other privileges' Rs 7 billion of the region's Rs 10 billion budget was spent, while 250,000 Azad Kashmiris were unemployed.²⁶⁶

The military's rapid imposition of this (very) recently retired soldier as Azad Kashmir's President disregarded established norms—if not legally, then in spirit. With little choice, Azad Kashmiris acquiesced. Sardar Qayyum was out of favour owing to his closeness to the unacceptable Nawaz Sharif. He claimed that he deferred to Anwar 'to uphold the national interest'—Anwar's 'election' came two weeks after, and possibly because of, the inconclusive India-Pakistan talks at Agra that had disenchanted Musharraf.²⁶⁷ Compellingly, with Anwar in place, Musharraf's Pakistan could maximise its control of Azad Kashmir while pursuing diplomacy with India and militant activities in Indian J&K. Anwar was qualified for this job given his military connections and apparent 'dedication to the liberation of Kashmir'.²⁶⁸ Nevertheless, his appointment weakened Azad Kashmir's democratic credentials and gave India some rare political 'ammunition' on J&K matters. On 24 October 2001, Manmohan Singh cuttingly commented about 'Pakistan-Occupied Kashmir': 'Recently there was an election [there], but the power was handed over to an army general'.²⁶⁹

Between the 2001 and 2006 elections, some politically important events occurred in Azad Kashmir. In March 2002, after 15 years in charge, Sardar Qayyum resigned as Muslim Conference President because of other commitments (such as chairing the National Kashmir Committee)[270] and health issues, and to allow for 'new blood', chiefly his son, Sardar Attique.[271] Coincidentally, difficulties between Azad Kashmir's President and Prime Minister surfaced at the same time: Anwar, the former general, could not accept his status as a mere titular head; Sikandar, the long-term politician, believed that, as Prime Minister, he was in charge.[272] In October, Islamabad tasked Azad Kashmir's Chief Secretary and the GOC Murree with resolving this 'row'.[273] On 31 July 2003, Sardar Ibrahim died, aged 88. This was almost the end of an era, except that his younger rival, Sardar Qayyum, aged 79, survived him. In April 2004, the Muslim Conference's Sikandar and Attique factions, after disputing power sharing arrangements,[274] reached a face-saving agreement, possibly 'worked out in Islamabad',[275] which included four dissident ministers and a dissident parliamentary secretary resigning.[276] Neither faction leader was fully popular with colleagues thereafter, with the ambitious Attique accused of having 'secured his personal interests' and Sikandar facing unrest until the 2006 elections,[277] including opposition from a 'forward bloc' of 11 members that sought his resignation in September 2004.[278] Sikandar's position was helped because the Opposition was disunited. In late 2005, Ishaq Zafar become PPPAK leader,[279] while Sultan Mahmood, supported by ten legislators,[280] launched his own party, the Peoples [sic] Muslim League-AJK (PML), ten weeks before the July 2006 elections.[281] In August 2005, religious parties formed the Muttahida Majlis-e-Amal (MMA, United Council of Action) to advance the Kashmir liberation movement and institute an Islamic system in Azad Kashmir.[282] Previously, in June 2005, Amanullah Khan's and Yasin Malik's JKLF factions supposedly reunited;[283] this action had little impact on Azad Kashmir.

Despite many challenges, Sardar Sikandar, who had political acumen and powerful supporters, completed his term. One supporter was General Musharraf. He wanted stability in Azad Kashmir while he dealt with India's responses to matters ranging from the negative 2001 terrorist attack on the Indian parliament to the positive 2004 India-Pakistan Composite Dialogue. While the GOC Murree 'curtailed' Sikandar's ability to operate freely,[284] few Azad Kashmiris were prepared to seriously destabilise him and earn Islamabad's wrath. Oddly, Sikandar considered removing the (very severe) constitutional requirement compelling election candidates to agree to J&K's accession to Pakistan,[285] possibly to enhance his democratic credentials or as a political gesture to Kashmiris in Indian J&K. Sikandar oversaw some historic events during his term. These included the first visit by journalists sponsored by the South Asia Free Media Association,[286] a visit by an All Parties Hurriyat Conference delegation from Kashmir,[287] and his inauguration of the momentous Muzaffarabad-Srinagar bus service on 5 April 2005.[288] In August 2005, the Azad Kashmir Government, without explanation, made Urdu Azad Kashmir's official language, with English used 'for official correspondence with Pakistan'.[289] This meant that Azad Kashmir had the same official language as Pakistan—and Indian J&K. Finally, all events paled into insignificance on 8 October 2005 when northern parts of Azad Kashmir experienced a devastating earthquake. The major task then became rescue, rebuilding and rehabilitation of the many thousands of affected Azad Kashmiris (and people in NWFP).

# THE UNTOLD STORY OF THE PEOPLE OF AZAD KASHMIR

## *2006 elections and Sardar Attique's defeat and return*

Despite the catastrophic earthquake, the 2006 Azad Kashmir elections were still scheduled to be held. Beforehand, the Muslim Conference had its usual factional issues, particularly the new breakaway Haqiqi faction.[290] The party had an ambitious party president and potential prime minister, Sardar Attique. His cause was helped when Sardar Sikandar stood aside to allow his 'aggressive and threatening young brother' to contest from their home town, Kotli.[291] The Election Commission banned 50 JKLF or All Party National Alliance candidates who refused to agree to support J&K's accession to Pakistan.[292] Some rivals were concerned that Sultan Mahmood Chaudhry's new party would benefit unfairly from his Jat connections.[293] Mahmood was friendly with the 'Chaudhrys of Gujrat': Chaudhry Shujaat Hussain, the influential Punjabi head of the strongly pro-Musharraf Pakistan Muslim League (Quaid faction) or 'King's Party', and Chaudhry Pervaiz Elahi, Punjab Chief Minister from the same party.[294] With ten of 12 refugee seats wholly in Punjab or with Punjabi voters, such connections might be useful.[295] Attique trumped Mahmood by also meeting with the 'Chaudhrys of Gujrat', and with General Musharraf and Prime Minister Shaukat Aziz. With his father's help, the 'shrewd' Attique openly—even blatantly—sought 'to remove all possible hurdles' to him becoming prime minister and to show voters and rivals, especially Mahmood, that he had Islamabad's imprimatur.[296] For Azad Kashmir's President, Anwar Khan, and some journalists railing against Pakistan favouring 'the ruling party',[297] these meetings 'on the eve of the polls put their transparency in doubt'.[298] The politicised Anwar's complaint involved 'sour grapes'; he was estranged from Attique's Muslim Conference and enchanted by Mahmood's Peoples Muslim League, for which he had considered being an electoral candidate.

Voting took place on 11 July 2006. There were now 41 directly-elected seats, with a new seat, Neelum I, created in the large Muzaffarabad District.[299] To reduce bogus voting, voters had to show their (Pakistan) National Identity Card, driver's licence, passport or original state subject certificate.[300] Voter turnout was over 60 per cent,[301] although some journalists believed it was lower as, following the earthquake, many people's lives had not returned to normal.[302] Similarly, some deceased voters' names appeared on electoral rolls, while the names of some living people did not.[303] To ensure peace and order at 'sensitive polling stations', 8,000 Pakistan Army soldiers, 20,000 paramilitary and various police assisted civil authorities. They did not prevent incidents of violence, mainly in refugee electorates, nor some alleged booth capturing and stuffing of ballot boxes in places like Karachi,[304] where the locally powerful Muttahida Qaumi Movement (MQM; United National Movement) representing *mohajir*s (refugees from India and their descendants) surprisingly won two refugee seats. The MQM's close links with a fellow *mohajir*, Pervez Musharraf, may have helped.

Similar allegations of serious vote rigging marred the 2006 polls. The PPPAK leader, Ishaq Zafar, claimed improper voting at some Muzaffarabad polling stations.[305] The MMA, which had expected to do well because of prominent support for earthquake victims,[306] did not win any seats and organised a post-election, multi-party conference to consider action against alleged rigging.[307] Sultan Mahmood's aggrieved party published a 24-page booklet that emotionally detailed

## ELECTIONS AND INTERNAL POLITICS SINCE 1970

'A Sordid Saga of Electoral Drama & Fraud'.[308] To show their disdain for the polls, Mahmood, his party's three prospective members and Sardar Khalid Ibrahim refused to take the legislator's oath in the Legislative Assembly.[309] The Muslim Conference's winning of seven (of 12) refugee seats while the PPPAK won none also suggested possible 'foul play'. Nevertheless, the Election Commissioner considered that the elections had been conducted 'in a free, fair and peaceful manner [without] any untoward incident[s]'.[310]

Political 'pundits' suggested the 2006 Azad Kashmir elections would deliver a 'hung parliament'.[311] However, the Muslim Conference won 22 seats (including seven refugee seats). Its nearest rival, the PPPAK, won six seats (no refugee seats). Six independents won seats (two refugee seats), the PML won four seats (one refugee seat); MQM won two seats (both refugee seats), and the J&K People's Party won one seat. This put the Muslim Conference in a powerful position to secure reserved seats, plus the Azad Kashmir prime ministership and presidency. In the indirect elections on 22 July 2006, it won a further six (of eight) seats, bringing its strength in the Legislative Assembly to a majority position of 28. PPPAK and Jamiat Ulmah Islam (JUI) won one reserved seat each. Sardar Attique was elected prime minister, obtaining 35 (of 43) votes. His PPPAK opponent, Ishaq Zafar, became leader of the opposition.[312] In the presidential election on 27 July 2006, the Muslim Conference's candidate, Raja Zulqarnain Khan, from Bhimber, secured 40 (of 48) votes against his PPPAK opponent, Sardar Qamaruz Zaman.[313] From 'a respectable and reputed political family', Zulqarnain had begun his political career in 1960 with K.H. Khurshid and the J&K Liberation League.[314] Unlike his presidential predecessor, Anwar, Zulqarnain was uncontroversial.

On 7 August 2006, the new Muslim Conference regime took office. The Prime Minister, Sardar Attique, and his large 16-member cabinet, plus three prime ministerial advisers and one assistant with ministerial rank, tellingly were sworn in at Kashmir House, Islamabad—not in Muzaffarabad. This suggested where Attique's loyalties, priorities and interests lay. His cabinet included members from Azad Kashmir's eight districts and from some refugee electorates, and one woman. Four of Kotli District's five elected members, all of whom represented the Muslim Conference, were made ministers.[315] This was possibly to appease Sardar Sikandar, whom the Muslim Conference had dropped as presidential candidate in favour of Raja Zulqarnain.[316] With Sikandar's defeat and the retirement of his father, Attique represented the new breed of Muslim Conference leader.

Apart from asking the bureaucracy 'to keep pace with him in serving the people',[317] Attique wanted to reinvigorate the freedom struggle (like many before him). Indeed, he unabashedly considered himself the Prime Minister of J&K: 'every citizen of the entire state of Kashmir has [the] right to call me his prime minister'.[318] Nevertheless, some of his stances on J&K were problematic. In late 2008, he openly supported the victory of the coalition government in Indian J&K led by Omar Abdullah of the National Conference—an irony, given that this party was once the Muslim Conference's great political rival. Similarly, Attique's support for a member of the despised 'toady' Abdullah family caused some offence.[319] So too did his readiness to support General Musharraf's equivocal 'out-of-the-box' thinking on ways to resolve the Kashmir dispute.[320] Finally, while Attique was close to APHC members in Srinagar, he did not clearly support pro-Pakistan members, such as Syed Ali Shah Gilani. Instead he favoured others, such as Mirwaiz Umar Farooq, whose stance on J&K joining Pakistan was less certain.[321] Two other issues plagued Attique to his political detriment. First, the political demise of his political patrons—Musharraf, Shaukat Aziz and the Gujrat Chaudhrys—throughout 2007–08, coupled with the March 2008 victory of the Pakistan People's Party which traditionally allied with non-Muslim Conference politicians, weakened Attique. Second and more important, some dissident Muslim Conference legislators formed a 'forward bloc', which gained the support of the alienated Sardar Sikandar and Sultan Mahmood, still bitter about the rigged elections. 'Burying the hatchet', these politicians plotted to remove Attique as Prime Minister. His 30-month term ended on 6 January 2009 when the Speaker of the Legislative Assembly, Shah Ghulam Qadir, another anti-Attique plotter,[322] allowed the 'forward bloc' leader, Raja Farooq Haider, to introduce a no-confidence motion against Attique. (Haider had become an Assembly member after winning a by-election following Ishaq Zafar's death in October 2006.)[323] Haider accused Attique of 'deviating from the ideology of the Muslim Conference'[324] and 'spending a great deal of time outside Azad Kashmir'.[325] Others, such as Qadir, accused Attique and his government of promoting 'nepotism, tribalism'.[326]

Seeking to defend himself, Attique accused Islamabad of interfering in Azad Kashmir affairs 'to create political instability'. But in a sign that he truly understood where real power lay, Attique also appealed to Pakistan's President and Prime Minister, Asif Ali Zardari and Yousaf Raza Gilani, 'to save Azad Kashmir from instability'.[327] In the ensuing no-confidence vote, 32 (of 48) Legislative Assembly members voted against Sardar Attique[328] (the 49th seat was vacant due to a death). These comprised 19 Muslim Conference members, seven PPPAK, four PML and two MQM.[329] The next day, the Azad Kashmir President, Raja Zulqarnain, swore in Sardar Mohammad Yaqoob Khan as Prime Minister.[330] Attique became opposition leader.[331] Yaqoob's unwieldy 23-member cabinet suggested this was a 'coalition government'. It was balanced politically and geographically to satisfy Yaqoob's desire—or need—to 'give representation to all areas as well as constituents of the coalition government'.[332]

Sardar Attique's defeat was historic. For the first time in Azad Kashmir, a no-confidence motion had defeated the leader of the government. Previously, only MKA action, military takeovers or, since 1970, elections had removed presidents and prime ministers. Attique accepted the members' decision, affirmed his desire for an inclusive political atmosphere in Azad Kashmir, and graciously congratulated his successor. In turn, Sardar Yaqoob thanked his supporters, pragmatically 'vowed to run the government with the help of senior parliamentarians', and pointedly suggested he would 'speak less and work more'. While Farooq Haider claimed that Islamabad was not involved in his motion, Pakistan's Prime Minister was quick to congratulate Sardar Yaqoob. Gilani hoped Yaqoob 'would perform his duties for the betterment of the AJK people'.[333]

The election of the 56-year-old 'Haji Muhammad Yaqoob Khan' was interesting. In 2001, when he was first elected to the Legislative Assembly, he had been a Muslim Conference member.[334] In 2006, he was elected to the assembly in seat 19, 'Poonch and Sudhnoti III', as an independent.[335] This suggested that Yaqoob might have issues with the Muslim Conference, or with its President, Sardar

Attique. Yaqoob was unlike any of his predecessors: he had not achieved fame as a result of anti-Maharaja and anti-Indian struggles (like Ibrahim and Qayyum); he was not apparently from a famous family (like Attique, Sikandar, Mahmood, Zulqarnain); he had no important religious position (like Mirwaiz Yusuf Shah) or useful family or political connections (like Hamid Khan and K.H. Khurshid) or important military connections (like Anwar and military-appointed chief executives). Indeed, apart from Yaqoob's position as a *sardar* or tribal leader, his background appeared to be—relatively speaking, when compared with previous prime ministers—ordinary. This was a major development in a region where lineage, rank and status play an excessively important part in politics. Alternatively, it suggested that Yaqoob was a compromise candidate acceptable to those with too much political 'baggage' or insufficient 'clout' at that stage to obtain the prime ministership themselves.

Sardar Yaqoob lasted less than 12 months as Prime Minister. Confronting a no-confidence motion that he was likely to lose, he resigned on 14 October 2009.[336] His downturn in popularity had resulted from an early inability to appoint a senior minister (to deputise for him while he was overseas), which suggested personal indecisiveness, distrust or political difficulties among his large cabinet. Equally, his appointment of the unelected Chaudhry Mohammad Yasin 'as adviser on local government … with the status of a minister having executive powers' was very unpopular with Farooq Haider's 'forward bloc' and Sultan Mahmood's PML.[337] Yaqoob's long overseas absence around September 2009 also enabled his opposition, unhindered, to plan his downfall. On 22 October 2009, in the vote to elect the new prime minister, Haider defeated Yaqoob by 29 votes to 19. Yaqoob received seven votes from PPPAK members, six from the dissident Muslim Conference 'Friends Group', four from PML, and two from MQM.[338] Haider, now in league with Sardar Attique, was the 'reunified' Muslim Conference's candidate. Apparently Attique and Sardar Sikandar, with Nawaz Sharif's strong support, had negotiated with senior figures in Islamabad to ensure that Haider obtained Islamabad's imprimatur, even though he was of a different political persuasion from the PPP Government.[339] As usual, Islamabad had the major say in deciding who would be Azad Kashmir's prime minister.

Raja Farooq Haider, a 54-year old Rajput elected from 'Muzaffarabad V',[340] was Azad Kashmir's third prime minister in 2009, and its first ever from Muzaffarabad District.[341] 'According to him, he had a political lineage: his father, mother, uncle and sister had also been Azad Kashmiri politicians.[342] To placate his supporters, Haider installed a 24-member cabinet comprising 21 Muslim Conference members, two independents and one JUI member.[343] Two cabinet members were women. Of Haider's seven priorities for Azad Kashmir,[344] three are worth noting. First, he wanted the 'Ascendancy of Islam', which seemed unnecessary given that Azad Kashmir's population was 99.48 per cent Muslim,[345] the 'State religion' was Islam,[346] and that democracy had 'emerged [there] only with the help of Allah'.[347] His appointment to cabinet of the JUI member representing religious scholars possibly reflected, or promoted, this aim. Second, he wanted to obtain 'The complete freedom of Kashmir and its annexation to Pakistan'. This was not unusual, except that Haider, who also saw himself as Prime Minister for Kashmiris, could, unusually, 'communicate in [the] Kashmiri language' with them.[348] Third, he wished to 'fortify' the Muslim Conference and 'make it more dynamic', which suggested Haider also had issues with the party or its ambitious President, Sardar Attique. After being sworn in and inclusively thanking Pakistan's Zardari, Gilani and Sharif, Haider stated that the 'politics of "bradrism [sic] and regionalism" was like cancer which had badly affected the region'.[349] He did not clarify his remarks.

The 'tug of war for political power' in Azad Kashmir continued on 29 July 2010 when the Legislative Assembly elected its fourth prime minister for the term, after Farooq Haider's had resigned rather than face a no-confidence motion.[350] Sardar Attique was the only candidate, winning 39 (of 49) votes, with ten abstentions. Haider's critics complained that he 'failed to carry out development work' and 'ignored the Kashmir cause'.[351] Haider claimed (correctly) that Pakistan's President, Prime Minister and Minister for Kashmir Affairs and Gilgit-Baltistan, Manzoor Wattoo, and Azad Kashmir's President, Raja Zulqarnain, and Sardar Attique 'had united against him' because of his steps 'to curb corruption'. Significantly, Haider removed the Chief Justice of the Azad Kashmir Supreme Court, Riaz Akhtar, whose 'sudden and mysterious elevation' to this position was not made on the basis of seniority, as the Interim Constitution required, but possibly as a reward for 'organising' the dubious 2006 elections while Election Commissioner. After Justice Manzoor Gilani, who should have become Chief Justice, took his case to the Pakistan Supreme Court—which, given Azad Kashmir's unresolved international status, possibly did not have jurisdiction for such a case—and after President Zulqarnain reinstated Akhtar, Islamabad became involved in this important 'judicial crisis'.[352] Wattoo played a 'central role' replacing the intransigent Haider, after which the (again) acceptable Attique regained power, albeit with little public fanfare.[353] Soon afterwards Haider's ally, Shah Ghulam Qadir, lost his job as Speaker, to Chaudhry Anwaarul Haq.[354] Like Yaqoob before him, Farooq intended to legally challenge his loss.[355]

The next Azad Kashmir elections are due in mid-2011. These will be conducted using new electoral rolls, provided the Election Commission can find sufficient funds and staff to compile them.[356] With Sardar Attique's Muslim Conference disunited—but with him likely to continue as leader—the PPPAK, which has been out power for ten years, may benefit, although it lacks a high profile leader.[357] Other parties likely to contest the elections include Sultan Mahmood's Peoples Muslim League and a branch of the Pakistan Muslim League (Nawaz) party in Azad Kashmir, which Farooq Haider started the day before Attique became Prime Minister again.[358]

*Conclusion*

Azad Kashmir's political system and its politicians are maturing. It is positive that elections have been held regularly since 1970, although military rule from 1978 to 1988 impaired genuine participatory politics. A two-party system appeared to be emerging by 2001. However, to entrench such a system, Azad Kashmir needs a more popular Pakistan People's Party-Azad Kashmir, or a stronger Peoples Muslim League, or a new party with a charismatic leader. Currently, the Muslim Conference dominates the region's politics, with the extraordinary four changes of prime minister in 2009–10 essentially being power struggles between ambitious politicians of that party engaging in traditional factional politics to obtain power. Positively, all of the prime ministerial changes occurred using established parliamentary rules and mechanisms, with politicians abiding by the results. Negatively, Pakistan, as usual, played a major part. In recent times under General Musharraf and, since March 2008, under the Pakistan People's Party government, Islamabad's interference in Azad Kashmir has been relatively more measured and subtle—with the exception of Musharraf's gross imposition of Sardar Anwar as Azad Kashmir President in 2001. Generally, Pakistanis now appear to accept having an Azad Kashmiri in charge in Azad Kashmir who is not of the same political persuasion as them. This suggests that the Azad Kashmir-Pakistan relationship also is maturing.

Nevertheless, Azad Kashmiris rarely determine—or rarely determine wholly—their own prime minister, or his longevity. As Attique, Yaqoob and Haider found in 2009–10, 'The road to ruling Muzaffarabad passes through Islamabad'.[359] Pakistan asserts itself in Azad Kashmir in many ways: through control of the Islamabad-based Azad Kashmir Council; via the money it distributes to the region; via its overwhelming military presence; by using ISI; and through its ongoing ability to 'influence' election results, particularly via easily manipulable refugee seats in Pakistan. Equally, Azad Kashmir politicians—who to all intents and purposes, but not legally, are Pakistanis—'play' Pakistan's 'game', thereby strengthening Islamabad's position. They accept that one cannot be in power in Azad Kashmir without Islamabad's seal of approval, and they 'toe the line' accordingly. This appears to be the natural, and accepted, order of things. As the former Prime Minister Sultan Mahmood believed: 'It's necessary to spend six out of seven days of a week in Islamabad to continue as a primer [sic] minister of [Azad] Kashmir'.[360] Pakistan's dominance of Azad Kashmir's electoral processes, politics and leadership is not a new phenomenon, nor will it end soon. Pakistan wants a pliant Azad Kashmir regime until J&K's international status is finally resolved. It needs a stable Azad Kashmir from which to mount operations against India in Indian J&K, when required. Islamabad will therefore continue to be the most significant political 'player' in Azad Kashmir politics. As long as this remains the case, Azad Kashmir's political system is a constrained, controlled and compromised 'democracy'.

# CONCLUSION

Part One of this book discussed two factors that are still important in attempts to resolve the dispute over J&K's international status. The first was J&K's inherent disunity. In 1947, the ruler of J&K, Maharaja Sir Hari Singh, was highly unpopular. His diverse domain also lacked unity. Following the withdrawal in August 1947 of the supportive British paramountcy, the princely state that Hari Singh's rule had previously compelled to cohere rapidly disintegrated. J&K quickly became undeliverable in its entirety to either India or Pakistan. Major divisions within J&K's disparate population were an important aspect of this process, especially within the Muslim 'community' that comprised 77 per cent of the princely state's population. Muslims were divided in their aspirations for J&K's international status. Many in Jammu Province and in northern locations such as Gilgit wanted the princely state to join Pakistan. Equally, many secular-minded Kashmiri Muslims in the Kashmir Valley, led by Sheikh Abdullah, preferred India. Ultimately, Maharaja Hari Singh was able to accede to India because of Muslims' division, coupled with strong support from his fellow Hindus. Had J&K Muslims been politically unified in 1947, it would have been very difficult for the ruler to do anything but join his Muslim-majority princely state with Pakistan. The people of J&K continue to differ in their aspirations for J&K's international status. However, one major change since 1947 is that some of them, particularly Muslims in the Kashmir Valley, now want independence for J&K.

The second factor that is still important in attempts to resolve the Kashmir dispute is the ramifications of the three significant actions taken by Jammuites before the Maharaja's accession to India in 1947. The first action was the Muslim uprising in Poonch. The second was the serious inter-religious violence throughout Jammu Province, with Muslims favouring J&K joining Pakistan, while Hindus and Sikhs wanted India. The third was the creation of Azad Kashmir. The ramifications of these actions are important. They show that, soon after Partition, Jammuites went from being passive subjects, previously placated by Maharaja Hari Singh, to active participants opposing him and each other. Their actions politically, then physically, divided princely J&K into areas predominantly populated by pro-Pakistan or pro-Indian elements. Most significantly, these actions show that people in J&K actually instigated the dispute over J&K's international status—and not Pukhtoon raiders from Pakistan as India has claimed, a claim in which Pakistan has surprisingly acquiesced. Two further actions in 1947 showed that people in J&K wanted to determine the fate of 'their' state. In late October-November, Kashmiris formed a people's militia to defend themselves against the invading

Pukhtoons who intended—after looting, raping and pillaging Kashmiris—to capture J&K for Pakistan; and then in early November, pro-Pakistan Gilgitis rebelled and sought to join Pakistan. All of these actions by the people of J&K show that they were active participants in 1947 in attempts to determine J&K's international status. Importantly, they confirm that the people of J&K are stakeholders in the unresolved Kashmir dispute. They strongly suggest that these people need to be included in serious attempts to resolve this issue.

Despite instigating the Kashmir dispute, the people of J&K have been so marginalised that this dispute has long appeared to involve only two parties: India and Pakistan. Since mid-1948, no J&K-ites (to coin a new term) have been seriously involved in attempts to resolve their state's contested international status. The plebiscite promised by India, agreed to by Pakistan and reiterated by the United Nations, to enable the people to resolve J&K's international status has never been held. Nor is it likely ever to be held.[1] In 1972, the Simla Agreement formalised the people's marginalisation by stating that all 'differences' between India and Pakistan, including the Kashmir dispute, were bilateral issues.[2] Despite the Pakistan Government's supposed desire that the people of J&K 'must be associated with the Pakistan-India dialogue process for arriving at a sustainable solution',[3] the people have not been involved in the comprehensive India-Pakistan Composite Dialogue that began in January 2004. This is despite one of the Dialogue's eight items for discussion being the Kashmir dispute, while most other items directly or indirectly relate to J&K.[4] Similarly, no J&K-ites were involved in the Musharraf-Singh talks that apparently came close in 2007 to resolving the Kashmir dispute (discussed below).

Given their significant roles instigating, then sustaining, the Kashmir dispute, why did the people of J&K so readily accept being marginalised from resolution attempts? This book's examination of Azad Kashmir provides one answer. Ever since the British announced in 1947 that Pakistan would be created as a homeland for Muslims, those J&K Muslims, who later became known as Azad Kashmiris, have always strongly wanted J&K to be part of this nation: '*Kashmir Bane ga Pakistan*: Kashmir must become Pakistan.' They fought for this cause.[5] After the 1949 ceasefire, Azad Kashmiris happily disbanded their people's militia and ceded all significant power, civil and military, to Pakistan's leaders in Karachi, including total responsibility for the Kashmir dispute. They did so because they wanted their region to be integrated into the new entity of Pakistan, which they believed would happen soon via the promised plebiscite. Their actions also emulated those of other subcontinentals seeking to join the dominion of their choice, with all of the rights, responsibilities and renunciations that this involved.

Part Two of this book has examined how people have fared in the 'liberated' area of J&K that they named Azad (Free) Jammu and Kashmir. It demonstrates that this area has a *de facto* legitimacy. People from the Poonch *jagir*, chiefly, but also from Mirpur and Muzaffarabad districts, established 'Azad Kashmir' on 24 October 1947. Since then, these Muslims, along with like-minded Muslim refugees from eastern Jammu and the Kashmir Valley who migrated or were forced to flee to Azad Kashmir, have sought to develop this region and join it politically, administratively and economically with Pakistan. They have succeeded, with Azad Kashmir now fully integrated into (and dependent upon) Pakistan, except legally in

## CONCLUSION

relation to its international status. Indeed, instead of being called 'Pakistan-Administered Kashmir', a better term for Azad Kashmir and Gilgit-Baltistan, which region Pakistan has totally subjugated since 1947, would be 'Pakistan-Integrated Kashmir'.[6] Generally most Azad Kashmiris have been, and are, happy being with Pakistan, as this is what they have long wanted. (The only serious dissenters are those wanting independence for J&K, such as JKLF members, whose exact popularity is uncertain.) The Azad Kashmir constitution reflects this situation: it is 'interim' because Azad Kashmiris expect to finally and fully join Pakistan. This is despite Pakistan, which is in the superior position in all ways, invariably treating Azad Kashmiris as supplicants.

The above discussion raises two questions. First, should Azad Kashmiris' *de facto* status as Pakistanis now be made *de jure*? Given Azad Kashmir's dependent, submissive and integrated position in relation to Pakistan, logic suggests that Azad Kashmir should be made a *de jure* part of Pakistan and that Azad Kashmiris should become *de jure* Pakistanis. So too does India's long-term lack of interest in them. Since 1949, New Delhi's 'pragmatic attitude' has been to let Pakistan administer 'Pakistan-Occupied Kashmir',[7] which Pakistan has been doing until the promised United Nations plebiscite is held. Even though India nominally claims Pakistan-Administered J&K because Maharaja Hari Singh acceded to India, New Delhi has shown scant interest in 'its' territory since the 1949 ceasefire, or in the people's welfare therein. While the Northern Areas offer India strategic opportunities in relation to China, economically backward Azad Kashmir offers none. Possibly, India also realised early on that to placate, then integrate, the martial, militant, anti-Indian Azad Kashmir Muslims would be a difficult—and undesirable—task. It was easier to blame Pakistan for 'occupying' this area, while concurrently leaving these rabidly pro-Pakistan elements 'free' from Indian control. For its part, Pakistan has not made Azad Kashmir a *de jure* part of the nation because the entire former princely state of Jammu and Kashmir is still in dispute—and Islamabad is hopeful of obtaining more of J&K, particularly Muslim-majority areas, either via the plebiscite or through the actions of proxy forces. For Pakistan to unilaterally settle the status of any of the people in Pakistan-Administered Kashmir would be to negate this possibility. Therefore, until India and Pakistan resolve their dispute over J&K, Azad Kashmiris must remain only *de facto* Pakistanis.

The second question is, should the people of J&K be included in attempts to resolve the Kashmir dispute? Before answering this question, it is important to note that, since 1947, there have been three subtle but important changes to the Kashmir dispute. The three are related. First, since the ceasefire line was demarcated in 1949—if not since fighting actually divided the princely state in 1947—J&K has been an imagined entity: something that only exists in people's minds.[8] Some electorally-untried JKLF members and *azadi*-seekers may have a vision of a reunified and independent J&K, but such people appear to be in the minority.[9] Conversely, Indian and Pakistani negotiators are not prepared to countenance the 'third option' of independence for J&K. Indeed, the only point that I have found on which India and Pakistan agree in their entire dispute over possession of the former princely state is that neither J&K, nor any part of it, can become independent. Confronting such unique India-Pakistan unanimity, people's desire for independence for J&K will be exceedingly difficult to achieve.

# THE UNTOLD STORY OF THE PEOPLE OF AZAD KASHMIR

My assertion that J&K is now an imagined entity relates to the second change in the Kashmir dispute: the former princely state is never likely to be reunified. Since 1947, the five regions of J&K have become heavily integrated with, and dependent on, their respective metropolitan powers. With the obvious exception of the disgruntled Kashmir Valley, J&K's other four regions appear to be reasonably content with this arrangement: Jammu and Ladakh want to be with India; Azad Kashmir and Gilgit-Baltistan appear happy being with Pakistan. India and Pakistan, also, do not want to lose any of the areas in J&K into which they have put substantial effort and resources since 1947. Equally, neither nation appears to want, and neither seeks to obtain, the (potentially hostile) areas of J&K 'occupied' by the other. That is, India does not want to obtain (Muslim) Azad Kashmir and (Shia Muslim) Gilgit-Baltistan; Pakistan does not want to acquire (Hindu-dominant) Jammu and remote (Buddhist/Shia) Ladakh. The only area both appear to want to possess is the (Muslim) Kashmir Valley—where, ironically, most people appear uninterested in joining either nation.[10] Finally, neither nation's military has the capability, or the will, to capture the entire state, including the hostile areas currently outside their control. To capture all of J&K is too difficult because of its size and challenging terrain, the difficulty of long and vulnerable supply lines, and the ability of entrenched incumbent forces to oppose vulnerable attacking forces. Furthermore, this task is now seemingly impossible—and undesirable—given that India-Pakistan military rivalry now includes a significant nuclear dimension. A divided, dis-aggregated J&K will therefore continue.

The famed Kashmir Valley is the only region of contestation in J&K. Since obtaining this 'prize' in 1947, India has expended significant effort and money to retain possession of this Muslim-majority area. This confirms its assertion that there is a place in secular India for people of all religions. Indian forces have also prevented aggressive Pakistani forces comprising irregular proxies (1947; 1965; after 1988) and regular army combatants (1948; 1965; 1971) from capturing the Kashmir Valley. For its part, Pakistan considers itself an Islamic republic. Its name is an acronym in which the 'k' stands for 'Kashmir'; Pakistan therefore feels incomplete without possessing this Muslim-majority region. Pakistan does administer an area that has the renowned term 'Kashmir' in its official title, Azad Jammu and Kashmir, but it does not yet legally possess this region. Furthermore, Azad Kashmir is not actually a part of the famous Kashmir region, which Pakistan feels a strong desire to obtain—or at least to have some effective access to. Hence, the greatest challenge for India and Pakistan is to agree a resolution of the Kashmir dispute that satisfies enough of their respective aspirations in regard to the highly contested Kashmir Valley region. This challenge has been made more complex by disenchanted Kashmiris' desire to be free from both nations. Many Kashmiris now want independence, as has become clear since they began their anti-Indian uprising in 1988.

These two changes have led to the third—and most important—change in the Kashmir dispute since 1947: it is now about India and Pakistan determining which parts of J&K each should possess. Their old zero sum, or winner-takes-all, 'game' of obtaining J&K in its entirety ended, at the latest, when both nations acquired nuclear capabilities. Discussions associated with the India-Pakistan Composite Dialogue confirm this situation, although both nations still revert to their hard-

# CONCLUSION

line positions at times.[11] Nevertheless, India appears to want to convert the Line of Control dividing J&K into the future international border. This minimalist solution might suit the long-separated people of J&K, provided that the border allows them easy, unregulated access to one another, something India seems prepared to allow. Pakistan has not accepted India's position, although Islamabad's stance on J&K did become less rigid during General Musharraf's tenure (October 1999-August 2008). He countenanced 'out of the box' possibilities to resolve the Kashmir dispute.[12] Consequently, India, under Dr Manmohan Singh's leadership, and Pakistan apparently came 'close to an agreement on all outstanding issues' in 2007, but Musharraf's 'judicial crisis' and his subsequent downfall 'halted that process'.[13] While significant, any such agreement, which had not been enunciated, may not have been implementable: neither leader had prepared his people—many of whom have an insidious mistrust or dislike of the 'other' nation and its people—by 'selling' their resolution beforehand.[14] Importantly, there was also no domestic pressure compelling any such resolution to occur. Without this compelling factor, another attempt to resolve the Kashmir dispute passed into oblivion. Since then, India continues to appear to favour the LOC as the future J&K border, while Pakistan seems willing to negotiate a solution. When both nations finally return to meaningful discussions about J&K, their task will still be to determine which parts of the former princely state each nation should possess.

If history shows us anything about the Kashmir dispute, it is this: India and Pakistan have totally failed to resolve it. Indian and Pakistani leaders have tried on more than one occasion—and have failed each time. Neither nation has had sufficient incentive or will, and neither has been compelled by its population, to resolve this dispute. Indeed, some organisations involved with this dispute—such as the Pakistan Army, particularly, and the Indian Army—have a stake in ensuring that it continues. To resolve the Kashmir dispute would be to diminish their status and the need to command large, potent and expensive forces. (General Musharraf's previous stance was atypical.) Surprisingly, there are still no large, vocal pressure groups in India and Pakistan—no compelling constituencies—encouraging and pressuring their leaders to resolve the Kashmir dispute. This may be because Indians and Pakistanis have not properly understood the indirect cost to them of this dispute. Since 1947, they have suffered as scarce national resources have been diverted from vitally-needed development and nation-building projects into creating massive and costly military machines, now with nuclear capabilities, to defend the India-Pakistan border and each nation's part of J&K.[15] Equally, the two nations' citizens have not fully understood what the long-suffering and politically peripheral people of J&K have endured since 1947, and so have not sought to change this. Similarly, the leaders of India and Pakistan have not felt compelled to consult the people of J&K in a comprehensive, inclusive and meaningful way about their international status. With senior Indians and Pakistanis now dominating the Kashmir dispute, one might think it was devoid of people. It is not—the people of J&K are at the centre of this dispute in every way.

There are numerous other reasons for India and Pakistan not being able—or not choosing—to resolve the Kashmir dispute. These include competing and irreconcilable ideas of nationhood, respectively based around the predominance of secularism or religion; opportunistic, suspicious and unbending national and individual egos expounding paternalistic and nationalistic rhetoric; and entrenched strategic, military and political rivalry and cultures not prepared 'to give an inch' to the other side on any issue at any time—the injection of troops onto the inhospitable Siachen Glacier in the early 1980s being a good example of such truculence. Pakistan's inferiority complex, causing many Pakistanis to believe (falsely) that India wants to re-integrate Pakistan, has not helped. Nor has Indian arrogance and intransigence arising from India's superior strategic position regionally and in J&K, with Indian capabilities being boosted as India's economy grows. To this mix we must add a deep and ongoing India-Pakistan 'trust deficit', developed by the above factors and reinforced by a variety of perceived or actual underhand activities—in the guise of the 'foreign hand'—directed against each other since Partition. This 'trust deficit' has been entrenched, then magnified, by an almost total lack of contact between the people who make up the bulk of these nations: ordinary (as against elite) Indian and Pakistanis. Despite sharing so much history, geography, culture, ethnicity, language etc., ordinary Indian and Pakistanis rarely, if ever, meet. Apart from one land crossing, the India-Pakistan border is closed and largely impenetrable. Travel between the two nations is exceedingly difficult, if one can get a visa at all. Owing to this ongoing lack of contact, the people of each nation are ill-informed or ignorant about each other—and they do not trust each other. (A pleasant fact, however, is that people in each nation are ever curious to know more about the other nation and its people.)

Finally, neither India and Pakistan has become emotionally reconciled to the 1947 Partition of the subcontinent. Neither nation has engaged in any type of individual, national or bilateral healing process to fully acknowledge what happened during 1947 to their dividing, dislocating and distraught peoples. Neither has sought to reconcile and heal the sorrow and sadness associated with this tumultuous and traumatic event. Neither has allowed itself to be consistently respectful and generous towards the other nation. The closed nature—both physically and psychologically—of the India-Pakistan border and LOC in J&K has prevented reconciliation and healing. Consequently, people on either side of this border, and in J&K, have not been able to share their Partition stories, to listen to these, to question and react, to respect these, learn from these, and to mutually grieve and understand that all major religious communities suffered in 1947. Not having grieved, they cannot move on, and have not moved on, emotionally. This is confirmed by the India-Pakistan relationship swinging like a pendulum between the states of poor, parlous and abysmal, and by the negligible contacts between Indians and Pakistanis. A deep and genuine process of acknowledgement, grieving and reconciliation needs to occur before India and Pakistan can move forward positively and resolve their differences, including their significant dispute over Jammu and Kashmir. This dispute will never be resolved while both nations remain spiteful and while each seeks to maximise its own position in J&K and to minimise that of its rival. Instead, it requires a spirit of generosity and honest cooperation.

India's and Pakistan's total inability to resolve the Kashmir dispute has two major ramifications. The first is that the J&K people have been subjected to ongoing hardships and sufferings since 1947. J&K-ites have been severely dislocated by the heavily-militarised ceasefire line/LOC that dissects most of J&K and makes meetings and mourning of the dead impossible for relatives and friends along this dividing line.[16] They have been traumatised by brutal and often arbitrary heavy exchanges of small arms and artillery fire across the ceasefire line/LOC. They have experienced disruptive India-Pakistan wars in 1948, 1965 and 1971. They have been deprived of access to traditional, shorter and more convenient trade and transport links. They have been motivated, moved or mauled by the anti-Indian uprising in the Kashmir Valley since 1988, which India has suppressed brutally and which Pakistan, using proxies, has equally brutally supported—and as a result of which tourism declined substantially in the Kashmir Valley, whilst the number of militants and Kashmiri refugees increased in Azad Kashmir. They have been impacted by the 1999 'skirmish' in Kargil between 'militants' and Indian forces, particularly people on both sides of the LOC located near this area. Furthermore, the international status of the people of Pakistan-Administered Kashmir is still unresolved, with people in Azad Kashmir and Gilgit-Baltistan effectively stateless. Both regions also suffer from flawed political systems in which Pakistan is paramount. In Indian J&K, frustrated Kashmiris are clearly disenchanted with being under heavy-handed, often insensitive Indian control. Conversely, neglected Jammuites and Ladakhis dislike the local, national and international attention given to Kashmiris, to their detriment.

The second ramification of the total inability of India and Pakistan to resolve the Kashmir dispute is that a third party is clearly needed to break this deadlock. A precedent exists for such involvement: during the late 1950s, the World Bank facilitated the significant 1960 Indus Waters Treaty that enabled the sharing of vital irrigation water between India and Pakistan.[17] This treaty continues to operate reasonably successfully. The challenge in relation to the Kashmir dispute is to find an acceptable third party. The United Nations Security Council is not interested. In 1996 (and 2010),[18] to Islamabad's chagrin, an attempt was made to take J&K off the 'list of matters of which the Security Council is seized', given that the Council had not looked at this question in the last five years. It had not actually looked at this issue since November 1965.[19] As far as I can determine, Islamabad must now formally, and annually, ask for the 'India-Pakistan question'—meaning Pakistan's dispute with India over J&K—to remain on this list.[20] Pakistan would actually like a nation such as the United States to act as a third-party mediator or facilitator on J&K. However, India will not countenance external interference in South Asia, especially any third nation involvement in the Kashmir dispute.[21] India's stance arises from the Simla Agreement whereby all India-Pakistan 'differences', including those over J&K, should be resolved 'through bilateral negotiations or by any other peaceful means mutually agreed upon between them'.[22]

Despite the respective positions of India and Pakistan, there is actually a third party that could resolve the Kashmir dispute and which would be acceptable to both nations: the people of J&K. Using the Simla Agreement, India and Pakistan could 'mutually agree' to devolve power to this third party and allow it to resolve this issue. The involvement of the people of J&K would seem logical, even imperative, given their position as inherent stakeholders in the Kashmir dispute, their differing desires for J&K's international status, and India's and Pakistan's total inability to resolve the dispute.

The people of J&K have sufficient knowledge, self-interest and understanding to resolve the Kashmir dispute. They also have sufficient empathy and experience to understand the dislocation, hardship and suffering caused by J&K's division since 1947. Having experienced these negative factors to varying degrees for more than sixty years, they have sufficient desire, or will, to want to resolve J&K's status. The people's involvement in resolving the Kashmir dispute also would satisfy natural justice. Although they initiated the dispute over J&K's international status, since mid-1948, these people have never been seriously consulted about what status they want for what, after all, are their homelands. By empowering them, the bitterness surrounding the Kashmir dispute could be diluted—and this seemingly intractable dispute might be solved. Any solution reached by the people of J&K could be implemented, as it would be what they wanted—India and Pakistan would not (again) be imposing their wills and desires in J&K. Importantly, an open, inclusive and public consultative process involving the people of J&K (as discussed below) would prepare the people of India and Pakistan for a resolution of the Kashmir dispute. Indian and Pakistani leaders usually forget to inform, and educate these important, frequently partisan, sometimes virulent, observers of the Kashmir dispute.

The idea of involving the people of Jammu and Kashmir in resolving the Kashmir dispute is not a new idea. When accepting Maharaja Hari Singh's accession in 1947, India first proposed that the people should determine the international status of their state via a plebiscite. The United Nations reaffirmed this aim of a people's plebiscite in its 1948 resolutions, and thereafter tried to organise for the poll to be held; Pakistan's long-held diplomatic position is that the people of J&K should determine whether their state, in its entirety, would join India or Pakistan via the UN-supervised plebiscite. (That said, one of the great ironies of the Kashmir dispute is that India, a nation highly regarded for its democratic achievements, has not wanted a people's plebiscite conducted in J&K, while Pakistan, a country frequently ruled undemocratically by its military, has wanted such a poll.) In August 1952, shortly before Sheikh Abdullah's fall, after which things started to go 'sour' for India in Indian J&K, India's Prime Minister, Jawaharlal Nehru, made two important speeches in the Indian Parliament about the Kashmir dispute. In his speech titled 'Our Pledge to Kashmir', Nehru stressed that:

it is only the people of Kashmir who can decide the future of Kashmir ... we would willingly leave Kashmir if it was made clear to us that the people of Kashmir wanted us to go. However sad we may feel about leaving, we are not going to stay against the wishes of the people. We are not going to impose ourselves on them on the point of the bayonet.[23]

In a broader speech entitled 'Let the People Decide', Nehru stated that, regarding 'the people of Jammu and Kashmir ... we will give them a chance to decide. We propose to stand by their decision in this matter'.[24] It is therefore not a new idea to make the (marginalised) people of J&K the focus of resolving the Kashmir dispute; it is only a lapsed proposition.

Having thought about the Kashmir dispute and a possible resolution process since at least 1996,[25] I believe that both nations should step aside and 'Let the People Decide' the international status of J&K. That is, India and Pakistan should enable and empower the people of J&K to come together and negotiate their own solution to the Kashmir dispute. The people should engage in this process for as long as it takes to resolve J&K's international status. They should also keep India

## CONCLUSION

and Pakistan, and their respective media, informed about their discussions and developments. Out of these meetings will come familiarity; out of this familiarity will come understanding; out of this understanding could come a resolution.

To encourage this process and debate about it, I offer the following rudimentary framework to 'Let the People Decide':[26]

*The Task:* Through an extended process of dialogue, the people of J&K will determine a resolution to the Kashmir dispute and the international status of its component regions.

*Participation from J&K:* The people of J&K should convene, by whatever means they see fit, a body that I have called the 'Council to Resolve the International Status of J&K' (hereafter, the 'Council'). It must be as inclusive as possible, with delegates from all of J&K's five regions. The role of this body is to provide a place where the people's delegates can engage in dialogue and discussions.

Possible methods of convening such an inclusive participation are:

1. The Chief Minister of Indian J&K and the Prime Minister of Azad Kashmir, along with the respective opposition leaders, could consult their greater communities and then appoint delegates to the initial Council. For those in Indian J&K, this would include consulting Hindu Pandits living outside the state; for Azad Kashmiris, this would include consulting people living in Gilgit-Baltistan.
2. Delegates could be members already elected to the Indian J&K Legislative Assembly or Legislative Council, the Azad Kashmir Legislative Assembly or the Azad Kashmir Council, and the Gilgit-Baltistan Legislative Assembly.[27] Delegates from among pro-independence state subjects should also be included in the Council.

It would be the prerogative of people from any region in J&K to decline to participate in the Council because they are satisfied with their particular region's current international status. Such non-participation would confirm that these people want their region's current *de facto* status made *de jure*.

*Participation of India and Pakistan:* India and Pakistan should provide non-partisan support that enables participants to form and operate the Council, to cross the LOC for meetings and discussions, and to engage in free, frank and unfettered discussions in, and throughout, J&K.

India and Pakistan should send observers to all Council meetings.

A higher-level body that I have called the 'India-Pakistan-J&K Committee' would be formed (hereafter, the 'Committee'). It would comprise a small representative group from the Council and senior Indian and Pakistani political leaders. It would meet on a regular, rotational basis in India, Pakistan and J&K. The role of this body would be to ensure that the Indian and Pakistan governments are officially informed about the Council's deliberations, to discuss various possible solutions, and to seek feedback and ideas.

*The process:* There are many steps in this process, from determining participants for the Council and Committee, agreeing rules and procedures for ongoing engagement, to reconciling the past, keeping the people informed, and ensuring that the process is transparent throughout. Delegates should be encouraged to retain an open mind until they have fairly considered all major points of view and options—no matter how distasteful, difficult or disingenuous these may appear to be. Agreements among delegates should, wherever possible, be by consensus.

# THE UNTOLD STORY OF THE PEOPLE OF AZAD KASHMIR

Once Council delegates have agreed an international status for J&K, the people of J&K should vote on this via an adult-suffrage poll, with existing electoral rolls used for this purpose. Neutral international electoral monitors could supervise and monitor all polls. Council delegates should openly discuss all proposals and can advocate these among voters as appropriate.

More than one poll may be required to determine the final will of the people of J&K. Indeed, it may be desirable to conduct a number of polls to enable a full and inclusive consultation process to occur and to reduce the range of options. The ultimate aim is to arrive at a single, agreed, majority position for J&K or, if polls are held in a specific region or regions, a majority position in each region for the specific proposal voted on.

*Communication:* Representatives from the Council and Committee should regularly brief local and national media about deliberations in order to inform—and prepare—the people of India, Pakistan and J&K for a resolution of the Kashmir dispute. This will, in turn, inform the international community.

*Timelines:* Delegates' meetings and discussions should go on for as long as it takes them to agree an international status for J&K as a whole or on a regional basis. This may entail updating membership of either body involved in the dialogue.

*Challenges:* Three possible challenges confront this resolution process. Foremost is getting India and Pakistan to agree to it. Both nations will need to be strongly encouraged and lobbied by subcontinentals of goodwill, by Indians and Pakistanis in the non-government sector who are already trying to improve India-Pakistan relations, by activists in J&K, by world leaders and elder statesmen, and by the international community at large, to allow this resolution process to take place. International incentives may also help. Most important, large numbers of people in J&K, India and Pakistan need to realise that a solution to the Kashmir dispute would benefit all parties involved. They should create 'compelling constituencies' that lobby strongly for such a process to be started, then continued for as long as it takes. It is in these peoples' interests to do so. All have suffered, directly or indirectly and to various extents, from the debilitating effects of India-Pakistan rivalry, at the core of which is the ongoing Kashmir dispute. All would benefit from the dispute's resolution.

Secondly, Council delegates may lack sufficient agreement to be able to formulate an international status or statuses for J&K. The international community could offer appropriately-trained facilitators to help with this process. (This may be of particular assistance in the process of reconciliation arising from issues from the past.) Equally, the people of J&K could elect new delegates, then recommence the process. Otherwise, if the people of J&K prove unable to reach a resolution, the issue should revert to being a bilateral one for India and Pakistan to resolve.

Thirdly, India and Pakistan may not accept the possible international status or statuses for J&K that the Council proposes, particularly should this say, involve independence for J&K or any part of it. To respond to this challenge, the international community should encourage both nations to engage with the process, and thereby possibly influence it. Equally, it should encourage India and Pakistan to accept the status, or statuses, that the Council proposes after its exhaustive consultations, especially if the people of J&K have accepted these via their various state or regional votes. Again, people in J&K, India and Pakistan should form constituencies to lobby India and Pakistan to accept the Council's proposals.

More importantly, the people of J&K need to be fully aware that the only point on which India and Pakistan agree in their entire dispute over J&K is that neither J&K nor any part of it can become independent. Hence, people in J&K desirous of independence will need to develop, and clearly enunciate, documents and policies that show how, and why, independence would be viable and sustainable for J&K or their region, and why India and Pakistan should accept this option. They will also need to successfully 'sell' this option to Indians and Pakistanis.

That said, the ongoing contact between delegates may uncover geo-strategic, political and economic difficulties and challenges that an independent J&K would confront, including potential India-Pakistan competition over an independent J&K. These may possibly make independence unacceptable. Equally, this contact may encourage delegates to determine other solutions for J&K that are more acceptable to India and Pakistan—and beneficial to themselves.

Nevertheless if some, or a majority, of the people of J&K—after exhaustive discussions, suitable consideration and deep reflection on the significant ramifications of independence—decide that it is the preferred option for the state as a whole, or for a specific region or regions within J&K, then India and Pakistan should recognise and accept this option.

My proposal to 'Let the People Decide' J&K's status is worth attempting. Any solution determined by the people of J&K would give them ownership of it, plus a strong sense of responsibility to ensure that it works. This could also be a win-win situation for India and Pakistan, if only because it would remove one of the major irritants in their relationship, thereby possibly allowing better relations to develop. The founding fathers of India and Pakistan, particularly Mahatma Gandhi and Muhammad Ali Jinnah, and their supporters, offer hope for my proposal. Their struggle to rid India of British control took almost a quarter of a century to achieve, but ultimately the tired British did 'quit' India. The same, I hope, will happen with J&K: one day, India and Pakistan will simply 'quit' their intractable bilateral dispute over J&K and allow J&K-ites to resolve this issue.

A final point that this book recommends therefore, is to 'Let the People Decide' the issue of the international status of the divided and contested state of Jammu and Kashmir. Apart from benefiting J&K-ites—and Indians and Pakistanis—this would resolve the status of Azad Kashmiris, about whom this book has been written. The people of J&K should decide their state's status because it was they who instigated the Kashmir dispute. Equally, given the poor India-Pakistan relationship, arguably only they can resolve it. Should the people succeed, Jammu and Kashmir could then become a bridge between India and Pakistan—not an item of contestation, an impenetrable division, and a major source of insecurity, instability and hostility. 'Let the People Decide'!

# APPENDIX I

## THE RELATIONSHIP BETWEEN THE RAJAS OF POONCH AND THE MAHARAJAS OF JAMMU AND KASHMIR[1]

This appendix on the vexed relationship between the rajas of Poonch and the maharajas of Jammu and Kashmir is based on (far from complete) correspondence between various rajas of Poonch and British officials between 1930 and 1945. While this is somewhat one-sided in that it does not cover any correspondence from the maharajas, the appendix serves to highlight the disgruntlement that the rajas of Poonch felt towards their Jammu cousins who ruled in the superior position as maharajas of Jammu and Kashmir. The maharajas inherited their position by dint of some clever manoeuvring by their forebear, Gulab Singh (see Table I.1: The rajas of Poonch and the maharajas of Jammu and Kashmir, below). Gulab did this at a time when the British were weak in Punjab and needed him, a situation that Gulab appears to have taken full advantage of. On their side the British, at this time, were more interested in shoring up their shaky position than in resolving local family disputes, and so took the easier position of maintaining the status quo that they helped establish. As a result, the British adopted a consistent position that Poonch was an inferior entity to, and a feudatory of, Jammu and Kashmir. The rajas of Poonch were unable to change this situation. One reason for their inability was that, at significant times, particularly in the early years of British rule in Punjab, they were young, inexperienced men whose cunning and divisive uncle, Gulab, was able to divide. The disgruntled feelings of the rajas of Poonch—who appear to have been relatively liberal when compared with their cousins in Jammu—are important in the context of this book, because their treatment also informed and influenced some of the disgruntlement that (non-regal) Poonchis held in 1947 towards Maharaja Hari Singh.

The rajas of Poonch were direct descendents of Dhyan Singh, the younger brother of Gulab Singh.[2] They were (all with the family name of Singh): Hira, Jawahir (or Jawahar, Jowahir), Moti, Baldev (or Baldeo), Sukhdev, Jagatdev and Shiv Ratandev. Gulab Singh was the first Maharaja of Jammu and Kashmir. The three Maharajas who followed him, Ranbir, Pratap and Hari, were all directly descended from Gulab Singh. Ranbir and Pratap were the eldest sons in the primogenitural line, while Hari was the eldest son of Pratap's youngest brother, Raja Amar Singh. This 'deviation' in the line occurred because Pratap died without issue, although this was another cause for unease between the two Dogra families

229

as, in November 1906, Pratap had adopted Sukhdev Singh, the son of Raja Baldev Singh of Poonch, as his legal heir.[3] Pratap sought to ensure that the boy succeeded him as Maharaja. Had this happened, Sukhdev would have inherited the throne and become the fourth Maharaja of Jammu and Kashmir (instead of Hari Singh). However, the British declined to recognise Sukhdev as Pratap's legal successor. Instead, the boy was allowed to be Pratap's spiritual heir, a position which conveyed certain rights and responsibilities in relation to Pratap's personal and spiritual matters only, including lighting his funeral pyre in accordance with Hindu rites and traditions.

Although younger than Gulab, Dhyan was the more influential of the two brothers. (There was also a third brother, Suchet, who was younger than Dhyan.) This was chiefly because, until his untimely death in 1843, Dhyan had been the 'favourite' Prime Minister of the great Sikh ruler, Maharaja Ranjit Singh.[4] Dhyan not only held an important political and administrative position in the empire, but also a well-rewarded one in which largesse could be obtained and dispensed. Not surprisingly, Dhyan Singh and his offspring were prosperous and influential people. While Dhyan also helped his brothers' careers to prosper, Dhyan would have been the wealthiest and most influential of the three brothers at the time of his death in 1843.

Disenchantment between the two related houses of Poonch and Jammu and Kashmir goes back to the time of Dhyan Singh's death, if not before. In 1827, Maharaja Ranjit Singh apparently gave Raja Dhyan Singh the 'Raj of Bhimbar,

Table I.1: The rajas of Poonch and the maharajas of Jammu and Kashmir.

| Poonch raja | Position | Born | Died | Ruled Poonch |
|---|---|---|---|---|
| Dhyan Singh | First raja | 22.8.1796 | 15.9.1843 | 1827–1843 |
| Hira Singh | Dhyan's son | 1816 | 21.12.1844 | 1843–1844 |
| Jawahir Singh | Dhyan's son | – | Deposed | 1844–1859 |
| Moti Singh | Dhyan's son | – | 1892 | 1859–1892 |
| Baldev Singh | Moti's son | – | September 1918 | 1892–1918 |
| Sukhdev Singh | Baldev's son | 1901 | October 1927 | 1918–1927 |
| Jagatdev Singh | Baldev's son | – | 1940 | 1928–1940 |
| Shiv Ratandev Singh | Jagatdev's son | April 1925 | – | 2 July 1940–? |
| J&K maharaja | Position | Born | Died | Ruled J&K |
| Gulab Singh | Dhyan's brother [Raja of Jammu] | 18.10.1792 – | 7.8.1857 – | 1846–1857 [1822–1846] |
| Ranbir | Gulab's son | 1832 | 12.9.1885 | 1857–1885 |
| Pratap Singh [Pratap Singh's powers limited] | Ranbir's son [Council of State; British Resident] | 1850 – | 25.9.1925 – | 1885–1925 [1889–1905] |
| Hari Singh | Son of Amar, Pratap's younger brother | 30.9.1895 | 26.4.1961 | 23.9.1925–20.6.1949 |

Source: Various, including www.uq.net.au/~zzhsoszy/ips/p/poonch.html and www.uq.net.au/~zzhsoszy/ips/j/jammukashmir.html [accessed 29 January 2007].

# APPENDIX I

Chibbal and Poonch as a personal gift to be enjoyed ... in perpetuity from generation to generation'.[5] This was when Poonch state first came into existence. This followed an apparent earlier gift in 1822 of the princely state (or '*raj*') of Jammu to three Dogra brothers, Gulab, Dhyan and Suchet. Because Dhyan did not want to be isolated from Lahore 'where he wielded enormous influence', an arrangement was agreed that Gulab would manage the state on behalf of the three brothers.[6] It is not known why Suchet agreed to this arrangement. According to a later raja of Poonch, 'The origin of the state of Jammu and Kashmir therefore [wa]s based on the grant of joint ownership of the State.'[7] While this claim to ownership was initially important to the rajas of Poonch, they generally appear over time to have come to accept that Gulab's descendants had, with strong, indeed unwavering, British approval and support, become the sole rulers of the princely state of Jammu and Kashmir. Conversely, however, the rajas of Poonch did not come to accept that J&K had suzerainty over Poonch or that Poonch was a subservient entity to J&K.

The death of Dhyan Singh was a significant turning point in the saga of the Poonch and J&K Dogras. Soon after Dhyan's death in 1843, Suchet, possibly inspired by his elder brother Gulab, was killed apparently while trying to claim the prime ministership in Lahore from Dhyan's eldest son, Hira Singh. As Suchet died without issue, this left Gulab as the sole remaining brother, with all of the status and influence as the elder family statesman that this position endowed. Hira Singh later died in 1844 at the hands of Sikh troops, but for reasons unknown. Around this time, Gulab apparently took advantage of the youth and inexperience of Hira's two younger brothers, Jawahir and Moti, to seize territory belonging to both of them (Jasrota, Basauli and other places) and to Gulab's deceased brother Suchet (Bandralta or Ramnagar). However, in 1844 the ambitious (then) Raja Gulab Singh apparently overextended himself and his capabilities, as a result of which the Sikhs marched on Jammu and defeated Gulab. Both Gulab and his property were saved when Gulab's forgiving nephew, Jawahir, who still had significant influence in the Sikh Durbar (kingdom) by virtue of being Dhyan's son, apparently paid a large sum of money to the Sikhs to assuage Gulab's defeat and to prevent the confiscation of his uncle's property and assets.[8] This meant that the Poonch family had a further claim to the Jammu *raj*.

In 1846, events started to go the way of the sole surviving brother, Raja Gulab Singh. In March, he was involved in two significant treaties. First, Gulab's good offices were used to bring about an 'understanding' between the British Government and the Sikh Durbar. This resulted in the Treaty of Lahore on 9 March 1846 between the then ruler of the Punjab, Maharaja Dhalip Singh, and the British. Among other things, Dhalip agreed to 'recognise the independent sovereignty of Raja Gulab Singh in such territories or Districts in the [Punjab] hills as may be made over to [him] by separate agreement...[with] the British Government, with the dependencies thereof *which may have been in the Raja's possession since the time of the late Maharaja Kharrak Singh*'.[9] Kharrak Singh, who was Dhalip's father, died in 1840 after a very short reign; Kharrak's father, the great Sikh emperor Ranjit Singh, had died the previous year. At the time of Kharrak's death, his influential Prime Minister, Dhyan Singh, was still alive. Seven days after the Lahore Treaty, Raja Gulab Singh also entered into an agreement with the British.[10] Known as

231

the Treaty of Amritsar, it was signed on 16 March 1846. In it, the British sold Gulab indefeasible title to hereditary and other lands that comprised his existing domain as Raja of Jammu,[11] to other land he held in Ladakh, and to the Kashmir Valley and other land located in what later came to be called the Frontier Districts Province of J&K. In return, Gulab Singh paid the British Rs. 7.5 million.

As a result of the Treaty of Amritsar, the entity now known as Jammu and Kashmir emerged. Or did it? For the rajas of Poonch, the (first) Treaty of Lahore had recognised that Poonch was a separate entity from Jammu and that it (Poonch) was under the suzerainty of the Sikh Durbar in Lahore, not the suzerainty of Raja Gulab Singh in Jammu. As a result, when the British annexed the Punjab and began to rule it in 1849, the rajas of Poonch believed that they (the British) had inherited—and therefore should have formally stepped into—the Sikh Durbar's position as the suzerain power for the separate entity of Poonch. Unfortunately for the Poonch rajas, the British, at a time of turmoil as they consolidated their position in Punjab, seemed oblivious to the existence of the Poonch *raj*. Hence Dhyan Singh's two remaining sons, Jawahir and Moti Singh, as rajas of Poonch believed that their domain existed as an entity separate from J&K. Furthermore, they also believed that, by virtue of their position as heirs to their father Dhyan, and because of his position as an equal joint ruler of the Jammu *raj* with his brothers, that they were still entitled to a share of the princely state of J&K. Indeed, not only were they legal shareholders of the Jammu *raj*, apparently they had also contributed a large sum of money—possibly as much as Rs. 5 million—'as their share' of the Rs. 7.5 million that Gulab needed to pay the British for his purchase of J&K.[12] This money came from cash reserves and from selling property, including Dhyan Singh's *haveli* (house) in Lahore.[13] Gulab encouraged both of his nephews to contribute as he (Gulab) 'had been acting on behalf of the family and entirely in their interests'.[14] While both of Dhyan's sons did, apparently, contribute a good deal of money, they also quizzed their uncle about what legal provision Gulab had made for them. In reply, Gulab apparently told them that they were to be treated as equal to Gulab's sole surviving son, Ranbir. However Jawahir, particularly, and Moti became suspicious of Gulab and made a representation to the British. The brothers wanted three matters settled in which they were in dispute with Gulab: first, their right to be exclusive owners to the territory of their late brother, Hira Singh; second, their right to half the territory of their uncle, Suchet Singh; and third, their right to have their names entered in the Treaty of Amritsar as grantees along with Gulab Singh.

As a result of the brothers' representation, the British delivered not one, but two significant judgments: a '*Robkar*' by Sir Frederick Currie in 1848 and a decision by the Punjab Board of Revenue in 1852. It is these determinations that the rajas of Poonch were contesting right up until the death of Raja Jagatdev Singh in 1940. In 1848 Currie, who was then British Resident in Lahore, issued a *Robkar*, or opinion. This essentially stated that Poonch had a right to exist as a separate entity but also that it was a feudatory state of Jammu and Kashmir. However, it also indicated that Poonch was internally sovereign with its own administration. The Punjab Board of Revenue decision was an arbitration to settle a dispute between Jawahir and Moti over their father's estate. As a result of this decision, the junior brother, Moti, inherited one third of Poonch, whose territory eventually

## APPENDIX I

came to comprise the 1947 territory of Poonch. In what seemed to be an unfair decision, Moti's elder brother Jawahir inherited two thirds of the estate. In 1857, Gulab Singh died. Two years later, the new Maharaja, Ranbir Singh, accused his cousin of 'some treacherous conspiracy with foreigners'.[15] The British clearly agreed and Jawahir was deposed and forced to live in Ambala in Punjab. Ranbir paid his cousin an allowance of Rs. 100,000 per annum until Jawahir's death, after which Ranbir incorporated Jawahir's lapsed territory into J&K as his cousin had died without issue. Jawahir's nephew, Baldev, believed that Jawahir's lands should have gone to his father, Moti, as these lands had originally been part of Dhyan's state, of which Moti was a direct descendant.[16] A contrary report by a British resident disputed that claim. It stated that Jawahir 'renounced his claims on being granted an allow[a]nce' by Ranbir Singh.[17] Once again, the rajas of Poonch had been thwarted.

After the deposing of Jawahir, relations between Raja Moti Singh of Poonch and Maharaja Ranbir Singh of Jammu and Kashmir were cordial, even close. This changed with the accession of Maharaja Pratap Singh in 1885. Pratap's administration apparently was so 'disorganised' that a 'Council of Administration' was imposed on J&K. Indeed, in 1889, the British compelled the possibly pro-Russian Pratap to institute a Council of State that severely limited his powers, made him a figurehead, and allowed the council to control his (alleged mal)administration until 1905.[18] The British dominated this council via the British resident, who was the 'final arbiter' in J&K's affairs.[19] Raja Amar Singh, one of Pratap's younger brothers, was the major figure in J&K involved. (Amar Singh was the father of Hari Singh, who eventually succeeded Pratap as ruler of J&K.) The ambitious and pro-British Amar did not always see eye to eye with his elder brother, Pratap. He also played a major role on the council. From the time of the establishment of the council, 'new ideas as to the status of Poonch began to be formed and an aggressive policy was set on foot',[20] while also 'came the first rush of appreciable encroachments on the rights, and attack on the status of Poonch'.[21] According to the then Raja of Poonch, Baldev, he had also been given the first ever '*Dastur ul Amal*', a high level instruction 'containing scores of conditions imposing limitations' by which the Kashmir Durbar sought to impose its will on Poonch.[22] However, in responding to the Raja's complaints, the British Resident followed the consistent British line established by Currie's *Robkar*: Poonch was a feudatory state of Jammu and Kashmir.

The reasons for the new aggression towards Poonch by the Council of State after 1889 were not given. However, Raja Amar Singh may have been a big part of the problem, given the future tensions between Poonch and J&K and given his proactive role in the council against his brother Pratap. (This brotherly antagonism may also explain why Pratap, who was without an heir, sought to adopt another child as his heir and successor, thus potentially sidelining Amar's son, Hari, from ascending to the J&K throne on Pratap's death.) As early as 1892, Raja Moti Singh attempted to 'have the matter out with the Kashmir Durbar'. He died before he could successfully do so.[23] Moti's successor, Baldev Singh, sent a long appeal to the British Resident, H.S. Barnes, in 1895. One of Baldev's complaints was that the J&K state had started to use the terms '*jagir*' and '*jagirdar*' in reference to Poonch and its Raja. However, the Raja of Poonch believed that his domain was a 'state' of which he was chief, although his state was 'subordinate', 'dependent' or a 'vassal' state to J&K. However, his state also communicated with its 'overlord' not directly, but indirectly via the 'Foreign Office of the Jammu State', which showed a distinct degree of separation.[24] These points were important for Baldev as 'The Poonch Rajas have never been termed or treated as mere "Jagirdars" by the Kashmir Government'.[25]

The issues of the status of Poonch came up in 1927, presumably in the intervening period between the death of Raja Sukhdev Singh some time in 1927 and the future succession of Jagatdev Singh, who became Raja some time in 1928.[26] A British official, Sir Evelyn Howell, provided the Government of India with two letters about this issue, dated 19 October and 21 November 1927. These followed a meeting between Howell and Maharaja Hari Singh 15 October 1927 in which Howell gave some non-committal opinions to Hari Singh that contradicted his clear advice to the Government of India, thus keeping open the latter's options in relation to controlling Hari Singh. Howell claimed that Currie's *Robkar* of 1848 had been 'accepted by the parties concerned' and that the 'most solvent features' of Currie's award were that Maharaja Gulab Singh had granted Poonch to Rajas Jawahir and Moti Singh after the treaty of 1846 'as an Ilaqa which may either mean a dependency or simply a tract of country. No mention was made that the grant was a Jagir'. This meant that the management of the maharaja's dominions, whether under his direct possession or indirect possession or control, rested with the maharaja. Furthermore, there were prescribed terms for the rajas of Poonch, Jawahir and Moti Singh, who were required to make certain annual payments to the maharaja and 'were forbidden to commit any important act without consulting Maharaja Gulab Singh'. This did not mean that Poonch necessarily was a *jagir*, but it certainly was a feudatory, although this also 'implied some measure of separate jurisdiction'. On the 9 February 1928, the Government of India wrote to Maharaja Hari Singh and informed him somewhat vaguely that Currie's 1848 award meant that the British had no role to play in the relations between the maharaja and the raja of Poonch, except if either party appealed to the Government of India 'to compel observance' of the terms of Currie's 1848 agreement.

To the Government of India however, Howell made it clear that the British were not justified in interfering in the domestic relationship between the raja of Poonch and the maharaja of J&K, except in its role as the paramount power to enforce its rights and obligations. Hence, if Maharaja Hari Singh wanted to alter the instruction (or *sanad*) given to the new Raja of Poonch, the Government of India did not need to express any opinion on this internal matter. Maharaja Hari Singh apparently went ahead and stated in the *sanad* (possibly also called a *patta*, as is discussed below) that Poonch was a *jagir* and that J&K had certain rights in Poonch. As a result, the 'young and inexperienced' Jagatdev Singh 'was forced to employ a number of Kashmir officials'. They encroached on his rights and powers—and eventually caused him to become disenchanted with Maharaja Hari Singh's provocative actions.

On 27 February 1936 the Raja of Poonch, Jagatdev Singh, sent a memorial to the Viceroy of India. It had been compiled with the help of a lawyer, B.B. Chaterjee.[27] In legal terms, a memorial is usually described as a written statement of facts or opinions presented to a sovereign or ruler. Although Jagatdev's memorial provided much of the historical information given above in this appendix, the significance of the Raja's memorial was that he went straight 'to the top'. Unlike his predecessor, Raja Baldev Singh, Jagatdev approached the British via the Government of India seeking a review of the relationship between Poonch and J&K. This put the British in a position in which they had to do something to address the Raja's petition. In what amounted to a 'scattergun' approach, Jagatdev Singh sought a number of things. These included being under British feudatory control, not J&K's control—the latter position being 'not justified by any legitimate rights'[28]—and wanting the 'Ruling house of Poonch' to be given the territories to which it was entitled and a 'legitimate share of the benefits of ownership [sic] of the State of Jammu and Kashmir'.[29] Furthermore, Jagatdev wanted the 'Kashmir Durbar' stopped from encroaching on the 'rights and privileges' of the ruler and chief of Poonch and the state of Poonch by trying first, to 'divest the Ruler of Poonch of his ultimate judicial authority' in Poonch; second, to subordinate the ruler and the Poonch treasury to 'the dictates and intervention of the Durbar through the Kashmir Legislative Assembly'; third, to impose officials on Poonch; and, fourth—and very importantly—to deprive 'the State and Rulers of Poonch of their due and legitimate Customs Revenue known as Kohala Ferry Rasoom'.[30] This latter was a significant source of revenue as all people and goods going into or coming out from J&K via the Jhelum Valley Road had to cross the Jhelum River at Kohala—and therefore pay a toll or customs fee. It is not surprising that the voracious Hari Singh wanted to obtain access to this valuable source of revenue.

Jagatdev's memorial appears to be the culmination of a steadily degenerating relationship between the Maharaja and his relative. Going back at least to 1928 when the Raja ascended the Poonch throne, the two men had not always had a good relationship. In that year, Maharaja Hari Singh apparently gave Jagatdev a 'very kind and generous letter' giving assurance to the Raja that he (Hari Singh) 'was ready to forget and forgive the [undetailed] past, and that he would do everything possible to help' Jagatdev. According to the British Resident, it was a 'great pity' that the relations between the two rulers had 'deteriorated so lamentably since then' (1928), particularly as the Resident believed that Hari Singh would leave Jagatdev Singh alone 'so long as he ruled Poonch with reasonable efficiency'.[31] Apart from—or perhaps because of—their personal dislike of one another, this deterioration was due, in part, to some incidents in 1930 when the Raja appeared to fail to observe appropriate protocols at some J&K state functions. For his part, the Raja wrote a 'provocative' letter to a 'Mr Wakefield', who was the J&K Foreign Minister, which the British, who clearly sided with Hari Singh, successfully encouraged Jagatdev to withdraw. Nevertheless, the Maharaja was apparently furious with the Raja and wanted to punish his feudatory severely.[32] A year later, the Raja again snubbed official protocol in an 'unpleasant incident' at a state function at which J&K 'nobles and jagirdars' had gathered to welcome back the Maharaja, who had just returned from England. According to the Resident, the Raja's 'ill-advised' action 'may have been due more to a desire to differentiate himself from the other jagirdars than to a deliberate intention to show disrespect to the Maharaja'. Jagatdev was apologetic and sought the Maharaja's forgiveness.[33]

However, he was banned from the Maharaja's palace for a time, after which, on 6 June 1931, Hari Singh reduced the Raja's salute of guns from thirteen to nine.[34] Various reports and file annotations suggest that the Raja of Poonch was apparently a tactless and somewhat inept man, that the Maharaja was apparently aggressive and sometimes discourteous towards him, and that there was certainly acrimony on both sides. By late 1931 Jagatdev had had enough. As he put it, despite pursuing a policy of 'patience and forbearance for a very long time' with Hari Singh's 'consistent series of acts of ... aggression', the Raja's patience had run out. He now intended to lay his grievances before the Government of India.[35] By 1936, this intention had transformed into his memorial.

In responding to the Raja of Poonch's memorial, the British invoked Currie's *Robkar*, which stated that Poonch had a right to exist but that it was a feudatory state of Jammu and Kashmir. Apart from agreeing with and reiterating Currie's position, the British also told the Raja—who disagreed both with Currie and with the British stance—that Jagatdev Singh should have presented his petition to the Kashmir Durbar, and not to the British via their Resident in Jammu and Kashmir. Equally, if the Raja wanted to present a review petition, he also would need to do so through the Kashmir Durbar. In response, the Raja informed the Political Secretary of the Government of India that he would send his memorial to the Secretary of State for India in London as a form of appeal against the order of the Government of India.[36] Nevertheless, the Political Secretary noted that 'No action' was needed in relation to Jagatdev's possible appeal.[37] This was because, as far as the British were concerned, all petitions and memorials from the Raja of Poonch should have been made 'through the proper channel, i.e. the Govt. of Jammu & Kashmir', which itself should then forward these to the Resident, or a higher authority, 'without any unavoidable delay'.[38] Following this procedure, the Resident had sent the Raja of Poonch's memorial of 27 February 1936, which had been (mis)addressed to the Resident, to the J&K Government for remarks before submission to the Government of India.[39] An earlier letter from the 'Resident in Kashmir', who thought that the Raja might be trying to 'outstrip his status', also stated that a British order of 9 February 1928 had 'definitely settled' the status of Poonch: its status was a 'subordinate Jagirdar of Kashmir'.[40] Relations between the Maharaja and the Raja were therefore a 'domestic matter' on which the Government of India did not need to comment.[41] As a *jagirdar*, the Raja therefore needed to submit all petitions and correspondence with the British through the J&K Government.

In correspondence after Jagatdev Singh's death in 1940, notes on British files also talk of a *patta* that Maharaja Hari Singh granted to the Raja of Poonch in 1928 at the time of the Raja's succession (although Jagatdev failed to mention it in any of his correspondence).[42] (This may be similar to, or the same as, the *sanad* discussed above.) The *patta* appears to have been an 'agreement' with at least eleven clauses that comprised rules that the young Raja (he was then less than twenty-six years old, given that his elder brother, Sukhdev, had been born in 1901) agreed to obey. The *patta* was based on Currie's 1848 *Robkar*. While it was an agreement solely between the Maharaja and the Raja, the British had been shown a version 'confidentially' and the document had been 'modified in several aspects on [their] advice'. Nevertheless, Hari Singh made 'several attempts' to interpret

# APPENDIX I

the agreement to his advantage and thereby obtain 'a larger measure of interference in the affairs of Poonch'. The British, through their Resident, had sought to 'regulate' the Kashmir-Poonch relationship to limit the Maharaja's interference in Poonch.[43] However, this had clearly not satisfied the Raja of Poonch, Jagatdev Singh, who made his memorial to the British in 1936.

However, with the death of Jagatdev in 1940, his only son, Shiv Ratandev Singh, became the new Raja. Shiv Ratandev was a minor to whom Maharaja Hari Singh granted the title of Raja. In relation to his succession to the *jagir* of Poonch, Hari Singh made a formal proclamation that stated that the Raja 'would not exercise any powers of the administration over Poonch until he attains [his] majority and is considered to be fit' to have an investiture in accordance with a *patta* to be granted by the Maharaja. In the meantime, Hari Singh appointed a guardian, who was his military secretary, to look after 'the minor Raja's person and property', while an administrator responsible directly to the Maharaja would look after 'the administration of the Jagir'.[44] The British deemed it 'hardly practicable' to object to the 'new' arrangements that the Maharaja had actually been seeking for some time, whereby Poonch's administration was to be carried out 'in conformity' with the J&K Constitution (which allowed the Maharaja to dominate J&K) and whereby Poonch's courts came under the control of, and allowed Poonchis to appeal to, the J&K High Court.[45] These arrangements were 'almost certainly an improvement' for the people of Poonch. On the other hand, the British would not accept any moves by Hari Singh to 'abolish the levy of a separate customs duty in the jagir' unless he paid the Raja 'adequate compensation'. This was probably a reference to Hari Singh's desire to secure the abovementioned lucrative Kohala Ferry Rasoom and other customs duties.

The Maharaja's proclamation and moves to bring Poonch under his total and direct control were not necessarily well received. The British felt no need to comment on, or to express any appreciation for, the arrangements that would be made by Hari Singh for the 'minority administration in Poonch, [e]xcept to the extent that they may conflict with Sir Frederick Currie's award'. The British also agreed that the Raja's widow, the Rani—'an extremely cantankerous and quarrelsome lady' who, the J&K Government feared, 'may contaminate her son (now aged fifteen) with disloyal ideas' about the J&K administration—should be excluded from the minority administration; this was because 'she [was] uneducated'.[46] A 'huge gathering' of the 'Poonch Public' passed a resolution on 30 July 1940 that expressed the gathering's 'profound sorrow and deep indignation and resentment' of the Maharaja's proclamation and his description of Poonch as a *jagir* and the Raja as a *jagirdar*. The resolution noted that the 'beloved' Raja and the 'Poonch public' had presented memorials to the paramount power against the J&K Durbar which, according to them, 'are yet pending'. It called on the people of Poonch 'to unite and continue the struggle in a constitutional and peaceful manner, until Poonch State is free from the bondage and absolutely unwarranted yoke and interference of the Kashmir durbar'.[47]

Hence, while the British were ambivalent about the new administrative arrangements between Poonch and J&K, some, perhaps many, of the Poonchis were displeased with them. For his part, Maharaja Hari Singh hoped that the arrangements that he ordered would 'ensure, during the minority of the Jagirdar, an efficient and progressive local administration with which the people of the Jagir will feel contented and happy'.[48] By 1945, however, the Maharaja's government was 'unpopular in Poonch, especially among the numerous service families who contrast their treatment with that enjoyed by servicemen in the Punjab, especially in the matter of land grants'. The Maharaja's government also felt it necessary to ban a meeting of the 'Jammu Muslim Conference Party' that was to be held at a village near Bagh, because of communal troubles.[49] The Poonchis' dislike of Maharaja Hari Singh that was to surface clearly and forcefully in 1947 was beginning to come to the fore. The circumstances discussed above between the rajas of Poonch and the maharajas of J&K partly explain why.

# APPENDIX II

## PHYSICAL, POLITICAL AND RELIGIOUS COMPOSITION OF J&K IN 1941

There are six tables in this appendix. Three tables (One, Three and Five) provide information about the area, population and religious majority of each of J&K's three provinces—Jammu, Kashmir and the Frontier Districts—on a district and *tehsil* (sub-district) basis. The other three tables (Two, Four, Six) provide details about the religious composition of each province on a district basis.

While some authors and publications (mainly pro-Pakistan) do not consider either the Gilgit (Leased Area) or the Gilgit Agency to have been part of the princely state of Jammu and Kashmir, the 1941 Census included statistics for these areas. The British administered these areas on behalf of the J&K Government[1] until they retroceded them to the Maharaja Hari Singh on 1 August 1947. On 28 July, he sent a governor to take over the administration of these areas from the withdrawing British.[2] Hence, on 15 August 1947, these areas were under Maharaja Hari Singh's direct, albeit tenuous, administration and control.

*Areas and symbols*

All areas in the tables in this appendix are in square miles unless otherwise specified.

The tables contain various symbols. These are used consistently between tables:

D: District
H: Hindus
M: Muslims
Pop.: Population.

Table II.1: Jammu Province in 1941: Area, Population and Religious Majority by District and Tehsil

| District: Tehsil | Area | 1941 Pop. | Majority* | Comments |
|---|---|---|---|---|
| Chenani Jagir | 95 | 11,796 | 81.22% H | Totally surrounded by Udhampur District |
| Jammu | 1,147 | 431,362 | 57.53% H | – |
| –Akhnoor | 317 | 88,821 | Hindu | – |
| –Jammu | 346 | 156,556 | Hindu | Included Jammu City |
| –Samba | 327 | 89,464 | Hindi | – |
| –Sri Ranbirsinghpura | 157 | 96,521 | Slightly H | Smallest tehsil in J&K |
| Kathua | 1,023 | 177,672 | 74.31% H | Smallest district in J&K |
| –Basohli | 614 | 70,624 | Hindu | – |
| –Jasmergarh | 185 | 59,670 | Hindu | – |
| –Kathua | 224 | 47,378 | Hindu | – |
| Mirpur | 1,627 | 386,655 | 80.41% M | – |
| –Bhimber | 698 | 162,503 | 64.79% M | – |
| –Kotli | 574 | 111,037 | Muslim | – |
| –Mirpur | 355 | 113,115 | Muslim | – |
| Poonch Jagir | 1,627 | 421,828 | >90% M | District total 1,000 greater than sum of tehsils |
| –Bagh | 321 | 101,091 | Muslim | Sikhs outnumber Hindus |
| –Haveli | 479 | 110,733 | Muslim | Included Poonch Town |
| [–Karloop Jagir] | [4] | – | – | Counted in Jammu and Ramnagar tehsils |
| –Mendhar | 479 | 100,704 | Muslim | – |
| –Sudhnoti | 348 | 108,300 | Muslim | Majority of Hindus live in Sudhnoti |
| Reasi | 1,789 | 257,903 | 68.06% M | Census states >67% Muslim |
| –Rampur Rajouri | 806 | 140,844 | 79.09% M | – |
| –Reasi | 983 | 117,059 | 54.80% M | – |
| Udhampur | 5,070 | 294,217 | 56.02% H | – |
| –Bhadrawah | 553 | 44,518 | Hindu | – |
| –Kishtwar | 3,021 | 60,893 | Muslim | – |
| –Ramban | 588 | 75,793 | Muslim | – |
| –Ramnagar | 525 | 60,076 | Hindu | – |
| –Udhampur | 383 | 52,937 | Hindu | – |
| Total JP | 12,378 | 1,981,433 | 61.19% M | – |

Source: *Census of India 1941*, Volume XXII, *Jammu & Kashmir State*, Part III, *Village Tables*, Srinagar, R.G. Wreford, Editor, Jammu and Kashmir Government, 1942.

Key: JP  Jammu Province.
  *  Percentages only specified where tehsil figures have been provided by census.

APPENDIX II

Table II.2: Muslims and Hindus in Jammu Province as Percentages of their Respective Districts, as Percentages of the Province and as Percentages of their Respective Communities.

| District | Muslims | %D | %JP | %M | Hindus | %D | %JP | %H | Pop.JP★ | %JP |
|---|---|---|---|---|---|---|---|---|---|---|
| Chenani | 2,205 | 18.70 | 0.11 | 0.18 | 9,581 | 81.22 | 0.48 | 1.30 | 11,796 | 0.60 |
| Jammu | 170,789 | 39.60 | 8.62 | 14.09 | 248,173 | 57.53 | 12.53 | 33.68 | 431,362 | 21.77 |
| Kathua | >45,000 | 25.33 | 2.27 | 3.71 | 132,022 | 74.31 | 6.66 | 17.91 | 177,672 | 8.97 |
| Mirpur | 310,900 | 80.41 | 15.69 | 25.64 | 63,576 | 16.44 | 3.21 | 8.63 | 386,655 | 19.51 |
| Poonch | 379,645 | >90.00 | 19.16 | 31.31 | 37,965 | 9.00 | 1.92 | 5.15 | 421,828 | 21.29 |
| Reasi | 175,539 | ±68.06 | 8.86 | 14.48 | 80,725 | 31.30 | 4.07 | 10.96 | 257,903 | 13.01 |
| Udhampur | 128,327 | 43.62 | 6.48 | 10.59 | 164,820 | 56.00 | 8.32 | 22.37 | 294,217 | 14.85 |
| Total JP | 1,212,405 | – | 61.19 | 100.00 | 736,862 | – | 37.19 | 100.00 | 1,981,433 | 100.00 |

Source: *Census of India 1941*, Volume XXII, *Jammu & Kashmir State*, Part III, *Village Tables*, Srinagar, R.G. Wreford, Editor, Jammu and Kashmir Government, 1942.

Key: JP Jammu Province.
± The census gives this figure as 'over 67 per cent' (p. 151).
★ Includes 27,896 Sikhs (1.41 per cent) and 4,270 Others: Indian Christians, Jains, Buddhists and unspecified others (0.21 per cent).

Table II.3: Kashmir Province in 1941: Area, Population and Religious Majority by District and Tehsil.

| District: Tehsil | Area | 1941 Pop. | Majority* | Comments |
|---|---|---|---|---|
| Anantnag | 2,814 | 851,606 | 91.49% M | – |
| –Anantnag | 1,034 | 203,827 | Muslim | – |
| –Khas | 743 | 333,881 | Muslim | Includes Srinagar City, population 207,787 |
| –Kulgam | 588 | 157,372 | Muslim | – |
| –Pulwama | 449 | 156,526 | Muslim | – |
| Baramulla | 3,317 | 612,428 | 96.49% M | Almost all Hindus are Pandits |
| –Baramulla | 590 | 162,903 | 95.23% M | – |
| –Sri Partapsinghpora | 488 | 174,583 | 97.29% M | Also known as Badgam |
| –Uttarmachipora | 2,239 | 274,942 | 96.73% M | Also known as Handwara |
| Muzaffarabad | 2,408 | 264,671 | 92.89 | 12,922 Sikhs and 5,846 Hindus in district |
| –Karnah | 1,342 | 58,863 | Muslim | – |
| –Muzaffarabad | 546 | 125,585 | Muslim | > two thirds of Sikhs and Hindus lived in tehsil |
| –Uri | 520 | 80,223 | Muslim | – |
| Total KP | 8,539 | 1,728,705 | 93.48% M | – |

Source: *Census of India 1941*, Volume XXII, *Jammu & Kashmir State*, Part III, *Village Tables*, Srinagar, R.G. Wreford, Editor, Jammu and Kashmir Government, 1942.

Key: KP  Kashmir Province.
* Percentages only specified where tehsil figures have been provided by census.

Table II.4: Muslims, Hindus, Sikhs and Others in Kashmir Province as Percentages of their Respective Districts and as Percentages of the Province.

| District | Muslims | % | Hindus | % | Sikhs | % | Others* | % | Total |
|---|---|---|---|---|---|---|---|---|---|
| Anantnag | 779,134 | 91.49 | 66,766 | 7.84 | 5,621 | 0.66 | 85 | 0.01 | 851,606 |
| Baramulla | 590,936 | 96.49 | 12,919 | 2.11 | 8,458 | 1.38 | 115 | 0.02 | 612,428 |
| Muzaffarabad | 245,858 | 92.89 | 5,846 | 2.21 | 12,922 | 4.88 | 45 | 0.01 | 264,671 |
| Total KP | 1,615,928 | 93.48 | 85,531 | 4.95 | 27,001 | 1.56 | 245 | 0.01 | 1,728,705 |

Source: *Census of India 1941*, Volume XXII, *Jammu & Kashmir State*, Part III, *Village Tables*, Srinagar, R.G. Wreford, Editor, Jammu and Kashmir Government, 1942.

Key: KP  Kashmir Province.
* Unidentified, except in Muzaffarabad District where most were Indian Christians.

# APPENDIX II

Table II.5: Frontier Districts Province in 1941: Area, Population and Religious Majority by District and Tehsil.

| District: Tehsil | Area | 1941 Pop. | Majority** | Comments |
|---|---|---|---|---|
| Astore | 1,632 | 17,026 | 100.00% M | Negligible, uncounted minority; 5,438 Shias |
| Gilgit Agency | 14,680 | 76,526 | 100.00% M | <100 non-Muslims, two thirds of whom in Chilas |
| –Chilas | *est 2,800 | ±15,364 | Muslim | *Actual area 1,635 |
| –Hunza | *est 3,900 | ±15,341 | Maulia | Followers of Agha Khan |
| –Ishkuman | *est 1,600 | ±4,282 | Maulia | *Actual area 1,018 |
| –Kuh-Ghizar | *est 1,980 | ±8,512 | Maulia | *Actual area 2,020 |
| –Nagar | *est 1,600 | ±14,874 | Shia | – |
| –Punial | *est 1,600 | ±8,164 | Maulia | *Actual area 632 sq. miles |
| –Yasin | *est 1,200 | ±9,989 | Maulia | *Actual area 872 |
| Gilgit (LA) | 1,480 | 22,495 | 100.00% M | Negligible, uncounted minority |
| Ladakh District | 47,762 | 195,431 | 79.05% M | Given in census as 195,282; difference 149 |
| –Kargil | 7,392 | 52,853 | 84.03% M | Majority of Muslims were Shia; remainder B |
| –Ladakh | 29,848 | 36,307 | 87.77% B | – |
| –Skardu | 8,522 | 106,271 | 99.74% M | 85,000 Muslims were Shia |
| Total FDP | 63,554 | 311,478 | 86.86% M | – |

Sources: 1) *Census of India 1941*, Volume XXII, *Jammu & Kashmir State*, Part III, *Village Tables*, Srinagar, R.G. Wreford, Editor, Jammu and Kashmir Government, 1942.
2) *Census of Azad Kashmir, 1951*, Murree?, Iftikhar Ahmad, Chief Enumeration Officer, Government of Azad Kashmir, 1952.

Key: B     Buddhist.
      FDP    Frontier Districts Province.
      LA     Leased Area.
      *      The *Survey of Pakistan* was able to make more accurate calculations of the size of the various districts. According to the 1951 Azad Kashmir Census, the figures given in the 1941 Census were 'rough estimates'. The figures given in the 1951 Azad Kashmir Census were 'good for practical purposes but do not carry the stamp of the Government'.[3] Figures for Hunza and Nagar were still estimates because the Hunza-China border was not firm and the Hunza-Nagar border had not been established.
      **     Not given in the 1941 Census. Calculated by working back from district figures with percentage increase figures provided in the 1951 Azad Kashmir Census.

Table II.6: (Non-Shia) Muslims, Shia Muslims, Buddhists and Others in the Frontier Districts Province as Percentages of their Tehsils in Ladakh District, as Percentages of the Other Districts, and as Percentages of the Province.

| District: Tehsil | Muslims | % | Shias | Buddhists | % | Others* | % | Total |
|---|---|---|---|---|---|---|---|---|
| Astore | 17,026 | 100 | 5,438 | – | – | neg | – | 17,026 |
| Gilgit Agency | 76,526 | 100 | – | – | – | *** <100 | – | 76,526 |
| Gilgit (LA) | 22,495 | 100 | np | – | – | neg | – | 22,495 |
| Ladakh District | | | | | | | | |
| –Kargil | 44,410 | 84.03 | 39,427 | 8,298 | 15.70 | 145 | 0.27 | 52,853 |
| –Ladakh | 4,086 | 11.25 | np | 31,866 | 87.77 | 355 | 0.98 | 36,307 |
| –Skardu | 105,996 | 99.74 | >85,000 | 0 | – | 275 | 0.26 | 106,271 |
| LD total | 154,492 | 79.05 | >124,427 | 40,164 | 20.55 | 775 | 0.40 | 195,431** |
| Total FDP | 270,539 | 86.86 | – | 40,164 | 12.89 | 775 | 0.25 | 311,478 |

Source: *Census of India 1941*, Volume XXII, *Jammu & Kashmir State*, Part III, *Village Tables*, Srinagar, R.G. Wreford, Editor, Jammu and Kashmir Government, 1942.

Key: FDP   Frontier Districts Province.
     LA    Leased Area.
     LD    Ladakh District.
     neg   Negligible. The whole population was Muslim 'except for a negligible minority'.
     np    Not provided in 1941 Census.
     *     'Others' comprised 562 Hindus, 135 Unspecified Others and 78 Sikhs.
     **   Figure given in the 1941 Census for District total was 195,282 (difference 149).
     ***  Not counted in total for Frontier Districts Province.

# APPENDIX III

## MAJORITY POSITION OF MUSLIMS IN 1941

For three reasons, the figures in Table 1.1 may moderately understate the majority position of Muslims in 1941.

1) The overall population figures would have been greater if the 1941 Census had not been taken in February 1941 when many men went from J&K to other districts, particularly to Punjab, mainly looking for work 'to supplement the meagre incomes they extract from their lands'.[1] They returned home in spring. This migration particularly affected districts in Jammu Province, especially Muslim-majority Mirpur and Poonch, where agricultural holdings were poor or small, and the Muslim-majority districts of Baramulla and Anantnag in Kashmir Province, which had severe winters. Men in the Frontier Districts also went to other areas of J&K and to Punjab looking for work, but not in the same sort of numbers as men from the other two provinces.

2) The population figures for all districts of Jammu Province would have been greater in 1941 but for the heavy recruiting of men from this province, where Muslims were in the majority, into the British Indian Army. When the census was taken in February 1941, many of these men, the majority of whom were most probably Muslims, would have been outside J&K. Counting some or all of them would have boosted the numerical position of Muslims in Jammu Province in 1941.

Only Jammu Province provided large numbers of soldiers who served outside J&K, although men in the Gilgit Agency did join the local, British-officered Gilgit Scouts. While the various districts of Jammu Province had been long-term suppliers of men to the British Indian Army, numbers were up in 1941 because of World War II. No specific figures are available, but estimates of the number of men from Jammu Province who served in the British Indian Army range from 50,000 to 100,000. A reasonable figure appears to be 50,000 (see Appendix IV).

Although the 1941 Census did not give any specific figures, it mentioned six of the seven districts of Jammu Province as providing men to either the British Indian Army or the J&K State Army. In discussing Jammu Province overall, it stated:

A good percentage of the population in all districts belongs to what may be termed, for the sake of convenience, the martial classes, mostly Rajputs, both Hindu and Muslim. These elements are recruited for the army both in the State and in British India and their absence from their homes on military duty has a small effect on the permanent population. As this census coincided with the war and considerable recruiting activity, the population of some villages and localities with military service connections may well have been affected more than usual.[2]

In Hindu-majority Jammu District, the census said:

While agriculture is the chief means of subsistence except in urban areas, the rural population has other sources of income. The Rajputs and other classes accustomed to join the army form a considerable part of the population and pensions and pay for military service constitute an appreciable addition to the family funds in many homes.[3]

Although these Rajputs would have been both Hindu and Muslim, many of the Hindus would have joined the J&K State Army. Jammu District was the district from which the Maharaja came and the loyalty of the Hindus would not have been in doubt. For the same reason, in terms of becoming a soldier, the British Indian Army was far more accessible to Muslims than the J&K State Army. The number of Muslims in the J&K Army was not large, possibly because the Maharaja doubted their loyalty. Out of 7,957 men in his army in 1926, a maximum of 2,000 were Muslims.[4] The rest were Hindu Dogras, apart from about 1,000 'Gorkas' [Gurkhas]. By 1939, the J&K State Army had grown to 9,078 men, although the ethno-religious mix was similar to that of 1926.[5]

In Hindu-majority Kathua District, the census stated that the whole district was almost entirely dependent on agriculture, although 'Rajputs from Kathua are recruited in fair numbers for the Indian Army'.[6]

In Hindu-majority Udhampur District: 'The large Rajput element, especially in Ramnagar, provides recruits for the military services in the State and the army in British India'.[7]

In Muslim-majority Reasi District: 'Considerable numbers of the Rajput elements join the State army and by this means relieve the straitened circumstances existing in the majority of homes'.[8]

In the Muslim-majority Mirpur District:

An unusual feature of the Mirpur Muslim community is that females exceed males; this is exceptional and indicates the large number of men out of the district at the time of the census earning a living elsewhere ... Agriculture in the Kotli and Mirpur Tehsils can not fully support the people who are strong and virile; there are no industries worth the name. The result is that large numbers of the adult male population of both tehsils, Mirpur in particular, leave the district for periods varying in length in search of employment of all kinds. They join the army in large numbers as well as the mercantile marine operating from Indian ports; some of them are found as traders and seamen all over the world. Bhimber is not affected to the same extent although many of its men join the army.[9]

For the Poonch *jagir*, the census stated:

The [population] increase is below the average for the whole State. This may be attributed partly to increased migration to the Punjab in the winter, when the census was taken, in search of employment and enlistment in various units of the Indian Army with which this district, especially tehsils Bagh and Sudhnoti, has a close and long established association. The percentage increase is lowest in the Sudhnoti Tehsil ... [due] to the fact that [it] is the tehsil nearest to the Punjab, and [is] probably most affected by movement in search of employment and by enlistment.[10]

## APPENDIX III

In Bagh and Sudhnoti *tehsi*ls of Poonch *jagir*, the census in particular continued:

... the average size of holdings is small, crops are uncertain and outturn [sic] inadequate to meet local requirements. The other tehsils are subject to the same difficulties but to a less extent. A considerable number of men from the Bagh and Sudhnoti Tehsils, and in smaller numbers from Haveli and Mendhar Tehsils, enlist in the various units of the Indian army and get employment in various civil departments, especially railways, in British India. Many of them get domestic service in one capacity or another. Most of these men return to their homes at varying intervals. They do not dispose of any land they may have. Few leave the area for good. It is reasonable to suppose that at the recent census a larger number of men than usual were away from their homes at the time of enumeration owing to increased enlistment and the increased demand for labour.[11]

3) The exact numbers of Muslims in the districts of Kathua and the Poonch *jagir* were unknown. The 1941 Census states that in Kathua District there were was a Muslim population of 'over 45,000'[12] and that in Poonch *jagir* 'over 90 per cent of the total population is Muslim'.[13] These appear to be minima only, thus understating the number of Muslims.

# APPENDIX IV

## INDIAN ARMY SOLDIERS FROM POONCH, MIRPUR

The (British) Indian Army was far more accessible to J&K Muslims than the J&K State Army, which was dominated by Hindus. The areas of J&K that provided the greatest numbers of recruits to the Indian Army were those districts of Jammu Province that had poor land or small, uneconomic holdings, particularly Poonch *jagir*. These areas were also located close to British India (that is, India under direct British rule) and major recruiting centres such as Rawalpindi and Sialkot. While large numbers of men from Jammu Province served in the Indian Army, Kashmiris were not considered a martial race and were not encouraged to join. Men in the Frontier Districts Province, particularly from Gilgit, joined the local, British-officered Gilgit Scouts; few appear to have served in the Indian Army.

Large numbers of Poonchis and Mirpuris served in both world wars as Indian Army soldiers. They enlisted as 'Punjabi Musalmans' (Muslims) mainly in the Punjab Regiment.[1] Part 2 of Appendix III details the mentions in the 1941 Census of enlistments into the (British) Indian Army of men from six of the Jammu Province's seven districts. The final three paragraphs of this section deal specifically with Mirpur District and the Poonch *jagir*.

*Other mentions of Poonchis, Mirpuris (in alphabetical order)*

*Annexure 4* contained in the 'Memorial from the Raja of Poonch' to the then Viceroy of India in 1936 states that of Poonch's 'total population of 3,33,386 souls [sic], there are 1,73,000 [sic] men and leaving aside the children, the old and the invalid the number of men of the [sic] fighting age comes to about 57,670. Owing to the Late Raja Sahibs untiring efforts and vast personal influence about 18,000 men joined the Indian army in various capacities during the [First World W]ar which approximately means one out of every three men of the fighting age of the state ... he inspired so much enthusiasm into the hearts of his warlike subjects. ... By sending every third man of the [sic] fighting age to the front he stands first amongst all the Indian chiefs of this Vast Empire'.[2] The *Census of Azad Kashmir, 1951*, Murree?, Iftikhar Ahmad, Chief Enumeration Officer, Government of Azad Kashmir, 1952, p. 5, states there were 'seventy thousand demobilised Muslim soldiers of the two World Wars' in the districts of Poonch, Mirpur and Muzaffarabad.

# THE UNTOLD STORY OF THE PEOPLE OF AZAD KASHMIR

*Kashmir's Fight for Freedom*, Department of Public Relations, Azad Kashmir Government, 1948, p. 1, states that 100,000 Muslims from J&K served in World War II. After war broke out, even though 'Moslems volunteered to take part in it on the side of the United Nations [sic]', they were not allowed to join Kashmir forces in large numbers. They had to join the British Indian Army. The number of these Moslem volunteers was 100,000, forming a force about ten times as large as the Kashmir army'. The figure of 100,000 may be overstated.

Sardar M. Ibrahim Khan, *The Kashmir Saga*, Lahore, Ripon Printing Press, 1965, p. 71, claims there were 'no less than 80,000 discharged soldiers from the old Indian Army in Poonch'. (This may include World War I veterans.) Ibrahim, a Poonchi, was the founder President of Azad (Free) Kashmir. On p. 52, he states that Maharaja Hari Singh had seen 'a great gathering of about forty thousand men, almost all ex-Servicemen of the British Army from Sudhnutti and Bagh Tehsils of Poonch, assembled to greet him on April 21, 1947 at Rawalakot'.

Josef Korbel, *Danger in Kashmir*, Princeton University Press, revised edition, 1966 [First edition 1954], pp. 54–5, citing a document published in Azad Kashmir (*Jammu: A Muslim Province*, Kashmir Publications, Muzaffarabad, Azad Kashmir, p. 13', no author or publication date given) states that in World War II, 71,667 citizens of J&K served in the Indian forces. Of these, 60,402 were Muslims. Korbel was a member of the United Nations Commission for India and Pakistan (UNCIP) 'during its early and critical days' (p. viii).

Alastair Lamb, *Birth of a Tragedy. Kashmir 1947*, Karachi, Oxford University Press, 1994, p. 60, states that 'over 20,000 of them [Poonchis] served in the Indian Army in World War I. In World War II, the number was far higher; at its end at least 60,000 ex-servicemen returned to the Jagir'.

Ian Stephens, *Pakistan*, London, Ernest Benn Limited, second (revised) edition, 1964, p. 199, relates that Indian recruiting authorities long ago noted the fighting qualities of the 'sturdy' Sudhans, one of the main Poonch tribes. According to Stephens, who was Editor of *The Statesman* in 1947, over 40,000 Sudhans served in the Indian Army during World War II.

G.M.D. Sufi, *Kashir. Being a History of Kashmir From the Earliest Times to Our Own*, Lahore, The University of Punjab, Volume II, 1949, p. 816, stated that J&K supplied 31,000 recruits to the British Indian Army out of which Punch (Poonch) was 'particularly prominent in … offering recruits'.

Richard Symonds, *The Making of Pakistan*, London, Faber and Faber, 1950, p. 157, confirms that the 'craggy, barren jagir' contributed the number of troops stated by Stephens (above).

Richard Symonds, *In the Margins of Independence; A Relief Worker in India and Pakistan (1941–1949)*, Karachi, Oxford University Press, 2001, p. 76, also states retrospectively but on the basis of diaries that he kept at the time (p. 4) that 70,000 Poonchis had served in the Indian Army 'during the [Second World W]ar'.

Hugh Tinker, *India and Pakistan. A Political Analysis*, New York, Frederick A. Praeger, 1962, p. 152, Footnote 1, notes that, before 1939, apart from Punjab, Nepal

# APPENDIX IV

and the United Provinces, 'Kashmir (Poonch Muslims)' was one of the 'other provinces' making 'important contributions' to recruitment for the Indian Army.

C.E. Tyndale Biscoe, *Kashmir in Sunlight & Shade*, London, Seeley, Service & Co., 'second and cheaper edition', 1925 [First published 1921?], p. 78, stated that 'Poonch state gave more recruits for the Indian army than any other part of the Indian Empire'. Biscoe was an educator in Srinagar.

Annex 7, 'Minutes of the Meeting with the Defence Minister of the "Azad Kashmir Government"', in United Nations Commission for India and Pakistan, 'Report of the Sub-committee on Western Kashmir', New York, Unpublished Restricted Document, 31 March 1949, pp. 70–1, states that, according to the Secretary to the [Azad Kashmir] Defence Department, 'Colonel [Mohammad] Hussein ... 65,000 Muslims from the [Azad Kashmir] State had fought in the Indian Army in World War II. 15,000 of these were now in the Pakistan Army'.

A reasonable figure for Poonchi and Mirpuri returnees from World War II seems to be at least 50,000. This is deduced from the evidence provided above.

# APPENDIX V

## PHYSICAL AND POLITICAL COMPOSITION
## OF J&K AFTER THE 1949 CEASEFIRE

The inconclusive fighting between Indian and pro-Pakistan forces over J&K ended with a United Nations-brokered ceasefire on 1 January 1949. Prior to this, India's military forces had mounted two major offensives in J&K in May 1948 and in late 1948, which gained it the upper hand and much territory. However, India failed to take possession of J&K's western and northern parts. Conversely, the pro-Pakistan forces comprising the Pakistan and Azad armies and residual Pukhtoons could not capture J&K's eastern and central portions. Indeed, one Azad Kashmiri believed that, had the pro-Pakistan forces not agreed to the ceasefire, they 'probably would have lost the rest of Poonch, Mirpur and Muzaffarabad' to Indian forces.[1] That is, they would have lost all of Azad Kashmir.

When the ceasefire on 1 January 1949 came into effect, fighting had divided the former princely state into Indian J&K and what I call Pakistan-Administered J&K. Indian J&K consisted of Jammu, the Kashmir Valley and Ladakh; Pakistan-Administered J&K comprised Azad Kashmir and the Northern Areas. While all of J&K nominally belonged to India as a result of Maharaja Hari Singh's accession, pro-Pakistan forces had obtained some 30,000 sq. miles of territory[2] while India had 'lost'—it had never actually possessed them physically—some 638 whole villages, forty-four part villages, four towns and 1.3 million people.[3] The area under Indian control was approximately 54,000 sq. miles, almost 70 per cent of which comprised Ladakh.

After the 1949 ceasefire, governments on both sides of the ceasefire line realigned the boundaries of various districts, and parts thereof, to incorporate changes forced on them by the loss or gain of territory and for administrative purposes. After these changes, Kathua District in (Indian) Jammu was the sole district with the same boundaries as at the time of the census of 1941. (The areas given in the tables below are in square miles.)

*Azad Kashmir*

The most obvious change to J&K was the creation of Azad Kashmir. It consisted of three districts: Mirpur, Poonch and Muzaffarabad. Poonch and Mirpur comprised territory from the former districts of Mirpur and Poonch Jagir in the former Jammu Province that had been liberated from Maharaja Hari Singh's control and then, subsequently, not lost to India. Muzaffarabad District comprised areas of Kashmir Province freed from the Maharaja's control and not recaptured by India. These included the former Muzaffarabad *tehsil* and a thin slice of Uri *tehsil*, both of which had been in Muzaffarabad District, plus some of the former Baramulla District.

Azad Kashmir did not extend to the other area of J&K under Pakistan's control: the liberated areas of Gilgit and Baltistan, later called the Northern Areas (NAs). This region was separated from Azad Kashmir around November 1947 and was directly administered by a political agent appointed by Pakistan. India claims Azad Kashmir and the Northern Areas. It calls them collectively Pakistan-Occupied Kashmir (POK), although it also sometimes uses this term to refer to Azad Kashmir exclusively.

Table V.1: Makeup of Azad Kashmir before and after 1947.

| District | 1941 size | New size | 1941 Pop. | New Pop.* | Comments |
|---|---|---|---|---|---|
| Muzaffarabad | 2,408 | 2,082 | 264,671 | 220,971 | New size had 260 sq. miles from Baramulla |
| Poonch# | 1,627 | 969 | 421,828 | 293,723 | – |
| Mirpur | 1,627 | 1,443 | 386,655 | 371,459 | – |
| Total | NIE | 4,494 | [1,073,154] | 886,153 | All Muslims, except 790 Hindus and others |

Sources: 1) *Census of India 1941*, Volume XXII, *Jammu & Kashmir State*, Part III, *Village Tables*, Srinagar, R.G. Wreford, Editor, Jammu and Kashmir Government, 1942;
2) *Census of Azad Kashmir, 1951*, Murree?, Iftikhar Ahmad, Chief Enumeration Officer, Government of Azad Kashmir, 1952.

Key: NIE  Not in existence.
　　 Pop.  Population, either of the whole district in 1941 or of the new, smaller district in 1951.
　　 *　　 According to the 1951 Azad Kashmir Census.
　　 #　　 Referred to as 'Punch' in the 1951 Azad Kashmir Census.

*Jammu Province*

Even though it had lost 2,412 sq. miles to Azad Kashmir, India still held the majority of Jammu Province after 1949. This was an area slightly larger than 10,000 sq. miles. (Indian) Jammu now comprised those districts that had a Hindu majority in 1947, plus Reasi District and those parts of the former Jammu Province's western districts of the *jagir* of Poonch and Mirpur that the Indian Army had recaptured from pro-Pakistan forces in bitter fighting. (Indian) Jammu also had an 'alternative' Poonch District, within which was located Poonch City, the major city in the former *jagir* of Poonch and the place to which many Hindus and Sikhs in western Jammu Province fled, after religious violence started in the province in 1947. India has always held Poonch City, despite it being heavily besieged

## APPENDIX V

by enemy elements in 1947–48. India's ability to use air power to resupply the city was the decisive factor in India's favour.

Major changes to Jammu Province's districts were made after the ceasefire. A new district called Doda was created out of Udhampur District's northern *tehsils* of Kishtwar and Bhaderwah, parts of the Chenani *jagir* and parts of Reasi *tehsil* in the former Reasi District. Doda was contiguous to Ladakh District and the Indian state of Himachal Pradesh. The much smaller Udhampur District inherited most of the Reasi *tehsil* and moved westwards to become the geographical heart of the province. Jammu District was enlarged by the inclusion of one village from Udhampur District and twenty-seven inhabited and nineteen uninhabited villages of Bhimber *tehsil* of Mirpur District. (India's) Poonch District became slightly larger with the inclusion of the former Reasi District's other *tehsil* of Rajauri and some residual parts of Kotli *tehsil* and Bhimber *tehsil*, previously in Mirpur District.

Table V.2: Makeup of (Indian) Jammu after the 1949 ceasefire.

| District** | 1941 size | New size | 1941 Pop. | New Pop.* | Comments |
|---|---|---|---|---|---|
| Jammu | 1,147 | 1,249 | 431,362 | 516,932 | – |
| Poonch | 1,627 | 1,689 | 421,828 | 326,061 | Old district lost 969 sq. miles to AK |
| Mirpur | 1,627 | In AK | 386,655 | See AK | Old district lost 1,443 sq. miles to AK |
| Udhampur | 5,070 | 1,732 | 294,217 | 254,061 | – |
| Reasi | 1,789 | NIE | 257,903 | NIE | To Poonch, Udhampur, Doda, Anantnag |
| Kathua | 1,023 | 1,023 | 177,672 | 207,430 | – |
| Chenani | 95 | Nil | 11,796 | NIE | To Doda and Udhampur |
| Doda | NIE | 4,380 | NIE | 268,403 | Newly created |
| Total JP | 12,378 | 10,073 | 1,981,433 | 1,572,887 | – |

Sources: 1) *Census of India 1941*, Volume XXII, *Jammu & Kashmir State*, Part III, *Village Tables*, Srinagar, R.G. Wreford, Editor, Jammu and Kashmir Government, 1942;
2) *Census of Azad Kashmir, 1951*, Murree?, Iftikhar Ahmad, Chief Enumeration Officer, Government of Azad Kashmir, 1952;
3) *Census of India 1961*, Volume VI, *Jammu and Kashmir*, Part I-A (i), *General Report*, Srinagar, M.H. Kamili, Superintendent of Census Operations Jammu and Kashmir, Census of India, 1968.

Key: AK   Azad Kashmir.
JP   Jammu Province.
NIE   Not in existence.
Pop.   Population, either of the whole district in 1941 or of the new district.
\*   Figures are from the 1961 Census of India.
\*\*   In descending order based on respective district populations in 1941 Census.

### Kashmir Province

As a result of fighting in Kashmir Province, India lost some 2,000 sq. miles of Muzaffarabad and Baramulla districts, mainly to Azad Kashmir, but also to Astore

# THE UNTOLD STORY OF THE PEOPLE OF AZAD KASHMIR

District in Pakistan's Gilgit and Baltistan region. There were also changes in (Indian) Kashmir after the ceasefire. A new district called Srinagar, based on the summer capital, was created. It comprised almost all of both the Khas *tehsil* of Anantnag District and the Badgam *tehsil* of Baramulla District, plus a small part of the Baramulla District's Baramulla *tehsil*. This was a logical move as Khas *tehsil* had previously been based around Srinagar City. Baramulla District picked up those areas of the Muzaffarabad District not in Azad Kashmir, plus a very small part of Anantnag District. Anantnag District acquired some villages from Udhampur District and a few villages from the Reasi *tehsil* of the defunct Reasi District.

Table V.3: Makeup of (Indian) Kashmir after the 1949 ceasefire.

| District | 1941 size | New size | 1941 Pop. | New Pop. | Comments |
|---|---|---|---|---|---|
| Baramulla | 3,317 | 2,536 | 612,428 | 604,659 | 260 sq. miles to AK; 276 to Astore |
| Anantnag | 2,814 | 2,097 | 851,606 | 654,368 | – |
| Muzaffarabad | 2,408 | In AK | 264,671 | See AK | 1,822 sq. miles to AK |
| Srinagar | NIE | 1,205 | NIE | 640,411 | Newly created |
| Total KP | 8,539 | 5,838 | 1,728,705 | 1,899,438 | – |

Sources: 1) *Census of India 1941*, Volume XXII, *Jammu & Kashmir State*, Part III, *Village Tables*, Srinagar, R.G. Wreford, Editor, Jammu and Kashmir Government, 1942;
2) *Census of Azad Kashmir, 1951*, Murree?, Iftikhar Ahmad, Chief Enumeration Officer, Government of Azad Kashmir, 1952;
3) *Census of India 1961*, Volume VI, *Jammu and Kashmir*, Part I-A (i), *General Report*, Srinagar, M.H. Kamili, Superintendent of Census Operations Jammu and Kashmir, Census of India, 1968.

Key: AK   Azad Kashmir.
      KP    Kashmir Province.
      NIE  Not in existence.
      Pop.  Population, either of the whole district in 1941 or of the new district.

*Frontier Districts Province*

There was no major reorganisation of the districts of the former Frontier Districts Province after the 1949 ceasefire. This was possibly due to their remoteness and their small populations. Another factor was that the only area really affected by fighting was the Kargil *tehsil* of Ladakh District. It had been divided by bitter clashes between pro-Pakistan forces and the Indian military to gain control of the strategic road from Srinagar to Leh, via Zoji La Pass, that went through the Kargil *tehsil*. Otherwise, India's Ladakh District still comprised one district, albeit reduced in size because of the loss of part of Kargil *tehsil* and all of Skardu *tehsil* to Pakistan-Administered Gilgit and Baltistan (later called the Northern Areas).

On the other (Pakistan-Administered) side of the former Frontier Districts Province, there was a minor adjustment to Astore District to include a former area of Baramulla District held by the pro-Pakistan forces. In the Gilgit Agency, the Survey of Pakistan was able to make more accurate calculations of the size of the

# APPENDIX V

Table V.4: Makeup of the Frontier Districts before and after 1947.

| District: Tehsil | 1941 size | New size | 1941 Pop. | New Pop. | Comments |
|---|---|---|---|---|---|
| Ladakh | ±45,762 | #I: 37,754 | 195,431 | I: 88,651 | 37,754 sq. miles under Indian control |
| –Ladakh | 29,848 | – | 36,307 | I: NP | All of tehsil under Indian control |
| –Kargil | 7,392 | I: NP | 52,853 | I: NP | Majority of tehsil under Indian control |
| | – | P: 1,596 | – | P: 14,579 | – |
| –Skardu | 8,522 | 8,522 | 106,271 | 110,583 | Tehsil under Pakistan administration |
| PAB total | – | 10,118 | – | 125,162 | Part Kargil Tehsil and all Skardu Tehsil |
| Astore | 1,632 | i) 1,690 | 17,026 | 22,258 | All below comprise PAG |
| | | ii) 276 | – | – | @From Baramulla District |
| Gilgit (LA) | 1,480 | 1,541 | 22,495 | 24,572 | |
| Gilgit Agency | | | | | |
| –Hunza | est 3,900 | est 3,900 | 15,341* | 15,691 | CEO sceptical of 'New Pop'. Figure |
| –Nagar | est 1,600 | est 1,600 | 14,874* | 18,353 | 10.11% increase over 1941 |
| –Punial | est 1,600 | 632 | 8,164* | est 8,990 | 16.18% increase over 1941 |
| –Ishkuman | est 1,600 | 1,018 | 4,282* | est 4,975 | Possibly not genuine: white ants ate |
| –Yasin | est 1,200 | 872 | 9,989* | 9,453 | 1,095 enumeration slips for both areas |
| –Kuh-Ghizar | est 1,980 | 2,020 | 8,512* | 8,249 | 4.53% increase over 1941 |
| –Chilas | est 2,800 | 1,635 | 15,364* | est 16,060 | |
| Agency total | 14,680 | 11,677 | 76,526 | 81,771 | 83,908?; 2,137 possibly missed in total |
| PAG total | – | 15,184 | 116,047 | 128,601 | – |
| Total | 63,554 | P: 25,302 | 311,478 | P: 253,763 | Census says 255,900; difference 2,137 |
| District | 1941 size | New size | 1941 Pop. | New Pop. | Comments |
| Ladakh | ±45,762 | #I: 37,754 | 195,431 | I: 88,651 | 37,754 sq. miles under Indian control |
| –Ladakh | 29,848 | – | 36,307 | I: NP | All of tehsil under Indian control |
| –Kargil | 7,392 | I: NP | 52,853 | I: NP | Majority of tehsil under Indian control |
| | – | P: 1,596 | – | P: 14,579 | – |

257

| | | | | | |
|---|---|---|---|---|---|
| –Skardu Tehsil | 8,522 | 8,522 | 106,271 | 110,583 | Tehsil under Pakistan administration |
| PAB total | – | 10,118 | – | 125,162 | Part Kargil Tehsil and all Skardu Tehsil |

Sources: 1) *Census of India 1941*, Volume XXII, *Jammu & Kashmir State*, Part III, *Village Tables*, Srinagar, R. G. Wreford, Editor, Jammu and Kashmir Government, 1942;
2) *Census of Azad Kashmir, 1951*, Murree?, Iftikhar Ahmad, Chief Enumeration Officer, Government of Azad Kashmir, 1952;
3) *Census of India 1961*, Volume VI, *Jammu and Kashmir*, Part I-A (i), *General Report*, Srinagar, M.H. Kamili, Superintendent of Census Operations Jammu and Kashmir, Census of India, 1968.

Key:
est   Estimate.
CEO   Chief Enumeration Officer.
I   India.
LA   Leased Area.
NP   Not provided.
P   Pakistan.
PAB   Pakistan–Administered Baltistan; in 1951, this region comprised Skardu Tehsil and that part of Kargil Tehsil not under Indian control.
PAG   Pakistan–Administered Gilgit; in 1951, this region comprised Astore, Gilgit (Leased Area) and the former Gilgit Agency as it existed in 1947.
Pop.   Population, either of the whole district in 1941 or of the new district.
*   Not given in the 1941 Census. Calculated by working back from district figures with percentage increase figures (given in 'Comments') provided in the 1951 Azad Kashmir Census.
#   1961 Indian estimate of territory under its control in the former Frontier Districts.
±   Revised by India in 1961 upwards by 1,555 sq. miles to 47,317 sq. miles.
@   According to the 1951 Azad Kashmir Census.

## APPENDIX V

various districts. According to the 1951 Azad Kashmir Census, the figures given in the 1941 Census were 'rough estimates'. The figures given in the 1951 Azad Kashmir Census were '... good for practical purposes but do not carry the stamp of the Government'.[4] Figures for Hunza and Nagar were still estimates because the Hunza-China border was not firm and the Hunza-Nagar border had not been established.

# APPENDIX VI

## CEASEFIRE LINE IN J&K

A United Nations-brokered ceasefire on 1 January 1949 ended the fighting in J&K between Indian and pro-Pakistan forces. In July 1949, Pakistan's and India's military representatives agreed a ceasefire line that formalised J&K's division. As described in more detail below, it snaked through J&K and divided Mirpur District and Poonch *jagir* in Jammu Province, Muzaffarabad and Baramulla districts in Kashmir Province, and Ladakh District in the Frontier Districts Province. While effective, the ceasefire line was also inefficient. According to the 1951 Azad Kashmir Census, 'Many areas are so torn between Azad Kashmir and India [sic] that the village habitation is on one side and its grazing grounds and sources of irrigation are on the other. Similarly, at places one has the forest and the other has the stream that served it for rafting timber.'[1] To observe military operations and violations along the ceasefire line, the United Nations sent a small group of observers, the United Nations Military Observer Group in India and Pakistan (UNMO-GIP).[2] It still monitors the line, which was renamed the Line of Control (LOC) after the 1971 India-Pakistan war.

*Ceasefire line described by the 1951 Azad Kashmir Census*[3]

'Starting in the bed of the seasonal stream immediately east of Dhuramdala village in Bhimber Tehsil, the cease-fire [sic] line ascends north, and turning west in the outer hills follows this direction until it sharply turns curves east near the village Siriah which is held by India. Dipping slightly into Kotli Tehsil it follows the course of the original boundary line between Punch and Reasi districts leaving which it plunges into Punch district taking away a large part of it, including the headquarters of the district [Punch Town] and of Mendhar Tehsil. Further on, it turns north-east until it touches the original boundary of Punch with Baramula [sic] district wherefrom it again zigzags due east to enter Uri Tehsil of which it brings a thin slice to Azad Kashmir until passing north of Pir Kanthi it descends to the river Jhelum following the course of the Urusa nullah. Across the river the line starts from a point almost opposite to the one at which it terminates on its left bank. Proceeding north-east the line passes over Chhota Qazinag and running for some distance the course of the boundary line between Muzaffarabad and

# THE UNTOLD STORY OF THE PEOPLE OF AZAD KASHMIR

Baramula [sic] districts drops abruptly to the left bank of the Kishenganga river at the point of Teethwal. Travelling north along the river for about six miles it leaves the river forming a bow the other end of which touches Keran. At Keran too the river takes the place of the cease-fire line for about the same length as at Teethwal. From Keran it zigzags east out of the limits of Muzaffarabad district emerging from which it dips deep into the north of Baramula [sic] district and passing over Chorwan (on the Gurez-Burzil-Astore route) it enters Ladakh district to bisect the Tehsil of Kargil. Taking a north-easterly course the line terminates over the glaciers of the Saltoro Range which is the western bulwark of the great Kara Korum [sic] Range'.

*Ceasefire line described by the 1961 Census of India*[4]

'[T]he Cease-fire Line, which starting from Kargil runs alongside the northern border of tehsil Sopore and enters Handwara detaching 14 1/2 of its villages. It then passes through Karnah intersecting the Domel-Uri Road and extends through Hajipir road to Haveli Tehsil. Beyond Heveli [sic], the line moves southwards splitting up the tehsils of Mendhar, Kotli and Bhimber.

'[The area under Indian control] was reduced by three districts, viz., Astore, Gilgit Leased Area and Gilgit Agency and five whole tehsils, viz., Muzaffarabad, Skardu, Mirpur, Bagh and Sudhnuti, as also 638 whole and forty-four part villages and four towns representing the residual parts of such of the tehsils which were split up by the Cease-fire Line. The aggregate area covered by these districts, tehsils and villages etc. as provisionally estimated stands at 32,358 sq. miles.

'The areas which fell on this side of the said line consisted of six whole districts, namely, Anantnag, Udhampur, Jammu, Kathua, Reasi and Chenani and district Baramulla less by 14 1/2 villages of Handwara tehsil, parts of district Muzaffarabad now constituting the tehsils of Uri and Karnah, part of district Ladakh consisting of tehsil Leh and a portion of Kargil tehsil, a part of tehsil Bhimber known as nayabat Chhamb and parts of split-up tehsils of Haveli, Mendhar and Kotli which together with the nayabat of Nowshera previously included in district Mirpur comprise the new Poonch district. In addition, village Mansar of tehsil Leh...[is occupied] by the Chinese.

'The Directorate of the Map Publications, Dehradun, have [sic] provisionally estimated the area on this side of the Cease-Fire Line at 53,664.9 square miles'.

*Area under Pakistan's administration*

The area of J&K under Pakistan's direct or indirect administration after the 1949 ceasefire included the entire districts of Astore, Gilgit (Leased Area) and Gilgit Agency and the entire tehsils of Muzaffarabad (Muzaffarabad District), Skardu (Ladakh District), Mirpur (Mirpur District) and Bagh and Sudhnoti (Poonch Jagir).[5] Pakistan's area also included land from:

- Kotli and Bhimber *tehsils* in Mirpur District and from Haveli and Mendhar *tehsils* in the Poonch *jagir*, both districts within Jammu Province;

# APPENDIX VI

- Uri and Karnah *tehsils* in Muzaffarabad District and Uttarmachipora (better known as Handwara) *tehsil* in Baramulla District, both districts within Kashmir Province;
- the Kargil *tehsil* of Ladakh District.

Astore, Gilgit (Leased Area), the Gilgit Agency and Skardu (Ladakh District) were directly administered by Pakistan as the Northern Areas. The other areas comprised Azad Kashmir, for which Pakistan officially controlled defence, foreign affairs, communications and coinage.

*Area under India's control*

India's area consisted of the other parts of those divided *tehsils* and districts that were not with Pakistan, plus the entire districts of Jammu, Kathua, Udhampur, Reasi and Chenani Jagir in Jammu Province, the entire district of Anantnag in Kashmir Province, and all of the Ladakh *tehsil* of Ladakh District in the Frontier Districts. India estimated this area to be 53,665 sq. miles.[6]

# APPENDIX VII

## MAIN OFFICE HOLDERS OF AZAD KASHMIR[1]

*Presidents (pre-'The Azad Jammu and Kashmir Government Act, 1970')*

| | |
|---|---|
| Sardar Muhammad Ibrahim Khan | 24 October 1947–31 May 1950 |
| Colonel (Retired) Ali Ahmad Shah | 31 May 1950–1 December 1951 |
| Mir Waiz Yusuf Shah | 5 December 1951–21 June 1952 |
| Colonel (Retired) Sher Ahmad Khan | 21 June 1952–31 May 1956 |
| Mir Waiz Yousuf Shah | 31 May 1956–6 September 1956 |
| Sardar Muhammad Abdul Qayyum Khan | 07 September 1956–13 April 1957 |
| Sardar Muhammad Ibrahim Khan | 13 April 1957–26 April 1959 |
| Mr K.H. Khurshid | 01 May 1959–5 August 1964 |
| Khan Abdul Hamid Khan | 07 August 1964–7 October 1969 |

*Chief Executive (appointed by General Yahya's martial law regime)*

| | |
|---|---|
| Major-General (Retired) Abdul Rehman Khan | 8 October 1969–11 November 1970 |

*President (and Chief Executive; operating under 'The Azad Jammu and Kashmir Government Act, 1970')*

| | |
|---|---|
| Sardar Muhammad Abdul Qayyum Khan | 12 November 1970–16 April 1975 |

(Qayyum lost office after a successful vote of no-confidence. The Speaker of the Legislative Assembly, Mr Manzar Masood, then acted as president until Sardar Muhammad Ibrahim Khan took office in May 1975. Concurrently, the political system in Azad Kashmir changed from a presidential system to a prime ministerial one.)

*President (titular head; operating under 'The Azad Jammu and Kashmir Interim Constitution Act, 1974', then during the start of General Zia's martial law regime)*

| | |
|---|---|
| Sardar Muhammad Ibrahim Khan | 29 May 1975–31 October 1978 |

# THE UNTOLD STORY OF THE PEOPLE OF AZAD KASHMIR

*Prime Minister (operating under 'The Azad Jammu and Kashmir Interim Constitution Act, 1974')*

Khan Abdul Hamid Khan					29 June 1975–11 August 1977

(Dismissed by President Ibrahim soon after Zia's regime took over in Pakistan.)

*Chief Executive and/or President (appointed by General Zia's martial law regime)*

| | |
|---|---|
| Major-General (Retired) Abdul Rehman Khan | 11 August 1977–30 October 1978 |
| Major-General (Retired) Muhd. Hayat Khan | 31 October 1978–February 1983 [sic] |
| Major-General (Retired) Abdul Rehman Khan | 01 February 1983–1 October 1985 |

*Prime Minister (operating post-General Zia's martial law regime under 'The Azad Jammu and Kashmir Interim Constitution Act, 1974')*

| | |
|---|---|
| Sardar Sikandar Hayat Khan | 17 June 1985–28 June 1990 |
| Raja Mumtaz Hussain Rathore | 29 June 1990–5 July 1991 |
| Sardar Muhammad Abdul Qayyum Khan | 29 July 1991–30 July 1996 |
| Barrister Sultan Mahmood Chaudhry | 30 July 1996–25 July 2001 |
| Sardar Sikandar Hayat Khan | 25 July 2001–23 July 2006 |
| Sardar Attique Ahmad Khan | 23 July 2006–6 January 2009 |
| Sardar Mohammad Yaqoob Khan | 6 January 2009–22 October 2009 |
| Raja Muhammad Farooq Haider Khan | 22 October 2009–26 July 2010 |
| Sardar Attique Ahmad Khan | 29 July 2010– |

*Presidents (titular heads; operating post-General Zia's martial law under 'The Azad Jammu and Kashmir Interim Constitution Act, 1974')*

| | |
|---|---|
| Sardar Muhammad Abdul Qayyum Khan | 01 October 1985–28 June 1990 |
| Sardar Muhammad Abdul Qayyum Khan | 26 August 1990–20 July 1991 |

(Ishaq Zafar and Abdur Rashir Abbassi respectively were interim presidents between Sardar Qayyum and Sardar Sikandar.)

Sardar Sikandar Hayat Khan			12 August 1991–25 August 1996

(End date not certain. Sikandar was re-elected president by the old electoral college just before the Legislative Assembly elections of 30 June 1996. He was ousted by a successful no-confidence motion at a joint sitting of the Azad Kashmir Council and the Azad Kashmir Legislative Assembly on 12 August 1996.)

| | |
|---|---|
| Sardar Muhammad Ibrahim Khan | 25 August 1996–25 August 2001 |
| Sardar Mohammed Anwar Khan★ | 25 August 2001–25 August 2006 |
| (★Major-General (Retired)) | |
| Raja Zulqarnain Khan | 25 August 2006– |

# APPENDIX VIII

## AZAD KASHMIR 'COUNCIL LEGISLATIVE LIST'

Under Section 31 (2), part (a) of *The Azad Jammu and Kashmir Interim Constitution Act, 1974*, the Azad Kashmir Council had 'exclusive power to make laws with respect to any matter in the Council Legislative List'.[1] This list comprised the Interim Constitution's 'Third Schedule, Council Legislative List' (given below).

Because Pakistan dominated the Azad Kashmir Council, this effectively gave Islamabad control over Azad Kashmir's affairs and a veto power on many issues, such as foreign affairs, nuclear matters and law and order issues. Under Section 31 (2), part (b), the Azad Kashmir Legislative Assembly (only) had the power to make laws with respect 'to any matter not enumerated in the Council Legislative list'.[2]

However, the powers of both the Azad Kashmir Legislative Assembly and the Azad Kashmir Council were also qualified by Section 31 (3) (provided at the end of this appendix). This denied both bodies the power to pass laws to do with foreign affairs (including UNCIP affairs), trade, defence and security, and currency. While it is unstated, these powers lie with Pakistan.

### *Third Schedule: Council Legislative List*[3]

1) Subject to the responsibilities of the Government of Pakistan under the UNCIP Resolutions, nationality, citizenship and [naturalisation], migration from or into Azad Jammu and Kashmir, and admission into, and emigration and expulsion from, Azad Jammu and Kashmir, including in relation thereto the regulation of the movements in Azad Jammu and Kashmir of persons not domiciled in Azad Jammu and Kashmir.
2) Post and Telegraphs, including Telephones, Wireless, Broad-casting [sic] and other like forms of Communication; Post Office Saving [sic] Bank.
3) Public debt of the Council, including the borrowing of money on the security of the Council Consolidated Fund.
4) Council public services and Council Public Service Commission.
5) Administrative courts for Council Subjects.
6) Council agencies and institutions for the following purposes, that is to say for research, professional or technical training, or for the promotion of special studies.

7) Nuclear energy, including: (a) mineral resources necessary for the generation of nuclear energy; (b) the production of nuclear fuels and the generation and use of nuclear energy; and (c) ionising radiations
8) Aircraft and air navigation, the provision of aerodromes; regulation and organization of air traffic and of aerodrome.
9) Beacons and other provisions for safety of aircraft.
10) Carriage of Passengers and goods by air.
11) Copyright, inventions, designs, trade marks and merchandise marks.
13) Opium so far as regards sale for export.
14) Banking, that is to say, the co-ordination with the Government of Pakistan of the conduct of banking business.
15) The law of insurance and the regulation of the conduct of insurance business.
16) Stock-exchange and future [sic] markets with object and business not confined to Azad Jammu and Kashmir.
17) Corporations, that is to say the incorporation, regulation and winding up of trading corporations including banking insurance and financial corporations, but not including corporations owned or controlled by Azad Jammu and Kashmir and carrying on business only within Azad Jammu and Kashmir or, co-operative societies, and of corporations, whether trading or not, with object not confined to Azad Jammu and Kashmir, but not including universities.
18) Planning for economic coordination, including planning and coordination of scientific and technological research.
19) Highways, continuing beyond the territory of Azad Jammu and Kashmir, excluding roads declared by the Government of Pakistan to be [of] strategic importance.
20) Council surveys including geological surveys and Council meteorological organizations.
21) Works, lands and buildings vested in, or in the possession of, the Council for the purposes of the Council (not being Military, Navel [sic] or air force works), but as regards property situate [sic] in Azad Jammu and Kashmir, subject always to law made by the Legislative Assembly, save in so far as law made by the Council otherwise provides.
22) Census.
23) Establishment of standards of weights and measures.
24) Extension of the powers and jurisdiction of members of a police force belonging to Azad Jammu and Kashmir or any Province of Pakistan to any area in such Province or Azad Jammu and Kashmir, but not so as to enable the police of Azad Jammu and Kashmir or such province to exercise powers and jurisdiction in such Province or Azad Jammu and Kashmir without the consent of the Government of that province or Azad Jammu and Kashmir; extension of the powers [of] jurisdiction of members of a police force belonging [to] the [sic] Azad Jammu and Kashmir or a Province of Pakistan to railway areas outside Azad Jammu and Kashmir or that province.
25) Election to the Council.

## APPENDIX VIII

26) The salaries, allowances and privileges of the members of the Council and [Advisors].
27) Railways.
28) Mineral [sic] oil natural gas; liquids and substances declared by law made by the Council to be dangerously inflammable.
29) Development of industries, where development under Council control is declared by law made by the Council to be expedient in the public interest.
30) Removal of prisoners and accused persons from Azad Jammu and Kashmir to Pakistan or from Pakistan to Azad Jammu and Kashmir.
31) Measures to combat certain offences committed in connection with matters concerning the Council and the Government and the establishment of [a] police force for that purpose [or the extension to Azad Jammu and Kashmir of the jurisdiction of a police force established in Pakistan for the investigation of offences committed in connection with matters concerning the Government of Pakistan.]
32) Prevention of the extension from Azad Jammu and Kashmir to Pakistan or from Pakistan to Azad Jammu and Kashmir of infections of contagious diseases or pests affecting men [sic], animals or plants.
33) Population planning and social welfare.
34) Boilers.
35) Electricity.
36) Newspapers, books and printing presses.
37) State Property.
38) Curriculum, syllabus, planning, policy, centers [sic] of excellence and standards of education.
39) Sanctioning of cinematograph films for exhibition.
40) Tourism.
41) Duties of customs, including export duties.
42) Taxes on income other than agricultural income.
43) Taxes on corporations.
44) Taxes on the capital value of the assets, not including taxes on capital gains on immovable property.
45) Taxes and duties on the production capacity of any plant, machinery, under taking [sic], establishment or installation in lieu of the taxes and duties specified in entries forty-two and forty-three or in lieu of either or both of them.
46) Terminal taxes on goods or passengers carried by railway or air; taxes on their fares and freights.
47) Fees in respect of any of the matters enumerated in this list, but not including fees taken in any court.
48) Jurisdiction and powers of all courts with respect to any of the matters enumerated in this list.
49) Offences against laws with respect to any of the matters enumerated in this list.
50) Inquiries and statistics for the purposes of any matters enumerated in this list.
51) Matters which under the Act are within the Legislative competence of the Council or relates to the Council.
52) Matters incidental or ancillary to any of the matters enumerated in this list.

*Section 31 (3)*[4]

Neither the Council nor the Assembly shall have the power to make any law concerning:

a) the responsibilities of the Government of Pakistan under the UNCIP Resolutions;
b) the defence and security of Azad Jammu and Kashmir;
c) the current coin or the issue of any bills, notes or other paper currency; or
d) the external affairs of Azad Jammu and Kashmir including foreign trade and foreign aid.

# APPENDIX IX

## COMPOSITION OF THE AZAD AND KASHMIR COUNCIL IN DECEMBER 2006*

| Member | Role | Period | |
|---|---|---|---|
| A) PM, Pakistan | Chairman | Ex officio | |
| B) President, AK | Vice Chairman | Ex officio | |
| C) PM, AK (or nominee) | Member | Ex officio | |
| D) Six AK members | Elected by AK Leg. Assembly | Date of Oath | Date of Expiry |
| 1) Raja Iftikhar Ayub | Member | 3.2.2006 | 2.2.2011 |
| 2) Sardar Naseim Ahmad Sarfaraz Khan | Member | 3.2.2006 | 2.2.2011 |
| 3) Sardar Farooq Sikandar | Member | 3.2.2006 | 2.2.2011 |
| 4) Mr Hamid Khan | Member | 3.2.2006 | 2.2.2011 |
| 5) Mr Ghulam Raza Shah Naqvi | Member | 9.9.2006 | 8.9.2011 |
| 6) Mr Parvaiz Ahkhtar | Member | 9.9.2006 | 8.9.2011 |
| E) Five Pakistan members** | PM Pakistan nominates | | Date of Nomination |
| 1) Major (Retired) Tahir Iqbal | Min. Kashmir Affairs and NAs | Ex officio | 25.4.2006 |
| 2) Mian Khurshid Mahmud Kasuri | Min. Foreign Affairs | | 2.9.2004 |
| 3) Mr Aftab Ahmad Khan Sherpao | Min. Interior | | 2.9.2004 |
| 4) Lt. Gen. (Retired) Javed Ashraf | Min. Education | | 2.9.2004 |
| 5) Sheikh Rashid Ahmad | Min. Railways | | 2.9.2004 |
| Advisors to the Chairman | PM Pakistan nominates | | Date of Nomination |
| 1) Raja Iftikhar Ayub | | | 9.9.2006 |
| 2) Sardar Naseim Ahmad Sarfaraz Khan | | | 9.9.2006 |
| 3) Sardar Farooq Sikandar | | | 9.9.2006 |

Source: *Composition of AJ&K Council*, no further publication details, obtained in Pakistan in December 2006.

# THE UNTOLD STORY OF THE PEOPLE OF AZAD KASHMIR

Key: AK      Azad Kashmir.
     Leg.     Legislative.
     Min.    minister.
     NAs    Northern Affairs.
     PM     prime minister.
     Retired  Retired
     *        The council composition will have changed after the election of the Pakistan People's Government at the 2008 Pakistan elections, although the Azad Kashmir representation may well still be the same.
     **      This shows only five Pakistan members when, according to Section 21 of *The Azad Jammu and Kashmir Interim Constitution Act, 1974*, there should be six: the five members nominated by the Pakistan prime minister, plus the ex-officio Minister for Kashmir Affairs and Northern Areas.

# APPENDIX X

## AZAD KASHMIR ADMINISTRATIVE SET-UP AND FUNCTIONS

Table X.1: Azad Kashmir Administration: as per the *Rules of Business 1985*.

| No. | Secretariat Department | Attached Departments | Head of Attached Department |
|---|---|---|---|
| 1 | Agriculture Department | i) Agriculture<br>ii) Animal Husbandry<br>iii) Hill Farming Technical Development Project | i) Director Agriculture<br>ii) Director Animal Husbandry<br>iii) Project Director, Hill Farming Technical Dev. Project |
| 2 | Cooperative Department | i) Co-operative [sic] Deptt.<br>★ii) A.K. Govt. Cooperative Bank Ltd. | i) Registrar Cooperative Societies<br>ii) ditto★★ |
| 3 | Communication & Works Department | i) P.W.D<br>★ii) Electricity Department | i) Chief Engineer, PWD<br>ii) Chief Engineer Electricity<br>iii) Electrical Inspector |
| 4 | Custodian Department | | Custodian |
| 5 | Education Department | i) Education Directorate Colleges<br>ii) Education Directorate Schools<br>★iii) A.K. Intermediate & Secondary Edu; Board Mirpur<br>★iv) University of Azad Jammu and Kashmir<br>v) Directorate of Sports | i) Director Education Colleges<br>ii) Director Education Schools<br>iii) Chairman A.K. Intermediate and Secondary Education Board Mirpur<br>iv) Vice Chancellor<br>v) Director Sports |
| 6 | Finance | i) Excise & Taxation<br>ii) Audit | i) Collector Excise & Taxation<br>ii) Accountant General |
| 7 | Forest Department | i) Forest Department<br>ii) Games [sic] Department<br>iii) Fisheries<br>iv) Tourism<br>v) Archeology [sic] | Chief Conservator of Forests<br>Director Tourism [sic] |
| 8 | Food Department | Food Directorate | Director Food |
| 9 | Health Department | Health Directorate | Director of Health Services |

| | | | |
|---|---|---|---|
| 10 | Home Department | i) Police<br>ii) Civil Defence<br>iii) Jails<br>iv) Armed Services Board<br>v) A.K.R.F. Affairs# | i) Inspector General of Police<br>ii) Director of Civil Defence<br>iii) Inspector General of Prisons<br>iv) Director Armed Services Board<br>v) do [sic] |
| 11 | Industries, Commerce, Mineral Resources and Labour Department | i) Industries<br>ii) Mineral Resources and Concessions<br>iii) Labour<br>iv) Printing & Stationery Deptt. | i) Director, Industries, Mineral Development and Labour Department<br>ii) Controller, Printing Press |
| 12 | Information Department | Information and Publicity | Director Information |
| 13 | Law Department | i) Law Occicers [sic]#<br>ii) Legislative Assembly<br>★iii) Supreme Court<br>★iv) High Court<br>★v) Shariat Court<br>vi) Council of Islamic Ideology | i) Secretary Law<br>ii) Secretary Assembly<br>iii) Chief Justice AJ&K<br>iv) Chief Justice<br>v) Chief Justice Shariat Court<br>vi) Chairman |
| 14 | Local Govt. and Social Welfare Department | i) Rural Development Programme<br>ii) Local Government<br>iii) Social Welfare | i) Director, Local Govt. and Social Welfare |
| 15 | Mangla Dam Affairs | Mangla Dam Affairs | Commissioner, Mangla Dam |
| 16 | Planning & Development Department | Planning & Development | Additional Chief Secretary/ Development Commissioner |
| 17 | Revenue Department | i) Revenue<br>ii) Land Settlement | i) Commissioner<br>ii) Commissioner Land Settlement |
| 18 | Rehabilitation | Rehabilitation | Rehabilitation Commissioner |
| 19 | Services and General Administration Department | i) A.K. Public Service Commission<br>★ii) Mirpur Development Authority<br>★iii) A.K.M.I.D.C#<br>★iv) AKLASC#<br>★v) Service Tribunal<br>vi) Mohtasib (Ombudsman)★★ | i) Chairman AK.P.S.C. [sic]<br>ii) Chairman M.D.A.<br>iii) Chairman A.K.M.I.D.C.<br>iv) Managing Director AKLASC<br>v) Chairman Service Tribunal.<br>vi) Mohtasib (Ombudsman) |
| 20 | Religious Affairs/ Auqaf, Ushar & Zakat Department | i) Religious Affairs/ Ammor-e-Dinya<br>ii) Auqaf<br>iii) Zakat & Ushar<br>★iv) zakat [sic] Council | i) Director Ammor-e-Dinya<br>ii) Director Auqaf<br>iii) Chief Administrator Zakat and Ushar<br>iv) Chairman Zakat Council |
| 21 | Transport Department | AJ&K Transport Authority | Chairman P.T.A.# |
| 22 | Anti-Corruption Department | Director Anticorruption [sic] | Director Anticorruption [sic] |

## APPENDIX X

| 23 | Prime Minister's Inspection Team | Prime Minister's Inspection Team | Chairman Prime Minister's Inspection Team |

\* These are Attached Departments for administrative [sic] and Financial purposes only otherwise these are not organs of Government but are independent bodies.

Source: 'Schedule I, List of Departments', *Rules of Business 1985*, Services & General Administration Department, Azad Government of the State of Jammu and Kashmir, Muzaffarabad, 1985, pp. 29–32.

Key: \*             asterisk contained in the original document.
    \*\*            Hand made alteration or addition in the original document.
    #             No further details available.
    AKLAS         Azad Kashmir Logging & Saw-Mills Corporation.
    A.K.M.I.D.C   Azad Kashmir Mineral and Industrial Development Corporation.
    A.K.R.F.      Azad Kashmir Regular Forces [see '15. HOME DEPARTMENT … No, 40' below].
    P.T.A.        Provincial Transport Authority.
    PWD/P.W.D.    Public Works Department.

Table X.2: Azad Kashmir Administration: as per the *Statistical Yearbook 1988* (as at 31.12.1988, with departments arranged in loose alphabetical order (as per the original), and with the total number of 'sanctioned posts' and four gradings given).

|    | Departments | Total | G 1–4 | G 5–15 | G 16 | G 17+ |
|----|---|---|---|---|---|---|
|    | Azad Kashmir | 47693 | 17316 | 26214 | 480 | 3683 |
|    | Percentage of the total | 100% | 36.31% | 54.96% | 1.01% | 7.72% |
| 1  | Agriculture | 963 | 561 | 331 | 1 | 70 |
| 2  | Accountant general | 370 | 55 | 267 | 25 | 23 |
| 3  | AKMIDC | 75 | 37 | 22 | 2 | 14 |
| 4  | Amoor-i-Dinia [Religious Affairs] | 86 | 33 | 30 | 1 | 22 |
| 5  | Animal Husband-ry [sic] | 914 | 636 | 194 | 3 | 81 |
| 6  | Assembly secretariat | 126 | 59 | 40 | 14 | 13 |
| 7  | Auqaf [Religious or Charitable Trusts] | 355 | 167 | 171 | 8 | 9 |
| 8  | Chairman Intermediate Board | 160 | 45 | 96 | 6 | 13 |
| 9  | Co-operative Societies | 139 | 42 | 87 | 2 | 8 |
| 10 | Civil Defence | 57 | 22 | 27 | 6 | 2 |
| 11 | Excise & Taxation | 229 | 122 | 94 | 3 | 10 |
| 12 | Education | 24063 | 3231 | 18510 | 119 | 2203 |
| 13 | Electricity | 2052 | 1254 | 742 | 10 | 46 |
| 14 | Election Commissioner | 35 | 13 | 17 | 1 | 4 |
| 15 | Election Commissioner (Local Bodies) | 8 | 3 | 4 | – | 1 |
| 16 | Finance | 65 | 18 | 33 | 3 | 11 |
| 17 | Food | 370 | 198 | 155 | 12 | 5 |
| 18 | Forestry | 1895 | 1173 | 597 | 52 | 73 |
| 19 | Health | 4257 | 2360 | 1518 | 36 | 343 |
| 20 | I.H.F.D.P. | 603 | 290 | 249 | 11 | 53 |
| 21 | Home Including Police & Jail Staff | 4473 | 3838 | 587 | 2 | 46 |
| 22 | Industries | 1050 | 573 | 430 | 25 | 22 |

| | | | | | | |
|---|---|---|---|---|---|---|
| 23 | Information | 62 | 19 | 30 | 4 | 9 |
| 24 | Judiciary | 412 | 196 | 167 | 12 | 37 |
| 25 | Local Govt. & Rrual [sic] Dev[elopment] | 602 | 139 | 410 | 4 | 49 |
| 26 | Law | 36 | 12 | 15 | 1 | 8 |
| 27 | M.D.A. | 157 | 62 | 76 | 4 | 15 |
| 28 | Printing Press | 108 | 55 | 51 | 1 | 1 |
| 29 | PWD | 1999 | 1334 | 559 | 16 | 90 |
| 30 | Planning & Dev[elopment] | 75 | 25 | 30 | 7 | 13 |
| 31 | Provincial Transport Authority | 21 | 7 | 12 | 2 | – |
| 32 | Public Service Commission | 21 | 8 | 9 | 2 | 2 |
| 33 | President Secretariat | 87 | 36 | 37 | 5 | 9 |
| 34 | Prime Minister Secretariat | 82 | 38 | 24 | 7 | 13 |
| 35 | Revenue | 566 | 274 | 233 | 36 | 33 |
| 36 | Services & General Administration | 106 | 49 | 31 | 7 | 19 |
| 37 | Supreme Court | 51 | 24 | 11 | 4 | 12 |
| 38 | Services Tribunal | 19 | 8 | 6 | 2 | 3 |
| 39 | Sports | 18 | 9 | 3 | 4 | 2 |
| 40 | Zakat & Ushar [Obligatory Payments for Muslims] | 84 | 28 | 45 | 5 | 6 |
| 41 | University of Azad Jammu & Kashmir | 842 | 263 | 264 | 25 | 290 |

Source: 'Table 99: Number of sanctioned posts by National pay scales groups and depaertments [sic] of the Azad Kashmir from 1985 to 1988', *Statistical Year Book 1988*, Muzaffarabad?, Planning & Development Department, Azad Government of the State of Jammu and Kashmir, 1989, pp. 216–18.

Key: +        Grade 17 and above.
  AKMIDC     Azad Kashmir Mineral and Industrial Development Corporation.
  G          Grade.
  I.H.F.D.P. Integrated Hill Farming Development Project.
  M.D.A.     Mangla Dam Authority.
  PWD/P.W.D. Public Works Department.

3) 'Distribution of business among Departments', as per *Rules of Business 1985*.[1]

Schedule—II.
(See Rule 3 (3)).
Distribution of business among Departments.

1. AGRICULTURE DEPARTMENT.

(a) Agriculture Education, Training and Research except University education.
(b) Experimental and demonstration farms;
(c) Improvement of Agricultural methods;
(d) Protection against insects and pests and prevention of plant diseases.
(e) Agricultural information and publications.
(2) [sic] Arbori cultural operations.
(3) Government gardens.
(4) Bee-keeping.

# APPENDIX X

(7) [sic] Service matters except those entrusted to Services and General Administration Department.
(5) [sic] Agriculture statistics.
(6) Hill Farming Technical Development Project.

## 2. ANIMAL HUSBANDRY.

(a) Improvement of livestock;
(b) Prevention of animal diseases;
(c) Veterinary training;
(d) Prevention of cruelty to animals;
(e) Dairy farming.

## 3. AUQAF DEPARTMENT.

(1) Administration of the Azad Kashmir Auqaf Act.
(2) Charitable and Religious Endowments.
(3) Religious Trusts.
(4) Mosques, Shrines and other religious institutions under the control of the Administrator Auqaf, Azad Kashmir.
(5) Religious Education Schemes.
(6) Publication of books on Islamyat [sic].
(7) Service matters, except those entrusted to Services and General Administration Department.

## 4. COMMUNICATIONS & WORKS DEPARTMENT.

(1) (a) Construction, equipment, maintenance, repairs and fixation of rent of all Government buildings, residential and non-residential, including Rest Houses, Circuit Houses and Government Guest Houses.
   (b) Public Health Engineering and Works pertaining to Government buildings.
(2) Construction, maintenance and repairs of roads, Bridges, Forries [sic], Tunnels, ropeways and causeways.
(3) Road fund.
(4) Laying standards and specification [sic] for various type [sic] of roads and Bridges for A.K.
(5) Inland waterways and inland navigation.
(6) Town planning.
(7) Town Development and housing.
(8) Irrigation:
   (a) tube-wells and other utilization schemes in areas;
   (b) embankments;
   (c) drainage;
   (d) storage of water and construction of reservoirs.
(9) Waterlogging schemes.
(10) Preparation of architectural plans, drawings of buildings of Azad Jammu and Kashmir Govt.
(11) Service matters, except those entrusted to Services and General Administration Department.

## 5. CUSTODIAN DEPARTMENT.

(1) Evacuee Property and Laws relating thereto.
(2) Control of Evacuee Funds.
(3) Service matters relating to the appointments and promotions etc. in the department to any extent i.e. at any level.
(4) Custodian shall be Ex-Officio Secretary of his Department.
(5) Grant of Proprietory [sic] Rights under the relevant laws.

## 6. CO-OPERATIVE DEPARTMENT.

(1) Co-operative Societies.
(2) Co-operative Banks.

## 7. COUNCIL OF ISLAMIC IDEOLOGY

(1) To make recommendations to the Government, the Assembly and the Council as to the ways and means of enabling and encouraging the Muslims of Jammu and Azad Kashmir to order their lives individually and collectively in all respects is [sic] accordance with the principles and concept of Islam as enunciated in the Holy Quran and Sunnah.
(2) To advise the Assembly, the Council and the President or the Government on any question referred to the Islamic Council as to whether a proposed law is or is not repugnant to the injunctions of Islam.
(3) To make recommendations as to the measures for bringing existing Laws into conformity with the injunctions of Islam and the Steps by which such measures should be brought into effect.
(4) To compile in a suitable form, for guidance of [sic] Assembly, the Council, the President and the Government such injunctions of Islam as can be given Legislative effect.

## 8. EDUCATION DEPARTMENT.

(1) School and College Education.-
  (a) Primary Education.
  (b) Secondary Education.
(2) University Education.
(3) Co-ordination of Schemes for higher studies abroad.
(4) Grant of Scholarships.
(5) Promotion of Art and literature.
(6) Technical Education and Research.
(7) Education of handicapped children specially, deaf, dumb and blind.
(8) Liberaries [sic].
(9) Historical or protected monuments maintained by or through the Azad Kashmir Government.
(10) Ancient manuscripts and historical records.
(11) Museums.
(12) Sports and physical culture.
(13) Youth and Culture.
(14) Service matters, except those entrusted to Services and General Administration Department.

## APPENDIX X

### 9. EXCISE AND TAXATION DEPARTMENT.
(1) Collection of Central Taxes.
(2) Collection of Provincial Taxes and Excise.

### 10. ELECTRICITY DEPARTMENT.
(1) Development, Generation supply and Distribution of hydel and thermal Power.
(2) Determination of rates of supply to consumers in bulk and otherwise prescribing tariffs.
(3) Acquisition and revocation of licences of electric undertakings.
(4) Administration of Electricity Act, 1910 [sic], as inforce [sic] in Azad Jammu and Kashmir and other Acts on the subject.
(5) Assessment and collection of revenue taxes on electricity.
(6) Preparation of Development Plans.
(7) Construction of Lt & Ht [sic] distribution lines and its [sic] maintenance.

### 11. FINANCE DEPARTMENT.
(1) Management of public funds i.e.-
   (a) supervision and control of Govt. finances;
   (b) preparation of Government budget;
   (c) preparation of supplementary estimates and demands for excess grants;
   (d) appropriation and re-appropriations; and
   (e) ways and Means.
(2) Public accounts and Public Accounts Committee.
(3) The framing of financial rules for guidance of Departments and supervision of maintenance of accounts.
(4) Floatation [sic] and administration of Public loans.
(5) Examination and advice on matters affecting directly or indirectly the finances of Azad Kashmir.-
(a) grants, contributions, other allowances and honoraria, contingencies, recoveries from and payment to Government departments and cases relating to money matters generally such as defalcations, embezzlements and other losses;
(b) emoluments, pensions and allowances;
(c) loans and advances to Government servants.
(6) Administration of public revenue save otherwise provided.
(7) Communication of financial sanctions.
(8) Examination of all proposals for the increase or reduction of taxation.
(9) Creation of new posts and Examination of Scehemes [sic] of new expenditure.
(10) Audit of receipt [sic] and expenditure.
(11) Public debt.
(12) The Local Audit Department.
(13) Treasuries and Sub-Treasuries.
(14) Service matters except those entrusted to Services and General Administration Department.

## 12. FOOD DEPARTMENT.

(1) Food procurement, Rationing and Distribution.
(2) Storage of food-grains.
(3) Civil Supplies.
(4) Control over the prices.
(5) Service matters except those entrusted to Services and General Administration Department.

## 13. FOREST DEPARTMENT.

(1) Forests (including Forest Protection, Forest Settlement, reforestation, erosion, denudat [sic] and Range Management.
(2) Levy of duty, fee [sic] etc on import of timber.
(3) Forest Production, import and export of forest products and recovery of dues.
(4) Budget and accounts statistics.
(5) Botanical Survey.
(6) Games.
(7) Protection of Wild birds, plants and animals.
(8) Fisheries.
(9) Tourism.
(10) Archeology [sic].
(11) Service matters, except those, [sic] entrusted to Services and General Administration Department.

## 14. HEALTH DEPARTMENT.

(1) Public health and sanitation.-
    (a) prevention and control of infectious and contigious [sic] diseases;
    (b) tuberculosis;
    (c) eradication/control of Malaria;
    (d) lepers [sic] Act;
    (e) treatment of patients bitten by rabid animals;
    (f) adultration [sic] of food stuffs;
    (g) mutrition [sic] surveys;
    (h) mutrition [sic] and publicity in regard to food;
    (i) vaccination and inocculation [sic];
    (j) maternity and child welfare; and
    (k) quarentine [sic].
(2) Medical Profession.-
    (a) regulation of medical and other professional qualification [sic] and standards;
    (b) medical registration;
    (c) indigenous system of medicines;
    (d) medical attendance on Government servants;
    (e) levy of fees by medical officers.
(3) Control of medical drugs, poisons and dangerous drugs (Drugs Act and Rules).
(4) Service matters, except those entrusted to Services and General Administration Department.

## APPENDIX X

### 15. HOME DEPARTMENT

(1) Public order and internal security.
(2) Political intelligence and censorship.
(3) Criminal Law and Criminal Law procedure.
(4) Criminal Lunatics.
(5) Evidence and Oaths.
(6) Arms, ammunition and military stores.
(7) Control of petroleum and explosives.
(8) Public amusement, control over places, performances and exhibitions.
(9) Crime reports.
(10) All matters connected with Police Establishment and administration including.-
  (a) police rules;
  (b) police Works;
  (c) grant of gallantry awards;
  (d) departmental examination of officers.
(11) Prisons, Remand Homes, transfer of prisoner [sic], State-political-prisoners, Good conduct, Prisoners and Probational Release Act.
(12) Extradition and deportation.
(13) Passports and permits.
(14) Civil Defence and A.R.P.[2]
(15) Compensation for loss of property or life due to civil commotion or while on duty.
(16) Rent control and requisitioning of property.
(17) Smuggling.
(18) Clubs.
(19) Collective fines.
(20) Hoarding and black-marketing.
(21) War Book.
(22) Civil Security Schemes.
(23) Commutation and remission of santences [sic]; and mercy petitions.
(24) Preventive detention and administration of press Laws.
(25) Presecution [sic] in respect of newspapers and other publication [sic].
(26) Border incidents including incidents where diplomatic action is required.
(27) Homeguard [sic] and territorial forces.
(28) Political prisoners.
(29) Recovery of missing persons.
(30) Prohibited maps.
(31) Matters connected with the Navy, Army or the Air Force of the Pakistan Marine service or any other armed forces.-
  (a) Territorial Force Act and Auxiliary Force Act;
  (b) varification [sic] of antecidents [sic] of persons employed in Defence Services;
  (c) camping ground; and
  (d) war injuries Scheme.
(32) Civil Armed Forces.
(33) Service matters, except those entrusted to Services and General Administration Department.

(34) Liason [sic] with Defence Authorities.
(35) Enforcement of provisions of Motor Vehicles Ordinance, 1971 and the Rules thereunder relating to control of traffic and inspection and checking of Motor Vehicles for the purpose of traffic control.
(36) Protection of key points and vital installations.
(37) Security Identity Cards.
(38) Armed Services, Board.
(39) Fauji Foundation.
(40) A.K.R.F. Affairs namely:-[3]

Recommendations for the grant of pensions, scholerships [sic] and gratuities etc. of A.K.R.F. personnel.

## 16. INDUSTRIES, COMMERCE & MINERAL RESOURCES AND LABOUR DEPARTMENT.

(1) Planning and Development of Industries, including Cottage Industries.
(2) Industries Research.
(3) Loan and subsidies to Industries.
(4) Industrial training, including Reavelling [sic] Demonstration parties.
(5) Industrial control.
(6) Control on the supplies and distribution of iron and steel.
(7) Industrial exhibition [sic] within the country.
(8) Survey of Industries.
(9) Trade and Commerce within Azad Kashmir, including Government Commercial undertakings, Merchandise Market Act, Insurance Act, Partnerships Act, Trade enquiries.
(10) All cases relating to Boilers Act, Patent and Designs Act, Explosive [sic] Act and Companies Act.
(11) Sericultures.
(12) Registration of Joint Stock Companies, Firms and Societies.
(13) Mines and Minerals.-
　(a) Development and Mineral Resources and regulation of Mines;
　(b) Minerals Rules; and
　(c) Grant and transfer of prospecting Licences and mining leases;
(14) Chambers and Associations of Commerce and Industry.
(15) Labour matters enclosing welfare of labour.
(16) Service matters, except those entrusted to Services and General Administration Department.

## 17. INFORMATION DEPARTMENT.

(1) publicity.
(2) public relations.
(3) production and distribution of films and documentaries of journals for educational interest in consultation with Department concerned.
(4) Service matters, except those entrusted of [sic] Services and General Administration Department.

## APPENDIX X

### 18. LAW DEPARTMENT.

(1) Conduct of Government litigation including.-
   (a) representations in criminal case;
   (b) appeals and applications for enhancement of sentences and convictions;
   (c) filing and defending civil suits against Government and public servants.
(2) Advice to Departments on all legal matters including interpretation of laws, rules and orders having the force of law.
(3) Government Law Officers, Advocate General, Public Prosecutors, Government Pleaders, Special Counsels, Appointment, transfer, leave, fee etc.
(4) Appointment of Notary Public.
(5) Matters relating to legal practitioners, including scale of fees.
(6) Matters relating to the approval of appointments of legal advisers and engagement of legal practitioners made by statutory bodies, payment of their fee and termination of their services.
(7) Defence of pauper [sic] accused in the courts and fees to pleader for such defence.
(8) Civil Law and Procedure.
(9) Matters relating to the Legislature including salaries, allowances and privileges of speaker, member, officials of the Assembly.
(10) Scrutnizing [sic] and drafting of bills, ordinances, notifications, rules, regulations, statutory orders and by-laws.
(11) Scrutiny of non official bills.
(12) Constitutional Legislation.
(13) Codification of laws and printing of Acts, Rules and Orders.
(14) All matters relating to Supreme Court, High Court, Shariat Court and Council of Islamic Ideology.
(15) Service matters, except those entrusted to the Services and General Administration Department.

### 19. LOCAL GOVERNMENT, RURAL DEVELOPMENT AND SOCIAL WELFARE DEPARTMENT.

(1) Matters relating to:-
   (a) district councils, Municipal Committees, Town Committes [sic], Union Councils, Halqa Councils and Illaqa Councils.
   (b) elections, Election Petitions, writ petitions and civil suits in regard to local bodies.
   (c) establishment and budget of Local Government and Rural Development Programme and Local Bodies except Grant-in-Aid for Hospital and Dispensaries.
   (d) directorate of Rural Development Programme and their subordinate officials.
   (e) local Taxation and Local Rates.
(2) Registration of Births, Deaths and Marriages by Local Councils and Local Bodies.
(3) Development Fund and Development Scheme Pertaining to Local Councils and Local Bodies.

(4) Grant-in-Aid for Local Councils and Local Bodies.
(5) Slaughter Houses under Local Councils and Local Bodies, (other than those in Cantonments).
(6) Local councils Service, including Engineering and Health Services under Local Government and Local Bodies.
(7) Framing of Rules, Regulations and by-laws under Municipal Act and other local laws.
(8) Ponds and prevention of cattle trespass.
(9) Census.
(10) Rural uplift.
(11) Burning grounds, burial grounds and Muslim graveyards not taken over by the Auqaf Department.
(12) Village Police.
(13) Co-ordination of Social Welfare Schemes.
(14) Urban community Development and other social Welfare projects, excluding Medical Social Welfare Projects.
(15) Orphanages.
(16) Eradication of Social Evils.
(17) Rehabilitation of handicapped and disabled adult-persons.
(18) Social Security.
(19) Water supply, drainage and sanitary Schemes.
(20) Co-ordination of the activities for the Welfare women-folk.
(21) Service matters, except those entrusted to Services and General Administration Department.

## 20. MANGLA DAM AFFAIRS.

(1) All matters such as administration, rehabilitation, compensation etc. of displaced persons from Mangla Dam areas.
(2) Problems of new towns and hamlets as a result of Mangla Dam.

## 21. PLANNING & DEVELOPMENT DEPARTMENT.

(1) Planning including policy and development.
(2) Co-ordination of technical assistance.
(3) Economic research.
(4) Co-ordination of statistics in general.
(5) Execution of all development schemes, programmes, and proposals submitted by other departments and making recommendations to Government thereon.
(6) To evaluate the progress of development schemes and their critical appraisal.
(7) Initiation of measures for giving suitable publicity to development Plan and educating the public on the results achieved from time to time.
(8) Service matters except those entrusted to Services and General Administration Department.

## 22. PRINTING AND STATIONERY DEPARTMENT.

(1) Government book department—Supply of official publications of the Azad Jammu and Kashmir Government and exchange of publications with Central and Provincial Governments of Pakistan.

(2) Establishment and Budget of Government Press and stationery office.
(3) Monthly income and expenditure statement of Government Press.
(4) Procurement of stationery (both indigenous and imported) and its supply to Department.
(5) Local purchase of stationery.
(6) Printing and stationery Mannual [sic].
(7) Printing, binding, private and Govt. press.
(8) Purchase, servicing, condemnation and disposal of waste paper.
(9) Allocation of stationery to Departments and disposal of waste paper.
(10) Procurement and Supply of Typewriters, Plain Paper Copiers, Calculators Adding and Accounting Machines to the Departments.
(11) Service matters, except those entrusted to Services and General Administration Department.

## 23. REHABILITATION DEPARTMENT.
(1) Rehabilitation of refugees.
(2) Evacuee property, its allotment etc. as warranted by Law.

## 24. REVENUE DEPARTMENT.
(1) Land Revenue administration.-
   (a) assessment and collection of revenue, development cess and surcharges thereon and agriculture income tax;
   (b) land surveys and record of rights, including restriction over transfer of title;
   (c) alienation of revenue;
   (d) laws regarding land tenures (Special remission of land revenue and remission under sliding scale).
   (e) religious endownment [sic] of land;
   (f) escheats; and
   (g) pre-emption Law.
(2) Scheme relating to grant of land to retired and retiring Government servants.
(3) Taccavi, land improvement and other agricultural loans.
(4) Compulsory acquisition of land, Land Acquisition Act and Rules made thereunder, rent control;
(5) Demarcation and rectangulation [sic] of land;
(6) Leases of ferries and bridges;
(7) Treasurer trove;
(8) Matters connected with the recruitment, training, pay, allowances, promotions, leave, posting and transfers of revenue field staff and district and Sub-Divisional establishment (Ministerial), except those entrusted to Services and General Administration Department.
(9) Copying Department;
(10) Stamps and Court fees, Jidicial [sic] and non judicial;
(11) Famine Relief Fund and relief for other natural calimities. [sic] e.g. earthquakes, floods and conflagrations;

(12) Debt Conciliation Boards;
(13) Land Laws;
(14) Settlement and re-assessment;
(15) Tenency [sic] Law and relations between landlord [sic] and tenants;
(16) Waterlogging and salinity other than schemes relating thereto.
(17) Unification of Land Laws.
(18) Budget and accounts.
(19) Territorial adjustments and changes.
(20) Boundary disputed [sic].
(21) Rehabilitation of war displaced persons.
(22) Lamberdars.
(23) Wages census.
(24) Location etc. of paidawar-e-Arazi (Usher).
(25) Questions of domicile and applications for state subject.
(26) Service matters except those entrusted to Services and General Administration Department.

## 25. RELIGIOUS AFFAIRS DEPARTMENT.

(1) Islamic laws.
(2) Religious Affairs.
(3) Advice to Departments on all Religious matters including interpretation of laws of Islam.
(4) Preaching of Islam.
(5) Nazam-e-Salaat.
(6) All matters relating to Hajj.
(7) Policy matters regarding syallbous [sic] and examination of Deni Maddaras (Religious Schools).
(8) Research work for Auqaf, Council of Islamic Ideology and Usher-o-Zakat Departments, and guidance in implementation of Islamic Laws as and when asked for.
(9) Service matters except those entrusted to Services and General Administration Department.

## 26. SERVICES AND GENERAL ADMINISTRATION DEPARTMENT.

(1) Cabinet work including.-
  (a) Cabinet—appointments, salaries and privileges of Ministers; and
  (b) all Secretarial work of Cabinet including convening of meetings.
(2) General co-ordination.
(3) Honours, awards and Sanads for public service.
(4) Sypher [sic] and other Codes.
(5) Ceremonials, including.-
  (a) warrant of precedents and table of precedence protocol [sic].,
  (b) Azad Kashmir Flag Rules;
  (c) Civil Uniforms;
  (d) liveries and clothing rules.
(6) Holidays.

# APPENDIX X

(7) Office management; including;-
   (a) civil secretariat and Government offices, generally;
   (b) secretariat standing orders; and
   (c) memorials and petitions standing orders.;
   (d) Azad Jammu and Kashmir Management Group Service.
(8) Preparation of civil list.
(9) service [sic] Rules relating to various Services and Posts, and interpretation thereof.
(10) Registration and Recognition of service Associations.
(11) Rights and interest of members of service.
(12) Subject to the Schedule VII,[4] matters connected with the recruitment, training, pay, allowances, promotion, leave, posting and powers of.-
   (i) the Ministerial establishment of the A.K. Secretariat; and
   (ii) the Azad Kashmir Secretariat Service; and
   (iii) All Pakistan unified grade/Deputationist [sic] etc.
(13) Re-employment of retired officers;
(14) appointment [sic] of commissions of inquiry or panel of officers in cases of misconduct of Government servants.
(15) Organization [sic] and method; including.-
   (a) periodic review of the organisation [sic], staff functions and procedure of the Departments, attached Departments and Subordinate officers, and suggestions for improvement thereof.,
   (b) improvement of General efficiency and economic execution of Government business.,
   (c) advice regarding proper utilization of stationery and Printing resources of the Government.
   (d) training in Organizations [sic] and Methods.
(16) Public Service Commission.
(17) Framing and alteration of Rules of Business for Azad Kashmir Government and allocation of business among Ministers.
(18) Inspection teams.
(19) Compilation of the list of persons debarred from further employment under [sic] the Azad Kashmir Government.
(20) Policy regarding expenditious [sic] disposal of land acquisition case.
(21) Departmental examinations;
(22) Inservice [sic]/pre-service training of ministerial employees and Section Officers (probationers).
(23) Matters connected with Training at the National Institution of Public Administration, Lahore and Karachi and Pakistan Academy for Rural Development Peshawar (Divisional Level Courses).
(24) Technical Assistance Recruitment Programme.
(25) Distribution of Provincial quota of motor cars.
(26) Official Language Committee.
(27) High Officers Reservations.
(28) Identity cards for civil officers.
(29) Compilation of the list of persons debarred from further employment under [sic] the Government for submission to the Government of Pakistan.

(30) Compilation of the statement showing protection of the interest of minority communities for submission to the Government of Pakistan.
(31) Absorption of surplus staff and allied matters.
(32) Expeditious finalization of delayed pension and G.P Fund cases (Pension cases disposal Committee).
(33) Training of staff dealing with the pension and G.P Fund cases.
(34) Employees Welfare Schemes.
(35) Employees Demands.
(36) Group Insurance Scheme.
(37) Selection Board for the Secretariat.
(38) Selection Board for Heads of Attached Department.
(39) Services Tribunal.
(40) West [sic] Pakistan Essential Services Maintenance Act.
(41) Observance of National Days.
(42) Provision of Official public address system.
(43) Redress of grievances of members of Public and Government employees against the Administration.

## 27. TRANSPORT DEPARTMENT.

(i) Administration of the Azad Kashmir Motor Vehicles Ordinance excepting enforcement of provisions relating to control of traffic and inspection and checking of Motor Vehicles for the purpose of traffic control.
(ii) Matters relating to Azad Jammu and Kashmir Transport Authority.

## 28. ZAKAT AND USHAR DEPARTMENT.

(1) Administration of Zakat and Ushar.
(2) Assessment and collection of Zakat and Ushar.
(3) Service matters except those entrusted to Services and General Administration Department.

## 29. ANTI-CORRUPTION DEPARTMENT.

Prevention of corruption under relevant laws.

## 30. PRIME MINISTER'S INSPECTION TEAM.

(1) Inspection of All Government Departments, Autonomous, Semi-autonomous and local bodies except the following:
(a) matters decided and awaiting disposal before a judicial Quasi/Judicial forum;
(b) any work of judicial/Quasi-Judicial nature.
(2) Cognizance of any important matter of public interest.
(3) To entertain complaints except those relating to service matter of Government Servants etc.
(4) Special assignments under the orders of the Prime Minister.
(5) Inspection of Development Projects.
(6) Review of the progress of ADP.[5]
(7) To put up recommendations to the Prime Minister.

Note: Any requisition made or assistance sought by the Chairman or by the Inspection Team in this regard shall be complied with promptly by all concerned.

# APPENDIX XI

## AZAD KASHMIR'S ACTUAL ADMINISTRATION AND POPULATION, 1988–2008

Table XI.1: Azad Kashmir administrative set up, populations 1988 and 2008, population growth rate 1988–2008, and population density.

| Division and area (sq kms) | Pop. 1998 Census | Districts, area (sq kms), %A | Pop. 1988 Census | Pop. 2008, projected* | %I | PD | Sub Districts |
|---|---|---|---|---|---|---|---|
| Muzaffarabad: 6,117 | 955,000 | Muzaffarabad: 2,496; 18.8% | 620,000 | 817,000 | 2.8 | 327 | Muzaffarabad Hattian Patika Leepa |
| | | Neelum: 3,621; 27.2% | 126,000 | 166,000 | 2.8 | 46 | Athmaqum Sharda |
| Poonch: 2,792 | 1,237,000 | Poonch: 855; 6.4% | 411,000 | 512,000 | 2.24 | 599 | Rawalakot Hajira Thorar Abbasput |
| | | Bagh: 1,368; 10.3% | 393,000 | 479,000 | 2.0 | 350 | Bagh Haveli Dhirkot Harigal |
| | | Sudhnuti: 569; 4.3% | 224,000 | 272,000 | 1.99 | 478 | Pallandri Mang Torarkhal Baloch |
| Mirpur: 4,388 | 1,490,000 | Mirpur: 1,010; 7.6% | 334,000 | 411,000 | 2.09 | 406 | Mirpur Dudyal |
| | | Bhimber: 1,516; 11.4% | 302,000 | 390,000 | 2.6 | 257 | Bhimber Barnala Samahni |
| | | Kotli: 1,862; 14% | 563,000 | 727,000 | 2.59 | 390 | Kotli Fatehpur-Thakiala Sehnsa Charhoi |
| Azad Kashmir: 13,297 | 3,682,000 | Total: 8: 13,297 | 2,973,000 | +3,774,000 | 2.41 | 284 | Total: 27 |

# THE UNTOLD STORY OF THE PEOPLE OF AZAD KASHMIR

Source: *Azad Kashmir at a Glance*, 2008, Muzaffarabad, Planning & Development Department, Azad Govt. of the State of Jammu & Kashmir, 2008, www.pndajk.gov.pk/glance.asp [accessed 15 September 2010].

Key: Pop. Population.
     PD   Population density per square kilometre.
     %A  District's area as a percentage of Azad Kashmir's area.
     %I   Percentage increase in population between 1998 and 2007.
     *    Projected from figures in 1998 Azad Kashmir Census.
     +    This figure given as 3,772,000 in original document.

# APPENDIX XII

## ASPECTS OF THE AZAD KASHMIR BUDGETS

Table XII.1: Azad Jammu & Kashmir Council Development Programme 2006–2007, Summary.

| | Sector | Ongoing projects | New projects | Total |
|---|---|---|---|---|
| 1 | Roads and Bridges | Rs. 162.8 million | Rs. 37.5 million | Rs. 200.3 million |
| 2 | Office Buildings | Rs. 9.4 million | Rs. 210 million | Rs. 219.4 million |
| 3 | Residential Buildings | Rs. 37 million | Rs. 30 million | Rs. 67 million |
| 4 | Community Uplift Schemes | Rs. 82.3 million | Rs. 4 million | Rs. 86.3 million |
| 5 | Education | Rs. 30 million | Rs. 18.2 million | Rs. 48.3 million |
| 6 | Package for Kashmiri Refugees | Rs. 38.7 million | Nil | Rs. 38.7 million |
| 7 | Members' Development Programme | Nil | Rs. 90 million | Rs. 90 million |
| 8 | Block Provision | Nil | Rs. 150 million | Rs. 150 million |
| Total | | Rs. 360.2 million | Rs. 539.7 million | Rs. 900 million |

Source: *Azad Jammu & Kashmir Council Development Programme 2006–07*, Development & Works Wing, Azad Jammu & Kashmir Council Secretariat, Islamabad, 2006?, p. 1.

Table XII.2: Comparison of revenue spent or accrued in 2005–06 (as per Revised Estimates), and budgeted to accrue or spend in 2006–07 (as per Budget Estimates), by Azad Kashmir Departments.

| Departments: Revenue | RE 2005–2006 | BE 2006–2007 | Departments: Spending | RE 2005–2006 | BE 2006–2007 |
|---|---|---|---|---|---|
| Excise Tax & Duty | 820.000 M | 950.000 M | General Admin | 846.951 M | 741.461 M |
| Revenue (nfd) | 6.400 M | 6.500 M | Land Revenue | 51.340 M | 52.640 M |
| Stamps | 127.000 M | 130.000 M | Stamps | 5.175 M | 5.013 M |
| Forest | 225.000 M | 400.000 M | Forest | 187.985 M | 244.665 M |
| Income from Registration | 2.800 M | 3.000 M | Information | 30.375 M | 26.885 M |
| Armed Services Board | 0 | 4.500 M | Armed Services Board | 14.013 M | 15.892 M |
| Admin of Justices | 10.000 M | 13.500 M | Admin of Justice | 138.950 M | 149.570 M |
| Police | 30.000 M | 30.000 M | Police | 988.060 M | 986.570 M |
| Prisons | 0.300 M | 0.300 M | Prisons | 44.740 M | 34.345 M |
| Education | 33.500 M | 40.000 M | Education | 3913.500 M | 4074.500 M |
| Health | 4.800 M | 6.000 M | Health | 943.450 M | 1025.460 M |
| Agriculture | 1.800 M | 2.500 M | Agriculture | 162.270 M | 166.710 M |
| Animal Husbandry | 4.000 M | 5.000 M | Animal Husbandry | 153.130 M | 159.725 M |
| Co-Operatives | 0 | 0.020 M | Co-Op Societies | 19.552 M | 20.692 M |
| Industries | 18.000 M | 19.000 M | Industries | 46.593 M | 50.008 M |
| Sericulture | 0.600 M | 0.600 M | Sericulture | 20.853 M | 21.868 M |
| Miscellaneous | 235.452 M | 48.000 M | Miscellaneous | 261.435 M | 413.210 M |
| Public Works Department | 65.000 M | 70.000 M | Public Works Department | 758.790 M | 702.090 M |
| Electricity | 2210.000 M | 2600.000 M | Electricity | 2689.350 M | 2987.120 M |
| Government Printing Press | 6.000 M | 6.000 M | Printing Press | 17.740 M | 19.590 M |
| Amoor-I-Dinia (Religious Affairs) | 13.000 M | 14.000 M | Amoor-I-Dinia (Religious Affairs) | 37.404 M | 39.016 M |
| Food | 160.000 M | 170.000 M | Food | 39.010 M | 44.990 M |
| Tourism/Wildlife | 1.200 M | 1.500 M | Tourism/Wildlife | 32.498 M | 35.533 M |
| Total 1 (AK Revenue) | 3974.852 M | 4520.420 M | Rehabilitation | 371.111 M | 372.587 M |
| Mangla Dam Royalty | 696.600 M | 663.300 M | LG&RD | 82.865 M | 88.475 M |
| 80% Share from AK Council | 2065.000 M | 2272.000 M | Pension | 610.000 M | 615.000 M |

| | | | | | |
|---|---|---|---|---|---|
| Share Of Federal Taxes | 2887.511 M | 3317.000 M | SW & Women Uplift | 63.590 M | 65.765 M |
| Federal Aid for Deficit Budget | 2765.767 M | 3158.080 M | Civil Defense | 16.680 M | 18.260 M |
| Net capital receipts | 915.270 M | Nil | Sports | 10.690 M | 11.260 M |
| Total 2 (Pak Revenue) | 9330.148 M | 9410.380 M | State Trading | 746.900 M | 741.900 M |
| Total Revenue | 13,305.000 M | 13,930.800 M | Total Spending | 13,305.000 M | 13,930.800 M |

Source: *Azad Kashmir at a Glance*, undated, Muzaffarabad, Planning & Development Department, Azad Govt. of the State of Jammu & Kashmir, 2007?, www.pndajk.gov.pk/glance.asp [accessed 25 February 2009], p. 1, [subsection] 'Budget 2007': [Unnumbered Table] 'Total General Revenue Receipts in AJK 2005–06 & 2006–07 Rs. (Millions)' and [Unnumbered Table] 'Total General Estimates & Revised Estimates of Normal Expenditures in 2005–06 & 2006–07 Rs. (Millions)'.

Key: Admin Administration.
AK Azad Kashmir.
BE Budget Estimate (2006–2007).
LG&RD Local Government and Rural Development.
M Million/s.
nfd no further details.
Pak Pakistan.
RE Revised Estimate (2005–2006).
SW Unknown: Social Work?

# APPENDIX XIII

## CROSSING PROCESS BETWEEN AZAD KASHMIR AND INDIAN J&K[1]

Number of people who have officially crossed the Line of Control from 15 November 2005 until 28 November 2006:
- from Azad Kashmir to Indian J&K: 2,134;
- from Indian J&K to Azad Kashmir: 2,020.

From 15 November 2005 until 28 November 2006, 4,785 applied in Azad Kashmir to cross the LOC:
- 3,882 applications approved by the Azad Kashmir authorities were passed to Indian J&K authorities for their clearance/approval;
- 3,965 applications were passed by the Indian J&K authorities to Azad Kashmir authorities for clearance/approval.

Allowable purposes/reasons to cross the LOC:
- visit to relatives;
- visit to friends;
- for religious purposes;
- for tourism.

Azad Kashmir Government servants are not permitted to cross the LOC.

Crossing points:[2]
1. Chilehana-Tithwal [Nauseri-Tithwal]; Neelum Valley, Muzaffarabad District;
2. Chakothi-Uri; Muzaffarabad District (popular);
3. Haji Pir-Silikot [Hajipur-Uri]; Bagh District;
4. Rawalakot-Poonch; Poonch District (popular);
5. Tattapani [-Poonch]; Poonch District: located about 8 kms further south than the Rawalakot-Poonch crossing point; it was not operational in December 2006 owing to rain washing out the road; people from Kotli, Mirpur and Bhimber would normally use this crossing.

The process:
- five designated crossing authorities in Azad Kashmir for each crossing point:
- the local crossing authority is an officer of 17/18 grade in the Azad Kashmir Government, usually from the Revenue Department, but the officer at Rawalakot is the District Veterinary Officer;

- applicants must complete a simple form comprising: name; address; name and address of relative/contact on the other side of the LOC; number of days away;
- completed forms are recorded, cleared and approved in Azad Kashmir;
- approved forms are then passed to the concerned authority in Indian J&K—and vice versa;
- it takes a month to clear a form in Azad Kashmir and in Indian J&K—but the whole approval process can take up to three months;
- a list of approved applicants is passed between authorities in Azad Kashmir and Indian J&K on a regular basis;
- the next crossing day after their application is approved by the other side, a successful applicant can cross at one of the approved crossing points;
- crossing days and times are determined by the respective designated crossing authority: apparently there are no set dates;
- people can change money at crossing points but usually they carry/use USD.

Table XIII.1: Cross-LOC Trade Items.

|   | *From Indian J&K* | *From Azad Kashmir* |
|---|---|---|
| 1 | Carpets | Rice |
| 2 | Rugs | Jahnamaz (prayer rugs) and Tusbies (prayer beads) |
| 3 | Wall Hangings | Precious Stones |
| 4 | Shawls and Stoles | Gabbas (wool floor coverings) |
| 5 | Namdas (cotton floor coverings) | Namdas |
| 6 | Gabbas | Peshawari leather chappals (footwear) |
| 7 | Embroidered items, including crewel | Medicinal Herbs |
| 8 | Furniture including walnut furniture | Maize and maize products |
| 9 | Wooden handicrafts | Fresh fruits and vegetables |
| 10 | Fresh fruits and vegetables | Dry fruits including walnuts |
| 11 | Dry fruits including walnuts | Honey |
| 12 | Saffron | Moongi (pulses) |
| 13 | Aromatic plants | Imli (tamarind) |
| 14 | Fruit bearing plants | Black Mushroom |
| 15 | Dhania (coriander), Moongi, Imli, Black Mushrooms | Furniture including walnut furniture |
| 16 | Kashmiri spices | Wooden handicrafts |
| 17 | Rajmah (pulses) | Carpets and rugs |
| 18 | Honey | Wall hangings |
| 19 | Paper Mache products | Embroidered items |
| 20 | Spring, Rubberised Coir/ Foam Mattresses cushions, pillows and quilts | Mattresses cushions, pillows and quilts |

# APPENDIX XIII

| 21 | Medicinal Herbs | Shawls and stoles |
|---|---|---|

Source: Smruti S. Pattanaik and Arpita Anant, *Cross-LoC Confidence Building Measures between India and Pakistan: A Giant Leap or a Small Step towards Peace?*, Institute for Defence Studies and Analyses, Issue Brief, February 2010, www.idsa.in/system/files/CrossLoCCBMbetweenIndiaandPakistan.pdf [accessed 20 March 2010].

Notes: Pattanaik and Anant's source is 'Standard Operating Procedure (SOP) for Cross-LoC Trade'. In their document, 'Indian J&K' is called 'J&K'; 'Azad Kashmir' is called 'Pakistan-Occupied Kashmir'.[3]

# APPENDIX XIV

## MATTERS RE AZAD KASHMIR ELECTIONS, PARTICULARLY IN 2006

Table XIV.1: Summation of Azad Kashmir Legislative Assembly Elections 2006.[1]

| | | | |
|---|---|---|---|
| Total voters | 2,407,467 | Total seats | 49 |
| Men voters | 1,286,016 | Directly elected seats | 41 |
| Women voters | 1,133,517 | Special (reserved) seats | 5 Women 3 Others |
| Constituencies | 29 in Azad Kashmir 12 in Pakistan for J&K Refugees | Total candidates: (per party below) | 369 |
| Parties | 17 | Muslim Conference | 40 |
| Polling stations | 3,746 | Peoples [sic] Muslim League | 37 |
| Polling booths | 5,442 | Pakistan People's Party–AK | 36 |
| Polling assistants | 14,428 | MMA | 33 |
| Polling officers | 7,214 | MQM | 23 |
| Presiding officers | 4,857 | Independents & Others | 200 |

Key: AK  Azad Kashmir.
     MMA  Muttahida Majlis-e-Amal (United Council of Action).
     MQM  Muttahida Qaumi Movement (United National Movement).

Table XIV.2: Candidates and Positions of Major Parties in 2006 Azad Kashmir Legislative Assembly.[2]

| Parties | MC | PML | PPPAK | MMA | MQM | Inds & Others |
|---|---|---|---|---|---|---|
| Candidates | 40 | 37 | 36 | 33 | 23 | 200 |
| Seats | 28 | 4 | 8 | Nil | 2 | 7 |

Key: Inds  Independents.
     MC  Muslim Conference.
     MMA  Muttahida Majlis-e-Amal (United Council of Action).
     MQM  Muttahida Qaumi Movement (United National Movement).
     PML  Peoples Muslim League-AJK.
     PPPAK  Pakistan People's Party–Azad Kashmir

# THE UNTOLD STORY OF THE PEOPLE OF AZAD KASHMIR

Table XIV.3: Breakdown of results for the 2006 Azad Kashmir election.[3]

| Party | Constituency (DE) | AKE | Non AKE | Constituency (IE) | Total |
|---|---|---|---|---|---|
| MC | 22 | 15 | 7 | 6 | 28 |
| PPPAK | 6 [7]* | 6 [7]* | – | 1 | 7 [8]* |
| PML | 4 | 3 | 1 | – | 4 |
| Independent | 6 [5]* | 4 [3]* | 2 | – | 6 [5]* |
| MQM | 2 | – | 2 | – | 2 |
| JKPP | 1 | 1 | – | – | 1 |
| JUI | – | – | – | 1 | 1 |
| Total | 41 | 29 | 12 | 8 | 49 |

Key: 
- AKE — Azad Kashmir electorates.
- DE — Constituency directly elected by voters on 11 July 2006.
- IE — Constituency indirectly elected by members of the Legislative Assembly on 21 July 2006.
- JKPP — Jammu & Kashmir People's Party.
- JUI — Jamiat Ulmah Islam [possibly the Pakistan Jamiat ulmah-i-Islam Jammu & Kashmir].
- MC — All Jammu and Kashmir Muslim Conference.
- MQM — Muttahida Qaumi Movement (United National Movement).
- Non AKE — Non Azad Kashmir electorates, i.e. electorates for J&K refugees in Pakistan.
- PML — Peoples Muslim League-AJK.
- PPPAK — Pakistan People's Party-Azad Kashmir.
- * — Figures in brackets refer to the official Azad Jammu and Kashmir website that shows that Seat 24 belongs to a PPPAK representative.

Table XIV.4: List of Members of the Azad Kashmir Legislative Assembly in 2006 as a result of the elections and one by-election and their possible *biradari*.[4]

| | Constituency (DE) | Name | Party | Biradari |
|---|---|---|---|---|
| 1 | Mirpur I | Chaudhry Muhammad Yousaf | MC | Jat |
| 2 | Mirpur II | Chaudhry Abdul Majeed | PPPAK | Jat |
| 3 | Mirpur III | Sultan Mahmood Chaudhry | PML | Jat |
| 4 | Mirpur IV | Rukhsar Ahmad | MC | Jat |
| 5 | Bhimber I | Muhammad Shafique Jarral | MC | Jarral or Mirza |
| 6 | Bhimber II | Ali Shan Chaudhry | Independent | Jat |
| 7 | Bhimber III | Chaudhry Anwar-ul-Haq | PML | Jat |
| 8 | Kotli I | Malik Muhammad Nawaz Khan | MC | Malik |
| 9 | Kotli II | Muhammad Naeem Khan | MC | Rajput |
| 10 | Kotli III | Raja Naseer Ahmad Khan | MC | Rajput |
| 11 | Kotli IV | Major (Retired) Munsaf Dad Khan | MC | Rajput |

## APPENDIX XIV

| | | | | |
|---|---|---|---|---|
| 12 | Kotli V | Raja Nisar Ahmad Khan | MC | Rajput |
| 13 | Bagh I | Sardar Attiq Ahmad Khan | MC | Abbasi |
| 14 | Bagh II | Raja Muhammad Nasim Khan | MC | Rajput |
| 15 | Bagh III | Sardar Qamar-uz-Zaman Khan | PPPAK | Mughal |
| 16 | Bagh IV | Chaudhry Muhammad Aziz | Independent | Gujjar |
| 17 | Poonch & Sudhnoti I | Sardar Abdul Qayyum | MC | Niazi or Sudhan |
| 18 | Poonch & Sudhnoti II | Sardar Ghulam Sadiq Khan | PPPAK | Sudhan |
| 19 | Poonch & Sudhnoti III | Haji Muhammad Yaqoob Khan | Independent | Sudhan |
| 20 | Poonch & Sudhnoti IV | Sardar Khalid Ibrahim Khan | JKPP | Sudhan |
| 21 | Poonch & Sudhnoti V | Dr Muhammad Najeeb Naqi Khan | MC | Sudhan |
| 22 | Poonch & Sudhnoti VI | Sardar Farooq Ahmad Tahir | MC | Sudhan |
| 23 | Neelum I | Abdul Waheed | PPPAK | Mughal |
| 24 | Muzaffarabad I | Begum Noreen Arif | Independent | Rajput |
| 25 | Muzaffarabad II | Syed Ghulam Murtaza Gillani | MC | Gillani |
| 26 | Muzaffarabad III | Muhammad Hanif Awan | PPPAK | Awan |
| 27 | Muzaffarabad IV | Chaudhry Latif Akbar | PPPAK | Gujjar |
| 28 | Muzaffarabad V★ | Raja Farooq Haider Khan | MC | Rajput |
| 29 | Muzaffarabad VI | Muhammad Rasheed | PML | Gujjar |
| 30 | Jammu & Others I | Muhammad Tahir Khokhar | MQM | Khokhar |
| 31 | Jammu & Others II | Chaudhry Muhammad Ismail | MC | Gujjar |
| 32 | Jammu & Others III | Hamid Raza | MC | Gujjar? |
| 33 | Jammu & Others IV | Chaudhry Muhammad Siddique | MC | Not known |
| 34 | Jammu & Others V | Muhammad Akbar Chaudhry | Independent | Gujjar |
| 35 | Jammu & Others VI | Raja Muhammad Siddique | MC | Rajput |
| 36 | Kashmir Valley I | Gul Muhammad Bhut | MQM | Kashmiri |
| 37 | Kashmir Valley II | Ghulam Mohi-ud-Din Dewan | PML | Kashmiri |
| 38 | Kashmir Valley III | Syed Shoukat Ali Shah | MC | Syed |
| 39 | Kashmir Valley IV | Shah Ghulam Qadir | MC | Syed |
| 40 | Kashmir Valley V | Muhammad Sanaullah Qadri | MC | Kashmiri or Qureshi |
| 41 | Kashmir Valley VI | Abdul Majid Khan | Independent | Pathan |

|    | Constituency (IE) | Name | Party*** | |
|----|---|---|---|---|
| 42 | Reserved for Women | Miss Shazia Khatoon | PPPAK | Not known |
| 43 | Reserved for Women | Mrs Shamin Ali | MC | Not known |
| 44 | Reserved for Women | Mrs Naheed Tariq | MC | Not known |
| 45 | Reserved for Women | Mrs Mehrul Nissa | MC | Not known |
| 46 | Reserved for Women | Mrs Nasreen Rani | MC | Not known |
| 47 | O/s J&K State Subjects | Mr Mahmood Riaz | MC | Not known |
| 48 | Technocrats & OP | Mr Abdul Rasheed Abbasi | MC | Not known |
| 49 | Religious Scholars** | Mr Pir Muhammad Atiq-ur-Rahman | JUI | Not known |

Sources: 1) Election details based on election documents obtained by me, and on Chief Election Commissioner, Azad Jammu & Kashmir Election Commission, H.# 256-A, ST.# 30, SEC.F-10/1, ISLAMABAD, *Notification [of election results] dated 15/07/2006* and *Notification [of election results] dated 19/07/2006*, unpublished election documents obtained by me while in Azad Kashmir in December 2006. Also available (with some variations, changes and updates) at 'List of Members Legislative Assembly 2006-Todate', *Azad Jammu and Kashmir Government*, http://www.ajk.gov.pk/site/index.php?option=com_content&task=view&id=2618&Itemid=142 [accessed 29 October 2007].

Key: 
- DE — Constituency directly elected by voters on 11 July 2006.
- IE — Constituency indirectly elected by members of the Legislative Assembly on 21 July 2006.
- JKPP — Jammu & Kashmir People's Party.
- JUI — Jamiat Ulmah Islam [possibly the Pakistan Jamiat ulma[h?]-i-Islam Jammu & Kashmir].
- J&K — Jammu and Kashmir.
- MC — All Jammu and Kashmir Muslim Conference.
- MQM — Muttahida Majlis-e-Amal (United Council of Action).
- OP — Other professionals, i.e., seat reserved for technocrats and other professionals.
- O/s — Overseas, i.e., seat reserved for J&K State Subjects residing overseas.
- PML — Peoples Muslim League-AJK.
- PPPAK — Pakistan People's Party-Azad Kashmir.
- * — Muzaffarabad V was initially won by Muhammad Ishaq Zafar (a Gujjar) of PPPAK. He died on 2 September 2006 while leader of the opposition in the Legislative Assembly.[5] The by-election held on 28 October 2006 was won by Raja Farooq Haider from the All Jammu and Kashmir Muslim Conference.[6]
- ** — Seat reserved for religious scholars, i.e. Ulema-e-Din or Mushaikh.
- *** — Party affiliations obtained from the official Azad Jammu and Kashmir website.[7]
- ~ — Possible only, as a result of a brief discussion by me while in Azad Kashmir in December 2006 with an electoral official. The official was very quickly able to nominate a *biradari* for each member based on his personal knowledge, although these details may not necessarily be accurate, as such details are not sought as part of the electoral process.

APPENDIX XIV

*Some discrepancies in the table XIV.4:*

The official Azad Jammu and Kashmir website, as updated on 4 November 2006, shows that:[8]

1) seats 17–20 are for representatives from Poonch; seats 21 and 22 are for representatives from Sudhnoti;
2) seat 23 is shown as one of those allocated to 'Muzaffrabad' [sic];
3) the member for Seat 24, 'Begum Naureen Arif', is a member of the PPPAK;
4) seat 36 is one of seven allocated to 'Jammu & Others'. It should be part of those allocated to the 'Kashmir Valley'. Both 'regions' have six seats each in the Azad Kashmir Legislative Assembly.

Table XIV.5: 2006 Azad Kashmir Legislative Assembly Candidates, Parties and Constituency-wise Details.[9]

| | Constituency | Total voters | Candidates | Party | Winner | Party | Votes |
|---|---|---|---|---|---|---|---|
| 1 | Mirpur I | 37987 | Ch. M. Yousaf | MC | Ch. M. Yousaf | MC | 6928 |
| | | | Ch. Umar Farooq | PPPAK | | | |
| | | | Afsar Shaid | PML | | | |
| | | | Masud ul Haq | MMA | | | |
| | | | Masaud Khalid | Ind | | | |
| 2 | Mirpur II | 35371 | Cap. r. Sarfaraz | MC | Abdul Majeed | PPPAK | 10154 |
| | | | Abdul Majeed | PPPAK | | | |
| | | | Ch. Arif | PML | | | |
| | | | Saud Iqbal | MMA | | | |
| | | | Nazir Inqalabi | Ind | | | |
| 3 | Mirpur III | 51802 | Arshid Mahmood G | MC | B. Sultan Mahmood | PML | 14937 |
| | | | Mirza Afzal Jiral | PPPAK | | | |
| | | | B. Sultan Mahmood | PML | | | |
| | | | Dr Riaz Ahmed | MMA | | | |
| | | | Imran Sheikh | MQM | | | |
| 4 | Mirpur IV | 46793 | Ch. Rukhsar Ahmed | MC | C. Rukhsar Ahmed | MC | 16150 |
| | | | Ch. Muhammad Shf | PPPAK | | | |
| | | | Ch. Arshad | PML | | | |
| | | | Hussain | MMA | | | |
| | | | Raja Mukhtar Abasi | Ind | | | |
| | | | Abdulaziz, Zulfeqar | | | | |
| 5 | Bhimber I | 63071 | Mirza Shafiq Jiral | MC | M. Shafiq Jiral | MC | 15443 |
| | | | Ch. Pervaiz Ashraf | PPPAK | | | |
| | | | Colonel Abdul Gani | PML | | | |
| | | | Lon | MQM | | | |
| | | | M. M. Zubair | | | | |
| 6 | Bhimber II | 57541 | Raja Raziq Ahmed | MC | Ali Shan Ch. | Ind | 15310 |
| | | | Ch. Waheed Akram | PPPAK | | | |
| | | | Ch. M. Rashid | PML | | | |
| | | | Tahir Mahmood | MMA | | | |
| | | | Ali Shan Ch. | Ind | | | |

| # | Constituency | Votes | Candidates | Party | Winner | Party | Votes |
|---|---|---|---|---|---|---|---|
| 7 | Bhimber III | 77099 | Ch. Tariq Farooq | MC | Ch. Anwar ul Haq | PML | 25140 |
| | | | Raja Qasir | PPPAK | | | |
| | | | Ch. Anwar ul Haq | PML | | | |
| | | | Ch. M. Ali Akhtar | MMA | | | |
| 8 | Kotli I | 75375 | Malik M. Nawaz | MC | Malik M. Nawaz | MC | 19314 |
| | | | Aftab Anjum | PPPAK | | | |
| | | | Malik Yousaf | PML | | | |
| | | | Malik Zarat | Ind | | | |
| 9 | Kotli II | 68744 | Sardar Naeem Khan | MC | S. Naeem Khan | MC | 22794 |
| | | | Sardar Khizar Hayat | PPPAK | | | |
| | | | Ch. Ilyas | PML | | | |
| | | | Mahmood Ahmed | MMA | | | |
| 10 | Kotli III | 74306 | Raja Nasir Ahmed | MC | Raja Nasir Ahmed | MC | 26539 |
| | | | Ch. Mazhar Hussain | PPPAK | | | |
| | | | Bashir Pahlwan | PML | | | |
| | | | Gulam Raza | MMA | | | |
| 11 | Kotli IV | 78474 | Mr Munsif Dad | MC | Maj. Munsif Dad | MC | 20227 |
| | | | Ch. M. Yasin | PPPAK | | | |
| | | | Shoukat Farid | PML | | | |
| | | | Raja Mushtaq | MMA | | | |
| 12 | Kotli V | 70504 | Raja Nisar Ahmed | MC | Raja Nisar Ahmed | MC | 16582 |
| | | | Matloob Inqalabi | PPPAK | | | |
| | | | Rafiq Naiar | PML | | | |
| | | | Habiburahman Afaqi | MMA | | | |
| | | | Shkeel Raza, G. Ra | Ind | | | |
| 13 | Bagh I | 73403 | Sardar Atiq A. Khan | MC | Sardar Atiq A Khan | MC | 21595 |
| | | | Ajaz Mubashir | PPPAK | | | |
| | | | Raja Sijad Ahmed | PML | | | |
| | | | M. Saleem Ajaz | MMA | | | |
| | | | Mr Khleeq Lateef | Ind | | | |
| 14 | Bagh II | 64481 | Raja Naseem Khan | MC | Raja Naseem Khan | MC | 10812 |
| | | | S. Qamaruzaman | PPPAK | | | |
| | | | S. Arshad Azad | PML | | | |
| | | | Rashid Turabi | MMA | | | |
| 15 | Bagh III | 54250 | S. Amir Akbar Khan | MC | S. Qamaru Zaman | PPPAK | 13082 |
| | | | S. Qamaruzaman | PPPAK | | | |
| | | | S. Amjid Yousaf | PML | | | |
| | | | Tanveer Anwar | MQM | | | |
| 16 | Bagh IV | 75069 | M. Alim Rizvi | MC | Ch. Abdul Aziz | Ind | 18120 |
| | | | R. Khursheed Rathor | PPPAK | | | |
| | | | F. Mumtaz Rathor | PML | | | |
| | | | Ali Raza Bukhari | MMA | | | |
| | | | Ch. Abdul Aziz | Ind | | | |
| 17 | Poonch I | 61612 | S.A. Qayoum Niazi | MC | S.A. Qayoum Niazi | MC | 11947 |
| | | | S. Asgar Afandi | PPPAK | | | |
| | | | Yasin Gulshan | PML | | | |
| | | | Gulam M. Minhas | MMA | | | |
| 18 | Poonch II | 58769 | Khan Bahdur Khan | MC | S. Gulam Sadiq | PPPAK | 14458 |
| | | | S. Gulam Sadiq | PPPAK | | | |

# APPENDIX XIV

|    |             |       |                    |       |                    |       |       |
|----|-------------|-------|--------------------|-------|--------------------|-------|-------|
|    |             |       | S. Hayat Khan      | PML   |                    |       |       |
|    |             |       | M. Kamaludin       | MMA   |                    |       |       |
| 19 | Poonch III  | 71832 | Sardar Tahir Anwar | MC    | Haji S. Yaqoub     | MCH   | 10909 |
|    |             |       | S. Ashraf Khan     | PPPAK |                    |       |       |
|    |             |       | S. Abid Hussain    | PML   |                    |       |       |
|    |             |       | S. Ajaz Afzil      | MQM   |                    |       |       |
|    |             |       | Haji S. Yaqoub     | MCH   |                    |       |       |
| 20 | Poonch IV   | 63219 | S. Sayab Khalid    | MC    | S. Khalid Ibrahim  | JKPP  | 9194  |
|    |             |       | S. Khalid Ibrahim  | JKPP  |                    |       |       |
|    |             |       | S. Tahir Akram     | PML   |                    |       |       |
|    |             |       | P. Abdul Razaq     | MMA   |                    |       |       |
|    |             |       | S. Sagir Chugtai   | Ind   |                    |       |       |
| 21 | Sudhnoti I  | 68798 | Dr Najeeb Naqi     | MC    | Dr. Najeeb Naqi    | MC    | 21160 |
|    |             |       | S. Abdul Majid     | PPPAK |                    |       |       |
|    |             |       | S. M. Hussain      | PML   |                    |       |       |
|    |             |       | Abdul Raouf Sabir  | MMA   |                    |       |       |
|    |             |       | S. Altaf           | MCH   |                    |       |       |
| 22 | Sudhnoti II | 64733 | S. Farooq Tahir    | MC    | S. Farooq A. Tahir | MC    | 17889 |
|    |             |       | S. Manzoor Asim    | PPPAK |                    |       |       |
|    |             |       | S. Rafiq           | PML   |                    |       |       |
|    |             |       | Malik M. Hussain   | MMA   |                    |       |       |
|    |             |       | S. Akhtar Rubani   | Ind   |                    |       |       |
| 23 | Neelum I    | 76760 | Gul e Khandan      | MC    | M. Abdul Waheed    | PPPAK | 21312 |
|    |             |       | Mian Abdul Waheed  | PPPAK |                    |       |       |
|    |             |       | Ch. Rasheed        | PML   |                    |       |       |
|    |             |       | S. Mazhar Hussain S| MMA   |                    |       |       |
|    |             |       | Shah Wali Awan     | MQM   |                    |       |       |
| 24 | Muzaffar-   | 58694 | Mir Ali Akbar      | MC    | Noreen Arif        | Ind   | 12608 |
|    | abad I      |       | Jawaid Ayoub       | PPPAK |                    |       |       |
|    |             |       | M.M. Hasan         | MMA   |                    |       |       |
|    |             |       | Noreen Arif, Ishtiaq | Ind |                    |       |       |
| 25 | Muzaffar-   | 48603 | Murtaza Gilani     | MC    | G. Murtaza Gilani  | MC    | 9290  |
|    | abad II     |       | Bazil Naqvi        | PPPAK |                    |       |       |
|    |             |       | Sajad Gilani       | PML   |                    |       |       |
|    |             |       | Mufti Bashir K     | MMA   |                    |       |       |
|    |             |       | Abdul Wahid        | Ind   |                    |       |       |
| 26 | Muzaffar-   | 45925 | Malik Arfan        | MC    | M. Hanif Awan      | PPPAK | 7841  |
|    | abad III    |       | M. Hanif Awan      | PPPAK |                    |       |       |
|    |             |       | Kh. Farooq Ahmed   | PML   |                    |       |       |
|    |             |       | S. Aqeel ur Rahman | MMA   |                    |       |       |
|    |             |       | Fida Rathor        | MQM   |                    |       |       |
| 27 | Muzaffar-   | 74644 | Raja Ibrar         | MC    | Ch. Latif Akbar    | PPPAK | 13599 |
|    | abad IV     |       | Ch. Latif Akbar    | PPPAK |                    |       |       |
|    |             |       | Ch. Shafqat        | PML   |                    |       |       |
|    |             |       | Q. Shahid Hameed   | MMA   |                    |       |       |
|    |             |       | Raja Abdul Qayoum  | Ind   |                    |       |       |
| 28 | Muzaffar-   | 67257 | R. Farooq Haider   | MC    | M. Ishaq Zafar     | PPPAK | 21793 |
|    | abad V      |       | M. Ishaq Zafar     | PPPAK |                    |       |       |
|    |             |       | Ch. Shahnawaz      | PML   |                    |       |       |

| # | Constituency | | Candidates | Party | Winner | Party | Votes |
|---|---|---|---|---|---|---|---|
| 29 | Muzaffar-abad VI | 61059 | Dewan Chugtai | MC | Ch. M. Rasheed | PML | 10332 |
| | | | Arif Mughal | PPPAK | | | |
| | | | Ch. Rasheed | PML | | | |
| | | | Hafiz Atiq Awan | MMA | | | |
| | | | Rafaqat Awan | Ind | | | |
| 30 | Jammu & Others I | 68076 | S. Abdul Aziz | MC | M. Tahir Khokhar | MQM | 18919 |
| | | | Dr Ahsan Manzar M | PPPAK | | | |
| | | | Maqsood uzaman | MMA | | | |
| | | | M. Tahir Khokhar | MQM | | | |
| 31 | Jammu & Others II | 106543 | Ch. M. Ismaeel | MC | Ch. M. Ismaeel | MC | 14105 |
| | | | Ch. Maqbool Ahmed | PML | | | |
| | | | S. Abdul Razaq | MMA | | | |
| 32 | Jammu & Others III | 120811 | Hafiz Hamid Raza | MC | Hafiz Hamid Raza | MC | 18850 |
| | | | Faiz Malik | PPPAK | | | |
| | | | Suhail Gujar | PML | | | |
| 33 | Jammu & Others IV | 96580 | Ch. Sadiq Bati | MC | Ch. Sadiq Bati | MC | 20863 |
| | | | M. Hussain | PML | | | |
| | | | Shahmim Akhtar | MMA | | | |
| 34 | Jammu & Others V | 78213 | Ch. Zubair | PPPAK | M. Akbar Ch. | Ind | 41402 |
| | | | Akbar Ibraheem | PML | | | |
| | | | M. Akbar Ch. | Ind | | | |
| 35 | Jammu & Others VI | 75808 | Raja Sadiq | MC | Raja Sadiq | MC | 11348 |
| | | | Akram Shah | PPPAK | | | |
| | | | Amin Chugtai | PML | | | |
| | | | Raja Jahangir | MMA | | | |
| | | | K. Mustfa, R. Mujhid | Ind | | | |
| 36 | Kashmir Valley I | 5944 | Abdul Manan | MC | Saleem But | MQM | 2859 |
| | | | M. Iqbal Kashmiri | PPPAK | | | |
| | | | Rustam Shaikh | PML | | | |
| | | | Saleem But | MQM | | | |
| 37 | Kashmir Valley II | 6662 | M. Yousaf Shah | MC | Gulam Mahioudin | PML | 1104 |
| | | | Gulam Mahioudin | PML | | | |
| 38 | Kashmir Valley III | 3789 | S. Shoukat Shah | MC | S. Shoukat Shah | MC | 775 |
| | | | S M Shah | PML | | | |
| | | | Gulam Sarwar | MMA | | | |
| 39 | Kashmir Valley IV | 5310 | Shah Gulam Qadir | MC | Shah Gulam Qadir | MC | 1094 |
| | | | Asim But | PPPAK | | | |
| | | | Iqbal Qurashi | PML | | | |
| | | | Iltaf Hussain | MMA | | | |
| 40 | Kashmir Valley V | 7509 | M. Sana Ulah Qadri | MC | M. Sana Ulah Qadri | MC | 2057 |
| | | | Iqbal Razaq But | PPPAK | | | |
| | | | Arif Shah | PML | | | |
| | | | Gulam Mustafa | MMA | | | |
| 41 | Kashmir Valley VI | 6042 | Abdul L. Salhariya | MC | Majid Khan | Ind | 1629 |
| | | | Muhamad Arshad | PML | | | |
| | | | Noor ul bari | MMA | | | |
| | | | Majid Khan | Ind | | | |

Key (not all abbreviations are spelt out):
Ch.     Chaudhry.

## APPENDIX XIV

| | |
|---|---|
| Ind | Independent. |
| JKPP | Jammu & Kashmir People's Party. |
| J&K | Jammu and Kashmir. |
| M | Muhammad. |
| MC | All Jammu and Kashmir Muslim Conference. |
| MCH | Muslim Conference (Haqiqi); political affiliation later given as an independent. |
| MMA | Muttahida Majlis-e-Amal (United Council of Action). |
| MQM | Muttahida Qaumi Movement (United National Movement). |
| PML | Peoples Muslim League–AJK. |
| PPPAK | Pakistan People's Party–Azad Kashmir. |
| S | Sardar. |

Table XIV.6: Differences in Electorate Sizes in Azad Kashmir in 1996, 2001, 2006.[10]

| Constituency Name* | ANE 1996# | ANE 2001# | ANE 2006+ |
|---|---|---|---|
| *Within Azad Kashmir* | | | |
| Mirpur I-IV** | 33,122 | 34,413 | 42,988 |
| Bhimber I-III | 45,570 | 57,716 | 65,904 |
| Kotli I-V | 44,733 | 57,716 | 65,904 |
| Bagh I-IV | 46,471 | 56,807 | 66,801 |
| Poonch & Sudhnoti I-VI | 43,023 | 57,850 | 64,827 |
| Neelum I*** | – | – | 76,860 |
| Muzaffarabad I-VI | 44,681 | 65,674 | 59,364 |
| Average Size of AK Constituency | 43,035 | 56,741 | 62,972 |
| Total Voters in Azad Kashmir | 1,204,965 | 1,588,753 | 1,826,180 |
| *Within Pakistan* | | | |
| Jammu & Others I-VI | 62,390 | 77,839 | 91,005 |
| Kashmir Valley I-VI | 5,543 | 5,313 | 5,876 |
| Average Size of Pak Constituency | 33,966 | 41,576 | 48,441 |
| Total Voters in Pakistan | 407,595 | 498,916 | 581,287 |
| *Azad Kashmir and Pakistan* | | | |
| Average Size of All Constituencies | 40,314 | 52,192 | 58,719 |
| Grand Total of Voters | 1,612,560 | 2,087,669 | 2,407,467 |

Key: ANE   Average Number of Electors per constituency.
      AK    Azad Kashmir.
      Pak   Pakistan.
      *     Listed in the order given by the Chief Election Commissioner of Azad Jammu and Kashmir.
      **    Mirpur apparently has smaller constituencies to accommodate and provide a 'cushion' for the 800,000 Mirpuris who live abroad, chiefly in the United Kingdom.
      ***   Neelum I was a new constituency for the 2006 election. It was created from Muzaffarabad District, whose electors had apparently had a longstanding demand to have another constituency for their district.

# THE UNTOLD STORY OF THE PEOPLE OF AZAD KASHMIR

\#     Voting took place in 40 constituencies: 28 in Azad Kashmir; 12 in Pakistan.
\+     Voting took place 41 constituencies: 29 In Azad Kashmir; 12 in Pakistan. The newly added constituency was Neelum I.

Table XIV.7: Delimitation of constituencies for 2001 Azad Kashmir elections.[11]

| Constituency | | Location within Azad Kashmir |
|---|---|---|
| 1 | Mirpur I | All of Dadyal Tehsil |
| 2 | Mirpur II | Part of Mirpur Tehsil |
| 3 | Mirpur III | Municipal Mirpur and part of Mirpur Tehsil |
| 4 | Mirpur IV | Part of Mirpur Tehsil |
| 5 | Bhimber I | Barnala Tehsil |
| 6 | Bhimber II | Samahni Tehsil |
| 7 | Bhimber III | Bhimber Tehsil |
| 8 | Kotli I | Part of Kotli Tehsil |
| 9 | Kotli II | Fatehpur Tehsil and part of Kotli Tehsil |
| 10 | Kotli III | Sehnsa Tehsil and part of Kotli Tehsil |
| 11 | Kotli IV | Part of Kotli Tehsil |
| 12 | Kotli V | Part of Kotli Tehsil |
| 13 | Bagh I | Almost all of Dhirkot Tehsil |
| 14 | Bagh II | Part of Bagh Tehsil and a very small part of Dhirkot Tehsil |
| 15 | Bagh III | Part of Bagh Tehsil |
| 16 | Bagh IV | Haveli Tehsil |
| 17 | Poonch & Sudhnoti I | Abbaspur Tehsil and part of Hajira Tehsil |
| 18 | Poonch & Sudhnoti II | Part of Hajira Tehsil and part of Pallandri Tehsil |
| 19 | Poonch & Sudhnoti III | Part of Rawalakot Tehsil |
| 20 | Poonch & Sudhnoti IV | Part of Rawalakot Tehsil |
| 21 | Poonch & Sudhnoti V | Part of Pallandri Tehsil |
| 22 | Poonch & Sudhnoti VI | Part of Pallandri Tehsil |
| 23 | Muzaffarabad I | Athmuqam Tehsil |
| 24 | Muzaffarabad II | Part of Muzaffarabad Tehsil |
| 25 | Muzaffarabad III | Part of Muzaffarabad Tehsil |
| 26 | Muzaffarabad IV | Part of Muzaffarabad Tehsil |
| 27 | Muzaffarabad V | Hattian Tehsil |
| 28 | Muzaffarabad VI | Part of Hattian Tehsil and part of Muzaffarabad Tehsil |
| | | *Location within Pakistan* |
| 29 | Jammu & Others I | Baluchistan Province; Sind Province; Bahawalpur, Multan, Dera Ghazi Khan, Faisalabad, Sargodha and Lahore divisions in Punjab Province |
| 30 | Jammu & Others II | Most of Gujranwala District; Hafizabad District; two tehsils of Sialkot District in Punjab Province |
| 31 | Jammu & Others III | Sialkot Tehsil of Sialkot District in Punjab Province |
| 32 | Jammu & Others IV | Narowal District in Punjab Province |
| 33 | Jammu & Others V | Wazirabad Tehsil of Gujranwala District; Gujrat District; Mandi Baha-ud-din District in Punjab Province |
| 34 | Jammu & Others VI | North-West Frontier Province; Rawalpindi Division in Punjab Province; Islamabad Capital Territory |
| 35 | Kashmir Valley I | Baluchistan Province and Sind Province |
| 36 | Kashmir Valley II | Lahore Division of Punjab Province |

## APPENDIX XIV

| SN | Constituency | Description |
|---|---|---|
| 37 | Kashmir Valley III | Bahawalpur, Multan, Dera Ghazi Khan, Gujranwala, Sargodha and Faisalabad divisions; Jhelum and Chakwal districts in Punjab Province |
| 38 | Kashmir Valley IV | Wards Nos. 15–50 within Rawalpindi Municipal Corporation (as these wards existed in 1985) |
| 39 | Kashmir Valley V | Wards Nos. 1–14 within Rawalpindi Municipal Corporation (as these wards existed in 1985); Cantonment ward Nos. 1–10; Rawalpindi District outside the Municipal Corporation; Islamabad Capital Territory; Attock District |
| 40 | Kashmir Valley VI | North-West Frontier Province |

Note: The Azad Kashmir Election Commission apparently determines and delimits electorates within Azad Kashmir, while the Pakistan Election Commission determines and delimits electorates in Pakistan. This is a feasible process, given that both bodies have offices in Islamabad.[12]

Table XIV.8: Voter turnouts in 1996, 2001 Legislative Assembly elections.[13]

| SN | Constituency | VT 1996 % | VT 2001 % | SN | WP 2006 %* |
|---|---|---|---|---|---|
| 1 | Mirpur I | 70 | 71 | 1 | 18 |
| 2 | Mirpur II | 85 | 70 | 2 | 29 |
| 3 | Mirpur III | 67 | 61 | 3 | 29 |
| 4 | Mirpur IV | 71 | 69 | 4 | 35 |
| 5 | Bhimber I | 90 | 61 | 5 | 25 |
| 6 | Bhimber II | 91 | 55 | 6 | 27 |
| 7 | Bhimber III | 72 | 59 | 7 | 33 |
| 8 | Kotli I | 75 | 53 | 8 | 26 |
| 9 | Kotli II | 84 | 52 | 9 | 33 |
| 10 | Kotli III | 77 | 59 | 10 | 36 |
| 11 | Kotli IV | 77 | 51 | 11 | 26 |
| 12 | Kotli V | 87 | 54 | 12 | 24 |
| 13 | Bagh I | 69 | 51 | 13 | 29 |
| 14 | Bagh II | 85 | 49 | 14 | 17 |
| 15 | Bagh III | 67 | 56 | 15 | 24 |
| 16 | Bagh IV | 90 | 54 | 16 | 24 |
| 17 | Poonch & Sudhnoti I | 87 | 49 | 17 | 19 |
| 18 | Poonch & Sudhnoti II | 79 | 47 | 18 | 25 |
| 19 | Poonch & Sudhnoti III | 59 | 50 | 19 | 15 |
| 20 | Poonch & Sudhnoti IV | 54 | 49 | 20 | 15 |
| 21 | Poonch & Sudhnoti V | 59 | 54 | 21 | 31 |
| 22 | Poonch & Sudhnoti VI | 69 | 48 | 22 | 28 |
|  | Neelum I |  |  | 23 | 28 |
| 23 | Muzaffarabad I | 68 | 51 | 24 | 21 |
| 24 | Muzaffarabad II | 61 | 49 | 25 | 19 |
| 25 | Muzaffarabad III | 67 | 54 | 26 | 17 |
| 26 | Muzaffarabad IV | 77 | 45 | 27 | 18 |
| 27 | Muzaffarabad V | 68 | 53 | 28 | 32 |
| 28 | Muzaffarabad VI | 71 | 48 | 29 | 17 |
|  | *Average AK seats★* | *74* | *54* |  | *25* |
| 29 | Jammu & Others I | 41 | 21 | 30 | 28 |

| | | | | | |
|---|---|---|---|---|---|
| 30 | Jammu & Others II | 64 | 31 | 31 | 13 |
| 31 | Jammu & Others III | 49 | 35 | 32 | 16 |
| 32 | Jammu & Others IV | 62 | 38 | 33 | 22 |
| 33 | Jammu & Others V | 58 | 41 | 34 | 53 |
| 34 | Jammu & Others VI | 53 | 33 | 35 | 15 |
| 35 | Kashmir Valley I | 66 | 41 | 36 | 48 |
| 36 | Kashmir Valley II | 56 | 26 | 37 | 17 |
| 37 | Kashmir Valley III | 72 | 55 | 38 | 20 |
| 38 | Kashmir Valley IV | 49 | 38 | 39 | 21 |
| 39 | Kashmir Valley V | 57 | 37 | 40 | 27 |
| 40 | Kashmir Valley VI | 55 | 58 | 41 | 27 |
| | *Average refugee seats*★ | *57* | *38* | | *25* |
| | *Overall average* | *69* | *49* | | *25* |

Key: AK    Azad Kashmir.
      SN    Seat number; the second column shows the inclusion of Neelum I.
      VT    Voter turnout as a percentage of voters enrolled, for the year stated.
      WP   Winner's Percentage of the vote as a percentage of the total registered vote (no voter turnout figures obtainable for 2006 elections, but considered to be over 60 per cent).
      ★     As calculated by me.

9. Azad Kashmir Political Parties, their Heads in 2006 and their location.[14]

1. All Jammu & Kashmir Muslim Conference (commonly called 'the Muslim Conference').
   - Sardar Attique Ahmed Khan, Rawalpindi.
2. Pakistan People's Party-Azad Kashmir.
   - Sahibzada Ishaq Zaffer, Muzaffarabad [now deceased].
3. Pakistan Muslim League Jammu & Kashmir.
   - Major General (Retired) Muhammad Hayat Khan, Rawalpindi.
4. Jammu & Kashmir Liberation League.
   - Justice (Retired) Abdul Majid Malik, Mirpur.
5. Jammu & Kashmir People's Party.
   - Sardar Khalid Ibrahim Khan, Islamabad.
6. Jamiat-ul-Ulema Azad Jammu & Kashmir.
   - Sahibzada Attiq-ur-Rehman Faizpuri, Mirpur
7. Jamiat-e-Islami Azad Jammu & Kashmir (associated with MMA: Muttahida Majlis-e-Amal).
   - Sardar Ejaz Afzal, Rawalpindi.
8. Millat Party Azad Jammu & Kashmir.
   - Muhammad Yousaf Awan, Islamabad.
9. People's Party Azad Jammu & Kashmir (Rathore Group).
   - Khwaja Atta Mohi-ud-Din Qadri, Kotli City.
10. All Jammu & Kashmir Justice Party.
    - Professor Maqsood Jaffri, Rawalpindi.
11. Jammu & Kashmir Awami Tehreek.
    - Sardar Mansoor Khan, Rawalpindi.

## APPENDIX XIV

12. Kashmir Freedom Movement.
    - Khaliq Hussain Chaudhry, Bhimber.
13. Jamiat-ul-Ulema-e-Islam Azad Jammu & Kashmir (associated with MMA: Muttahida Majlis-e-Amal).
    - Maulana Muhammad Yousaf, Pallandri.
14. Jammu & Kashmir Liberation Front.
    - Amanullah Khan, Rawalpindi.
15. Jammu & Kashmir National Liberation Front.
    - Shoukat Maqbool Butt, Muzaffarabad.
16. Azad Jammu & Kashmir Muslim League.
    - Raja Muhammad Azad Khan, Rawalpindi.
17. Islamic Democratic Party Azad Jammu & Kashmir (a Shia-based party).
    - Syed Ghulam Raza Naqvi, Kotli.
18. Jammu & Kashmir Mahaz—Raay—Shummari.
    - Syed Muhammad Saeed Shah Nazki, Lahore.
19. Kashmir Freedom Front.
    - Mufti Sana-ul-Haq Bukhari, Murree.
20. Jammu & Kashmir Milli Tehreek (associated with MMA: Muttahida Majlis-e-Amal).
    - Syed Muhammad Ali Raza Bukhari, Rawalpindi.
21. Pakistan People's Party (Shaheed Bhutto) Azad Jammu & Kashmir.
    - Munir Hussain Chaudhry, Mirpur.
22. Nazam-e-Mustafa Conference.
    - Sahibzada Syed Muhammad Nadeem Ahmad Gilani, Muzaffarabad.
23. Azad Jammu & Kashmir Awami Conference.
    - Chaudhry Maqbool Raza Rajorvi, Mirpur.
24. Pakistan Jamiat ulma[h]-i-Islam Jammu & Kashmir (associated with MMA: Muttahida Majlis-e-Amal).
    - Mufti Muhammad Younas Chaudhry, Mirpur.
25. Markazi Jamiat-e-Ahllay Hadees Azad Jammu & Kashmir (associated with MMA).
    - Maulana Muhammad Anwar Ruknudin, Bagh City.
26. Suni Tahrek Azad Jammu & Kashmir (associated with MMA: Muttahida Majlis-e-Amal).
    - Sardar Abdul Shakoor Ladhalvi, Kotli.
27. MMA [Muttahida Majlis-e-Amal] Azad Jammu & Kashmir.
    - Sardar Ijaz Afzal Khan, Rawalpindi.

N.B.: The Peoples Muslim League-AJK is not listed above. It (inexplicably) did not appear on the election documents given to me.

*Breakdown of locations:*

| *Inside Azad Kashmir:* | 15 | *Inside Pakistan:* | 12 |
| Bagh: | One | Islamabad: | Two |

# THE UNTOLD STORY OF THE PEOPLE OF AZAD KASHMIR

| Bhimber: | One | Lahore: | One |
|---|---|---|---|
| Kotli: | Three | Rawalpindi: | Nine |
| Mirpur: | Five | | |
| Murree: | One | | |
| Muzaffarabad: | Three | | |
| Pallandri: | One | | |

10. Qualifications and disqualifications for being a member of the Azad Kashmir Legislative Assembly

Authorities in Azad Kashmir and Pakistan can ensure that suitable people are elected to the Azad Kashmir Legislative Assembly—or, indeed, fail to actually get to the candidate stage—via criteria listed in the 'Qualifications and disqualifications for being a member' section of the Azad Kashmir election laws.[15] These comprise six qualifications for a person to be able to qualify as a member and twenty-five disqualifications. The qualifications are: being a state subject; being over twenty-five years old; being on the electoral roll; being of good character, including not being 'commonly known as one who violates Islamic Injunction'; having 'adequate knowledge of Islamic teachings', practicing obligatory Islamic duties, and abstaining from 'major [but undefined] sins'; and being 'sagacious, righteous, honest, ameen [sic] and not profligate'. The Islamic criteria do not apply to non-Muslims; instead, they must have 'a good moral reputation'. Disqualifications include insanity, insolvency, having a criminal record, being employed by the government, misconduct, corruption, membership of an illegal political party, 'having a bad reputation or [being] known to be morally corrupt', threatening or using force and inflicting injury, not completing electoral returns for expenses, tax defaulting, possessing unjustifiable assets, and making false statements.

There are two further important disqualifications. First, a person can be disqualified if 'he is propagating any opinion or acting in any manner, prejudicial to the ideology of Pakistan, the ideology of [the] State's accession to Pakistan or the sovereignty, integrity of Pakistan or security of Azad Jammu and Kashmir or Pakistan or morality'. Avoiding disqualification under this clause includes maintaining public order and not defaming the judiciary of Azad Kashmir or Pakistan or 'the Armed Forces of Pakistan'. A further—but discriminatory—criterion was added in 2001 by Act XXVII of 2001 of the Legislative Assembly:[16] a person can be disqualified if 'he does not have academic qualifications of matriculation or equivalent from a recognized institution'. What comprises a 'recognized institution' is not defined; in Pakistan for the 2002 elections conducted there, this also included *madrassa*s.

# NOTES

## INTRODUCTION

1. Only a few books have been written about Azad Kashmir, mostly by Azad Kashmiris. However, only the former Azad Kashmiri jurist, Yusuf Saraf, discusses events and conditions in Azad Kashmir since 1947 in any detail: Muhammad Yusuf Saraf, *Kashmiris Fight—For Freedom*, Volume I (1819–1946), Lahore, Ferozsons, 1977; Volume II (1947–1978), Lahore, Ferozsons, 1979. The second volume is the most comprehensive book ever published about Azad Kashmir. Both volumes are almost impossible to obtain.
2. Ahmad Hassan, 'Northern Areas renamed Gilgit-Baltistan; Poll for assembly, CM in November; Regional groups unhappy: Autonomy package for NAs approved', *Dawn*, 30 August 2009.
3. 'NWFP name change to cost treasury Rs. 8 billion', *Dawn*, 10 April 2010.
4. United Nations Commission for India and Pakistan, *Report of the Sub-committee on Western Kashmir*, Unpublished Restricted Document (S/AC.12/WK/1), New York, 31 March 1949. Hereafter referred to as UNCIP, *Report of the Sub-committee on Western Kashmir*. I am indebted to my British colleague, Alexander Evans, for access to this invaluable primary source. It has greatly enhanced my scholarship—and this book.
5. *Census of Azad Kashmir, 1951*, Murree?, Iftikhar Ahmad, Chief Enumeration Officer, Government of Azad Kashmir, 1952, pp. 1–2. I am indebted to the Azad Kashmir official who allowed me to photocopy this rare document that was invaluable to my research.
6. *Rules of Business 1985*, Services & General Administration Department, Azad Government of the State of Jammu and Kashmir, Muzaffarabad, 1985. I am thankful to the Azad Kashmir official who gave me this document.
7. Little of significance about Azad Kashmir's administration has appeared since Yusuf Saraf's 1979 publication, *Kashmiris Fight—For Freedom*, Volume II.

## 1. J&K: DISUNITED PEOPLE—UNDELIVERABLE STATE

1. See Clause 7 of the 'Indian Independence Act, 18 July 1947', in Sarwar K. Hasan and Zubeida Hasan, Editors, *Documents on the Foreign Relations of Pakistan. The Kashmir Question*, Karachi, Pakistan Institute of International Relations, 1966, pp. 10–11. Others have argued that, after the British departed the Indian subcontinent, the new dominions, especially India, inherited British paramountcy, with the result that no princely state was

independent, theoretically or otherwise. See, for example, A.G. Noorani, 'C.P. and independent Travancore', *Frontline*, Volume 20, Issue 13, 21 June–4 July 2003.
2. V.P. Menon, *The Story of the Integration of the Indian States*, Bombay, Orient Longman, 1961, various pages, particularly p. 376 in relation to J&K.
3. While both rulers and their states would later prove problematic, they are largely outside the scope of this book.
4. Information about the three roads is from S.N. Dhar, *Kashmir: Eden of the East*, Allahabad, Kitab Mahal, 1945, pp. 120–24.
5. General Sir Frank Messervy, 'Kashmir', *Asiatic Review*, Volume 45, Number 161, 1949, p. 474.
6. O.H.K. Spate and A.T.A. Learmonth, *India and Pakistan. A General and Regional Geography* London?, Methuen, Revised Third Edition, 1967, p. 439.
7. Saraf, *Kashmiris Fight—For Freedom*, Volume I, p. 17.
8. M. Ganju, *This is Kashmir (With Special Reference to U.N.O.)*, Delhi, S. Chand & Co., 1948, p. ix.
9. M.R. Imrany, *Paradise Under the Shadow of Hell. India's War on Kashmir As Seen By Non-Muslims and Neutral Observers*, Lahore, No publisher details, 1948, p. 192.
10. *Census of India 1941*, Volume XXII, *Jammu & Kashmir State*, Part III, *Village Tables*, Srinagar, R.G. Wreford, Editor, Jammu and Kashmir Government, 1942, p. 346.
11. Z.H. Zaidi, Editor-in-Chief, *Quaid-i-Azam Mohammad Ali Jinnah Papers*, Volume V, Islamabad, Government of Pakistan, Cabinet Division, 2000, p. 540. The original telegram from Janak Singh, the J&K Prime Minister is at p. 538. Lord Birdwood, *Two Nations and Kashmir*, London, Robert Hale, 1956, p. 45, notes that the Standstill Agreement was telegraphically agreed but never actually signed. A former British official, Birdwood 'encountered' Maharaja Hari Singh a number of times (p. 31).
12. Saraf, *Kashmiris Fight—For Freedom*, Volume II, p. 771.
13. Sisir Gupta, *Kashmir. A Study in India-Pakistan Relations*, Bombay, Asia Publishing House, 1966, p. 103.
14. Saraf, *Kashmiris Fight—For Freedom*, Volume II, p. 771.
15. Birdwood, *Two Nations and Kashmir*, p. 46.
16. *White Paper on Jammu & Kashmir* Delhi, Government of India, 1948, p. 2.
17. See Appendix II: Physical, Political and Religious Composition of J&K in 1941, for detailed information on a provincial basis about the makeup of J&K in 1947.
18. The figures in Table 1.1 may moderately understate the majority position of Muslims in J&K. See Appendix III: Majority Position of Muslims in 1941.
19. Author unknown, 'Jammu and Kashmir State 1947', p. 2, in *Powell Collection, Papers and Correspondence*, dated 1947–1960, of Richard Powell (1889–1961), Indian Police Force 1908–1947, Inspector-General of Police Jammu and Kashmir 1946–1947, Indian Office Records, MSS EUR D862 [accessed at National Document Centre, Islamabad, December 2004].
20. 'Copy of Note by R.C. Kak, Jammu and Kashmir State in 1946–47, Part VII. 2-Maharaja Harisingh [sic]', in *Powell Collection, Papers and Correspondence*, p. 12, states that Maharaja Hari Singh and the 'highly influential' Swami Santdev (mentioned below), who supposedly had supernatural powers, believed that an independent 'Dogristan'

could be formed. It would comprise J&K, 'the districts of Kangra and the States and areas now mostly included in the [sic] Himachal Pradesh'. Menon, *The Story of the Integration of the Indian States*, pp. 376–7, stated that the Maharaja, despite contrary advice by the Viceroy, Lord Mountbatten, 'was toying with … an "Independent Jammu and Kashmir"'.

21. According to Pakistanis, this was a conspiracy. For a discussion of Gurdaspur, see Alastair Lamb, *Kashmir, A Disputed Legacy, 1846–1990*, Karachi, Oxford University Press, Second Impression, 1994, various pages.
22. *CMG*, 29 July 1947, reported that the J&K Government (presciently) intended to metal the Kathua Road and 'thus connect Jammu State' with India 'through Pathankot'.
23. Karan Singh, *Autobiography*, Delhi, Oxford University Press, 1994, pp. 41–2, 48.
24. Article 10, 'Amritsar Treaty, 1846', in K.M. Panikkar, *The Founding of the Kashmir State. A Biography of Maharaja Gulab Singh, 1792–1858*, London, George Allen & Unwin, 1953, p. 114. The entire treaty comprises pp. 111–15. It was concluded on 16 March 1846.
25. *Memoranda on the Indian States 1940*, Delhi, The Manager of [Indian Government] Publications, 1940, pp. 163–4. The Sikh ruler, Maharaja Ranjit Singh, had apparently awarded Gulab Singh the principality of Jammu in 1820.
26. J.E. Schwartzberg, 'Who are the Kashmiri People? Self-identification as a Vehicle for Self-determination', *Environment and Planning A*, Volume 29, 1997, p. 2248.
27. For a full description of the creation and consolidation of J&K, see Lamb, *Kashmir, A Disputed Legacy*.
28. Panikkar, *The Founding of the Kashmir State*, pp. 124–5.
29. Balraj Puri, *Jammu and Kashmir. Triumph and Tragedy of Indian Federalisation*, New Delhi, Sterling Publishers, 1981, Appendix B, pp. 204–5, contains the 'Edict of "Abdication"' which Pratap Singh issued on 8 March 1889. According to it, for five years, 'the Maharaja will not interfere and will have no voice in the administration of the public affairs of the State, but he will continue to enjoy the rights and position of Maharaja'.
30. Lamb, *Kashmir, A Disputed Legacy*, pp. 13, 29–30.
31. Birdwood, *Two Nations and Kashmir*, p. 31. Karan Singh, *Autobiography*, p. 20, states that, in 1947, the resident lived in Srinagar in summer and in Sialkot in winter (not in Jammu City). His father had insisted on this arrangement owing to his mistrust of the British.
32. Ian Copland, 'Islam and Political Mobilization in Kashmir, 1931–34', *Pacific Affairs*, Volume 54, Number 2, 1981, p. 231.
33. Copland, 'Islam and Political Mobilization in Kashmir', p. 241. On p. 244, Copland relates that, after the 1931 uprising, Hari Singh accepted a British officer, Colonel Colvin, to run his administration. On p. 254, he states that Colvin handed back 'the reins of power' to the Maharaja in March 1935, by which time the situation in J&K had stabilised.
34. Sir Reginald Coupland, *India: A Re-Statement*, London, Oxford University Press, 1945, p. 179.
35. Puri, *Jammu and Kashmir. Triumph and Tragedy*, pp. 45–6.
36. *The Times*, 20 November 1947.

37. Manzoor Fazili, *Kashmir Government and Politics*, Srinagar, Gulshan Publishers, 1982, p. 63.
38. Saraf, *Kashmiris Fight—For Freedom*, Volume I, p. 328. *Memoranda on the Indian States*, p. 163, states that, by 1940, this force comprised 3,400 men. While the overall religious imbalance may have been partially, or even substantially, rectified by then, the Maharaja's ambivalence about employing Muslims in positions of authority meant that it was unlikely that many would have been in senior positions.
39. Lieutenant-General Sir George MacMunn, *The Indian States and Princes*, London, Jarrolds, 1936, p. 130.
40. Major K. Brahma Singh, *History of Jammu and Kashmir Rifles 1820–1956*, New Delhi, Lancer International, 1990, p. 169.
41. Calculated from figures given in Singh, *History of Jammu and Kashmir Rifles*, p. 145.
42. Prem Nath Bazaz, *Inside Kashmir*, Mirpur, Verinag Publishers, 1987 [First Published by Kashmir Pub. [sic] Company, Srinagar, 1941], p. 200.
43. P.N. Chopra, Chief Editor, *India's Struggle for Freedom: Role of Associated Movements*, Volume Four, Delhi, Agam Prakashan, 1985, pp. 735–6. Chopra's source is a press note from the Government of the Maharaja. G.M.D. Sufi, *Kashir. Being a History of Kashmir From the Earliest Times to Our Own*, Volume II, Lahore, University of Punjab, 1949, p. 828, confirms that only 'Hindu Dogras' were allowed arms.
44. Copland, 'Islam and Political Mobilization in Kashmir', p. 234.
45. Mridu Rai, *Hindu Rulers, Muslim Subjects: Islam, Rights and the History of Kashmir*, London, Hurst & Company, 2004, p. 213.
46. Rai, *Hindu Rulers, Muslim Subjects*, p. 274.
47. Schedule II, 'General Constituencies', and Schedule III, 'Special Constituencies', in Document Number 9, 'The Jammu and Kashmir Constitution Act No. XIV of 22nd Bahadon, 1996 ([7th] September 1939', in Mirza Shafique Hussain, Compiler, *History of Kashmir: A Study in Documents 1916–1939*, Islamabad, National Institute of Historical and Cultural Research, 1992, pp. 243–5.
48. Document 9, Hussain, *History of Kashmir: A Study in Documents*, pp. 228–9.
49. Document Number 8, 'Administration Report of the Praja Sabha Department of Jammu and Kashmir Government for the Year 1938', in Hussain, *History of Kashmir: A Study in Documents*, pp. 215, 217.
50. Author unknown, 'Jammu and Kashmir State 1947', in *Powell Collection, Papers and Correspondence*, p. 1.
51. *CMG*, 7 August 1947.
52. Interview between Mountbatten and Nehru, 24 June 1947, *Constitutional Relations Between Britain and India, The Transfer of Power 1942–7*, Volume XI, London, Nicholas Mansergh, Editor-in-Chief, Her Majesty's Stationery Office, 1982, p. 592.
53. Kashmir Resident to Abell, 13 August 1947, *Constitutional Relations Between Britain and India, The Transfer of Power 1942–7*, London, Nicholas Mansergh, Editor-in-Chief, Volume XII, Her Majesty's Stationery Office, 1983, p. 696.
54. These newspapers included: *Civil & Military Gazette* (*CMG*, Lahore); *Dawn* (New Delhi until around 15 August 1947, then production ceased for a time while it relocated to Karachi); *The New York Times* (*NYT*, New York); *The Times* (London); *The*

*Times of India* (*TOI*, Bombay); and *The Statesman* (Calcutta). Owing to its location in Lahore, the *CMG* carried the most news about J&K, although many newspapers had local correspondents and stringers in J&K, or used reports from news agencies with local sources. While the newspapers generally carried 'hard' news on the situation in J&K with little analysis, their editorials tended to be 'influenced' by the politics of the nation in which the newspaper was located. Hence Indian-based papers were pro-Indian, Pakistani-based papers were pro-Pakistan. See Ian Stephens, *Horned Moon. An Account of a Journey through Pakistan, Kashmir, and Afghanistan*, London, Chatto & Windus, 1953, pp. 18–20, 113–15. Apart from *CMG*, all other newspapers are still operating. Hugh Tinker, *India and Pakistan. A Political Analysis*, New York, Frederick A. Praeger, 1962, p. 181, states that *CMG* was a Hindu-owned paper that 'ran into trouble' after Partition. As far as I can determine, it ceased publication in September 1963.

55. *CMG*, 28 October 1947.
56. *The Times*, 20 November 1947.
57. Mohammad Ishaq Khan, *Experiencing Islam*, New Delhi, Sterling Publishers, 1997, pp. 92–3, discusses this relic.
58. *Census of India 1941*, various pages.
59. *The Times*, 20 November 1947.
60. Pandit Anand Koul, *Geography of the Jammu and Kashmir State*, Mirpur, Verinag Publishers, 1991, p. 37 [No previous publication details, but a Reprint of the Second Edition, 1925; see Bibliography], p. vi.
61. I.S. Jehu, Editor, *The India and Pakistan Year Book 1948*, Bombay, Bennett, Coleman & Co., 1948, p. 25. Rawalpindi's population then was 181,000; Sialkot's was 138,000.
62. Also sometimes spelt Baramula.
63. Dhar, *Kashmir: Eden of the East*, p. 19.
64. *Census of India 1941*, p. 443.
65. This book does not examine the plebiscite idea. For such an examination, see Christopher Snedden, 'Would a Plebiscite Have Resolved the Kashmir Dispute?', *South Asia: Journal of South Asian Studies*, Volume XXVIII, Number, 1, April 2005.
66. Rai, *Hindu Rulers, Muslim Subjects*, p. 225, footnote 2, states that she found 'no evidence' for the word Kashmiriyat being used before 1947. It appears to have come into widespread use after the Kashmiris began their anti-Indian uprising in 1988.
67. Raju G.C. Thomas, 'Reflections on the Kashmir Problem', in Raju G.C. Thomas, Editor, *Perspectives on Kashmir. The Roots of Conflict in South Asia*, Boulder, Westview Press, 1992, p. 39.
68. Riyaz Punjabi, 'Kashmir: The Bruised Identity', in Thomas, *Perspectives*, p. 149.
69. Sufi, *Kashir. Being a History of Kashmir*, Volume II, p. 41.
70. *Nund Rishi. Unity in Diversity* [B.N. Parimoo, Translator], Srinagar, J&K Academy of Art, Culture and Languages, 1984, p. 156.
71. Mohammad Ishaq Khan, *History of Srinagar 1846–1947. A study in Socio-Cultural Change*, Srinagar, Aamir Publications, 1978, pp. 119–20.
72. Bazaz, *Inside Kashmir*, p. 177.
73. Mir Qasim, *My Life and Times*, New Delhi, Allied Publishers, 1992, p. 31.
74. 'Sheikh Abdullah's Speech in the Constituent Assembly, Jammu and Kashmir, on 5

November, 1951, Calling upon People to Perform their Duties', quoted in Qasim, *My Life and Times*, Appendix II, p. 188.
75. Prem Nath Bazaz, *Azad Kashmir: A Democratic Socialist Conception*, Mirpur, Verinag, 1992 [First Published by Ferozsons, Lahore, 1951], pp. 13–14.
76. 'Statement showing the Results of the [1947] Elections', in *The Jammu and Kashmir Praja Sabha Debates*, Volume XVIII, Thursday 3rd April 1947/21 Chet 2004, March–April Session of the 3rd J&K Praja Sabha, Jammu, Dewan Press, 1947, p. 3. Bazaz stood for the seat of 'Srinagar City South (Hindu)', but was soundly defeated by the winner, 'P[andit] Amar Nath Kak'. Out of a possible 8,907 votes, 4,184 were cast; Kak obtained 3,650 votes, 'P[andit] Prem Nath Bazaz' 372 votes, and a third candidate, 'Dr. Shamboo Nath Peshin', 162 votes.
77. *The Statesman*, 17 October 1947.
78. Bazaz, *Azad Kashmir*, p. 20.
79. Sheikh Mohammad Abdullah, *Flames of the Chinar* [Khushwant Singh, Translator], New Delhi, Viking, 1993, pp. 87, 91; Mehr Chand Mahajan, *Looking Back*, New Delhi, Har-Anand Publications, 1994 [First published 1963?], p. 131.
80. Saraf, *Kashmiris Fight—For Freedom*, Volume II, p. 753. Author unknown, 'Jammu and Kashmir State 1947', p. 1, in *Powell Collection, Papers and Correspondence*, p. 3. Birdwood, *Two Nations and Kashmir*, p. 47, states that Kak, 'while fostering independence, was certainly closer to Pakistan than to India in an identity of broad policy'.
81. Somnath Tikku, *Kashmir Speaking*, Srinagar, Raina's News Agency, 1946?, p. 167. A state subject was a local person of J&K who had a legitimate right to be in the princely state. This issue is discussed in Chapter 2.
82. Karan Singh, *Autobiography*, p. 55.
83. The (now deceased) Kashmiri political activist and journalist Mir Abdul Aziz, who fled Srinagar soon after the accession to avoid persecution by National Conference elements, informed me in Rawalpindi on 24 March 1999 that Kak told him and Mirwaiz Yusuf Shah, a rival of Sheikh Abdullah, on 6 August 1947 that Hari Singh was going to accede to India and that he (Kak) was resigning.
84. 'Copy of Note by R.C. Kak, Jammu and Kashmir State in 1946–47', pp. 14–15, in *Powell Collection, Papers and Correspondence*.
85. 'Copy of Note by R.C. Kak, Jammu and Kashmir State in 1946–47', p. 16, in *Powell Collection, Papers and Correspondence*.
86. Birdwood, *Two Nations and Kashmir*, p. 46.
87. Abdullah, *Flames of the Chinar*, p. 13.
88. Ibid., various pages.
89. Copland, 'Islam and Political Mobilization in Kashmir', p. 231.
90. Bazaz, *Inside Kashmir*, p. 183.
91. 'The Kashmir Crisis', Despatch Number 13 to US Secretary of State by R.D. Gatewood, American Consul, Lahore, 4 November 1947, p. 2, in *Confidential U.S. State Department Central Files, India: Internal Affairs, 1945–1949, Part I, Political, Governmental, and National Defense Affairs*, Frederick, MD, University Publications of America, Reel Number 9.
92. S.M. Abdullah, 'Introduction', in *Jammu & Kashmir 1947–50. An Account of Activities of*

*First Three Years of Sheikh Abdullah's Government*, Jammu, Government of Jammu and Kashmir?, The Ranbir Government Press, 1951, p. i.
93. Abdullah, *Flames of the Chinar*, pp. 56–7, 83.
94. Ibid., pp. 47, 83.
95. Ian Copland, 'The Princely States, the Muslim League, and the Partition of India in 1947', *The International History Review*, Volume XIII, Number 1, February 1991, p. 53. According to UNCIP, *Report of the Sub-committee on Western Kashmir*, p. 5, the Muslim Conference had 'a total claimed membership of 300,000 (including Gilgit and Ladakh' in 1949. This was probably overstated to boost the Muslim Conference's credibility. Owing to the turbulent events in J&K soon after Partition, the National Conference's membership would almost certainly have risen also.
96. Author unknown, 'Jammu and Kashmir State 1947', in *Powell Collection, Papers and Correspondence*, p. 4.
97. Abdullah, *Flames of the Chinar*, p. 49.
98. A.H. Suharwardy, *Tragedy in Kashmir*, Lahore, Wajidalis, 1983, p. 40.
99. Sardar M. Ibrahim Khan, *The Kashmir Saga*, Lahore, Ripon Printing Press, 1965, p. 25.
100. Puri, *Jammu and Kashmir. Triumph and Tragedy*, pp. 52–3.
101. Sardar M. Ibrahim Khan, *The Kashmir Saga*, p. 25.
102. Zaheer Masood Quraishi, *Elections & State Politics of India (A Case-Study of Kashmir)*, Delhi, Sundeep Prakashan, 1979, p. 45.
103. Quraishi, *Elections & State Politics of India*, p. 46. According to Quraishi, there were 707,419 people eligible to vote in the 1947 J&K elections. Of these, 182,800 actually voted, giving a 26 per cent turnout. However, 'only 8 per cent votes were cast in the Muslim constituencies in the [Kashmir] Valley'. These low turnouts may suggest the National Conference's influence.
104. *CMG*, 30 September 1947.
105. *The Times*, 10 October 1947.
106. Ibid., 29 October 1947.
107. *CMG*, 21 October 1947.
108. Abdullah, *Flames of the Chinar*, p. 83.
109. *The Statesman*, 22 October 1947.
110. *The Sunday Statesman*, 12 October 1947.
111. Balraj Puri, *Jammu—A Clue to Kashmir Triangle*, Delhi, self-published, 1966, p. 13. According to Puri, Jammu was possibly 'the strongest hold of the Hindu Sabha in the country'.
112. Balraj Puri, *Simmering Volcano*, New Delhi, Sterling Publishers, 1983, p. 11. On pp. 12–13, Puri states that the Hindu Sabha, better understanding 'the implications of independence and its lack of viability in view of growing Muslim hostility to the idea', passed a broad resolution in May 1947 extending its support to the Maharaja 'whatever he was doing or might do on the issue of the accession'. According to Puri, p. 13, this later changed to supporting the Maharaja's accession to India at an 'appropriate time'.
113. *CMG*, 3 July 1947.
114. Mahajan, *Looking Back*, p. 162.

115. *The Times*, 10 October 1947.
116. *Dawn*, 11 May 1947.
117. Ibid., 22 May 1947.
118. Mir Abdul Aziz, 'Internal Kashmir Affairs—A Practicable Solution, Kashmiristan?', p. 2, in a proposal attached to a letter to 'The Hon'ble Minister for Kashmir Affairs, Pakistan (Rawalpindi)', by Mir Abdul Aziz, 'Member General Council, All Jammu and Kashmir Muslim Conference', 5 May 1950, pp. 53–61, contained in File No. 13 (5)-PMS/50, Volume 10, 'Government of Pakistan, Prime Minister's Secretariat, All Jammu & Kashmir Muslim Conference', held at the National Documentation Centre, Cabinet Building, Islamabad, Pakistan. File accessed on 27–29 December 2006.
119. *Dawn*, 22 June 1947.
120. Ibid., 22 May 1947.
121. Ibid., 22 July 1947; *CMG*, 24 July 1947.
122. Ibid., 29 July 1947.
123. Chaudhri Muhammad Ali, *The Emergence of Pakistan*, New York, Columbia University Press, 1967, pp. 287, 297.
124. Interview between Mountbatten and Jinnah, 5 July 1947, *Constitutional Relations Between Britain and India*, Volume XI, p. 936.
125. Jinnah on Kashmir Situation, Extract from India News, 13 July 1947, *Constitutional Relations Between Britain and India*, Volume XII, p. 128.
126. *CMG*, 24 July 1947; Saraf, *Kashmiris Fight—For Freedom*, Volume II, pp. 711–12.
127. *The Statesman*, 22 October 1947.
128. Qasim, *My Life and Times*, p. 31.
129. Information on Muslim Conference in this paragraph from Ian Copland, 'The Abdullah Factor: Kashmiri Muslims and the Crisis of 1947', in D.A. Low, Editor, *The Political Inheritance of Pakistan*, Basingstoke, Macmillan, 1991, pp. 235–6.
130. Qasim, *My Life and Times*, p. 31.
131. Copland, 'The Abdullah Factor', p. 234.
132. Viceroy's Personal Report No. 15, 1 August 1947, *Constitutional Relations Between Britain and India*, Volume XII, p. 449. Author unknown, 'Jammu and Kashmir State 1947', in *Powell Collection, Papers and Correspondence*, p. 5, claims the Kak and Nehru families had had a feud for 'many years'.
133. Karan Singh, *Autobiography*, 1982, p. 40.
134. Letter from Vallabhbhai Patel to Pandit Ramchandra Kak, 15 August 1946, in Durga Das, Editor, *Sardar Patel's Correspondence 1945–50, Volume I, New Light on Kashmir*, Ahmedabad, Navajivan Publishing House, 1971, pp. 11–12.
135. *Memoranda on the Indian States*, pp. 270, 274.
136. Based on information in *Census of India 1941*, pp. 232–4.
137. Alastair Lamb, *Birth of a Tragedy. Kashmir 1947*, Karachi, Oxford University Press, 1994, pp. 54–63, also discusses this issue.
138. Charles Ellison Bates, Compiler, *A Gazetteer of Kashmir*, Mirpur, Verinag Publishers, Reprinted (No publication date; first published 1873?], p. 313.
139. Sardar M. Ibrahim Khan, *The Kashmir Saga*, p. 9. Lamb, *Birth of a Tragedy*, pp. 55–6 quotes the impression of 'a contemporary British observer, G.T. Vigne' about this flaying.

140. Sardar M. Ibrahim Khan, *The Kashmir Saga*, Mirpur, Verinag, Second Edition, 1990, pp. 78–86. In a new, additional chapter titled the 'Sudhan Revolt', Ibrahim quotes extensively from Major G. Carmichael Smith, *The Reigning Family of Lahore*, Calcutta, W. Thacker and Co., St. Andrew's Library, 1847.
141. On 5 March 1999, on a return trip to Muzaffarabad from Rawalakot, I was informed at a river we crossed that this was the place where Gulab Singh had flayed alive the Poonchis.
142. Bazaz, *Inside Kashmir*, p. 230. Unless otherwise stated, the rest of this paragraph is based on Appendix I: The Relationship between the Rajas of Poonch and the Maharajas of Jammu and Kashmir. It explains their dislike, disputes and the system of 'dual control'.
143. HGS, 'Poonch 1937—1947', in *Powell Collection, Papers and Correspondence*, p. 1.
144. Appendix I: The Relationship; Memoranda on the Indian States, p. 167.
145. *Census of India 1941*, p. 231, confirms that the new Raja was a minor.
146. Appendix I: The Relationship.
147. Bazaz, *Inside Kashmir*, p. 230.
148. *Census of India 1941*, p. 231.
149. HGS, 'Poonch 1937—1947', p. 1, in *Powell Collection, Papers and Correspondence*.
150. Bates, *A Gazetteer of Kashmir*, pp. 312–13.
151. *Census of India 1941*, p. 231.
152. Appendix I: The Relationship; Memoranda on the Indian States, p. 166.
153. Bazaz, *Inside Kashmir*, p. 230.
154. *Census of India 1941*, p. 232.
155. Richard Symonds, *In the Margins of Independence; A Relief Worker in India and Pakistan (1941–1949)*, Karachi, Oxford University Press, 2001, p. 78.
156. *Memoranda on the Indian States*, p. 166.
157. According to Ian Stephens, *Pakistan*, London, Ernest Benn, Second (Revised) Edition, 1964, p. 187, Symonds was the 'best authority' on Poonch in 1947. Richard Symonds, *In the Margins of Independence*, pp. 76–82, states that he (Symonds) was a non-combatant who had previously been in the Poonch area from about 21 to 26 November 1947. During, or around, this time, he also met many of the leading military and political figures involved in Azad Kashmir. Richard Symonds, *The Making of Pakistan*, London, Faber and Faber, 1950, p. 10, states that he (Symonds) later served on the Secretariat for the United Nations Commission for India and Pakistan.
158. Symonds, *In the Margins of Independence*, pp. 78–9.
159. Mohd. Hafizullah, *Towards Azad Kashmir*, Lahore, Bazam-i-Froghi-i-Adab, 1948, p. 53.
160. Symonds, 'With the Rebel Forces of Poonch', *The Statesman*, 4 February 1948.
161. Symonds, *In the Margins of Independence*, p. 79.
162. Author unknown, *Copy of Poonch Services*, p. 3, Annexure No. 4 to Letter from Jagatdev Singh, Raja of Poonch, to 'His Excellency the Right Honourable Freeman [sic] Freeman-Thomas, Earl of Wellingdon [sic], G.M.S.I., G.M.I.E., G.C.M.G., C.B.E., Viceroy and Governor General of India', dated 27 February 1936, as contained in the 'Memorial from the Raja of Poonch, Kashmir State', File No. 452-P(S)/37 of 1937, Political Department, 'Political' Branch, Government of India, as accessed at the National Documentation Centre, Cabinet Building, Islamabad, 29 December 2006.

163. Bazaz, *Inside Kashmir*, p. 230, stated that the *jagir*'s income was Rs. 984,000; *Memoranda on the Indian States*, p. 166, stated that it was 'about Rs. 9,50,000'.
164. This paragraph based on information contained in HGS, 'Poonch 1937—1947', pp. 1–4, in *Powell Collection, Papers and Correspondence*. All quotations in this paragraph are from this source.
165. Michael Brecher, *The Struggle for Kashmir*, New York, Oxford University Press, 1953, p. 26.
166. 'Liquidation of Landlordism in Jammu & Kashmir', in Suresh K. Sharma and S.R. Bakshi, Editors, *Encyclopedia of Kashmir*, New Delhi, Anmol Publications, 1995, Volume 10, *Economic Life of Kashmir*, p. 130.
167. Mirza Mohammad Afzal Beg, 'On the Way to Golden Harvests—Agricultural Reforms in Kashmir' [First Published in Jammu, 1950], in Sharma and Bakshi, *Encyclopedia of Kashmir*, Volume 10, p. 212.
168. Beg, 'On the Way to Golden Harvests', pp. 212–13.
169. Brecher, *The Struggle for Kashmir*, p. 26.
170. Singh, *History of Jammu and Kashmir Rifles*, pp. 206–7.
171. Messervy, 'Kashmir', pp. 469, 475.
172. See Appendix III: Majority Position of Muslims in 1941, point 2.
173. Sufi, *Kashir. Being a History of Kashmir*, Volume II, p. 816.
174. Appendix IV: Indian Army Soldiers from Poonch, Mirpur, substantiates this figure.
175. Singh, *History of Jammu and Kashmir Rifles*, p. 169.
176. According to S.N. Prasad and Dharm Pal, *History of Operations in Jammu & Kashmir (1947–48)* New Delhi, History Division, Ministry of Defence, Government of India, 1987?, pp. 19–20.
177. Annex 7, 'Minutes of the Meeting with the Defence Minister of the "Azad Kashmir Government"', in UNCIP, *Report of the Sub-committee on Western Kashmir*, p. 71.
178. Sardar M. Ibrahim Khan, *The Kashmir Saga*, p. 15.
179. Note from Resident, Srinagar, on 'Communal Trouble in Poonch, to 'Griffin', 9 June 1945, pp. 4–5, in File No. 15 (12) P(S)/45 of 1945, Political Department, Pol Branch [Government of India] states that 'The Maharaja's Government [sic] is as you know unpopular in Poonch, especially among the numerous Service families who contrast their treatment with that enjoyed by Servicemen in the Punjab, especially in the matter of land grants'.
180. Singh, *History of Jammu and Kashmir Rifles*, p. 215.
181. Suharwardy, *Tragedy in Kashmir*, p. 98.
182. Sardar M. Ibrahim Khan, *The Kashmir Saga*, p. 35.
183. D.F. Karaka, *Betrayal in India*, London, Victor Gollancz, 1950, p. 179.
184. Subrata K. Mitra, 'Nehru's Policy Towards Kashmir: Bringing Politics Back in Again', *The Journal of Commonwealth and Comparative Politics*, Volume 35, Number 2, July 1997, p. 57.
185. Nehru, 'Introductory Essay', in Dhar, *Kashmir: Eden of the East*, pp. xvii-xviii.
186. Letter to Begum Abdullah, 4 June 1947, in S. Gopal, General Editor, *Selected Works of Jawaharlal Nehru*, Volume 3, New Delhi, Jawaharlal Nehru Memorial Fund, 1985, p. 197.

187. Nehru to Mountbatten, 17 June 1947, *Constitutional Relations Between Britain and India*, Volume XI, pp. 442–8. Quotations in next sentence from pp. 442–3.
188. Nehru to Mountbatten, 17 June 1947, *Constitutional Relations Between Britain and India*, Volume XI, p. 448.
189. Viceroy's Sixth Miscellaneous Meeting, 22 April 1947, *Constitutional Relations Between Britain and India, The Transfer of Power 1942–7*, Volume X, London, Nicholas Mansergh, Editor-in-Chief, Her Majesty's Stationery Office, 1981, p. 365.
190. *The Times*, 1 November 1947.
191. 'Report submitted by the United Nations Representative for India and Pakistan, Sir Owen Dixon, to the Security Council, 15 September 1950', in Sarwar K. Hasan and Zubeida Hasan, Editors, *Documents on the Foreign Relations of Pakistan*, p. 277.
192. *The Times*, 13 January 1948.
193. *Organiser*, New Delhi, 21 November 1999, stated that the Maharaja's former private secretary, Captain Dewan Singh, at the time an octogenarian, had said that the maharaja 'could never think of joining Pakistan—a theocratic state'.

2. THE PEOPLE: DIVIDING J&K—INSTIGATING THE KASHMIR DISPUTE

1. Bazaz, *Azad Kashmir*, p. 11, writing in 1951, stated that his party actually coined the term 'Azad Kashmir' at a party gathering in Anantnag on 12 May 1946. However, his book was not about the actual region of Azad Kashmir. Its purpose was to convey his and his party's conception of what a free Kashmir should comprise of. Santosh Kaul, *Freedom Struggle In Jammu and Kashmir*, New Delhi, Anmol Publications, 1990, pp. 177–8, states that the Muslim Conference at a 'Special Convention' held in Srinagar from 27–30 July 1946 made a series of demands for 'political reforms' in J&K via its '"Azad Kashmir" Manifesto'. I have not been able to obtain a copy of this manifesto.
2. Symonds, *In the Margins of Independence*, p. 57.
3. While preparations for this invasion must have been going on in Pakistan before this date, that contentious matter is outside the scope of this book.
4. See, for example, the Enclosure titled 'Note of a talk with Mr. Liaquat Ali Khan at Lahore on 1 November 1947', in a letter from Lord Mountbatten to Sardar Patel, 2 November 1947, in Das, *Sardar Patel's Correspondence*, p. 75; A. De Mhaffe, *Road to Kashmir*, Lahore, Ripon Printing Press, 1948?, p. 170; Shaikh Izzatullah, *Kashmir-Plebiscite* [sic], Lahore, Iqbal Company Limited, 1949?, p. 74; Ziaul Islam, *The Revolution in Kashmir*, Karachi, Pakistan Publishers, 1948, p. 55.
5. Copland, 'Islam and Political Mobilisation in Kashmir', p. 231.
6. Joseph Schechtman, *The Refugee in the World: Displacement and Integration*, New York, A.S. Barnes, 1963, p. 108, quotes figures revealing that, from mid-August to mid-November 1947, about 10.2 million people migrated from, or to, West Pakistan. They comprised 4.4 million Hindus and Sikhs who went to India and 5.8 million Muslims who went to Pakistan. The violence and privations associated with this upheaval resulted in large numbers from all communities being killed or abducted, or dying. No exact fatality figures are available. Schechtman states that estimates range from 1 million provided by 'authoritative circles in New Delhi' to a (surely incorrect) figure of 'twenty or thirty thousand' given by Nehru.

7. See Christopher Snedden, 'What Happened to Muslims in Jammu? Local Identity, "'the Massacre' of 1947" and the Roots of the "Kashmir Problem"', *South Asia: Journal of South Asian Studies*, Volume XXIV, Number 2, December 2001.
8. *The Times*, 10 October 1947.
9. Ian Stephens, *Horned Moon. An Account of a Journey through Pakistan, Kashmir, and Afghanistan*, London, Chatto & Windus, 1953, p. 108. Stephens was editor of *The Statesman*, Calcutta and New Delhi, from 1942 to 1949.
10. *CMG*, 8 October 1947.
11. Ibid., 18 October 1947. The paper's report followed the arrest of the editor of the *Kashmir Times* on 17 October when he was attempting to leave J&K.
12. *The Times*, 10 October 1947. *The Times* confirmed most of the activities described beforehand, including the closure of the *Kashmir Times*.
13. *CMG*, 21 October 1947.
14. *TOI*, 20 October 1947.
15. A typical example is contained in the (emotively-titled) book: Jasjit Singh, Editor, *Pakistan Occupied Kashmir Under the Jackboot*, New Delhi, Siddhi Books, 1995, pp. vi, 3.
16. Chapters 4 and 6 discuss events in Gilgit. While significant, these events took place after, and possibly because of, Maharaja Hari Singh's accession to India.
17. Brecher, *The Struggle for Kashmir*, p. 25. Brecher himself also only devotes four paragraphs to the Poonch uprising.
18. Symonds, *In the Margins of Independence*, p. 77.
19. HGS, 'Poonch 1937—1947', in *Powell Collection, Papers and Correspondence*, p. 4.
20. Annex 7, 'Minutes of the Meeting with the Defence Minister of the "Azad Kashmir Government"', in UNCIP, *Report of the Sub-committee on Western Kashmir*, p. 71, and Appendix I, 'Extracts from Pamphlets "Military Background of the Kashmir Liberation Movement" and "Annual Administration Report of the Ministry of Defence"', attached to Annex 7, p. 73.
21. Sardar M. Ibrahim Khan, *The Kashmir Saga*, p. 52.
22. Singh, *History of Jammu and Kashmir Rifles*, p. 219. *Kashmir Before Accession*, Lahore, [No Publisher Details [Printed by the Superintendent, Government Printing, West Punjab]], 1948, various pages, also talks of Poonchis being disarmed.
23. I have no figures for the number of Poonchis in the Pakistan Army in 1947 but, according to Messervy, 'Kashmir', p. 475, 'some 15,000' Poonchis were in it in 1949. Messervy was Commander-in-Chief of the Pakistan Army from 15 August 1947 to 15 February 1948.
24. Sardar M. Ibrahim Khan, *The Kashmir Saga*, p. 55.
25. *Kashmir Before Accession*, p. 21. India and Pakistan obtained independent dominion status at midnight on 14 August. For Pakistan, 'independence day' is 14 August; for India, it is 15 August. Each dominion became completely independent of all British ties (apart from membership of the Commonwealth) after adopting their own constitution on 'republic day': 26 January 1950 for India; 23 March 1956 for Pakistan
26. *Kashmir Before Accession*, p. 11; pp. 17–20 has interviews with Poonchis describing their 'sufferings' at the hands of these elements.
27. Suharwardy, *Tragedy in Kashmir*, p. 203.

28. Sardar Muhammad Abdul Qayyum Khan, *The Kashmir Case* Rawalpindi?, Al-Mujahid Academy?, 1992, p. 2.
29. Sardar M. Ibrahim Khan, *The Kashmir Saga*, p. 45; Lamb, *Kashmir, A Disputed Legacy*, p. 123, also states that it began in June; Birdwood, *Two Nations and Kashmir*, p. 49, states that the campaign began in the spring of 1947. Lamb, *Birth of a Tragedy*, p. 61, claims that, by 14–15 August, this 'essentially separatist movement had spread beyond Poonch into Mirpur and parts, even, of Jammu'.
30. *Kashmir Before Accession*, p. 12; Sardar M. Ibrahim Khan, *The Kashmir Saga*, p. 45.
31. Ibid., p. 12.
32. Imrany, *Paradise Under the Shadow of Hell*, p. v.
33. De Mhaffe, *Road to Kashmir*, p. 170.
34. Zaidi, *Jinnah Papers*, Volume V, pp. 571–2.
35. Izzatullah, *Kashmir-Plebiscite*, p. 72.
36. Saraf, *Kashmiris Fight—For Freedom*, Volume II, p. 848.
37. *Kashmir's Fight for Freedom*, Washington, Department of Public Relations, Azad Kashmir Government, 1948, p. 2. Also Symonds, 'With the Rebel Forces of Poonch' and Symonds, *In the Margins of Independence*, p. 78.
38. Prasad and Pal, *History of Operations in Jammu & Kashmir (1947–48)*, p. 13. This official Indian publication does not discuss the Poonch uprising—it mentions 'Punch' in relation to alleged cross-border raids into J&K.
39. Symonds, *In the Margins of Independence*, p. 78.
40. Symonds, 'With the Rebel Forces of Poonch'.
41. *Kashmir's Fight for Freedom*, Washington, Department of Public Relations, Azad Kashmir Government, p. 3.
42. Later a prominent political leader in Azad Kashmir.
43. *CMG*, 19 February 1948. According to this report, the Maharaja's government had once offered a Rs. 5,000 reward for Qayyum's capture 'dead or alive'. At that stage, Qayyum also believed that the anti-Indian forces would triumph in J&K: 'As to the end, it is a certainty. We must win.' Sardar Muhammad Abdul Qayyum Khan, *The Kashmir Case*, p. 12, states that people call him 'Mujahid-e-Awwal' (the first *mujahid* or freedom fighter, crusader, warrior—all are given as translations in his book), for 'initiat[ing] an armed struggle against the Dogra Raj, in the State of Jammu and Kashmir. Whether you call it a conspiracy, rebellion or movement, it was I who started it'.
44. Symonds, 'With the Rebel Forces of Poonch'.
45. Messervy, 'Kashmir', p. 469.
46. *White Paper on Jammu & Kashmir*, pp. 6–12.
47. Singh, *History of Jammu and Kashmir Rifles*, p. 222.
48. *Defending Kashmir*, Appendix I, Delhi, The Publications Division, Ministry of Information and Broadcasting, Government of India, 1949, pp. 159–62.
49. *White Paper on Jammu & Kashmir*, p. 6. According to Rakesh Ankit, 'The Forgotten Soldier of Kashmir', *Epilogue*, 12 May 2010, www.epilogue.in/detailnews.aspx?mwid=781 [accessed 1 August 2010], Scott served in this position from 1936 to September 1947.
50. *Census of India 1941*, p. 232.

51. Izzatullah, *Kashmir-Plebiscite*, pp. 73–4.
52. *CMG*, 22 October 1947. A press note dated 24 October in *The Statesman*, 26 October 1947, also spoke of 'incidents' in Sialkot district 'by raiders from across the Sialkot-Jammu border'.
53. Appendix I, 'Extracts from Pamphlets "Military Background of the Kashmir Liberation Movement" and "Annual Administration Report of the Ministry of Defence"', attached to Annex 7, 'Minutes of the Meeting with the Defence Minister of the "Azad Kashmir Government"', in UNCIP, *Report of the Sub-committee on Western Kashmir*, p. 73.
54. Symonds, 'With the Rebel Forces of Poonch'. I can confirm this steepness.
55. HGS, 'Poonch 1937—1947', p. 1, in *Powell Collection, Papers and Correspondence*.
56. Izzatullah, *Kashmir-Plebiscite*, p. 72.
57. Sardar M. Ibrahim Khan, *The Kashmir Saga*, pp. 69–70.
58. Suharwardy, *Tragedy in Kashmir*, p. 107.
59. Sardar M. Ibrahim Khan, *The Kashmir Saga*, p. 84.
60. Suharwardy, *Tragedy in Kashmir*, p. 135.
61. Victoria Schofield, *Kashmir in the Crossfire*, London, I.B. Tauris, 1996, p. 134, 311, footnote 64.
62. Annex 7, 'Minutes of the Meeting with the Defence Minister of the "Azad Kashmir Government"', in UNCIP, *Report of the Sub-committee on Western Kashmir*, pp. 70–71.
63. Appendix I, 'Military Matters', attached to Annex 3, 'Questionnaire and Answers of Azad Authorities', in UNCIP, *Report of the Sub-committee on Western Kashmir*, p. 51.
64. Leutenant General Sardar F.S. Lodi, '50 Years of Azad Kashmir Regiment', *The Nation*, 14 October 1997.
65. Annex 7, 'Minutes of the Meeting with the Defence Minister of the "Azad Kashmir Government"', in UNCIP, *Report of the Sub-committee on Western Kashmir*, p. 70. According to Lieutenant Colonel (Retired) M.A. Haq Mirza, Sher-i-Jang, *The Withering Chinar*, Islamabad, Institute of Policy Studies, 1991?, p. 21, Colonel Ali Ahmad Shah was only a major in 1948.
66. Appendix I, 'Military Matters', attached to Annex 3, 'Questionnaire and Answers of Azad Authorities', in UNCIP, *Report of the Sub-committee on Western Kashmir*, p. 49.
67. Appendix 1, 'Extracts from Pamphlets "Military Background of the Kashmir Liberation Movement" and "Annual Administration Report of the Ministry of Defence"', attached to Annex 3, 'Minutes of the Meeting with the Defence Minister of the "Azad Kashmir Government"', in UNCIP, *Report of the Sub-committee on Western Kashmir*, pp. 70–71.
68. Annex 7, 'Minutes of the Meeting with the Defence Minister of the "Azad Kashmir Government"', in UNCIP, *Report of the Sub-committee on Western Kashmir*, p. 70. In 1949, this pay was increased to Rs. 20 per month.
69. Appendix I, 'Military Matters', attached to Annex 3, 'Questionnaire and Answers of Azad Authorities', in UNCIP, *Report of the Sub-committee on Western Kashmir*, p. 49.
70. Appendix I, 'Extracts from Pamphlets "Military Background of the Kashmir Liberation Movement" and "Annual Administration Report of the Ministry of Defence"', attached to Annex 7, 'Minutes of the Meeting with the Defence Minister of the "Azad

Kashmir Government'", in UNCIP, *Report of the Sub-committee on Western Kashmir*, pp. 70–71.
71. Sardar Muhammad Abdul Qayyum Khan, *The Kashmir Case*, p. 103.
72. Ibid., p. 115.
73. Ibid., p. 70.
74. UNCIP, *Report of the Sub-committee on Western Kashmir*, p. 13.
75. Hafizullah, *Towards Azad Kashmir*, p. 97; Sardar M. Ibrahim Khan, *The Kashmir Saga*, Second Edition, 1990, p. 103.
76. Hasan Zaheer, *The Times and Trials of the Rawalpindi Conspiracy 1951*, Karachi, Oxford University Press, 1998, pp. 29–160, details the events in J&K that encouraged Khan.
77. Sardar M. Ibrahim Khan, *The Kashmir Saga*, p. 74.
78. Lamb, *Kashmir, A Disputed Legacy*, p. 129.
79. Sardar M. Ibrahim Khan, *The Kashmir Saga*, p. 74.
80. Hafizullah, *Towards Azad Kashmir*, p. 93. The RSS (National Self-Service Society) was a right-wing Hindu organisation.
81. Suharwardy, *Tragedy in Kashmir*, p. 110.
82. *The Times*, 8 September 1947.
83. *CMG*, 2 October 1947.
84. Ibid., 19 October 1947.
85. Ibid., 21 October 1947.
86. Ibid., 28 October 1947.
87. *The Times*, 25 October 1947.
88. Ibid., 30 October 1947.
89. *CMG*, 23 October 1947.
90. *The Times*, 28 October 1947.
91. Bazaz, *Inside Kashmir*, pp. 202, 204.
92. Rai, *Hindu Rulers, Muslim Subjects*, p. 243.
93. *The Azad Jammu and Kashmir Interim Constitution Act, 1974 (Amended upto* [sic] *date) May 1997*, Muzaffarabad, Azad Goverment of the State of Jammu & Kashmir (Law, Justice and Parliamentary Affairs Department), 1997, p. 4, states that this was the 'late Government of the State of Jammu and Kashmir Notification No. 1-L/84, dated the 20th April, 1927'.
94. According to Fazili, *Kashmir Government and Politics*, pp. 131–3, all persons resident in J&K before 1885 were Class I State Subjects; those who came between 1885 and 1911, were Class II State Subjects; those who came after 1911 and before 31 January 1927 and had obtained a concession or permission to purchase immovable property were Class III State Subjects. Class IV State Subjects related to companies. In my interview with Sardar Ibrahim at Rawalakot on 4 March 1999, he told me that Chaudhry Ghulam Abbas's forebears were from Jullundur in Punjab and that Abbas was a Class III state subject.
95. Riyaz Punjabi, 'Kashmiriyat: The Mystique of an Ethnicity', *Indian International Centre Quarterly*, Volume 17, Number 2, 1990, p. 114.
96. In December 2004, in Lahore, Rawalpindi and Sialkot, my wife, Diane Barbeler, and I interviewed a number of Muslims who were living in Jammu Province in 1947 and

heard terrible stories about how Hindus and Sikhs had wreaked death and destruction on Muslims and their communities. In Jammu City in December 2004–January 2005, I heard more of the same from Muslims who had remained in Indian J&K. Equally, I heard terrible stories from Hindus who had lived in Mirpur and Muzaffarabad in 1947 about how Muslims had wreaked similar death and destruction on Hindus. All communities suffered in 1947.

97. Author unknown, 'Jammu and Kashmir State 1947', p. 1, in *Powell Collection, Papers and Correspondence*. The author further states that 'in a single [unnamed] month no less than 100,000 [refugees] passed through Jammu Province'.
98. *CMG*, 17 September 1947, quoting a report from their Jammu correspondent dated 4 September.
99. Ibid., 20 September 1947. *Census of India 1961*, Volume VI, *Jammu and Kashmir*, Part I-A (i), *General Report*, Srinagar, M.H. Kamili, Superintendent of Census Operations Jammu and Kashmir, Census of India, 1968, p. 157, states that, in 1961, Indian J&K had 68,291 immigrants who had lived there less than sixteen years. Two-thirds of these comprised 'displaced persons from West Pakistan'. Part I-A (ii), pp. 76–77, states that almost all of these immigrants had settled in Jammu.
100. *CMG*, 17 September 1947.
101. *Kashmir's Fight for Freedom*, [Washington], Deppartment of Public Relations, Azad Kashmir Government, pp. 2–3; *Kashmir Before Accession*, Foreword; De Mhaffe, *Road to Kashmir*, p. 169.
102. Hafizullah, *Towards Azad Kashmir*, pp. 55, 83; Islam, *The Revolution in Kashmir*, pp. 7–8.
103. *Kashmir's Fight for Freedom* [Washington], Department of Public Relations, Azad Kashmir Government, pp. 5–6.
104. *Kashmir Before Accession*, pp. 29–53, discusses and provides accounts of anti-Muslim activities in Jammu. Appendix C, pp. viii-xx, provides 'Details regarding the Loss of Life and Property of Muslims in Jammu and Kashmir States [sic]'. Its figures were probably calculated from information obtained from 'persons displaced' from J&K who had successfully made an 'entry into Pakistan'.
105. Ibid., various pages. It is impossible to state exact figures as, in a number of cases, a date range is given, e.g. Incident fifty-eight (p. xiv) took place between the dates '20th to 29th October 1947'.
106. Hafizullah, *Towards Azad Kashmir*, pp. 83–90; De Mhaffe, *Road to Kashmir*, pp. 169–81, 188–94; Izzatullah, *Kashmir-Plebiscite*, pp. 71–3; Islam, *The Revolution in Kashmir*, pp. 20–1, 25–6; Imrany, *Paradise Under the Shadow of Hell*, pp. 20–23.
107. UNCIP, *Report of the Sub-committee on Western Kashmir*, p. 16.
108. Annex 9, 'Tour Diary, Mirpur District', in UNCIP, *Report of the Sub-committee on Western Kashmir*, p. 87. Interestingly, the *zaildar*, whose name was not given, was 'produced' by a 'Mr. Mainprice'. For further information about this man, see below.
109. *CMG*, 26 September 1947.
110. Ibid., 14 and 17 September 1947.
111. Ibid., 8 October 1947.
112. Ibid., 19, 21, 22, 23 (two reports), 24, 25 (two reports), 26, 27 October 1947.
113. Ibid., 22 October 1947.

114. Ibid., 26 October 1947. Information in this paragraph is from this report.
115. Appendix D, *Kashmir Before Accession*, pp. xxi–xxix, also provides details of thirty-eight cross-border 'raids' by elements from J&K (usually comprising 'Dogra troops' and 'non-Muslim civilians') into the adjoining Gujrat and Sialkot districts of Pakistan.
116. Information and quotations in this paragraph are from *CMG*, 28 October 1947.
117. *The Times*, 17, 18, 20 November 1947; *TOI*, 28 October 1947.
118. *CMG*, 21 November 1947.
119. *NYT*, 26 November 1947.
120. *CMG*, 18 December 1947. Also published in *Dawn*, Karachi, 23 December 1947.
121. It is probable the 'Englishmen' were Horace Alexander and Richard Symonds. In his article 'With the Rebel Forces in Poonch', *The Statesman*, 4 February 1948, Symonds mentioned that, around the end of November 1947, Alexander was given 'facilities' by the governments of India and J&K and had 'gone to investigate the condition of Muslims in Jammu' while he (Symonds) had gone to 'visit concentrations of Hindus and Sikhs' in Azad Kashmir. Richard Symonds, *In the Margins of Independence*, various references, also discusses how both men, as members of the [Society of] Friends Ambulance Unit and later as volunteers for India and Pakistan, witnessed and investigated the effects of inter-religious in J&K in 1947. On p. 55, Symonds states that, on 23 October 1947, he met the 'British assistant editor' of *CMG* in Lahore who was 'apologetic' that *CMG* had 'unfortunately described Horace and myself as agents of Nehru and had not indicated that we had been appointed jointly by both sides'.
122. Aziz Beg, *Captive Kashmir*, Lahore, Allied Business Corporation, 1957, p. 32. *Kashmir Before Accession*, pp. 22–50, had similar reports by survivors of anti-Muslim violence in Jammu.
123. *The Times*, 17 November 1947.
124. This paragraph based on *CMG*, 18 December 1947.
125. Ibid.
126. *White Paper on Jammu & Kashmir*, pp. 65–6.
127. *CMG*, 2 December 1947.
128. *White Paper on Jammu & Kashmir*, p. 71.
129. *CMG*, 17 December 1947.
130. Abdullah, *Flames of the Chinar*, p. 97.
131. Birdwood, *Two Nations and Kashmir*, p. 51.
132. Similar stories were related to me by two Azad Kashmiris. The Azad Kashmir Mohtasib (Ombudsman), Tariq Masud, who was nine years old in 1947, told me during a number of meetings with him on visits to Muzaffarabad from December 1997 to January 1998 and in March 1999 that, around October-November 1947, he and his family were part of a convoy going to Pakistan that was stopped by Sikhs and other non-Muslims. The Muslims fled through fields towards Sialkot. Masud, his parents and his three siblings all reached Pakistan alive. On 13 March 1999 in Muzaffarabad, Malik Rashid, former head of the Kashmir Liberation Cell, Muzaffarabad, told me he was nineteen years old in Reasi in 1947. He left Jammu in December after, and because of, the killing of Muslims. Hindus killed his father, all his brothers (except his eldest brother) and his wife. According to Rashid, the Maharaja's Hindu-majority armed

forces made the difference, otherwise it would have been a local, and far more equal, fight between Hindus and Muslims. In December 2004–January 2005, my wife and I also interviewed Jammu Muslims—and Hindus—who experienced the terrible turmoil and violence of 1947. Their stories provide further support for the evidence reported by the Englishmen.

133. Symonds, 'With the Rebel Forces of Poonch'.
134. Horace Alexander, 'India-Pakistan I', *The Spectator*, London, Issue 180, 16 January 1948, pp. 66–7.
135. Alexander, 'India-Pakistan I', p. 66. Alexander had met Gandhi on 1 November 1947.
136. 'Speech at a Prayer Meeting, November 27, 1947', in *The Collected Works of Mahatma Gandhi*, Volume XC (November 11, 1947–January 30, 1948), New Delhi, Publications Division, Ministry of Information and Broadcasting, Government of India, 1984, p. 115.
137. 'Speech at Guru Nanak Birthday Function, November 28, 1947', in *The Collected Works of Mahatma Gandhi*, Volume XC, p. 123.
138. Abdullah, *Flames of the Chinar*, p. 98.
139. 'Speech at a Prayer Meeting, New Delhi, December 25, 1947', in *The Collected Works of Mahatma Gandhi*, Volume XC, p. 299.
140. *CMG*, 27 December 1947.
141. Stephens, *Pakistan*, p. 200.
142. Abdullah, *Flames of the Chinar*, p. 99.
143. This paragraph is based on, with all quotations taken from, *The Times*, 10 August 1948. This was the Special Correspondent's second report on 'The Fate of Kashmir'. The first, subtitled 'An India-Pakistan Battleground', appeared on 9 August 1948.
144. Consultations in July–August 2000 with Mr Nick Mays, Deputy Archivist at News International, London, and Dr Kevin Greenbank, Centre of South Asian Studies, University of Cambridge, reveal that the 'Special Correspondent' was Frederick Paul Mainprice. (The Centre of South Asian Studies holds Mainprice's papers.) An officer of the Indian Civil Service, Mainprice was Assistant Political Agent, Gilgit, until August 1947. From 14 June 1948, he holidayed in Kashmir but was expelled on 13 September, possibly for pro-Pakistan leanings. Given that *The Times* adhered strongly to a policy of protecting author anonymity, Mr Mays is confident that the Indian J&K Government would not have known Mainprice had written *The Times*' articles that had appeared during his stay in the Kashmir Valley. Mainprice's figures may need to be taken with 'a grain of salt' as he later worked for the Pakistan Government on the Kashmir problem. Indeed, a 'Mr. Mainprice' is mentioned in Annex 9, 'Tour Diary, Mirpur District', in UNCIP, *Report of the Sub-committee on Western Kashmir*, p. 80, as being 'Deputy Secretary, Government of Pakistan'.
145. Discussions in December 1997, January 1998 and March 1999 in Islamabad, Rawalpindi and Muzaffarabad with people who left Jammu Province or Kashmir Province in 1947, or soon thereafter, either for Azad Kashmir or Pakistan.
146. Hafizullah, *Towards Azad Kashmir*, p. 119.
147. M.A. Gurmani, *Kashmir: A Survey*, Rawalpindi?, Public Relations Directorate, Ministry of Kashmir, Government of Pakistan, 1952?, p. 38.

148. This rest of this paragraph based on *Dawn*, 2 January 1951.
149. Balraj Madhok, *Kashmir: Centre of New Alignments*, New Delhi, Deepak Prakashan, 1963, p. 76. Far more research is needed on the neglected subject of Muslim violence against Hindus and Sikhs in Mirpur, Poonch, Muzaffarabad and other places in J&K in 1947.
150. *White Paper on Jammu & Kashmir*, pp. 27–8.
151. Jyoti Bhusan Das Gupta, *Jammu and Kashmir*, The Hague, Martinus Nijhoff, 1968, p. 97, quoting 'Balraj Madhok, *Kashmir, Center* [sic] *of New Alignments* (New Delhi 1963), 70–5'. Balraj Madhok, *Kashmir: Centre of New Alignments*, pp. 70–75, does discuss anti-Hindu violence in Bhimber, Rajauri, Kotli, Mirpur, Deva Vatala and Poonch town. However, Professor Madhok's credentials on this issue are questionable. His book's back cover states that he 'collaborated' with Dr Shyama Prasad Mukherjee (who died tragically in 1953 while in custody in an Indian J&K jail) in forming the right-wing, Hindu-nationalist 'Bhartiya [sic] Jan [sic] Sangh' party. More pointedly, Madhok's back cover also states that he had 'a distinguished academic career'. Despite this, he does not provide any substantiating sources, references or bibliography for his (rather serious) case.
152. Sardar M. Ibrahim Khan, *The Kashmir Saga*, pp. 49–50. Sardar Ibrahim confirmed (sadly) that Hindus had been killed when I interviewed him at Rawalakot on 4 March 1999. H.L. Bhagotra, 'Foreword', in C.P. Gupta, *The Directory of Mirpur Mahajan Families Settled in Jammu*, Jammu, Mirpur Mahajan Sabha, 1997, claims that after Mirpur fell in November 1947, 'not less than 20,000 citizens of Mirpur … lost their lives, about 2500 were captured by the enemy and the remaining about 2500 migrated to different parts of India'. Later in this publication, Gupta, who is both a Mirpur victim/survivor and a member of the Mirpur Mahajan Sabha community (as is Bhagotra, its president), gives an account entitled 'Mirpur (How it fell to Pakistan [sic] in 1947)', unnumbered pages. Gupta and other Mirpuris told me in Jammu City in 2005 that, much to their chagrin, they are still seeking to be classified as internally displaced people within J&K (i.e. internal refugees).
153. UNCIP, *Report of the Sub-committee on Western Kashmir*, p. 3.
154. For the post-ceasefire structure of divided J&K, see Appendix V: Physical and Political Composition of J&K after the 1949 Ceasefire.
155. *Census of Azad Kashmir, 1951*, p. 12.
156. Snedden, 'What Happened to Muslims in Jammu?', p. 127.
157. 'Extracts from the translation of a diary captured at Uri by 161 Bde and forwarded to H.Q. Delhi, and Eastern Command Secretariat, February, 1948', *White Paper on Jammu & Kashmir*, p. 31, states that 'nearly 22,000 Hindus and Sikhs were killed in villages *en route* from Kohala to Uri' which, if true, is (another) extraordinary statistic in the list of violence that occurred in J&K in 1947.
158. *Census of India 1961*, pp. 272, 360. In January 2005, I also interviewed a number of non-Muslims (Hindus, predominantly) who had fled with their families from Mirpur, Muzaffarabad and Poonch and had ended up living in Jammu City.
159. Snedden, 'What Happened to Muslims in Jammu?', p. 127.
160. *Census of India 1961*, p. 359.

161. *Kashmir's Fight for Freedom*, Washington, Department of Public Relations, Azad Kashmir Government, p. 2.
162. Hafizullah, *Towards Azad Kashmir*, pp. 55, 83.
163. *Kashmir's Fight for Freedom*, Washington, Department of Public Relations, Azad Kashmir Government, p. 3. I am unable to confirm where martial law was imposed. This may have been done locally in areas such as Poonch. Otherwise, the Maharaja's troops were severely extended in 1947, which would have made an imposition of martial law throughout J&K unenforceable.
164. Sardar M. Ibrahim Khan, *The Kashmir Saga*, p. 56.
165. *Kashmir's Fight for Freedom*, Washington, Department of Public Relations, Azad Kashmir Government, p. 3.
166. Prem Nath Bazaz, *The History of Struggle for Freedom in Kashmir*, Karachi, National Book Foundation, 1976 [First published by Kashmir Publishing [sic] Company, New Delhi, 1954], p. 620.
167. *CMG*, 8 October 1947. *CMG* stated that 'Mr. Anwar is a prominent member of the Kashmir Muslim Conference'. Bazaz, *The History of Struggle for Freedom in Kashmir*, p. 621, revealed that 'Mr. Anwar' was Ghulam Nabi Gilkar, a member of the working committee of the Muslim Conference. This was confirmed by C. Bilqees Taseer, *The Kashmir of Sheikh Muhammad Abdullah*, Lahore, Ferozsons, 1986, p. 317, who stated that Gilkar had once been a 'very loyal worker' of Sheikh Abdullah.
168. Bazaz, *The History of Struggle for Freedom in Kashmir*, p. 620.
169. Ibid., pp. 620–21. Taseer, *The Kashmir of Sheikh Muhammad Abdullah*, p. 317.
170. Saraf, *Kashmiris Fight—For Freedom*, Volume II, pp. 1286–7.
171. Bazaz, *The History of Struggle for Freedom in Kashmir*, p. 621.
172. Prasad and Pal, *History of Operations in Jammu & Kashmir (1947–48)*, p. 21.
173. Saraf, *Kashmiris Fight—For Freedom*, Volume II, pp. 891–2.
174. The tribesmen should have been prevented from entering J&K. *CMG*, 23 October 1947, published a communiqué by the NWFP Government on 22 October that stated that: 'Elaborate precautionary measures have been taken all along the border [with J&K] to prevent tribesmen and local inhabitants going into Kashmir state'. *CMG*, 28 October 1947, stated that the 'gathering of tribesmen near Peshawar was known some days before the lashkar began to move'. These reports suggest complicity by some Pakistani officials in the Pukhtoon invasion.
175. Although not Sardar Ibrahim, it seems. In *The Kashmir Saga*, pp. 80–81, he states the tribals were skilled in ambush and hand-to-hand combat ('dagger fighting'), but they lacked the discipline and skills to fight an organised enemy, to capture territory quickly or to engage in conventional warfare.
176. Bazaz, *The History of Struggle for Freedom in Kashmir*, p. 622.
177. Appendix VII: Main Office Holders of Azad Kashmir.
178. Birdwood, *Two Nations and Kashmir*, p. 81.
179. Sardar M. Ibrahim Khan, *The Kashmir Saga*, p. 51; 'Statement showing the Results of the [1947] Elections', in *The Jammu and Kashmir Praja Sabha Debates*, p. 4. There were '16,229' possible votes in the 'Bagh Sadnooti Muslim' constituency.
180. Saraf, *Kashmiris Fight—For Freedom*, Volume II, p. 1288.

181. *CMG*, 24 July 1947.
182. Saraf, *Kashmiris Fight—For Freedom*, Volume II, p. 712. This 'historic' resolution is on pp. 711–12.
183. *CMG*, 3 July 1947.
184. HGS, 'Poonch 1937- -1947', in *Powell Collection, Papers and Correspondence*, p. 3.
185. Saraf, *Kashmiris Fight—For Freedom*, Volume II, p. 1288.
186. 'Statement showing the Results of the [1947] Elections', in *The Jammu and Kashmir Praja Sabha Debate*, p. 3, shows that 'Ch. Hamid Ullah' obtained 1,357 votes of the 1,925 votes cast out of a possible 3,104 votes to beat three other candidates and be elected for the 'Jammu City (Muslim)' constituency in the Praja Sabha.
187. Bazaz, *The History of Struggle for Freedom in Kashmir*, p. 626.
188. Islam, *The Revolution in Kashmir*, p. 7.
189. Sardar M. Ibrahim Khan, *The Kashmir Saga*, pp. 61, 62.
190. Saraf, *Kashmiris Fight—For Freedom*, Volume II, pp. 1288–9.
191. Sardar M. Ibrahim Khan, *The Kashmir Saga*, p. 98.
192. *CMG*, 25 October 1947.
193. *TOI*, 28 October 1947.
194. Saraf, *Kashmiris Fight—For Freedom*, Volume II, p. 1288.
195. *CMG*, 25 October 1947, reported this communiqué in its entirety.
196. *CMG*, 1 November 1947, reported 'a communiqué issued by the Azad Kashmir Government'.
197. *Keesing's Contemporary Archives*, London, Longman, Volume VI (1947), p. 8931.
198. *The Times*, 1 November 1947.
199. *CMG*, 28 October 1947.
200. Hafizullah, *Towards Azad Kashmir*, p. 105.
201. *CMG*, 29 October 1947. Curiously, the Azad Kashmir Government also requested 'India and Pakistan not to use the Kashmir aerodrome [i.e. Srinagar] because it is unsafe'.
202. Sardar M. Ibrahim Khan, *The Kashmir Saga*, Second Edition, pp. 209–210, states in an added new chapter, 'Some Blunders Committed in Kashmir', that, in November 1947, he wanted Pakistan to accept an accession from the Government of Azad Jammu and Kashmir, a 'parallel' (or rival) government in J&K that 'had liberated at least half of the state'. This would have given Pakistan 'a good enough legal coverage' to allow the Pakistan Army then to enter J&K. Jinnah 'almost adopted' this position in November 1947, but Liaquat Ali Khan rejected it. According to Ibrahim, had the Pakistan Army entered J&K then, 'things would have turned in our favour'. Instead, Pakistan committed a 'grave error'.

## 3. INDIA AND PAKISTAN: NEGATING THE PEOPLE'S ACTIONS

1. Ian Talbot, *Pakistan: A Modern History*, London, Hurst & Company, 1998, p. 115, footnote 86, believes that the 'balance of evidence seems to indicate that the Pakistan Government did not instigate the tribal incursion which was a spontaneous *jihad*', although

NWFP and Punjab officials and politicians 'sympathised with the action and on occasion assisted the transit of the tribesmen'. Andrew Whitehead, *A Mission in Kashmir*, New Delhi, Penguin Viking, 2007, various pages, who meticulously discusses the Pukhtoons' invasion of J&K, suggests that at the very least Pakistanis, including Jinnah, knew what was going on. On p. 51, Whitehead states that 'The Pakistani authorities have persistently denied that they gave substantial material help to the tribal invasion … but the evidence of published memoirs and in the archives points in the other direction.' Interestingly, the Chief Minister of NWFP in 1947, Khan Abdul Qayyum (Qayum/Qaiyum) Khan, who was involved in organising and supporting the tribal invasion of Kashmir Province in October 1947, was the elder brother of a later President and Prime Minister of Azad Kashmir, Khan Abdul Hamid Khan. According to Ian Talbot, *Pakistan: A Modern History*, London, Hurst & Company, Third Edition, 2009, p. 462, Khan Abdul Qayyum Khan was 'born in Chitral of Kashmiri origin'. Saraf, *Kashmiris Fight—For Freedom*, Volume II, pp. 791, 1344, confirms the brothers' relationship and states that Qayyum Khan was from 'village Wanigam, in Baramula district', where he had land and a house. He also had 'a house in Baramula town', where, as we shall see, Pukhtoon tribesmen committed excesses in 1947.
2. Prem Nath Bazaz, *Truth About Kashmir*, Delhi, The Kashmir Democratic Union, 1950, p. 5.
3. Abdullah, *Flames of the Chinar*, pp. 90, 97–9.
4. 'Telegram dated 31st October 1947, from Foreign, New Delhi, to Punsg, Lahore, Foreign, Karachi' in *White Paper on Jammu & Kashmir*, p. 50.
5. Nehru to Patel, 30 December 1947, in Gopal, *Selected Works of Jawaharlal Nehru*, p. 414.
6. Patel to Maharaja of Jammu and Kashmir, 2 October 1947, in P.N. Chopra, Chief Editor, *The Collected Works of Sardar Vallabhbhai Patel*, Delhi, Volume XII, Konark Publishers, 1998, p. 211.
7. *White Paper on Jammu & Kashmir*, pp. 7–8.
8. Gopal, *Selected Works of Jawaharlal Nehru*, p. 265.
9. Patel to Mahatma Gandhi, 30 August 1947, in Chopra, *The Collected Works of Sardar Vallabhbhai Patel*, p. 193.
10. Ibid., 21 April 1947.
11. Letter to M.C. Mahajan, 21 October 1947, in Gopal, *Selected Works of Jawaharlal Nehru*, p. 272.
12. This paragraph based on Enclosure, Nehru to Patel, 5 October 1947, in Das, *Sardar Patel's Correspondence*, p. 54.
13. *CMG*, 23 October 1947.
14. Ibid..
15. Nehru to Abdullah, 10 October 1947, Gopal, *Selected Works of Jawaharlal Nehru*, p. 270.
16. They had not yet had their titles changed to chief minister.
17. G. Parthasarathi, General Editor, *Jawaharlal Nehru: Letters to Chief Ministers 1947–1964*, New Delhi, Jawaharlal Nehru Memorial Fund, 1985, p. 7.
18. Gopal, *Selected Works of Jawaharlal Nehru*, p. 341.
19. Jawaharlal Nehru, *India's Foreign Policy, Selected Speeches, September 1946—April 1961*,

New Delhi, Publications Division, Ministry of Information and Broadcasting, Government of India, 1961, p. 444.
20. Gopal, *Selected Works of Jawaharlal Nehru*, pp. 350–51.
21. Ibid., p. 416.
22. Ibid., p. 364.
23. Ibid., p. 400.
24. Except where otherwise stated, all references in this paragraph from Das, *Sardar Patel's Correspondence*, pp. 45–7. This letter is also in Gopal, *Selected Works of Jawaharlal Nehru*, pp. 263–5.
25. Nehru, *India's Foreign Policy*, p. 443.
26. Sardar Patel to Sardar Baldev Singh, 7 October 1947, in Das, *Sardar Patel's Correspondence*, p. 59.
27. Nehru, *India's Foreign Policy*, pp. 443–46.
28. *CMG*, 4 November 1947, reported the text of Nehru's broadcast. Quotations in this paragraph are from that report. It is also in *White Paper on Jammu & Kashmir*, pp. 52–5, although it gives the date of the speech as 2 November.
29. *TOI*, 28 October 1947.
30. *White Paper on Jammu & Kashmir*, p. 3.
31. *CMG*, 2 November 1947.
32. 'Hindustan Times, 11th November 1947. By a correspondent of the United Press of America', in *White Paper on Jammu & Kashmir*, p. 40.
33. Messervy, 'Kashmir', p. 475; Annex 7, 'Minutes of the Meeting with the Defence Minister of the "Azad Kashmir Government"', in UNCIP, *Report of the Sub-committee on Western Kashmir*, p. 71.
34. *Defending Kashmir*, p. 8.
35. Ibid., Appendix I, p. 161.
36. 'Appendix IV: Attacks on Sialkot-Jammu border', *The Sikhs in Action*, Lahore, Government of Punjab?, 1948, pp. xxi–xxix. This (possibly partisan) document records thirty-three incidents that took place in East Punjab and thirty incidents in West Punjab from 16 September 1947 to 21 November 1947.
37. Karaka, *Betrayal*, pp. 173–4.
38. Information in this paragraph from *White Paper on Jammu & Kashmir*, various pages.
39. *White Paper on Jammu & Kashmir*, Foreword.
40. Ibid., p. 6.
41. Ibid., p. 3.
42. This is one reason why Pukhtoons invaded J&K via the all-weather Jhelum Valley Road, even though the aggression against Muslims was in (difficult-to-reach) Jammu Province.
43. *White Paper on Jammu & Kashmir*, pp. 22–3.
44. Singh, *History of Jammu and Kashmir Rifles*, p. 145.
45. *White Paper on Jammu & Kashmir*, p. 33.
46. Whitehead, *A Mission in Kashmir*, discusses events in Baramulla in detail.
47. 'Extracts from the translation of a diary captured at Uri by 161 Bde and forwarded to H.Q. Delhi, and Eastern Command Secretariat, February, 1948', *White Paper on Jammu & Kashmir*, p. 31.

48. Sardar M. Ibrahim Khan, *The Kashmir Saga*, Second Edition, 1990, p. 55.
49. *NYT*, 11 November 1947. *White Paper on Jammu & Kashmir*, p. 24, had a similar (the same?) report by Robert Trumbull, *NYT*, sent from Baramulla on 10 November 1947.
50. *The Times*, 4 November 1947.
51. *NYT*, 11 November 1947. Robert Trumbull, *As I See India*, London, Cassell, 1957, p. 91, who wrote the *NYT* story, states, somewhat sensationally, that the only removable object left in Baramulla was 'an old cover picture from *Life*'.
52. Lamb, *Kashmir, A Disputed Legacy*, p. 143, footnote 26.
53. *NYT*, 17 November 1947.
54. 'Eyewitness Account of Fighting in Vicinity of Baramula [sic], Kashmir', Despatch Number 355 to US Secretary of State by Howard Donovan, Counsellor of the US Embassy, New Delhi, 22 November 1947, in *Confidential U.S.*, Reel Number 10.
55. Lamb, *Kashmir, A Disputed Legacy*, p. 143, footnote 26.
56. Stephens, *Pakistan*, p. 200.
57. *The Times*, 17 November 1947.
58. *White Paper on Jammu & Kashmir*, pp. 65–6.
59. Ibid., p. 70.
60. Parthasarathi, *Jawaharlal Nehru: Letters*, p. 14.
61. *The Times*, 13 January 1948.
62. Ibid.
63. Ibid., 1 January 1948.
64. Kingsley Martin, 'As Pakistan Sees It', *New Statesman and Nation*, Issue 35, London, 6 March 1948, p. 188.
65. Hafizullah, *Towards Azad Kashmir*, p. 103.
66. Zaidi, *Jinnah Papers*, Volume V, *passim* (particularly after p. 540).
67. 'G. Mohamed to Liaquat Ali Khan', in Zaidi, *Jinnah Papers*, Volume V, pp. 561–71.
68. Zaidi, *Jinnah Papers*, Volume V, pp. 571–2.
69. Ibid., Volume V, p. 594.
70. Ibid., Volume V, p. 621. Also reported in *CMG*, 2 October 1947.
71. 'Quaid-i-Azam Refutes Kashmir Government's "*X Parte*" Allegations', in M. Rafique Afzal, editor, *Speeches and Statements of the Quaid-i-Azam Mohammad Ali Jinnah (1911–35 and 1947–48)*, Lahore, Research Society of Pakistan, University of Punjab, 1966, p. 446. This refutation is very similar to a telegram from Jinnah to the Maharaja of J&K on 20 October 1947 in *White Paper on Jammu & Kashmir*, pp. 10–11.
72. 'Telegram to the Prime Minister of Kashmir and Jammu [sic] State', in M. Rafique Afzal, editor, *Speeches and Statements of Quaid-i-Millat Liaquat Ali Khan (1941–51)*, Lahore, Research Society of Pakistan, University of Punjab, 1967, p. 130.
73. Enclosure, Mountbatten to Patel, 2 November 1947, in Das, *Sardar Patel's Correspondence*, p. 75.
74. *White Paper on Jammu & Kashmir*, pp. 57–8.
75. 'Telegram, dated the 4th (received 5th) December 1947, from Punsg, Lahore, to Foreign, New Delhi', in *White Paper on Jammu & Kashmir*, p. 72.
76. *White Paper on Jammu & Kashmir*, pp. 62–5.
77. Conversely, according to *The Times*, 10 November 1947, if the tribesmen had been

assisted by 'another country', that is, by Pakistan, 'they would have captured Srinagar within three days of the crossing the border'.

78. For example, in relation to the timing of the accession, *The Kashmir Dispute and Its Solution. Statement in Parliament by M.A. Gurmani* Karachi, Government of Pakistan, 1951, p. 15, makes the point that 'when the tribesmen went into Kashmir in response to the appeal of the oppressed people of the State, [J&K] had not acceded to India, and India, therefore, had no *locus standi*'. The Maharaja's accession changed that situation and thereafter Pakistan had to justify having a *locus standi* in J&K. For this argument, see Ijaz Hussain, *Kashmir Dispute. An International Law Perspective*, Islamabad, Quaid-i-Azam University, 1998, pp. 54–8.
79. *White Paper on Jammu & Kashmir*, pp. 62–5.
80. Ibid., pp. 56–60.
81. *Kashmir Questions. Extracts from Sir Zafrulla Khan's Speech Before the Security Council, February 1950*, New York, Pakistan Permanent Delegation to the United Nations, 1950, p. 5. (Also spelt as Zafrullah).
82. *Kashmir Questions*, pp. 14–15.
83. Gurmani, *Kashmir: A Survey*, pp. 17–19. In 1965, an official publication, *Story of Kashmir* Karachi, The Department of Films and Publications, Government of Pakistan, 1968, Revised Edition, pp. 7–8, followed the same line.
84. *White Paper on Jammu & Kashmir*, p. 81. Conversely, L.F. Rushbrook Williams, *The State of Pakistan*, London, Faber and Faber, Second (Revised) Edition, 1966, p. 85, states that he was told that 'some Pakistani regulars troops were stationed, early in 1948, just inside Azad Kashmir territory to give the local forces confidence; they were ordered to take no part in the actual fighting against Indian units'.
85. 'Report submitted by the United Nations Representative', p. 257.
86. Part D, 'Proceedings on the sub-continent', First Interim Report of the United Nations Commission on India and Pakistan, in M.S. Deora and R. Grover, Editors, *Documents on Kashmir Problem*, Volume X, New Delhi, Discovery Publishing House, 1991, p. 28.
87. 'Resolution of the [United Nations] Commission [for India and Pakistan] of August 13, 1948', in Josef Korbel, *Danger in Kashmir*, Princeton University Press, Revised Edition, 1966 [First Edition, 1954], p. 364.
88. *Defending Kashmir*, p. 7.
89. *Kashmir's Fight for Freedom*, Washington, Department of Public Relations, Azad Kashmir Government, p. 3.
90. 'Part III—Complicity of Pakistan in the Invasion of Kashmir', *White Paper on Jammu & Kashmir*, pp. 33–4.
91. 'Resolution Adopted by the UNCIP, 13 August 1948 (S/1100, Para 75)', in Sarwar K. Hasan and Zubeida Hasan, Editors, *Documents on the Foreign Relations of Pakistan*, p. 180.

4. PAKISTAN: INTEGRATING THE REGION

1. Zaidi, *Jinnah Papers*, Volume V, p. 540.
2. Part D, 'Proceedings on the sub-continent', First Interim Report of UNCIP, in M.S. Deora and R. Grover, Editors, *Documents on Kashmir Problem*, Volume X, p. 28.

3. Part II, A, 'Resolution adopted by the UNCIP, 13 August 1948', in Sarwar K. Hasan and Zubeida Hasan, Editors, *Documents on the Foreign Relations of Pakistan*, p. 182.
4. 'Letter of the Representative of India Addressed to the President of the Security Council, 1 January 1948', in Sarwar K. Hasan and Zubeida Hasan, Editors, *Documents on the Foreign Relations of Pakistan*, pp. 107–113.
5. 'Resolution adopted by the UNCIP, 5 January 1949', in Sarwar K. Hasan and Zubeida Hasan, Editors, *Documents on the Foreign Relations of Pakistan*, pp. 212–14. In terms of the various force reductions in J&K, this resolution referred back to Part II, A and B, of 'Resolution adopted by the UNCIP, 13 August 1948', in Sarwar K. Hasan and Zubeida Hasan, Editors, *Documents on the Foreign Relations of Pakistan*, pp. 180–83.
6. The UN Security Council (UNSC) discussed the Kashmir dispute often in its early years, but not since 1965. See S/1996/603*, 22 August 1996, *United Nations Security Council*, http://domino.un.org/UNISPAL.NSF/3822b5e39951876a85256b6e00 58a478/c0924183a7f95851852563a900544efa!OpenDocument [accessed 18 July 2007]. One reason was the dispute's intractability. A second was that the Soviet Union (until its demise), with which India enjoyed a close relationship from the late 1950s and which was a permanent UNSC member, either vetoed or threatened to veto discussion of this issue. In 1971, the UNSC discussed the India-Pakistan war in East Pakistan, but the Kashmir dispute was not specifically mentioned. In 1996, a major change in the UNSC's treatment of the Kashmir dispute occurred. To Pakistan's chagrin, J&K was removed from the 'list of matters of which the Security Council is seized' because it had not looked at J&K in the last five years. (The 'Hyderabad question' was also on this list, even though UNSC had not discussed it since 24 May 1949.) As far as I can determine, Islamabad must now formally and annually ask for the 'India-Pakistan question'—that is, Pakistan's dispute with India over J&K—to remain on this list. See S/1996/704, 29 August 1996, *United Nations Security Council*, http://daccessdds.un.org/doc/UNDOC/GEN/N96/223/44/PDF/N9622344.pdf?OpenElement [accessed 18 July 2007].
7. *Story of Kashmir*, Karachi, Revised Edition, p. 3.
8. Stephen Phillip Cohen, *The Idea of Pakistan*, Lahore, Vanguard, 2005, p. 220.
9. *The Times*, 31 October 1947. *CMG*, 8 October 1947, stated that 'there is already a movement' in Gilgit for J&K's accession to Pakistan. A seemingly informed report by the 'Peshawar Correspondent' in *The Times*, 2 January 1948, spoke of an 'underground movement [being] at work' in the Gilgit area before the Maharaja's accession to India.
10. *The Times*, 2 January 1948.
11. *NYT*, 2 November 1947.
12. Ahmad Hasan Dani, *History of Northern Areas of Pakistan*, Islamabad, National Institute of Historical and Cultural Research, 1991, p. 410.
13. *The Times*, 2 January 1948.
14. *NYT*, 2 November 1947 and 5 November 1947.
15. *The Times*, 2 January 1948. Dani, *History of Northern Areas of Pakistan*, p. 414.
16. Birdwood, *Two Nations and Kashmir*, p. 129.
17. *The Times*, 2 January 1948. Birdwood, *Two Nations and Kashmir*, pp. 129–30, although Birdwood calls him 'Captain Brown'.

18. *The Times*, 2 January 1948 and Birdwood, *Two Nations and Kashmir*, p. 129.
19. UNCIP, *Report of the Sub-committee on Western Kashmir*, p. 13.
20. *NYT*, 1 December 1947, informed that Gilgitis may also have resisted 'troublesome elements' helped by Swatis having 'a high time raiding and looting in Gilgit'.
21. Sardar M. Ibrahim Khan, *The Kashmir Saga*, p. 70.
22. See Chapter 6: A Significant 'Loss': the Northern Areas.
23. *Administration Report of the Jammu and Kashmir State for S. 2005* [sic] *(13th April 1948– 12th April 1949)*, Jammu, Ranbir Government Press, 1951, p. 3. The year 2005 was based on a Hindu calendar used by the Dogra maharajas and their initial successor regime in Indian J&K
24. *The Times*, 1 November 1947.
25. Ibid., 30 October 1947.
26. Ibid., 28 October 1947.
27. Abdullah, *Flames of the Chinar*, pp. 93–4.
28. *The Times*, 3 November 1947. According to Mir Qasim, *My Life and Times*, p. 39, the Indian Army got off to a bad start when some soldiers seeking revenge for events in Punjab killed some Muslims at Srinagar Airport. The 'shocked and infuriated' locals were talked out of making a procession with their dead to Srinagar's major mosque, an act that could have created 'an uncontrollable situation and turned the people's anger against India instead of the invaders and perhaps could have given a different direction to the history of Kashmir'.
29. Parthasarathi, *Jawaharlal Nehru: Letters*, p. 8.
30. *The Times*, 1 November 1947.
31. Mahajan, *Looking Back*, p. 155. The first condition was that the Maharaja should accede to India with regard to defence, external affairs and transport. The second was that a new constitution should be framed and J&K's internal administration democratised.
32. *The Times*, 1 November 1947.
33. Mahajan, *Looking Back*, p. 156.
34. The composition of the 23-man 'Emergency Council' is contained in 'Chief Secretariat (General Department), Emergency Administration Order No. 176-H of 1947, 30th October, 1947', in S.R. Bakshi, *Kashmir Through Ages—4, Kashmir: Political Problems*, New Delhi, Sarup & Sons, 1997, pp. 72–4.
35. *The Statesman*, 15 May 1948.
36. Mahajan, *Looking Back*, p. 156.
37. Abdullah, *Flames of the Chinar*, p. 103; Mahajan, *Looking Back*, p. 171–3.
38. Parthasarathi, *Jawaharlal Nehru: Letters*, p. 87.
39. *Jammu & Kashmir 1947–50. An Account of Activities of First Three Years of Sheikh Abdullah's Government, Jammu*, Government of Jammu and Kashmir?, The Ranbir Government Press, 1951, p. ii.
40. *The Statesman*, 12 March 1948.
41. See Appendix V: Physical and Political Composition of J&K after the 1949 Ceasefire.
42. Jawaid Alam, Editor, *Jammu and Kashmir 1949–64: Select Correspondence between Jawaharlal Nehru and Karan Singh*, New Delhi, Penguin Viking, 2006, p. 36, footnote 1.
43. *Census of India 1961*, p. 35.

44. For the composition of Indian J&K and Pakistan-Administered J&K see Appendix V: Physical and Political Composition of J&K after the 1949 Ceasefire.
45. Lamb, *Kashmir, A Disputed Legacy*, pp. 163–4. For a description of the ceasefire line, see Appendix VI: Ceasefire Line in J&K.
46. Sardar M. Ibrahim Khan, *The Kashmir Saga*, p. 145, states that at 'the end of 1949', he attended a meeting of the UN Security Council 'as a representative of the Azad Kashmir Government'. He had also attended a Security Council meeting in 1948.
47. UNCIP, *Report of the Sub-committee on Western Kashmir*, p. 3.
48. Ibid., *Report of the Sub-committee on Western Kashmir*, p. 11. Muhammad Ayub Khan, *Friends Not Masters. A Political Autobiography*, London, Oxford University Press, 1967, p. 31, claims 'some 50,000 men under arms, of varying military quality'.
49. Ayub Khan, *Friends Not Masters*, p. 31. There is still an Azad Kashmir regiment that is part of the Pakistan Army, although its headquarters are at Mansar in Punjab. See Lieutenant General Sardar F.S. Lodi, '50 Years of Azad Kashmir Regiment', *The Nation*, 14 October 1997 and Cloughley, *A History of the Pakistan Army*, Second Edition, p. 19. According to Mirza, *The Withering Chinar*, p. 27, it was only in '1979 when Azad Kashmir regular forces were converted into [the] Azad Kashmir Regiment of Pakistan Army', which seems rather late.
50. UNCIP, *Report of the Sub-committee on Western Kashmir*, p. 11.
51. Annex 7, 'Minutes of the Meeting with the Defence Minister of the "Azad Kashmir Government"', in UNCIP, *Report of the Sub-committee on Western Kashmir*, p. 71.
52. Hafizullah, *Towards Azad Kashmir*, p. 106.
53. *Dawn*, 31 May 1949.
54. Hasan, *Documents on the Foreign Relations of Pakistan*, pp. 177, 180.
55. Part V, 'Analysis of the Main Problems, Third Interim Report of the United Nations Commission on India and Pakistan', in Deora, *Documents on Kashmir Problem*, p. 274.
56. This section partly based on an interview with Mr Akram Zamir, Director, South Asia Section, Pakistan Ministry of Foreign Affairs, Islamabad, 25 March 1999.
57. Sardar M. Ibrahim Khan, *The Kashmir Saga*, p. 101.
58. Similarly, Pakistan did not accept accessions made by the rulers of Hunza and Nagar in early November 1947. See Chapter 6: 'A Significant 'Loss': the Northern Areas'.
59. *The Constitution of the Republic of Pakistan*, Karachi, Government of Pakistan, 1962, pp. 86, 115.
60. 'Article 257, Provision relating to the State of Jammu and Kashmir, Part XII (contd), Miscellaneous, Chapter 4. General', *The Constitution of the Islamic Republic of Pakistan*, www.pakistani.org/pakistan/constitution/part12.ch4.html [accessed 18 March 2009]. This also was Article 203 in the 1956 Constitution: see Sisir Gupta, *Kashmir. A Study in India-Pakistan Relations*, Bombay, Asia Publishing House, 1966, pp. 405–06.
61. Sardar M. Ibrahim Khan, *The Kashmir Saga*, p. 106.
62. Parthasarathi, *Jawaharlal Nehru: Letters to Chief Ministers*, p. 88.
63. Sardar M. Ibrahim Khan, *The Kashmir Saga*, p. 106.
64. 'Resolution of the Commission of August 13, 1948', in Korbel, *Danger in Kashmir*, p. 364. Korbel has the entire resolution in Appendix II, pp. 362–6.
65. Part V, 'Analysis of the Main Problems, Third Interim Report of the United Nations Commission on India and Pakistan', in Deora, *Documents on Kashmir Problem*, p. 274.

66. Interview with Justice Majid Mallick (Retired), Muzaffarabad, 11 March 1999.
67. *Dawn*, 17 March 1970, states that this irked some Azad Kashmiri leaders until 1970.
68. Chaudhri Muhammad Ali, *The Emergence of Pakistan*, p. 246. Ali states that he was secretary-general directly responsible to the prime minister. In this position, he had set up an organisation 'to deal with the various aspects of the Kashmir problem ... and it was only after more than a year that a separate ministry for Kashmir affairs [sic] was formed'.
69. Chaudhri Muhammad Ali, *The Emergence of Pakistan*, p. 242.
70. According to *Dawn*, 16 March 1949, 'it was learnt' in Karachi that the MKA had been established.
71. *Five Years of Pakistan (August 1947–August 1952)*, Karachi, Pakistan Publications 1952?, p. 241, states that 'The main function of the Ministry of Kashmir Affairs ... is negotiation and liaison with U.N. Representatives and implementation of agreements on Kashmir resulting from negotiations with [UNCIP] and the U.N. Representatives. Among the subsidiary functions ... [is] the administration of Gilgit and Baltistan, provision of requisite relief to Muslim refugees from India-occupied [sic] areas ... and assistance and technical advice to the Azad Kashmir Government in the discharge of their [sic] normal administrative responsibilities'.
72. *Dawn*, 16 March 1949. This report also stated that the 'United Nations Commission Liaison Office in Karachi had been merged with the Ministry for Kashmir Affairs'. One of the officers within the MKA was also the 'Chief Plebiscite Officer'.
73. *Dawn*, 16 March 1949.
74. Sardar Muhammad Abdul Qayyum Khan, *The Kashmir Case*, p. 73.
75. *Dawn*, 16 March 1949.
76. *CMG*, 11 January 1949; *CMG*, 13 January 1949; *CMG*, 18 January 1949. The latter report had a photo of Gurmani titled 'New Minister with Azad Government'.
77. Annex 18, UNCIP, *Report of the Sub-committee on Western Kashmir*, p. 120.
78. *Dawn*, 14 April 1950, noted that Gurmani was promoted to Minister for Kashmir Affairs. According to Ayesha Jalal, *The State of Martial Rule: The Origins of Pakistan's Political Economy of Defence*, Lahore, Sang-e-Meel Publications, 1999, p. 138, footnote 6, Gurmani served in this position until November 1951, when he became Pakistan's Interior Minister. *Dawn*, 21 November 1951, reported that Dr Mahmud Hussain replaced Gurmani. Hussain was elevated into the cabinet and based in (distant) Karachi, a situation that may have helped MKA bureaucrats to assert themselves over Azad Kashmiris. *Dawn*, 11 May 1953, reported that Shuaib Qureshi had become Minister for Kashmir Affairs.
79. Saraf, *Kashmiris Fight—For Freedom*, Volume II, p. 1292.
80. Taseer, *The Kashmir of Sheikh Muhammad Abdullah*, p. 261.
81. Ayesha Jalal, *The State of Martial Rule*, p. 138, footnote 6.
82. Jalal, *The State of Martial Rule*, pp. 128, 178.
83. Sardar Muhammad Abdul Qayyum Khan, *The Kashmir Case*, p. 22.
84. Saraf, *Kashmiris Fight—For Freedom*, Volume II, p. 1310.
85. See Appendix VII: Main Office Holders of Azad Kashmir.
86. Saraf, *Kashmiris Fight—For Freedom*, Volume II, p. 1334.

87. Letter from Ghulam Abbas to 'Hon'ble Mr. Liaquat Ali Khan, Prime Minister of Pakistan, Government House, Peshawar [sic], October 26, 1950', contained in 1950: File No. 13 (10)-Pris/50, Government of Pakistan, Cabinet Secretariat, 'Correspondence with the Supreme Head of Azad Kashmir Movement', held at the National Documentation Centre, Cabinet Building, Islamabad, Pakistan. File accessed on 27–29 December 2006.
88. Khalid Hassan, 'Khurshid: A Life', Introduction to Khalid Hassan, Editor, *K.H. Khurshid. Memories of Jinnah*, Karachi, Oxford University Press, 1990, p. xvi. Hassan was the brother-in-law of K.H. Khurshid.
89. Rose, 'The Politics of Azad Kashmir', in Thomas, *Perspectives*, p. 238.
90. Hassan, 'Khurshid: A Life', p. xvi. This 'appalling treatment' was confirmed during an interview with President Sardar Ibrahim Khan, at his ancestral home in Rawalakot, Azad Kashmir, on 4 March 1999.
91. The entire agreement is reproduced in The High Court of Judicature, Azad Jammu and Kashmir, *Verdict on Gilgit and Baltistan (Northern Area)*, Mirpur, Kashmir Human Rights Forum, 1993?, pp. 134–139. On p. 134, this book states that the agreement 'appears to have been executed on April 28, 1949'. At the time it was signed, the agreement was either a secret document or poorly reported. *Dawn* carries no reports of it being signed. *The Kashmir Saga*, by Sardar M. Ibrahim Khan, who was a signatory, does not deal with it. Syed Manzoor H. Gilani, *Constitutional Development in Azad Jammu & Kashmir*, Lahore, National Book Depot, 1988, whose Introduction details Azad Kashmir's relations with Pakistan, does not discuss it. However, the agreement is reproduced, without any date of signature, as 'Appendix XVIII: Karachi Agreement' in Justice Syed Manzoor Hussain Gilani, *The Constitution of Azad Jammu & Kashmir (In the historical backdrop with corresponding Pakistan, India & Occupied Jammu and Kashmir Constitutions)*, Islamabad, National Book Foundation, 2008, pp. 674–5. The abovementioned Syed Manzoor H. Gilani (hereafter 'Gilani') and Justice Syed Manzoor Hussain Gilani (hereafter 'Justice Gilani') are the same person.
92. The High Court of Judicature, *Verdict on Gilgit and Baltistan*, 'Heads of Agreement' document, p. 138.
93. Ibid., pp. 138–9.
94. Interview with Sardar Ibrahim, Rawalakot, 4 March 1999.
95. Sardar M. Ibrahim Khan, *The Kashmir Saga*, p. 70.
96. Saraf, *Kashmiris Fight—For Freedom*, Volume II, p. 1292.
97. 'The Rules of Business of Azad Kashmir 1950', Gilani, *Constitutional Development in Azad Jammu & Kashmir*, Appendix III, Appendixes Section, pp. 45–74.
98. *The Azad Jammu and Kashmir Interim Constitution Act, 1974*, Preface.
99. 'Office of the Supreme Head of the Azad Kashmir Movement (Murree), [Order] No. 1/RS-AKM/50, December 28, 1950', in Gilani, *Constitutional Development in Azad Jammu & Kashmir*, Appendix III, Appendixes Section, p. 45.
100. Bazaz, *The History of Struggle for Freedom in Kashmir*, p. 637, quoting Mir Abdul Aziz, in a pamphlet entitled 'Dictatorship in Azad Kashmir'.
101. Gilani, *Constitutional Development in Azad Jammu & Kashmir*, Appendix III, Appendixes Section, p. 47.

102. Gilani, *Constitutional Development in Azad Jammu & Kashmir*, p. vii.
103. 'The Rules of Business of Azad Kashmir 1952' are in Gilani, *Constitutional Development in Azad Jammu & Kashmir*, Appendix IV, Appendixes Section, pp. 77–103.
104. Saraf, *Kashmiris Fight—For Freedom*, Volume II, p. 1310.
105. H.N. Kaul, 'The Azad Kashmir Cauldron', in *Kashmir Today*, Volume 6, Number 2, March 1962, p. 8.
106. Gilani, *Constitutional Development in Azad Jammu & Kashmir*, Appendixes Section, p. 78.
107. *The Azad Jammu and Kashmir Interim Constitution Act, 1974*, Preface.
108. 'Pakistan's Constitutional Position on Jammu and Kashmir's Status', Islamabad, Institute of Policy Studies, unpublished.
109. *Census of India 1941*, p. 231.
110. Saraf, *Kashmiris Fight—For Freedom*, Volume II, pp. 1292, 1313.
111. Jalal, *The State of Martial Rule*, p. 136. Each man was either Pakistan's head of state (governor-general; later president) or prime minister during this period. Nazimuddin served in both positions at different times.
112. Ian Talbot, *Pakistan: A Modern History*, Third Edition, p. 441.
113. Stephen Phillip Cohen, *The Idea of Pakistan*, p. 7.
114. Khalid B. Sayeed, *The Political System of Pakistan*, Boston, Houghton Mifflin, 1967, pp. 179–80.
115. Khalid B. Sayeed, *The Political System of Pakistan*, pp. 65–6.
116. Stephen Phillip Cohen, *The Idea of Pakistan*, p. 220.
117. Khalid B. Sayeed, *The Political System of Pakistan*, pp. 60–1.
118. Mir Qasim, *My Life and Times*, p. 75.
119. *Administration Report of Jammu and Kashmir for the years, 2011* [sic] *(13th April 1954– 12th April 1955)*, Srinagar?, Jammu and Kashmir Government, 1955?.
120. Abdullah, *Flames of the Chinar*, p. 115.
121. Fazili, *Kashmir Government and Politics*, p. 167. The whole of Article 370 is Appendix VI, pp. 167–9.
122. Karan Singh, *Autobiography*, p. 162.
123. Lamb, *Kashmir, A Disputed Legacy*, p. 189. Lamb states that there was 'evidence ... that in 1951 [Sheikh Abdullah] was in touch with Chaudhri [sic] Ghulam Abbas. Unfortunately, he does not provide any details of this 'evidence'. In the 'Report Submitted by the United Nations Representative for India and Pakistan, Sir Owen Dixon, to the Security Council, 15 September 1950', in Sarwar K. Hasan and Zubeida Hasan (eds), *Documents on the Foreign Relations of Pakistan. The Kashmir Question*, p. 265, Dixon interestingly stated that that he had 'inquired' of the Prime Ministers of India and Pakistan about the 'possibility ... of bringing into existence a coalition government, that is either a coalition brought about by a meeting of Sheikh Abdullah and Mr. Ghulam Abbas, Supreme Head of the Azad Kashmir movement, or by placing certain portfolios at the disposal of the respective parties'. This may have encouraged Abdullah and Abbas to try to meet—or encouraged speculation about them being in contact with each other. Mir Abdul Aziz, 'Internal Kashmir Affairs—A Practicable Solution, Kashmiristan?', p. 1, in a proposal attached to a letter to 'The Hon'ble Minister for Kashmir Affairs, Pakistan (Rawalpindi)', by Mir Abdul Aziz, 'Member General

Council, All Jammu and Kashmir Muslim Conference', 5 May 1950, pp. 53–61 (contained in File No. 13 (5)-PMS/50, Volume 10, 'Government of Pakistan, Prime Minister's Secretariat, All Jammu & Kashmir Muslim Conference', held at the National Documentation Centre, Cabinet Building, Islamabad, Pakistan [file accessed on 27–29 December 2006]), pondered whether both men wanted to create an 'independent buffer State' of 'Kashmiristan'.

124. *Dawn*, 19 April 1950. An earlier suggestion by Abbas was that 'a force be raised district-wise from the entire state in such a manner that it should proportionately represented [sic] the state's population'.
125. *Dawn*, 11 May 1953, reported requests made in the presence of Abbas at a Muslim Conference meeting for the Pakistan Government to 'make an early arrangement for the [sic] meeting of Chaudhry Ghulam Abbas and Sheikh Abdullah'. *Dawn*, 21 May 1953, reported that Abdullah 'had a secret telephone talk' with Nehru on 'Abbas's suggestion for meeting'. Abdullah was told 'not to indulge in such international affairs'. He was 'sacked and arrested' soon after, as reported by *Dawn*, 10 August 1953.
126. *The Testament of Sheikh Abdullah*, New Delhi, Palit and Palit, 1974, p. 83.
127. *Dawn*, 3 January 1951, reported that Sardar Qayyum and Mr Abdul Hamid had tendered their resignations to the Working Committee of the Muslim Conference. There were also 'heated discussions' at a meeting of the Working Committee about the 'United Nations' indifferent attitude towards the solution of the Kashmir dispute', with a 'majority of members' pressing for 'the resumption of direct and active liberation movement in Kashmir'. *Dawn*, 26 January 1951, reported (hopefully) that Muslim Conference leaders 'have decided to sink their differences to strengthen the freedom movement'.
128. *Dawn*, 26 April 1952, reported that, on 10 March, Sheikh Abdullah, had 'declared the Poonch border open and suggested that Muslim refugees might return to their homes'. There was little traffic, with most of it in the 'reverse direction' to Azad Kashmir.
129. According to Rushbrook Williams, *The State of Pakistan*, pp. 94–5, the ceasefire line was 'crossed by mountain paths which [we]re not always strictly patrolled, and a certain amount of coming and going [wa]s winked at by the authorities—at least on the Azad Kashmir side. My impression, after visiting both fronts, is that the Azad Kashmir forces do not stop any genuine peasant who has good reason—for example, the recapture of a straying animal—from crossing into their territory: and, on the Azad Kashmir side, cultivation goes on undisturbed right up to the line ... [Conversely,] the Indian authorities were not allowing cultivation—as contrasted, perhaps, with mere grazing—within two or three miles of their [side of the ceasefire] line'.
130. Sardar M. Ibrahim Khan, *The Kashmir Saga*, various pages.
131. Alexander Evans, 'Kashmiri Exceptionalism', in T.N. Madan and Aparna Rao, Editors, *The Valley of Kashmir: The Making and Unmaking of a Composite Culture*, New Delhi, Manohar, 2008, pp. 733–5.
132. Abdullah, *Flames of the Chinar*, pp. 158–60.
133. The information about Abdullah's visit comes from Abdullah, *Flames of the Chinar*, pp. 152–155, and Saraf, *Kashmiris Fight—For Freedom*, Volume II, pp. 1244–7.

134. Saraf, *Kashmiris Fight—For Freedom*, Volume II, p. 1247.
135. Sardar Muhammad Abdul Qayyum Khan, *The Kashmir Case*, p. 108.
136. Julian Schofield and Reeta Tremblay, 'Why Pakistan Failed: Tribal Focoism in Kashmir', *Small Wars & Insurgencies*, Volume 19, Number 1, 2008, pp. 26, 31–32. The '*jihadis*' were 'trained and led by SSG [Special Services Group; Pakistan's main commando force] and Azad Kashmir and Jammu officers'. Training camps were established 'in March 1965 at Kotli, Mongburji near Rawlakot [sic], Shinkiari and Ratu in Gilgit, to train ten force units'.
137. Sardar Muhammad Abdul Qayyum Khan, *The Kashmir Case*, pp. 12, 20–21.
138. Hasan Zaheer, *The Times and Trials of the Rawalpindi Conspiracy 1951*, p. 252, states that Sardar Qayyum told Major-General Akbar Khan in early 1951 that Azad Kashmiris 'had decided to start the war of liberation of Kashmir, even without the help of Pakistan and asked him to prepare a plan of action for them'. Saraf, *Kashmiris Fight—For Freedom*, Volume II, p. 1306, states that Qayyum was arrested in 1952 for 'having planned a coup d'état'. He was jailed in Pakistan for 'more than two years'.
139. *Dawn*, 24 April 1952. This convention was held in Lahore.
140. *Dawn*, 19 May 1952.
141. *Dawn*, 11 July 1952. As early as January 1951 at a three-day 'Kashmir Convention' of 250 delegates of leaders and workers of the 'Kashmir Liberation Movement', Ibrahim had been elected 'convenor' of a 'proposed All-Pakistan Kashmir Liberation Movement'. According to *Dawn*, 22 January 1951, at this event, a resolution urged the Pakistan Government 'to give their [sic] urgent and earnest consideration to the question of giving representation to "a large section of the Kashmir people" who were not represented on the Azad Kashmir Cabinet'.
142. Jalal, *The State of Martial Rule*, pp. 180, 182.
143. *All Parties Conference on Kashmir 1955, Opening Speech by The Hon'ble [sic] Mr Mohamad [sic] Ali, Prime Minister of Pakistan*, Karachi, Ferozsons, 1956?. In the speech, Chaudhry Muhammad Ali rehearsed, in great and tedious detail to an already informed audience, Pakistan's stance on the Kashmir dispute.
144. Sardar Muhammad Abdul Qayyum Khan, *The Kashmir Case*, p. 149.
145. Ibid., pp. 136, 149.
146. Saraf, *Kashmiris Fight—For Freedom*, Volume II, p. 1311.
147. Sardar Muhammad Abdul Qayyum Khan, *The Kashmir Case*, p. 136.
148. Saraf, *Kashmiris Fight—For Freedom*, Volume II, p. 1311.
149. Ibid., p. 1317; Mir Abdul Aziz, Rawalpindi, 19 March 1999, told me that the Awami League branch started in 1956.
150. Bazaz, *The History of Struggle for Freedom in Kashmir*, p. 628.
151. 'Memorandum by Ministry of Kashmir Affairs, Government of Pakistan, 10 February 1950', in Raja Abbas Khan, *Real Azad Kashmir*, Appendix A, Srinagar, Anu Kashmir Publications, 1969, p. 34.
152. Sardar M. Ibrahim Khan, *The Kashmir Saga*, title page.
153. Sardar Muhammad Abdul Qayyum Khan, *The Kashmir Case*, various pages.
154. Saraf, *Kashmiris Fight—For Freedom*, Volume II, p. 1292.
155. Sardar M. Ibrahim Khan, *The Kashmir Saga*, Second Edition, p. 206.

156. Saraf, *Kashmiris Fight—For Freedom*, Volume II, p. 1313.
157. Khalid B. Sayeed, *The Political System of Pakistan*, p. 92.
158. *CMG*, 16 November 1947. Khurshid was first arrested for violating a curfew and fined a rupee some time before he was rearrested on 15 November 1947. *Dawn*, 23 December 1948, reported that he was released from jail earlier in December and had gone to Pakistan.
159. Talbot, *Pakistan: A Modern History*, Third Edition, p. 160.
160. Hassan, 'Khurshid: A Life', p. xvi.
161. M.H. Askari, 'Kashmir Through the Looking Glass', *The Herald*, August 1991, p. 86. The Chief Secretary was Amanullah Khan Niazi.
162. Saraf, *Kashmiris Fight—For Freedom*, Volume II, pp. 1340–41.
163. M.H. Askari, 'Kashmir Through the Looking Glass', *The Herald*, August 1991, p. 86.
164. 'The Rules of Business of Azad Kashmir 1958' are in Gilani, *Constitutional Development in Azad Jammu & Kashmir*, Appendix V, Appendixes Section, pp. 107–135.
165. Gilani, *Constitutional Development in Azad Jammu & Kashmir*, has these two acts. 'The Azad Jammu and Kashmir Government Act, 1964' is Appendix VI, Appendixes Section, pp. 139–45; 'The Azad Jammu and Kashmir Government Act, 1968' is Appendix VII, Appendixes Section, pp. 149–60. This paragraph is based on these two references.
166. Saraf, *Kashmiris Fight—For Freedom*, Volume II, p. 1369.
167. In other Azad Kashmir legal documents, the word 'advisor' is spelt 'adviser'.
168. Justice Gilani, *The Constitution of Azad Jammu & Kashmir*, p. 115.
169. Talbot, *Pakistan: A Modern History*, Third Edition, p. 178.
170. Stephen Phillip Cohen, *The Idea of Pakistan*, p. 73.
171. Saraf, *Kashmiris Fight—For Freedom*, Volume I, p. 52.
172. Information in this paragraph about political parties is from Talbot, *Pakistan: A Modern History*, Third Edition, pp. 179–83, 482, 484, 491–5.
173. Stephen Phillip Cohen, *The Idea of Pakistan*, p. 74.
174. Justice Gilani, *The Constitution of Azad Jammu & Kashmir*, p. 115. Saraf, *Kashmiris Fight—For Freedom*, Volume II, pp. 1369–70, discusses these demonstrations.
175. Saraf, *Kashmiris Fight—For Freedom*, Volume II, p. 1370.
176. Interview with Sardar Ibrahim at Rawalakot on 4 March 1999; Mir Abdul Aziz, *Freedom Struggle in Kashmir*, Lahore, Research Society of Pakistan, University of the Punjab, 2000, p. 366.
177. *Dawn*, 8 October 1969.
178. Saraf, *Kashmiris Fight—For Freedom*, Volume II, p. 1345. On p. 1349, Saraf states that Rehman was promoted to major-general in recognition of his Azad Kashmir service. Major-General Rehman later served twice as Chief Executive of Azad Kashmir during Zia's martial law regime. See Appendix VII: Main Office Holders of Azad Kashmir.
179. *Dawn*, 9 October 1969.
180. The major episodes discussed very briefly in this paragraph are based on Talbot, *Pakistan: A Modern History*, Third Edition, pp. 185, 195, 200–213.
181. *Dawn*, 21 November 1969.
182. Talbot, *Pakistan: A Modern History*, Third Edition, p. 212.

183. 'The Azad Jammu and Kashmir Government Act, 1970', is in Gilani, *Constitutional Development in Azad Jammu & Kashmir*, Appendix VIII, Appendixes Section, pp. 165–204.
184. Information about this instruction from 'Cabinet Division, D.O. No. 8/9/70-Coord. I., Government of Pakistan, Rawalpindi, May 11, 1971', in Justice Gilani, *The Constitution of Azad Jammu & Kashmir*, Appendix LVIII, pp. 834–5.
185. Justice Gilani, *The Constitution of Azad Jammu & Kashmir*, p. 820. The 'Government Order' was 'No. Admin/15132-78/SS/70'.
186. Gilani, *Constitutional Development in Azad Jammu & Kashmir*, p. x.
187. Ibid., 'The Azad Jammu and Kashmir Government Act, 1970', Appendix VIII, Appendixes Section, pp. 171, 177.
188. According to Saraf, *Kashmiris Fight—For Freedom*, Volume II, p. 1371, when Brigadier Abdul Rehman took over as Chief Executive of Azad Kashmir in late 1969, 'His first task was to give Azad Kashmir a Constitution', which Saraf apparently drafted and of which 'over 70 per cent' was incorporated in the 'Government Act of 1970'.
189. Gilani, *Constitutional Development in Azad Jammu & Kashmir*, 'The Azad Jammu and Kashmir Government Act, 1970', Appendix VIII, Appendixes Section, pp. 201–03.
190. Sardar Muhammad Abdul Qayyum Khan, *The Kashmir Case*, p. 107. Kaul, 'The Azad Kashmir Cauldron', in *Kashmir Today*, p. 10, states that Ghulam Abbas, who died in 1968, was also accused 'in high Pakistani circles of secretly propagating the concept of independent Kashmir'.
191. Sardar Muhammad Abdul Qayyum Khan, *The Kashmir Case*, pp. 92–4.
192. Brian Cloughley, *A History of the Pakistan Army*, Oxford University Press, Second Edition, 2000, pp. 222–38, provides a good discussion of the 'War in the West', including operations in J&K. India appeared to do better than Pakistan in J&K.
193. Talbot, *Pakistan: A Modern History*, Third Edition, p. 229.
194. Saraf, *Kashmiris Fight—For Freedom*, Volume II, p. 1372.
195. Justice Gilani, *The Constitution of Azad Jammu & Kashmir*, p. 116.
196. Gowher Rizvi, 'India, Pakistan, and the Kashmir Problem, 1947–1972', in Thomas, *Perspectives*, p. 73; Sardar Muhammad Abdul Qayyum Khan, *The Kashmir Case*, pp. 82, 107, 111.
197. Sardar Muhammad Abdul Qayyum Khan, *The Kashmir Case*, pp. 82–4.
198. 'Simla Agreement July 2, 1972', *Kashmir Information Network*, www.kashmir-information.com/LegalDocs/SimlaAgreement.html [accessed 20 March 2010].
199. Sardar Muhammad Abdul Qayyum Khan, *The Kashmir Case*, p. 81.
200. Theoretically, Azad Kashmiris wanted to liberate Indian J&K, then administer it. Khalid Hassan, 'Khurshid: A Life', p. xvi, states that, during K.H. Khurshid's time, 'the "forward camp" of the entire State's liberation' was used. Sardar Muhammad Abdul Qayyum Khan, *The Kashmir Case*, p. 121, in a section entitled 'Azad Kashmir A Base Camp', states that 'It is our belief that Azad Kashmir is the Base Camp for the Freedom Movement and it should remain as such till the Kashmir issue is resolved'. Addressing the Muzaffarabad Press Club in 1998, the Azad Kashmir Prime Minister, Sultan Mahmood, described Azad Kashmir as 'the base camp for the liberation of occupied territory'.

201. 'Part I, Introductory', *The Constitution of the Islamic Republic of Pakistan*, www.pakistani.org/pakistan/constitution/part1.html [accessed 3 March 2010].
202. Sarfaraz Hussain Mirza, Editor, *Pakistan-India Kashmir Dispute. A Chronology of Important Events (1947–1990)*, Lahore, Pakistan Study Centre, 1994, p. 86. As the source, Mirza quotes *Pakistan Horizon*, Volume XXVII, Number 4, IV Quarter 1974.
203. Talbot, *Pakistan: A Modern History*, Third Edition, p. 224. The Pakistan Army suppressed an uprising in Baluchistan from 1973 to 1977.
204. Talbot, *Pakistan: A Modern History*, Third Edition, p. 4.
205. Sardar Muhammad Abdul Qayyum Khan, *The Kashmir Case*, pp. 111, 112.
206. Saraf, *Kashmiris Fight—For Freedom*, Volume II, p. 1372; Mir Abdul Aziz, *Freedom Struggle in Kashmir*, p. 366.
207. *The Azad Jammu and Kashmir Interim Constitution Act, 1974*, p. 1. Gilani, *Constitutional Development in Azad Jammu & Kashmir*, pp. 1–305, details and extensively discusses this act.
208. Justice Gilani, *The Constitution of Azad Jammu & Kashmir*, p. 117. This book also contains the Interim Constitution and Gilani's extensive commentary on it.
209. Saraf, *Kashmiris Fight—For Freedom*, Volume II, p. 1372.
210. According to M.H. Askari, 'Kashmir Through the Looking Glass', *The Herald*, August 1991, p. 86, the Interim Constitution Act, 1974, was mainly drawn up in 1974 by Hafiz Pirzada, the PPP's Minister for Provincial Coordination. A draft was presented to a 'cross-section' of Azad Kashmir leaders in Rawalpindi on 19 August 1974, at a meeting which Bhutto apparently addressed. Some Azad Kashmiris apparently had reservations about the (autonomy-weakening) constitution, but it was passed five days later 'by consensus'.
211. Stephen Phillip Cohen, *The Idea of Pakistan*, p. 52.
212. *The Azad Jammu and Kashmir Interim Constitution Act, 1974*, pp. 52–5.
213. Section 4, 'Fundamental Rights', Sub-section 4, 'The Rights', point 7, 'Freedom of association', in *The Azad Jammu and Kashmir Interim Constitution Act, 1974*, p. 6.
214. Lamb, *Kashmir, A Disputed Legacy*, pp. 287–94.
215. Rose, 'The Politics of Azad Kashmir', in Thomas, *Perspectives*, p. 241. While I have written most of this section using the past tense, much of the information concerning the Interim Constitution still currently applies.
216. *The Azad Jammu and Kashmir Interim Constitution Act, 1974*, p. 1.
217. Justice Gilani, *The Constitution of Azad Jammu & Kashmir*, p. 325.
218. Quoted in the judgment 'Abdul Bari v. Government of Azad Jammu and Kashmir PLJ 1977 AJK 63', in Justice Gilani, *The Constitution of Azad Jammu & Kashmir*, p. 360.
219. On occasions, I have been told that Nawaz Sharif's mother is an ethnic Kashmiri from the northern Leepa Valley. When I interviewed Sardar Ibrahim at Rawalakot on 4 March 1999, he confirmed Sharif's lineage and that he is from an 'old' Kashmir family (like Nehru's). This lineage did not necessarily endear Azad Kashmir to Sharif.
220. Details of Azad Kashmir Council from *The Azad Jammu and Kashmir Interim Constitution Act, 1974*, pp. 16–19.
221. Formerly the Minister for Kashmir Affairs; later the Minister for Kashmir Affairs and Northern Affairs. The title is now the Minister for Kashmir Affairs and Gilgit-Bal-

tistan. See *Ministry of Kashmir Affairs and Gilgit-Baltistan* website, www.kana.gov.pk/ [accessed 25 March 2010].
222. *The Azad Jammu and Kashmir Interim Constitution Act, 1974*, pp. 3, 10.
223. *Composition of AJ&K Council*, no further publication details, document obtained in Islamabad in December 2006.
224. Based on an interview with a senior official of the Azad Kashmir Council in Pakistan in December 2006.
225. Justice Gilani, *The Constitution of Azad Jammu & Kashmir*, pp. 325–7.
226. Section 21, Sub-section 13, *The Azad Jammu and Kashmir Interim Constitution Act, 1974*, p. 19. This section remains valid.
227. 'AJ&K Council' [subsection], 'Who we are', in *Azad Jammu and Kashmir Council*, www.ajkcouncil.com/AJKCouncilintroduction.asp [accessed 26 March 2010].
228. Ibid., 'Powers', www.ajkcouncil.com/AJKCouncilPowers.asp [accessed 26 February 2009].
229. Rose, 'The Politics of Azad Kashmir', in Thomas, *Perspectives*, p. 240.
230. Azad Kashmir 'Third Schedule [See section 31 (2)] Council Legislative List', *The Azad Jammu and Kashmir Interim Constitution Act, 1974*, pp. 56–9. Appendix VIII: Azad Kashmir 'Council Legislative List' specifies the fifty-two matters.
231. 'Fourth Schedule [Article 70 (4)] Legislative Lists', *The Constitution of the Islamic Republic of Pakistan*, www.pakistani.org/pakistan/constitution/schedules/schedule4.html [accessed 28 February 2010].
232. Point No. 25, 'Third Schedule [See section 31 (2)] Council Legislative List', *The Azad Jammu and Kashmir Interim Constitution Act, 1974*, p. 58.
233. *The Azad Jammu and Kashmir Interim Constitution Act, 1974*, p. 26.
234. This schedule is given in its entirety in Appendix X: Azad Kashmir Administrative Setup and Functions, part 3, 'Distribution of business among Departments', as per *Rules of Business 1985*.
235. *The Azad Jammu and Kashmir Interim Constitution Act, 1974*, p. 26.
236. Gilani, *Constitutional Development in Azad Jammu & Kashmir*, p. 293.
237. Section 53, *The Azad Jammu and Kashmir Interim Constitution Act, 1974*, pp. 48–9.
238. All information on Section 53-A from Gilani, *Constitutional Development in Azad Jammu & Kashmir*, p. 287.
239. Cloughley, *A History of the Pakistan Army*, Second Edition, p. 269.
240. See Talbot, *Pakistan: A Modern History*, Third Edition, pp. 239–43.
241. Sections altered and/or added to via the '5th Amendment Act, 1977' were 21 (14), 22 (1), 25 (1), 28 (1) and (2), and 53-A. See *The Azad Jammu and Kashmir Interim Constitution Act, 1974*, pp. 19, 20, 22, 23, 49.
242. This party is also called: Azad Kashmir People's Party; AK People's Party; Pakistan People's Party, Azad Jammu and Kashmir; Pakistan People's Party A.K., etc. I use its official name in 2006: 'Pakistan People's Party-Azad Kashmir' or 'PPPAK'.
243. Gilani, *Constitutional Development in Azad Jammu & Kashmir*, Appendix IX, Appendixes Section, p. 208. The 'Heads of Agreement' is at pp. 207–08.
244. Sub-section 14 of Section 21, *The Azad Jammu and Kashmir Interim Constitution Act, 1974*, p. 19. This sub-section is still current.

245. Gilani, *Constitutional Development in Azad Jammu & Kashmir*, Appendix IX, Appendixes Section, pp. 207, 209–210.
246. Gilani, *Constitutional Development in Azad Jammu & Kashmir*, Appendix IX, Appendixes Section, pp. 214–15. According to Nasir Malick, 'Kashmir: The Other Battle', *The Herald*, May 1990, pp. 38–9, Hayat Khan was a Sudhan. He later led the Tehrik-i-Amal Party in Azad Kashmir.
247. Alexander Evans, 'Kashmiri Exceptionalism', p. 732.
248. Chaudry Mohammad Sharif Tariq, *Kashmir in Strangulation*, Mirpur, Self Published, 1991, p. 21.
249. Malik Muhammad Saeed, Chief Editor, *The All Pakistan Legal Decisions. Azad J&K High Court*, Volume XLI, Lahore, PLD Publishers, 1989, pp. 1–28.
250. Malik Muhammad Saeed, Chief Editor, *The All Pakistan Legal Decisions. Azad J&K Supreme Court*, Volume XLII, Lahore, PLD Publishers, 1990, pp. 23–68. According to Sardar Ibrahim when I interviewed him at Rawalakot on 4 March 1999, he received 'Rs. 18 lakhs [Rs. 1,800,000] in compensation'.
251. Gilani, *Constitutional Development in Azad Jammu & Kashmir*, Appendix IX, Appendixes Section, p. 209.
252. Gilani, *Constitutional Development in Azad Jammu & Kashmir*, pp. 287–9.
253. Talbot, *Pakistan: A Modern History*, Third Edition, p. 256.
254. Sarfaraz Hussain Mirza, *Pakistan-India Kashmir Dispute*, p. 141. Mirza's source is *Pakistan Horizon*, Volume XXX, Numbers 3–4, III-IV Quarters 1977.
255. *The Azad Jammu and Kashmir Interim Constitution Act, 1974*, p. 49, footnote 2.
256. Gilani, *Constitutional Development in Azad Jammu & Kashmir*, p. 294.
257. *The Azad Jammu and Kashmir Interim Constitution Act, 1974*, p. 50.
258. Mir Abdul Aziz, 'Azad Kashmir Government: A Chronology', *The Muslim*, Islamabad, 13 August 1996.
259. Aziz, 'Azad Kashmir Government: A Chronology'.
260. *The Azad Jammu and Kashmir Interim Constitution Act, 1974*, p. 50.
261. Justice Gilani, *The Constitution of Azad Jammu & Kashmir*, p. 555.
262. Stephen Phillip Cohen, *The Idea of Pakistan*, p. 10.
263. Talbot, *Pakistan: A Modern History*, Third Edition, pp. 310, 327–8, 348–9.
264. Pervez Musharraf, *In the Line of Fire: A Memoir*, New York, Free Press, 2006, pp. 101–140. According to Musharraf, Nawaz Sharif staged the first 'coup' on 12 October 1999 by replacing Musharraf as Chief of the Pakistan Army without consultation and while Musharraf was outside Pakistan. The aircraft flying Musharraf back to Pakistan from Sri Lanka, despite running low on fuel, was not allowed to land in Pakistan. The Pakistan military mounted a 'counter-coup' to enable the aircraft to land, thereby saving its chief's life. According to Talbot, *Pakistan: A Modern History*, Third Edition, p. 376, 'Musharraf echoed earlier justifications of coups, claiming that the army had intervened because of [Sharif's] political mismanagement which had weakened the economy, encouraged provincial disharmony and undermined state institutions'.
265. Khizar Hayat Abbasi, 'Anwar Khan elected AJK president', *The News*, 2 August 2001.
266. *Report on the Seventh General Elections in Azad Jammu & Kashmir*, Muzaffarabad, Azad Jammu & Kashmir Election Commission, 2002, p. 115.

267. 'President's Vision [of former president, Anwar Khan]', *Government of Azad Jammu & Kashmir* website, www.ajk.gov.pk/main/president/vision.html [accessed 21 August 2009].
268. *Azad Jammu and Kashmir Council*, www.ajkcouncil.com/AJKCouncilintroduction.asp [accessed 26 February 2009]. It has little information about the Council or its members.
269. Information in this paragraph based on *Composition of AJ&K Council* (no further publication details) obtained in Islamabad in December 2006, and on a conversation with a senior official of the Azad Kashmir Council in Islamabad in December 2006. See also Appendix IX: Composition of the Azad Jammu and Kashmir Council in December 2006.
270. The structure of the Secretariat is available at 'Organizational Chart of Azad Jammu and Kashmir Council Secretariat', *Azad Jammu & Kashmir Council*, www.ajkcouncil.com/AJKCouncilSect.asp [accessed 2 March 2010].
271. *Azad Jammu and Kashmir Council*, www.ajkcouncil.com/AJKCouncilPowers.asp [accessed 14 January 2008].
272. Conversation held with a senior official of the Azad Kashmir Council while in Pakistan in December 2006. Confirmed by *Azad Jammu and Kashmir Council*, www.ajkcouncil.com/AJKCouncilPowers.asp [accessed 14 January 2008].
273. 'Rs 524.408m allocated for development projects in AJK', *The News*, 19 August 2001.
274. *Azad Jammu and Kashmir Council*, www.ajkcouncil.com/AJKCouncilPowers.asp [accessed 14 January 2008].
275. 'Rs 524.408m allocated for development projects in AJK', *The News*, 19 August 2001.
276. *Azad Jammu and Kashmir Council*, www.ajkcouncil.com/AJKCouncilPowers.asp [accessed 14 January 2008].
277. Conversation held with a senior official of the Azad Kashmir Council while in Pakistan in December 2006.
278. 'Rs 524.408m allocated for development projects in AJK', *The News*, 19 August 2001.
279. This paragraph largely based on the *Azad Jammu & Kashmir Council Development Programme 2006–07*, Development & Works Wing, Azad Jammu & Kashmir Council Secretariat, Islamabad, 2006?.
280. Conversation held with a senior official of the Azad Kashmir Council while in Pakistan in December 2006.
281. See Table XII 1, 'Azad Jammu & Kashmir Council Development Programme 2006–07, Summary', in Appendix XII: Aspects of the Azad Kashmir Budgets.
282. *Azad Jammu & Kashmir Council Development Programme 2006–07*, pp. 7, 9.
283. *Dawn*, 15 April 1951, reported that the Azad Kashmir Government had taken possession of 'about 400 acres of land in village "purab" [sic] in Sheikhupura district, about twenty-five miles from Lahore' and 'another twelve villages spread over 1,800 acres of arable but un-cultivable land in the Sultan-Rahmanpura area about ten miles to the east of Lahore'. Both areas had been 'the "Maharaja's" property in Pakistan', for which the Pakistan Government had decided that the Azad Kashmir Government was the 'true heir'.

284. Saraf, *Kashmiris Fight—For Freedom*, Volume II, p. 1304.
285. *The Azad Jammu and Kashmir Interim Constitution Act, 1974*, p. 6.

5. THE POLITICAL SYSTEM: DEMOCRATIC SHORTCOMINGS

1. Also spelt *biraderi*, as in some quotations in this chapter. It is pronounced 'brard-ree'.
2. Bazaz, *The History of Struggle for Freedom in Kashmir*, p. 628.
3. *Administration Report of Jammu and Kashmir for the years, 2011* [sic] *(13th April 1954–12th April 1955)*, Srinagar?, Jammu and Kashmir Government, 1955?.
4. *Dawn*, 6 April 1950.
5. *Dawn*, 3 August 1953, stated that the Muslim Conference had been 'revived' in Indian J&K. Maulvi Mohammad Amin, a younger brother of Mirwaiz Yusuf Shah, was President.
6. Based on information in *The Azad Jammu and Kashmir Interim Constitution Act*, Preface.
7. *Dawn*, 25 January 1949.
8. William Clark, 'A Journey to "Free Kashmir"', *The Listener*, Volume 51, 20 May 1954.
9. *The Azad Jammu and Kashmir Interim Constitution Act*, Preface.
10. Jammu and Kashmir Editors' Conference, *The Neglected and Ignored Press of Azad Kashmir*, Rawalpindi [published by] Kh. Sanaullah But [sic], 1956, p. 4.
11. Saraf, *Kashmiris Fight—For Freedom*, Volume II, pp. 1310–11. See also Chapter 4.
12. Sardar Muhammad Abdul Qayyum Khan, *The Kashmir Case*, p. 128.
13. Discussion with Mir Abdul Aziz, Rawalpindi, 23 January 1998.
14. Indeed, according to Sardar Muhammad Abdul Qayyum Khan, *The Kashmir Case*, p. 137, 'We were of the opinion that by holding elections our freedom movement would be irreparably damaged, and that the territory of Azad Kashmir instead of being the Base Camp of the freedom movement would become a settled territory in which there was democracy, the elections, and the governments being made and unmade. Our people would remain busy in baseless and fruitless activities'. Sardar Ibrahim opposed this stance.
15. Saraf, *Kashmiris Fight—For Freedom*, Volume II, pp. 1317–18.
16. Ibid., Volume II, p. 1345.
17. Discussion with Mir Abdul Aziz, Rawalpindi, 19 March 1999.
18. Saraf, *Kashmiris Fight—For Freedom*, Volume II, pp. 1344–45.
19. See Appendix VII: Main Office Holders of Azad Kashmir.
20. A number of Azad Kashmiris told me reverentially about Khurshid's death on a public bus in 1988, apparently with only Rs. 2 in his pocket. For them, this was a sign that Khurshid, unlike some others, had not exploited the political system for personal gain.
21. Sardar Muhammad Abdul Qayyum Khan, *The Kashmir Case*, p. 107.
22. Saraf, *Kashmiris Fight—For Freedom*, Volume II, p. 1335.
23. Jyoti Bhusan Das Gupta, *Jammu and Kashmir*, p. 243.
24. *The Freedom Monthly*, 10 June 1958, p. 1.
25. Figures from Saraf, *Kashmiris Fight—For Freedom*, Volume II, p. 1302. On p. 1301, Saraf states that, 'towards the end of 1948', the Pakistan Government 'agreed to place at the disposal of' Ghulam Abbas Rs. 100,000 per month 'for distribution among unem-

ployed political workers'. Apparently Abbas only distributed this among political workers 'on his own side in the internal power struggle [with Sardar Ibrahim] which naturally created bad blood', after which lobbying started for MKA involvement in Azad Kashmir.

26. *The Freedom Monthly*, 10 October 1958, p. 2.
27. Luv Puri, 'Across the LOC: a Political Conundrum', *Economic & Political Weekly*, 30 October 2010, Volume xlv, Number 44, p. 10.
28. *The Freedom Monthly*, 10 June 1958, p. 1.
29. Sardar M. Ibrahim Khan, *The Kashmir Saga*, p. 111.
30. Saraf, *Kashmiris Fight—For Freedom*, Volume II, p. 1311. Saraf states that 'Mr. Abdus Salam Yatu and his Kisan Mazdoor Conference was the first [party] to demand a representative Assembly' in Azad Kashmir and the party 'consistently campaigned for it … in [the] early fifties'. Bazaz, *The History of Struggle for Freedom in Kashmir*, p. 637, confirms this, stating that 'Abdul [sic] Salam Yatu' had been expelled from Indian J&K to Azad Kashmir in March 1951, where Yatu then started to call for 'the immediate establishment of a legislative assembly to be elected on the basis of adult franchise'. Mir Abdul Aziz, *Freedom Struggle in Kashmir*, pp. 352–61, also discusses 'Political Parties in Azad Kashmir.' One party that had a short existence in late 1947 in the Kashmir Valley, then in Rawalpindi and Azad Kashmir, was the 'Kashmir Freedom League' involving Mirwaiz Yusuf Shah and 'some other refugees from Kashmir'.
31. Sardar Muhammad Abdul Qayyum Khan, *The Kashmir Case*, p. 21.
32. Saraf, *Kashmiris Fight—For Freedom*, Volume II, p. 1317. Interview with Mir Abdul Aziz, Rawalpindi, 19 March 1999.
33. Ibid., Volume II, p. 1306. Hussain was the father of a later Azad Kashmir Prime Minister, Barrister Sultan Mahmood Chaudhry (1996–2001).
34. Mir Abdul Aziz, *Freedom Struggle in Kashmir*, p. 354.
35. *The Freedom Monthly*, Rawalpindi, 10 June 1958, p. 1.
36. George Thomson, MP, 'The Two Kashmirs', *Aspect*, Volume 8, London, September 1963, p. 14.
37. Quoted in Mehtab Ali Shah, 'The Kashmir Problem: a View from Four Provinces of Pakistan', *Contemporary South Asia*, Volume 4, Number 1, March 1995, p. 103. Sardar Muhammad Abdul Qayyum Khan, *The Kashmir Case*, various pages, uses this slogan often throughout his book, both in Urdu and English. Also written as '*Kashmir Banega Pakistan*' or '*Kashmir Baneyga Pakistan*'.
38. Saraf, *Kashmiris Fight—For Freedom*, Volume II, p. 1320.
39. Peer Giyasuddin, 'Main Trends of the History of the Kashmir Freedom Struggle', in Mohammad Yasin and A. Qaiyum Rafiqi, Editors, *History of the Freedom Struggle in Jammu & Kashmir*, New Delhi, Light & Life, 1980, pp. 82–3. Giyasuddin says this rallying cry was used in pre-Partition times (1931–38) by members of the Majlis-i-Ahrar, a 'militant anti-British Muslim Nationalist organisation based in Punjab [many of whose] important leaders were Kashmiri Muslims residing in Lahore, Sialkot and Amritsar'.
40. Taseer, *The Kashmir of Sheikh Muhammad Abdullah*, p. 185.
41. Aziz, 'Azad Kashmir Government: A Chronology'.

42. In January 1990, Sardar Ibrahim attempted a similar crossing, possibly with similar motives in mind.
43. Nazir Tabassum, 'AJK Govt [sic]: Clearing the Confusion', *The News International*, Islamabad/Rawalpindi, 6 July 1992. Tabassum made the same point when I had discussions with him in Mirpur on 21 March 1999.
44. Sheikh Abdullah freed Abbas after Abbas apparently agreed to try and convince Jinnah of the necessity and desirability of J&K becoming an independent state. Bazaz, *The History of Struggle for Freedom in Kashmir*, p. 626, states that Abbas 'failed in his mission'.
45. Saraf, *Kashmiris Fight—For Freedom*, Volume II, p. 1371.
46. *CMG*, 19 February 1948.
47. Saraf, *Kashmiris Fight—For Freedom*, Volume II, p. 1370, states that Qayyum was leading the Muslim Conference on 5 August 1968.
48. Interestingly, Sardar M. Ibrahim Khan, *The Kashmir Saga* (first and second editions), does not mention Qayyum. Conversely, Sardar Muhammad Abdul Qayyum Khan, *The Kashmir Case*, mentions Ibrahim over thirty times, not always positively. This may reflect each man's personality: Ibrahim wanted to be on the national and international stage; Qayyum was focused on events within J&K, particularly Azad Kashmir.
49. The two *sardars*, Qayyum and Ibrahim, were still politically active in Azad Kashmir in 2001. Sardar Ibrahim, then in his eighties, was President of Azad Kashmir. I interviewed him at his ancestral home in Rawalakot, which is located about 120 kms and four hours by road from Muzaffarabad, on 4 March 1999, and interviewed him again in the President's Residence, Muzaffarabad, on 17 March 1999. He died on 31 July 2003. Sardar Qayyum, who was in his seventies, was the immediate past Prime Minister of Azad Kashmir. His party, the All Jammu Kashmir Muslim Conference (Qayyum faction)—in true Azad Kashmiri style, the Muslim Conference has split into two factions—was part of the opposition in the Azad Kashmir Legislative Assembly. I interviewed him in the Prime Minister's Residence at Muzaffarabad on 3 March 1996, and again in Rawalpindi on 24 March 1999. I met him again when I interviewed his son, Sardar Attique Ahmad Khan, Azad Kashmir's then Prime Minister, in Islamabad on 16 December 2006. Although Sardar Qayyum no longer holds any public position, he is now the 'elder statesman' of Azad Kashmiri politics.
50. Saraf, *Kashmiris Fight—For Freedom*, Volume II, p. 1289.
51. Ibid., p. 700.
52. Age is still important in Azad Kashmir. *The Azad Jammu and Kashmir Interim Constitution Act*, p. 21, states that a person cannot become a member of the Legislative Assembly unless 'he' is over twenty-five years of age. On p. 10, it states that a person cannot become president unless 'he' is a Muslim over thirty-five. Had this age stipulation been in place in 1947, the then thirty-two-year-old 'Founder-President of Azad Kashmir', Sardar Ibrahim, would not have qualified to take office.
53. Bazaz, *The History of Struggle for Freedom in Kashmir*, p. 627.
54. Saraf, *Kashmiris Fight—For Freedom*, Volume II, p. 1290.
55. *CMG*, 30 December 1947.
56. Saraf, *Kashmiris Fight—For Freedom*, Volume II, p. 1291.

57. A title used by Sardar Ibrahim to describe himself. Interview with Sardar Ibrahim, Rawalakot, 4 March 1999.
58. *CMG*, 30 December 1947.
59. Ibid. 31 December 1947, carried a brief report from the Muslim Conference Publicity Bureau, Lahore, describing the previous day's press report as 'fantastic'. There was 'absolute unanimity' between the two organisations.
60. Hasan, *Documents on the Foreign Relations of Pakistan*, p. 179.
61. *Dawn*, 10 April 1948.
62. Bazaz, *The History of Struggle for Freedom in Kashmir*, p. 627.
63. *Dawn*, 10 April 1948.
64. Ibid.
65. *Dawn*, 15 April 1948. It is unlikely that this crowd was 10,000. The *Census of Azad Kashmir, 1951*, p. 2, stated that Muzaffarabad's population in 1951 was 'a little less than 5,000'.
66. *Dawn*, 15 April 1948.
67. Bazaz, *The History of Struggle for Freedom in Kashmir*, p. 628.
68. Saraf, *Kashmiris Fight—For Freedom*, Volume II, p. 1291.
69. *The Freedom Monthly*, Rawalpindi, 10 June 1958. Saraf, *Kashmiris Fight—For Freedom*, Volume II, p. 1303. Taseer, *The Kashmir of Sheikh Muhammad Abdullah*, p. 268, states that Abbas's own daughter, abducted around October 1947 in Jammu, was only 'restored to her father in 1954'.
70. Mir Abdul Aziz, 'Internal Kashmir Affairs—A Practicable Solution, Kashmiristan?', pp. 5–6, in a proposal attached to a letter to 'The Hon'ble Minister for Kashmir Affairs, Pakistan (Rawalpindi)' by Mir Abdul Aziz, 'Member General Council, All Jammu and Kashmir Muslim Conference', 5 May 1950, pp. 53–61, contained in File No. 13 (5)-PMS/50, Volume 10, 'Government of Pakistan, Prime Minister's Secretariat, All Jammu & Kashmir Muslim Conference'.
71. Bazaz, *The History of Struggle for Freedom in Kashmir*, p. 626.
72. Ibid., p. 628.
73. Sardar Muhammad Abdul Qayyum Khan, *The Kashmir Case*, p. 62.
74. Saraf, *Kashmiris Fight—For Freedom*, Volume II, p. 1307.
75. Mir Abdul Aziz, 'Internal Kashmir Affairs—A Practicable Solution, Kashmiristan?', p. 3.
76. Saraf, *Kashmiris Fight—For Freedom*, Volume II, p. 1297.
77. *Dawn*, 25 January 1949.
78. Saraf, *Kashmiris Fight—For Freedom*, Volume II, p. 1292.
79. Ibid., pp. 1292, 1297.
80. 'Azad Kashmir Government Reconstituted: Sardar Ibrahim replaced by Ali Ahmad Shah', *The Pakistan Times*, 31 May 1950. Saraf, *Kashmiris Fight—For Freedom*, Volume II, p. 1297, states that in mid-1949, Liaquat Ali Khan had ordered Ibrahim to resign, which Ibrahim did. However, Ghulam Abbas reinstated Ibrahim 'to establish that the Azad Kashmir President was *his* nominee [italics as per the original]'.
81. *Dawn*, 31 May 1950.
82. Letter from M.A. Gurmani to 'Chaudhry Ghulam Abbas Sahib, 26th May, 1950', contained in 1950: File No. 13 (10)-Pris/50, Government of Pakistan, Cabinet Secre-

tariat, 'Correspondence with the Supreme Head of Azad Kashmir Movement', p. 83, held at the National Documentation Centre, Cabinet Building, Islamabad, Pakistan [file accessed on 27–29 December 2006].
83. Saraf, *Kashmiris Fight—For Freedom*, Volume II, p. 1298. Aziz, *Freedom Struggle in Kashmir*, p. 355. According to Saraf, this unknown rank equated to a Spanish full general.
84. *Dawn*, 14 April 1950. Prior to this, Gurmani had been Minister of State without portfolio.
85. 'Report Submitted by the United Nations Representative for India and Pakistan, Sir Owen Dixon, to the Security Council, 15 September 1950', in Hasan, *Documents on the Foreign Relations of Pakistan*, p. 252.
86. Mir Abdul Aziz, 'Internal Kashmir Affairs—A Practicable Solution, Kashmiristan?', p. 2.
87. 'Azad Kashmir Government Reconstituted: Sardar Ibrahim replaced by Ali Ahmad Shah', *The Pakistan Times*, 31 May 1950.
88. Interview with Sardar Khalid Ibrahim Khan, son of Sardar Mohammad Ibrahim Khan and Head of the Jammu & Kashmir People's Party, Islamabad, 17 December 2006.
89. Bazaz, *The History of Struggle for Freedom in Kashmir*, p. 635.
90. Jyoti Bhusan Das Gupta, *Jammu and Kashmir*, p. 236.
91. *The Times*, 18 September 1950.
92. Ibid., 10 May 1955.
93. Jammu and Kashmir Editors' Conference, *The Neglected and Ignored Press of Azad Kashmir*, Rawalpindi, [published by] Kh. Sanaullah But [sic], 1956, pp. 3–4. I have not been able to access any of these Azad Kashmiri newspapers.
94. Jammu and Kashmir Editors' Conference, *The Neglected and Ignored Press of Azad Kashmir*, pp. 3–8.
95. Bazaz, *The History of Struggle for Freedom in Kashmir*, p. 637, quoting Mir Abdul Aziz, in a pamphlet entitled *Dictatorship in Azad Kashmir*.
96. 'The Rules of Business of Azad Kashmir 1950', Gilani, *Constitutional Development in Azad Jammu & Kashmir*, Appendix III, Appendixes Section, pp. 45–74.
97. Interview with Sardar Ibrahim at Rawalakot on 4 March 1999.
98. Sardar Muhammad Abdul Qayyum Khan, *The Kashmir Case*, p. 130.
99. Ibid., p. 24.
100. Interview with Sardar Ibrahim at Rawalakot on 4 March 1999.
101. Saraf, *Kashmiris Fight—For Freedom*, Volume II, p. 1298.
102. *Dawn*, 31 May 1950.
103. Saraf, *Kashmiris Fight—For Freedom*, Volume II, p. 1306.
104. *Dawn*, 5 June 1950.
105. Bazaz, *The History of Struggle for Freedom in Kashmir*, pp. 633–4.
106. Saraf, *Kashmiris Fight—For Freedom*, Volume II, p. 1297.
107. Ibid., Volume II, p. 1298.
108. *The Times*, 18 September 1950.
109. Aziz, 'Azad Kashmir Government: A Chronology'.
110. Saraf, *Kashmiris Fight—For Freedom*, Volume II, p. 1298.
111. Jyoti Bhusan Das Gupta, *Jammu and Kashmir*, p. 236.

112. In an interview with Sardar Khalid Ibrahim Khan, Islamabad, 17 December 2006, he claimed that the Pakistan Army had to quell this uprising and that there was a parallel government operating in Azad Kashmir for twelve months from around the time his father, Sardar Ibrahim, was sacked. Interestingly, Ibrahim does not mention this uprising in either edition of his book, *The Kashmir Saga*. Considerably more work needs to be done on this—and other—important displays of Sudhan displeasure in the 1950s.
113. Saraf, *Kashmiris Fight—For Freedom*, Volume II, p. 1298.
114. Sisir Gupta, *Kashmir. A Study in India-Pakistan Relations*, p. 403.
115. Aziz, 'Azad Kashmir Government: A Chronology'. According to Mir Abdul Aziz, Rawalpindi, 19 March 1999, he (Aziz) was appointed General Secretary of the parallel Muslim Conference.
116. Bazaz, *The History of Struggle for Freedom in Kashmir*, p. 634.
117. Jamna Das Akhtar, *Political Conspiracies in Pakistan. Liaquat Ali's Murder to Ayub Khan's Exit*, Delhi, Punjabi Pustak Bhandar, 1969, p. 119. Akhtar's source is *Daily Tej*, New Delhi, 19 August 1950.
118. Cloughley, *A History of the Pakistan Army*, Second Edition, p. 111.
119. Jamna Das Akhtar, *Political Conspiracies in Pakistan*, p. 119.
120. The rest of this paragraph based on 'Sudhan Defiance and Compromise', Saraf, *Kashmiris Fight—For Freedom*, Volume II, pp. 1298–1300.
121. See, for example, *Dawn*, 14 July 1950; *Dawn*, 25 August 1950; *Dawn*, 10 October 1950; *Dawn*, 25 October 1950; 27 November 1950; *Dawn*, 21 January 1951.
122. Bazaz, *The History of Struggle for Freedom in Kashmir*, p. 628.
123. *Dawn*, 29 November 1951.
124. Sisir Gupta, *Kashmir. A Study in India-Pakistan Relations*, p. 403.
125. *Dawn*, 2 December 1951.
126. Ibid., 15 December 1951.
127. Ibid., 2 December 1951. Abbas's resignation and Mirwaiz's appointment were announced on the same day and, clearly, were linked.
128. Ibid., 24 April 1952
129. Ibid., 5 December 1951.
130. Ibid., 19 May 1952.
131. Ibid., 20 June 1952.
132. Ibid., 23 June 1952.
133. Ibid., 22 June 1952.
134. Saraf, *Kashmiris Fight—For Freedom*, Volume II, p. 1306. Jyoti Bhusan Das Gupta, *Jammu and Kashmir*, p. 238.
135. *Dawn*, 22 June 1952.
136. Bazaz, *The History of Struggle for Freedom in Kashmir*, pp. 641–2.
137. *Dawn*, 26 June 1952.
138. Ibid.
139. Saraf, *Kashmiris Fight—For Freedom*, Volume II, pp. 1305–6.
140. *Dawn*, 5 July 1952.
141. 'The Rules of Business of Azad Kashmir 1952', Gilani, *Constitutional Development in Azad Jammu & Kashmir*, Appendix IV, Appendixes Section, pp. 77–103.

142. *Dawn*, 12 August 1952.
143. Saraf, *Kashmiris Fight—For Freedom*, Volume II, pp. 1310–11.
144. '"Azad Kashmir" is Neither Azad nor Kashmiri', *Organiser*, Volume 19, Number 7, Delhi, 26 September 1965.
145. Jyoti Bhusan Das Gupta, *Jammu and Kashmir*, p. 239.
146. Saraf, *Kashmiris Fight—For Freedom*, Volume II, p. 1311.
147. '"Azad Kashmir" is Neither Azad nor Kashmiri', *Organiser*. Jyoti Bhusan Das Gupta, *Jammu and Kashmir*, pp. 239–40.
148. Interview with Sardar Ibrahim at Rawalakot on 4 March 1999.
149. Sardar Muhammad Abdul Qayyum Khan, *The Kashmir Case*, pp. 136–7.
150. Lal Khan, Kashmir's Ordeal, www.marxist.com/kashmir-ordeal-six.htm [accessed 11 July 2008], p. 16.
151. Saraf, *Kashmiris Fight—For Freedom*, Volume II, p. 1307; Sardar Muhammad Abdul Qayyum Khan, *The Kashmir Case*, p. 132.
152. Ghulam Mohammad, Publicity Secretary, All-Jammu and Kashmir Muslim Conference, *Memorandum to Members of the Pakistan Constituent Assembly*, no original publication details July 1955?, as published in *Conditions in Pakistan-Occupied Kashmir*, Information Service of India, New Delhi, 1956?.
153. *CMG*, 3 July 1955, as quoted in Jyoti Bhusan Das Gupta, *Jammu and Kashmir*, p. 240.
154. Saraf, *Kashmiris Fight—For Freedom*, Volume II, p. 1307. Ayub was Commander-in-Chief of the Pakistan Army.
155. *Conditions in Pakistan-Occupied Kashmir*, Information Service of India, New Delhi, 1956?, comprising: 1) Ghulam Mohammad, Publicity Secretary, All-Jammu and Kashmir Muslim Conference, *Memorandum to Members of the Pakistan Constituent Assembly*, no original publication details, July 1955?; 2) (Khwajah) Sanaullah Butt, (Khwajah) Abdus Salam Yatu, (Khwajah) Ghulam Nabi Gilkar Anwar and Mir Abdul Aziz, 'Humble Appeal' to the Members of the Constituent Assembly of Pakistan, no original publication details, July 1955.
156. Sisir Gupta, Kashmir. *A Study in India-Pakistan Relations*, p. 405, footnote 103.
157. *The Pakistan Times*, 30 June 1950.
158. Sardar Muhammad Abdul Qayyum Khan, *The Kashmir Case*, pp. 132–3.
159. Ibid., p. 24.
160. Ibid., pp. 130–31.
161. Ibid., pp. 24, 133.
162. *The Times*, 17 July 1956.
163. Saraf, *Kashmiris Fight—For Freedom*, Volume II, p. 1306.
164. Jyoti Bhusan Das Gupta, *Jammu and Kashmir*, pp. 239–40. 'Khwaja Ghulam Mohammad' may be 'Ghulam Mohammad, "Publicity Secretary"' mentioned above.
165. Bazaz, *The History of Struggle for Freedom in Kashmir*, p. 644.
166. Jyoti Bhusan Das Gupta, *Jammu and Kashmir*, p. 241.
167. Aziz, *Freedom Struggle in Kashmir*, p. 356.
168. Saraf, *Kashmiris Fight—For Freedom*, Volume II, pp. 1312, 1314.
169. Ibid., p. 1314; Aziz, *Freedom Struggle in Kashmir*, p. 356.

170. *The Times*, 17 July 1956.
171. Sardar Muhammad Abdul Qayyum Khan, *The Kashmir Case*, p. 139. Saraf, *Kashmiris Fight—For Freedom*, Volume II, p. 1314.
172. Saraf, *Kashmiris Fight—For Freedom*, Volume II, p. 1314.
173. Sardar Muhammad Abdul Qayyum Khan, *The Kashmir Case*, pp. 25–6.
174. Ibid., pp. 139–40, 145–7. Saraf, *Kashmiris Fight—For Freedom*, Volume II, p. 1316.
175. Sardar Muhammad Abdul Qayyum Khan, *The Kashmir Case*, p. 140.
176. Saraf, *Kashmiris Fight—For Freedom*, Volume II, pp. 1316–17.
177. *The Times*, 15 April 1957.
178. Saraf, *Kashmiris Fight—For Freedom*, Volume II, p. 1318.
179. Ibid., p. 1319.
180. Aziz, 'Azad Kashmir Government: A Chronology'.
181. *The Freedom Monthly*, 10 June 1958, p. 2.
182. Unless otherwise indicated, this paragraph based on Aziz, *Freedom Struggle in Kashmir*, pp. 355–6; *The Freedom Monthly*, 10 October 1958, p. 2. 'United Nations Security Council Official Records, 796th Meeting, 9th October 1957', UNdemocracy.com, www.undemocracy.com/S-PV-796.pdf [accessed 10 March 2010], p. 16, mentions the existence of the 'Jammu and Kashmir "United Front"'. India's representative, Krishna Menon, made the mention, although he believed Pakistan was involved with this body.
183. Bazaz, *The History of Struggle for Freedom in Kashmir*, p. 621. Taseer, *The Kashmir of Sheikh Muhammad Abdullah*, p. 317.
184. Saraf, *Kashmiris Fight—For Freedom*, Volume II, p. 1377.
185. Rao A. Rashid, *The Smiling Face of Azad Kashmir*, Karachi, Din Muhammadi Press, 1963, p. 2. According to Saraf, *Kashmiris Fight—For Freedom*, Volume II, p. 1327, a Rao Abdul Rashid was Inspector-General of Police in Azad Kashmir around 1959.
186. Sadia Dehlvi, 'Conversation [with Sardar Qayyum]: "We Want India to Attack Us … That Will Decide Matters For Ever"', *Sunday*, 9–15 February 1986, p. 26.
187. Saraf, *Kashmiris Fight—For Freedom*, Volume I, p. 46.
188. *Census of Azad Kashmir, 1951*, p. 33.
189. Alexander Evans, 'Kashmiri Exceptionalism', in T.N. Madan and Aparna Rao, Editors, *The Valley of Kashmir: The Making and Unmaking of a Composite Culture*, New Delhi, Manohar, 2008, pp. 715–43, and particular pp. 729–33 on *biradari*.
190. Alexander Evans, 'Kashmiri Exceptionalism', pp. 729–31.
191. 'With Friends Like These…'; *Human Rights Violations in Azad Kashmir*, Human Rights Watch, Volume 18, Number 12, September 2006, p. 12.
192. R. Hussain, 'The Effect of Religious, Cultural and Social Identity on Population Genetic Structure among Muslims in Pakistan', *Annals of Human Biology*, Volume 32, Number 2, March–April 2005, p. 148.
193. For a very useful description of *biradari*, see 'Traditional Kinship Patterns' in Peter Blood, Editor, *Pakistan: A Country Study*, Washington, GPO for the Library of Congress, 1994, http://countrystudies.us/pakistan/30.htm [accessed 15 March 2010].
194. A Kashmiri informed me that *biradari* marriages are justified by Surah 11, verse 177, of the Koran: '… righteous is he who … giveth his wealth, for love of Him, to kins-

folk and to orphans and the needy and the wayfarer and to those who ask …'. See Marmaduke Pickthall, Translator, *The Meaning of the Glorious Koran*, New York, Alfred A. Knopf, 1930 [First published by Everyman's Library, 1909 and 1992], pp. 45–6. While this verse mentions various receivers, 'kinsfolk', i.e. *biradari*, is first in the list.
195. Figures from R. Hussain, 'The Effect of Religious, Cultural and Social Identity on Population Genetic Structure, p. 145.
196. Ibid., p. 151.
197. 'Traditional Kinship Patterns' in Peter Blood, *Pakistan: A Country Study*.
198. Rasul B. Rais, 'Elections in Pakistan: Is Democracy Winning?', *Asian Affairs*, Volume 12, Number 3, Fall 1985, p. 47.
199. Hasan-Askari Rizvi, 'Dynamics of campaigning', *Daily Times*, 20 January 2008.
200. Mughees Ahmed, 'Role of Biradari in Punjab Politics', *Journal of Research (Humanities)*, Volume 27, 2007, p. 21.
201. Indians sometimes say that 'Sudans', by which they appear to mean Muslims from Sudan, are also fighting alongside other Muslims in the anti-Indian uprising in the Kashmir Valley. These 'Sudans' most probably are Sudhans from Azad Kashmir.
202. *Population Census of Azad Kashmir 1972. District Census Report Poonch*, Islamabad, Ministry of Interior, States and Frontier Regions, 1972, p. 1.
203. *Census of Azad Kashmir, 1961, District Census Report, Muzaffarabad District*, Rawalpindi, Government of Pakistan Press, 1964, Parts I-V, pp. 11–12.
204. Zaffar Abbas, 'Kashmir: The Rocky Road Ahead', *The Herald*, February 1990, p. 65.
205. Akram Malik, 'PML-N has an edge over others in Gujranwala city', *Dawn*, 3 October 2002, noted that, for the 2002 Pakistan elections, there were various *biradari*s in the Gujranwala district: 'Kashmiri, Arain, Ansari, Shaikh and Kamboh in the city, while Jat Cheema, Rana Rajput, Arain, Chattha and Virk [were] in rural and remote areas'.
206. Alexander Evans, 'Kashmiri Exceptionalism', p. 733.
207. Roger Ballard, 'Kashmir Crisis: View from Mirpur', *Economic & Political Weekly*, Bombay, 2–9 March 1991, p. 513.
208. *The Azad Jammu and Kashmir Interim Constitution Act*, p. 4. On p. 7, the constitution states that 'every State subject has the right to profess and practice his [sic] own religion'; 'every religious denomination and every sect thereof has the right to establish, maintain and manage its places of worship'. While this is extremely liberal, there are no obvious signs of non-Muslims congregating in Azad Kashmir.
209. *Census of Azad Kashmir, 1951*, p. 35.
210. *1998 Census Report of Azad Kashmir*, Population Census Organization, Statistics Division, Government of Pakistan, July 2001, p. 25. It is marked 'For Official Use Only'.
211. This paragraph is based on the *1998 Census Report of Azad Kashmir*, pp. 24–5, 29. At the time of writing, this is the most recent census of Azad Kashmir. Note also that Azad Kashmir's districts have changed in size over time, as discussed in Chapter 6, with Poonch, by 2009, being both a division and a district within that division.
212. *The Azad Jammu and Kashmir Interim Constitution Act*, 1974, p. 10, states that, in Azad Kashmir, 'Untouchability is abolished, and its practice in any form is forbidden'.
213. *1998 Census Report of Azad Kashmir*, p. 29.
214. See Table XIV 3: List of Members of the Azad Kashmir Legislative Assembly in 2006

as a result of the elections and one by-election, and their possible *biradaris*, in Appendix XIV: Matters re Azad Kashmir Elections, particularly in 2006. In the two List[s] of Returned Candidates During [1970 and 1975], Annex 'E' or the three List[s] of Contesting Candidates During [1985, 1990, 1991], Annex 'E' obtained in Azad Kashmir in December 2006, there was a column for each candidate's 'Tribe', although this did not have any entries for any year.

215. Nasir Malick, 'Calling it Splits', *The Herald*, June 1990, p. 27.
216. Talbot, *Pakistan: A Modern History*, pp. 157–8. Talbot states that the Basic Democracy system was introduced in Azad Kashmir before Pakistan, and that presidential and State Council elections took place in October/November 1961.
217. Kaul, 'The Azad Kashmir Cauldron', p. 9.
218. Saraf, *Kashmiris Fight—For Freedom*, Volume II, p. 1339.
219. Ibid., Volume II, p. 1340.
220. Khan, *Real Azad Kashmir*, p. 4.
221. Rose, 'The Politics of Azad Kashmir', in Thomas, *Perspectives*, p. 244.
222. Nasir Malick, 'Kashmir: The Other Battle', *The Herald*, pp. 38–9.
223. Rose, 'The Politics of Azad Kashmir', in Thomas, *Perspectives*, p. 242.
224. Nasir Malick, 'Calling it Splits', *The Herald*, p. 28.
225. Chaudry Mohammad Sharif Tariq, *Kashmir in Strangulation*, p. 21.
226. Nasir Malick, 'Kashmir: The Other Battle', *The Herald*, p. 37.
227. The rest of this paragraph is based on Rose, 'The Politics of Azad Kashmir', in Thomas, *Perspectives*, pp. 243–4.
228. Information about refugees from 'The Azad Jammu and Kashmir Legislative Assembly Ordinance, 1970', in *The Election Laws (As Amended up to March, 2002)*, Azad Jammu & Kashmir Election Commission, Islamabad [sic], 2002, p. 105.
229. *The Azad Jammu and Kashmir Interim Constitution Act*, p. 4. There also exists the 'Azad Jammu and Kashmir State Subject Act, 1980 (Act XIII of 1980)', which gives the Azad Kashmir Council permission to grant state subject status to a person or deprive him or her of it. It does so via rules stipulated in the subsequent 'Notification'. Both documents are in Justice Gilani, *The Constitution of Azad Jammu & Kashmir*, Appendix LXI, pp. 838–44.
230. Gilani, *Constitutional Development in Azad Jammu & Kashmir*, p. 138.
231. Conversation with electoral official in Azad Kashmir in December 2006.
232. Nasir Malick, 'Kashmir: The Other Battle', *The Herald*, p. 39. A.G. Noorani, 'The Betrayal of Kashmir: Pakistan's Duplicity and India's Complicity', in Thomas, *Perspectives*, p. 266.
233. 'The Azad Jammu and Kashmir Legislative Assembly Ordinance, 1970 (Ordinance VI of 1970)', in *The Election Laws*, p. 105.
234. Nasir Malick, 'Calling it Splits', *The Herald*, p. 28.
235. Section 13, 'The Azad Jammu and Kashmir Legislative Assembly (Elections) Ordinance 1970 (Amended Upto [sic] 2002)', in *The Election Laws*, p. 99.
236. 'Former Members', Legislative Assembly of Azad Jammu and Kashmir, www.ajkassembly.gok.pk/former_members.htm [accessed 15 March 2010].
237. Based on conversations with various officials in Azad Kashmir in December 2006.

238. Table XIV 7: Delimitation of constituencies for 2001 Azad Kashmir elections, in Appendix XIV: Matters re Azad Kashmir Elections, particularly in 2006.
239. 'Former Members', Legislative Assembly of Azad Jammu and Kashmir; 'Members AJK Legislative Assembly 2006 till now', Legislative Assembly of Azad Jammu and Kashmir, www.ajkassembly.gok.pk/current_members.htm [accessed 15 March 2010].
240. 'The Azad Jammu and Kashmir Legislative Assembly (Elections) Ordinance 1970 (Amended Upto [sic] 2002)', in *The Election Laws*, pp. 121–7, dealing with 'Qualifications and disqualifications for being a member' is unclear about this issue.
241. Gilani, *Constitutional Development in Azad Jammu & Kashmir*, Appendix VII, Appendixes Section, p. 150.
242. *Statistical Year Book 1988*, Muzaffarabad?, Planning & Development Department, Azad Government of the State of Jammu and Kashmir, 1989, p. 182.
243. Jyoti Bhusan Das Gupta, *Jammu and Kashmir*, p. 243.
244. Saraf, *Kashmiris Fight—For Freedom*, Volume II, p. 1369.
245. Ibid.
246. Gilani, *Constitutional Development in Azad Jammu & Kashmir*, Appendix VII, Appendixes Section, p. 150.
247. Information obtained from a document entitled *List of Returned Candidates during 1970*, Annex 'E', no further publication details available, obtained in Azad Kashmir in December 2006.
248. Handwritten addition in 'The Azad Jammu and Kashmir Electoral Rolls Ordinance 1970 (Amended Upto [sic] 2002', in *The Election Laws*, p. 105.
249. Noorani, 'The Betrayal of Kashmir: Pakistan's Duplicity and India's Complicity', in Thomas, *Perspectives*, p. 266.
250. *Dawn*, 21 November 1969.
251. Conversation with electoral official in Azad Kashmir in December 2006.
252. For further details, see Table XIV 8: Voter turnouts in 1996, 2001 Legislative Assembly elections, in Appendix XIV: Matters re Azad Kashmir Elections, particularly in 2006.
253. Gilani, *Constitutional Development in Azad Jammu & Kashmir*, p. 138.
254. Conversation with electoral official in Azad Kashmir in December 2006.
255. Information on the eight indirectly elected members from *The Azad Jammu and Kashmir Interim Constitution Act*, pp. 19–20. Quotations from 'The Azad Jammu and Kashmir Legislative Assembly Ordinance, 1970', in *The Election Laws*, p. 106.
256. Based on documents obtained, and on conversations with various officials, in Azad Kashmir in December 2006.
257. 'List of Members Legislative Assembly 2006–Todate [sic]', Azad Jammu and Kashmir Government, www.ajk.gov.pk/site/index.php?option=com_content&task=view&id=2618&Itemid=142 [accessed 4 November 2007].
258. Sardar Muhammad Abdul Qayyum Khan, *The Kashmir Case*, pp. 118–21.
259. M.H. Askari, 'Kashmir Through the Looking Glass', *The Herald*, August 1991, p. 85.
260. Rose, 'The Politics of Azad Kashmir', in Thomas, *Perspectives*, p. 244.
261. Interview with Tariq Masud, Ombudsman, Azad Kashmir Government, Muzaffarabad, 8 January 1998. One thing that has noticeably changed since my first visit to Muzaffarabad in 1996 is the obvious presence of Kashmir Valley refugees uprooted by the

anti-Indian insurgency. Previously one had to search for, or be taken to, refugee camps for Kashmiris on Muzaffarabad's outskirts. By 1999, these camps were clearly visible in Muzaffarabad.

262. Interview with Sardar Ibrahim, Rawalakot, 4 March 1999.
263. Saraf, *Kashmiris Fight—For Freedom*, Volume II, pp. 1369–70.
264. *Dawn*, 9 October 1969.
265. Interview with Sardar Ibrahim at Rawalakot on 4 March 1999.
266. *Dawn*, 9 October 1969.
267. Gilani, *Constitutional Development in Azad Jammu & Kashmir*, p. x.
268. List of Returned Candidates during 1970, Annex 'E'.
269. Saraf, *Kashmiris Fight—For Freedom*, Volume II, p. 1372.
270. Ibid., p. 1352.
271. Schofield, *Kashmir in the Crossfire*, p. 179.
272. Information in this paragraph from Saraf, *Kashmiris Fight—For Freedom*, Volume II, p. 1353, and Tariq, *Kashmir in Strangulation*, p. 20.
273. *The Azad Jammu and Kashmir Interim Constitution Act*, p. 15.
274. The Preface to *Report on the Third General Election in Azad Jammu and Kashmir 1985*, Islamabad, Azad Jammu and Kashmir Election Commission, 1987, p. i, states that 'The second [Azad Kashmir] general election in 1974 [sic; it was 1975] was also held under the 1970 Act. Shortly thereafter, the Act was repealed by the A.J.&K. Interim Constitution Act, 1974 ... However, by a deeming provision, the repealing Act provided that the President then in office and [the] Legislative Assembly then existing would nevertheless, continue to function as if elected and established under the new dispensation'.
275. Saraf, *Kashmiris Fight—For Freedom*, Volume II, p. 1355.
276. Aziz, *Freedom Struggle in Kashmir*, p. 357.
277. On 17 December 2003, the President of Pakistan, General Pervez Musharraf, told a journalist that Pakistan had 'left aside' the United Nations Security Council resolutions that deal with his nation's dispute with India over J&K, including the conducting of a plebiscite in J&K. While Pakistan was in favour of the UN resolutions, Musharraf conceded that 'both sides need to talk to each other with flexibility, coming beyond stated positions, meeting halfway somewhere'. See *Dawn*, Karachi, 19 December 2003.

## 6. THE ADMINISTRATION: LARGE AND OVERSEEN

1. Rose, 'The Politics of Azad Kashmir', in Thomas, *Perspectives*, p. 237.
2. Bazaz, *The History of Struggle for Freedom in Kashmir*, p. 624.
3. *Five Years of Pakistan (August 1947–August 1952)*, Karachi, Pakistan Publications, 1952?, p. 237.
4. *Dawn*, 26 November 1947.
5. *Five Years of Pakistan*, p. 237.
6. Ibid., p. 237.

7. Sardar M. Ibrahim Khan, *The Kashmir Saga*, pp. 101–02. Pulandri, Pulandari and Pallandri are variations of this place name. Justice Gilani, *The Constitution of Azad Jammu & Kashmir*, p. 53, states that after moving from Rawalpindi, the headquarters of the provisional Azad Kashmir Government were at 'Junjal Hill in Pallandri'.
8. *CMG*, 13 November 1947.
9. Sardar M. Ibrahim Khan, *The Kashmir Saga*, p. 102. Trarkhal and Tarakhel are variations.
10. Saraf, *Kashmiris Fight—For Freedom*, Volume II, p. 1289. Bazaz, *The History of Struggle for Freedom in Kashmir*, p. 624, states that a 'Secretariat' was established in the 'Chadda Buildings at Rawalpindi'.
11. *CMG*, 25 October 1947.
12. *Dawn*, 9 February 1949. Annex 6, 'Minutes of Meetings with Officials of the "Azad Kashmir Government"', UNCIP, *Report of the Sub-committee on Western Kashmir*, p. 59.
13. Gilani, *Constitutional Development in Azad Jammu & Kashmir*, Appendix III, Appendixes Section, p. 45.
14. *Five Years of Pakistan*, p. 237.
15. Suharwardy, *Tragedy in Kashmir*, p. 129.
16. Annex 3, 'Questionnaire and Answers of Azad Authorities', UNCIP, *Report of the Sub-committee on Western Kashmir*, p. 21.
17. Symonds, 'With the Rebel Forces of Poonch'; UNCIP, *Report of the Sub-committee on Western Kashmir*, p. 16.
18. UNCIP, *Report of the Sub-committee on Western Kashmir*, p. 8.
19. *Dawn*, 2 January 1951.
20. Saraf, *Kashmiris Fight—For Freedom*, Volume II, p. 1290.
21. Bazaz, *The History of Struggle for Freedom in Kashmir*, p. 624.
22. Saraf, *Kashmiris Fight—For Freedom*, Volume II, p. 1290.
23. Sardar M. Ibrahim Khan, *The Kashmir Saga*, pp. 102–03.
24. This paragraph largely based on Suharwardy, *Tragedy in Kashmir*, pp. 132–3. A discussion with A.M. Salaria, Lahore, 29 March 1999, confirmed some details. From March 1947, Salaria was a forestry officer in the Maharaja's administration, then in the Azad Kashmir Government, from which he retired in 1972 as Chief Conservator of Forests.
25. Saraf, *Kashmiris Fight—For Freedom*, Volume II, p. 1289.
26. Sardar M. Ibrahim Khan, *The Kashmir Saga*, pp. 102–03.
27. *Dawn*, 9 May 1948.
28. Ibid.
29. Ibid., 20 May 1948.
30. *Census of Azad Kashmir, 1951*, refers throughout to the 'Northern Areas' area as 'Gilgit & Baltistan'. Dani, *History of Northern Areas of Pakistan*, p. 410, infers that the title 'Northern Areas' was in use in 1947.
31. See Appendix V: Physical and Political Composition of J&K after the 1949 Ceasefire.
32. *Census of India 1941*, p. 527.
33. *CMG*, 29 July 1947, announced the 'Retrocession of Gilgit to Kashmir'. *CMG*, 2 August 1947, confirmed this action: 'Gilgit Retroceded to Kashmir'.
34. Dani, *History of Northern Areas of Pakistan*, p. 410.
35. *The Times*, 2 January 1948 and Dani, *History of Northern Areas of Pakistan*, p. 415.

36. UNCIP, *Report of the Sub-committee on Western Kashmir*, p. 13.
37. *Census of Azad Kashmir, 1951*, p. 13.
38. Dani, *History of Northern Areas of Pakistan*, pp. 410, 414.
39. *Census of Azad Kashmir, 1951*, p. 12.
40. *Census of India 1961*, p. 144.
41. *Census of Azad Kashmir, 1951*, p. 10.
42. Before fighting and the ceasefire line divided J&K, the easiest land route to Gilgit had been the Srinagar-Gilgit 'road'. While describing this as a road, *Census of India 1941*, pp. 527–8, noted that there was no wheeled transport in the Gilgit Agency or Ladakh. There was another 'road' to Gilgit from Chitral in NWFP and a 'track' from Rawalpindi to Chilas along the Indus River through formerly British-controlled territory. This track was later made into the Karakoram Highway from Havelian, NWFP, to Kashgar, in Xinjiang in China.
43. Sardar M. Ibrahim Khan, *The Kashmir Saga*, p. 70.
44. *The Times*, 19 May 1949.
45. Ibid., 2 January 1948. Justice Gilani, *The Constitution of Azad Jammu & Kashmir*, Appendixes XIV-XVII, pp. 666–73, has each 'Document of accession in favour of Pakistan' for 'Raja Mir Mehboob Ali Khan, Governor Yasin' (document translated from Urdu), 'Raja Muhammad Anwar, Governor Pooniyal' (document translated from Urdu), 'Shoukat Ali, Walie-Nagar Pakistan [sic]' (document translated from Urdu but signed in English), and the 'Mir of Hunza' (document in English).
46. Two newspapers reported that the Mirs had actually acceded to Pakistan: *The New York Times*, 5 November and *CMG*, 6 November 1947. According to *The Times*, 3 November 1947, the Mehtar of nearby Chitral (NWFP) on 2 November had 'repudiated the nominal suzerainty of the Maharaja of Kashmir and had declared his accession to Pakistan'.
47. Government of Pakistan, Prime Minister's Secretariat, Declassified File No. 13 (5)-PMS/50, *All Jammu & Kashmir Muslim Conference*, 'Resolution Adopted by the Working Committee of the Jammu and Kashmir Muslim Conference on the 10th of January 1950', p. 46.
48. Government of Pakistan, Prime Minister's Secretariat, Declassified File No. 13 (5)-PMS/50, *All Jammu & Kashmir Muslim Conference*, 'Letter from Ghulam Abbass [sic], All Jammu & Kashmir Muslim Conference, Rawalpindi, to The Hon'ble Liaquat Ali Khan, 9 March 1950', p. 45.
49. The High Court of Judicature, *Verdict on Gilgit and Baltistan*, pp. 1–3. The petition was made by Malik Muhammad Miskeen and Haji Amir Jan, from District Diamir in the Northern Areas, and Shaikh Abdul Aziz, from Muzaffarabad.
50. The High Court of Judicature, *Verdict on Gilgit and Baltistan*, p. 30.
51. The decision is in 'Civil Appeals Nos. 37 and 34 of 1993, decided on 14th September, 1994, PLD 1995 Supreme Court (AJ&K) 1', in *The All Pakistan Legal Decisions. Supreme Court (AJ&K)*, Volume XLVII, Lahore, PLD Publishers, 1995, pp. 1–30.
52. 'Civil Appeals Nos. 37 and 34 of 1993, decided on 14th September, 1994, PLD 1995 Supreme Court (AJ&K) 1', p. 26.
53. While little has changed in the Northern Areas since 1947, on 23 October 2007 General Musharraf announced that 'all administrative and financial authority would be

shifted to [the] Northern [A]reas from [the] Ministry of Kashmir Affairs[,] Islamabad'. Prior to this announcement, the Northern Areas Legislative Council had, to all intents and purposes, been a limited advisory body only. See 'NA Legislative Council given Legislative Assembly status', *Pak Tribune*, Islamabad, 23 October 2007, www.paktribune.com/news/index.shtml?192618.
54. On 1 January 1949, J&K had three administrations: the Azad Kashmir administration; the Indian J&K administration, over which an increasingly marginalised Maharaja Hari Singh was exercising limited oversight; and the Pakistani political agent in Northern Areas.
55. Rashid, *The Smiling Face of Azad Kashmir*, p. 3.
56. Ibid.
57. *The Azad Jammu and Kashmir Interim Constitution Act*, p. 1.
58. UNCIP, *Report of the Sub-committee on Western Kashmir*, p. 3.
59. Annex 5, 'Minutes of the Meeting With Sardar Ibrahim, President of the "Azad Kashmir Government"', in UNCIP, *Report of the Sub-committee on Western Kashmir*, p. 57.
60. UNCIP, *Report of the Sub-committee on Western Kashmir*, p. 5.
61. Ibid., p. 4.
62. Annex 3, 'Questionnaire and Answers of Azad Authorities', UNCIP, *Report of the Sub-committee on Western Kashmir*, p. 7.
63. Appendix A, 'The Civil Secretariat', to Annex 3, 'Questionnaire and Answers of Azad Authorities', UNCIP, *Report of the Sub-committee on Western Kashmir*, p. 25.
64. UNCIP, *Report of the Sub-committee on Western Kashmir*, p. 4.
65. The rest of this paragraph based on UNCIP, *Report of the Sub-committee on Western Kashmir*, pp. 6–7.
66. Rashid, *The Smiling Face of Azad Kashmir*, p. 6.
67. *Dawn*, 9 February 1949. This article also stated that the Muslim Conference was shifting its headquarters from Sialkot to Rawalpindi. Both these moves had been made to 'facilitate political work during the plebiscite' in J&K.
68. Discussion with Mir Abdul Aziz, Rawalpindi, 23 January 1998.
69. Rashid, *The Smiling Face of Azad Kashmir*, p. 6.
70. Ibid.
71. Dhar, *Kashmir: Eden of the East*, pp. 120–22. Even though the Jhelum Valley Road was closed from 1947 to 2005 (and is now only open to residents of J&K able to obtain the necessary permissions), a sign at Domel, on Muzaffarabad's outskirts, for many years has shown 'Srinagar, 183 kms'. Since April 2005, India and Pakistan have initiated a limited fortnightly Srinagar-Muzaffarabad passenger bus service that traverses this road.
72. *Census of Azad Kashmir, 1951*, p. 2.
73. *Dawn*, 17 December 1947.
74. Annex 9, 'Tour Diary, Mirpur District', UNCIP, *Report of the Sub-committee on Western Kashmir*, pp. 80–81.
75. Clark, 'A Journey to "Free Kashmir"'.
76. Information on the 1950 Rules of Business from Khalil Ahmed Qureshi, *The Annual Volume of Azad Jammu & Kashmir Laws, 1948*, Muzaffarabad, Law Department, Azad Government of the State of Jammu and Kashmir, 1980?, Preface, p. B.

77. Gilani, *Constitutional Development in Azad Jammu & Kashmir*, Appendix III, Appendixes Section, p. 46.
78. Ibid., Appendix IV, Appendixes Section, pp. 77–102.
79. Ibid., Appendix V, Appendixes Section, pp. 107–135.
80. Ibid., Appendix V, Appendixes Section, p. 109.
81. Ibid., Appendix V, 'Schedule—IV. Procedure in Regard to the Proceedings of the Council', Appendixes Section, p. 135.
82. Ibid., Appendix V, Appendixes Section, p. 108.
83. The rest of this paragraph based on Gilani, *Constitutional Development in Azad Jammu & Kashmir*, Appendix V, 'Schedule—IV. Procedure in Regard to the Proceedings of the Council', Appendixes Section, pp. 132–5.
84. Qureshi, *The Annual Volume of Azad Jammu & Kashmir Laws, 1948*, Preface, p. B.
85. Gilani, *Constitutional Development in Azad Jammu & Kashmir*, Appendix VI, Appendixes Section, pp. 139–43.
86. Ibid., Appendix VII, Appendixes Section, pp. 149–60.
87. Qureshi, *The Annual Volume of Azad Jammu & Kashmir Laws, 1948*, Preface, p. B.
88. Gilani, *Constitutional Development in Azad Jammu & Kashmir*, Appendix IV, Appendixes Section, pp. 82, 87.
89. Ibid., Appendix IV, Appendixes Section, p. 102.
90. Ibid., Appendix IV, Appendixes Section, p. 79.
91. *Census of India 1941*, p. 231.
92. UNCIP, *Report of the Sub-committee on Western Kashmir*, p. 4.
93. Saraf, *Kashmiris Fight—For Freedom*, Volume II, p. 1291.
94. Ibid., Volume II, p. 1309.
95. Gilani, *Constitutional Development in Azad Jammu & Kashmir*, Appendix IV, Appendixes Section, pp. 88–9.
96. Saraf, *Kashmiris Fight—For Freedom*, Volume II, p. 1309, and 'Facilities for retired AJK officials opposed', *Dawn*, 26 June 2006, which calls the latter position 'additional chief secretary (development)'.
97. Gilani, *Constitutional Development in Azad Jammu & Kashmir*, Appendix IV, Appendixes Section, p. 90.
98. Ibid., Appendix IV, Appendixes Section, pp. 100, 103.
99. *Pakistan's Constitutional Position on Jammu and Kashmir's Status*, Islamabad, Institute of Policy Studies, unpublished.
100. Gilani, *Constitutional Development in Azad Jammu & Kashmir*, Appendix IV, Appendixes Section, p. 82.
101. 'A Guide to Performance Evaluation', Director General, *Pakistan Public Administration Research Centre*, Islamabad, 2004, www.pakistan.gov.pk/divisions/establishment-division/media/PEGuide.pdf [accessed 20 March 2009], p. 33.
102. Item number twelve (of eighteen), 'Job Description Section Officer. (*Kashmir*)' in an unnamed, undated document containing various position descriptions, *Kashmir Affairs Division*, www.pakistan.gov.pk/divisions/kashmiraffairs-division/media/WorkDistribution.pdf [accessed 20 March 2009], p. 6.
103. 'Facilities for retired AJK officials opposed', *Dawn*, 26 June 2006.

104. This paragraph based on Charles H. Kennedy, *Bureaucracy in Pakistan*, Karachi, Oxford University Press, 1987, pp. 187–8, 193–15.
105. Qureshi, *The Annual Volume of Azad Jammu & Kashmir Laws, 1948*, Preface, p. B.
106. *The Land Laws of Azad Jammu and Kashmir (As Amended up to 31st March 1996)*, Muzaffarabad, Ch. Mukhtar Hussain, Compiler and Editor, Board of Revenue, Azad Jammu and Kashmir Government, 1996, p. 34. Two of the laws adopted were the Punjab Land Revenue Act, 1887, and the Tenancy Act, 1887.
107. Qureshi, *The Annual Volume of Azad Jammu & Kashmir Laws, 1948*, Preface, p. C, includes the Code of Criminal Procedure, Penal Code, Evidence Act, Arms Act, Code of Civil Procedure, Police Act, Shariat Act, and Courts Act.
108. *The Land Laws of Azad Jammu and Kashmir*, p. 34. This act was amended in 1959 and 1988.
109. *Azad Kashmir On [The] Road To Progress*, Muzaffarabad, Mohammad Iqbal, Compiler and Editor, Information Directorate, Azad Government of Jammu and Kashmir State, 1965, p. 47. This may have been the 1959 amendment to the 'Adaptation of Laws Act, 1948'.
110. *Azad Kashmir On [The] Road To Progress*, p. 47.
111. This paragraph based on UNCIP, *Report of the Sub-committee on Western Kashmir*, pp. 8–9, and Appendix F, 'Rough Budget Estimates for the Year 1949–1950', to Annex 3, 'Questionnaire and Answers of Azad Authorities', UNCIP, *Report of the Sub-committee on Western Kashmir*, pp. 46–7.
112. *Azad Kashmir On [The] Road To Progress*, p. 40.
113. *Census of Azad Kashmir, 1951*, p. 15.
114. UNCIP, *Report of the Sub-committee on Western Kashmir*, p. 8.
115. Annex 6, 'Minutes of Meetings with Officials of the "Azad Kashmir Government"', UNCIP, *Report of the Sub-committee on Western Kashmir*, p. 62.
116. *Azad Kashmir On [The] Road To Progress*, p. 40.
117. Gilani, *Constitutional Development in Azad Jammu & Kashmir*, Appendix IV, Appendixes Section, p. 88.
118. *Census of Azad Kashmir, 1951*, pp. 2, 11.
119. *Azad Kashmir On [The] Road To Progress*, pp. 39–40.
120. Gilani, *Constitutional Development in Azad Jammu & Kashmir*, Appendix IV, Appendixes Section, pp. 98–9.
121. *Azad Kashmir On [The] Road To Progress*, page immediately after Contents page.
122. Ibid., p. 123, final paragraph of the report.
123. Rashid, *The Smiling Face of Azad Kashmir*, p. 2.
124. Gilani, *Constitutional Development in Azad Jammu & Kashmir*, Appendix V, Appendixes Section, pp. 126–9.
125. Rashid, *The Smiling Face of Azad Kashmir*, p. 2.
126. Ibid., p. 2.
127. I only have partial information from the 1972 and 1981 censuses.
128. *Azad Kashmir at a Glance 1995*, Muzaffarabad, Planning & Dev. [sic] Department, Azad Govt. [sic] of the State of Jammu & Kashmir, 1996?. The first year I have of this publication is 1995, although it was published earlier: *Azad Kashmir Statistical Year Book*

1990, Muzaffarabad?, Statistics Section, Planning & Development Department, Azad Government of the State of Jammu & Kashmir, 1992, Preface, refers to a '1991 version'.

129. See, for example, *Azad Jammu and Kashmir Government,* www.ajk.gov.pk/site/index.php?option=com_frontpage&Itemid=1, *Prime Minister Secretariat of Azad Government of the State of Azad Jammu & Kashmir,* www.pmajk.gov.pk/home.asp, *Legislative Assembly of Azad Jammu &Kashmir,* www.ajkassembly.gok.pk/, and *Planning & Development [of Azad Kashmir Government],* www.pndajk.gov.pk/default.asp [all accessed 19 March 2009].
130. *Azad Kashmir Statistical Year Book 1988,* p. 182.
131. *Azad Kashmir Statistical Year Book 1990,* p. 6.
132. Ibid., p. 2.
133. Ibid., p. 9.
134. Ibid., p. vii.
135. *Rules of Business 1985,* Services & General Administration Department, Azad Government of the State of Jammu and Kashmir, Muzaffarabad, 1985, p. 1. I have not been able to obtain a copy of the Rules of Business, 1975.
136. Section 58, *The Azad Jammu and Kashmir Interim Constitution Act,* p. 51.
137. *Rules of Business 1985,* p. 1.
138. Ibid., pp. 1, 28, 60.
139. 'Business Rules', *Azad Jammu and Kashmir Government,* www.ajk.gov.pk/site/index.php?option=com_content&task=view&id=79&Itemid=94 [accessed 19 March 2009]. This site has an extract from the 'Rules of Business 1985 (amended June 2002)'.
140. Some, but not all, of these rules were available by doing a search on the Azad Jammu and Kashmir Government's website: www.ajk.gov.pk/site/index.php?option=com_frontpage&Itemid=1 [accessed 1 April 2010].
141. While the Rules of Business 1985 are still currently in operation in Azad Kashmir, I have written about them in the past tense.
142. *Rules of Business 1985,* pp. i–iii.
143. Unless otherwise stated, the information in the rest of this paragraph is from ibid., pp. 1–6.
144. 'To rule for ever', editorial in *Daily Excelsior,* 6 July 2007, states that 'of thirty-seven chief secretaries of "Azad" Kashmir after 1947 only one has risen from the local services'.
145. *Rules of Business 1985,* pp. 29–32, 33–52. Schedule II is listed entirely in Appendix X: Azad Kashmir Administrative Setup and Functions, part 3) 'Distribution of business among Departments', as per *Rules of Business 1985.*
146. *Rules of Business 1985,* pp. 58–62.
147. Ibid., pp. 51–2.
148. Ibid., pp. 6.
149. The rest of the information in this paragraph is from ibid., pp. 54–5.
150. Ibid., pp. 52–4.
151. Ibid., p. 52.
152. Ibid., p. 5.

153. 'Cabinet Division, D.O. No. 8/9/70-Coord. I., Government of Pakistan, Rawalpindi, May 11, 1971', in Justice Gilani, *The Constitution of Azad Jammu & Kashmir*, Appendix LVIII, p. 834.
154. *Rules of Business 1985*, pp. 29–32.
155. *Azad Kashmir Statistical Year Book 1990*, p. vii.
156. Ibid., Map of Azad Jammu & Kashmir immediately before Preface and p. 8. Figures rounded to the nearest hundred.
157. Figures on Azad Kashmir education from *Statistical Year Book 1988*, pp. 221–5.
158. *Azad Kashmir Statistical Year Book 1990*, p. vii. The figures were from the *1981 Census of Azad Kashmir*. By 1996, the estimated literacy rate was 44 per cent.
159. *Census of Azad Kashmir, 1951*, pp. 19–20. Page 20 noted that 'Female education presents more than the usual problems, because a girls' school in each village is a hope which is difficult to realize and parents in the country side have not an unjustifiable [sic] objection to permitting growing girls to undertake alone the everyday journey to and from schools which are not situated in villages of their own residence'.
160. Figures on Azad Kashmir health from *Statistical Year Book 1988*, p. 235.
161. Ibid., pp. 243, 374.
162. Ibid., pp. 247, 316.
163. 'Table 1.1: Detail of Changes Taken Place in the Boundary of Administrative Units After 1981, Azad Kashmir', *1998 Census of Azad Kashmir*, p. 2. The table doesn't state when the various changes were made.
164. *Azad Kashmir at a Glance 1995*, pp. 2, 7.
165. *Azad Kashmir at a Glance 1996*, Muzaffarabad, Planning & Dev. [sic] Department, Azad Gov. [sic] of the State of Jammu & Kashmir, 1997?, p. 7.
166. All information in this paragraph from *Azad Kashmir at a Glance*, 2008, Muzaffarabad, Planning & Development Department, Azad Government of the State of Jammu & Kashmir, 2008, www.pndajk.gov.pk/glance.asp [accessed 15 September 2010], [no page numbers]. Also see Appendix XI: Azad Kashmir's Actual Administration and Population, 1988–2008, for administration and population details.
167. This paragraph is based on *Azad Kashmir at a Glance*, 2007, Muzaffarabad, Planning & Development Department, Azad Government of the State of Jammu & Kashmir, www.pndajk.gov.pk/ajk_glance2007.asp#DDSDAJK [accessed 19 March 2009], no page numbers.
168. All figures on the Azad Kashmir Administration for 1988 calculated from statistics in *Statistical Year Book 1988*, pp. 216–18. For the forty-one divisions of the Azad Kashmir administration, see Appendix X: Azad Kashmir Administrative Setup and Functions.
169. All figures on government employees from *1998 Census Report of Azad Kashmir*, pp. 150–55.
170. Calculated from 'Police Strength' in *1998 Census Report of Azad Kashmir*, p. 32.
171. Annexure D, 'Definitions and Concepts', *1998 Census Report of Azad Kashmir*, p. x.
172. *Azad Kashmir at a Glance 2005*, Muzaffarabad, Planning & Development Department, Azad Government of the State of Jammu & Kashmir, 2006?, p. 1.
173. Figures on the Azad Kashmir Administration calculated from statistics in *Statistical Year Book 1988*, pp. 216–18. There also are details about Azad Kashmir's 'sanctioned posts'

in Table X 2: Azad Kashmir Administration: as per the *Statistical Yearbook 1988*, in Appendix X: Azad Kashmir Administrative Setup and Functions.
174. *Statistical Year Book 1988*, p. 370.
175. These were the departments of Amoor-i-Dinia (Religious Affairs), Auqaf (Religious/charitable trusts) and Zakat & Usher (regarding Muslims' obligatory payments).
176. 1985 information from *Rules of Business 1985*, pp. 58–62. 1952 information from Gilani, *Constitutional Development in Azad Jammu & Kashmir*, Appendix IV, Appendixes Section, pp. 88–9.
177. *Census of Azad Kashmir, 1951*, p. 12.
178. *Azad Kashmir at a Glance*, 2007, no page numbers. *Azad Kashmir at a Glance*, 2008, various page numbers.
179. Part 3) 'Distribution of business among Departments', as per Rules of Business 1985, in Appendix X: Azad Kashmir Administrative Setup and Functions.
180. Muhammad Aslam, 'Industrialization in Azad Kashmir—An Assessment', *Economic Review*, Volume 10, Number 11, November 1979, p. 33.
181. 'Table 82: Density of Population in Azad Kashmir Districtwise in 1972 Census' and 'Table 83: Density of Population in Azad Kashmir Districtwise in 1981 Census', *Statistical Year Book 1988*, pp. 187, 188.
182. *Statistical Year Book 1988*, p. ii.
183. *Five Years of Pakistan*, p. 237.
184. On my first trip to Azad Kashmir in 1996, I met the Inspector-General of Police. In 1999, I met the Chief Secretary, Inspector-General of Police, Finance Secretary and Accountant-General. In 2006, I met the Chief Secretary and Inspector-General of Police. While filling the most senior positions in Azad Kashmir, these Pakistani lent officers often were keen to get back to their (less remote) homes and positions in Pakistan.

7. THE ECONOMY: POOR AND DEPENDENT

1. Azad Kashmir at a *Glance 1995*, p. 2. *Azad Kashmir at a Glance*, 2008, p. 4.
2. Annex 3, 'Questionnaire and Answers of Azad Authorities', in UNCIP, *Report of the Sub-committee on Western Kashmir*, p. 17.
3. Hafizullah, *Towards Azad Kashmir*, p. 170.
4. Ibid., pp. 162–3.
5. Ibid., p. 170.
6. *Census of Azad Kashmir, 1951*, p. 6.
7. An alternative road to Domel came from Havelian rail terminus in NWFP, via Abbottabad and Muzaffarabad.
8. Dhar, *Kashmir: Eden of the East*, p. 120.
9. Ganju, *This is Kashmir*, p. ix.
10. Saraf, *Kashmiris Fight—For Freedom*, Volume I, p. 17.
11. *Census of Azad Kashmir, 1951*, p. 6.
12. S. Amjad Ali, 'Economic Aspects of Kashmir Problem', *The Pakistan Times* Magazine, 11 June 1950.

13. Messervy, 'Kashmir', p. 474.
14. Spate and Learmonth, *India and Pakistan*, p. 439. Such blockages still regularly occur in winter, which isolate the Kashmir Valley (and Ladakh) from the subcontinent.
15. The Jhelum Valley Road does close owing to landslides and snow, but such closures are usually brief—hours, as against days.
16. Ganju, *This is Kashmir*, p. 53.
17. S. Amjad Ali, 'Economic Aspects of Kashmir Problem', *The Pakistan Times* Magazine, 11 June 1950.
18. Dhar, *Kashmir: Eden of the East*, pp. 121, 125, 126.
19. Spate and Learmonth, *India and Pakistan*, p. 439.
20. Ganju, *This is Kashmir*, p. ix.
21. Ibid., p. 42.
22. A similar claim and the same term are used by Khan, *Real Azad Kashmir*, p. 2.
23. Aslam, 'Industrialization in Azad Kashmir', p. 35.
24. *Pakistan 1953–1954*, Pakistan Publications, Karachi, 1954?, p. 274.
25. All distances given in this paragraph are from *Census of Azad Kashmir, 1951*, p. 32.
26. *Azad Kashmir On [The] Road To Progress*, p. 123.
27. Roger Ballard, 'Kashmir Crisis: View from Mirpur', p. 513.
28. *Dawn*, 18 September 1949.
29. Maneck B. Pithawalla, *An Introduction to Kashmir. Its Geology and Geography*, Muzaffarabad, Kashmir Publications, 1953, p. 84.
30. Unless otherwise stated, the rest of this paragraph is based on *Azad Kashmir On [The] Road To Progress*, pp. 42–3.
31. Aslam, 'Industrialization in Azad Kashmir', p. 43.
32. *Census of Azad Kashmir, 1951*, p. 33.
33. UNCIP, *Report of the Sub-committee on Western Kashmir*, p. 9.
34. Annex 3, 'Questionnaire and Answers of Azad Authorities', in UNCIP, *Report of the Sub-committee on Western Kashmir*, p. 16.
35. *Census of Azad Kashmir, 1951*, p. 33.
36. Ibid., *1951*, pp. 15–16.
37. *Azad Kashmir Statistical Year Book 1990*, pp. vii-viii.
38. *Census of Azad Kashmir, 1951*, p. 33.
39. Ibid., p. 15.
40. *Azad Kashmir at a Glance*, undated, Muzaffarabad, Planning & Development Department, Azad Government of the State of Jammu & Kashmir, 2007?, www.pndajk.gov.pk/glance.asp [accessed 25 February 2009], p. 1 [subsection] 'Economic survey of Pakistan 2005–2006'.
41. Qudssia Akhlaque, 'AJK: a journey of discovery', *The Nation*, 20 April 1995.
42. *Statistical Year Book 1988*, pp. 24–5.
43. Pakistan introduced the metric system in 1966, and its use became compulsory in 1979. I provide imperial and metric measures, as per the respective source of the information.
44. Figures for yields for 1982–87 calculated from information in *Statistical Year Book 1988*, pp. 3–11, and for 1997–98 from *1998 Census Report of Azad Kashmir*, pp. 8–9.

45. *1998 Census Report of Azad Kashmir*, pp. 8–10.
46. *Azad Kashmir at a Glance*, undated, p. 1.
47. *1998 Census Report of Azad Kashmir*, p. 11, shows that Azad Kashmir also cropped *bajra* (millet; 9,600 hectares), grams (5,200 hectares) *jawar (sorghum;* 2,700), rape seed and mustard (3,000), potatoes (285), and unspecified 'others' (11,000). A horticultural industry produced a range of fruit, nuts and vegetables, chiefly guavas (390,000 tonnes), walnuts (352,000 tons) and pears (174,000 tonnes).
48. This paragraph based on *Census of Azad Kashmir, 1951*, p. 34.
49. This is still the quickest and easiest route between Azad Kashmir's two major cities.
50. Figures calculated from information in *Statistical Year Book 1988*, pp. 9–11, 169.
51. *Census of Azad Kashmir, 1951*, pp. 6, 34. Page 6 states these figures were given by Sheikh Abdullah in his Introduction to *Jammu and Kashmir, 1947–50*, no publication details provided. This was probably Abdullah's Introduction to *Jammu & Kashmir 1947–50. An Account of Activities of First Three Years of Sheikh Abdullah's Government*, Jammu, The Ranbir Government Press, 1951.
52. *Census of Azad Kashmir, 1951*, pp. 33–4.
53. Rounded figures from ibid., *1951*, p. 12.
54. Ibid., p. 34.
55. *1998 Census Report of Azad Kashmir*, p. 29.
56. *Statistical Year Book 1988*, pp. 186, 196.
57. Ibid., p. 179.
58. Discussion with A.M. Salaria, Lahore, 29 March 1999.
59. *Azad Kashmir On [The] Road To Progress*, p. 78.
60. *Census of Azad Kashmir, 1961*, p. 6.
61. *Azad Kashmir Statistical Year Book 1990*, p. viii.
62. *1998 Census Report of Azad Kashmir*, pp. 10–11. While the Census date is 1998, on p. 11, the date for the 'Source' for Table 1.7 that provides data on Azad Kashmir's 'Area Under Different Types of Forests …' is '2000'.
63. *Census of Azad Kashmir, 1951*, p. 33.
64. UNCIP, *Report of the Sub-committee on Western Kashmir*, p. 8.
65. Rashid, *The Smiling Face of Azad Kashmir*, p. 3.
66. *Census of Azad Kashmir, 1961*, p. 6.
67. Ibid., p. 15.
68. Messervy, 'Kashmir', p. 475. Annex 7, 'Minutes of the Meeting with the Defence Minister of the "Azad Kashmir Government"', in UNCIP, *Report of the Sub-committee on Western Kashmir*, p. 71.
69. *Pakistan 1953–1954*, Pakistan Publications, Karachi, 1954?, p. 274.
70. *Five Years of Pakistan*, p. 239.
71. Thomson, 'The Two Kashmirs', p. 14.
72. *Azad Kashmir On [The] Road To Progress*, p. 40.
73. Ibid., p. 96.
74. Ibid., p. 123.
75. Nasir Ahmad Farooki, 'Through the valley and plains of Azad Kashmir-1', in *Dawn*, 1 August 1950, noted that 'Muzaffarabad has started well on its industrial progress in a

small way'. Farooki had a second piece in *Dawn*, 24 August 1950. Both may have been publicity pieces as 'the Azad Kashmir Government had asked [him] to tour' the region.

76. *Reports of the Advisory Panels for the Fourth Five-Year Plan*, Planning Commission, Government of Pakistan, Volume II, Islamabad, July 1970, p. 374.
77. *Azad Kashmir Statistical Year Book 1990*, p. viii.
78. *Azad Kashmir Statistical Year Book 1988*, p. 337.
79. Discussion with Sardar Mohammad Sadiq Khan, Chief Economist, Development Department, Azad Kashmir Government, Muzaffarabad, 16 January 1998.
80. *Azad Kashmir at a Glance 1995*, p. 2.
81. *Azad Kashmir at a Glance 2003*, Muzaffarabad, Planning & Dev. [sic] Department, Azad Govt. [sic] of the State of Jammu & Kashmir, 2004?, p. 2. *Azad Kashmir at a Glance*, 2008, p. 4.
82. 'Cabinet Division, D.O. No. 8/9/70-Coord. I., Government of Pakistan, Rawalpindi, May 11, 1971', in Justice Gilani, *The Constitution of Azad Jammu & Kashmir*, Appendix LVIII, pp. 834–5.
83. Thomson, 'The Two Kashmirs', p. 14.
84. 'Rs 9728m allocated for AJK uplift', *Dawn*, 16 April 1993. Sardar Muhammad Abdul Qayyum Khan, *The Kashmir Case*, p. 124, states that, when he became President in 1970, he 'established the planning and development department in Azad Kashmir'.
85. Discussion with Sardar Mohammad Sadiq Khan, Muzaffarabad, 16 January 1998.
86. *Federal Government's Contribution to the progress of Azad Kashmir*, Islamabad, Ministry of Information & Broadcasting, Government of Pakistan, 1976, pp. 3–4. These areas were hardly 'remote': a photo on the document's front cover shows Bhutto, Sardar Ibrahim and Hamid Khan striding forth wearing dress shoes, collars and ties, and full lounge suits with coats buttoned.
87. See *Azad Kashmir at a Glance 1995*, p. 24 and Table 7.2.
88. *Federal Government's Contribution to the progress of Azad Kashmir*, p. 4. All figures in this paragraph are from p. 4 of this publication.
89. *Azad Kashmir at a Glance 1995*, p. 24.
90. *Azad Kashmir On [The] Road To Progress*, p. 122.
91. *Reports of the Advisory Panels for the Fourth Five-Year Plan*, p. 372.
92. Rose, 'The Politics of Azad Kashmir', in Thomas, *Perspectives*, p. 247.
93. *Public Sector Development Programme 2006–2007*, Muzaffarabad, Planning & Development Department, Azad Government of the State of Jammu and Kashmir, 2007?, p. v.
94. *Public Sector Development Programme for the Year 1997–98 of Azad Government of the State of Jammu & Kashmir*, Muzaffarabad, Planning & Development Department, Azad Government of the State of Jammu & Kashmir, 1997?, first page of Preface.
95. Table XII 2: Comparison of revenue spent or accrued in 2005–2006 (as per Revised Estimates), and budgeted to accrue or spend in 2006–07 (as per Budget Estimates), by Azad Kashmir Departments, in Appendix XII: Aspects of the Azad Kashmir Budgets.
96. *Azad Kashmir at a Glance 2003*, p. 27. In *Azad Kashmir at a Glance 2005*, p. 29, it appears as 'Mangla Dame Royalty'.
97. 'Protest over release of Rs 1.4 billion to WAPDA; AJK Council discontinues developmental activities', *The Nation*, 4 October 2000.

98. This paragraph based on Presentation on *Economic Features*, Azad Jammu and Kashmir Government, 2006, unpublished handout obtained in Azad Kashmir in December 2006, pp. 3–4.
99. The India-Pakistan ceasefire on the LOC from November 2003 to about November 2008 improved this situation.
100. Colonel (Retired) B. Malik, 'The development of AJ&K: A rejoinder to information minister', *The Muslim*, 13 December 1995 and 'New AJK Government', *The Nation*, 27 July 2001.
101. 'Sikandar warns against neglect in uplift projects', *Dawn*, 1 February 2002.
102. This paragraph based on Presentation on *Economic Features*, Azad Jammu and Kashmir Government, pp. 8–11.
103. *1998 Census Report of Azad Kashmir*, pp. 36–42.
104. Ibid., p. 1.
105. Ibid., pp. iii, v.
106. Ibid., Islamabad, Population Census Organization, Statistics Division, Government of Pakistan, July 2001. Both the 'Third Schedule: Council Legislative List' and the *Rules of Business 1985* list 'census' as one of their responsibilities. See Appendixes VIII and X respectively.
107. Ibid., p. 29.
108. Ibid., p. 106.
109. Ibid., pp. 132–46.
110. Ibid., cover page.
111. Ibid., p. 104.
112. *Census of Azad Kashmir, 1951*, p. 12.
113. *1998 Census Report of Azad Kashmir*, p. 104.
114. Migration figures from ibid., pp. 132–3, 144–5.
115. Ibid., p 27.
116. Ibid., pp. 13–20. Seven of eight tables in this section had information from the Azad Kashmir Planning and Development Department for 2000.
117. Industry figures from *1998 Census Report of Azad Kashmir*, pp. 15–16. On p. 15, the total figure for 'Districtwise Number of Industries' was 915; on p. 16, the figures for 'Industrial Units' totalled 916.
118. This paragraph based on ibid., pp. 61–8.
119. Annexure D, 'Definitions and Concepts', ibid., p. ix.
120. *Azad Kashmir at a Glance 2005*, p. 1.
121. 'New AJK Government', *The Nation*, 27 July 2001.
122. *1998 Census Report of Azad Kashmir*, pp. 8–13.
123. *Azad Kashmir at a Glance*, undated, p. 1.
124. M.H. Naqvi, '46th Foundation Day of Azad Government of the State of Jammu and Kashmir being observed with fresh enthusiasm for reconstruction', *The Nation*, 24 October 1992.
125. Tariq Naqash, 'Avalanche kills thirty-two in Neelum Valley', *Dawn Wire Service*, Week Ending 21 March 1996, www.lib.virginia.edu/area-studies/SouthAsia/SAserials/Dawn/1996/21Mar96.html [accessed 15 December 2006].

126. Andrew Wilder, *Perceptions of the Pakistan Earthquake Response: Humanitarian Agenda 2015 Pakistan Country Study*, Feinstein International Center, Medford, 2008, p. 9. I acknowledge that my coverage of the 2005 earthquake is scant, factual and somewhat clinical. It certainly does not deal with the emotions and sadness that Azad Kashmiris had to contend with. However, the earthquake is generally outside the scope of this book—partly because it is highly deserving of a book on its own.
127. Mumtaz Hamid Rao, 'Rains, Snow swell Miseries: Deaths by Quake up over 55,000 in Pakistan', *Pakistan Times*, 16 October 2005, http://pakistantimes.net/2005/10/16/top.htm, [accessed 6 February 2008].
128. *Earthquake Damage (Compiled by AJK Government* [sic]*), Dated 26.10.2005*, unpublished handout, copy obtained in Azad Kashmir in December 2006.
129. This rest of this paragraph based on *State Earthquake Reconstruction & Rehabilitation Agency (SERRA)*, Government of AJ&K [sic], 2006, unpublished handout, copy obtained in Azad Kashmir in December 2006, pp. 2–3.
130. Unless otherwise stated, this paragraph based on *State Earthquake Reconstruction & Rehabilitation Agency (SERRA)*, pp. 2, 4. SERRA is subordinate to ERRA.
131. Andrew Wilder, *Perceptions of the Pakistan Earthquake Response*, p. 47. Chapter 8 briefly discusses the earthquake relief roles of 'militant *jihadi* groups'.
132. Siddharth Srivastava, 'Nature forces back terror', *Asia Times Online*, 18 October 2005, www.atimes.com/atimes/South_Asia/GJ18Df03.html [accessed 19 October 2005].
133. *State Earthquake Reconstruction & Rehabilitation Agency (SERRA)*, pp. 2, 4, 5, 13.
134. Noor Aftab, 'Motorists get trapped on Murree Expressway', *The News*, 8 August 2009. A first stage of the N-75 project is the 'Islamabad-Murree Dual Carriage Way (IMDCW)'.
135. Arshad Dogar, 'Motorway police to man Islamabad-Murree road', *The News*, 28 March 2010.
136. *Azad Kashmir at a Glance*, undated, p. 2.
137. Unless otherwise stated, this paragraph based on *State Earthquake Reconstruction & Rehabilitation Agency (SERRA)*, pp. 2, 4, 5, 13.
138. Moosa Kaleem and Zulfiqar Ali, 'Homeless and Adrift: Revisiting the quake zone a year after 8/10', *The Herald*, 31 October 2006, p. 62.
139. Iftikhar A. Khan, 'Attique offers gas to held [sic] Kashmir', *Dawn*, 11 February 2007.
140. *Azad Kashmir at a Glance*, undated, p. 2. In the document's table titled 'Quality Of Life Indices-2006', the unemployment rate is given as 65 per cent.
141. This paragraph based on 'Liberalization of Telecom Sector In AJK & NAs', in *Annual Report 2008*, Pakistan Telecommunication Authority, Islamabad, 2008, pp. 69–74, www.pta.gov.pk/annual-reports/annrep0708/ch_07.pdf [accessed 23 March 2009].
142. 'Telecom Deregulation In Azad Jammu & Kashmir And Northern Areas', Pakistan Telecommunication Authority, in *Annual Report 2007*, Pakistan Telecommunication Authority, Islamabad, 2007, Chapter 7, www.pta.gov.pk/annual-reports/annrep0607/chapter_8.pdf [accessed 23 March 2009], p. 96.
143. 'New AJK Government', *The Nation*, 27 July 2001.
144. *Pakistan 1955–1956*, Pakistan Publications, Karachi, 1956, p. 360.
145. Ballard, 'Kashmir Crisis: View from Mirpur', p. 514.

146. *Pakistan 1955–1956*, p. 360.
147. For details of India's protest, see 'Mangla Dam Project' in Sharma and Bakshi, *Encyclopaedia of Kashmir*, Volume 8, pp. 176–203.
148. Mumtaz Hamid Rao, 'The Mangla Dam', *Pakistan Times*, 14 January 2005, http://pakistantimes.net/2005/01/14/oped3.htm [accessed 2 March 2009].
149. 'Letter Dated 11 September, 1959 from the Acting Permanent Representative of Pakistan A. Shahi Addressed to the President of the Security Council', in Sharma and Bakshi, *Encyclopaedia of Kashmir*, Volume 8, p. 188.
150. Saraf, *Kashmiris Fight—For Freedom*, Volume II, pp. 1308–09.
151. Ballard, 'Kashmir Crisis: View from Mirpur', p. 514.
152. Sultan Ahmed, 'Rise in power rates to accentuate inflation', *Dawn Wire Service*, Week Ending 21 March 1998, www.lib.virginia.edu/area-studies/SouthAsia/SAserials/Dawn/1998/21Mar98.html [accessed 15 December 2006].
153. Sabihuddin Ghausi, 'Wapda blames Sindh for big default', *Dawn Wire Service*, Week Ending 12 February 2000, www.lib.virginia.edu/area-studies/SouthAsia/SAserials/Dawn/2000/12feb00.html [accessed 15 December 2006].
154. 'Protest over release of Rs 1.4 billion to WAPDA; AJK Council discontinues developmental activities', *The Nation*, 4 October 2000.
155. *Dawn*, 26 June 1957, quoted in 'Letter dated 21 August 1957 from the representative of India Arthur S. Lall to the President of the Security Council', in Sharma, *Encyclopaedia of Kashmir*, Volume 8, *Kashmir and United Nations*, p. 176.
156. *Dawn*, 6 September 1957, quoted in 'Letter dated 24 January 1958 from the representative of Pakistan Agha Shahi to the President of the Security Council', in Sharma and Bakshi, *Encyclopaedia of Kashmir*, Volume 8, p. 183. Khan, *Real Azad Kashmir*, had a dissenting view.
157. Discussion with Sardar Mohammad Sadiq Khan, Muzaffarabad, 16 January 1998.
158. Rose, 'The Politics of Azad Kashmir', in Thomas, *Perspectives*, p. 247.
159. 'Azad Kashmir budget', *Dawn*, 25 June 1998.
160. 'Work to begin: Mangla Dam raising project in May', *Dawn*, 28 February 2004.
161. Khalid Mustafa, 'IRSA okays Mangla Dam raising', *Daily Times*, 15 September 2002. IRSA is the Indus River System Authority, 'a body to regulate the distribution of water amongst [Pakistan's] four federating units'. IRSA stated that WAPDA also needed to get the support of the Azad Kashmir Government for this project.
162. Mumtaz Hamid Rao, 'The Mangla Dam', *Pakistan Times*, 14 January 2005.
163. Ihtasham ul Haque, 'Mangla dam reservoir slowly "dying": water, power crisis looms', *Dawn*, 19 September 2007.
164. 'Agreement inked to begin raising Mangla Dam height', *Dawn*, 28 June 2003.
165. 'Work to begin: Mangla Dam raising project in May', *Dawn*, 28 February 2004.
166. *An Introduction to the Hydroelectric Potential of Azad Jammu & Kashmir*, AJK Hyro Electric Board, Muzaffarabad, 2006?, www.pmajk.gov.pk/pdf_files/hydropower_potential.pdf [accessed 2 March 2009].
167. 'Half of AJK development allocation remains unutilized', *Dawn*, 29 April 2004.
168. Aslam, 'Industrialization in Azad Kashmir', p. 34.
169. Discussion with Sardar Mohammad Sadiq Khan, Muzaffarabad, 16 January 1998. The

5,000 MW figure is confirmed by Presentation on *Economic Features*, Azad Jammu and Kashmir Government, p. 5. 7,170 MW figure from Engr Hussain Ahmad Siddiqui, 'Speeding up hydropower generation', *Dawn*, 30 August 2010.
170. Presentation on *Economic Features*, Azad Jammu and Kashmir Government, p. 5.
171. 'Gigantic Jagran Power project to be inaugurated next month', *The Nation*, 7 May 2000.
172. Engr Hussain Ahmad Siddiqui, 'Speeding up hydropower generation', *Dawn*, 30 August 2010. These were Jagran (30.4 MW capacity), Kathai (3.2 MW), Kundal Shahi (2 MW), Leepa (1.6 MW), Kel (0.4 MW), Changan (0.05 MW) and Patikka (0.05 MW).
173. *Azad Kashmir at a Glance*, 2008, p. 8. This page had a complete list of Azad Kashmir's hydel projects.
174. Adil Hasan Khan, 'Neelum-Jhelum Project: No Smooth Sailing For Pakistan', *Institute of Peace and Conflict Studies*, New Delhi, 21 April 2006, www.ipcs.org/article/pakistan/neelum-jhelum-project-no-smooth-sailing-for-pakistan-1996.html [accessed 24 April 2006].
175. Appendix VIII: Azad Kashmir 'Council Legislative List'.
176. Rose, 'The Politics of Azad Kashmir', in Thomas, *Perspectives*, p. 247.
177. Discussion with Sardar Sikandar Hayat Khan, Kotli, 21 March 1999.
178. This paragraph is based on Ballard, 'Kashmir Crisis: View from Mirpur', pp. 514–17. Quotations are from p. 514. My discussions with Mirpuris in Mirpur, March 1999 generally confirmed the information in this and the following paragraphs.
179. Appendix V: Physical and Political Composition of J&K after the 1949 Ceasefire. Appendix XI: Azad Kashmir's Actual Administration and Population, 1988–2008.
180. *Census of India 1941*, p. 182.
181. Ballard, 'Kashmir Crisis: View from Mirpur', pp. 515, 516.
182. *Statistical Year Book 1988*, pp. 183–4.
183. Ballard, 'Kashmir Crisis: View from Mirpur', p. 514.
184. Dinesh Kumar, 'Pakistan's proxy war in Kashmir is no longer a secret', *TOI*, Mumbai, 21 July 1998.
185. 'Table No. 9, Country Wise Workers' Remittances', *State Bank of Pakistan*, www.sbp.org.pk/Ecodata/Homeremit_arch.xls [accessed 11 March 2009]. UK remittances were lower than those from the United States (US$1.76 billion), Saudi Arabia ($1.21 billion) and the United Arab Emirates ($1.09 billion).
186. Abid Qaiyum Suleri and Kevin Savage, *HPG Background Paper-Remittances in crises: a case study from Pakistan*, Overseas Development Institute, London, November 2006, www.odi.org.uk/resources/hpg-publications/background-papers/2006/remittances-crises-pakistan.pdf [accessed 13 January 2007], pp. 7, 14.
187. Ballard, 'Kashmir Crisis: View from Mirpur', p. 514.
188. *Azad Kashmir at a Glance*, undated, pp. 1, 2.
189. Appendix VIII: Azad Kashmir 'Council Legislative List'.
190. Home, *Bank of Azad Jammu & Kashmir*, www.bankajk.com/res.php?sgv=010001 [accessed 16 September 2010]. I thank Ershad Mahmud for confirming this situation.
191. 'Agricultural Loans Scheme-Comprehensive Circular', *State Bank of Pakistan*, www.

sbp.org.pk/acd/C2096.htm [accessed 11 March 2009]. The State Bank of Pakistan called it the 'Azad Jammu & Kashmir Provincial Cooperative Bank Ltd'.
192. *Azad Kashmir On [The] Road To Progress*, pp. 103–4.
193. *Statistical Year Book 1988*, p. 352.
194. Afshan Subohi, 'Workers' remittances build a new city', *Dawn*, 23 February 2009.
195. Ballard, 'Kashmir Crisis: View from Mirpur', p. 515.
196. *Statistical Year Book 1988*, pp. 182, 258, 286, 288.
197. 'Plan chalked out to promote investment in Azad Kashmir', *Dawn*, 18 May 2003.
198. *Reports of the Advisory Panels for the Fourth Five-Year Plan*, Planning Commission, Government of Pakistan, Volume II, Islamabad, July 1970, p. 369.
199. 'Plan chalked out to promote investment in Azad Kashmir', *Dawn*, 18 May 2003.
200. 'Comprehensive plan for industrialisation of AJK', *The Nation*, 12 November 2003.
201. Afshan Subohi, 'Workers' remittances build a new city', *Dawn*.
202. *The JKLF Roadmap For Peace & Prosperity in South Asia*, Rawalpindi, Jammu Kashmir Liberation Front, 2003, p. 7.
203. Interview with Amanullah Khan, Chairman, Jammu Kashmir Liberation Front, Rawalpindi, 22 December 2006.
204. *The JKLF Roadmap For Peace & Prosperity in South Asia*, pp. 9, 12.
205. Srinagar, Muzaffarabad and Jammu City have airports, but only Srinagar's is international, though with limited services. Muzaffarabad has a domestic airport only, and flights to it have not occurred for many years—I flew there in 1996, but have been unable to do so since.
206. Section 31 (3), *The Azad Jammu and Kashmir Interim Constitution Act*, p. 26.
207. Commissioner Relief & Rehabilitation AJK Board of Revenue, Azad Jammu and Kashmir Government, www.ajk.gov.pk/site/index.php?option=com_content&task=view&id=2900&Itemid=94 [accessed 12 March 2009]. One of the functions of the Relief Department is 'Relief to the affectees and internally displaced persons living along LOC'.
208. 'Internally Displaced People: Exiled in their Homeland', United Nations Office for the Coordination of Humanitarian Affairs, 2007?, http://ochaonline.un.org/NewsInFocus/InternallyDisplacedPeopleIDPs/tabid/5132/language/en-US/Default.aspx [accessed 15 September 2009].
209. Interview with an Azad Kashmir Government official on 5 December 2006 in Muzaffarabad. The presence of IDPs was not obvious in Muzaffarabad when I first visited in February 1996; indeed, they appeared to be 'hidden' in remoter locations. They only became obvious in later years via clearly observable camps built close to Muzaffarabad.
210. 'Refugee camps in Azad Kashmir', *Jammu and Kashmir* website, www.gharib.demon.co.uk/refugees/camps.htm [accessed 12 March 2009]. A note at the bottom states that 'Details reproduced with the kind permission of Government of Azad Jammu & Kashmir, Department of Rehabilitation, Muzaffarabad. Figures correct as of 31 January 1997.'
211. The rest of this paragraph based on an interview with an Azad Kashmir Government official on 5 December 2006 in Muzaffarabad. All figures are for 2006.

212. Syeda Viquar-un-nisa Hashmi, 'The plight of refugees', *Dawn Magazine*, 5 May 2002.
213. Zafar Meraj, 'So close, yet so far', *Newsline*, January 2005, www.newsline.com.pk/NewsJan2005/sprep2jan2005.htm [accessed 11 November 2005].
214. Rounded figures calculated from 'Details of Refugee Camps in AJK', Commissioner Relief & Rehabilitation AJK Board of Revenue.
215. 'Kashmiri DPs to get more facilities', *Dawn*, 30 October 2002.
216. 'Details of the facilities offered to Refugees in the Camps', Commissioner Relief & Rehabilitation AJK Board of Revenue.
217. Zafar Meraj, 'So close, yet so far', *Newsline*, January 2005.
218. See Appendix XII: Aspects of the Azad Kashmir Budgets.
219. *Azad Jammu & Kashmir Council Development Programme 2006–07*.
220. 'Refugee Camps in Azad Kashmir', *Jammu and Kashmir* website.
221. 'Kashmir Dispute: Background', *Ministry of Foreign Affairs, Pakistan*, [undated], www.mofa.gov.pk/Pages/Brief.htm [accessed 8 August 2008].
222. 'Tearful reunion as Kashmiris cross LoC', *Dawn*, 8 April 2005.
223. 'Sonia to flag off Poonch-Rawalkot [sic] bus', *Indian Express*, 19 June 2006.
224. 'Joint Statement issued after Foreign Minister level Review of the Fourth Round of Composite Dialogue, Islamabad, 21 May 2008', *Indian Ministry of External Affairs*, New Delhi, meaindia.nic.in/ [accessed 25 May 2008].
225. 'Pak-India talks on Kashmir CBMs may be held next week', *The News*, 12 July 2008.
226. Appendix XIII: Crossing Process between Azad Kashmir-Indian J&K.
227. 'Joint Statement issued after Foreign Minister level Review of the Fourth Round of Composite Dialogue, Islamabad, 21 May 2008'.
228. 'Trade across LoC begins today', *The News*, 21 October 2008. For a list of the 21 items, see Table XIII 1: Cross-LOC Trade Items in Appendix XIII: Crossing Process between Azad Kashmir-Indian J&K.
229. Nirupama Subramanian, 'PoK eyes cross-LoC trade for economic progress on its side', *The Hindu*, 22 September 2008.
230. Subramanian, 'PoK eyes cross-LoC trade for economic progress on its side'.

## 8. ELECTIONS AND INTERNAL POLITICS SINCE 1970

1. Saraf, *Kashmiris Fight—For Freedom*, Volume II, pp. 1346, 1347. Tariq, *Kashmir in Strangulation*, pp. 21–2.
2. Tariq, *Kashmir in Strangulation*, p. 19.
3. Saraf, *Kashmiris Fight—For Freedom*, Volume II, pp. 1347–48.
4. Ibid., p. 1347.
5. Aziz, 'Azad Kashmir Government: A Chronology'.
6. Saraf, *Kashmiris Fight—For Freedom*, Volume II, p. 1347.
7. Note at the bottom of the document: *List of Returned Candidates during 1970, Annex 'E'*.
8. *List of Returned Candidates during 1970, Annex 'E'*.
9. Saraf, *Kashmiris Fight—For Freedom*, Volume II, p. 1347.
10. Samuel Baid, 'Politics in "Azad Kashmir"', in Jasjit Singh, Editor, *Pakistan Occupied Kashmir Under the Jackboot*, New Delhi, Siddhi Books, 1995, p. 111.

11. *List of Returned Candidates during 1975, Annex 'E'*.
12. Saraf, *Kashmiris Fight—For Freedom*, Volume II, p. 1355.
13. *Report on the Third General Election in Azad Jammu and Kashmir 1985*, Islamabad, Azad Jammu and Kashmir Election Commission, 1987, p. 46.
14. Results in this paragraph from *List of Returned Candidates during 1975, Annex 'E'*.
15. Saraf, *Kashmiris Fight—For Freedom*, Volume II, pp. 1355–7. Bhutto may also have been indirectly referring to New York City's corrupt Tammany Hall Democratic politics.
16. Baid, 'Politics in "Azad Kashmir"', p. 112.
17. Rose, 'The Politics of Azad Kashmir', in Thomas, *Perspectives*, p. 241.
18. Baid, 'Politics in "Azad Kashmir"', p. 112.
19. Saraf, *Kashmiris Fight—For Freedom*, Volume II, pp. 1357–8.
20. *Report on the Third General Election in Azad Jammu and Kashmir 1985*, p. 99.
21. Ibid., Preface, p. i.
22. Gilani, *Constitutional Development in Azad Jammu & Kashmir*, Appendix IX, Appendixes Section, pp. 209–210.
23. *Report on the Third General Election in Azad Jammu and Kashmir 1985*, pp. 14–16, 32.
24. Ibid., p. 17.
25. Ibid., p. 32.
26. Ibid., pp. 25, 39.
27. Rose, 'The Politics of Azad Kashmir', in Thomas, *Perspectives*, p. 241.
28. *Report on the Third General Election in Azad Jammu and Kashmir 1985*, p. 41.
29. Ibid., p. 27.
30. Ibid., p. 41.
31. Ibid., pp. 26, 41, 43.
32. B.K. Bangroo, 'Pakistan Occupied Kashmir: People In Turmoil', *Onlooker*, 15 May 1986, p. 26.
33. Tariq, *Kashmir in Strangulation*, p. 21.
34. Rose, 'The Politics of Azad Kashmir', in Thomas, *Perspectives*, p. 241.
35. *Report on the Third General Election in Azad Jammu and Kashmir 1985*, p. 63.
36. *Report on the Third General Election in Azad Jammu and Kashmir 1985*, p. 53.
37. Figures rounded from *Report on the Third General Election in Azad Jammu and Kashmir 1985*, p. 35.
38. A.J.&K. Election Commission, Muzaffarabad, 'Figure—01', *Four Figures to do with Polling Turnouts* [author's title], no further publication details, obtained in Azad Kashmir in December 2006.
39. *Report on the Third General Election in Azad Jammu and Kashmir 1985*, pp. 116–17.
40. *Report on the Third General Election in Azad Jammu and Kashmir 1985*, pp. 76, 80.
41. *Report on the Third General Election in Azad Jammu and Kashmir 1985*, p. 111.
42. Rose, 'The Politics of Azad Kashmir', in Thomas, *Perspectives*, p. 242.
43. Section 8-A, Political Parties Ordinance, as discussed in *Report on the Third General Election in Azad Jammu and Kashmir 1985*, p. 53. Rose, 'The Politics of Azad Kashmir', in Thomas, *Perspectives*, p. 242.
44. *Report on the Third General Election in Azad Jammu and Kashmir 1985*, pp. 78–9.
45. Ibid., p. 86.

## NOTES

46. Rose, 'The Politics of Azad Kashmir', in Thomas, *Perspectives*, p. 242. I have been unable to determine the independent's name.
47. *Report on the Third General Election in Azad Jammu and Kashmir 1985*, p. 88.
48. Information on the Azad Kashmir presidential election from *Report on the Third General Election in Azad Jammu and Kashmir 1985*, pp. 91–3.
49. *The Azad Jammu and Kashmir Interim Constitution Act*, pp. 18, 50.
50. Sadia Dehlvi, 'Conversation [with Sardar Qayyum]', p. 25.
51. M.H. Askari, 'Kashmir Through the Looking Glass', *The Herald*, August 1991, p. 85.
52. B.K. Bangroo, 'Pakistan Occupied Kashmir: People In Turmoil', p. 24.
53. Sadia Dehlvi, 'Conversation [with Sardar Qayyum]', p. 24. Sardar Muhammad Abdul Qayyum Khan, *The Kashmir Case*, p. 125.
54. Rose, 'The Politics of Azad Kashmir', in Thomas, *Perspectives*, p. 242.
55. Baid, 'Politics in "Azad Kashmir"', pp. 117–18.
56. Rose, 'The Politics of Azad Kashmir', in Thomas, *Perspectives*, p. 242.
57. Tariq, *Kashmir in Strangulation*, p. 21.
58. Zaffar Abbas, 'Kashmir: The Rocky Road Ahead', *The Herald*, February 1990, p. 64. The anti-Indian militancy in Indian J&K is outside the scope of this book. It is covered well by Alexander Evans, 'The Kashmir Insurgency: As Bad as it Gets', *Small Wars & Insurgencies*, Volume 11, Number 1, 2000, pp. 69–81.
59. *The JKLF Roadmap For Peace & Prosperity in South Asia*, pp. 13–14.
60. Interview with Amanullah Khan, Rawalpindi, 22 December 2006.
61. Lamb, *Kashmir, A Disputed Legacy*, pp. 291–3, 335–6.
62. Ibid., p. 292.
63. Saraf, *Kashmiris Fight—For Freedom*, Volume II, pp. 1377–8. *The JKLF Roadmap For Peace & Prosperity in South Asia*, p. 13.
64. Lamb, *Kashmir, A Disputed Legacy*, p. 291.
65. Snedden, 'Would a Plebiscite Have Resolved the Kashmir Dispute?', p. 77.
66. Saraf, *Kashmiris Fight—For Freedom*, Volume II, p. 1378.
67. See Lamb, *Kashmir, A Disputed Legacy*, pp. 291–3, 335–6.
68. *The JKLF Roadmap For Peace & Prosperity in South Asia*, p. 13.
69. Victoria Schofield, *Kashmir in Conflict*, London, I.B. Tauris, 2000, p. 116.
70. Yoginder Sikand, 'The Emergence and Development of the Jama'at-i-Islami of Jammu and Kashmir (1940s–1990)', *Modern Asian Studies*, Volume 36, Number 3, 2002, p. 746.
71. *The JKLF Roadmap For Peace & Prosperity in South Asia*, p. 13.
72. Yoginder Sikand, 'The Emergence and Development of the Jama'at-i-Islami …', p. 746.
73. Lamb, *Kashmir, A Disputed Legacy*, pp. 292, 336.
74. *The JKLF Roadmap For Peace & Prosperity in South Asia*, p. 13.
75. Julian Schofield and Reeta Tremblay, 'Why Pakistan Failed: Tribal Focoism in Kashmir', p. 33.
76. Victoria Schofield, *Kashmir in Conflict*, p. 157.
77. *The JKLF Roadmap For Peace & Prosperity in South Asia*, pp. 13–14.
78. 'Kashmir Dispute: Background', *Ministry of Foreign Affairs, Pakistan*, website, undated, www.mofa.gov.pk/Pages/Brief.htm [accessed 19 March 2010].
79. Sardar Muhammad Abdul Qayyum Khan, *The Kashmir Case*, p. 126.

80. Ibid., p. 114.
81. C. Christine Fair, 'Who Are Pakistan's Militants and Their Families?', *Terrorism and Political Violence*, Volume 20, Number 1, January 2008, p. 53. Fair surveyed '141 Pakistani families of slain militants … [and] collected data about the militants and their households'.
82. Brian Cloughley, 'Pakistan's Army and National Stability', *Pakistan Security Research Unit*, Brief Number 47, 22nd April 2009, http://spaces.brad.ac.uk:8080/download/attachments/748/Brief+47.pdf [accessed 22 May 2009], p. 4.
83. Cloughley, 'Pakistan's Army and National Stability', pp. 4–5.
84. The rest of this paragraph based on Hasan Abbas, *Pakistan's Drift into Extremism: Allah, the Army and America's War on Terror*, Armonk, N.Y., M.E. Sharpe, 2004, pp. 210, 212–14. There are various spellings for the names of anti-Indian militant groups.
85. 'India and the war on terrorism', *Strategic Comments*, Volume 7, Number 9, November 2001, p. 1. The reputable International Institute for Strategic Studies publishes *Strategic Comments*.
86. Musharraf, *In the Line of Fire*, p. 201.
87. 'Joint Statement issued after Foreign Minister level Review of the Fourth Round of Composite Dialogue'.
88. 'Pakistan admits India attack link', *BBC News*, 12 February 2009, http://news.bbc.co.uk/2/hi/south_asia/7885261.stm [accessed 14 February 2009].
89. This paragraph is adapted from Rajat Pandit, 'Forty-two operational terror camps in Pak, PoK', *TOI*, 19 June 2009, http://timesofindia.indiatimes.com/articleshow/msid-4673319,prtpage-1.cms [accessed 18 March 2010]. Pandit does not say how he got access to this information.
90. These included: 'Jangal Mangal, Andher Bela, Shinkiari and Jalo Gali, with other NWFP camps including Boi, Oghi and Attar Shisha'.
91. Mumtaz Alvi, 'Musharraf uprooted training camps: Qayyum', *The News*, 4 May 2007.
92. 'No change in Kashmir policy pledged', *Dawn*, 20 July 2002.
93. Musharraf, *In the Line of Fire*, p. 249. Musharraf displays some confusion about Azad Kashmir. On p. 57, he calls Muzaffarabad the capital of 'Independent Kashmir'; on p. 249, he uses the term 'Azad (Independent) Kashmir'. By 'independent', he presumably means 'independent' from India, not 'independent' from Pakistan. Also on p. 57, he notes that the 'Kishenganga River … enters Pakistan [sic] at Kekrun, where its name becomes the Neelum River'. The Kishenganga/Neelum enters Azad Kashmir, not Pakistan; it also flows only through Azad Kashmir (joining the Jhelum at Domel), not through Pakistan. In one photo (unnumbered page), Musharraf incorrectly locates 'Mangla [Dam]' as being in 'North Punjab'—it is in Azad Kashmir.
94. 'Pakistan is Always Seen as the Rogue: SPIEGEL Interview with Pervez Musharraf (Interview conducted by Susanne Koelbl)', *Spiegel*, 4 October 2010, www.spiegel.de/international/world/0,1518,721110,00.html [accessed 6 October 2010].
95. *'With Friends Like These…'*, Human Rights Watch, p. 8.
96. Andrew Wilder, *Perceptions of the Pakistan Earthquake Response*, pp. 13, 48.
97. *'With Friends Like These…'*, Human Rights Watch, pp. 23, 25.
98. 'Support to Kashmiris pledged', *Dawn*, 6 February 1997. 'Complete support shown to Kashmiris', *Dawn*, 7 February 1998.

99. Zaffar Abbas, 'Kashmir: The Rocky Road Ahead', *The Herald*, p. 68.
100. Nazir Ahmad Shawl, 'Change in Pakistan & the AJK government', *The Nation*, 4 November 1999.
101. Based on publications the Kashmir Liberation Cell gave me in Muzaffarabad in 1999.
102. B. Raman, 'The Omens from Muzaffarabad', *South Asia Analysis Group*, Paper No. 286, 30 July 2001, www.southasiaanalysis.org/papers3/paper286.html [accessed 24 March 2010], stated that General Musharraf planned to revive the Kashmir Liberation Cell 'abolished during the second tenure of Nawaz Sharif as the Prime Minister'.
103. 'The Prime Minister of Azad Jammu and Kashmir Raja Muhammad Farooq Haider Khan emphasized that Kashmir Liberation Cell should be made more active', *Prime Minister* [sic] *Secretariat of Azad Government of the State of Azad Jammu & Kashmir*, 8 January 2010, www.pmajk.gov.pk/news2.asp?id=44 [accessed 19 March 2010].
104. Victoria Schofield, *Kashmir in Conflict*, pp. 179–80.
105. Also called the Muttahida Jihad (or Jehad) Council. According to K.P.S. Gill, 'J&K: Shifting Strategy of Subversion', *South Asia Terrorism Portal*, South Asia Intelligence Review, Volume 2, Number 33, 1 March 2004, www.satp.org/satporgtp/sair/Archives/2_33.htm [accessed 24 March 2010], the UJC was shifted from Islamabad to Muzaffarabad.
106. This paragraph is based on *With Friends Like These...*', Human Rights Watch, p. 22. On p. 7, the report states that it 'documents incidents of torture by the ISI, and by Azad Kashmir police acting at the ISI's and the army's behest' undertaken with 'the purpose of "punishing" errant politicians, political activists and journalists'. I was told similar stories about ISI's strong role in Azad Kashmir on visits to Muzaffarabad in 1996 and 1999.
107. *With Friends Like These...*', Human Rights Watch, p. 8.
108. 'Kashmir: Confrontation and Miscalculation', *International Crisis Group*, Islamabad / Brussels, Asia Report No. 35, 11 July 2002, p. 6.
109. Syed Salahuddin is a *nom de guerre* based on Saladin, who fought the Christian Crusaders; Salahuddin's birth name is (the less glamorous) Mohammed Yusuf Shah.
110. Nicholas Howenstein, 'The Jihadi Terrain in Pakistan: An Introduction to the Sunni Jihadi Groups in Pakistan and Kashmir', Research Report 1, *Pakistan Security Research Unit*, 5 February 2008, http://spaces.brad.ac.uk:8080/download/attachments/748/resrep1.pdf [accessed 22 March 2009], pp. 8, 12.
111. 'Kashmir: Confrontation and Miscalculation', *International Crisis Group*, p. 6.
112. 'Muttahida Jehad Council (Also known as the United Jehad Council)', *South Asia Terrorism Portal*, www.satp.org/satporgtp/countries/india/states/jandk/terrorist_outfits/mjc.htm [accessed 22 March 2010].
113. *With Friends Like These...*', Human Rights Watch, p. 8.
114. Sumita Kumar, 'Pakistan's Jehadi Apparatus: Goals and Methods', *Strategic Analysis*, Volume 24, Number 12, 2001, p. 2192.
115. Yoginder Sikand, 'The Emergence and Development of the Jama'at-i-Islami ...', pp. 706, 751.
116. All Parties Hurriyat Conference is an umbrella body for Kashmiri nationalist groups.
117. Navnita Chadha Behera, *Demystifying Kashmir*, Washington DC, Brookings Institution Press, 2006, pp. 53, 159, 245.

118. Zulfiqar Ali, 'No Fruitful Talks can Take Place without Taking us into Confidence', *The Herald Annual*, January 2001, p. 89. 'Muttahida Jehad Council (Also known as the United Jehad Council)', *South Asia Terrorism Portal*.
119. 'Twelve envoys visit AJK: OIC efforts to continue for solution of Kashmir issue', *Dawn*, 30 June 1997.
120. *With Friends Like These…*', Human Rights Watch, p. 21.
121. Syed Shoaib Hasan, 'Why Pakistan is "boosting Kashmir militants"', *BBC News*, 3 March 2010, http://news.bbc.co.uk/2/hi/south_asia/4416771.stm [accessed 19 March 2010].
122. Mazhar Tufail, 'United Jihad Council says talks are Indian ploy', *The News*, 1 March 2010, www.thenews.com.pk/daily_detail.asp?id=226559 [accessed 4 March 2010].
123. 'Hardliners vow jihad to liberate Kashmir', *Dawn*, 24 March 2010. Anita Joshua, 'Jihad only way to liberate Kashmir, say Lashkar and Jaish', *The Hindu*, 25 March 2010.
124. 'Pakistan-India talks must cover Kashmir: Hizb chief', *Dawn*, 11 February 2010,
125. 'Muttahida Jehad Council (Also known as the United Jehad Council)', *South Asia Terrorism Portal*.
126. 'Pakistan-India talks must cover Kashmir: Hizb chief', *Dawn*.
127. Howenstein, 'The Jihadi Terrain in Pakistan', various pages.
128. Section 31 (3) (b) and Item 1 of the Third Schedule; see Appendix VIII: Azad Kashmir 'Council Legislative List'.
129. Tariq Naqash, 'Masood's entry into AJK banned', *Dawn*, 15 May 2003.
130. Tariq Naqash, 'Two soldiers killed: Baitullah's suicide foray into AJK', *Dawn*, 28 June 2009.
131. Tariq Naqash, 'Suicide attack on mourners in Muzaffarabad', *Dawn*, 28 December 2009.
132. Amir Mir, 'Lashkar-e-Zil behind Azad Kashmir suicide hits', *The News*, 12 January 2010.
133. *Pakistan Body Count*, www.pakistanbodycount.org/bla.php [accessed 23 August 2010].
134. Tariq Naqash, 'Two soldiers killed: Baitullah's suicide foray into AJK', *Dawn*.
135. Amir Mir, 'Lashkar-e-Zil behind Azad Kashmir suicide hits', *The News*.
136. Hamid Mir, 'How an ex-Army commando became a terrorist', *The News*, 20 September 2009.
137. V.K. Dethe, 'POK front plans protest week', *TOI*, Bombay, 27 September 1989.
138. Z.A. [Zaffar Abbas], 'There is no military solution to the Kashmir problem—[interview with] Amunallah Khan[,] Chairman JKLF', *The Herald*, February 1990, p. 74. The other five points were: to support in 'all possible ways' the Kashmiris' struggle; that J&K should not be treated as a property right of any one area; to ensure that J&K remained a united entity; to stop (perceived) Indian attempts to make the Muslim majority in J&K into a minority; and, to ensure that Gilgit and Baltistan were considered part of J&K.
139. Ihtashamul Haque, 'Taking Charge', *The Herald*, February 1990, p. 44.
140. 'The Kashmiri Struggle: A Who's Who', *The Herald*, February 1990, pp. 81–2.
141. Victoria Schofield, *Kashmir in Conflict*, pp. 174–5.
142. Based on an assessment of five articles in *The Herald*, February 1990, pp. 64–86, which issue gave major coverage to the Kashmiris' anti-Indian uprising.

143. Ihtashamul Haque, 'Taking Charge', *The Herald*, p. 44.
144. I. Haque, '"Every second man in Pakistan and Azad Kashmir is prepared to join my commando force"', *The Herald*, February 1990, p. 79.
145. Zaffar Abbas, 'Kashmir: The Rocky Road Ahead', *The Herald*, p. 77.
146. 'Meanwhile on the Battlefront', *The Herald*, May 1990, p. 34.
147. Zaffar Abbas, 'Kashmir: The Rocky Road Ahead', *The Herald*, pp. 69 [incorrectly given as p. 81 in original], 71.
148. Zaffar Abbas, 'Kashmir: The Rocky Road Ahead', *The Herald*, p. 65.
149. Nasir Malick, 'Taking Refuge', *The Herald*, May 1990, p. 39.
150. Z[affar] A[bbas], '"We cannot remain silent while our brothers are being massacred"', *The Herald*, February 1990, p. 80.
151. Zaffar Abbas, 'Kashmir: The Rocky Road Ahead', *The Herald*, p. 65.
152. M.H. Askari, 'Kashmir: The Struggle Continues', *The Herald*, April 1990, p. 47.
153. Members of the Special Committee for Oversight of Elections 2006, Peoples [sic] Muslim League, *Azad Kashmir Elections Hijacked. Why?*, Jammu & Kashmir Peoples Muslim League, 2006, p. 2.
154. *'With Friends Like These…'*, Human Rights Watch, p. 21.
155. This paragraph based on Nasir Malick, 'Kashmir: The Other Battle', *The Herald*, pp. 37–9.
156. This was/is not a law. It was a 1987 amendment to 'The Azad Jammu and Kashmir Legislative Assembly (Elections) Ordinance 1970 (Amended Upto [sic] 2002)', in *The Election Laws*, p. 130, as a result of which the Election Commissioner 'may at any time … make such alterations in the [electoral] programme … as may in his opinion be necessary'.
157. Hereafter called Sultan Mahmood.
158. As listed in *List of Contesting Candidates During 1990, Annex 'E'*, no further publication details, obtained in Azad Kashmir in December 2006, p. 1.
159. 'Qualification and Dis-qualification', *The Azad Jammu and Kashmir Legislative Assembly (Elections) Ordinance 1970 and Rules 1970 (Amended Upto [sic] May, 2006)*, Azad Jammu and Kashmir Election Commission, Muzaffarabad, 2006, p. 6. See also 'Qualifications and disqualifications to be a member of the Legislative Assembly', in Appendix XIV: Matters re Azad Kashmir elections, particularly in 2006.
160. Navnita Chadha Behera, *Demystifying Kashmir*, p. 196.
161. Nasir Malick, 'Calling it Splits', p. 28.
162. Calculated from figures contained in *List of Contesting Candidates During 1990, Annex 'E'*, pp. 1–5.
163. A.J. & K. Election Commission, Muzaffarabad, 'Figure—01', *Four Figures to do with Polling Turnouts* [author's title].
164. Nasir Malick, 'Calling it Splits', *The Herald*, pp. 26, 27.
165. Nasir Malick, 'Calling it Splits', *The Herald*, p. 27.
166. Rose, 'The Politics of Azad Kashmir', in Thomas, *Perspectives*, p. 242.
167. 'Dismissal of Bhutto Government', *Keesing's Record of World Events (formerly Keesing's Contemporary Archives)*, Volume 36, August 1990, p. 37655.
168. I. Haque, '"Sahibzada Yaqub Khan doesn't know the ABC of the Kashmir issue"— [interview with] Amanullah Khan', *The Herald*, July 1990, p. 37.

169. This paragraph based on Ihtashamul Haque, 'Leading from the Front', *The Herald*, July 1990, p. 36.
170. Nasir Malick, 'Smooth Operator', *The Herald*, April 1991, p. 87.
171. Rose, 'The Politics of Azad Kashmir', in Thomas, *Perspectives*, p. 242.
172. 'AJK Assembly dissolution', *Dawn*, 2 April 1991.
173. M. Mirza, 'Azad Kashmir Assembly: Why Dissolution?', *Pakistan Illustrated Weekly*, Volume 3, Numbers 9 and 10, 20 April 1991, p. 12.
174. 'Fall of Azad Kashmir Assembly', *The Frontier Post*, 2 April 1991. M. Mirza, 'Azad Kashmir Assembly: Why Dissolution?', p. 11.
175. 'AJK Assembly dissolution', *Dawn*.
176. M. Mirza, 'Azad Kashmir Assembly: Why Dissolution?', *Pakistan Illustrated Weekly*.
177. Nasir Malick, 'The Great Escape', *The Herald*, May 1991, p. 67.
178. 'Fall of Azad Kashmir Assembly', *The Frontier Post*.
179. Ahmed Rashid, 'The Summer of Discontent', *The Herald*, June 1991, p. 34.
180. 'Putting the AJK house in order', *The News*, 28 April 1991.
181. 'The "Azad" Kashmir mess', *The Frontier Post*, 4 July 1991.
182. 'AJK Assembly dissolution', *Dawn*. 'Fall of Azad Kashmir Assembly', *The Frontier Post*. 'Labyrinthine politics of AJK', *The News*, 2 April 1991.
183. 'Labyrinthine politics of AJK', *The News*.
184. 'Putting the AJK house in order', *The News*.
185. Nasir Mallick [sic], 'Trouble in Paradise', *The Herald*, July 1991, pp. 83–5.
186. 'The "Azad" Kashmir mess', *The Frontier Post*.
187. A.J. & K. Election Commission, Muzaffarabad, 'Figure—01', *Four Figures to do with Polling Turnouts* [author's title].
188. A.A. Salaria, 'The Enigma of AJK Polls', *Dawn*, 11 July 1996.
189. M.H. Askari, 'Kashmir Through the Looking Glass', *The Herald*, p. 85.
190. Nasir Mallick [sic], 'Trouble in Paradise', *The Herald*, p. 84.
191. 'PoK crisis grows worse', *TOI*, 22 July 1991.
192. 'The "Azad" Kashmir mess', *The Frontier Post*.
193. 'A matter for court', *The Muslim*, 4 July 1991.
194. Nasir Mallick [sic], 'Trouble in Paradise', *The Herald*, p. 84.
195. Unless stated otherwise, this paragraph based on Nasir Mallick [sic], 'Trouble in Paradise', *The Herald*, pp. 83–5.
196. Nasir Mallick [sic], 'Trouble in Paradise', *The Herald*, p. 83.
197. M.H. Askari, 'Kashmir Through the Looking Glass', *The Herald*, pp. 85–6.
198. Sardar Ibrahim, who was dismissed as President by Zia in October 1978, finally won his court case challenging this action in 1990. See Chapter 4.
199. Zaffar Abbas, 'A Sardar for all Seasons', *The Herald*, June 1996, p. 15.
200. Section 7, *The Azad Jammu and Kashmir Interim Constitution Act*, p. 11.
201. Conversation with Justice Manzoor Hussain Gilani, Justice of the Azad Kashmir Supreme Court, in Rawalpindi, 23 October 2008.
202. 'Khan's victory', *The Economist*, 15 February 1992.
203. Bearing in mind, of course, that the Northern Areas administered by Pakistan also had no democracy or self rule at that time (a situation that has changed little since 1947).

204. Zaffar Abbas, 'A Sardar for all Seasons', *The Herald*, p. 15.
205. A.A. Salaria, 'The Enigma of AJK Polls', *Dawn*.
206. Zaffar Abbas, 'A Sardar for all Seasons', *The Herald*, p. 15.
207. This information is from A.A. Salaria, 'The Enigma of AJK Polls', *Dawn*, and Ghulam Ahmad Pandit, 'The President of AK government back in saddle', *The Muslim*, 1 September 1996.
208. Zaffar Abbas, 'Elective Affinities', *The Herald*, June 1996, p. 60.
209. Ghulam Ahmad Pandit, 'The President of AK government back in saddle', *The Muslim*.
210. Tariq Butt, 'Lack of homework gives Sultan a new lease of life', *The News*, 27 December 1997.
211. 'Votes Obtained by Political Parties and Independent Candidates during General Elections June 30 1996 and List of the Candidates During Elections 1996', no further publication details, obtained in Azad Kashmir in December 2006, p. 1.
212. A.A. Salaria, 'The Enigma of AJK Polls', *Dawn*.
213. Zaffar Abbas, 'Elective Affinities', *The Herald*, p. 59.
214. Ibid., pp. 59–60.
215. Tariq Naqash, 'AJK president ousted through no-trust vote', *Dawn*.
216. 'All Jammu & Kashmir Muslim Conference (AJKMC)', *Global Security*, www.globalsecurity.org/military/world/pakistan/ajkmc.htm [accessed 10 November 2005].
217. 'Azad Kashmir affairs', *The Nation*, 21 December 1997.
218. Abdul Rashid Malik, 'Rathore victim of betrayal', *The Nation*, 23 June 1998.
219. 'AJK premier dissolves cabinet', *Dawn*, 15 January 2000. One ministry member later died and another resigned in September 1999.
220. 'PPP cancels Rathore's basic membership', *Dawn*, 5 January 1998.
221. Abdul Rashid Malik, 'Rathore victim of betrayal', *The Nation*.
222. Tariq Butt, 'Lack of homework gives Sultan a new lease of life', *The News*.
223. Tariq Naqash, 'Politics of Supposition', *Dawn*, 23 June 1998.
224. Abdul Rashid Malik, 'Public rallies race in Azad Kashmir', *The Nation*, 17 December 1998.
225. Tariq Naqash, 'Politics of Supposition', *Dawn*.
226. Tariq Naqash, 'Cosmetic reforms by AJK government', *Dawn*, 26 October 1999. According to Brian Cloughley, *A History of the Pakistan Army*, Second Edition, pp. 376–7, almost all of these 'militants' were actually soldiers from the Pakistan-commanded Northern Light Infantry which is based in, and whose soldiers come from, the Northern Areas.
227. Zaffar Abbas, 'A Sardar for all Seasons', *The Herald*, p. 15.
228. Tariq Naqash. 'AJK PM spends most of his time in Islamabad', *Dawn*, 8 October 1999; Hafizur Rahman, 'Long-distance government', *The News*, 4 December 1999.
229. Tariq Naqash, 'Cosmetic reforms by AJK government', *Dawn*.
230. Abdul Rashid Malik, 'Public rallies race in Azad Kashmir', *The Nation*.
231. 'Unconstitutional change in AJK opposed', *Dawn*, 25 October 1999.
232. Tariq Butt, 'Qualification condition a serious jolt to Qayyum', *The News*, 22 May 2001.
233. 'AJK premier dissolves cabinet', *Dawn*.

234. Tariq Naqash, 'Cosmetic reforms by AJK government', *Dawn*.
235. Hafizur Rahman, 'Long-distance government', *The News*.
236. Khizar Hayat Abbasi, 'Major changes expected on AJK political chessboard', *The News*, 14 March 2001.
237. Tariq Naqash, 'Sardar's changed stance toward Sultan', *Dawn*, 24 November 1999.
238. 'Accountability Bureau for delaying elections in AJK', *The News*, 26 April 2001.
239. By chance, my wife and I met the Chairman, Azad Kashmir Ehtesab Bureau, Major General (Retired) Sarfraz Iqbal, in December 2004 on our way into Azad Kashmir.
240. Aslam Khan, 'AJK to have either prime minister or president', *The News*, 10 May 2001.
241. Khizar Hayat Abbasi, 'Matric qualification fixed for assembly candidates', *The News*, 12 May 2001. Musharraf later imposed a similar requirement in Pakistan.
242. Tariq Butt, 'Qualification condition a serious jolt to Qayyum', *The News*.
243. *Report on the Seventh General Elections in Azad Jammu & Kashmir*, Muzaffarabad, Azad Jammu & Kashmir Election Commission, 2002, p. 83.
244. Khizar Hayat Abbasi, 'Matric qualification fixed for assembly candidates', *The News*.
245. Khizar Hayat Abbasi, 'AJK candidates' assets declaration made public', *The News*, 20 June 2001.
246. Based on discussions held with Azad Kashmiris in Lahore, Islamabad and Muzaffarabad in December 2004.
247. *Report on the Seventh General Elections in Azad Jammu & Kashmir*, pp. 81, 96, 137–8.
248. Quoted in Ershad Mahmud, 'Azad Kashmir's struggle for fair poll', *The News*, 15 May 2005.
249. Election results calculated from *Report on the Seventh General Elections in Azad Jammu & Kashmir*, pp. 83–4, 141–51.
250. 'AJK Polls', *The Nation*, 7 July 2001.
251. Tariq Naqash, 'Sikandar Hayat elected AJK PM', *Dawn*, 25 July 2001.
252. Khizar Hayat Abbasi, 'MC wins six, PPAJK secures two reserved seats', *The News*, 21 July 2001.
253. Ahmed Hassan, 'Power game in AJK begins', *Dawn Wire Service*, 14 July 2001. According to Hassan, Sardars Sikandar, Qayyum and Attique, and Sultan Mahmood all met Major-General Aziz on separate occasions on or before 13 July 2001. The 'military government … won laurels for showing absolute impartiality' in the Azad Kashmir polls.
254. Tariq Naqash, 'Sikandar Hayat elected AJK PM', *Dawn*.
255. 'Sikandar Hayat trounces Sultan Mehmood [sic] in AJK', *The Herald*, p. 28.
256. M Gulzar Khan, 'Reading into AJK polls', *The News*, 9 July 2001.
257. *Report on the Seventh General Elections in Azad Jammu & Kashmir*, p. 96. Tariq Butt, 'Electorate introduce two party system in AJK', *The News*, 7 July 2001.
258. 'Spanner in the works?', *The Nation*, 31 July 2001.
259. 'New AJK Government', *The Nation*.
260. 'Bio-data of new President', *The Nation*, 26 August 2001.
261. Khizar Hayat Abbasi, 'Anwar Khan elected AJK president', *The News*, 2 August 2001.
262. *Report on the Seventh General Elections in Azad Jammu & Kashmir*, p. 115. This change then applied to all ex-military and government officials.

263. Khizar Hayat Abbasi, 'Anwar Khan elected AJK president', *The News*.
264. 'President's Vision [of former president, Anwar Khan]', *Government of Azad Jammu & Kashmir* website, www.ajk.gov.pk/main/president/vision.html [accessed 21 August 2009].
265. 'Spanner in the works?', *The Nation*, 31 July 2001.
266. 'Perform or quit, AJK president tells officers', *Dawn*, 17 September 2001.
267. 'Anwar chosen president as compromise: Qayyum', *Dawn*, 5 October 2002. 'Agra summit at a glance', *BBC News*, 21 July 2001, http://news.bbc.co.uk/2/hi/south_asia/1430367.stm [accessed 24 July 2009].
268. 'President's Vision [of former president, Anwar Khan]'. Two months after Anwar became Azad Kashmir President, militants attacked Indian J&K's Legislative Assembly on 1 October 2001, which was the first major terrorist attack after '9/11', and India's parliament on 13 December 2001. It is not known if Anwar was involved in either action.
269. Quoted in Ershad Mahmud, 'Azad Kashmir's struggle for fair poll', *The News*. Retired senior army officers, General Krishna Rao and Lieutenant General S.K. Sinha, had been governors of Indian J&K, but New Delhi appointed them, they were not elected. See 'Chronology of Governors', *Raj Bhawan J&K*, http://jkrajbhawan.nic.in/His%20Excellency/previous.htm [accessed 24 March 2010].
270. The National Kashmir Committee was established in 2002 to publicise Pakistan's position in the Kashmir dispute. Since February 2008, it has become the 'Special Committee of the Parliament on Kashmir', *National Assembly of Pakistan*, www.na.gov.pk/sp_kashmir.html [accessed 11 November 2010].
271. Khizar Hayat Abbasi, 'Qayyum quits MC presidentship Tuesday, Attique may be new chief', *The News*, 17 March 2002.
272. Khizar Hayat Abbasi, 'Premier Sikandar Hayat in a difficult dilemma', *The News*, 14 March 2002.
273. Shaiq Hussain, 'AJK Chief Secy tasked to end Anwar-Sikandar row', *The Nation*, 17 October 2002.
274. 'Crisis in AJK', *The News*, 29 February 2004.
275. Tariq Naqash, 'Sikandar, Attique told to patch up', *Dawn*, 6 March 2004.
276. 'Sikandar, Attique resolve AJK crisis', *The Nation*, 14 April 2004.
277. 'Dissenting lawmakers join hands to secure political interests', *Dawn*, 7 July 2004.
278. 'AJK premier loses support of eleven legislators', *Dawn*, 10 September 2004; 'Political crisis resurfaces with Qayyum's return', *The Nation*, 28 September 2004.
279. Khizar Hayat Abbasi, 'Cracks emerge in PPPAJK', *The News*, 1 September 2005.
280. Tariq Naqash, 'MC wins seven out of eight special seats, taking its strength to thirty-one in forty-nine member house', *muzaffarabadak.com* website, www.muzaffarabadak.com/ajkelection2006.htm, [accessed 15 August 2008].
281. Rashid Malik, 'Mute election campaign in AJK', *The Nation*, 16 May 2006.
282. 'AJK religious parties form alliance', *The News*, 1 September 2005.
283. 'Kashmiri separatist group unites', *BBC News*, http://news.bbc.co.uk/1/hi/world/south_asia/4077122.stm, [accessed 14 August 2008].
284. Ershad Mahmud, 'Forthcoming AJK elections: emerging realities', *The News*, 23 May 2006.

285. Raja Asghar, 'Accession clause to be abolished: Sikandar', *Dawn*, 26 November 2004.
286. Ibid.
287. Abdul Rashid Malik, 'Pakistan visit biggest achievement, says Mirwaiz', *The Nation*, 17 June 2005.
288. 'Tearful reunion as Kashmiris cross LoC', *Dawn*, 8 April 2005.
289. Khizar Hayat Abbasi, 'Urdu is declared the official language of AJK', *The News*, 21 August 2005. However, in 1988, *Statistical Year Book 1988*, p. iii, stated that Urdu was the official language of Azad Kashmir.
290. Irfan Ghauri, 'Hung parliament likely in Azad Kashmir', *Daily Times*, 10 July 2006. The Muslim Conference (Haqiqi faction) fielded two candidates and won one seat: see Appendix XIV: Matters re Azad Kashmir elections, particularly in 2006.
291. Tariq Butt, 'Attique to be AJK premier if Muslim Conference wins', *The News*, 3 July 2006.
292. 'Elections held for forty-one seats of AJK Assembly', *The News*, 12 July 2006. 'India slams polls in PoK', *The Statesman*, New Delhi, 13 July 2006.
293. Tariq Butt, '"Attique to be AJK premier if Muslim Conference wins"', *The News*.
294. Ershad Mahmud, 'Forthcoming AJK elections: emerging realities', *The News*; Ershad Mahmud, 'Refugee seats vital in AJK political setting', *The News*, 11 June 2006.
295. See Table XIV 7: Delimitation of constituencies for 2001 Azad Kashmir elections, in Appendix XIV: Matters re Azad Kashmir elections, particularly in 2006.
296. Tariq Butt, '"Attique to be AJK premier if Muslim Conference wins"', *The News*.
297. 'AJK elections', *The Nation*, 13 July 2006.
298. 'AJK poll results', *The News*, 14 July 2006. 'AJK elections', *The Nation*.
299. For detailed information about the 2006 elections—results, parties, constituency sizes and locations, candidates, party heads, etc.—see Appendix XIV: Matters re Azad Kashmir elections, particularly in 2006.
300. '2.4 million voters to use right of franchise today in AJK', *The Nation*, 11 July 2006. The *1998 Census Report of Azad Kashmir*, p. 70, states that, in 1998, 71 per cent of Azad Kashmiris had obtained a National Identity Card. By 2006, this percentage would have been higher. Identity cards had to be produced on demand and in order to vote. Musharraf, *In the Line of Fire*, p. 249, states that the identity of a man who attempted to assassinate him in 2003, 'Mohammad Jamil', was found partly by accessing information on the National Database and Registration Authority that stores all National Identity Card data.
301. 'MC gets majority seats in AJK polls', *The News*, 13 July 2006.
302. 'Azad Kashmir poll results', *Dawn*, 14 July 2006.
303. 'AJK elections', *The Nation*.
304. '2.4 million voters to use right of franchise today in AJK', *The Nation*; 'Elections held for forty-one seats of AJK Assembly', *The News*; 'AJK elections', *The Nation*, 13 July 2006.
305. 'Muslim Conference wins AJK elections', *Daily Times*, 13 July 2006.
306. 'MC gets majority seats in AJK polls', *The News*.
307. Raja Asghar, 'AJK opposition plans protest campaign', *Dawn*, 20 July 2006.
308. Members of the Special Committee for Oversight of Elections 2006, Peoples [sic] Muslim League, *Azad Kashmir Elections Hijacked. Why?*

309. 'Zulqarnain of MC to face PPP's Qamar in AJK polls', *Dawn*, 27 July 2006. According to the report 'Azad Kashmir MLA takes oath' in *Dawn*, 6 March 2009, Khalid Ibrahim resigned from the Legislative Assembly on 6 January 2009.
310. 'MC gets majority seats in AJK polls', *The News*.
311. Irfan Ghauri, 'Hung parliament likely in Azad Kashmir', *Daily Times*. Raja Asghar, 'AJK opposition plans protest campaign'.
312. 'Attique sworn in as new PM', *The Nation*, 25 July 2006.
313. 'Zulqernain [sic] new AJK president', *The News*, 28 July 2006.
314. 'President's profile', *Azad Jammu & Kashmir* [Government] website, www.ajk.gov.pk/main/president/profile.html, [accessed 14 August 2008].
315. 'sixteen-member AJK cabinet sworn in', *Dawn*, 8 August 2006.
316. 'Zulqarnain of MC to face PPP's Qamar in AJK polls', *Dawn*.
317. 'Attique sworn in as new PM', *The Nation*. After a meeting with Sardar Attique in December 2006, I spoke with one of his two personal assistants, who was a friend of mine. He told me that Attique had two personal assistants from the Azad Kashmir administration, as one alone could not keep up with his blistering pace and work rate. This later caused Attique credibility problems: he moved fast, made many promises, but delivered on few.
318. 'I am PM of both Kashmirs', *Dawn*, 17 August 2008.
319. 'Change of government in Azad Kashmir', *Daily Times*, 8 January 2009.
320. 'Musharraf thinks out-of-box to resolve Kashmir', *The Financial Express*, 26 January 2006.
321. When I met Sardar Attique at the Prime Minister's Residence, Muzaffarabad, on 19 December 2006, he proudly told me that he had to leave our dinner discussions to take a phone call from Mirwaiz Umar Farooq.
322. On 24 October 2008, I met Shah Ghulam Qadir in Islamabad. He informed me that Attique would soon face a no-confidence motion and (incorrectly) that he (Qadir) would be nominated as the replacement prime minister.
323. 'Farooq to take oath on Saturday', *Dawn*, 10 November 2006.
324. 'Change of government in Azad Kashmir', *Daily Times*.
325. Tariq Naqash, No-trust vote topples AJK PM Attique, *Dawn*, 7 January 2009.
326. 'Sardar Attique blamed for division of ruling MC', *KashmirWatch.com*, www.kashmirwatch.com/showajnk.php?subaction=showfull&id=1231937369&archive=&start_from=&ucat=18&var1news=value1news [accessed 16 April 2009].
327. Tariq Naqash, No-trust vote topples AJK PM Attique, *Dawn*.
328. 'AJK PM Attique voted out', *The News*, 7 January 2009.
329. 'Change of government in Azad Kashmir', *Daily Times*.
330. 'Sardar Yaqoob vows to serve AJK masses with new zeal', *The News*, 8 January 2009.
331. Photo of 'Prime Minister of Azad Jammu and Kashmir Sardar Muhammad Yaqoob Khan while exchanging views with the Opposition leader Sardar Attique Ahmed Khan during the session of AJK Legislative Assembly', *Prime Minister* [sic] *Secretariat, Azad Government of the State of Jammu & Kashmir*, www.pmajk.gov.pk/picgallery2.asp?id=1 [accessed 9 April 2009].
332. 'Cabinet of AJK', *Prime Minister* [sic] *Secretariat, Azad Government of the State of Azad*

*Jammu & Kashmir*, www.pmajk.gov.pk/cabinet%20of%20AJK.asp [accessed 16 April 2009].

333. 'AJK PM Attique voted out', *The News*.
334. Azad Jammu & Kashmir Election Commission, *Tabulated & Graphic Presentation Of* [sic] *Election Returns-2001*, Azad Jammu & Kashmir Election Commission Secretariat, Muzaffarabad, 2001, p. 5.
335. See Appendix XIV: Matters re Azad Kashmir elections, particularly in 2006. The 'Profile of Sardar Muhammad Yaqoob Khan, Prime Minister of Azad Jammu & Kashmir' on *Prime Minister* [sic] *Secretariat, Azad Government of the State of Jammu & Kashmir*, www.pmajk.gov.pk/profile.asp [accessed 9 April 2009], stated that his 'Political Affiliation' is 'All Jammu and Kashmir Muslim Conference'.
336. 'Sardar Yaqoob resigns as prime minister of AJK', *Dawn*, 15 October 2009.
337. Zahid Rashid, 'AJK politics in 2009—A review', *The Frontier Post*. Appendix IV shows that a 'Ch. M. Yasin' was an unsuccessful Pakistan People's Party, Azad Kashmir candidate for the seat of Kotli IV in the 2006 Azad Kashmir Legislative Assembly elections.
338. Tariq Naqash, 'Farooq Haider elected AJK prime minister', *Dawn*, 23 October 2009.
339. Tariq Naqash, 'Political crisis in PaK', *Rising Kashmir*, 10 October 2009, www.risingkashmir.com/index.php?option=com_content&task=view&id=17730&Itemid=1 [accessed 12 October 2009].
340. 'Farooq to take oath on Saturday', *Dawn*.
341. Tariq Naqash, 'Farooq Haider elected AJK prime minister', *Dawn*.
342. 'Home page [for The Prime Minister of Azad Jammu & Kashmir Raja Muhammad Farooq Haider Khan]', *The Azad Government of the State of Jammu & Kashmir*, www.pmajk.gov.pk/home.asp [accessed 5 January 2010].
343. The document 'Cabinet Of [sic] AJK', *The Azad Government of the State of Jammu & Kashmir*, www.pmajk.gov.pk/cabinet%20of%20AJK.asp [accessed 5 January 2009], does not provide the various cabinet members' party affiliations. I have determined these using information in Appendix XIV: Matters re Azad Kashmir elections, particularly in 2006.
344. 'Profile of the Prime Minister of Azad Jammu & Kashmir Raja Muhammad Farooq Haider Khan', *The Azad Government of the State of Jammu & Kashmir*, www.pmajk.gov.pk/profile.asp [accessed 5 January 2010].
345. *1998 Census Report of Azad Kashmir*, p. 104.
346. *The Azad Jammu and Kashmir Interim Constitution Act, 1974*, p. 4.
347. Sardar Muhammad Abdul Qayyum Khan, *The Kashmir Case*, p. 126.
348. Tariq Naqash, 'If you respect Kashmiri opinion then the borders will have to be changed', *Rising Kashmir*, undated (October 2009?), www.risingkashmir.com/index.php?option=com_content&task=view&id=18620&Itemid=37 [accessed 5 January 2010].
349. Tariq Naqash, 'Farooq Haider elected AJK prime minister', *Dawn*.
350. Tariq Naqash, 'Kashmiri refugees threaten to cross LoC', *Dawn*, 11 August 2010.
351. 'Sardar Attique elected new AJK PM', *Dawn*, 29 July 2010.
352. Ershad Mahmud, 'Another judicial impasse', *The News on Sunday*, 11 April 2010.
353. Raja Riaz, 'The road to ruling Muzaffarabad passes through Islamabad', *Daily Times*, 28 July 2010.

354. Tariq Naqash, 'Anwaarul Haq elected AJK speaker unopposed', *Dawn*, 15 August 2010.
355. Amir Wasim, 'Raja Farooq to challenge new PM's election', *Dawn*, 28 July 2010.
356. Tariq Naqash, 'AJK government, EC to compile new voters' rolls', *Dawn*, 11 June 2010.
357. Ershad Mahmud, 'Extending wings', *The News on Sunday*, 13 Sept 2009.
358. Amir Wasim, 'Raja Farooq to challenge new PM's election', *Dawn*, 28 July 2010.
359. Raja Riaz, 'The road to ruling Muzaffarabad passes through Islamabad', *Daily Times*.
360. Ibid.

CONCLUSION

1. Whether the plebiscite would have resolved the Kashmir dispute is a moot point. See Christopher Snedden, 'Would a Plebiscite Have Resolved the Kashmir Dispute?'.
2. 'Simla Agreement July 2, 1972', *Kashmir Information Network*.
3. 'Kashmir Dispute: Background', *Ministry of Foreign Affairs, Pakistan*, www.mofa.gov.pk/Pages/Brief.htm [accessed 22 April 2009]. A search of 'All Sections' of the *Indian Ministry of External Affairs* website, http://meaindia.nic.in/searchhome.htm [accessed 22 April 2009], reveals that India has no such obvious desires or compunctions in relation to what is, for India, generally termed 'an internal affair'.
4. Seven of the eight items in the India-Pakistan Composite Dialogue directly or indirectly relate to J&K: 1) peace and security, including confidence building measures (CBMs); 2) the Kashmir dispute; 3) Siachen Glacier; 4) the Wullar Barrage/Tulbul Navigation project (in the Kashmir Valley); 5) terrorism and drug-trafficking; 6) economic and commercial cooperation; and, 7) the promotion of friendly exchanges. The eighth issue is Sir Creek, on the India-Pakistan coastline, which does not relate to J&K.
5. As did J&K Muslims in the Northern Areas.
6. In August 2009, Pakistan renamed the Northern Areas 'Gilgit-Baltistan'. I use both terms in the Conclusion, depending on the context.
7. Ershad Mahmud, 'Status of AJK in Political Milieu', *Policy Perspectives*, Volume 3, Number 2, July–December 2006, Institute of Policy Studies, http://ips-pk.org/content/view/449/259/ [accessed 24 February 2010].
8. For an explanation of this concept, see Benedict Anderson, *Imagined Communities: Reflections on the Origin and Spread of Nationalism*, London, Verso, 1963.
9. Robert W. Bradnock, *Kashmir: Paths to Peace*, London, Chatham House, 2010, pp. 16–19, shows that, in an survey conducted in truncated J&K—which excluded the Indian J&K districts of Doda, Pulwara and Kupwara, the Azad Kashmir district of Neelum, and the entire Gilgit-Baltistan—in September–October 2009, on average, 44 per cent of the 1,400 Azad Kashmiris surveyed and 43 per cent of 2,374 people in Indian J&K surveyed favoured independence for J&K. Importantly, the 'Proportion who would vote for the whole of Kashmir to become independent' were a majority in the Indian J&K districts of Anantnag (74 per cent), Badgam (75 per cent), Baramula (95 per cent) and Srinagar (82 per cent), all of which districts are in the Kashmir Valley, and, surprisingly, in Azad Kashmir's Poonch District (58 per cent). Conversely, there was zero support for inde-

pendence for 'Kashmir' in all of Jammu's districts except for Jammu District, where support for independence was one per cent.

10. Robert W. Bradnock, *Kashmir: Paths to Peace*, pp. 16, 17, 19. Support for India was ten per cent or less, except in Anantnag District (22 per cent); support for Pakistan was seven per cent or less in all districts polled.
11. On 28 September 2010, at the UN General Assembly's sixty-fifth Session, Makhdoom Shah Mehmood Qureshi, Pakistan's Minister for Foreign Affairs, mentioned that the 'Kashmir dispute is about the exercise of the right to self-determination by the Kashmiri people through a free, fair and impartial plebiscite under the UN auspices'. The next day, S.M. Krishna, India's Minister of External Affairs, spoke of J&K being 'an integral part of India'. For both speeches, see: http://gadebate.un.org/View/SpeechView/tabid/85/smid/411/ArticleID/261/Default.aspx; http://gadebate.un.org/View/SpeechView/tabid/85/smid/411/ArticleID/281/Default.aspx [both statements accessed 5 October 2010].
12. 'Musharraf thinks out-of-box to resolve Kashmir', *The Financial Express*, 26 January 2006.
13. Jawed Naqvi, 'Kashmir deal was nearly clinched, says Kasuri', *Dawn*, 22 February 2009. 'Pakistan, India were close to pact two years back: Singh', *The News*, 3 May 2009. Musharraf confirmed Singh's claim in 'Musharraf: India, Pakistan were close to agreement on three issues [Kashmir, Siachen and Sir Creek]', *The Hindu*, 18 July 2009.
14. See Steve Coll, 'The Back Channel', *The New Yorker*, 2 March 2009.
15. Such development and nation-building projects include: providing more education and educational facilities, at all levels; the raising of literacy standards; providing more health facilities, particularly for women; social welfare and poverty alleviation programmes; economic and infrastructure development; providing potable water, electricity, better housing; etc. The list is a long one.
16. The LOC ends at map point NJ 980420 in north-eastern J&K. Beyond is the Saltoro Range and the disputed Siachen Glacier, on which India and Pakistan have stationed forces.
17. 'The Indus Waters Treaty', *The Henry L. Stimson Center*, www.stimson.org/southasia/?sn=sa20020116300 [accessed 8 October 2008].
18. 'India welcomes exclusion of J&K from U.N. list', *The Hindu*, 15 November 2010. 'UN removes Jammu and Kashmir from list of disputes', *Daily Times*, 16 November 2010.
19. S/1996/603*, 22 August 1996, *United Nations Security Council*, http://domino.un.org/UNISPAL.NSF/3822b5e39951876a85256b6e0058a478/c0924183a7f95851852563a900544efa!OpenDocument [accessed 18 July 2007]. The 'Hyderabad question' also remained on the 'list of matters of which the Security Council is seized', even though it had not been discussed by the Security Council since 24 May 1949!
20. S/1996/704, 29 August 1996, *United Nations Security Council*, http://daccessdds.un.org/doc/UNDOC/GEN/N96/223/44/PDF/N9622344.pdf?OpenElement [accessed 18 July 2007].
21. 'No scope for third-party mediation on Kashmir: India', *Indian Express*, 22 September 2010.
22. Section 1. (ii), 'Simla Agreement July 2, 1972'.

23. Jawaharlal Nehru, 'Our Pledge To Kashmir', Speech in Parliament, New Delhi, 7 August, 1952, in *Jawaharlal Nehru's Speeches 1949–1953*, The Publications Division, Ministry of Information and Broadcasting, Government of India, Delhi, 1954, pp. 338–9.
24. Jawaharlal Nehru, 'Let the People Decide', Speech in Parliament, New Delhi, 7 August, 1952, in *Jawaharlal Nehru's Speeches 1949–1953*, p. 353. Although the date given in the publication is 7 August 1952, this speech appears to have been given a few days later.
25. I have actually been studying and thinking about the Kashmir dispute since I began working on South Asia matters in 1984 as a politico-strategic intelligence analyst. Indeed, the first brief that I delivered was on India's hanging of Maqbool Butt in February 1984.
26. This 'framework' is partly based on Christopher Snedden, 'The India-Pakistan Peace Process: Overcoming the "Trust Deficit"', *Pakistan Security Research Unit*, Brief Number 20, 2 October 2007, http://spaces.brad.ac.uk:8080/download/attachments/748/Brief+20.pdf [accessed 4 October 2007].
27. Formerly the Northern Areas Legislative Council. See 'PPP gets mandate to rule Gilgit-Baltistan', *Dawn*, 14 November 2009.

## APPENDIX I. THE RELATIONSHIP BETWEEN THE RAJAS OF POONCH AND THE MAHARAJAS OF JAMMU AND KASHMIR

1. This appendix based on information contained in microfilmed files of the (British) Government of India held at the National Documentation Centre, Cabinet Building, Islamabad, Pakistan. With the assistance of NDC staff, I accessed various files on 27–29 December 2006.
2. For details, where available, of their births, deaths and period of rule, see Table I.1.
3. Letter from Jagatdev Singh, Raja of Poonch, to 'His Excellency the Right Honourable Freeman Freeman-Thomas, Earl of Wellingdon [sic], G.M.S.I., G.M.I.E., G.C.M.G., C.B.E., Viceroy and Governor General of India', 27 February 1936, p. 21, in File No. 452-P(S)/37 of 1937, 'Memorial from the Raja of Poonch, Kashmir State', Political Department, 'Political' Branch, [Government of India].
4. Letter from Jagatdev Singh, Raja of Poonch, to 'His Excellency the Right Honourable Freeman Freeman-Thomas, Earl of Wellingdon [sic]', p. 5.
5. Ibid. Chibball is also sometimes spelt Chhibbal; Bhimbar is sometimes spelt Bhimber.
6. Ibid.
7. Ibid.
8. Ibid., p. 7.
9. Raja Sir Baldeo Singh, *The Poonch State Case*, p. 8, Annexure No. 1 to Letter from Jagatdev Singh, Raja of Poonch, to 'His Excellency the Right Honourable Freeman Freeman-Thomas, Earl of Wellingdon [sic]', italics as per the original. Baldeo Singh's undated 1895? twenty-eight-page document was originally written to 'H.S. Barnes, Esq., Resident in Kashmir'. It was (later?) printed at 'The Public Printing Press, Lahore', although it is not clear whether this printing was done by Baldev or by his second son, Jagatdev Singh, to whose memorial it was annexed.

10. The 'Amritsar Treaty, 1846' is contained in K.M. Panikkar, *The Founding of the Kashmir State. A Biography of Maharaja Gulab Singh, 1792–1858*, London, George Allen & Unwin, 1953, pp. 111–15.
11. *Memoranda on the Indian States 1940*, Delhi, The Manager of [Indian Government] Publications, 1940, pp. 163–4.
12. Raja Sir Baldeo Singh, *The Poonch State Case*, p. 10, Annexure No. 1 to Letter from Jagatdev Singh, Raja of Poonch, to 'His Excellency the Right Honourable Freeman Freeman-Thomas, Earl of Wellingdon [sic]'.
13. Ibid.
14. Raja Sir Baldeo Singh, *The Poonch State Case*, p. 9, Annexure No. 1 to Letter from Jagatdev Singh, Raja of Poonch, to 'His Excellency the Right Honourable Freeman Freeman-Thomas, Earl of Wellingdon [sic]'.
15. Letter from Jagatdev Singh, Raja of Poonch, to 'His Excellency the Right Honourable Freeman Freeman-Thomas, Earl of Wellingdon [sic]', p. 11.
16. Raja Sir Baldeo Singh, *The Poonch State Case*, p. 14, Annexure No. 1 to Letter from Jagatdev Singh, Raja of Poonch, to 'His Excellency the Right Honourable Freeman Freeman-Thomas, Earl of Wellingdon [sic]'.
17. H.S. Barnes, Resident in Kashmir, 4 December 1895, *The Punch* [sic] *Case*, p. 4, Annexure No. 2 to Letter from Jagatdev Singh, Raja of Poonch, to 'His Excellency the Right Honourable Freeman Freeman-Thomas, Earl of Wellingdon [sic]'.
18. Balraj Puri, *Jammu and Kashmir. Triumph and Tragedy of Indian Federalisation*, New Delhi, Sterling Publishers, 1981, Appendix B, pp. 204–5, contains the 'Edict of "Abdication"' that Pratap Singh issued on 8 March 1889.
19. Lamb, *Kashmir, A Disputed Legacy*, pp. 12–13, 29–30.
20. Raja Sir Baldeo Singh, *The Poonch State Case*, p. 24, Annexure No. 1 to Letter from Jagatdev Singh, Raja of Poonch, to 'His Excellency the Right Honourable Freeman Freeman-Thomas, Earl of Wellingdon [sic]'.
21. Letter from Jagatdev Singh, Raja of Poonch, to 'His Excellency the Right Honourable Freeman Freeman-Thomas, Earl of Wellingdon [sic]', p. 11.
22. Raja Sir Baldeo Singh, *The Poonch State Case*, p. 16, Annexure No. 1 to Letter from Jagatdev Singh, Raja of Poonch, to 'His Excellency the Right Honourable Freeman Freeman-Thomas, Earl of Wellingdon [sic]'.
23. Letter from Jagatdev Singh, Raja of Poonch, to 'His Excellency the Right Honourable Freeman Freeman-Thomas, Earl of Wellingdon [sic]', pp. 11–12.
24. Raja Sir Baldeo Singh, *The Poonch State Case*, pp. 17–18, Annexure No. 1 to Letter from Jagatdev Singh, Raja of Poonch, to 'His Excellency the Right Honourable Freeman Freeman-Thomas, Earl of Wellingdon [sic]'. pp. 73–4.
25. Letter from Jagatdev Singh, Raja of Poonch, to 'Lieutenant Colonel, L.E. Lang, C.I.E., M.C., Resident, Kashmir. Sialkot, 26 January 1937, p. 3, in 'Memorial from the Raja of Poonch, Kashmir State'.
26. This paragraph and the following paragraph based on Author unknown [Lieutenant Colonel L.E. Lang, Resident in Kashmir?], 'Untitled note about the Memorial from the Raja of Poonch', in File No. 452-P(S)/37 of 1937, 'Memorial from the Raja of Poonch, Kashmir State', Political Department, 'Political' Branch, [Government of India].

27. File No. 452-P(S)/37 of 1937, 'Memorial from the Raja of Poonch, Kashmir State', Political Department, 'Political' Branch, [Government of India].
28. Letter from Jagatdev Singh, Raja of Poonch, to 'His Excellency the Right Honourable Freeman Freeman-Thomas, Earl of Wellingdon [sic]', pp. 18–19.
29. Ibid., pp. 20–21.
30. Ibid., p. 22.
31. Letter from G.D. Ogilvie, Resident, Kashmir, to 'The Hon'ble Sir Charles Watson, K.C.I.E., C.S.I., Political Secretary to the Government of India in the Foreign and Political Department, New Delhi', 8 February 1930, pp. 3–4, in File No. 58-P (Secret), 1930, 'Strained relations between His Highness the Maharaja of Kashmir and his feudatory the Raja of Poonch', Government of India, Foreign and Political Department, Political.
32. Letter from G.D. Ogilvie, Resident, Kashmir, to 'The Hon'ble Sir Charles Watson, K.C.I.E., C.S.I., Political Secretary to the Government of India in the Foreign and Political Department', 18 May 1931, pp. 1–3, in File No. 58-P (Secret), 1930, 'Strained relations between His Highness the Maharaja of Kashmir and his feudatory the Raja of Poonch', Government of India, Foreign and Political Department, Political.
33. Letter from G.D. Ogilvie, Resident, Kashmir, to 'The Hon'ble Sir Charles Watson, K.C.I.E., C.S.I., Political Secretary to the Government of India in the Foreign and Political Department, New Delhi', 17 January 1931, pp. 3–4, in File No. 286-P (Secret), 1931, 'Strained relations between H.H. the Maharaja of Kashmir and his feudatory the Raja of Poonch', Government of India, Foreign and Political Department, Political.
34. Letter from the Resident, Kashmir, to 'The Hon'ble Sir Charles Watson, K.C.I.E., C.S.I., Political Secretary to the Government of India in the Foreign and Political Department, Simla', 11 June 1931, p. 1, in File No. 286-P (Secret), 1931, 'Strained relations between H.H. the Maharaja of Kashmir and his feudatory the Raja of Poonch', Government of India, Foreign and Political Department, Political.
35. Note on file [by E.M. Howell?] about a visit from Raja Jagat Deo [sic] Singh on 28 November 1931, in File No. 286-P (Secret), 1931, 'Strained relations between H.H. the Maharaja of Kashmir and his feudatory the Raja of Poonch', Government of India, Foreign and Political Department, Political.
36. Copy of letter from Jagat Dev Singh, Raja of Poonch, to 'Lieutenant Colonel L.E. Lang, C.I.E., M.C., The Hon'ble Resident in Kashmir, Srinagar', 24 June 1937, p. 3, in File No. 452-P(S)/1937, 'Memorial from the Raja of Poonch, Kashmir State', Political Department?, Political Branch?, Government of India.
37. Letter from Jagat Dev Singh, Raja of Poonch, to 'C.L. Corfield Esq., M.C., the Hon'ble Political Secretary, Government of India, Simla', 28 June 1937, in File No. 452-P(S)/1937, 'Memorial from the Raja of Poonch, Kashmir State', Political Department?, Political Branch?, Government of India. Corfield's handwritten note of two words is dated '3.7.37'.
38. Letter from P. Gaisford, D.S. (P) Deputy Secretary (Political)? to 'The Resident in Kashmir' on the subject of the 'Memorial from the Raja of Poonch', 12 October 1937, p. 2, in File No. 416 P(S)/34, 1936, 'Memorial from the Raja of Poonch praying for enquiry into political status of Poonch and decision whether there has been encroach-

ment on the rights of the Jagir by the Kashmir Government', Political Department, Political Branch, [Government of India].

39. 'Letter from Lieutenant Colonel L.E. Lang C.I.E., M.C., Resident in Kashmir, to The Secretary to His Excellency the Crown Representative, Political Department, Simla', 18th September 1937, p. 3, in File No. 452-P(S)/1937, 'Memorial from the Raja of Poonch, Kashmir State', Political Department?, Political Branch?, Government of India.

40. Letter from the Resident in Kashmir, No. D 424-C/37, 18 September 1937, in File No. 416 P(S)/34, 1936, 'Memorial from the Raja of Poonch praying for enquiry into political status of Poonch and decision whether there has been encroachment on the rights of the Jagir by the Kashmir Government', Political Department, Political Branch, [Government of India]. Underlined word as per the original.

41. Author unknown, untitled five page note on 'the question of the succession of the late Raja Jagat Dev Singh of Poonch', 10 August 1940, p. 1, in File No. 3 (13)—P(S)/40, Part II, 1940, 'Poonch Affairs. Death of Raja Jagat Dev Singh of Poonch. Administrative arrangements in Poonch during the minority of the present Raja of Poonch', Political Department, 'Political' Branch, [Government of India].

42. Author unknown, untitled five page note on 'the question of the succession of the late Raja Jagat Dev Singh of Poonch', 10 August 1940, p. 1, in File No. 3 (13)—P(S)/40, Part II, 1940.

43. Author unknown, untitled five page note on 'the question of the succession of the late Raja Jagat Dev Singh of Poonch', 10 August 1940, p. 1, in File No. 3 (13)—P(S)/40, Part II, 1940.

44. 'New Raja of Poonch', *The Tribune*, 20 July 1940, in File No. 3 (13)—P(S)/40, Part II, 1940, 'Poonch Affairs. Death of Raja Jagat Dev Singh of Poonch. Administrative arrangements in Poonch during the minority of the present Raja of Poonch', Political Department, 'Political' Branch, [Government of India].

45. Unless otherwise stated, the rest of this paragraph based on Author unknown, untitled five page note on 'the question of the succession of the late Raja Jagat Dev Singh of Poonch', pp. 4–5, in File No. 3 (13)—P(S)/40, Part II, 1940, 'Poonch Affairs. Death of Raja Jagat Dev Singh of Poonch. Administrative arrangements in Poonch during the minority of the present Raja of Poonch', Political Department, 'Political' Branch, [Government of India].

46. Author unknown [the British Resident in J&K?], untitled file note regarding a conversation with the 'Prime Minister of Kashmir' about the Rani of Poonch, 21 February 1941, in File No. 3 (13)—P(S)/40, Part II, 1940, 'Poonch Affairs. Death of Raja Jagat Dev Singh of Poonch. Administrative arrangements in Poonch during the minority of the present Raja of Poonch', Political Department, 'Political' Branch, [Government of India].

47. Abdulla Khan, 'English translation of the Resolution passed by the Poonch Public on 30 July 1940 at Murree' in File No. 3 (13)—P(S)/40, Part II, 1940, 'Poonch Affairs. Death of Raja Jagat Dev Singh of Poonch. Administrative arrangements in Poonch during the minority of the present Raja of Poonch', Political Department, 'Political' Branch, [Government of India].

48. 'Proclamation of His Highness the Maharaja Bahadur of Jammu & Kashmir, dated the 5th of Sawan 1997 19 July 1940 Relating to Poonch Jagir', in *The Jammu & Kashmir Government Gazette*, Volume 52, Srinagar Friday The [sic] 5th Sawan 1997 = 19 July 1940, No. 39 a, p. 3, in File No. 3 (13)—P(S)/40, Part II, 1940, 'Poonch Affairs. Death of Raja Jagat Dev Singh of Poonch. Administrative arrangements in Poonch during the minority of the present Raja of Poonch', Political Department, 'Political' Branch, [Government of India].
49. Letter from the Resident, 9 June 1945, to 'Griffin', in 'Poonch Affairs. 2. Communal Trouble in Poonch', in File No. 5 (12) P(S)/45, 1945, Political Department, Pol Branch, [Government of India].

## APPENDIX II. PHYSICAL, POLITICAL AND RELIGIOUS COMPOSITION OF J&K IN 1941

1. *Census of India 1941*, p. 527.
2. *CMG*, 29 July 1947.
3. *Census of Azad Kashmir, 1951*, p. 11.

## APPENDIX III. MAJORITY POSITION OF MUSLIMS IN 1941

1. *Census of India 1941*, p. 66.
2. Ibid., p. 3.
3. Ibid., p. 4.
4. Calculated from figures given in Singh, *History of Jammu and Kashmir Rifles*, p. 145.
5. Singh, *History of Jammu and Kashmir Rifles*, p. 169.
6. *Census of India 1941*, p. 66.
7. Ibid., p. 98.
8. Ibid., p. 153.
9. Ibid., p. 182.
10. Ibid., p. 232.
11. Ibid., p. 233.
12. Ibid., p. 66.
13. Ibid., p. 232.

## APPENDIX IV. INDIAN ARMY SOLDIERS FROM POONCH, MIRPUR

1. Messervy, 'Kashmir', pp. 469, 475.
2. Author unknown, *Copy of Poonch Services*, pp. 2–3, Annexure No. 4 to Letter from Jagatdev Singh, Raja of Poonch, to 'His Excellency the Right Honourable Freeman Freeman-Thomas, Earl of Wellingdon [sic], G.M.S.I., G.M.I.E., G.C.M.G., C.B.E., Viceroy and Governor General of India', dated 27 February 1936, as contained in the 'Memorial from the Raja of Poonch, Kashmir State', File No. 452-P(S)/37 of 1937, Political Department, 'Political' Branch, Government of India, as accessed at the National Documentation Centre, Cabinet Building, Islamabad, 29 December 2006. The Raja of Poonch at the time was Jagatdev Singh.

## APPENDIX V. PHYSICAL AND POLITICAL COMPOSITION OF J&K AFTER THE 1949 CEASEFIRE

1. Sardar M. Ibrahim Khan, *The Kashmir Saga*, p. 155. Equally, the Azad Kashmir politician (and former pro-Pakistan freedom fighter in 1947) Sardar Abdul Qayyum Khan told me in Rawalpindi on 24 March 1999, that he was 'shocked' when he first heard of the ceasefire only on the day it came into effect. He (optimistically) believed that the Azad Army would have been in control of J&K by the end of February or in March 1949 had its efforts not been thwarted by the 1949 ceasefire.
2. *Census of India 1961*, p. 147.
3. P.L. Lakhanpal, *Essential Documents and Notes on Kashmir Dispute*, Second Edition, Delhi, International Books, 1965, p. 10.
4. *Census of Azad Kashmir, 1951*, p. 11.

## APPENDIX VI. CEASEFIRE LINE IN J&K

1. *Census of Azad Kashmir, 1951*, p. 8.
2. Pauline Dawson, *The Peacekeepers of Kashmir*, London, Hurst & Company, 1994, p. 29.
3. *Census of Azad Kashmir, 1951*, p. 8.
4. Ibid., pp. 145–6.
5. Ibid., p. 146.
6. Ibid.

## APPENDIX VII. MAIN OFFICE HOLDERS OF AZAD KASHMIR

1. Various sources. For the period up until 1996, the chief source is notes positioned underneath photographs located in the Khurshid Library, Muzaffarabad, of various office holders in Azad Kashmir. I took these notes during a research trip to Muzaffarabad in January 1998. For the post-1996 period, a major source has been various pages within the Azad Jammu and Kashmir Government website, www.ajk.gov.pk/site/index.php?option=com_frontpage&Itemid=1 [accessed 6 November 2007].

## APPENDIX VIII. AZAD KASHMIR 'COUNCIL LEGISLATIVE LIST'

1. *The Azad Jammu and Kashmir Interim Constitution Act*, p. 26.
2. Ibid.
3. Azad Kashmir 'Third Schedule [See section 31 (2)] Council Legislative List', *The Azad Jammu and Kashmir Interim Constitution Act*, pp. 56–9. Except for my various insertions of 'sic' in the list, the other square brackets in the text were amendments to the Third Schedule.
4. *The Azad Jammu and Kashmir Interim Constitution Act*, p. 26.

## APPENDIX X. AZAD KASHMIR ADMINISTRATIVE SET-UP AND FUNCTIONS

1. *Rules of Business 1985*, pp. 33–52. All numbering throughout as per the original document. Some, but not all, of these rules also are available by doing a search on the Azad

Jammu and Kashmir Government's website at: www.ajk.gov.pk/site/index.php?option=com_frontpage&Itemid=1.
2. A.R.P.: Air Raid Precautions?
3. Azad Kashmir Regular Forces.
4. 'Schedule—VII (See Rule 21) Cases Relating to Appointments and Promotions to posts (Approval of Prime Minister to be obtained before issue of Orders)', in *Rules of Business 1985*, pp. 55–7.
5. ADP: Area Development Project?

## APPENDIX XIII. CROSSING PROCESS BETWEEN AZAD KASHMIR AND INDIAN J&K

1. Based on documents obtained, and on conversations with various officials, in Azad Kashmir in December 2006.
2. The names of these crossing points vary slightly from those given in Chapter 7, and, where different, the version in Chapter 7 is provided in the brackets.
3. I thank Smruti Pattanaik for her help translating some of the names of the trade items.

## APPENDIX XIV. MATTERS RE AZAD KASHMIR ELECTIONS, PARTICULARLY IN 2006

1. Table based on information contained at *Muzaffarabadak.com*, http://www.muzaffarabadak.com/ajkelection2006.htm [accessed 5 November 2007].
2. Ibid.
3. Table based on information contained in Table XIV 4.
4. For current information, see 'Members AJK Legislative Assembly', *Legislative Assembly of Azad Jammu & Kashmir*, www.ajkassembly.gok.pk/current_members.htm [accessed 16 April 2009]. Unfortunately, this site does not provide members' political affiliations.
5. 'Ishaq Zafar dies of heart attack', *Dawn*, Karachi, 3 September 2006, http://www.dawn.com/2006/09/03/top17.htm [accessed 29 October 2007].
6. 'Farooq to take oath on Saturday', *Dawn*, Karachi, http://www.dawn.com/2006/11/10/nat21.htm [accessed 29 October 2007].
7. *Azad Jammu and Kashmir Government*, URL as above [accessed 29 October 2007].
8. Ibid.
9. First three columns based on information in 'Statement Showing Constituency[-]Wise Difference in Number of Electors in 1996, 2001 & 2006', no further publication details, obtained by me while in Azad Kashmir in 2006. The rest based on information contained at *Muzaffarabadak.com*, http://www.muzaffarabadak.com/ajkelection2006.htm [accessed 5 November 2007].
10. Based on election documents obtained by me, and on conversations that I had with various officials, while in Azad Kashmir in December 2006.
11. *Report on the Seventh General Elections in Azad Jammu & Kashmir 2001*, Muzaffarabad, Azad Jammu & Kashmir Election Commission, 2002, pp. 26–35. These constituencies would have been similar for the 2006 election with the exception of the newly-created

Neelum I constituency, which comprised much, perhaps all, of Athmuqam *tehsil* in Muzaffarabad District.

12. Based on a conversation that I had with an Azad Kashmir election official, December 2006.
13. Figures for 1996 (rounded) and for 2001 are from 'Comparative statement showing difference in overall turnout during General Elections 1996 and 2001 to the Azad Jammu and Kashmir Legislative Assembly' in Comparative *Report on the Seventh General Elections in Azad Jammu & Kashmir 2001*, Muzaffarabad, Azad Jammu & Kashmir Election Commission, 2002, p. 104. Figures for 2006 are my calculations based on 'Table XIV 5: 2006 Azad Kashmir Legislative Assembly Candidates, Parties and Constituency-wise Details' above.
14. Based on election documents obtained by me, and on conversations that I had with various officials, while in Azad Kashmir in December 2006.
15. The remainder of this paragraph and the next paragraph are based on 'The Azad Jammu and Kashmir Legislative Assembly (Elections) Ordinance 1970 (Amended Upto [sic] 2002)', in *The Election Laws (As Amended up to March, 2002)*, Azad Jammu & Kashmir Election Commission, Islamabad [sic], 2002, pp. 121–7.
16. *The Election Laws (As Amended up to March, 2002)*, p. 126.

# BIBLIOGRAPHY

*Note on names: although many people in the subcontinent do not have the equivalent of Western last names, for the sake of convenience I have listed authors' names alphabetically based on a person's final name. Titles without authors are listed alpha-numerically.*

*Public or Official Documents or Websites*

*(Princely) Jammu and Kashmir*

'Statement showing the Results of the [1947] Elections', in *The Jammu and Kashmir Praja Sabha Debates*, Volume XVIII, Thursday 3rd April 1947/21 Chet 2004, March–April Session of the third J&K Praja Sabha, Jammu, Dewan Press, 1947.

*Azad Kashmir*

*An Introduction to the Hydropower Potential of Azad Jammu & Kashmir*, AJK Hydro Electric Board, Muzaffarabad, 2006, www.pmajk.gov.pk/pdf_files/hydropower_potential.pdf [accessed 2 March 2009].

*Azad Jammu and Kashmir Council*, www.ajkcouncil.com/AJKCouncilintroductionasp [accessed 26 February 2009].

*Azad Jammu and Kashmir Government*, www.ajk.gov.pk/site/index.php (and various subsections) [accessed 19 March 2009].

*Azad Jammu and Kashmir Supreme Court Recorder*, Muzaffarabad?, Shaikh Manzoor Ahmad, Editor, Supreme Court of Azad Jammu and Kashmir, 1995.

Azad Jammu & Kashmir Election Commission, *Tabulated & Graphic Presentation Of [sic] Election Returns-2001*, Azad Jammu & Kashmir Election Commission Secretariat, Muzaffarabad, 2001.

*Azad Jammu & Kashmir Govt [sic] Financial Code, Volume II*, Rawalpindi, Hamdard Steam Press, 1954.

*Azad Kashmir at a Glance 1995*, Muzaffarabad, Planning & Dev. [sic] Department, Azad Govt. [sic] of the State of Jammu & Kashmir, 1996?.

*Azad Kashmir at a Glance 1996*, Muzaffarabad, Planning & Dev. [sic] Department, Azad Govt. [sic] of the State of Jammu & Kashmir, 1997?.

*Azad Kashmir at a Glance 2002*, Muzaffarabad, Planning & Dev. [sic] Department, Azad Govt. [sic] of the State of Jammu & Kashmir, 2003?.

*Azad Kashmir at a Glance 2003*, Muzaffarabad, Planning & Dev. [sic] Department, Azad Govt. [sic] of the State of Jammu & Kashmir, 2004?.

*Azad Kashmir at a Glance 2004*, Muzaffarabad, Planning & Development Department, Azad Government of the State of Jammu & Kashmir, 2005?.

# BIBLIOGRAPHY

*Azad Kashmir at a Glance 2005*, Muzaffarabad, Planning & Development Department, Azad Government of the State of Jammu & Kashmir, 2006?.

*Azad Kashmir at a Glance*, 2007, Muzaffarabad, Planning & Development Department, Azad Government of the State of Jammu & Kashmir, www.pndajk.gov.pk/ajk_glance2007.asp#DDSDAJK [accessed 19 March 2009].

*Azad Kashmir at a Glance*, undated, Muzaffarabad, Planning & Development Department, Azad Government of the State of Jammu & Kashmir, 2007?, www.pndajk.gov.pk/glance.asp [accessed 25 February 2009].

*Azad Kashmir at a Glance*, 2008, Muzaffarabad, Planning & Development Department, Azad Government of the State of Jammu & Kashmir, 2008, www.pndajk.gov.pk/glance.asp [accessed 15 September 2010].

*Azad Kashmir On [The] Road To Progress*, Muzaffarabad, Mohammad Iqbal, Compiler and Editor, Information Directorate, Azad Government of Jammu and Kashmir State, 1965.

*Azad Kashmir Statistical Year Book 1990*, Muzaffarabad?, Statistics Section, Planning & Development Department, Azad Government of the State of Jammu & Kashmir, 1992.

Aziz, Mir Abdul, 'Internal Kashmir Affairs—A Practicable Solution, Kashmiristan?', p. 1, in a proposal attached to a letter to 'The Hon'ble Minister for Kashmir Affairs, Pakistan (Rawalpindi)', by Mir Abdul Aziz, 'Member General Council, All Jammu and Kashmir Muslim Conference', 5 May 1950, pp. 53–61, contained in File No. 13 (5)-PMS/50, Volume 10, 'Government of Pakistan, Prime Minister's Secretariat, All Jammu & Kashmir Muslim Conference', held at the National Documentation Centre, Cabinet Building, Islamabad, Pakistan [file accessed on 27–29 December 2006].

*Bank of Azad Jammu & Kashmir*, www.bankajk.com/res.php?sgv=010001 [accessed 16 September 2010].

*Census of Azad Kashmir, 1951*, Murree?, Iftikhar Ahmad, Chief Enumeration Officer, Government of Azad Kashmir, 1952.

Commissioner Relief & Rehabilitation AJK Board of Revenue, *Azad Jammu and Kashmir Government*, www.ajk.gov.pk/site/index.php?option=com_content&task=view&id=2900&Itemid=94 [accessed 12 March 2009].

*Earthquake Damage (Compiled by AJK Governament* [sic]*)*, Dated 26 October 2005, unpublished handout, copy obtained in Azad Kashmir in December 2006.

'Former Members', *Legislative Assembly of Azad Jammu and Kashmir*, www.ajkassembly.gok.pk/former_members.htm [accessed 15 March 2010].

*Kashmir's Fight for Freedom*, Washington, Department of Public Relations, Azad Kashmir Government, 1948.

*Legislative Assembly of Azad Jammu &Kashmir*, www.ajkassembly.gok.pk/ [accessed 19 March 2009].

'Members AJK Legislative Assembly 2006 till now', *Legislative Assembly of Azad Jammu and Kashmir*, www.ajkassembly.gok.pk/current_members.htm [accessed 15 March 2010].

'Organizational Chart of Azad Jammu and Kashmir Council Secretariat', *Azad Jammu & Kashmir Council*, www.ajkcouncil.com/AJKCouncilSect.asp [accessed 2 March 2010].

*Planning & Development [of Azad Kashmir Government]*, www.pndajk.gov.pk/default.asp [accessed 19 March 2009].

*Prime Minister* [sic] *Secretariat of Azad Government of the State of Azad Jammu & Kashmir*, www.pmajk.gov.pk/home.asp [accessed 19 March 2009].

*Public Sector Development Programme for the Year 1997–98 of Azad Government of the State of Jammu & Kashmir*, Muzaffarabad, Planning & Development Department, Azad Government of the State of Jammu & Kashmir, 1997?.

# BIBLIOGRAPHY

*Public Sector Development Programme 2006–2007*, Planning & Development Department, Azad Government of the State of Jammu and Kashmir, Muzaffarabad, 2007?.

Qureshi, Khalil Ahmed, *The Annual Volume of Azad Jammu & Kashmir Laws, 1948*, Muzaffarabad, Law Department, Azad Government of the State of Jammu and Kashmir, 1980?.

*Report on the Third General Election in Azad Jammu and Kashmir 1985*, Azad Jammu and Kashmir Election Commission, Islamabad, 1987.

*Report on the Seventh General Elections in Azad Jammu & Kashmir 2001*, Azad Jammu & Kashmir Election Commission, Muzaffarabad, 2002.

*Rules of Business 1985*, Services & General Administration Department, Azad Government of the State of Jammu and Kashmir, Muzaffarabad, 1985.

*Statistical Year Book 1988*, Muzaffarabad?, Planning & Development Department, Azad Government of the State of Jammu and Kashmir, 1989.

*The Azad Jammu and Kashmir Interim Constitution Act, 1974 (Amended upto [sic] date) May 1997*, Muzaffarabad, Azad Government of the State of Jammu & Kashmir (Law, Justice and Parliamentary Affairs Department), 1997.

*The Azad Jammu and Kashmir Legislative Assembly (Elections) Ordinance 1970 and Rules 1970 (Amended Upto [sic] May, 2006.)*, Azad Jammu and Kashmir Election Commission, Muzaffarabad, 2006.

*The Election Laws (As Amended up to March, 2002)*, Azad Jammu & Kashmir Election Commission, Islamabad [sic], 2002.

*The Land Laws of Azad Jammu and Kashmir (As Amended up to 31st March 1996)*, Muzaffarabad, Ch. Mukhtar Hussain, Compiler and Editor, Board of Revenue, Azad Jammu and Kashmir Government, 1996.

'The Prime Minister of Azad Jammu and Kashmir Raja Muhammad Farooq Haider Khan emphasized that Kashmir Liberation Cell should be made more active', *Prime Minister* [sic] *Secretariat of Azad Government of the State of Azad Jammu & Kashmir*, 8 January 2010, www.pmajk.gov.pk/news2.asp?id=44 [accessed 19 March 2010].

*Documents to do with various aspects of the Azad Kashmir Legislative Assembly and elections to this body.*

*The documents listed below were obtained while in Azad Kashmir in December 2006. They are extracts from unspecified official documents for which I have no further publication details.*[1]

- A.J & K. Election Commission document containing 'Figure-01: Percentage of Total Polling During Elections (1985–90–91–96)'; 'Figure-02: Party-wise Percentage of Total Obtained Votes in Azad Kashmir and Pakistan during Elections 1996, for "40" Constituencies of Legislative Assembly A.J.& K.'; 'Figure-03: District (Unit) Wise [sic] Percentage of Polling during General Elections (June 30, 1996)'; 'Figure-04: Increase in Percentage of Polling During Elections (1985–90–91–96)'.
- 'Brief' [discussing the first seven Legislative Assemblies, i.e. 1) 1971–1975; 2) 1975–1977; 3) 1985–1990; 4) 1990–1991; 5) 1991–1996; 6) 1996–2001; 7) 2001–2006] and 'List of Members 2006 till now'.

---

[1] I acknowledge the help, support and encouragement of the Azad Kashmiris who helped me to obtain these highly useful documents and some other electoral reports.

# BIBLIOGRAPHY

- Chief Election Commissioner, Azad Jammu & Kashmir Election Commission, H.# 256-A, ST.# 30, SEC.F-10/1, ISLAMABAD, *Notification [of election results]* dated 15 July 2006 and *Notification [of election result]* dated 19 July 2006.
- Chief Election Commissioner, 'Notification [of returned candidates for directly-elected seats in the 2006 election]', Azad Jammu & Kashmir Election Commission, Islamabad [sic].
- Detailed Breakdown of the AJ&K Legislative Assembly Seats [for 1991, by number of votes (only)].
- List of Returned Candidates During 1970, Annex 'E'.
- List of Returned Candidates During 1975, Annex 'E'.
- List of Contesting Candidates [by Party Name only] during 1985, Annex 'E'.
- List of Returned Candidates of Elections 1985, Appendix IV.
- List of Contesting Candidates [by Party Name only] during 1990, Annex 'E'.
- List of Contesting Candidates [by Party Name only] during 1991, Annex 'E'.
- Particulars of Various Parties Registered in AJ&K, 1996.
- Partywise Summary of the Candidates who Participated During 1985, 1990 and 1991 Election, Annex.
- Political Party Heads in Azad Jammu and Kashmir, 2006.
- 'Statement Showing Constituency Wise Difference in Number of Electors in 1996, 2001 & 2006'.
- Votes Obtained by Political Parties and Independent Candidates during General Elections 30 June 1996 and List of the Candidates During Elections 1996.

*India, before 15 August 1947*

*Census of India 1941*, Volume XXII, *Jammu & Kashmir State*, Part III, *Village Tables*, Srinagar, R.G. Wreford, Editor, Jammu and Kashmir Government, 1942.

Copies of microfilmed files (various) of the (British) Government of India held at the National Documentation Centre, Cabinet Building, Islamabad, Pakistan.

*Memoranda on the Indian States 1940*, Delhi, The Manager of [Indian Government] Publications, 1940.

*India, after 15 August 1947*

*Census of India 1951*, Volume VI, *India*, Part I-A, *The Land and the People-1951*, New Delhi, R.A. Gopalswami, Registrar-General, Census of India, 1953.

*Census of India 1961*, Volume VI, *Jammu and Kashmir*, Part I-A (i), *General Report*, Srinagar, M.H. Kamili, Superintendent of Census Operations Jammu and Kashmir, Census of India, 1968.

Chagla, M.C., *Kashmir 1947–1965*, Delhi, Publications Division, Ministry of Information and Broadcasting, 1965.

*Conditions in Pakistan-Occupied Kashmir*, Information Service of India, New Delhi, {1956?}, comprising: 1) Ghulam Mohammad, Publicity Secretary, All-Jammu and Kashmir Muslim Conference, *Memorandum to Members of the Pakistan Constituent Assembly*, no original publication details, July 1955?, and Sanaullah Butt, (Khwajah) Abdus Salam Yatu, (Khwajah) Ghulam Nabi Gilkar Anwar and Mir Abdul Aziz, *'Humble Appeal' to the Members of the Constituent Assembly of Pakistan*, no original publication details, July 1955. (See also *Kashmir Documents 1–7* below.)

# BIBLIOGRAPHY

*Defending Kashmir*, Delhi, The Publications Division, Ministry of Information and Broadcasting, Government of India, 1949.

'Joint Statement issued after Foreign Minister level Review of the Fourth Round of Composite Dialogue, Islamabad, 21 May 2008', *Indian Ministry of External Affairs*, New Delhi, meaindia.nic.in/ [accessed 25 May 2008].

*Kashmir Documents 1–7*, New Delhi, Information Service of India, 1956?. [This bound volume contains seven leaflets: 1) Pakistan Aggression in Kashmir, [First Published 1949?]; 2) Pakistan's Call To War On India; 3) Conditions in Pakistan-Occupied Kashmir; 4) Kashmir's Accession To India; 5) United Nations Assurances To India; 6) Sadiq-Abdullah Correspondence; and, 7) Sheikh Abdullah's Address To Kashmir Assembly. It is held in the Fisher Library, University of Sydney.]

*Indian Ministry of External Affairs* website, http://meaindia.nic.in/searchhome.htm [accessed 22 April 2009].

Prasad, S.N. and Dharm Pal, *History of Operations in Jammu & Kashmir (1947–48)*, New Delhi, History Division, Ministry of Defence, Government of India, 1987?.

*White Paper on Jammu & Kashmir*, Delhi, Government of India, 1948.

### Indian Jammu and Kashmir

*Administration Report of the Jammu and Kashmir State for S. 2005* [sic] *(13th April 1948–12th April 1949)*, Jammu, Ranbir Government Press, 1951. [The year 2005 was based on a Hindu calendar used by the Dogra maharajas and their initial successor regime in Indian J&K.]

*Administration Report of Jammu and Kashmir for the years, 2011* [sic] *(13th April 1954–12th April 1955)*, Srinagar?, Jammu and Kashmir Government, 1955?. [The year 2005 was based on a Hindu calendar used by the Dogra maharajas and their initial successor regime in Indian J&K.]

'Chronology of Governors', *Raj Bhawan J&K*, http://jkrajbhawan.nic.in/His%20Excellency/previous.htm [accessed 24 March 2010].

*Jammu & Kashmir 1947–50. An Account of Aactivities of First Three Years of Sheikh Abdullah's Government*, Jammu, Government of Jammu and Kashmir?, The Ranbir Government Press, 1951.

### Pakistan

'A Guide to Performance Evaluation', Director General, Pakistan Public Administration Research Centre, Islamabad, 2004, www.pakistan.gov.pk/divisions/establishment-division/media/PEGuide.pdf [accessed 20 March 2009].

'Agricultural Loans Scheme-Comprehensive Circular', *State Bank of Pakistan*, www.sbp.org.pk/acd/C2096.htm [accessed 11 March 2009].

Ali, Mohamad, *All Parties Conference on Kashmir 1955, Opening Speech by The Hon'ble* [sic] *Mr Mohamad* [sic] *Ali, Prime Minister of Pakistan*, Karachi, Ferozsons, 1956?.

'Article 257, Provision relating to the State of Jammu and Kashmir, Part XII (contd), Miscellaneous, Chapter 4. General', *The Constitution of the Islamic Republic of Pakistan*, www.pakistani.org/pakistan/constitution/part12.ch4.html [accessed 18 March 2009].

*Census of Azad Kashmir, 1961, District Census Report, Muzaffarabad District*, Rawalpindi, Government of Pakistan Press, 1964.

# BIBLIOGRAPHY

*Federal Government's Contribution to the progress of Azad Kashmir*, Islamabad, Ministry of Information & Broadcasting, Government of Pakistan, 1976.

'Fourth Schedule [Article 70 (4)] Legislative Lists', *The Constitution of the Islamic Republic of Pakistan*, www.pakistani.org/pakistan/constitution/schedules/schedule4.html [accessed 28 February 2010].

Gurmani, M.A., *Kashmir: A Survey*, Rawalpindi?, Public Relations Directorate, Ministry of Kashmir, Government of Pakistan, 1952?.

*Inside Occupied Kashmir Today*, Washington DC, Information Division, Embassy of Pakistan, 1965.

'Job Description Section Officer. (*Kashmir*)' in an unnamed, undated document containing various position descriptions, *Kashmir Affairs Division*, www.pakistan.gov.pk/divisions/kashmiraffairs-division/media/WorkDistribution.pdf [accessed 20 March 2009].

'Kashmir Dispute: Background', *Ministry of Foreign Affairs, Pakistan, website*, undated, www.mofa.gov.pk/Pages/Brief.htm [accessed 8 August 2008].

'Kashmir Dispute: Background', *Ministry of Foreign Affairs, Pakistan*, website, undated, www.mofa.gov.pk/Pages/Brief.htm [accessed 19 March 2010].

*Kashmir Questions. Extracts from Sir Zafrulla Khan's Speech Before the Security Council, February 1950*, New York, Pakistan Permanent Delegation to the United Nations, 1950.

Letter from M.A. Gurmani to 'Chaudhry Ghulam Abbas Sahib, 26th May, 1950', contained in 1950: File No. 13 (10)-Pris/50, Government of Pakistan, Cabinet Secretariat, 'Correspondence with the Supreme Head of Azad Kashmir Movement', p. 83, held at the National Documentation Centre, Cabinet Building, Islamabad, Pakistan [file accessed on 27–29 December 2006].

'Liberalization of Telecom Sector In AJK & NAs', in *Annual Report 2008*, Pakistan Telecommunication Authority, Islamabad, 2008, Chapter 7, www.pta.gov.pk/annual-reports/annrep0708/ch_07.pdf [accessed 23 March 2009].

*Ministry of Kashmir Affairs and Gilgit-Baltistan* website, www.kana.gov.pk/ [accessed 25 March 2010].

'Part I, Introductory', *The Constitution of the Islamic Republic of Pakistan*, www.pakistani.org/pakistan/constitution/part1.html [accessed 3 March 2010].

*Population Census of Azad Kashmir 1972. District Census Report Poonch*, Islamabad, Ministry of Interior, States and Frontier Regions, 1972.

*Reports of the Advisory Panels for the Fourth Five-Year Plan*, Volume II, Islamabad, Planning Commission, Government of Pakistan, July 1970.

Saeed, Malik Muhammad, Chief Editor, *The All Pakistan Legal Decisions. Azad J&K High Court*, Volume XLI, Lahore, PLD Publishers, 1989.

———, Chief Editor, *The All Pakistan Legal Decisions. Azad J&K Supreme Court*, Volume XLII, Lahore, PLD Publishers, 1990.

'Special Committee of the Parliament on Kashmir', *National Assembly of Pakistan*, www.na.gov.pk/sp_kashmir.html [accessed 11 November 2010].

*Story of Kashmir*, Karachi, Revised Edition, The Department of Films and Publications, Government of Pakistan, 1968.

'Table No. 9, Country Wise Workers' Remittances', *State Bank of Pakistan*, www.sbp.org.pk/Ecodata/Homeremit_arch.xls [accessed 11 March 2009].

'Telecom Deregulation In Azad Jammu & Kashmir And Northern Areas', Pakistan Telecommunication Authority, in *Annual Report 2007*, Pakistan Telecommunication Au-

# BIBLIOGRAPHY

thority, Islamabad, 2007, Chapter 7, www.pta.gov.pk/annual-reports/annrep0607/chapter_8.pdf [accessed 23 March 2009].

*The Constitution of the Republic of Pakistan*, Karachi, Government of Pakistan, 1962.

*The Constitution of the Islamic Republic of Pakistan*, www.pakistani.org/pakistan/constitution/part12.ch4.html [accessed 18 March 2009].

*The Kashmir Dispute and Its Solution. Statement in Parliament by M.A. Gurmani*, Karachi, Government of Pakistan, 1951.

*1998 Census Report of Azad Kashmir*, Islamabad, Population Census Organization, Statistics Division, Government of Pakistan, July 2001.

## Other

Confidential U.S. State Department Central Files, India: Internal Affairs, 1945–1949, Part I, *Political, Governmental, and National Defense Affairs*, Frederick, Maryland, University Publications of America, Reel Numbers 9–10.

*Constitutional Relations Between Britain and India, The Transfer of Power 1942–7*, Volume X, 22 March–30 May 1947, London, Nicholas Mansergh, Editor-in-Chief, Her Majesty's Stationery Office, 1981.

———, Volume XI, 31 May–7 July 1947, 1982.

———, Volume XII, 8 July–15 August 1947, 1983.

'Internally Displaced People: Exiled in their Homeland', *United Nations Office for the Co-ordination of Humanitarian Affairs*, 2007?, http://ochaonline.un.org/NewsInFocus/InternallyDisplacedPeopleIDPs/tabid/5132/language/en-US/Default.aspx [accessed 15 September 2009].

'Kashmir: New Hopes for Agreement on Future Autonomy', *Australian Foreign Affairs Record*, Volume 45, Number 8, Canberra, August 1974.

'Report submitted by the United Nations Representative for India and Pakistan, Sir Owen Dixon, to the Security Council, 15 September 1950', in Hasan, Sarwar K., and Hasan, Zubeida, Editors, *Documents on the Foreign Relations of Pakistan. The Kashmir Question*, Karachi, Pakistan Institute of International Relations, 1966.

'Simla Agreement 2 July 1972', *Kashmir Information Network*, www.kashmir-information.com/LegalDocs/SimlaAgreement.html [accessed 20 March 2010].

'The Indus Waters Treaty', *The Henry L. Stimson Center*, www.stimson.org/southasia/?sn=sa20020116300 [accessed 8 October 2008].

United Nations Commission for India and Pakistan, *Report of the Sub-committee on Western Kashmir*, New York, Unpublished Restricted Document, 31 March 1949.

'United Nations Security Council Official Records, 796th Meeting, 9 October 1957', *UNdemocracy*, www.undemocracy.com/S-PV-796.pdf [accessed 10 March 2010].

## Reference Documents and Collected Works

Afzal, M. Rafique, Editor, *Selected Speeches and Statements of the Quaid-i-Azam Mohammad Ali Jinnah (1911–34 and 1947–48)*, Lahore, Research Society of Pakistan, University of the Punjab, 1966.

———, *Speeches and Statements of Quaid-i-Millat Liaquat Ali Khan (1941–51)*, Lahore, Research Society of Pakistan, University of the Punjab, 1967.

Agarwal, S.P., General Editor, *Modern History of Jammu and Kashmir*, Volume 2, New Delhi, Concept Publishing, 1995.

# BIBLIOGRAPHY

Alam, Jawaid, Editor, *Jammu and Kashmir 1949–64: Select Correspondence between Jawaharlal Nehru and Karan Singh*, New Delhi, Penguin Viking, 2006.

Bakshi, S.R., *Kashmir Through Ages—4, Kashmir: Political Problems*, New Delhi, Sarup & Sons, 1997.

Chopra, P.N., Chief Editor, *The Collected Works of Sardar Vallabhbhai Patel*, Delhi, Volume XII, Konark Publishers, 1998.

Das, Durga, Editor, *Sardar Patel's Correspondence 1945–50*, Volume I, *New Light on Kashmir*, Ahmedabad, Navajivan Publishing House, 1971.

Deora, M.S., and R, Grover, Editors, *Documents on Kashmir Problem*, Volume X, New Delhi, Discovery Publishing House, 1991. Gopal, S., General Editor, *Selected Works of Jawaharlal Nehru*, Volume 3–6, New Delhi, Jawaharlal Nehru Memorial Fund, 1985–1987.

Grover, Verinder and Ranjana Arora, Editors, *Political System in Pakistan, Volume 10, Political Events in Pakistan: A Chronology*, New Delhi, Deep & Deep, 1995.

Guimbretiere, A., and Mohibul Hasan, 'Kashmir', in Van Danzel, Lewis and Pellat, Editors, *The Encyclopedia of Islam*, Volume IV, Leiden, E.J. Brill, 1978.

Hasan, Sarwar K., and Zubeida Hasan, Editors, *Documents on the Foreign Relations of Pakistan. The Kashmir Question*, Karachi, Pakistan Institute of International Relations, 1966.

Hussain, Mirza Shafique, Compiler, *History of Kashmir: A Study in Documents 1916–1939*, Islamabad, National Institute of Historical and Cultural Research, 1992.

Jehu, I.S., Editor, *The India and Pakistan Year Book 1948*, Bombay, Bennett, Coleman & Co., 1948.

Jehu, I.S., *The India & Pakistan Year Book and Who's Who 1949*, Bombay, Bennett, Coleman & Co., 1950?.

*Keesing's Record of World Events (formerly Keesing's Contemporary Archives)*, London, Longman.

Lakhanpal, P.L., *Essential Documents and Notes on Kashmir Dispute*, Delhi, International Books, Second Edition, 1965.

Mirza, Sarfaraz Hussain, Editor, *Pakistan-India Kashmir Dispute. A Chronology of Important Events (1947–1990)*, Lahore, Pakistan Study Centre, 1994.

Nehru, Jawaharlal, *India's Foreign Policy, Selected Speeches, September 1946—April 1961*, New Delhi, Publications Division, Ministry of Information and Broadcasting, Government of India, 1961.

———, 'Our Pledge To Kashmir', Speech in Parliament, New Delhi, 7 August, 1952, in *Jawaharlal Nehru's Speeches 1949–1953*, The Publications Division, Ministry of Information and Broadcasting, Government of India, Delhi, 1954.

Parthasarathi, G., General Editor, *Jawaharlal Nehru: Letters to Chief Ministers 1947–1964*, New Delhi, Jawaharlal Nehru Memorial Fund, 1985.

Pickthall, Marmaduke, Translator, *The Meaning of the Glorious Koran*, New York, Alfred A. Knopf, 1930 [First published by Everyman's Library, 1909 and 1992].

Poplai, S.L., Editor, *India: 1947–50, Volume I, Internal Affairs*, London, Oxford University Press, 1959.

*Powell Collection, Papers and Correspondence, dated 1947–1960, of Richard Powell (1889–1961), Indian Police Force 1908–1947, Inspector-General of Police Jammu and Kashmir 1946–1947*, Indian Office Records, MSS EUR D862 [accessed at National Document Centre, Islamabad, December 2004]. In particular:

——— Author unknown [HG Scott?], 'Jammu and Kashmir State 1947';

# BIBLIOGRAPHY

——— 'Copy of Note by R.C. Kak, Jammu and Kashmir State in 1946–47, Part VII. 2-Maharaja Harisingh [sic]';

——— HGS, 'Poonch 1937—1947'.

Sharma S.R., and S.R. Bakshi, Editors, *Encyclopedia of Pakistan*, Volumes 5, New Delhi, Rima Publishing, 1994.

Sharma, Suresh K., and S.R. Bakshi, Editors, *Encyclopedia of Kashmir*, Volumes 10, New Delhi, Anmol Publications, 1995.

———, Editors, *Encyclopedia of Kashmir*, Volume 10, *Economic Life of Kashmir*, New Delhi, Anmol Publications, 1995.

Sharma, Usha, Editor, *Heritage of Jammu, Kashmir and Ladakh*, Volumes 5, New Delhi, Radha Publications, 1996.

*The Collected Works of Mahatma Gandhi*, Volume LXXXIX (1 August 1947-November 10, 1947), New Delhi, Publications Division, Ministry of Information and Broadcasting, Government of India, 1983.

———, Volume XC (11 November 1947–30 January 1948), 1984.

*The JKLF Roadmap For Peace & Prosperity in South Asia*, Jammu Kashmir Liberation Front, Rawalpindi?, 2003.

Zaidi, Z.H., Editor-in-Chief, *Quaid-i-Azam Mohammad Ali Jinnah Papers*, Volume V, Islamabad, Government of Pakistan, Cabinet Division, 2000.

*Books, Chapters and Pamphlets*

Abbas, Hasan, *Pakistan's Drift into Extremism: Allah, the Army and America's War on Terror*, Armonk, NY, M.E. Sharpe, 2004.

Abdullah, Sheikh Mohammad, *Flames of the Chinar* [Khushwant Singh, Translator], New Delhi, Viking, 1993.

Ahmad, Mushtaq, *The Economy of Pakistan*, Karachi, Pakistan Institute of International Affairs, 1950.

Akbar, M.J., *Kashmir: Behind the Vale*, New Delhi, Viking, 1991.

Akhtar, Jamna Das, *Political Conspiracies in Pakistan Liaquat Ali's Murder to Ayub Khan's Exit*, Delhi, Punjabi Pustak Bhandar, 1969.

Ali, Chaudhri Muhammad, *The Emergence of Pakistan*, New York, Columbia University Press, 1967.

Amin, Tahir, *Mass Resistance in Kashmir, Origins, Evolution, Options*, Islamabad, Institute of Policy Studies, 1995.

Anderson, Benedict, *Imagined Communities: Reflections on the Origin and Spread of Nationalism*, London, Verso, 1963.

Ayub Khan, Muhammad, *see under* Khan, Muhammad Ayub.

Aziz, Mir Abdul, *Freedom Struggle in Kashmir*, Lahore, Research Society of Pakistan, University of the Punjab, 2000.

Bamzai, Prithivi Nath Kaul, *A History of Kashmir*, Delhi, Metropolitan Book Co., 1962.

———, 'Introduction', in Koul, Pandit Anand, *Geography of the Jammu and Kashmir State*, Mirpur, Verinag Publishers, 1991.

Banerji, J.N., *I Report on Kashmir*, Calcutta, The Republic Publications, 1948?.

Bates, Charles Ellison, Compiler, *A Gazetteer of Kashmir*, Mirpur, Verinag Publishers, Reprinted [No Publication Date; First Published 1873?].

## BIBLIOGRAPHY

Bazaz, Prem Nath, *Azad Kashmir: A Democratic Socialist Conception*, Mirpur, Verinag Publishers, 1992 [First Published by Lahore, Ferozsons, 1951].

———, *Inside Kashmir*, Mirpur, Verinag Publishers, 1987 [First Published by Kashmir Pub. [sic] Company, Srinagar, 1941].

———, *The History of Struggle for Freedom in Kashmir*, Karachi, National Book Foundation, 1976 [First Published by Kashmir Pub.[sic] Company, New Delhi, 1954].

———, *Truth About Kashmir*, Delhi, The Kashmir Democratic Union, 1950.

Bedi, B.P.L., and Freda Bedi, *Sheikh Abdulla* [sic]. *His Life and Ideals*, Srinagar [No Publisher Details], 1949.

Beg, Aziz, *Captive Kashmir*, Lahore, Allied Business Corporation, 1957.

Beg, Mirza Mohammad Afzal, 'On the Way to Golden Harvests—Agricultural Reforms in Kashmir' [First Published in Jammu, 1950], in Berindranath, Dewan, 'Azad Kashmir, Problems and Perspectives', article from *Mainstream*, New Delhi, Published as a Separate Pamphlet, No Publication Details, 1968?.

Behera, Navnita Chadha, *Demystifying Kashmir*, Washington DC, Brookings Institution Press, 2006.

Birdwood, Lord, *Two Nations and Kashmir*, London, Robert Hale, 1956.

Brecher, Michael, *The Struggle for Kashmir*, New York, Oxford University Press, 1953.

Chand, Attar, *Islamic Nations and Kashmir Problem*, Delhi, Raj Publications, 1994.

———, *Pakistan Terrorism in Punjab & Kashmir*, Delhi, Amar Prakashan, 1993?.

Chari, A.S.R., *The Kashmir Problem*, New Delhi, M. Kalimulla, 1965.

Chopra, P.N., Chief Editor, *India's Struggle for Freedom: Role of Associated Movements*, Volume 4, Delhi, Agam Prakashan, 1985.

Chopra, V.D. and M. Rasgotra, Editors, *Genesis of Regional Conflicts: Kashmir, Afghanistan, West Asia, Cambodia, Chechnya*, New Delhi, Gyan Publishing, 1995.

Cloughley, Brian, *A History of the Pakistan Army*, Oxford University Press, Second Edition, 2000.

Cohen, Maurice, *Thunder over Kashmir*, Hyderabad, Orient Longman, 1955.

Cohen, Stephen P., *The Indian Army*, Delhi, Oxford University Press, 1990.

———, *The Pakistan Army*, Berkeley, University of California Press, 1984.

———, *The Idea of Pakistan*, Lahore, Vanguard, 2005.

Copland, Ian, 'The Abdullah Factor: Kashmiri Muslims and the Crisis of 1947', in D.A. Low, Editor, *The Political Inheritance of Pakistan*, Basingstoke, Macmillan, 1991.

———, *The Princes in the Endgame of Empire, 1917–1947*, Cambridge University Press, 1997.

Coupland, Sir Reginald, *India: A Re-Statement*, London, Oxford University Press, 1945.

Dani, Ahmad Hasan, *History of Northern Areas of Pakistan*, Islamabad, National Institute of Historical and Cultural Research, 1991.

Dar, Mohammad Ali, *Trade and Commerce During Dogra Rule in Kashmir (A.D. 1846–1947)*, Faridabad, Om Publications, 1999.

Dawson, Pauline, *The Peacekeepers of Kashmir*, London, Hurst & Company, 1994.

De Mhaffe, A., *Road to Kashmir*, Lahore, Ripon Printing Press, 1948?.

Dhar, S.N., *Kashmir: Eden of the East*, Allahabad, Kitab Mahal, 1945.

Evans, Alexander, 'Kashmiri Exceptionalism', in T.N. Madan and Aparna Rao, Editors, *The Valley of Kashmir: The Making and Unmaking of a Composite Culture*, New Delhi, Manohar, 2008.

# BIBLIOGRAPHY

Fazili, Manzoor, *Kashmir Government and Politics*, Srinagar, Gulshan Publishers, 1982.

Fazili, Manzoor A., *Socialist Ideas & Movements in Kashmir (1919–1947)*, New Delhi, Eureka Publications, 1980.

*Five Years of Pakistan (August 1947–August 1952)*, Karachi, Pakistan Publications, 1952?.

*Free Kashmir Calling:Yih Chhuh Azad Kashmir Radio*, Muzaffarabad?, Azad Kashmir Radio, 1950?.

Ganju, M., *This is Kashmir (With Special Reference to U.N.O.)*, Delhi, S. Chand & Co, 1948.

Gilani, Syed Manzoor Hussain, *Administration of Justice in Azad Kashmir*, Rawalpindi, Nazco Art Printers, 2002.

Gilani, Syed Manzoor H., *Constitutional Development in Azad Jammu & Kashmir*, Lahore, National Book Depot, 1988.

Gilani, Justice Syed Manzoor Hussain, *The Constitution of Azad Jammu & Kashmir (In the Historical Backdrop with Corresponding Pakistan, India & Occupied Jammu and Kashmir Constitutions)*, Islamabad, National Book Foundation, 2008.

Giyasuddin, Peer, 'Main Trends of the History of the Kashmir Freedom Struggle', in Mohammad Yasin and A. Qaiyum Rafiqi, Editors, *History of the Freedom Struggle in Jammu & Kashmir*, New Delhi, Light & Life, 1980.

Gupta, C.P., *The Directory of Mirpur Mahajan Families Settled in Jammu*, Jammu, Mirpur Mahajan Sabha, 1997.

Gupta, Jyoti Bhusan Das, *Jammu and Kashmir*, The Hague, Martinus Nijhoff, 1968.

Gupta, Sisir, *Kashmir. A Study in India-Pakistan Relations*, Bombay, Asia Publishing House, 1966.

Hafizullah, Mohd., *Towards Azad Kashmir*, Lahore, Bazam-i-Froghi-i-Adab, 1948.

Hasan, Khalid, Editor, *Azadi. Kashmir Freedom Struggle 1924–1998*, Lahore, Printing Professionals, 1999.

Hassan, Khalid, 'Khurshid: A Life', Introduction to Hassan, Khalid, Editor, *K.H. Khurshid. Memories of Jinnah*, Karachi, Oxford University Press, 1990.

High Court of Judicature, Azad Jammu and Kashmir, *Verdict on Gilgit and Baltistan (Northern Area)*, Mirpur, Kashmir Human Rights Forum, 1993?.

Hewitt, Vernon, *Reclaiming the Past?*, London, Portland Books, 1995.

Hodson, H.V., *The Great Divide*, London, Hutchinson, 1969.

Hussain, Ijaz, *Kashmir Dispute. An International Law Perspective*, Islamabad, Quaid-i-Azam University, 1998.

Hutchison, J., and J. Ph. Vogel, *History of the Panjab* [sic] *Hill States*, Himachal Pradesh, Department of Languages, 1982.

Imrany, M.R., *Paradise Under the Shadow of Hell. India's War on Kashmir As Seen By Non-Muslims and Neutral Observers*, Lahore, No Publisher Details, 1948.

*Inside Indian-Held Kashmir*, Muzaffarabad, Kashmir Publications, 1960?.

Iqbal, S.M., Editor, *The Culture of Kashmir*, Karachi, Wahid Publications, 1991.

Irfani, Suroosh, Editor, *Fifty Years of the Kashmir Dispute*, Muzaffarabad, University of Azad Jammu and Kashmir, 1997.

Islam, Ziaul, *The Revolution in Kashmir*, Karachi, Pakistan Publishers, 1948.

Izzatullah, Shaikh, *Kashmir-Plebiscite* [sic], Lahore, Iqbal Company, 1949?.

Jammu and Kashmir Editors' Conference, *The Neglected and Ignored Press of Azad Kashmir*, Rawalpindi, [published by] Kh. Sanaullah But [sic], 1956.

415

# BIBLIOGRAPHY

*Jammu and Kashmir Pamphlets, 1964–1968*, No Publication Details. [This is a collection of pamphlets bound into a single volume by Sydney University. It is held in the Fisher Library, University of Sydney.]

Jeffrey, Robin, Editor, *People, Princes and Paramount Power*, Delhi, Oxford University Press, 1978.

Jha, Prem Shankar, *Kashmir, 1947. Rival Versions of History*, Delhi, Oxford University Press, 1996.

Kapur, M.L., *History and Culture of Kashmir*, Jammu, Kashmir History Publications, 1976.

———, *History of Jammu and Kashmir State, Volume I, The Making of the State*, Jammu, Kashmir History Publications, 1980.

———, Editor, *Maharaja Hari Singh (1895–1961)*, New Delhi, Har-Anand Publications, 1995.

Karaka, D.F., *Betrayal in India*, London, Victor Gollancz, 1950.

'Kashmir—A Statistical Survey', in Suresh K. Sharma and S.R. Bakshi, Editors, *Encyclopedia of Kashmir*, Volume 10, *Economic Life of Kashmir*, New Delhi, Anmol Publications, 1995.

*Kashmir Before Accession*, Lahore, No Publisher Details [Printed by the Superintendent, Government Printing, West Punjab], 1948.

*Kashmir in [The] Security Council*, Srinagar, Lalla Rookh Publications, 1953.

*Kashmir Slides Into Slavery. India Defies United Nations*, Muzaffarabad, Kashmir Publications, 1965.

Kaul, Santosh, *Freedom Struggle In Jammu and Kashmir*, New Delhi, Anmol Publications, 1990.

Kennedy, Charles H., *Bureaucracy in Pakistan*, Karachi, Oxford University Press, 1987.

*Keys to Kashmir*, Srinagar, Lalla Rookh, 1957.

Khan, Amanullah, *Free Kashmir*, No Publisher Details, 1970.

Khan, G.H., *Freedom Movement in Kashmir 1931–1940*, New Delhi, Light & Life, 1980.

Khan, Mohammad Ishaq, *Experiencing Islam*, New Delhi, Sterling Publishers, 1997.

———, *History of Srinagar 1846–1947. A Study in Socio-Cultural Change*, Srinagar, Aamir Publications, 1978.

———, *Kashmir's Transition to Islam: The Role of Muslim Rishis*, New Delhi, Manohar, 1994.

———, *Perspectives on Kashmir: Historical Dimensions*, Srinagar, Gulshan Publishers, 1983.

———, 'The Significance of the Dargah of Hazratbal in the Socio-Religious and Political Life of Kashmiri Muslims', in Christian W. Troll, Editor, *Muslim Shrines in India*, Delhi, Oxford University Press, 1989.

Khan, Major-General (Retired) Muhammad Akbar, *Raiders in Kashmir*, Lahore, Jang Publishers, 1992.

Khan, Muhammad Ayub, *Friends Not Masters. A Political Autobiography*, London, Oxford University Press, 1967.

Khan, Raja Abbas, *Real Azad Kashmir*, Srinagar, Anu Kashmir Publications, 1969.

Khan, Sardar M. Ibrahim, *The Kashmir Saga*, Lahore, Ripon Printing Press, 1965.

———, *The Kashmir Saga*, Mirpur, Verinag Publishers, Second Edition, 1990.

Khan, Sardar Muhammad Abdul Qayyum, *The Kashmir Case*, Rawalpindi?, Al-Mujahid Academy?, 1992.

———, *In Search of Freedom*, Volume I, No Publication Details, 1994?.

Korbel, Josef, *Danger in Kashmir*, Princeton University Press, Revised Edition, 1966 [First Edition, 1954].

# BIBLIOGRAPHY

Koul, Pandit Anand, *Geography of the Jammu and Kashmir State*, No Publisher Details, Printed. by Thacker, Spink & Co., Calcutta, Second Edition, 1925 [First Published 1913].

———, *Geography of the Jammu & Kashmir State*, Mirpur, Verinag Publishers, 1991 [No Previous Publication Details but a Reprint of the Second Edition, 1925; see Record Immediately Above].

Lamb, Alastair, *Birth of a Tragedy. Kashmir 1947*, Karachi, Oxford University Press, 1994.

———, *Incomplete Partition: The Genesis of the Kashmir Dispute 1947–1948*, Hertingfordbury, Roxford Books, 1997.

———, *Kashmir, A Disputed Legacy, 1846–1990*, Karachi, Oxford University Press, Second Impression, 1994.

MacMunn, Lieutenant-General Sir George, *The Indian States and Princes*, London, Jarrolds, 1936.

Madhok, Balraj, *Kashmir: Centre of New Alignments*, New Delhi, Deepak Prakashan, 1963.

Mahajan, Mehr Chand, *Looking Back*, New Delhi, Har-Anand Publications, 1994 [First Published 1963?].

Members of the Special Committee for Oversight of Elections 2006, Peoples [sic] Muslim League, *Azad Kashmir Elections Hijacked. Why?*, Jammu & Kashmir Peoples Muslim League, 2006.

Menon, V.P., *The Story of the Integration of the Indian States*, Bombay, Orient Longman, 1961.

Mirza, Lieutenant-Colonel (Retired) M.A. Haq, Sher-i-Jang, *The Withering Chinar*, Islamabad, Institute of Policy Studies, 1991?.

Mughal, Amirullah Khan, and Ch. Mukhtar, Hussain Compilers, *The Judicial System in Azad Jammu & Kashmir (As Modified up to 30-4-1994)*, Muzaffarabad, National Book Depot, 1994.

Musharraf, Pervez, *In the Line of Fire: A Memoir*, New York, Free Press, 2006.

Nehru, Pandit Jawaharlal, 'Introductory Essay on Kashmir', in S.N. Dhar, *Kashmir: Eden of the East*, Allahabad, Kitab Mahal, 1945.

Noorani, A.G., *The Kashmir Question*, Bombay, Manaktalas, 1964.

*Nund Rishi. Unity in Diversity* [B.N. Parimoo, Translator], Srinagar, J&K Academy of Art, Culture and Languages, 1984.

*Pakistan 1953–1954*, Karachi, Pakistan Publications, 1954?.

*Pakistan 1955–1956*, Karachi, Pakistan Publications, 1956.

Panikkar, K.M., *Indian States*, Second Edition, Bombay, Oxford University Press, 1943.

———, *The Founding of the Kashmir State. A Biography of Maharaja Gulab Singh, 1792–1858*, London, George Allen & Unwin, 1953.

Pirzada, Syed Sharifuddin, *Foundations of Pakistan. All-India Muslim League Documents: 1906–1947*, New Delhi, Metropolitan Book Comapany, 1982.

Pithawalla, Maneck B., *An Introduction to Kashmir. Its Geology and Geography*, Muzaffarabad, Kashmir Publications, 1953.

Puri, Balraj, *Jammu—A Clue to Kashmir Triangle*, Delhi, self-published, 1966.

———, *Jammu and Kashmir. Triumph and Tragedy of Indian Federalisation*, New Delhi, Sterling Publishers, 1981.

———, *Simmering Volcano*, New Delhi, Sterling Publishers, 1983.

Qasim, Mir, *My Life and Times*, New Delhi, Allied Publishers, 1992.

Quraishi, Zaheer Masood, *Elections & State Politics of India (A Case-Study of Kashmir)*, Delhi, Sundeep Prakashan, 1979.

# BIBLIOGRAPHY

Rai, Mridu, *Hindu Rulers, Muslim Subjects: Islam, Rights and the History of Kashmir*, London, Hurst & Company, 2004.

Raina, N.N., *Kashmir Politics and Imperialist Manoeuvres 1846–1980*, New Delhi, Patriot Publishers, 1988.

Rashid, Rao A., *The Smiling Face of Azad Kashmir*, Karachi, Din Muhammadi Press, 1963.

Raza, Maroof, *Wars and No Peace Over Kashmir*, New Delhi, Lancer Publishers, 1996.

Rushbrook Williams, L.F., *The State of Pakistan*, Second Edition (Revised), London, Faber and Faber, 1966.

Sahni, J.N., *The Kashmir Problem*, New Delhi, The Foreign Relations Society of India, 1951.

Samad, Yunus, *A Nation in Turmoil. Nationalism and Ethnicity in Pakistan, 1937–1958*, New Delhi, Sage Publications, 1995.

Sarabhai, Mridula, *Letters from Constitution House*, Muzaffarabad, Kashmir Publications, 1957?.

Saraf, Muhammad Yusuf, *Kashmiris Fight—For Freedom*, Volume I (1819–1946), Lahore, Ferozsons, 1977; Volume II (1947–1978), Lahore, Ferozsons, 1979.

Sayeed, Khalid B., *The Political System of Pakistan*, Boston, Houghton Mifflin, 1967.

Saxena, H.L., *The Tragedy of Kashmir*, New Delhi, Nationalist Publishers, 1975.

Schechtman, Joseph, *The Refugee in the World: Displacement and Integration*, New York, A.S. Barnes, 1963.

Schofield, Victoria, *Kashmir in Conflict*, London, I.B. Tauris, 2000.

———, *Kashmir in the Crossfire*, London, I.B. Tauris, 1996.

Sen, Lt. General L.P., *Slender was the Thread*, Hyderabad, Orient Longman, 1988 [First Published 1969].

Sharma, B.L., *Kashmir Awakes*, Delhi, Vikas Publications, 1971.

Sharma, P.N., *Inside Pak Occupied Kashmir*, New Delhi, Delhi Press, 1958?.

Singh, Jaswant, *Jammu and Kashmir. Political and Constitutional Development*, New Delhi, Har-Anand Publications, 1996.

Singh, Jasjit, Editor, *Pakistan Occupied Kashmir Under the Jackboot*, New Delhi, Siddhi Books, 1995.

Singh, Karan, *Autobiography*, Delhi, Oxford University Press, 1994 [First Published in Two Volumes: *Heir Apparent, An Autobiography*, Delhi, Oxford University Press, 1982; *Sadar-I-Risayat, An Autobiography*, Volume II (1953–1967), Delhi, Oxford University Press, 1985].

Singh, Major K. Brahma, *History of Jammu and Kashmir Rifles 1820–1956*, New Delhi, Lancer International, 1990.

Singh, Nirmal K., *Inter-Communal Relations in Jammu & Kashmir (1846 to 1931)*, Jammu, Jay Kay Book House, 1991.

Spate, O.H.K. and Learmonth, A.T.A., *India and Pakistan. A General and Regional Geography* London?, Methuen, Revised Third Edition, 1967.

Stephens, Ian, *Horned Moon. An Account of a Journey through Pakistan, Kashmir, and Afghanistan*, London, Chatto & Windus, 1953.

———, *Pakistan*, London, Ernest Benn, Second (Revised) Edition, 1964.

*Struggle for the Right of Self Determination*, Mirpur, Jummu [sic] Kashmir Liberation League, 1998.

Sufi, G.M.D., *Islamic Culture in Kashmir*, New Delhi, Light & Life, 1979.

———, *Kashir. Being a History of Kashmir From the Earliest Times to Our Own*, Volume I, Lahore, University of Punjab, 1948.

# BIBLIOGRAPHY

———, Volume II, 1949.
Suharwardy, A.H., *Kashmir. The Incredible Freedom-Fight*, Lahore, Jang Publishers, 1991.
———, *Tragedy in Kashmir*, Lahore, Wajidalis, 1983.
Suleri, Abid Qaiyum and Kevin Savage, *HPG Background Paper-Remittances in Crises: a Case Study from Pakistan*, Overseas Development Institute, London, November 2006, www.odi.org.uk/resources/hpg-publications/background-papers/2006/remittances-crises-pakistan.pdf [accessed 13 January 2007].
Symonds, Richard, *The Making of Pakistan*, London, Faber and Faber, 1950.
———, *In the Margins of Independence; A Relief Worker in India and Pakistan (1941–1949)*, Karachi, Oxford University Press, 2001.
Talbot, Ian, *Pakistan: A Modern History*, London, Hurst & Company, 1998; Third Edition, 2009.
Tariq, Ch. Mohammad Sharif, *Kashmir in Strangulation*, Mirpur, self-published, 1991.
Taseer, C. Bilqees, *The Kashmir of Sheikh Muhammad Abdullah*, Lahore, Ferozsons, 1986.
*The Kashmir Question*, Lucknow, The Lucknow University, 1950.
*The Testament of Sheikh Abdullah*, New Delhi, Palit and Palit, 1974.
Thomas, Raju G.C., Editor, *Perspectives on Kashmir. The Roots of Conflict in South Asia*, Boulder, Westview Press, 1992. In particular:
——— Noorani, A.G., 'The Betrayal of Kashmir: Pakistan's Duplicity and India's Complicity';
——— Punjabi, Riyaz, 'Kashmir: The Bruised Identity';
——— Rizvi, Gowher, 'India, Pakistan, and the Kashmir Problem, 1947–1972';
——— Rose, Leo E., 'The Politics of Azad Kashmir'.
Tikku, Somnath, *Kashmir Speaking*, Srinagar, Raina's News Agency, 1946?.
Trumbull, Robert, *As I See India*, London, Cassell, 1957.
Tyndale Biscoe, C.E., *Kashmir in Sunlight & Shade*, London, Seeley Service, Second Edition, 1925 [First Published 1921?].
———, *Tyndale-Biscoe of Kashmir. An Autobiography*, London, Seeley Service, 1951?.
Wani, G.A., *Kashmir History and Politics 1846–1994. A Select Annotated Bibliography*, Second Edition, Srinagar, Tariq Enterprises, 1996.
Weekes, Richard V., *Pakistan. Birth and Growth of a Muslim Nation*, Princeton, D. Van Nostrand, 1964.
Whitehead, Andrew, *A Mission in Kashmir*, New Delhi, Penguin Viking, 2007.
*Whither Kashmir?*, London, The Diplomatic Press and Publishing Company, 1950.
Wilder, Andrew, *Perceptions of the Pakistan Earthquake Response: Humanitarian Agenda 2015 Pakistan Country Study*, Feinstein International Center, Medford, 2008.
Wirsing, Robert, *India, Pakistan, and the Kashmir Dispute*, Calcutta, Rupa & Company, 1995.
Yasin, Mohammad and Qaiyum A. Rafiqi, Editors, *History of the Freedom Struggle in Jammu & Kashmir*, New Delhi, Light & Life, 1980.
Zaheer, Hasan, *The Times and Trials of the Rawalpindi Conspiracy 1951*, Karachi, Oxford University Press, 1998.
*1947–1997 The Kashmir Dispute at Fifty: Charting Paths to Peace*, New York, Kashmir Study Group, 1997.

# BIBLIOGRAPHY

*Articles and Periodicals*

Ahmed, Mughees, 'Role of *Biradari* in Punjab Politics', *Journal of Research (Humanities)*, Volume 27, 2007.
Alexander, Horace, 'India-Pakistan I', *The Spectator*, Issue 180, London, 16 January 1948.
'All Jammu & Kashmir Muslim Conference (AJKMC)', *Global Security*, www.globalsecurity.org/military/world/pakistan/ajkmc.htm [accessed 10 November 2005].
Ankit, Rakesh, 'The Forgotten Soldier of Kashmir', *Epilogue*, 12 May 2010, www.epilogue.in/detailnews.aspx?mwid=781 [accessed 1 August 2010].
Aslam, Muhammad, 'Industrialization in Azad Kashmir—An Assessment', *Economic Review*, Volume 10, Number 11, November 1979.
'"Azad Kashmir" is Neither Azad nor Kashmiri', *Organiser*, New Delhi, Volume 19, Number 7, 26 September 1965.
Aziz, Mir Abdul, 'Azad Kashmir Government: A Chronology', *The Muslim*, Islamabad, 13 August 1996.
Ballard, Roger, 'Kashmir Crisis: View from Mirpur', *Economic & Political Weekly*, Bombay, 2–9 March 1991.
Baid, Samuel, 'Politics in "Azad Kashmir"', in Jasjit Singh, Editor, *Pakistan Occupied Kashmir Under the Jackboot*, New Delhi, Siddhi Books, 1995.
Baid, Samuel, 'Self-Determination for Kashmiris: A Camouflage for Pak's [sic] own Claim', *Strategic Analysis*, Volume 13, Number 3, June 1990.
Bangroo, B.K., 'Pakistan Occupied Kashmir: People In Turmoil', *Onlooker*, 15 May 1986.
Bhat, Roop Krishen, 'The Plebiscite Front: It's [sic] Organisation, Strategy and Role in Kashmir's Politics', *Political Science Review*, Volume 10, Numbers 3–4, 1971.
Bradnock, Robert W., *Kashmir: Paths to Peace*, London, Chatham House, 2010.
Clark, William, 'A Journey to "Free Kashmir"', *The Listener*, Volume 51, 20 May 1954.
Cloughley, Brian, 'Pakistan's Army and National Stability', *Pakistan Security Research Unit*, Brief Number 47, 22nd April 2009, http://spaces.brad.ac.uk:8080/download/attachments/748/Brief+47.pdf [accessed 22 May 2009].
Coll, Steve, 'The Back Channel', *The New Yorker*, 2 March 2009.
*Contemporary South Asia*, Volume 4 [Kashmir Special Issue], Number 1, March 1995.
Copland, Ian, 'Islam and Political Mobilization in Kashmir, 1931–34', *Pacific Affairs*, Volume 54, Number 2, 1981.
———, 'The Princely States, the Muslim League, and the Partition of India in 1947', *The International History Review*, Volume XIII, Number 1, February 1991.
Dehlvi, Sadia, 'Conversation [with Sardar Qayyum]: "We Want India to Attack Us ... That Will Decide Matters For Ever"', *Sunday*, 9–15 February 1986.
Evans, Alexander, 'Kashmir: A Tale of Two Valleys', *Asian Affairs*, Volume XXXVI, Number 1, March 2005.
Evans, Alexander, 'The Kashmir Insurgency: As Bad as it Gets', *Small Wars & Insurgencies*, Volume 11, Number 1, 2000.
Fair, C. Christine, 'Who Are Pakistan's Militants and Their Families?', *Terrorism and Political Violence*, Volume 20, Number 1, January 2008.
*Frontline*, Madras/Chennai.
Gill, K.P.S., 'J&K: Shifting Strategy of Subversion', *South Asia Terrorism Portal*, South Asia Intelligence Review, Volume 2, Number 33, 1 March 2004, www.satp.org/satporgtp/sair/Archives/2_33.htm [accessed 24 March 2010].

# BIBLIOGRAPHY

Hardgrave, Robert L., Editor, 'Kashmir 1947: Burdens of the Past, Options for the Future—Four Perspectives', *Commonwealth & Comparative Politics*, Volume 36, Number 1, March 1998.

Hoq, Abdul, 'Azad Kashmir—Story of Repression and Tyranny', *Kashmir Scene (Srinagar)*, Volume 1, Number 6, October 1966.

Howenstein, Nicholas, 'The Jihadi Terrain in Pakistan: An Introduction to the Sunni Jihadi Groups in Pakistan and Kashmir', Research Report 1, *Pakistan Security Research Unit*, 5 February 2008, http://spaces.brad.ac.uk:8080/download/attachments/748/resrep1.pdf [accessed 22 March 2009].

Husain, Ita'at, 'The Ordeal of Kashmir', *Pakistan Quarterly*, Volume 13, Numbers 2 and 3, Autumn/Winter 1965.

Hussain, R., 'The Effect of Religious, Cultural and Social Identity on Population Genetic Structure among Muslims in Pakistan', *Annals of Human Biology*, Volume 32, Number 2, March–April 2005.

'India and the War on Terrorism', *Strategic Comments*, Volume 7, Number 9, November 2001.

'Kashmir: Confrontation and Miscalculation', *International Crisis Group*, Islamabad/Brussels, Asia Report No. 35, 11 July 2002.

Kaul, H.N., 'The Azad Kashmir Cauldron', *Kashmir Today*, Volume 6, Number 2, March 1962.

Khan, Adil Hasan, 'Neelum-Jhelum Project: No Smooth Sailing For Pakistan', *Institute of Peace and Conflict Studies*, New Delhi, 21 April 2006, www.ipcs.org/article/pakistan/neelum-jhelum-project-no-smooth-sailing-for-pakistan-1996.html [accessed 24 April 2006].

Khan, Lal, *Kashmir's Ordeal*, www.marxist.com/kashmir-ordeal-six.htm [accessed 11 July 2008].

Khan, Mohammad Ishaq, 'Kashmiri Response to Islam (A.D. 1320–1586)', *Islamic Culture*, Volume 61, Number 1, January 1987.

Korbel, Josef, 'The Kashmir Dispute After Six Years', *International Organization*, Volume 7, Number 4, November 1953.

Kumar, Sumita, 'Pakistan's Jehadi Apparatus: Goals and Methods', *Strategic Analysis*, Volume 24, Number 12, 2001.

*Link*, New Delhi.

Lyon, Peter, 'Kashmir', *International Relations: Journal of David Davies Memorial Institute of International Studies*, Volume 3, Number 2, October 1966.

Mahmud, Ershad, 'Status of AJK in Political Milieu', *Policy Perspectives*, Volume 3, Number 2, July–December 2006, Institute of Policy Studies, http://ips-pk.org/content/view/449/259/ [accessed 24 February 2010].

Martin, Kingsley, 'As Pakistan Sees It', *New Statesman and Nation*, London, Issue 35, 6 March 1948.

Meraj, Zafar, 'So Close, Yet So Far', *Newsline*, January 2005, www.newsline.com.pk/NewsJan2005/sprep2jan2005.htm [accessed 11 November 2005].

Messervy, General Sir Frank, 'Kashmir', *Asiatic Review*, Volume 45, Number 161, 1949.

Mirza, M., 'Azad Kashmir Assembly: Why Dissolution?', *Pakistan Illustrated Weekly*, Volume 3, Numbers 9 and 10, 20 April 1991,

# BIBLIOGRAPHY

Mitra, Subrata K., 'Nehru's Policy Towards Kashmir: Bringing Politics Back in Again', *The Journal of Commonwealth and Comparative Politics*, Volume 35, Number 2, July 1997.

'Muttahida Jehad Council (Also known as the United Jehad Council)', *South Asia Terrorism Portal, New Statesman and Nation*, London, www.satp.org/satporgtp/countries/india/states/jandk/terrorist_outfits/mjc.htm [accessed 22 March 2010].

Noorani, A.G., 'C.P. and independent Travancore', *Frontline*, Volume 20, Issue 13, 21 June–4 July 2003.

Om, Hari, 'The Forgotten Kashmiris', *The Kashmir Times*, 12 July 1999, www.jammukashmir.com/archives/archives1999/99july12a.html [accessed 19 March 2099].

*Organiser*, New Delhi.

'Pakistan is Always Seen as the Rogue: SPIEGEL Interview with Pervez Musharraf (Interview conducted by Susanne Koelbl)', *Spiegel*, 4 October 2010, www.spiegel.de/international/world/0,1518,721110,00.html [accessed 6 October 2010].

Pattanaik, Smruti S., and Arpita Anant, *Cross-LoC Confidence Building Measures between India and Pakistan: A Giant Leap or a Small Step towards Peace?*, Institute for Defence Studies and Analyses, Issue Brief, February 2010, www.idsa.in/system/files/CrossLoCCBMbetweenIndiaandPakistan.pdf [accessed 20 March 2010].

*Political Impact of the Earthquake, Asia Briefing No. 46*, International Crisis Group, March 2006, www.crisisgroup.org/home/index.cfm?id+4023&1=1 [accessed 4 March 2009].

Prakash, Siddartha, 'The Political Economy of Kashmir Since 1947', *Contemporary South Asia*, Volume 9, Number 3, 2000.

Punjabi, Riyaz, 'Kashmiriyat: The Mystique of an Ethnicity', *Indian International Centre Quarterly*, Volume 17, Number 2, 1990.

Puri, Luv, 'Across the LOC: a Political Conundrum', *Economic & Political Weekly*, 30 October 2010, Volume xlv, Number 44.

Rais, Rasul B., 'Elections in Pakistan: Is Democracy Winning?', *Asian Affairs*, Volume 12, Number 3, Fall, 1985.

Raman, B., 'The Omens from Muzaffarabad', *South Asia Analysis Group*, Paper No. 286, 30 July 2001, www.southasiaanalysis.org/papers3/paper286.html.

Schofield, Julian and Reeta Tremblay, 'Why Pakistan Failed: Tribal Focoism in Kashmir', *Small Wars & Insurgencies*, Volume 19, Number 1, 2008.

Schwartzberg, J.E., 'Who are the Kashmiri People? Self-identification as a Vehicle for Self-determination', *Environment and Planning A*, Volume 29, 1997.

Shah, Mehtab Ali, 'The Kashmir Problem: a View from Four Provinces of Pakistan', *Contemporary South Asia*, Volume 4, Number 1, March 1995.

Shahabuddin, Syed, 'Cutting the Gordian Knot Over Kashmir. An Imperative for the Sub-Continent', *Politics India*, Volume 1, Number 6, December 1996.

Sikand, Yoginder, 'The Emergence and Development of the Jama'at-i-Islami of Jammu and Kashmir (1940s–1990)', *Modern Asian Studies*, Volume 36, Number 3, 2002.

Sinha, Lieutenant General S.K., 'Jammu and Kashmir: Past, Present, Future', *Journal of the United Services Institution of India*, Volume CXXXV, Number 560, April-June 2005.

Snedden, Christopher, 'The India-Pakistan Peace Process: Overcoming the "Trust Deficit"', *Pakistan Security Research Unit*, Brief Number 20, Pakistan Security Research Unit, 2 October 2007, http://spaces.brad.ac.uk:8080/downloads/attachments/748/Brief+20.pdf [accessed 4 October 2007].

# BIBLIOGRAPHY

———, 'The India-Pakistan "Peace Process"': Stronger but with Some Interference', in *South and Central Asia: Building Economic and Political Linkages*, Islamabad, Institute of Regional Studies, 2009.

———, 'What Happened to Muslims in Jammu? Local Identity, "'the Massacre' of 1947" and the Roots of the "Kashmir Problem"', *South Asia: Journal of South Asian Studies*, Volume XXIV, Number 2, December 2001.

———, 'Would a Plebiscite Have Resolved the Kashmir Dispute?', *South Asia: Journal of South Asian Studies*, Volume XXVIII, Number 1, April 2005.

Symonds, Richard, 'With the Rebel Forces of Poonch', *The Statesman*, Calcutta, 4 February 1948.

Tabassum, Nazir, 'AJK Govt [sic]: Clearing the Confusion', *The News International*, Islamabad/Rawalpindi, 6 July 1992.

*The Economist*, London.

*The Herald*, Karachi.

*The Freedom Monthly*, Rawalpindi, 1957–1960.

*The Spectator*, London.

Thomson, George, MP, 'The Two Kashmirs', *Aspect*, Volume 8, London, September 1963.

*Thought*, New Delhi.

'Traditional Kinship Patterns' in Peter Blood, Editor, *Pakistan: A Country Study*, Washington, GPO for the Library of Congress, 1994, http://countrystudies.us/pakistan/30.htm [accessed 15 March 2010].

'With Friends Like These…'; *Human Rights Violations in Azad Kashmir*, Human Rights Watch, Volume 18, Number 12, September 2006.

### Newspapers

*Asia Times Online*, www.atimes.com.

*Civil and Military Gazette (CMG)*, Lahore.

*Daily Excelsior*, Jammu City

*Daily Times*, Lahore.

*Dawn*, New Delhi, then some time after Partition (September 1947?), Karachi.

*Dawn Magazine*, Karachi.

*Dawn Wire Service*, Karachi.

*Indian Express*, New Delhi.

*Pak Tribune*, Islamabad.

*Pakistan Times*, Islamabad.

*The Financial Express*, New Delhi.

*The Frontier Post*, Peshawar.

*The Hindu*, Madras/Chennai.

*The Muslim*, Islamabad.

*The Nation*, Islamabad.

*The News*, Islamabad.

*The News on Sunday*, Islamabad.

*The New York Times (NYT)*, New York.

*The Pakistan Times*, Lahore.

# BIBLIOGRAPHY

*The Statesman*, Calcutta.
*The Sunday Statesman*, Calcutta.
*The Times*, London.
*The Times of India (TOI)*, Bombay/Mumbai.

*Unpublished Papers*

Hussain, Rifaat, 'Pakistan's Relations with Azad Kashmir' [much of which has since been published under the same title in R. Dassani and H. Rowen, *Prospects for Peace in South Asia*, Stanford University Press, 2005].

Presentation on *State Earthquake Reconstruction & Rehabilitation Agency (SERRA)*, Government of AJ&K [sic], 2006, unpublished handout obtained in Azad Kashmir in December 2006.

Presentation on *Economic Features*, Azad Jammu and Kashmir Government, 2006, unpublished handout obtained in Azad Kashmir in December 2006.

'Pakistan's Constitutional Position on Jammu and Kashmir's Status', Islamabad, Institute of Policy Studies, unpublished.

*Interviews, Discussions*

*In Azad Kashmir*

Afaqi, Professor Jabir, former academic, Azad Kashmir University, Muzaffarabad, 13 January 1998.

Ahmad, Pirzada Irshad, Assistant Director, Azad Jammu and Kashmir Tourism, Muzaffarabad, 12 January 1998 and 17 March 1999.

Ali, Chaudhry Sultan, Minister for Law, Azad Kashmir Government, 13 March 1999.

Ashraf, Choudhry Mohammad, Chief Secretary, Azad Kashmir Government, Muzaffarabad, 8 March 1999.

Arshad, Raja Raza, Secretary, Finance Department, Azad Kashmir Government, Muzaffarabad, 3 and 10 March 1999.

Bela, Lieut. Colonel, Pakistan Army Medical Corps, Muzaffarabad, 28 February 1996.

Durrani, Qayoom, Editor, Azad Kashmir Legislative Assembly, Muzaffarabad, 17 January 1998.

Hayat, Malik Asif, Inspector-General, Azad Kashmir Police Force, Muzaffarabad, 3 and 10 March 1999.

Khan, Professor Mirza Zaman, Director of Kashmir Studies, Azad Kashmir University, Muzaffarabad, 3 March 1996 and 8 January 1998.

Khan, Mohammad Habib, Inspector-General, Azad Kashmir Police Force, Muzaffarabad, 28 and 29 February 1996.

Khan, Sardar Attique, (then) Prime Minister of Azad Kashmir, at the Prime Minister's Residence, Muzaffarabad, 19 December 2006.

Khan, Sardar Abdul Qayyum, (then) Prime Minister of Azad Kashmir, at the Prime Minister's Residence, Muzaffarabad, 3 March 1996.

Khan, Sardar Khalid Ibrahim, son of Sardar Mohammad Ibrahim Khan and Head of Jammu & Kashmir People's Party, Islamabad, 17 December 2006.

Khan, Sardar Mohammad Ibrahim, President of Azad Kashmir, at his ancestral home in Rawalakot, 4 March 1999, and at the President's Residence, Muzaffarabad, on 17 March 1999.

# BIBLIOGRAPHY

Khan, Sardar Mohammad Sadiq, Chief Economist, Development Department, Azad Kashmir Government, Muzaffarabad, 16–17 January 1998, and as Secretary, Department of Local Government and Rural Development, Azad Kashmir Government, Muzaffarabad, 5–7 March 1999.

Khan, Sardar Sikandar Hayat, former Azad Kashmir prime minister and president and President, Muslim Conference (Sikandar Faction), Kotli, 21 March 1999.

Majid, Chaudhry Abdul, Speaker (PPP), Azad Kashmir Legislative Assembly, Muzaffarabad, 8 and 9 March 1999.

Mallick, Justice (Retired) Abdul Majeed, President, Kashmir Liberation League, and retired Chief Justice, Azad Kashmir High Court, Muzaffarabad on 11 March 1999.

Masud, Tariq, Mohtasib (Ombudsman), Azad Kashmir Government, Muzaffarabad, 8 January 1998 and 8, 10, 11 March 1999.

Rashid, Malik, former Head, Kashmir Liberation Cell, Muzaffarabad, 9 January 1998 and 13 March 1999.

Shah, S. Sajjad, Director, Khurshid National Library, Muzaffarabad, 6 January 1998 and 5 March 1999.

Tabassum, Professor Nazir, Professor of English, Government College, Mirpur, 21 March 1999.

Tariq, M. Sharif, presidential candidate in 1970, author of *Kashmir in Strangulation* and a leading figure in the Kashmir Liberation League, Mirpur, 21 March 1999.

Unnamed official of the Azad Kashmir Government on 5 December 2006 in Muzaffarabad about refugees from Indian J&K.

Zaffer, Sahibzada Ishaq, Senior Minister (PPP), Azad Kashmir Government, Muzaffarabad, 9, 10 and 12 March 1999.

*In Pakistan*

Ahmed, Mirwaiz Muhammed, son of the late Mirwaiz Yusuf Shah, Rawalpindi, 22 January 1998.

Aziz, Mir Abdul, resident in Srinagar in 1947, journalist and former Muslim Conference member, Rawalpindi, 23 January 1998 and 19, 24 March 1999.

Chaudhry, Barrister Sultan Mahmood, Head of Peoples Muslim League—AJK, Islamabad, 27 October 2008.

Gilani, Justice Manzoor Hussain, Justice of the Azad Kashmir Supreme Court, Rawalpindi, 23 October 2008.

Hussain, Professor Ijaz, Chairman, Department of International Relations, Quaid-i-Azam University, and author of *Kashmir Dispute. An International Law Perspective*, Islamabad, 31 December 1997.

Khan, Amanullah, Chairman, Jammu Kashmir Liberation Front, Rawalpindi, 22 December 2006.

Khan, Sardar Abdul Qayyum, former Azad Kashmir prime minister and president and President, Muslim Conference (Qayyum Faction), Rawalpindi, 24 March 1999.

Khan, Sardar Attique, Prime Minister of Azad Kashmir, with his father, Sardar Abdul Qayyum Khan, former Azad Kashmir prime minister and president, at Kashmir House, Islamabad on 16 December 2006.

Mahmud, Ershad, former employee of Institute of Policy Studies, Islamabad, and journalist, in Islamabad and Rawalpindi on various occasions between 2004 and 2009.

# BIBLIOGRAPHY

Mahmud, Professor Khalid, Research Analyst, Centre for Regional Studies, Islamabad, 1 January 1998 and 27 March 1999.

Masud, Tariq, Mohtasib (Ombudsman), Azad Kashmir Government, Muzaffarabad, Islamabad 27 March 1999 and at various other times.

Qadir, Shah Ghulam, Speaker of the Azad Kashmir Legislative Assembly, Islamabad, 24 October 2008.

Parthasarathy, Gopalaswami, High Commissioner, High Commission of India, Islamabad, 25 March 1999.

Rahman, Khalid, Executive Director, Institute of Policy Studies, Islamabad, 1 January 1997.

Safi, Ghulam Mohammad, General Secretary, and Nasim, Syed Yousuf, Advocate, All Parties Hurriyat Conference (APHC) Sub Office, Islamabad, 21 January 1998.

Salaria, A.M., Forestry Officer in Maharaja's Government and Former Chief Conservator of Forests (retired 1972), Azad Kashmir Government, Lahore, 29 March 1999.

Siddiqi, Jalees Ahmad, Senior Joint Secretary, Azad Jammu & Kashmir Council Secretariat, Islamabad, 21 January 1998.

Zamir, Akram, Director, South Asia Section, Pakistan Ministry of Foreign Affairs, Islamabad, 25 March 1999.

*Other*

Aziz, Sartaj, Former Pakistan Foreign Minister, Melbourne, 17 October 2000.

*Websites, URLs*

*BBC News*: http://news.bbc.co.uk.
*KashmirWatch.com*: www.kashmirwatch.com/index.php.
*Pakistan Body Count*: www.pakistanbodycount.org/bla.php
'Refugee Camps in Azad Kashmir', *Jammu and Kashmir* website: http://www.pbase.com/hgharibwww.gharib.demon.co.uk/refugees/camps.htm [accessed 12 March 2009].
*Rising Kashmir*: www.risingkashmir.com/index.php.
*SANA (South Asian News Agency)*: www.sananews.net/english/.

# INDEX

Abbas, Chaudhry Ghulam: 90, 94, 96, 115, 119, 125, 128, 131–2, 147; background of, 23; death of (1968), 117; imprisonment of (1946), 25, 27, 60, 118; President of All J&K Muslim Conference, 90, 118, 120; rumours of contact with Sheikh Abdullah (1951), 94; sacking of Sardar Ibrahim (1950), 121; Supreme Head of Azad Kashmir Movement, 92, 114, 122, 150
Abbasi, Mehtab: Minister for Kashmir Affairs, Pakistan, 203
Abdullah, Begum: family of, 33
Abdullah, Omar: 211
Abdullah, Sheikh Mohammad: 17, 22, 24–5, 34, 55, 62, 66–7, 117, 224; appointed as Chief Emergency Administrator, 86, 97; Article 370, 94; autobiography of, 21; boycott of Praja Sabha elections (1947), 23; family of, 33; leader of All J&K National Conference, 12, 17, 21, 23, 46, 73; Prime Minister of J&K, 21, 86; sacking of (1953), 94; supporters of, 11
Afghanistan: borders of, 11, 146
Ahmadiyya: 'apostasy', 93
Akali Dal: 73
Akbar, Emperor: 17
Akbar, Chaudhry Latif: 208
Akhtar, Riaz: Chief Justice of Azad Kashmir Supreme Court, 214
Al-Badr Mujahideen: 199
Al Fatah: 199
Al Jehad: 199
Al Umar Mujahideen: 199

Ali, Chaudhry Muhammad: 93, 95; Prime Minister of Pakistan, 127
Ali, Chaudhry Sohbat: 191
All-India States Peoples' Conference: 67
All J&K Jamiat-e-Ulema-e-Islam: 201
All J&K Muslim Conference: 22, 26–7, 33–4, 42, 44, 47, 51, 61, 66, 91–2, 96, 98, 101, 105, 114–15, 118, 136–7, 121, 123, 125, 132, 145, 189, 192–3, 201, 205, 207, 212; affiliate of Muslim League, 12, 20, 107, 132–3; electoral performance (1991), 203; electoral performance (2006), 136; formation of (1932), 21; members of, 26, 60–1, 95, 113, 142, 189; revival of (1941), 22–3; supporters of, 112; Working Committee, 96, 124, 147
All J&K National Conference: 15, 22, 24, 27, 34, 74, 78; ideology of, 17, 23, 120, 161; led by Sheikh Mohammad Abdullah, 12, 17, 21, 23, 46, 73; members of, 22–3, 67; 'Quit Kashmir' campaign (1946), 26, 62
All Parties Hurriyat Conference (APHC): 198
Anjuman-i-Naujvanan-i-Kashmir: led by Sheikh Muhammad Iqbal Jafari, 128
Ansari, Abdul Khaliq: 194; leader of Azad Kashmir Awami Conference, 127
Anwar, Sardar: see Khan, Major-General (Retd.) Sardar Mohammed Anwar
Attique, Sardar: see Khan, Sardar Attique Ahmad
Awami League: 96, 99; branches of, 116; ideology of, 98

427

# INDEX

Azad Army: 44, 45, 59, 62, 91, 121, 141, 143–144, 147, 148

Azad Kashmir: 2–3, 29, 37–8, 40, 43, 49, 56–7, 59, 83, 87, 94, 99–101, 110, 161, 163, 167–9, 176, 183, 188, 196–7, 223; Bagh, 144, 154, 158, 177, 185, 200; Basic Democracies Act (1960), 134; Basic Democracy elections (1961), 131; Census (1951), 128, 160; Census (1972), 154; Census (1981), 154; Census (1998), 130–1, 159, 169, 176–7; civil secretariat of, 149; Constitution (1970), 99, 189; Council, 102–5, 107–8, 134, 137–8, 150, 152, 155, 157, 162, 175, 180–2, 191, 205–6, 215, 223, 225; creation of (1947), 62–3, 218; economy of, 164, 175–6, 178, 187, 207; Ehtesab Bureau, 206–7; Election Commission, 135, 193, 207, 214; earthquake, 178–180; elections (1990), 199; foreign remittances, 163, 170, 171, 183–184; Forest Department, 169–70; Government of, 62, 75, 85, 88, 90–3, 97, 106, 108–9, 118, 123–5, 133, 141–2, 144–7, 149, 152, 154, 159–60, 166–7, 170, 172, 176, 178, 181–6, 194–5, 197, 199, 204–5, 209; Hajira, 144; High Court, 106, 148, 156, 193, 202, 204; hydro-electricity (hydel), 163, 171, 175–176, 180–182, 187; Interim Constitution (1974), 102–7, 109, 131, 137–8, 148, 151, 155, 185, 191, 204, 214; Internally Displaced People (IDPs) in, 185–6, 200; Kotli, 144, 154, 159, 177, 183, 200, 211; lack of strategic depth, 143; legal system of, 152; Legislative Assembly, 103–6, 131, 133–5, 137, 155–7, 190–1, 201, 205–7, 211, 225; Mangla Dam, 180–1, 184, 187, 206; Mirpur, 153–4, 158–9, 168, 170–1, 181, 183, 185, 190, 196, 200, 206, 218; Muslim population of (1998), 213; Muzaffarabad, 9, 15, 17, 43, 45, 48, 51, 57, 59–60, 72, 86, 89, 95, 102, 115, 119, 123, 127, 130–1, 135, 141–2, 144, 149, 153–5, 158–9, 164, 166, 170, 177, 179, 183, 185–7, 190, 196–8, 200–1, 203, 205–6, 209, 211, 215, 218; Poonch, 153–5, 158, 165–6, 185, 187, 190, 218; Presidential Election Act (1960), 151; Regiment, 199, 208; Rules of Business (1950), 92–3, 98, 100, 104, 122, 144, 149, 161; Rules of Business (1975), 155, 161; Rules of Business (1985), 155–7, 161; Shariat Court, 156; State Council, 98; Supreme Court, 148, 156, 214; telecommunications sector, 179; Trarkhel, 119, 143–145, 199; unemployment rate, 178; Urdu official language, 209

Azad Kashmir Awami Conference: led by Abdul Khaliq Ansari, 127

Aziz, Major-General Shahid: General Officer Commanding Murree, 207, 209

Aziz, Shaukat: 212; Prime Minister of Pakistan, 210

Baghis: 130

Bahadur, Sardar Khan: 191

Bangladesh: 99; Independence of (1971), 101

Baramulla: 17, 86; brutalities in, 72–74

Bazaz, Prem Nath: 77, 119; leader of Kashmir Kisan Mazdoor Conference, 20, 24

*Begaar*: 32

Bhutto, Benazir: 193, 202, 206; Prime Minister of Pakistan, 132; re-election of (1993), 204; sacking of (1990), 106, 132

Bhutto, Zulfikar Ali: 95, 101–2, 106, 113, 172, 190, 191, 200; administration of, 172; elections (1970), 99; execution of (1979), 139; founder of PPP (1967), 98; implementation of prime ministerial system in Azad Kashmir (1974), 136, 137; Prime Minister of Pakistan, 107, 132, 136

*Biradari*: 131–2; concept of, 128–30; political significance of, 129, 139

Bogra, Muhammad Ali: 93, 95

Buddhism: 34–5, 220

Ceasefire (1949): 63, 76, 85, 86–87, 95, 96, 113, 142, 148, 161, 218, 219

Ceasefire line: 116–117, 127, 163, 165, 166, 222, 223

# INDEX

Chaudhry, Barrister Sultan Mahmood: 132, 201, 202, 210, 212; leader of Peoples [sic] Muslim League: 209–10, 213, 214; leader of PPPAK, 204; Prime Minister of Azad Kashmir, 201, 205–207, 215
Chenab River: 9, 28, 49, 57
China: 11, 35, 146, 219
Chundrigar, Ibrahim Ismail: 93

Dixon, Sir Owen: UN Representative for India and Pakistan, 94–5, 121, 123
Dogras: 13, 26–7, 34, 42, 51, 53, 70, 86, 142, 149, 176; influence of, 14; negativity about, 24, 28–9, 32

Elahi, Chaudhry Pervaiz: 210
'Englishmen': reports of violence against Muslims, 52–54
Farooq, Mirwaiz Umar: 212

Gandhi, Mahatma: 15, 55, 227; assassination of (1948), 55
Gilani, Justice Manzoor: 214
Gilani, Syed Ali Shah: 212
Gilani, Yousaf Raza: Prime Minister of Pakistan, 212
Gilgit: 13, 17, 32, 40, 45, 91, 217; pro-Pakistan uprising, 77, 83, 85, 112, 146–147, 218; separate from Azad Kashmir, 91
Gilgit Scouts: 45, 85, 146
Gilgit-Baltistan: 2, 219, 220, 223; Legislative Assembly, 225
Gilkar, Khwaja Ghulam Nabi: 127–8; leader of Kashmir Republican Party, 127
Graham, Frank P.: UN Representative for India and Pakistan, 94, 123
Gul, Hamid: former ISI chief, 198
Gurmani, Mushtaq Ahmad: Minister for Interior, 123; Minister for Kashmir Affairs, 77, 89–91, 93, 97, 120, 124

Haider, Raja Farooq: 197, 212; background of, 213; Prime Minister of Azad Kashmir, 213; resignation of (2010), 214

Hamidullah, Chaudhry: 60–1, 116, 118, 124, 127, 145; acting President of All J&K Muslim Conference, 25; 'Chief Rebel', 61
Haq, Chaudhry Anwaarul: Speaker of Legislative Assembly, 214
Harkat-ul-Ansar: 199
Harkat-ul-Jihad al-Isalmi (Huji): led by Commander Ilyas Kashmiri, 199
Hazratbal shrine: 16
Hinduism: 11, 16, 18, 34–5, 41, 47, 68, 153, 217; caste system of, 130; *jati, varna,* 130; violence against followers, 56–7, 72
Hizb-ul-Momineen: 199
Hizb-ul-Mujahideen: 199
Hizbullah: 199
Hussain, Chaudhry Shujaat: 210
Hussain, Chaudhry Noor: 116, 124, 127; leader of Azad Muslim Conference, 105, 190
Hussain, Dr Mahmud: Minister for Kashmir Affairs, 124

Ibrahim, Sardar: see Khan, Sardar Muhammad Ibrahim
Ibrahim, Sardar Khalid: 205, 211

Independent Party: founded by Sardar Abdul Qayyum Khan (1951), 95
India: 2, 24, 40–1, 46, 62, 65–6, 77, 86, 107, 110, 113, 217, 221, 225–7; Amritsar, 67; Bombay, 9, 28, 69; borders of, 222; Calcutta, 9, 39; Calcutta riots (1946), 13; Cochin, 28; Constituent Assembly, 33, 68–9, 73, 112; Cooch Behar, 28; Government of, 10, 21, 42–3, 66, 69–71, 225; Hyderabad, 8, 65, 76; Independence of (1947), 8–9; Junagadh, 58, 65; military of, 30–1, 41, 44, 60, 68, 71, 76, 85, 99, 117, 163, 165–6, 220; Moplah rebellion (1921), 13; Mumbai attacks (2008), 196; New Delhi, 10, 62, 65, 67, 69, 75–6, 78, 101, 219; Partition (1947), 1, 7, 16, 22, 34, 36, 38, 63, 165, 217, 222; Royal Indian Air Force (RIAF), 143, 149, 164

429

# INDEX

India-Pakistan Composite Dialogue: 209, 220; beginning of (2004), 186, 218
Indian J&K: 2, 26, 85–8, 95–6, 101, 107, 112, 116–17, 120–1, 123, 127, 131, 133, 139, 141–2, 144, 146, 148, 153, 161, 163, 165, 178, 187, 193–5, 203, 206, 211, 224; Constituent Assembly election (1951), 94; food imports, 169; isolation of Azad Kashmir from, 185; Kashmiri population of, 134, 223; lack of democracy in, 201, 204; militant activity in, 198, 208, 215; population of, 48, 57, 111, 130, 185–6; smuggling networks active in, 197
India-Pakistan War (1948): 223
India-Pakistan War (1965): 223
India-Pakistan War (1971): 200, 223; impact on Azad Kashmir politics, 139, 142, 154, 171
Indian National Congress: 21–2, 27, 33, 38; led by Jawaharlal Nehru, 12; members of, 59; Working Committee, 27
Indus Waters Treaty (1960): 182, 223
Inter-religious violence: 12, 37, 38, 47–57, 66–70, 75
Iqbal, Muhammad: ancestors of, 17
Islam: 11, 16, 136, 156; conversions to, 14, 18, 130; Haj, 95; Ramadan, 200; Shia, 220; Sufism, 16; Sunnism, 16; violence against followers, 74–5

J&K Liberation League: 98, 136, 202; led by K.H. Khurshid, 137, 189, 211
J&K People's Conference: led by Abdul Majeed Malik, 127
J&K People's National Party: 201
J&K People's Party: electoral performance (2006), 211
J&K Plebiscite Front: led by Muhammad Sharif Tariq, 189
Jafari, Sheikh Muhammad Iqbal: leader of Anjuman-i-Naujvanan-i-Kashmir, 128
Jaish-e-Mohammed: 196, 198–9
Jamiat-e-Ulema J&K: 201
Jamiat-i-Islami: 192–3, 198
Jamiat-ul-Mujahideen: 199
Jamiat Ulmah Islam (JUI): electoral performance (2006), 211; members of, 213

Jammu Kashmir Islamic Front: 199
Jammu and Kashmir (J&K): 2, 7, 24, 32, 35, 58, 63, 66–7, 69, 74, 79, 87–8, 101, 109, 117, 154, 219–20, 224; Banihal Pass, 9; borders of, 44, 68, 70; Buddhist population of, 35; Census (1941), 16; Constituent Assembly, 94; Constitution of, 15; construction of (1846), 12; direct British rule of (1889–1905), 13; economy of, 9; Frontier Districts Province, 10, 13, 17, 24, 85, 92, 146–7, 152; Government of, 9, 42, 51–2, 59, 75–6; Hindu population of, 11, 16, 34, 56–7, 72; international status of, 1, 215, 224, 226; Jammu City, 8–9, 29, 39, 43, 53, 145, 164–5, 185; Jammu Province, 8, 10–12, 15–16, 18, 21–2, 27–8, 35, 38–40, 42, 45, 48–9, 51–2, 54–8, 74, 77, 83, 141, 217; Kashmir Province, 9–10, 17–18, 24, 38–40, 45, 47–8, 55, 57, 62, 68, 72–3, 83, 85–6, 133, 141, 164–5; Kashmir Valley, 8, 13, 16–18, 20, 22–4, 27–8, 31, 33–4, 48, 52, 59, 62, 74, 86, 119, 128–9, 136, 164, 177, 185, 189, 192, 194–5, 217–18, 220; Kathua District, 11, 51–2, 55, 57; Ladakh, 13, 16, 35, 47, 86, 91, 220; Line of Control (LOC), 94, 130–1, 163, 175, 180, 185–7, 195, 203–4, 221–3, 225; Mirpur District, 16, 43, 56–7, 69, 127, 149; Muslim population of, 10, 20, 33, 35, 46, 48, 56, 65, 70–1, 74, 76; Poonch, 16, 27, 29–30, 41–2, 44–6, 63, 67, 69–70, 74–5, 93, 96, 122–3, 125–7, 142, 145, 149, 151, 217; Praja Sabha, 14, 20, 23, 60, 112; Provisional Republican Government of Kashmir State, 59; Pukhtoon invasion of (1947), 12; Sikh population of, 11, 56–7, 72; Srinagar, 9, 15–16, 21, 23, 33, 39, 51, 61, 67, 72, 85, 125, 149, 164–5, 185–7, 200, 209, 211; State Forces, 31–2, 41, 43, 54; Tourism, 9, 40, 165, 185; Udhampur District, 55, 57
Jammu Kashmir Liberation Front (JKLF): 184–5, 194–5, 199, 202, 210, 219; re accession to Pakistan, 201, 207, 210; led by Yasin Malik, 200; supporters of, 185

430

# INDEX

Jammuites: 1, 119, 130, 217; political support for Chaudhry Ghulam Abbas, 128; three significant actions taken by, 1

Jehangir, Emperor: family of, 17

Jhelum River: 8, 9, 43, 44, 59, 165, 167, 180; as border with British India, 28; flow of, 182

Jhelum Valley Road: 8–9, 40, 46, 51, 59, 68, 149, 163–165

Jinnah, Muhammad Ali: 15, 21, 26, 42, 46, 120, 227; family of, 97; Governor-General of Pakistan, 75; leader of Muslim League, 12, 112

Kachru, Dwarkanath: Secretary of All-India States Peoples' Conference, 67

Kak, Ramchandra: 11; Prime Minister of J&K, 20, 27, 40

Kashmir Kisan Mazdoor Conference (Peasants and Workers Conference): led by Prem Nath Bazaz, 20, 24; supporters of, 24

Kashmir Liberation Alliance: formation of (1989), 199

Kashmir Liberation Army: 194

Kashmir National Liberation Front: 102, 194

Kashmir Republican Party: led by Khwaja Ghulam Nabi Gilkar, 127

Kashmiris: 131, 144; 'old' Kashmiris, 17; political support for Mirwaiz Yusuf Shah, 128

Kashmiri, Commander Ilyas: leader of Harkat-ul-Jihad al-Islami (Huji), 199

Kashmiriyat/Kashmiriness: 18

Khan, Abdul Hamid: 213; former Chief Justice of Azad Kashmir High Court, 115; President of Azad Kashmir, 99, 115, 138; Prime Minister of Azad Kashmir, 154, 191

Khan, Sardar Abdul Qayyum: 42, 96, 99–100, 105, 117, 131, 136, 193, 196, 200, 207, 209; background of, 124; elected as Prime Minister of Azad Kashmir (1991), 136, 199, 201, 204–5; family of, 107, 209; founder of Independent Party, 95; President of Azad Kashmir, 127

Khan, Brigadier (Retd.), later Major-General (Retd.), Abdul Rehman: Chief Executive or President of Azad Kashmir, 99, 106, 137, 155, 191, 192

Khan, Colonel Akbar: military career of, 45

Khan, Amanullah: 194, 195; commemoration of Maqbool Butt's execution (1992), 204; leader of JKLF faction, 200, 201, 209

Khan, Sardar Attique Ahmad: 212–13; electoral victory of (2001), 133; Prime Minister of Azad Kashmir, 211, 214

Khan, General Ayub Muhammad: 93, 95, 97, 125, 127, 150; Chief of Pakistan Army, 98; Government Act (1968), 137; regime of, 113

Khan, Ghulam Ishaq: Chairman of Pakistan Senate, 107; Cabinet Secretary, Pakistan, 100

Khan, Liaquat Ali: 76, 122, 147; assassination of (1951), 95, 123; background of, 75; Prime Minister of Pakistan, 66, 73

Khan, Major-General (Retd.) Sardar Mohammed Anwar: imposed as President of Azad Kashmir (2001), 215; President of Azad Kashmir, 107, 208

Khan, Sardar Mohammad Yaqoob: Prime Minister of Azad Kashmir, 212–13

Khan, Air Marshal Muhammad Asghar: founder of Tehrik-i-Istiqlal, 98

Khan, Brigadier (later Major-General Retd.) Muhammad Hayat: 192; Chief Executive or President of Azad Kashmir, 106, 191, 192; President of Tehrik-I-Amal, 192, 200

Khan, Sardar Muhammad Ibrahim: 61, 90, 92, 96, 99, 118–19, 122, 125, 127–9, 131, 136, 189, 211; background of, 60; foundation President of Azad Kashmir, 42; President of All J&K Muslim Conference, 123, 189; President of Azad Kashmir, 88, 90, 105–6, 117, 123, 145, 148, 150, 191; Proclamation (1977), 105; removed from power (1950), 94, 121; revision of Rules of Business (1958), 150

# INDEX

Khan, Shah Rais: 85
Khan, Colonel Sher Ahmad: 117; background of, 122; President of Azad Kashmir, 92
Khan, Sardar Sikandar Hayat: 106, 107, 199, 201, 206, 211, 212, 213; contested refugee seat, 133; Prime Minister of Azad Kashmir, 155, 182, 193, 204–5, 207, 209
Khan, General Yahya: 101; Chief of Pakistan Army, 98; granting of constitution to Azad Kashmir (1970), 99; regime of, 106, 113, 138, 189
Khan, Zafrullah: Foreign Minister of Pakistan, 77, 93, 95
Khanam, Saeeda: 190
Khurshid, K.H.: 99, 116, 132, 136, 190, 213; leader of J&K Liberation League, 137, 189, 211; President of Azad Kashmir, 90, 97, 115, 127
Khyber Pakhtunkhwa: 2
Koran/Quran: 23, 130, 186

Lashkar-e-Taiba: 199; role in Mumbai attacks (2008), 196
Lashkar-e-Zil: 199
Leghari, Farooq: dismissal of Zulfikar Ali Bhutto (1996), 107

Mahajan, Mehr Chand: 20; Prime Minister of J&K, 25, 86
Malhotra, Jagmohan: Governor of Indian J&K, 203
Malik, Abdul Majeed: leader of J&K People's Conference, 127
Malik, Rehman: Interior Minister of Pakistan, 196
Malik, Yasin: leader of JKLF faction, 200, 209
Markaz Dawat-ul-Irshad (MDI): Lashkar-i-Taiba, 195, 198
Masood, Manzar: Speaker of Legislative Assembly, 138
'Massacre' of Muslims: 39, 47–49, 52, 55, 58, 63, 75, 77
Ministry of Kashmir Affairs (MKA): see Pakistan

Mirpuris: 29, 41, 47–8, 57, 69–70, 96–7, 120, 124, 127, 130, 170, 181, 183–5, 207; electorates of, 134; foreign remittances, 183–184; in merchant navy, 28, 170, 183; military service during Second World War (1939–45), 31; support for JKLF, 185; UK-based population, 130, 134, 177
Mirza, Iskander: 93
Mohammed, Bakshi Ghulam: Prime Minister of Indian J&K, 21
Mohammad, Khwaja Ghulam: 127
Mountbatten, Lord Louis: Viceroy of India, 15, 33; Governor-General of India, 68, 75
Muhammad, Ghulam: 93
Muhammad, Prophet: 16
Musharraf, General Pervez: 107, 196–7, 207–11, 215, 218; Chairman of Azad Kashmir Council, 206; imposition of Sardar Anwar as President of Azad Kashmir (2001), 215; regime of, 138, 189, 221; resignation of (2008), 187; rise to power (1999), 206
Muslim Janbaz Force: 199
Muslim League: 21, 26, 47, 73, 132; affiliates of, 12, 20, 33, 107, 132–3; electoral performance (1996), 205; Lahore Resolution (1940), 23; led by Muhammad Ali Jinnah, 12, 112
Muttahida Qaumi Movement (MQM): 210, 212
Muzaffarabadis: 130

Nazimuddin, Khwaja: 93; Prime Minister of Pakistan, 95, 123–4
Neelum River: 167, 198; formerly Kishenganga, 164; flow of, 182
Nehru, Jawaharlal: 2, 15, 22, 32–34, 54, 66, 68–9, 95, 112; assumption that circumstances in Srinagar reflected affairs in J&K, 17; background of, 33; death of (1964), 95; leader of Indian National Congress, 12; lover of Kashmir, 17; Prime Minister of India, 11, 27, 66–7, 73, 86, 224; speeches of, 224; visit to Srinagar (1940), 23

# INDEX

Nehru, Motilal: 33
Noon, Firoz Khan: 93
Noor-ud-Din, Sheikh: 18
Northern Areas: 2, 83, 84, 86, 87, 88, 92, 95, 101, 109, 112, 120, 139, 146, 165, 171, 196; 'loss' to Azad Kashmir, 146–148; strategic importance, 146, 219

PaK [Pakistan-Administered J&K]: 197
Pakistan: 12, 24, 40–2, 52, 65, 70, 77–8, 83, 87, 94, 107, 110–11, 141, 143, 162, 167, 169, 175–6, 188, 191, 218–19, 221, 225–7; Abbottabad, 180; Azad Jammu and Kashmir Interim Constitution Act (1974), 102; Baluchistan, 93, 133; borders of, 44, 68, 222; Central Superior Services, 152; Civil Service, 98; Constitution (1962), 88, 98, 104; Directorate for Inter-Services Intelligence (ISI), 194–5, 198, 215; East Bengal, 93, 99; Election Commission, 135; Federally Administered Tribal Areas, 101, 152; Government of, 9–10, 46, 51, 56, 65, 68, 78, 84–5, 89, 91, 95, 100, 102, 127, 137, 143, 148, 150, 153, 157, 175, 194, 207, 225; Gujrat, 54; Independence of (1947), 1, 7–8, 16, 22, 34, 36, 38, 63, 217, 222; Islamabad, 84, 101, 104, 107–8, 111, 133, 135, 147, 172, 179, 203–4, 206, 208–9, 211–15; Karachi, 17, 76, 86, 93, 95–6, 120–1, 123–5, 147, 161, 173, 175, 185; Khairpur, 93; Lahore, 28, 43, 46, 75, 147, 165; military of, 41, 63, 70, 77, 87, 94, 101, 105, 107, 116–17, 122–3, 125–6, 132, 136, 143, 148, 163, 170, 189, 195, 197, 199–200, 202–3, 208, 210, 220–1; Ministry of Kashmir Affairs (MKA), 84, 89–93, 96–9, 109, 114, 116, 121, 124–5, 127, 138–9, 147–8, 150–2, 155, 161, 193, 212; Murree, 144, 164–5; National Assembly, 98; National Bank of, 170; North-West Frontier Province (NWFP), 2, 9, 16, 28, 32, 43–4, 68–9, 71–2, 93, 101, 143–4, 152, 163, 165, 191, 196–7, 209; Pathankot, 39; Planning Commission, 171–2, 184; Rawalpindi, 9, 28, 43, 75, 84, 89, 92, 98, 115, 122, 127, 144, 147, 164–5; Sialkot, 8, 9, 31, 37, 39, 43, 51, 52, 53, 56, 75, 128, 144–5; Sind, 93, 101, 133; Supreme Court, 214; Telecommunications Authority, 180; Water and Power Development Authority (WADPA), 180–2
Pakistan-Administered J&K: 2, 91, 165, 171, 219; lack of democracy in, 112; population of, 219, 223
Pakistan-Administered Kashmir: 128, 171, 219, 223
Pakistan-Integrated Kashmir: 219
Pakistan Muslim League (Nawaz): 206, 214
Pakistan Muslim League (Quaid): 210
Pakistan-Occupied Kashmir (POK): 2
Pakistan People's Party (PPP): 99, 129, 132, 190, 200–1, 212–13, 215; factions of, 101; formation of (1967), 98
Pakistan People's Party-Azad Kashmir (PPPAK): 105, 132, 190–2, 199, 201–2, 208, 211–12, 214; electoral performance (1991), 133, 203; electoral performance (1996), 205; led by Ishaq Zafar, 209; members of, 192, 213
Palandri: 70, 122, 124, 125, 143, 144
Patel, Sardar: 27, 66–68, 86
Plebiscite: 24, 56, 68, 76, 84, 87, 88, 91, 92, 94, 101, 114, 122, 148, 224; direct action re, 124; no longer an option, 139, 171
Poonch uprising (1947): 12, 37, 38, 41–47, 63, 72, 75
Poonch, uprising in (1950): 96, 122–123;
Poonch, uprising in (1955): 124–125
Poonchis: 28–32, 41–44, 47–48, 57, 60, 67–71, 73, 77, 96, 97, 119, 124, 130, 131, 170; Muslim, 37; military service during Second World War (1939–45), 31; political support for Sardar Ibrahim, 128; presence in Pakistan military, 170; Sudhans, 97; taxation of, 30
Pukhtoons: 1, 15, 43, 63, 73, 78, 84, 143; invasion of J&K (1947), 12, 46, 48, 59, 61–2, 66–72, 74, 79, 86, 217–18; Muslim, 38; Pakistani, 65

# INDEX

Punjab: 39, 58, 93; agricultural industry of, 168; Gurdaspur District, 11; Pakistan, 9, 16, 101, 133, 143, 163

Punjabi: 16, 18, 31, 38–9, 43, 47, 74, 90, 130, 185, 210; dialects of, 28, 176; presence in Pakistan military, 101

'Punjabisation' of Pakistan: 101

Qadir, Shah Ghulam: Speaker of Legislative Assembly, 212, 214

Qasim, Mir: Chief Minister of Indian J&K, 26

Qayyum, Sardar: see Khan, Sardar Abdul Qayyum

Rahman, Sheikh Mujibur: leader of Awami League, 98–9

Rajputs: 12, 14, 16, 53, 68, 128, 130, 131, 213

Rashtriya Swayamsevak Sangh (RSS): 73; members of, 48, 51

Rasool, Mian Ghulam: 191

Rathore, Mumtaz Hussain: 133, 191, 201–2, 204; Prime Minister of Azad Kashmir, 106; Speaker of Legislative Assembly, 205

Reddy, G.K.: editor of *Kashmir Times*, 15

Refugees: 37, 39, 48–49, 57, 91, 96, 144, 186, 218; *biradari*, 132; J&K refugees in Pakistan, 99, 106, 107, 109, 121, 139; Hindus and Sikhs, 35, 43, 48, 54, 55, 73; Kashmir Refugees Committee, 119; Muslim, 52, 56, 75; seats for in Azad Kashmir Legislative Assembly, 133–136, 190, 191, 192, 201, 203, 205, 207, 210, 211

Salahuddin, Syed: Chairman of United Jihad Council, 198

Santdev, Swami: influence of, 20

Saudi Arabia: 95

Scott, Major-General: 45, 71; Chief of Staff of J&K State Forces, 43

Shah, Colonel Ali Ahmad: Azad Kashmir Defence Minister, 44, 120, 149; President of Azad Kashmir, 120, 128

Shah, Mirwaiz Yusuf: 95, 97, 120, 128, 131; background of, 23; Health and Education Minister of Azad Kashmir, 149; President of Azad Kashmir, 97

Shah, Syed Nazir Hussain: Finance Minister of Azad Kashmir, 122, 149

Shaheen, Farhat, 190

Sharif, Begum Zamurd: 190

Sharif, Nawaz: 105, 132, 202, 206; leader of Muslim League, 107; regime of, 103, 106, 132–3, 202–4

Sialkot-Jammu-Pathankot corridor: 37, 39

Sikandar, Sardar: see Khan, Sardar Sikandar Hayat

Sikhs: 11, 18, 34–5, 41, 47, 49, 51, 70, 73, 217; violence against followers, 56–7, 72

Simla Agreement: 148, 171, 223; finalisation of (1972), 137; provisions of, 101, 218

Singh, Gansara: 85

Singh, Karan: 27, 86; re his father, Maharaja Hari Singh, 12

Singh, Maharaja Gulab: imposition of Dogra rule, 29; role in construction of J&K (1846), 12; signing of Treaty of Amritsar (1846), 12

Singh, Maharaja Pratap: 29, 47; accusation of maladministration (1889), 13

Singh, Maharaja Ranbir: 13

Singh, Maharaja Sir Hari: 10–11, 13, 15, 20, 34, 47, 58, 60, 68, 84, 92, 99, 109, 115; accession to India (1947), 8, 16–17, 25, 27, 33–5, 37, 39, 41, 45, 55, 62, 65–6, 69, 75, 78, 85–6, 116, 142, 146, 219, 224; demotion of Raja Jagatdev Singh as ruler of Poonch (1928), 29; family of, 12, 54; lack of popularity, 1, 8; military career of, 32; possible involvement in inter-religious violence, 52, 53, 54, 55; regime of, 8, 13–14, 133, 146, 149, 217

Singh, Manmohan: 208, 221

Singh, Raja Jagatdev: instituted as ruler of Poonch (1928), 29

Singh, Shiv Ratandev: minor ruler of Poonch, 29

Singh, Sardar Baldev: Indian Defence Minister, 68

# INDEX

Standstill Agreement (1947): impact of, 9; provisions of, 83
State subject: 20, 31, 37, 38, 47, 63, 67, 68, 69, 70, 71, 74, 78, 100, 112, 13, 136, 153, 210, 225; 1927 law re, 47
Sudhan: 29, 30, 43, 60, 71, 92, 97, 106, 120, 132, 139, 208; *biradari*, 128–31; uprising in 1938, 30; uprising in 1950, 96, 122–123; uprising in 1955, 124–125
Suhrawardy, H.S.: 93, 121; Prime Minister of Pakistan, 96, 115–16, 127

Taliban: 196
Tamman, Hayat Muhammad Khan: Political Adviser to Zulfikar Ali Bhutto, 138, 190
Tariq, Muhammad Sharif: J&K Plebiscite Front presidential candidate (1970), 189
Tehrik-e-Jehad: 199
Tehrik-i-Ahmal Party: 192–3
Tehrik-i-Istiqlal: founded by Air Marshal Muhammad Asghar Khan, 98
Tehrik-i-Taliban: 199
Tehrik-ul-Mujahideen: 199
'Timber' curtain: 165
Treaty of Amritsar (1846): language of, 12
Trumbull, Robert, correspondent for *The New York Times*: 72–3

United Jihad Council (UJC): 197; creation of (1994), 198; members of, 198
United Kingdom (UK): 183–4; construction of J&K (1846), 12; direct rule of J&K (1889–1905), 13; Government of, 12; military of, 41; Mirpuri Jat population of, 130, 134, 177; Pakistan population of, 183; withdrawal from India (1947), 8, 27, 36, 38–9, 227
United Nations (UN): 1, 63, 76, 85, 87, 91, 95, 109, 116, 118, 139, 148, 161, 218–19, 224; Commission for India and Pakistan (UNCIP), 3, 49, 51, 77, 84, 88–9, 91, 100, 104, 149, 153, 167, 170; personnel of, 94; Security Council (UNSC), 84, 88, 180, 223
United States of America (USA): 9/11 attacks, 196; military of, 94

Wani, Ghulam-ud-Din: Revenue Minister of Azad Kashmir, 149
World Bank: 179–80, 223
World War I (1914–18): 31, 124
World War II (1939–45): 30–2, 124; UK labour shortage during, 183

Yasin, Chaudhry Mohammad: 213

Zafar, Ishaq: 210–11; death of (2006), 212; leader of PPPAK, 209
Zardari, Asif Ali: President of Pakistan, 212
Zia-ul-Haq, General: 105, 129; Chairman of Azad Kashmir Council, 191; death of (1988), 106–7, 157, 193; invocation of Section 56 of Interim Constitution (1978), 106; regime of, 103, 136, 138, 191; rise to power (1977), 148
Zulqarnain, Raja: 211–13; President of Azad Kashmir, 214